Get the eBook FREE!

(PDF, ePub, Kindle, and liveBook all included)

We believe that once you buy a book from us, you should be able to read it in any format we have available. To get electronic versions of this book at no additional cost to you, purchase and then register this book at the Manning website.

Go to https://www.manning.com/freebook and follow the instructions to complete your pBook registration.

That's it!
Thanks from Manning!

grokking
functional programming

Michał Płachta

MANNING
SHELTER ISLAND

For online information and ordering of this and other Manning books, please visit
www.manning.com. The publisher offers discounts on this book when ordered in quantity.
For more information, please contact

    Special Sales Department
    Manning Publications Co.
    20 Baldwin Road, PO Box 761
    Shelter Island, NY 11964
    Email: orders@manning.com

Many of the designations used by manufacturers and sellers to distinguish their products are claimed
as trademarks. Where those designations appear in the book, and Manning Publications was aware of a
trademark claim, the designations have been printed in initial caps or all caps.

♾ Recognizing the importance of preserving what has been written, it is Manning's policy to have the books
   we publish printed on acid-free paper, and we exert our best efforts to that end. Recognizing also our
   responsibility to conserve the resources of our planet, Manning books are printed on paper that is at least
   15 percent recycled and processed without the use of elemental chlorine.

The author and publisher have made every effort to ensure that the information in this book was correct
at press time. The author and publisher do not assume and hereby disclaim any liability to any party for
any loss, damage, or disruption caused by errors or omissions, whether such errors or omissions result
from negligence, accident, or any other cause, or from any usage of the information herein.

 Manning Publications Co.
20 Baldwin Road
Shelter Island, NY 11964

Development editor: Jennifer Stout
Technical development editor: Josh White
Review editor: Aleksandar Dragosavljević
Production editor: Keri Hales
Copy editor: Christian Berk
Proofreader: Katie Tennant
Technical proofreader: Ubaldo Pescatore
Typesetter: Dennis Dalinnik
Cover designer: Leslie Haimes

ISBN: 9781617291838
Printed and bound by CPI Group (UK) Ltd, Croydon, CR0 4YY

• •

To my dear family: Marta, Wojtek, and Ola,
for all the good vibes and inspiration.

To my parents: Renia and Leszek, for all the
opportunities you've given me.

contents

4 Functions as values   71

6   Error handling   173

7 Requirements as types   229

8 IO as values   269

10 Concurrent programs 365

preface

Hello! Thanks for purchasing *Grokking Functional Programming*. I've spent the last decade talking with programmers about the approach to programming, its maintainability, and how functional programming concepts are slowly being adopted by mainstream languages. Many of those professional developers say it's still very difficult to learn functional concepts from existing sources, which are either too simplistic or too complex. That's the gap this book is trying to fill. It aims to provide a step-by-step practical guide for programmers who want to get the full picture of fundamental functional programming concepts.

People learn best from examples, and that's why this book is heavy with them. Theory always comes second. After finishing this introductory book, you'll be able to write fully featured programs using functional programming and comfortably dive into its theoretical foundations.

You'll get the most benefit from this book if you've already created some non-trivial applications using an imperative object-oriented language like Java or Ruby. It's a big plus if you've worked on a team who struggled with lots of bugs and maintainability issues, because this is where functional programming shines the most.

I hope you'll enjoy reading the chapters and solving the exercises as much as I enjoyed writing them. Thanks again for your interest in the book!

—Michał Płachta

acknowledgments

I'd like to first of all thank the Scala community for its continuous pursuit of tools and techniques that help build maintainable software. All of the ideas presented in the book are the result of countless hours of code reviews, discussions, multiple back-and-forth blog articles, hot-take presentations, and production outage postmortems. Thank you all for your passion.

I'd like to thank my family, especially my wife Marta, for supporting me during the writing of this book with huge amounts of encouragement and love. Many thanks go to my wonderful kids, Wojtek and Ola, for making sure I don't sit at the computer for too long.

This book has been the work of many people. I'd like to thank the staff at Manning: Michael Stephens, acquisitions editor; Bert Bates, editor; Jenny Stout, development editor; Josh White, technical development editor; Christian Berk, copy editor; Keri Hales, production editor; Ubaldo Pescatore, technical proofreader; Katie Tennant, proofreader; and all of the behind-the-scenes folks who helped get this book into print.

To all the reviewers: Ahmad Nazir Raja, Andrew Collier, Anjan Bacchu, Charles Daniels, Chris Kottmyer, Flavio Diez, Geoffrey Bonser, Gianluigi Spagnuolo, Gustavo Filipe Ramos Gomes, James Nyika, James Watson, Janeen Johnson, Jeff Lim, Jocelyn Lecomte, John Griffin, Josh Cohen, Kerry Koitzsch, Marc Clifton, Mike Ted, Nikolaos Vogiatzis, Paul Brown, Ryan B. Harvey, Sander Rossel, Scott King, Srihari Sridharan, Taylor Dolezal, Tyler Kowallis, and William Wheeler, thank you; your suggestions helped make this a better book.

about this book

Who should read this book

The book assumes that the reader has at least one year of commercial experience developing software using a mainstream object-oriented programming language like Java. Examples use Scala as the teaching language, but this is not a Scala book. No prior knowledge of Scala or functional programming is required.

How this book is organized: A road map

The book is divided into three parts. The first part lays the foundation. We will learn tools and techniques that are ubiquitous in functional programming (FP). In chapter 1, we will discuss how to learn FP with this book. In chapter 2, we will show the difference between pure and impure functions. In chapter 3, we will introduce the immutable value. Finally, in chapter 4, we will show how pure functions are just immutable values and demonstrate all the superpowers that we get from this fact.

In the second part of the book, we will use only immutable values and pure functions to solve real-world problems. In chapter 5, we will introduce the most important function in FP and show how it helps in building sequential values (and programs) in a concise and readable way. In chapter 6, we will learn how to build sequential programs that may return errors. We will use chapter 7 to learn about functional software design. Chapter 8 will teach you how to deal with an impure, external, side-effectful world in a safe and functional way. Then, we will introduce streams and streaming systems in chapter 9. We will build streams of hundreds of thousands of items using the functional approach. In chapter 10, we will finally create some functional and safe concurrent programs.

In the third part we will implement a real-world functional application that uses Wikidata as a data source. We will use it to highlight everything we learned in the previous parts. In chapter 11, we will need to create an immutable-based data model and use proper types, including IO, to integrate with Wikidata, use caching and multiple threads to make the application fast. We will wrap all of these concerns in pure functions and additionally show how we can reuse our object-oriented design intuitions in the functional world. In chapter 12, we will show how to test the application we developed in chapter 11 and how easy it is to maintain, even in the presence of big requirement changes.

Finally, we will wrap up the book with a final set of exercises that will make sure you grokked functional programming.

About the code

This book contains many examples of source code both in numbered listings and in line with normal text. In both cases, source code is formatted in a `fixed-width font like this` to separate it from ordinary text. Sometimes code is also **in bold** to highlight code that has changed from previous steps in the chapter, such as when a new feature adds to an existing line of code.

In many cases, the original source code has been reformatted; we've added line breaks and reworked indentation to accommodate the available page space in the book. Code annotations accompany many of the listings, highlighting important concepts.

You can get executable snippets of code from the liveBook (online) version of this book at https://livebook.manning.com/book/grokking-functional-programming. The complete code for the examples in the book is available for download from the Manning website at https://www.manning.com/books/grokking-functional-programming, and from GitHub at https://github.com/miciek/grokkingfp-examples. All book resources, including bonus materials, are available at https://michalplachta.com/book/.

liveBook discussion forum

Purchase of *Grokking Functional Programming* includes free access to liveBook, Manning's online reading platform. Using liveBook's exclusive discussion features, you can attach comments to the book globally or to specific sections or paragraphs. It's a snap to make notes for yourself, ask and answer technical questions, and receive help from the author and other users. To access the forum, go to https://livebook.manning.com/book/grokking-functional-programming/discussion. You can also learn more about Manning's forums and the rules of conduct at https://livebook.manning.com/discussion.

Manning's commitment to our readers is to provide a venue where a meaningful dialogue between individual readers and between readers and the author can take place. It is not a commitment to any specific amount of participation on the part of the author, whose contribution to the forum remains voluntary (and unpaid). We suggest you try asking the author some challenging questions lest his interest stray! The forum and the archives of previous discussions will be accessible from the publisher's website as long as the book is in print.

about the author

MICHAŁ PŁACHTA is an experienced software engineer and an active contributor to the functional programming community. He regularly speaks at conferences, runs workshops, organizes meetups, and blogs about creating maintainable software.

Part 1
The functional toolkit

The first part of *Grokking Functional Programming* lays the foundation. We will learn tools and techniques that are ubiquitous in functional programming. Everything we learn in this part will be reused in the remaining chapters and the rest of your career.

In **chapter 1**, we will discuss the basics and make sure we are on the same page regarding the approach to teaching this book embraces. We will set up our environment, write some code, and solve some first exercises.

In **chapter 2**, we will discuss the difference between pure and impure functions. We will use some imperative examples to show the dangers and functional snippets that help mitigate them.

In **chapter 3**, we will introduce the pure function's dancing partner: the immutable value. We will present how one cannot live without the other and that both of them define what functional programming is.

Finally, in **chapter 4**, we will show how pure functions are just values and demonstrate all the superpowers that we get from this fact. This will allow us to connect all the dots together and assemble our first full-fledged functional toolkit.

In this chapter

you will learn

- who this book is for

- what a function is

- how useful functional programming is

- how to install needed tools

- how to use this book

> 66 I can only approach you by particular
> examples and let you infer what it is. 99
>
> —RICHARD HAMMING, "LEARNING TO LEARN"

Perhaps you picked up this book because …

You are curious about functional programming

1

You heard about functional programming, read the Wikipedia entry, and looked at a few books too. Maybe you rolled your eyes at the mathy explanations behind all the code, but you still remained curious about it.

> I dreamed about writing the least intimidating functional programming book ever. This is it: entry-level, practical, and with as little eye-rolling as possible.

You tried to learn functional programming before

2

You have tried learning functional programming more than once and still don't get it. Just when you understand one key concept, the next obstacle waits around the corner. And this obstacle requires understanding many more things before even approaching it.

> Learning functional programming should be enjoyable. This book encourages you to take small steps and assumes that your endorphins will keep you going.

You are still on the fence

3

You have been programming for many years in an object-oriented or imperative programming language. You have experienced the buzz of functional programming, read some blog posts, and tried coding a bit. Still, you cannot see how it makes your programming life better.

> This book is heavily focused on practical applications of functional programming. It will add some functional concepts to your mental toolbox. You will be able to use them—no matter what language you use.

Or maybe something else?

Whatever your reasons, this book tries to address them differently. It focuses on learning through **experimentation and play**. It encourages you to ask questions and come up with answers by coding. It will help you grow to new levels as a programmer. I hope you'll enjoy the ride.

What do you need to know before we start?

We assume that you have been developing software in any of the popular languages, such as Java, C++, C#, JavaScript, or Python. This is a very vague statement, so here are some quick checklists that will help us make sure we are on the same page.

You will follow along comfortably if

— You are familiar with basic object-orientation concepts like classes and objects.

— You are able to read and comprehend code like this:

```java
class Book {
  private String title;
  private List<Author> authors;

  public Book(String title) {
    this.title = title;
    this.authors = new ArrayList<Author>();
  }

  public void addAuthor(Author author) {
    this.authors.add(author);
  }
}
```

Book has a title and a list of Author objects.

Constructor: Creates a new Book object with a title and no authors

Adds an Author for this instance of Book

You will get maximum benefits if

— You have had problems with stability, testability, regression or integration of your software modules.

— You have experienced problems debugging code like this:

```java
public void makeSoup(List<String> ingredients)  {
  if(ingredients.contains("water")) {
    add("water");
  } else throw new NotEnoughIngredientsException();
  heatUpUntilBoiling();
  addVegetablesUsing(ingredients);
  waitMinutes(20);
}
```

It probably isn't going to be the best soup you've ever tasted ...

You don't need to

— Be an expert in object orientation

— Be a Java/C++/C#/Python master

— Know anything about any functional programming language, such as Kotlin, Scala, F#, Rust, Clojure, or Haskell

What do functions look like?

Without further ado, let's jump right into some code! We don't really have all the necessary tools set up yet, but this won't stop us, will it?

Here are a bunch of different functions. All of them have something in common: **they get some values as inputs, do something, and maybe return values as outputs**. Let's see:

```
public static int add(int a, int b) {
    return a + b;
}
```
Gets two ints, adds them, and returns the sum

```
public static char getFirstCharacter(String s) {
    return s.charAt(0);
}
```
Gets a String and returns its first character

```
public static int divide(int a, int b) {
    return a / b;
}
```
Gets two ints, divides the first by the second one, and returns the result

```
public static void eatSoup(Soup soup) {
    // TODO: "eating the soup" algorithm
}
```
Gets the Soup object, does something with it, and returns nothing

Why all the public statics?

You probably wonder about the `public static` modifier in each definition. Well, it's there on purpose. Functions we use in this book are all static (i.e., they don't need any object instance to be executed). They are free—they can be called by anybody from anywhere, as long as the caller has the input parameters they require. They work only with the data the caller provides—nothing more.

This has, of course, some major ramifications, which we will address later in the book. For now, let's remember that when we say **function**, we mean a `public static` function that can be called from anywhere.

Quick exercise

Implement the two functions below:

```
public static int increment(int x) {
    // TODO
}
public static String concatenate(String a, String b) {
    // TODO
}
```

Answers:
```
return x + 1;
return a + b;
```

Meet the function

As we've seen, functions come in different flavors. Basically, each function consists of a signature and a body, which implements the signature.

```
public static int add(int a, int b) {
  return a + b;        ← Signature
}                      Body
```

In this book **we will focus on functions which return values** because, as we shall see, these functions are at the heart of functional programming. We won't use functions that return nothing (i.e., void).

Input value → | ʄ | → Output value

We can treat a function as a box that gets an input value, does something with it, and returns an output value. Inside the box is the *body*. Types and names of input and output values are part of the *signature*. So we can represent the add function as follows:

int a →
int b → | add | int →

Signature vs. body

In the diagrams above, the implementation of the function, its body, is hidden inside the box, while the signature is publicly visible. This is a very important distinction. If the signature alone is enough to understand what's going on inside the box, it is a **big win for the programmers who read the code** because they don't need to go inside and analyze how it's implemented before they use it.

> **THIS IS BIG!**
> In FP, we tend to focus more on signatures than bodies of functions we use.

Quick exercise

Draw a function diagram for the function below. What's inside the box?

```
public static int increment(int x)
```

Answer:
There is a single arrow going in, named int x, and a single arrow going out, named int. The implementation is return x + 1;

When the code lies …

Some of the most difficult problems a programmer encounters happen when a code does something it's not supposed to do. These problems are often related to the signature telling a different story than the body. To see this in action, let's briefly revisit the four functions we've seen earlier:

```java
public static int add(int a, int b) {
  return a + b;
}

public static char getFirstCharacter(String s) {
  return s.charAt(0);
}

public static int divide(int a, int b) {
  return a / b;
}

public static void eatSoup(Soup soup) {
  // TODO: "eating a soup" algorithm
}
```

Surprisingly, three of the above four functions lie.

> **Q** So functions can lie?
>
> **A** Unfortunately, yes. Some of the functions above lie with a straight face. It usually boils down to the signature not telling the whole story about the body.

getFirstCharacter promises that when we provide a String, it will give us a char in return. However, sneaky as we are, when we provide an empty String, it will not give us any char, it will throw an exception!

divide will not provide a promised int if we give it 0 as b.

eatSoup promises to eat the soup we provide, but when we do, it does nothing and returns void. This is probably what most children have as the default implementation.

add, on the other hand, will return an int, no matter what we provide as a and b—as promised! We can count on such functions!

In this book, we will focus on functions that don't lie. We want their signatures to tell the whole story about the body. **You will learn how to build real-world programs using only these kinds of functions.**

After reading this book, rewriting your functions to their trustworthy functional counterparts will be a piece of cake for you!

THIS IS BIG!
Functions that don't lie are very important features of FP.

Imperative vs. declarative

Some programmers divide programming languages into two main paradigms: imperative and declarative. Let's try to grasp the difference between these two paradigms by going through a simple exercise.

Imagine we are tasked with creating a function that calculates a score in some word-based game. A player submits a word, and the function returns a score. One point is given for each character in the word.

Calculating the score imperatively

```java
public static int calculateScore(String word) {
  int score = 0;
  for(char c : word.toCharArray()) {
    score++;
  }
  return score;
}
```

Developer reads:

To calculate the score for a word, first initialize score as 0, then go through word's characters, and for each character increment the score. Return the score.

Imperative programming focuses on how the result should be computed. It is all about defining specific steps in a specific order. We achieve the final result by providing a detailed step-by-step algorithm.

Calculating the score declaratively

```java
public static int wordScore(String word) {
  return word.length();
}
```

Developer reads:

The score for a word is its length.

The declarative approach focuses on what needs to be done—not how. In this case we are saying we need a length of this string, and we return this length as the score for this particular word. That's why we can just use the length method from Java's String to get the number of characters, and we don't care how it was computed.

We also changed the name of the function from calculateScore to wordScore. This may seem like a minor difference, but using a noun makes our brain switch into the declarative mode and focus on what needs to be done rather than the details of how to achieve it.

By the way, SQL is also a mostly declarative language. You usually state what data you need, and you don't really care how it's fetched (at least during development).

Declarative code is usually more succinct and more comprehensible than imperative code. Even though many internals, like the JVM or CPUs, are strongly imperative, we, as application developers, can heavily use the declarative approach and hide imperative internals, just like we did with the length function. In this book, **you will learn how to write real-world programs using the declarative approach**.

Coffee break:
Imperative vs. declarative

Welcome to the very first coffee break exercise section of the book! We'll try to make sure you have grasped the difference between imperative and declarative approaches.

> **What are coffee breaks in this book?**
>
> There are several types of exercises in the book. You've already encountered the first one: *quick exercise*. They are marked using a big question mark and scattered around the book. They should be pretty straightforward to solve without any paper or computer access.
>
> The second type of exercise is the coffee break. Here, we assume that you have some time with a piece of paper or a computer, and you'd like to be stretched a little bit. During coffee breaks, we'll try to bring a particular topic home. They are critical to the learning process.
>
> Some of the coffee breaks may be harder for you, but don't worry if you are stuck. There is always an answer and an explanation on the next page. But before you read it, make sure you've been trying to solve an exercise for around 5–10 minutes. This is crucial to gain the understanding of the topic at hand, even if you can't figure it out.

You learn the most when you struggle at first!

In this exercise, we need to enhance our imperative `calculateScore` and declarative `wordScore` functions. The new requirement says that the score of the word should now be equal to the number of characters that are different than 'a'. **Here's your task. You are given the code below**:

```
public static int calculateScore(String word)  {
  int score = 0;
  for(char c : word.toCharArray()) {
    score++;
  }
  return score;
}

public static int wordScore(String word)  {
  return word.length();
}
```

make sure to think about the solution for a bit before checking the next page. The best way to do this is to write your answer on a piece of paper or using a computer.

Change the functions above so that the following are true:

```
calculateScore("imperative") == 9      wordScore("declarative") == 9
calculateScore("no") == 2              wordScore("yes") == 3
```

Coffee break explained: Imperative vs. declarative

I hope you've enjoyed your first coffee break. Now it's time to check your answers. Let's start with the imperative solution.

Imperative solution

The imperative approach strongly encourages us to directly implement the algorithm—the "how." So we need to get the word, go through all the characters in this word, increment the score for each character that is different than 'a', and return the final score when finished.

```java
public static int calculateScore(String word)  {
  int score = 0;
  for(char c : word.toCharArray()) {
    if(c != 'a')
      score++;
  }
  return score;
}
```

And that's it! We just added an if clause inside the for loop.

Declarative solution

The declarative approach focuses on the *what*. In this case, the requirement was already defined declaratively: *"The score of the word should now be equal to the number of characters that are different than 'a'."* We can almost directly implement this requirement as

```java
public static int wordScore(String word)  {
  return word.replace("a", "").length();
}
```

Alternatively, we can introduce a helper function.

```java
public static String stringWithoutChar(String s, char c) {
  return s.replace(Character.toString(c), "");
}

public static int wordScore(String word)  {
  return stringWithoutChar(word, 'a').length();
}
```

You may have come up with a different solution. Its is acceptable if it focuses on the string without as (*what*), instead of fors and ifs (*how*).

> **THIS IS BIG!**
> In FP, we focus on *what* needs to happen more often than *how* it should happen.

How useful is learning functional programming?

Functional programming is programming using functions with

— Signatures that don't lie
— Bodies that are as declarative as possible

In this book, we'll dive deeper into these topics, step by step, and eventually we will be able to build real-world programs without even thinking about the old habits. This alone will be a game changer. However, the benefits don't stop here. There are other useful side effects you acquire when learning functional programming with this book.

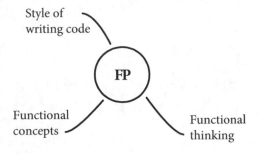

It's a style of writing code in any language

So far, we have used Java to write functions, even though it is considered an object-oriented imperative language. It turns out the techniques and features of declarative and functional programming are making their way into Java and other traditionally imperative languages. You can already use some of the techniques in your language of choice.

Functional concepts are the same in FP languages

This book focuses on general, universal features and techniques of functional programming. This means that if you learn a concept here, using Scala, you will be able to apply it in many other functional programming languages out there. We are focusing on things that are common between many FP languages, not on single-language specifics.

Functional and declarative thinking

One of the most important skills you will learn is the different approach to solving programming problems. By mastering all those functional techniques, you will add another, very powerful, tool to your software engineer toolbox. This new perspective will definitely help you grow in your profession, no matter how your story has unfolded so far.

Leaping into Scala

The majority of examples and exercises in this book use Scala. If you don't know this language, don't worry, you will learn all the necessary basics very soon.

> **Q** Why Scala?
>
> **A** This is a pragmatic choice. Scala has all the functional programming features, while its syntax is still similar to one of the mainstream imperative languages. This should smoothen the learning process. Remember, we want to spend the minimum amount of time focusing on syntax. We want to learn just enough Scala to allow us to talk about bigger concepts in functional programming. We want to learn just enough syntax to be able to solve big, real-world programming problems functionally. Finally, we treat Scala as just a teaching tool. After reading this book, you will decide on your own whether Scala is enough for your daily programming tasks or you want to pick up any other functional programming language, with crazier syntax but the same concepts.

We will still use some Java to present the imperative examples. The intention is to use Scala only for the completely functional code snippets.

Meet the function ... in Scala

Earlier in this chapter, we met our first function, written in Java. The function accepted two integer parameters and returned the sum of them.

```
public static int add(int a, int b) {
    return a + b;
}
```

It's time to rewrite this function in Scala and learn some new syntax.

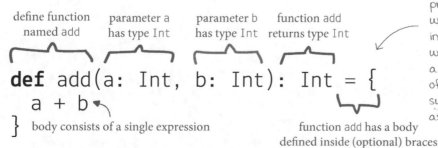

define function named add — parameter a has type Int — parameter b has type Int — function add returns type Int

```
def add(a: Int, b: Int): Int = {
    a + b
}
```

body consists of a single expression

function add has a body defined inside (optional) braces

Scala allows us to omit braces (they are optional). If a programmer doesn't include braces, then the compiler assumes that the indentation is significant, like in Python. You can use this feature if you prefer it. However, we will include braces in this book because we want to spend a minimum amount of time focusing on syntax differences, as mentioned.

Practicing functions in Scala

Now that we know the syntax of a function in Scala, we can try to rewrite some of our previous Java snippets in Scala. Hopefully, this will make the transition a little easier.

> ### What are *practicing ... * sections in this book?
>
> There are three types of exercises in the book. You've already encountered two of them: *quick exercise* (small exercises marked with a big question mark and easy to solve in your head) and *coffee breaks* (longer and harder and aimed to make you think about a concept from a different perspective, using a piece of paper or a computer).
>
> The third type is a *practicing ...* exercise. This is the most tedious of the three because it's heavily based on repetition. Usually, you are tasked with three to five exercises that are solved in exactly the same way. This is done on purpose—to train your muscle memory. The things you learn in those sections are used extensively in the book, so it's important to get them into your system as quickly as possible.

Your task is to rewrite the three functions below from Java to Scala:

We haven't talked about the tools we need to install on our computers to write Scala, so please do this one on a piece of paper.

```java
public static int increment(int x) {
    return x + 1;
}

public static char getFirstCharacter(String s) {
    return s.charAt(0);
}

public static int wordScore(String word)  {
    return word.length();
}
```

Notes:
– String in Scala has exactly the same API as String in Java.
– Character type in Scala is Char.
– Integer type in Scala is Int.
– We don't need semicolons in Scala.

Answers

```scala
def increment(x: Int): Int = {
    x + 1
}

def getFirstCharacter(s: String): Char = {
    s.charAt(0)
}

def wordScore(word: String): Int = {
    word.length()
}
```

Getting your tools ready

It's time to start writing some functional Scala code on the actual computer. To do that, we need to install some things. As each computer system is different, please follow these steps with caution.

Download the book's companion source code project

First and foremost: each piece of code that you see in this book is also available in the book's companion Java/Scala project. Download or check it out by going to https://michalplachta.com/book. The project comes with a README file that has all the up-to-date details on how to get started.

Install the Java Development Kit (JDK)

Let's make sure you have the JDK installed on your computer. This will allow us to run Java and Scala (which is a JVM language) code. If you are unsure, please run `javac -version` in your terminal, and you should get something like `javac 17`. If you don't, please visit https://jdk.java.net/17/.

Install sbt (Scala build tool)

sbt is a build tool used in the Scala ecosystem. It can be used to create, build, and test projects. Visit https://www.scala-sbt.org/download.html to get the instructions of how to install the sbt on your platform.

Run it!

In your shell, you will need to run an `sbt console` command, which will start the Scala **read–evaluate–print loop (REPL)**. This is the preferred tool to run examples and do exercises in this book. It allows you to write a line of code, press Enter, and get feedback immediately. If you run this command inside the book's source code folder, you will additionally get access to all exercises, which should come in handy, especially later in the book, when they get more complicated. Let's not get ahead of ourselves, though, and start playing around with the REPL itself. Have a look below to get some intuition on how to use this tool. After running sbt console:

```
Welcome to Scala 3.1.3
Type in expressions for evaluation. Or try :help.

scala>

scala> 20 + 19
val res0: Int = 39
```

The version of Scala we use

This is the Scala prompt where we enter commands and the code. Go ahead, write some mathematical expression, and press Enter!

The expression was evaluated to a value named res0 that has type Int and is 39.

If you fancy a more automatic way of installing the JDK/Scala or you prefer to use Docker or a web interface, make sure to visit the book's website to learn about alternative ways of coding exercises in the book.

JDK 17 is the latest long-term-support (LTS) version as of writing this book. Other LTS versions should be fine too.

Note:
We recommend using the REPL (sbt console) with this book, especially at the beginning, because it works out of the box, and you won't get distracted. You will be able to load all exercises directly into your REPL. However, when you get familiar with the way exercises work, you are free to switch to an IDE. The most beginner-friendly one is IntelliJ IDEA. After installing Java, you can download this IDE from https://www.jetbrains.com/idea/.

Getting to know the REPL

Let's do a quick REPL session together and learn some new Scala tricks
along the way!

```
scala> print("Hello, World!")
Hello, World!
```

Type code here, and press the Enter Key to execute it immediately.

The REPL prints the output to the console.

val is a Scala keyword that defines a constant value. Note that val is part of the language and not a REPL command.

```
scala> val n = 20
val n: Int = 20
```

The REPL created n as an Int with the value 20. This value will be in the scope for the duration of the REPL session.

We can reference any value that was previously defined.

```
scala> n * 2 + 2
val res1: Int = 42
```

Whenever we don't assign a name to the result, the REPL will generate a name for us. In this case, res1 is a name that the REPL created. It is of type Int and has the value 42.

We can reference any REPL-generated value just like any other value.

```
scala> res1 / 2
val res2: Int = 21
```

Here, the REPL generates another value named res2 of type Int.

Just input the previously defined name to inspect its value.

```
scala> n
val res3: Int = 20
```

You can :load any Scala file from the book's companion repository. Here, we load the chapter 1 code. The REPL shows what was loaded: the three functions you wrote in the previous exercise! Make sure to confirm it by viewing this file in a text editor.

```
scala> :load src/main/scala/ch01_IntroScala.scala
def increment(x: Int): Int
def getFirstCharacter(s: String): Char
def wordScore(word: String): Int
// defined object ch01_IntroScala
```

All commands to the REPL itself (not code) are preceded with a :colon. Use :quit or :q to quit the REPL.

```
scala> :quit
```

Useful REPL commands

:help Show all the commands with descriptions
:reset Forget everything and start fresh
:quit End the session (quit the REPL)

Useful keyboard shortcuts

up/down arrows Cycle through previous entries
tab Reveal auto-completion options, if any

Writing your first functions!

The time has come! This is the moment when you write (and use!) your first functions in Scala. We'll use the ones we are already familiar with.

Fire up the Scala REPL (sbt console), and write

```scala
scala> def increment(x: Int): Int = {
     |    x + 1
     | }
def increment(x: Int): Int
```

The | character appears in the REPL output whenever you press Enter while writing a multi-line expression.

As you can see, the REPL responded with a line of its own. It said that it understood what we typed: the name is increment, and it is a function that gets a parameter x of type Int and returns an Int back. Let's use it!

```scala
scala> increment(6)
val res0: Int = 7
```

We called our function by applying 6 as the argument. The function returned 7, as expected! Additionally, the REPL named this value res0.

> **Using code snippets from this book**
>
> To make the code listings as readable as possible, we won't be printing the REPL prompt scala> in this book anymore. We also won't print detailed responses from the REPL. The example above is what you should do in your REPL session. However, in the book we'll only print
>
> ```scala
> def increment(x: Int): Int = {
>   x + 1
> }
>
> increment(6)
> → 7
> ```
>
> As you can see, we denote answers from the REPL using →. It means, "After entering the code above and pressing Enter, the REPL should respond with a value 7."

Now, let's try to write and call another function we met earlier:

```scala
def wordScore(word: String): Int = {
  word.length()
}

wordScore("Scala")
→ 5
```

> We will use this graphic to indicate that you should try to write code in your own REPL session.

Again, this is how the snippet on the left may look in your REPL.

```scala
scala> wordScore("Scala")
val res1: Int = 5
```

How to use this book

Before we wrap up this chapter, let's first go through all the ways this book can and should be used. Remember, this is a technical book, so do not expect to read it from cover to cover in one sitting. Instead, keep the book at your desk, working with it next to your keyboard and a few sheets of paper to write on. Shift your perspective from being a receiver of thoughts to being an active participant. Following are some additional tips.

Do the exercises

Make the commitment to do every exercise. Resist the temptation to cut and paste code or absentmindedly transfer it from the book into the REPL.

Don't look up answers, especially for coffee breaks. It may feel good to solve an exercise very quickly, but it impedes your long-term learning success.

Quick exercises, coffee breaks, and practicing . . . sections

There are three types of exercises in the book:

- *Quick exercises* are small exercises that can be completed without any external tools—in your head.
- *Coffee breaks* are longer and harder and aimed to make you think about a concept from a different perspective. This usually requires you to use a piece of paper or a computer.
- *Practicing ...* sections are based heavily on repetition. They are used to train your muscle memory in concepts and techniques that are critical in the rest of the book.

Create a space to learn

Keep some paper nearby and a few pencils or pens of different colors. Sharpies or flip chart markers are good too. We want you to work in a space that radiates information—not a dull, sterile place.

Don't rush

Work at a pace that is comfortable. It's OK to not have a consistently steady pace, too. Sometimes we run; other times we crawl. Sometimes we do nothing. Rest is very important. Remember that some topics may be harder than others.

On the other hand, if it feels easy, you're not learning.

Write code and lots of it

This book has hundreds of snippets that you can transfer directly into your REPL session. Each chapter is written as a "REPL story," but you are encouraged to play with the code, write your own versions, and just have fun!

Remember that all the code you encounter in this book is available in the book's companion source code repository.

Summary

In this chapter you learned five very important skills and concepts, which we'll use as a foundation in the rest of the book.

Who is this book for?

We started by defining you—the reader. There are three main reasons you may have chosen this book: maybe you are just curious about FP or you didn't have enough time or luck to learn it properly before, or maybe you learned it before and didn't like it very much. Whatever the reasons, our reader is a programmer who wants to learn some new ways of creating real-world applications and do so by experimentation and play. We require that you are acquainted with an object-oriented language like Java.

What is a function?

Then, we introduced our protagonist, the *function*, and talked a little bit about signatures and bodies. We also touched on a problem that we encounter when signatures are not telling the whole story about the body and how it makes programming such a difficult endeavor.

How useful is functional programming?

We talked about the difference between imperative and declarative programming, defining, roughly, what functional programming is and how it can help you grow as a software professional.

> REPL sessions are marked with this graphic throughout the book. Remember to :reset your session before starting a new chapter.

Installing needed tools

We installed `sbt` and used the Scala REPL to write our first functions in Scala. We learned how the code snippets from the book work in the REPL and how we use → to denote REPL responses in code snippets.

CODE: CH01_*
Explore this chapter's source code by looking at ch01_* files in the book's repository.

Learning how to use this book

Finally, we went through all the administrative features of the book. We described three types of exercises (*quick exercises*, *coffee breaks*, and *practicing...* sections), discussed how to prepare your workspace to learn as much as possible, and described how to work with the code snippets. You can copy and paste them into your REPL session, transfer them manually, or :load them from the Scala files included in the book's repository. Remember to get the source code by going to https://michalplachta.com/book. There is also a README file there that will help you set everything up.

In this chapter

you will learn

- why we need pure functions

- how to pass copies of the data

- how to recalculate instead of storing

- how to pass the state

- how to test pure functions

66 Sometimes, the elegant implementation is just 99
a function. Not a method. Not a class. Not a
framework. Just a function.

—JOHN CARMACK

Why do we need pure functions?

In the last chapter we learned about functions that don't lie. Their signatures tell the whole story about their body. We concluded that these are the *functions we can trust*: the fewer surprises there are when we code, the fewer bugs there will be in the applications we create. In this chapter we will learn about the most trustworthy of all the functions that don't lie: a *pure function*.

> **THIS IS BIG!**
> Pure functions are the foundation of functional programming.

Shopping cart discounts

Let's start by looking at an example that doesn't use pure functions. We'll go through its problems and try to solve them intuitively first. **Our task is to write a "shopping cart functionality" that is able to calculate discounts based on the current cart contents.**

> **Requirements: Shopping cart**
> 1. Any item (modeled as a `String`) can be added to the cart.
> 2. If any book has been added to the cart, the discount is 5%.
> 3. If no book has been added, the discount is 0%.
> 4. Items in the cart can be accessed at any time.

We can design a solution that is a direct encoding of the requirements above. Here's a diagram of the ShoppingCart class responsible for handling them:

Note that we sometimes omit types and other details in drawings to make them as clear as possible. Here, we omitted the String type in the addItem parameter list.

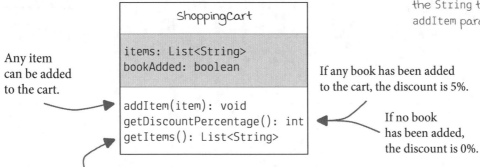

Any item can be added to the cart.

```
ShoppingCart

items: List<String>
bookAdded: boolean

addItem(item): void
getDiscountPercentage(): int
getItems(): List<String>
```

If any book has been added to the cart, the discount is 5%.

If no book has been added, the discount is 0%.

Items in the cart can be accessed any time.

Before we dive into the implementation and real code, let's briefly go through the diagram above. The ShoppingCart class has two fields, items and bookAdded, which are used as an internal state. Then, each requirement is implemented as a single method. The three methods are being used as a public interface by the rest of the world (class clients).

Coding imperatively

We designed a solution for our problem by coming up with some state fields and public interface methods. **Warning!** The design of ShoppingCart has some very serious problems! We will discuss them shortly. If you have already spotted them, good for you! If not, please keep thinking about all the possible ways this design and the code below may be misused.

ShoppingCart
items: List<String> bookAdded: boolean
addItem(item): void getDiscountPercentage(): int getItems(): List<String>

Now, it's time to write some code.

```java
public class ShoppingCart {
    private List<String> items = new ArrayList<>();
    private boolean bookAdded = false;

    public void addItem(String item) {
        items.add(item);
        if(item.equals("Book")) {
            bookAdded = true;
        }
    }

    public int getDiscountPercentage() {
        if(bookAdded) {
            return 5;
        } else {
            return 0;
        }
    }

    public List<String> getItems() {
        return items;
    }
}
```

Here's the diagram that represents the code snippet at the bottom of the page. The gray area represents state (i.e., variables that will change over time).

Remember that this is only a small example, which aims to showcase some non-obvious problems that do exist in real codebases and are much harder to detect.

Looks reasonable, right? If a book is added to the cart, we set the bookAdded flag to true. This in turn is used in getDiscountPercentage to return the proper discount percentage. **Both items and bookAdded are called** *state* because these values change over time. Now, let's look at how we could use this class.

```java
ShoppingCart cart = new ShoppingCart();
cart.addItem("Apple");
System.out.println(cart.getDiscountPercentage());
console output: 0
cart.addItem("Book");
System.out.println(cart.getDiscountPercentage());
console output: 5
```

Breaking the code

Even though all the code we've seen so far looks good, the implementation of the ShoppingCart class is still incorrect. And this has a lot to do with the *state*: items and bookAdded fields. Let's look at one possible flow in the program to see this problem.

```java
class ShoppingCart {
  private List<String> items = new ArrayList<>();
  private boolean bookAdded = false;
  public void addItem(String item) {
    items.add(item);
    if(item.equals("Book")) {
      bookAdded = true;
    }
  }
  public int getDiscountPercentage() {
    if(bookAdded) {
      return 5;
    } else {
      return 0;
    }
  }
  public List<String> getItems() {
    return items;
  }
}
```

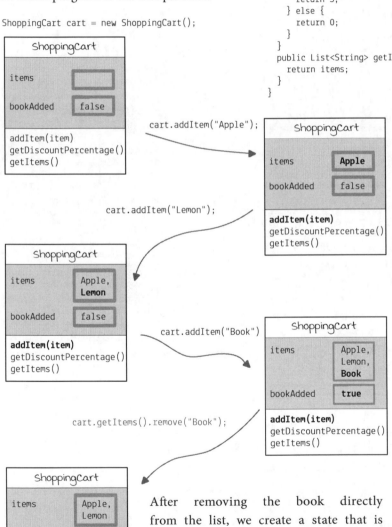

```
ShoppingCart cart = new ShoppingCart();
```

cart.addItem("Apple");

cart.addItem("Lemon");

cart.addItem("Book")

cart.getItems().remove("Book");

Yes, we didn't plan for this kind of usage of getItems, but remember that if it is possible, it will most likely be used by someone in the future. When programming, we need to think about all the possible usages to confirm we guard the internal state the best we can.

After removing the book directly from the list, we create a state that is corrupted: there is no book in the cart, but getDiscountPercentage() returns 5. This problematic outcome arises because **the state is handled improperly.**

By the way, using getItems().add would also cause problems! Experienced developers may be quick to disregard this example as an obvious code smell, but rest assured that such problems happen quite often!

Passing copies of the data

The problem we hit in the previous example can easily be fixed by **returning a copy of the List** when somebody calls getItems.

```java
public class ShoppingCart {
  private List<String> items = new ArrayList<>();
  private boolean bookAdded = false;

  public void addItem(String item) {
    items.add(item);
    if(item.equals("Book")) {
      bookAdded = true;
    }
  }

  public int getDiscountPercentage() {
    if(bookAdded) {
      return 5;
    } else {
      return 0;
    }
  }
  public List<String> getItems() {
    return items;
  }
}
```

> We are not returning the current items state but making a copy and returning it instead. This way nobody will be able to corrupt it.

```java
public List<String> getItems() {
    return new ArrayList<>(items);
}
```

We will explain why we are using copies instead of Collections .unmodifiableList in chapter 3.

This may not seem like a big change but **passing copies of data is one of the fundamental things done in functional programming**! We will cover this technique in depth very soon. But first, we need to make sure the whole ShoppingCart class is correct—no matter how it's used.

> **THIS IS BIG!**
> We pass copies of data in FP instead of changing the data in place.

Removing an item

Let's assume a client of our class, surprisingly, needs an additional functionality that was not specified at the beginning. We learned about it the hard way when our code misbehaved. Here's requirement #5:

> 5. Any item previously added to the cart can be removed.

Since we are now returning a copy of items, to satisfy this requirement we need to add another public method:

```java
public void removeItem(String item) {
  items.remove(item);
  if(item.equals("Book")) {
    bookAdded = false;
  }
}
```

Is this the end of our problems? Is the code *correct* now?

Breaking the code . . . again

We started returning a copy of items and added the removeItem method, which improved our solution a lot. Can we call it a day? It turns out we can't. Surprisingly, there are even more problems with ShoppingCart and its internal state than one might have anticipated. Let's look at another possible flow in the program to see a new problem.

```java
class ShoppingCart {
  private List<String> items = new ArrayList<>();
  private boolean bookAdded = false;

  public void addItem(String item) {
    items.add(item);
    if(item.equals("Book")) {
      bookAdded = true;
    }
  }

  public int getDiscountPercentage() {
    if(bookAdded) {
      return 5;
    } else {
      return 0;
    }
  }
  public List<String> getItems() {
    return new ArrayList<>(items);
  }
  public void removeItem(String item) {
    items.remove(item);
    if(item.equals("Book")) {
      bookAdded = false;
    }
  }
}
```

```java
ShoppingCart cart = new ShoppingCart();
```

We added two books and removed only one of them. That's how we created a state that is corrupted: there is a book in the cart, but getDiscountPercentage() returns 0! This problematic outcome arises because, again, **the state is handled improperly**.

Recalculating instead of storing

The problem we hit in the previous example can be fixed by taking a step back and rethinking our main objective.

We were tasked with creating a shopping cart functionality that is able to calculate a discount. We trapped ourselves by trying to keep track of all the additions and removals and imperatively deciding whether a book has been added or not. Instead, we could just **recalculate the discount every time** it's needed by going through the whole list.

```
public class ShoppingCart {
  private List<String> items = new ArrayList<>();
  private boolean bookAdded = false;

  public void addItem(String item) {
    items.add(item);
    if(item.equals("Book")) {
      bookAdded = true;
    }
  }

  public int getDiscountPercentage() {
    if(bookAdded) {
      return 5;
    } else {
      return 0;
    }
  }

  public List<String> getItems() {
    return new ArrayList<>(items);
  }

  public void removeItem(String item) {
    items.remove(item);
    if(item.equals("Book")) {
      bookAdded = false;
    }
  }
}
```

> We are removing the bookAdded state and moving the logic that calculates it from addItem/removeItem to getDiscountPercentage.

```
public int getDiscountPercentage() {
  if(items.contains("Book")) {
    return 5;
  } else {
    return 0;
  }
}
```

> getDiscountPercentage calculates the discount by going through the list each time the discount is needed.

What a change! Our code is much safer and less problematic now. All the logic related to discounts is now in getDiscountPercentage. We don't have the bookAdded state, which caused us so many problems. The only downside of this change is that for very large shopping lists, the discount may take a long time to calculate. **We are trading corner-case performance for readability and maintainability.**

we will come back to this topic in chapter 3.

Focusing on the logic by passing the state

Let's look at the final solution and think a bit about what it really does.

```
class ShoppingCart {
  private List<String> items = new ArrayList<>();      ⟵      items is our internal state
                                                                that we need to tiptoe
                                                                around.
  public void addItem(String item) {                   ⟵      addItem is just a wrapper
    items.add(item);                                            around List's add method.
  }

  public int getDiscountPercentage() {
    if(items.contains("Book")) {                       ⟵      This function is the only
      return 5;                                                 original one. It fulfills our
    } else {                                                    requirements.
      return 0;
    }
  }

  public List<String> getItems() {                            getItems is just a wrapper
    return new ArrayList<>(items);                     ⟵      that we need to guard
  }                                                           the List by always
                                                              returning its copy.

  public void removeItem(String item) {               ⟵      removeItem is just a
    items.remove(item);                                        wrapper around List's
  }                                                            remove method.
}
```

The problem with the solution above is that we need lots of boilerplate code to make sure the state can't be accessed outside of the class. At the same time the most important function, from the business-requirements perspective, is getDiscountPercentage. In fact, this is the only functionality that's needed!

We can get rid of all the wrapper functions around items by requiring it to be passed as an argument.

```
class ShoppingCart {
  public static int getDiscountPercentage(List<String> items) {
    if(items.contains("Book")) {
      return 5;
    } else {
      return 0;
    }
  }
}
```

We use the static keyword to indicate that the function doesn't need any instance to be useful.

And **this is the functional solution to this problem!**

Where did the state go?

You are probably worried about the latest change in the ShoppingCart class. How can we just remove all the state and leave one function there? What about the remaining requirements? The three below are still not satisfied by getDiscountPercentage in its current form:

— Any item (modeled as a String) can be added to the cart.
— Items in the cart can be accessed at any time.
— Any item previously added to the cart can be removed.

However, when you look closer, these requirements can be satisfied by any list-like class! And there are plenty to choose from in the standard library. Even if we didn't have any in the standard library, we could write our own that doesn't know anything about discounts.

```
List<String> items = new ArrayList<>();
items.add("Apple");
System.out.println(ShoppingCart.getDiscountPercentage(items));
console output: 0
items.add("Book");
System.out.println(ShoppingCart.getDiscountPercentage(items));
console output: 5
```

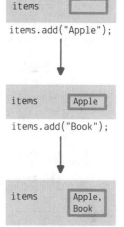

As you see, we don't have any state, we just pass a list of items to our discount-calculation function. We still have all the powers we had before, but now we have less code!

We will spend more time on this topic later in the book, particularly in chapters 8 and 11.

Separation of concerns

We split the requirements into two separate sets that are fulfilled by different pieces of code! This way we have smaller, independent functions and classes, which means they are easier to read and write. In software engineering, this is called a *separation of concerns*: every piece of code has its own responsibility and is concerned only about it. To see it in action, let's go through all the requirements and see how they are fulfilled.

THIS IS BIG!
In FP, we separate concerns into different functions.

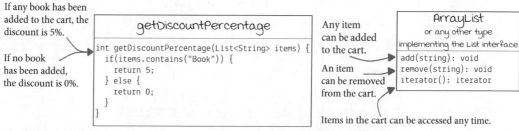

As you can see, **all state handling is now done in the ArrayList class**.

The difference between impure and pure functions

We've come a long way from an imperative to a fully functional solution. Along the way, we fixed some bugs and discovered some patterns. It's about time to list those patterns and, finally, meet the protagonist of this chapter. It turns out that the latest version of the `getDiscountPercentage` function has all the characteristics of a **pure function**.

Imperative

```java
class ShoppingCart {
  private List<String> items = new ArrayList<>();
  private boolean bookAdded = false;

  public void addItem(String item) {
    items.add(item);
    if(item.equals("Book")) {
      bookAdded = true;
    }
  }
}
```

❌ Function doesn't return a value

❌ Function mutates existing values

```java
  public int getDiscountPercentage() {
    if(bookAdded) {
      return 5;
    } else {
      return 0;
    }
  }
```

❌ Function calculates the return value based on more than just arguments

```java
  public List<String> getItems() {
    return items;
  }
}
```

❌ Function calculates the return value based on more than just arguments

Functional

```java
class ShoppingCart {
  public static int getDiscountPercentage(List<String> items) {
    if(items.contains("Book")) {
      return 5;
    } else {
      return 0;
    }
  }
}
```

✔️ Function always returns a single value

✔️ Function calculates the return value based only on its arguments

✔️ Function doesn't mutate any existing values

On the left side you can see the imperative solution we started with. It looked quite OK, but then we analyzed it more deeply and found some problems. We intuitively solved those problems and accidentally ended up with a class with a single static function (on the right).

Then, we analyzed the differences between those functions. We noticed three characteristics that the functional `ShoppingCart` has, which are missing in the imperative `ShoppingCart` class. **These are the main rules we should all follow when programming functionally.** We don't really need intuition to solve our problems. Following these rules alone will highlight problems in our code and suggest refactorings. We will discuss this deeply very soon, but first I will let you use these three rules to do a refactoring of your own.

THIS IS BIG!
We use three rules to create pure functions, which are less buggy.

Coffee break:
Refactoring to a pure function

Now it's your turn to refactor imperative code into a pure function, but in a totally different piece of code. You are going to refactor the TipCalculator class that can be used by a group of friends to calculate a tip based on the amount of people involved. The tip is 10% if the number of people splitting the bill is from one to five. If a group is larger than five people, the tip is 20%. We also cover the corner case of dining and dashing—when there are no people, then the tip is obviously 0%.

Here's the code. **Your task is to refactor the class below, so each function satisfies the three rules of a pure function.**

```java
class TipCalculator {
  private List<String> names = new ArrayList<>();
  private int tipPercentage = 0;

  public void addPerson(String name) {
    names.add(name);
    if(names.size() > 5) {
      tipPercentage = 20;
    } else if(names.size() > 0) {
      tipPercentage = 10;
    }
  }

  public List<String> getNames() {
    return names;
  }

  public int getTipPercentage() {
    return tipPercentage;
  }
}
```

Rules of a pure function
1. Function always returns a single value.
2. Function calculates the return value based only on its arguments.
3. Function doesn't mutate any existing values.

Remember the three techniques we learned about: *recalculating instead of storing*, *passing the state as an argument*, and *passing copies of data*.

Coffee break explained: Refactoring to a pure function

It looks like the `TipCalculator` class suffers from some problems we are very familiar with. We know exactly what we should do.

First, let's see which rules are broken by functions in `TipCalculator`.

```
class TipCalculator {
  private List<String> names = new ArrayList<>();
  private int tipPercentage = 0;

  public void addPerson(String name) {
    names.add(name);
    if(names.size() > 5) {
      tipPercentage = 20;
    } else if(names.size() > 0) {
      tipPercentage = 10;
    }
  }

  public List<String> getNames() {
    return names;
  }

  public int getTipPercentage() {
    return tipPercentage;
  }
}
```

addPerson doesn't return any value. A pure function should always return a single value.

addPerson mutates existing values: names and tipPercentage. A pure function should never mutate any values, it can only create new ones.

getNames calculates its return value based on the external state (the names variable). A pure function should only use arguments to create the return value.

getTipPercentage calculates its return value based on the external state (the tipPercentage variable). A pure function should only use arguments to create the return value.

Recalculating instead of storing

Let's fix getTipPercentage first. It calculates its value based on the tipPercentage field, which is an external variable and not passed as an argument. The tipPercentage field is calculated and stored by the addPerson function. To fix the getTipPercentage function, we will need to use two techniques. The first one is **recalculating instead of storing**.

```
public int getTipPercentage() {
  if(names.size() > 5) {
    return 20;
  } else if(names.size() > 0) {
    return 10;
  }
  return 0;
}
```

getTipPercentage still calculates its return value based on an external state, but we are one step closer to making it pure.

Passing state as an argument

The getTipPercentage function calculates a discount instead of using the stored value, but it still uses the external names value to do the calculation. We need to **pass the state as an argument** and make the getTipPercentage function pure. Others, however, are still not pure.

```
class TipCalculator {
  private List<String> names = new ArrayList<>();

  public void addPerson(String name) {
    names.add(name);
  }

  public List<String> getNames() {
    return names;
  }

  public static int getTipPercentage(List<String> names) {
    if(names.size() > 5) {
      return 20;
    } else if(names.size() > 0) {
      return 10;
    } else return 0;
  }
}
```

addPerson still doesn't return any value.

addPerson mutates an existing value: names.

getNames calculates its return value based on the external state.

Since this function is pure, it only uses arguments to calculate the return value. It now recalculates the tip each time getTipPercentage is called with the current list of names. It is much safer than the original version. We don't have an additional moving part of mutable state, and we can reason about getTipPercentage in isolation.

Passing copies of data

To fix addPerson, we need it to stop mutating any existing values and start **returning** modified **copies** as return values.

```
class TipCalculator {
  public List<String> addPerson(List<String> names,
                                String name) {
    List<String> updated = new ArrayList<>(names);
    updated.add(name);
    return updated;
  }

  public static int getTipPercentage(List<String> names) {
    if(names.size() > 5) {
      return 20;
    } else if(names.size() > 0) {
      return 10;
    } else return 0;
  }
}
```

addPerson is now a pure function because it doesn't mutate any existing values. However, we can also just remove it because it's only a wrapper around the add method of ArrayList.

Note that we specifically asked to refactor three functions. However, we slightly changed the API in the process and ended up with two (or just one?) functions. This is how pure function rules can guide us to better and safer APIs!

And that's a wrap! We transformed imperative functions into pure ones just by following the three rules. Our code is now easier to comprehend and therefore more maintainable.

In pure functions we trust

We started this chapter by going through a real-world example that had tricky bugs. We were able to refactor it into a pure function by following three simple rules. It goes without saying that we could also fix the bugs using an imperative approach. However, the point here is that programmers tend to create fewer bugs just by trying to write pure functions than when they follow the requirements and directly encode them as classes and methods.

We say that pure functions are "easy to reason about." We don't have to build large models of state transitions in our brains to understand them. Everything a function can do is right there in its signature. It takes some arguments and returns a value. Nothing else matters.

> **THIS IS BIG!**
> Pure functions are the foundation of functional programming.

Mathematical functions are pure

Pure functions' existence in programming is inspired by mathematical functions, which are always pure. Let's say we need calculate the final price of a discounted item we want to buy. The discount is 5%. We get our calculator out and input the price, $20, then press *, then 95 (100% - 5%) and then we get rid of percentages by pressing / 100. After pressing =, we get our final price: $19. What we just did, mathematically speaking, is

```
f(x) = x * 95 / 100
```
← *If the price is $20, we will pay only $19 after the discount! Pretty cool!*

For any given price x, the function f above will give us a discounted price back. So, if we give 20, 100, or 10 as x, calling f will give us the correct answers:

```
f(20)  = 19
f(100) = 95
f(10)  = 9.5
```

f is a pure function because it has three important characteristics:

— It always returns a single value.

— It calculates the return value based only on its arguments.

— It doesn't mutate any existing values.

These three characteristics are the main focus of this chapter. We have already applied them in our real programming tasks and seen that we can trust more in our code if it's built in a pure way.

Now, it's time to discuss the characteristics and rules of a pure function in depth. We'll learn how to detect pure functions and what programming language primitives are needed to write them.

Pure functions in programming languages

This is the pure mathematical function that calculates a discounted price:

```
f(x) = x * 95 / 100
```

Math

It can be easily translated to Java:

```
static double f(double x) {
    return x * 95.0 / 100.0;
}
```

Java

Both snippets do the same thing: they calculate 95% of a given value.

Most importantly, nothing was lost in translation. This function, written in Java, still has the three characteristics of the pure function.

It returns only a single value

The Java version of the function, as its mathematical counterpart, exists to do one thing and one thing only: it always returns exactly one value.

It calculates the return value based on its arguments

The Java version of the function, exactly like the math version, takes one argument and calculates the result based solely on this argument. Nothing more is used by the function.

It doesn't mutate any existing values

Both the Java and math versions of the function don't change anything in their environment. They don't mutate any existing values, and they don't use nor change any state fields. We can call them many times, and we will get the same result when we provide the same list of arguments. No surprises!

Note that a list is also a single value, although it can hold multiple values inside. That's OK! The main point here is that a function always returns a value.

> ### Pure function
>
> More generally, we say that a function is pure if
>
> — It returns only a single value.
> — It calculates the return value based only on its arguments.
> — It doesn't mutate any existing values.

Quick exercise

Let's quickly test your intuitions. Are these functions pure?

```
static int f1(String s) {        static double f2(double x) {
    return s.length() * 3;            return x * Math.random();
}                                }
```

Answers:
f1: yes, f2: no.

Difficulty of staying pure ...

Now we know how we can write pure functions in our programming languages. Assuming they make our programming life better, why aren't they more prevalent? The short answer is this: because we are not constrained to use them—languages we use don't require us to.

The long answer, however, needs some background. Let's go back to the function that calculates the price we'll pay after a 5% discount.

```
static double f(double x) {
    return x * 95.0 / 100.0;
}
```

We already know that it's pure. However, Java doesn't constrain us at all: **we could get away with a different, not-so-pure implementation**. Math, on the other hand, requires us to write only pure functions.

Math	Programming
We are constrained a lot more when writing or changing mathematical functions. We can't add "something more" to the function. If somebody uses our function f, they may safely assume that it returns a number when given a number. Math restricts the implementation from doing anything surprising.	In most mainstream languages, we can change and add anything we want almost anywhere we want. In the function f, we could ```double f(double x) {\n spaceship.goToMars();\n return x * 95.0 / 100.0;\n}``` And suddenly our promise to the user of f is broken.

← This function is no longer pure. Even worse! It is lying to us because it may not return a double if this mars mission fails with an exception.

The difficulty of staying pure comes from the fact that programming languages are usually a lot more powerful and elastic than math. However, *with great power comes great responsibility*. We are responsible for creating software that solves real problems and is maintainable at the same time. Unfortunately, our powerful tools can backfire—and often, they do.

Let's be more like math ...

We already know that the choice between writing pure functions and impure functions is ours to make. We know that we can transfer some of our knowledge of math to our programming endeavors. To do that, **we need to focus on three characteristics of a pure function and try to follow them wherever we go.**

Pure functions and clean code

We discovered what rules we should follow to make functions pure. It turns out that all three rules have some specific effects on the way we work. They make our code cleaner. But wait! Their benefits don't stop here. There are more!

> **Pure function**
>
> ☑ Returns a single value
>
> ☑ uses only its arguments
>
> ☑ Doesn't mutate existing values

Single responsibility

When a function can return only a single value and can't mutate any existing values, it can only do one thing and nothing more. In computer science, we say that it has a single responsibility.

No side effects

When a function's only observable result is the value it returns, we say that the function doesn't have any side effects.

> Q what is a side effect?
>
> A Anything a function does besides computing its return value based on its arguments is a side effect. So if your function does an HTTP call, it has side effects. If it changes a global variable or an instance field, it also has side effects. If it inserts something into a database, then yes, it has side effects! If it prints to the standard output, logs something using a logger, creates a thread, throws an exception, draws something on the screen, then ... you guessed it! Side effect, side effect, and side effect as well.

Don't worry, it doesn't mean you can't do those things in a functional program! We will do many of them later in this book.

Referential transparency

When we can call a function many times—at different times of day and night but with exactly the same parameters we get exactly the same answer. No matter what thread, what state the application is in, whether the database is up or down—f(20), f(20), f(20) will return 19, 19, 19. This property is called *referential transparency*.

   If you have a referentially transparent function, you could substitute a function call, say f(20), with its result, 19, without changing the program's behavior. If the function uses only its arguments to compute a value, and it doesn't mutate any existing values, it automatically becomes referentially transparent.

Coffee break: Pure or impure?

Before we move on to refactoring some impure functions, let's make sure you understand the three characteristics of a pure function.

Your task is to judge if a given function has zero, one, two, or three of the pure function characteristics. Zero means the function is impure; three means the function is pure. Any other value means the function is impure with some pure characteristics. For example:

```
static double f(double x) {
  return x * 95.0 / 100.0;
}
```

Three characteristics are present (it's a pure function).

Now it's your turn. Make sure you analyze each function thoroughly before answering. Use the pure function checklist to guide you.

> **Pure function**
> ☐ Returns a single value
> ☐ Uses only its arguments
> ☐ Doesn't mutate existing values

```
static int increment(int x) {
  return x + 1;
}

static double randomPart(double x) {
  return x * Math.random();
}

static int add(int a, int b) {
  return a + b;
}

class ShoppingCart {
  private List<String> items = new ArrayList<>();

  public int addItem(String item) {
    items.add(item);
    return items.size() + 5;
  }
}

static char getFirstCharacter(String s) {
  return s.charAt(0);
}
```

Coffee break explained: Pure or impure?

To solve this, we need to ask three questions about each function:

1. Does it always return a single value?
2. Does it compute its value based only on the data provided as arguments?
3. Does it stay away from mutating any existing values?

```
static int increment(int x) {
  return x + 1;
}
```

Yes, yes, and yes! It's a pure function.

```
static double randomPart(double x) {
  return x * Math.random();
}
```

Yes, no, and yes. This one returns only one value and doesn't mutate any existing values, but it uses `Math.random()` to generate random data based on something more than the provided arguments (side effects).

```
static int add(int a, int b) {
  return a + b;
}
```

Yes, yes, and yes again! Another pure function!

```
public int addItem(String item) {
  items.add(item);
  return items.size() + 5;
}
```

Yes, no, and no. This is an impure function. It returns just one value, but it doesn't compute it based only on arguments (it uses `items` state, which may contain various values), and it doesn't stay away from mutating existing values (again, it adds an item to the `items` state value).

```
static char getFirstCharacter(String s) {
  return s.charAt(0);
}
```

This one may be controversial because it's an isolated example. most often, exceptions are treated as another program flow. We'll come back to this topic in chapter 6.

No, yes, and yes. Another impure one. It doesn't always return a value. It returns the first character of a given `String` or throws an exception (for the empty `String`). It uses only data passed as an argument and doesn't mutate any existing values.

Using Scala to write pure functions

It's time for more coding! So far, we've seen that we can use Java to write simple pure functions without much hassle. This is also true in many other mainstream languages that support basic functional programming features and allow writing pure functions. However, some functional features that we are going to discuss later in the book have not gone mainstream (yet!), and we will use Scala to present them.

We will show some code from different languages, not just Java, throughout the book. The main reason for that is to prove that techniques presented here are universal. Additionally, many of them are being introduced into traditionally imperative mainstream languages.

Thus, before we dive deeper, let's stop for a moment and practice writing pure functions in Scala. Here's the functional Java version:

```java
class ShoppingCart {
  public static int getDiscountPercentage(List<String> items) {
    if(items.contains("Book")) {
      return 5;
    } else {
      return 0;
    }
  }
}
```

In Scala, we use the object keyword to create a single program-wide instance of an object. We use it as a container for pure functions. The Scala equivalent of the Java function above looks like this:

```scala
object ShoppingCart {
  def getDiscountPercentage(items: List[String]): Int = {
    if (items.contains("Book")) {
      5
    } else {
      0
    }
  }
}
```

object contains functions.
def marks a function.

There is no return key word because if in Scala and other FP languages is an expression. The last expression in the function is used as the return value.

Using this function is a little bit different than in Java, because **Lists in Scala are immutable,** which means that once they are created, they cannot be changed. Surprisingly, this helps a lot when programming functionally.

We will focus on immutable values in the next chapter, so treat this as a sneak peek.

```scala
> val justApple = List("Apple")
ShoppingCart.getDiscountPercentage(justApple)
→ 0
val appleAndBook = List("Apple", "Book")
ShoppingCart.getDiscountPercentage(appleAndBook)
→ 5
```

Practicing pure functions in Scala

Your task is to rewrite the code below from Java to Scala.

```java
class TipCalculator {
  public static int getTipPercentage(List<String> names) {
    if(names.size() > 5) {
      return 20;
    } else if(names.size() > 0) {
      return 10;
    } else return 0;
  }
}

List<String> names = new ArrayList<>();
System.out.println(TipCalculator.getTipPercentage(names));
```
console output: 0

```java
names.add("Alice");
names.add("Bob");
names.add("Charlie");
System.out.println(TipCalculator.getTipPercentage(names));
```
console output: 10

```java
names.add("Daniel");
names.add("Emily");
names.add("Frank");
System.out.println(TipCalculator.getTipPercentage(names));
```
console output: 20

Notes:

- List in Scala is created by using the constructor `List(...)` and passing all the items as comma-separated parameters.
- You can create an empty list by calling a special function called `List.empty`.
- List in Scala can't be modified, so you need to create an instance for each case.
- In Scala, a list of strings is written as `List[String]`.

Note that in Java snippets we use `println` to show the value a function returns, while in Scala we just call the function and see the result as a REPL response. If you like this way better, you can try using `jshell` for Java expressions.

Answer

```scala
object TipCalculator {
  def getTipPercentage(names: List[String]): Int = {
    if (names.size > 5) 20
    else if (names.size > 0) 10
    else 0
  }
}

TipCalculator.getTipPercentage(List.empty)
→ 0
val smallGroup = List("Alice", "Bob", "Charlie")
TipCalculator.getTipPercentage(smallGroup)
→ 10
val largeGroup = List("Alice", "Bob", "Charlie", "Daniel", "Emily", "Frank")
TipCalculator.getTipPercentage(largeGroup)
→ 20
```

`List.empty` returns the empty list. Here, we pass an empty list as an argument.

Testing pure functions

One of the biggest benefits of working with pure functions is their
testability. Easy testing is key to writing readable and maintainable
production code.

Functional programmers often strive to have as many critical
functionalities implemented as pure functions as possible. This way, we
are able to test them using a very straightforward unit test approach.

> Testing topics have
> their own chapter in
> this book (12), but we
> will briefly discuss some
> testing approaches and
> techniques before we
> get there to additionally
> highlight their importance.

> **Reminder: Using code snippets from this book**
>
> We have been using **>** at the beginning of code listings. Please remember
> it's a sign that you should execute Scala REPL in your terminal
> (**sbt console**) and then follow the listing. Code listings that contain
> Scala REPL responses are marked as →.

```
> def getDiscountPercentage(items: List[String]): Int = {
    if (items.contains("Book")) {
      5
    } else {
      0
    }
  }
  → getDiscountPercentage
  getDiscountPercentage(List.empty) == 1
  → false
  getDiscountPercentage(List.empty) == 0
  → true
  getDiscountPercentage(List("Apple", "Book")) == 5
  → true
```

> We don't use any testing
> library here—just raw
> assertions (Boolean
> expressions). Since we
> are in the REPL, we can
> immediately get the
> result of an assertion.

> You get false in the REPL
> if your assertion is invalid.

> We will use this style of
> assertions throughout the
> book.

Note that pure function–based assertions are stunningly similar to real
usage code. You just call a function! This helps a lot with writing better
tests. A single line describes both the input and the expected output.
Compare the three pure function tests above with a test you'd need to
write for the imperative ShoppingCart we started with (in Java):

```
ShoppingCart cart = new ShoppingCart();
cart.addItem("Apple");
cart.addItem("Book");
assert(cart.getDiscountPercentage() == 5);
```

> This test has multiple
> lines of the test setup
> code, which doesn't help
> readers understand
> what's being tested as
> quickly as a single-line
> pure function call. This
> approach gets even more
> complicated when we test
> bigger classes.

As you can see, imperative code usually needs more test code because you
need to set up all the state before making assertions.

Coffee break:
Testing pure functions

When we use pure functions, we tend to make fewer mistakes. But the benefits don't end there. Testing is far easier when using pure functions. The last coffee break of the chapter helps you write better unit tests.

Your task is to write some unit tests for each of the pure functions below. Try to write at least two assertions per function, with each one testing a different requirement. To write the best possible tests, do not look at implementations; just look at signatures and their requirements.

```
def increment(x: Int): Int = {
  x + 1
}

def add(a: Int, b: Int): Int = {
  a + b
}

def wordScore(word: String): Int = {
  word.replaceAll("a", "").length
}
```

Treat the definition of the word score as a business requirement for a word game.

The wordScore function gets a string and returns the score of a given word in a word game. The score of the word is defined as the number of characters that are different than **'a'**.

```
def getTipPercentage(names: List[String]): Int = {
  if (names.size > 5) 20
  else if (names.size > 0) 10
  else 0
}
```

The getTipPercentage function gets a list of names and outputs a tip that should be added to the bill. For small groups (up to five people), the tip is 10%. For larger groups, 20% should be returned. If the list of names is empty, the answer should be 0.

```
def getFirstCharacter(s: String): Char = {
  if (s.length > 0) s.charAt(0)
  else ' '
}
```

The function gets a String and returns its first character. In case an empty String is passed, the space character (' ') should be returned.

Coffee break explained: Testing pure functions

Here are some examples of valid tests. This list is by no means complete! Your tests are most certainly different, and that's OK. The most important thing is to get acquainted with the difference between old-school stateful tests and functional tests of pure functions (plus some REPL exposure).

```
> def increment(x: Int): Int = {
    x + 1
  }
  increment(6) == 7
  increment(0) == 1
  increment(-6) == -5
  increment(Integer.MAX_VALUE - 1) == Integer.MAX_VALUE
```

Four tests should be enough to test different corner cases, such as incrementing positive value, negative value, 0, and a value close to the maximum integer.

```
  def add(a: Int, b: Int): Int = {
    a + b
  }
  add(2, 5) == 7
  add(-2, 5) == 3
```

Here are some cases with adding positive and negative values. We should also test maximum and minimum values as we did for increment.

```
  def wordScore(word: String): Int = {
    word.replaceAll("a", "").length
  }
  wordScore("Scala") == 3
  wordScore("function") == 8
  wordScore("") == 0
```

A word with a's, a word without them, and an empty word.

```
  def getTipPercentage(names: List[String]): Int = {
    if (names.size > 5) 20
    else if (names.size > 0) 10
    else 0
  }
  getTipPercentage(List("Alice", "Bob")) == 10
  getTipPercentage(List("Alice", "Bob", "Charlie",
                        "Danny", "Emily", "Wojtek")) == 20
  getTipPercentage(List.empty) == 0
```

A case for each requirement should be written: a small group, a large group, and the empty list.

```
  def getFirstCharacter(s: String): Char = {
    if (s.length > 0) s.charAt(0)
    else ' '
  }
  getFirstCharacter("Ola") == 'O'
  getFirstCharacter("") == ' '
  getFirstCharacter(" Ha! ") == ' '
```

A case for each requirement should be written: a normal word and an empty word. Additionally it's good to confirm that words starting with a space will have the same answer as empty words (corner case).

I hope you enjoyed writing one-line, fast, and stable tests.

Summary

That's it! Let's summarize everything we learned about pure functions.

> **Pure function**
> — It returns only a single value.
> — It calculates the return value based only on its arguments.
> — It doesn't mutate any existing values.

Why do we need pure functions?

We started with a simple, imperative solution to a real-world problem. It turned out that the solution had some problems, which were connected to handling the state. We concluded that even simple, stateful, imperative computations may present some surprising challenges.

Passing copies of data

The first problem appeared when users of our class started using the `remove()` function on the `ArrayList` we returned. We learned that we can deal with such problems by passing and returning copies of data.

Recalculating instead of storing

There was one more problem left. Even after adding the `removeItem` API method (which turned out to be missing before), we didn't handle state updates correctly, which left us with a corrupted state. We learned that we can remove some of the state and just recalculate the discount based on current cart contents every time the discount is needed.

Passing the state

We ended up with a class with five methods, four of which were just simple wrappers around `ArrayList` methods. We decided to remove this boilerplate and pass a `List` value directly to the `getDiscountPercentage` function instead. We ended up with a single small function that solves our problem.

Testing pure functions

Finally, we briefly talked about another big benefit of pure functions: how easy it is to test them. Testing is important because it doesn't only ensure the correctness of a solution, but it also acts as its documentation. However, to achieve that, tests need to be concise and understandable. We will come back to this topic and discuss testing in depth in chapter 12.

In this chapter
you will learn

- why mutability is dangerous

- how to fight mutability by working with copies

- what shared mutable state is

- how to fight mutability by working with immutable
  values

- how to use immutable APIs of `String` and `List`

> 66 *Bad programmers worry about the code. Good* 99
> *programmers worry about data structures*
> *and their relationships.*
>
> —LINUS TORVALDS

The fuel for the engine

In the last chapter we met the pure function, which is going to be our best friend throughout the rest of the book. We introduced and briefly discussed some caveats regarding values that may change—mutable states. This chapter focuses on problems with mutable states and explains why pure functions can't use them in the majority of cases. We are going to learn about immutable values, which are used extensively in functional programming. The relation between a pure function and an immutable value is so strong that we can define functional programming using just two concepts.

> **Functional programming**
> is programming using *pure functions* that manipulate *immutable values*.

If pure functions make up the engine of functional programs, immutable values are its fuel, oil, and fumes.

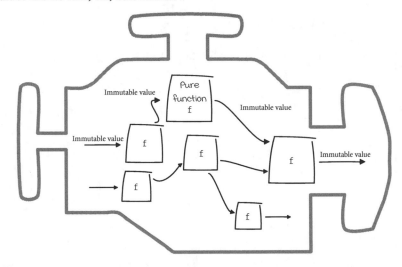

Q How is it even possible to write fully working applications using only pure functions and values that can never change?

A The short answer is this: pure functions make copies of data and pass them along. We need specific constructs in the language to be able to easily program using copies. You can find out more by reading the longer answer in this and the following chapters.

Another case for immutability

We've already seen some problems a mutable state can cause when we met the pure function. Now it's time to reiterate what we have learned and introduce even more potential problems.

The European trip

The context of our next example is a trip itinerary. Suppose we want to plan a trip around European cities: from Paris to Kraków. We draft the first plan:

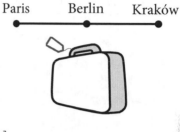

```
List<String> planA = new ArrayList<>();
planA.add("Paris");
planA.add("Berlin");
planA.add("Kraków");
System.out.println("Plan A: " + planA);
console output: Plan A: [Paris, Berlin, Kraków]
```

But then we learn that one of our friends is a big fan of Mozart and insists on visiting Vienna before going to Kraków:

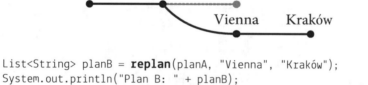

```
List<String> planB = replan(planA, "Vienna", "Kraków");
System.out.println("Plan B: " + planB);
console output: Plan B: [Paris, Berlin, Vienna, Kraków]
```

Our task is to write the replan function that will return an updated plan. It will need three parameters:

— A plan that we want to change (e.g., [Paris, Berlin, Kraków])

— A new city we want to add (e.g., Vienna)

— A city before which the new one should be added (e.g., Kraków)

Based on this specification and the usage example, we may conclude that the replan function should have the following signature:

```
static List<String> replan(List<String> plan,
                           String newCity,
                           String beforeCity)
```

return it as a new plan.

We take a given plan, insert newCity before beforeCity, and ...

Can you trust this function?

Let's look at one of the possible implementations of the replan function. We will explain this implementation by going through our original example, adding Vienna before Kraków at the end:

```
List<String> planA = new ArrayList<>();
planA.add("Paris");
planA.add("Berlin");
planA.add("Kraków");
List<String> planB = replan(planA, "Vienna", "Kraków");
```

The code on the left is represented graphically using the diagram below. We use the gray area on the left to visualize variables and how they change over time (read top down).

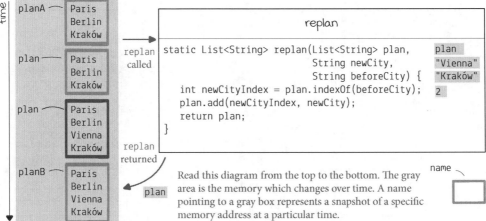

Read this diagram from the top to the bottom. The gray area is the memory which changes over time. A name pointing to a gray box represents a snapshot of a specific memory address at a particular time.

As you can see, we first create planA, which is our original plan. Then, we call the replan function and request adding Vienna before Kraków.

Then, inside the replan function, we first figure out before which index the new city (Vienna) should be added (Kraków has index 2). We add Vienna at this index, moving all the other cities one index forward and expanding the list. Finally, we return and save the result as planB. We get the desired result, but we can't celebrate just yet.

It turns out that although planB seems to be correct, when we try to print our original planA, it's different than what we created.

```
System.out.println("Plan A: " + planA);
console output: Plan A: [Paris, Berlin, Vienna, Kraków]
```

How did Vienna sneak into the original planA, if we had only added them in planB?

What happened? Have a look at the top of the page where we created planA. It only had three cities then. How did Vienna sneak into the original plan if we had only added it in planB? Unfortunately, the replan function doesn't behave as promised. It does more than just return a new plan with a new city. **It mutates more than just the returned list.**

Mutability is dangerous

When we use a function that takes a List and returns a List, we assume that a new List is returned. But nothing stops this function from modifying the list it received as a parameter.

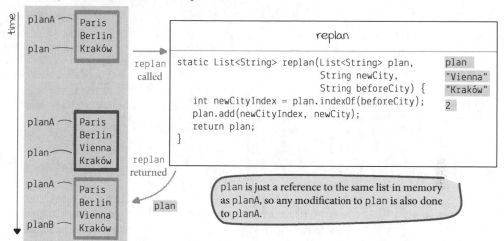

```
static List<String> replan(List<String> plan,
                           String newCity,
                           String beforeCity) {
    int newCityIndex = plan.indexOf(beforeCity);
    plan.add(newCityIndex, newCity);
    return plan;
}
```

plan is just a reference to the same list in memory as planA, so any modification to plan is also done to planA.

Now we know what happened! Unfortunately, replan lied to us. Even though the returned result is OK, the replan function additionally changed the list that we'd given it as an argument! plan inside the replan function pointed to the same list in the memory as planA outside the function. It promised to return a new value (the List return type suggests so), but instead it just mutated the list we'd given it as an argument! Changes to plan were applied to planA ...

Using mutable values is very dangerous. The replan is just a three-line function, so it's possible to quickly look at the implementation and understand that it mutates the incoming argument, but there are far bigger functions that require us to pay a lot of attention to avoid introducing such a sneaky bug. There are many more things you need to focus on, and they are not related to the business problem at hand.

Experienced developers may be quick to disregard this example as an obvious code smell, but again, please bear in mind that these problems are harder to detect in larger codebases.

THIS IS BIG! Avoiding mutability lies at the heart of functional programming.

Functions that lie ... again

To solve the problem with the `replan` function, we need to quickly recall what we discussed in chapter 2: *pure functions*. This information should give us additional insight into this particular problem we encountered and, hopefully, even more problems related to mutable values.

Is `replan` a pure function?

Pure function
— It returns only a single value.
— It calculates the return value based only on its arguments.
— It doesn't mutate any existing values.

```
static List<String> replan(List<String> plan,
                           String newCity,
                           String beforeCity) {
  int newCityIndex = plan.indexOf(beforeCity);
  plan.add(newCityIndex, newCity);
  return plan;
}
```

`replan` returns only one value and calculates it based on the provided arguments. But, as it turned out, it mutates existing values (in this case it mutates a list provided as the first argument: `plan`). So the answer is this: **no, replan is not a pure function**. Even worse! We needed to look at the implementation to be able to figure it out! At first, we just looked at its signature and assumed that it was a pure function. Then, we used it accordingly. That's how bugs are introduced.

Such functions are the worst because they mess with our intuitions. To understand this better, let's have a look at other mutating functions we can find in the `List` API and try to guess which ones are mutating something and may cause us similar headaches.

Intuition is very important in programming. The more intuitive the API you work with, the more effective you will be and the fewer bugs you will make. That's why we strive to use intuition to our advantage.

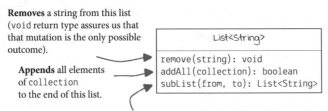

Removes a string from this list (void return type assures us that that mutation is the only possible outcome).

Appends all elements of collection to the end of this list.

```
List<String>

remove(string): void
addAll(collection): boolean
subList(from, to): List<String>
```

Returns a list which is a **view** to the this list (it doesn't mutate directly, but if the returned view is modified, then the mutation is also visible in this list).

Again, these are three methods of the `List` class from the standard Java library. As you can see, **all three of them use different approaches to mutations**. This is very counterintuitive and leaves us error prone.

Fighting mutability by working with copies

To solve the problem we need to make sure that our `replan` function doesn't mutate any existing values. We need to make sure that it is pure. Now that we know that users of our function expect us not to mutate values they provide as arguments, we can implement `replan` differently. We don't need to change the API—just the internals:

```
static List<String> replan(List<String> plan,
                           String newCity,
                           String beforeCity) {
    int newCityIndex = plan.indexOf(beforeCity);
    List<String> replanned = new ArrayList<>(plan);
    replanned.add(newCityIndex, newCity);
    return replanned;
}
```

Mutating values inside the pure function

Did you notice how we made a copy of the incoming argument, named it `replanned`, then mutated it using `add`? How's that not violating pure function rules?

To answer this question, please remember how the third rule of a pure function is constructed. ⟶

Pure functions don't mutate any existing values. They can't modify anything from the argument list or the global scope. **However, they can mutate locally created values.** In our case, `replan` creates a mutable `List`, modifies this list, then returns it. This is what we did in the `replan` function. Note that the Java programming language supports only mutable collections. However, we can still use the power of pure functions by mutating newly created copies inside functions. After this small change, the `replan` function behaves as expected, and we don't have any surprises waiting for us.

```
System.out.println("Plan A: " + planA);
console output: Plan A: [Paris, Berlin, Kraków]
List<String> planB = replan(planA, "Vienna", "Kraków");
System.out.println("Plan B: " + planB);
console output: Plan B: [Paris, Berlin, Vienna, Kraków]
System.out.println("Plan A: " + planA);
console output: Plan A: [Paris, Berlin, Kraków]
```

Remember referential transparency? If we call the `replan` function multiple times with the same arguments, do we always get the same result? Before the refactoring, we didn't. After this refactoring, we do! Our `replan` function is now referentially transparent!

> **Pure function**
> — It returns only a single value.
> — It calculates the return value based only on its arguments.
> — It doesn't mutate any *existing* values.

We will show very soon that in functional languages we don't have to mutate anything—even inside functions. Still, it's good to know that many functional techniques can be used in traditionally imperative languages, like Java, without any additional functional libraries.

Coffee break:
Getting burned by mutability

It's your turn to face the dangers of mutability. Here's another problematic example that uses a different mutable method of List.

Lap times

The most important things that are measured in motorsport are lap times. Cars or bikes are going around the circuit and try to record the best possible lap time. The quicker, the better! Here are two functions:

```java
static double totalTime(List<Double> lapTimes) {
  lapTimes.remove(0);
  double sum = 0;
  for (double x : lapTimes) {
    sum += x;
  }
  return sum;
}

static double avgTime(List<Double> lapTimes) {
  double time = totalTime(lapTimes);
  int laps = lapTimes.size();
  return time / laps;
}
```

And here's a sample usage of the functions above that generates a problem:

```java
ArrayList<Double> lapTimes = new ArrayList<>();
lapTimes.add(31.0); // warm-up lap (not taken into calculations)
lapTimes.add(20.9);
lapTimes.add(21.1);
lapTimes.add(21.3);

System.out.printf("Total: %.1fs\n", totalTime(lapTimes));
System.out.printf("Avg: %.1fs", avgTime(lapTimes));
```

Think for a while about what could possibly go wrong there. Can you list as many potential problems as possible? Which part is the most suspicious? The code above, unfortunately, prints incorrect values:

```
Total: 63.3s
Avg: 21.2s
```

Your task is to figure out what the correct result should be and fix totalTime and/or avgTime accordingly.

> **totalTime requirements**
>
> — totalTime should return a total running time for all laps, excluding the first lap, which is an incomplete warm-up lap used to prepare the car and tires.
>
> — Only lists with a minimum of two laps will be passed.

> **avgTime requirements**
>
> — avgTime should return average lap time, excluding the warm-up lap.
>
> — Only lists with a minimum of two laps will be passed.

A list is created, and four lap times are added as doubles (in seconds).

We print the results of the functions with 0.1 precision.

Coffee break explained: Getting burned by mutability

First, let's figure out what the correct result should be. We can try to calculate average and total time in our heads.

```
ArrayList<Double> lapTimes = new ArrayList<>();

lapTimes.add(31.0); // warm-up lap
lapTimes.add(20.9);
lapTimes.add(21.1);
lapTimes.add(21.3);

System.out.printf("Total: %.1fs\n", totalTime(lapTimes));
System.out.printf("Avg: %.1fs", avgTime(lapTimes));
```

total	laps	avg
0.0	0	-
20.9	1	20.9
42.0	2	21.0
63.3	**3**	**21.1**

If the functions had been written according to the specification, the code above would have printed

```
Total: 63.3s
Avg: 21.1s
```

But when we run it, we get the following:

```
Total: 63.3s
Avg: 21.2s
```

Why is there 21.2 instead of 21.1 that we calculated manually?! What happened?

OK, so we got the proper result from totalTime (63.3). But why did we get a different average time (21.2) than the one we calculated manually (21.1)? Was it a rounding error? Or just a bug in the function we missed?

Debugging mutations in totalTime

Let's find out by debugging both functions, starting with totalTime.

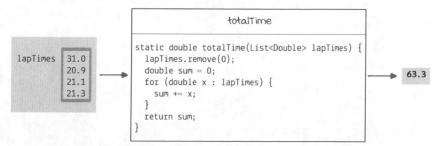

The totalTime function gets a list of four lap times, removes the first one, then adds all the remaining doubles together, returning it back to the caller. It all seems reasonable, and indeed, we get the right result when we run it. So far so good.

Debugging mutations in `avgTime`

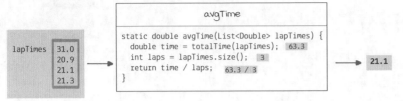

We can see that when we run `avgTime` in isolation, we get the correct result of 21.1. So why did we get 21.2 when we run the code below? This is still a big mystery, but let's not lose hope just yet.

```
System.out.printf("Total: %.1fs\n", totalTime(lapTimes));
```
console output: Total: 63.3s

```
System.out.printf("Avg: %.1fs", avgTime(lapTimes));
```
console output: Avg: **21.2s**

Debugging mutations in both `totalTime` and `avgTime`

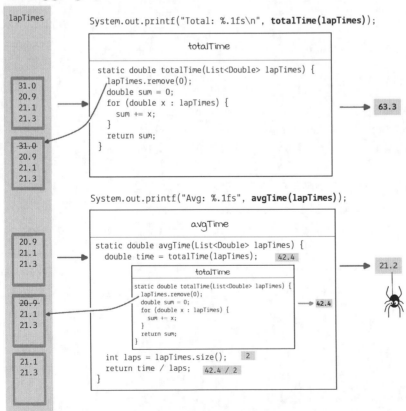

As you can see, the bug is not presenting itself when we use each function individually. **It appears only when we use those functions in a bigger program.** Mutation tricked us!

Making functions pure by mutating copies

We already learned how to deal with these kinds of problems. totalTime and avgTime are not pure functions because they mutate an existing value—in this case, lapTimes. To fix it, we need to work on a copy of the lapTimes inside both functions.

```
static double totalTime(List<Double> lapTimes) {
  List<Double> withoutWarmUp = new ArrayList<>(lapTimes);
  withoutWarmUp.remove(0); // remove warm-up lap
  double sum = 0;
  for (double x : withoutWarmUp) {
    sum += x;
  }
  return sum;
}

static double avgTime(List<Double> lapTimes) {
  double time = totalTime(lapTimes);
  List<Double> withoutWarmUp = new ArrayList<>(lapTimes);
  withoutWarmUp.remove(0); // remove warm-up lap
  int laps = withoutWarmUp.size();
  return time / laps;
}
```

Now, both functions are completely pure: they return a single value, which is computed based only on the arguments, and both of them don't mutate any existing values. We can now trust those functions more because they behave more predictably. Again, this feature is called *referential transparency*. Our functions will return exactly the same value when we provide them exactly the same arguments—no matter what.

If we can call a function multiple times with the same set of arguments and we always get the same result back, we say that this function is referentially transparent.

Can we do better?

Some of you probably wonder about the code duplication we introduced in the solution. Removing the warm-up lap functionality is duplicated in both functions. This is a slightly different problem, which violates a very popular rule: *don't repeat yourself* (DRY). We will address the problem and the rule later in this book because we need another tool to solve it functionally.

If you tried to solve this problem while doing the exercise and came up with a working solution that still doesn't mutate any existing values, good for you! If not, however, don't worry because you will learn how to do it soon enough. Right now, we need to focus only on avoiding mutability.

Introducing shared mutable state

The problem that hit us in our previous examples is just one of many that are related directly to using and manipulating a *shared mutable state*.

What is shared mutable state?

A *state* is an instance of a value that is stored in one place and can be accessed from the code. If this value can be modified, we have a *mutable state*. Furthermore, if this mutable state can be accessed from different parts of the code, it's a *shared mutable state*.

shared	mutable	state
This value can be accessed from many parts of the program.	This value can be modified in place.	This value is stored in a single place and is accessible.

Note how we change our focus from functions that operate on data (i.e., add or remove) to the data itself (i.e., plan and lapTimes).

Let's go through our problematic examples and define which parts caused us headaches and could be categorized as a shared mutable state.

List<String> plan

— This is a *state* because it can be accessed.

— It's *mutable*.

— It's *shared* (used and modified by replan and inside the main program).

```
                        replan
static List<String> replan(List<String> plan,
                           String newCity,
                           String beforeCity) {
  int newCityIndex = plan.indexOf(beforeCity);
  plan.add(newCityIndex, newCity);
  return plan;
}
```

Here, the mutable shared state is the plan parameter! replan is not a pure function because of it.

List<Double> lapTimes

— This is a *state* because it can be accessed.

— It's *mutable*.

— It's *shared* (by avgTime, totalTime and main program).

```
                       totalTime
static double totalTime(List<Double> lapTimes) {
  lapTimes.remove(0);
  double sum = 0;
  for (double x : lapTimes) {
    sum += x;
  }
  return sum;
}
```

As you probably remember, imperative programming is all about following some step-by-step procedures. These procedures usually work on mutable states (e.g., sorting algorithms modify the arrays in place).

As you can see, both plan and lapTimes are shared mutable states.

Shared mutable state is the building block of imperative programming. It may take different forms: a global variable, an instance field in a class, or any kind of read–write storage like a database table or a file. It can also be passed as an argument. Most importantly, as we have just witnessed, it can cause some serious problems.

State's impact on programming abilities

A programmer's brain gets easily overloaded. While programming, we need to keep many things in mind. The more things we need to take care of, the higher the probability is of missing something or getting something wrong. This problem isn't directly related to the mutable state, but programming in general. However, mutable state is a starting point to the rest of the discussion.

Firstly, if we need to keep many things in mind to solve a programming problem—and usually we do—the problem gets a lot harder if these things can change anytime, such as between function calls or even between two lines of code (programming using threads).

Secondly, if these ever-changing things are additionally shared, there's a problem of ownership and responsibility for them. We need to constantly ask ourselves: "Can I safely change this value?" "What other parts of the program use this value?" and "If I change this value, what entity should I notify about this change?"

Thirdly, if many entities can change a given state, we may have problems identifying all possible values of this state. It's very tempting to assume that this state has values that can be generated only by the code at hand. But it's a false assumption if this state is shared! Remember how we assumed that once a plan has been created, it cannot be changed because the replan function returns a new plan?

Mutable shared states are *moving parts* that we need to pay attention to while programming. Each part can *move* independently and non-deterministically. This is what makes mutable shared states hard.

All these moving parts add to the complexity of our program. The bigger the codebase is, the harder all the above problems get! You have probably encountered a very common issue: changing a value in one place of the source code caused all sorts of hellish problems in another, seemingly very distant, place. This is the complexity of a shared mutable state in action.

The more things we need to keep track of, the higher the cognitive load of a task is.

In the previous example, we had a replan function that took a plan as a parameter and returned a new plan. Even though we used planA as an input to replan and planB to store the result of calling the replan function, we were operating on the same mutable object the whole time!

Dealing with the moving parts

Finally, we can talk about techniques that directly deal with the *moving parts*, or shared mutable states. We'll introduce three approaches: the approach used when we fixed the replan function, an object-oriented approach, and a functional approach.

Our approach

```
                          replan

static List<String> replan(List<String> plan,
                           String newCity,
                           String beforeCity) {
  int newCityIndex = plan.indexOf(beforeCity);
  List<String> replanned = new ArrayList<>(plan);
  replanned.add(newCityIndex, newCity);
  return replanned;
}
```

This is a pure function. It returns a single value, which is calculated based only on the arguments. It also doesn't mutate any existing values.

We need to **make sure it doesn't mutate any existing values** by creating a totally new list and copying elements from the incoming list.

This function can be trusted. You will always get the same result if you provide the same arguments.

Object-oriented approach

In object-oriented programming (OOP) we'd probably use *encapsulation* to guard the changing data.

Encapsulation

Encapsulation is a technique that isolates a mutable state, usually inside an object. This object guards the state by making it private and making sure that all mutations are done only through this object's interface. Then, the code responsible for manipulating the state is kept in one place. All the moving parts are hidden.

```
                          Itinerary

private List<String> plan = new ArrayList<>();

public void replan(String newCity, String beforeCity) {
  int newCityIndex = plan.indexOf(beforeCity);
  plan.add(newCityIndex, newCity);
}

public void add(String city) {
  plan.add(city);
}

public List<String> getPlan() {
  return Collections.unmodifiableList(plan);
}
```

If we allow mutations, we need to explicitly expose them as separate methods.

In object-oriented programming, data and methods that change this data are coupled together. Data is private; it can be mutated only by methods.

This method returns void because it mutates data in place. **We lose the previous version of the plan.** Additionally, **it can't be trusted** because the result of calling it with the same arguments may be different (depending on the state).

We need to be very **careful not to leak the internal data** to the users of the class. We need to return a copy or a view to make sure nobody else mutates our state (i.e., it doesn't become shared). The bigger the class is, the more taxing and error-prone this becomes.

Dealing with the moving parts using FP

The time has come to introduce the second very important piece of our functional toolkit. We danced a long time around this topic, meeting all the mutable and impure villains along the way. We know that OOP uses encapsulation to fight them. What does FP have to say?

Functional approach   (but used in OO code as well, and getting popular)

The functional approach takes a different perspective: it tries to minimize the amount of moving parts—and ideally get rid of them completely. Functional codebases don't use shared mutable states, they use *immutable states*, or simply immutable values that act as states.

> ### Immutable values
>
> A technique that guarantees that once a value is created, it can never be changed. If a programmer needs to change even the slightest portion of a value (e.g., add a string to a list), a new value needs to be created and the old one left intact.

> **THIS IS BIG!**
> We don't use mutable states in FP—we use immutable ones instead.

Using immutable values instead of mutable ones eliminates a whole bunch of issues we have been discussing in this chapter. It also deals with the problem we encountered in our `replan` function.

So where's the catch? Well, it's a brand-new world; we need to learn how to use immutable values in a more practical setting. We will need to use Scala, where immutable collections, including lists, are built in.

Sneak peek at the functional approach in Scala

Over the following pages, we will learn the fully functional approach that embraces immutable values. We will implement the `replan` function in Scala. As a sneak peek, have a look at the final solution below. Don't worry if you don't get it yet—we will explain all the details along the way.

replan

```
def replan(plan: List[String],
           newCity: String,
           beforeCity: String): List[String] = {
  val beforeCityIndex = plan.indexOf(beforeCity)
  val citiesBefore = plan.slice(0, beforeCityIndex)
  val citiesAfter = plan.slice(beforeCityIndex, plan.size)
  citiesBefore.appended(newCity).appendedAll(citiesAfter)
}
```

List in Scala is immutable. Every operation returns a new List, always. Here, we use the combination of `List.slice`, `List.appended`, and `List.appendedAll` to add a given new city before the specified city. This works as intended and doesn't mutate any values.

Immutable values in Scala

If we want to design functions that use immutability, we need to use tools that are well suited for this. As we saw in our last example, Java's `List` and `ArrayList` are mutable, and we need to do some tricks to use the powers of a pure function. These tricks work fine, but there is still room for improvement. It's about time we get back to coding in Scala. And the reason is that **Scala has native support for immutability.** For example, the `List` type in Scala is immutable by default; we can't mutate it in place.

The same can be said about any other functional language. No matter what functional language you choose, you can expect that immutability is built in.

> ### Reminder: Using code snippets from this book
>
> It's been a while since we last touched Scala and the REPL, so I owe you a quick reminder of the convention we use in the book. Whenever you see a code snippet with **>** on the left, it means that we expect you to follow the code in your Scala REPL session (type "`sbt console`" in the terminal). Press Enter after each line, and your REPL should give you an answer similar to the one you see in the book after the → sign.

Make sure you use the correct version of Scala before proceeding. If you have any issues, please refer to the guide in chapter I.

Checking out `List` in Scala REPL

Let's prove that these are not just empty promises, and Scala really has built-in support for immutability. Fire up the Scala REPL, and write

Make sure you use the Scala version we installed in chapter I. If you have problems finding the appended function, you may be working with an old Scala version.

```
> val appleBook = List("Apple", "Book")
  → List("Apple", "Book")

  val appleBookMango = appleBook.appended("Mango")
  → List("Mango", "Apple", "Book")

  appleBook.size
  → 2

  appleBookMango.size
  → 3
```

This function adds an element at the end of this List. Note that this is not the idiomatic way of adding items to a List in Scala, due to its lacking performance (it needs to copy the whole original list), but it works fine for small lists.

As you can see, we have `appended` (i.e., added at the end) a *Mango* to a `List` that already included an *Apple* and a *Book*. We named this list, rather uninspiringly, `appleBookMango`. Then, we checked sizes of both `List`s, and it turned out that our original `appleBook` list didn't change after appending a new element! The size was still exactly 2. That means we got a new `List` back! Truth is, **Scala's `List` cannot be mutated.** Each operation returns a new `List`, no matter what.

Building our intuition about immutability

It's time to move into the immutable world. Let's do it gently, though. We will be using Scala's List API, which is immutable. But before we start using it to solve the problem with the replan function, let's practice using the immutable API we all already know well: String! Let's compare Scala's List API with Java's String API.

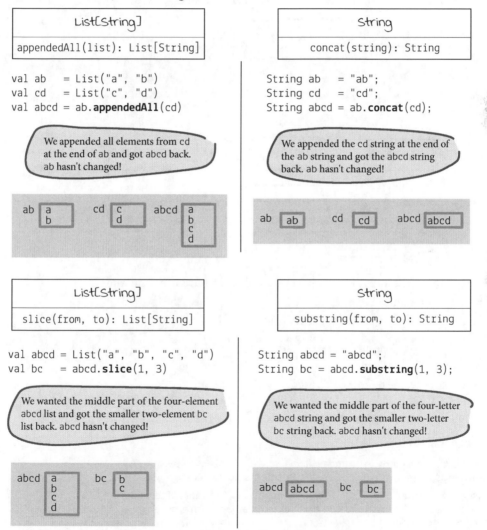

String is immutable. If you understand how String works, you will be able to grasp immutable collections with ease. If not, don't worry: we will play with String a bit before moving on.

Coffee break:
The immutable String API

Let's play with Java's String API, but in ... Scala! Scala uses the same String class as Java, so treat this as a gentle introduction to using immutable APIs and a way of practicing Scala.

Your task is to implement the abbreviate function that takes a String consisting of a full name and returns an abbreviated version.

String → abbreviate → String

Alonzo Church was a mathematician who developed the lambda calculus—the foundation of FP.

The abbreviate function should get one String as an argument and return a new one with the result. So if we call it with "Alonzo Church", we should get "A. Church" back.

"Alonzo Church" → String → abbreviate → String → "A. Church"

"A. Church" → String → abbreviate → String → "A. Church"

"A Church" → String → abbreviate → String → "A. Church"

Remember that the abbreviate function should be a pure function and manipulate only immutable values. No mutations! Use the power of creating new values based on some existing ones.

> ### Pure function
> — It returns only a single value.
> — It calculates the return value based only on its arguments.
> — **It doesn't mutate any existing values.**

Here are a few additional hints:

— Scala's String is exactly the same as Java's, so you can use your existing knowledge or go through String's documentation to implement abbreviate.

— Java's String has an immutable API, so if you just restrain yourself to using String's methods, you can be sure that your implementation is pure and you don't mutate anything.

— Please use Scala in this exercise. As a quick reminder, functions are defined using the def keyword:

```
def function(stringParameter: String): String = { ... }
```

Coffee break explained: The immutable `String` API

First, let's define manually what we need to achieve.

separator is the index of the first occurrence of the space character in the `name`.

Alonzo Church

`initial` is a substring from the beginning of the `name` that takes just one letter.

`lastName` is a substring of the name: from the index after the `separator` until the end of the `name`.

Note how we focused on defining relations between the incoming values and values we need to create. Using *is* in requirements is important and very helpful because we can easily encode each of them as immutable values.

Look how we focus on what needs to be done and not how it's done. It's declarative programming.

initial is a substring from the beginning of the name that has just one letter. → `val initial = name.substring(0, 1)`

separator is the index of the first occurrence of the space character in the name. → `val separator = name.indexOf(' ')`

lastName is a substring of the name from the index after the separator until the end of the name. → `val lastName = name.substring(separator + 1)`

name — `Alonzo Church`

initial — `A`

separator — `6`

lastName — `Church`

So the final implementation could look like this:

```scala
def abbreviate(name: String): String = {
  val initial   = name.substring(0, 1)
  val separator = name.indexOf(' ')
  val lastName  = name.substring(separator + 1)
  initial + ". " + lastName
}
```

Remember that we don't use the `return` *keyword in Scala. The result of the last expression is automatically returned.*

Note that we ignored error handling. We'll take care of it in chapter 6.

Of course, this is just one of the possible implementations. The most important thing is to make sure that your code doesn't mutate values.

Hold on ... Isn't this bad?

Functional programming is all about pure functions that manipulate immutable values. This means that every expression creates a new object, either from scratch or by copying parts of another object. **No values can be mutated.** Here are some questions you may have about this approach:

> **THIS IS BIG!**
> In FP, we just pass immutable values around!

Q Isn't copying bad in terms of performance?

A Yes, it's worse than just modifying things in place. However, we can argue that it's usually not relevant in the majority of applications. This means that in many cases readability and maintainability of the codebase far exceeds a potential performance drop.

Q So, if I'm using functional programming, my applications will be slow?

A Not necessarily. The best approach to performance analysis is, firstly, making sure that you are optimizing the right thing. You need to find the bottleneck and only then try to optimize it. If you are sure that an immutable operation is the main culprit, you still have several options. For example, if your problem is that you are frequently adding something to a very big list, then instead of appended you can use the prepended, function that adds an element at the beginning in constant time without copying or changing the old one.

Another way to look at both problems is that mutability can be used as an optimization technique in some scenarios. You can still use mutability and hide it inside a pure function, as we did earlier. Most importantly, you do this only in exceptional cases after a deliberate performance analysis of your program.

We'll discuss recursive values in chapter 9.

Q Why can't I just use Java's Collections.unmodifiableList?

A unmodifiableList takes a List as a parameter and returns a List, which is just a "view" of the original List. This view acts as a List, but it cannot be modified. The add method is still there and can be called... but it will result in a runtime exception, which violates our trust. Additionally, even if we return an "unmodifiable" List to our user, we can still mutate the original one! Hence, the user doesn't have any guarantees about the returned value, and all the shared mutable state problems we have discussed can still appear.

We'll discuss exception handling in chapter 6.

Purely functional approach to shared mutable state

We have almost all the tools we need to solve the `replan` problem (and many more similar ones) using a purely functional approach in Scala.

Here's the last version we implemented.

```
                            replan
static List<String> replan(List<String> plan,
                           String newCity,
                           String beforeCity) {
  int newCityIndex = plan.indexOf(beforeCity);
  List<String> replanned = new ArrayList<>(plan);
  replanned.add(newCityIndex, newCity);
  return replanned;
}
```

This is a pure function. It returns a single value, which is calculated based only on the arguments. It also doesn't mutate any existing values.

*We need to **make sure it doesn't mutate any existing values** by creating a totally new list and copying elements from the incoming list.*

This function can be trusted. You will always get the same result if you provide the same arguments.

Now we are able to deal with the highlighted problem because Scala, like any other FP language out there, has built-in support for immutable collections. If we use Scala's `List`, we don't have to worry about any potential mutations. It's just not possible to mutate anything!

Focusing on relations between values

Before implementing anything, let's stop for a moment and see how we can analyze such problems and arrive at purely functional solutions to them in the future. The trick is to **always start with listing all known relations between the incoming values and the value we want to produce**.

> **THIS IS BIG!**
> Immutability makes us focus on relations between values.

Cities that should go before the `newCity` are all the cities that are before `beforeCityIndex` in the `plan` list.

Cities that should go after the `newCity` are all the cities that are after `beforeCityIndex` in the `plan` list.

plan ⌐ `[Paris, Berlin, Kraków]`

newCity ⌐ `Vienna`

beforeCity ⌐ `Kraków`

`beforeCityIndex` is the index of `beforeCity` in the `plan` list.

Transforming relations into expressions

When we have all the relations between the incoming values and the
desired result, we can try to encode them as Scala expressions.

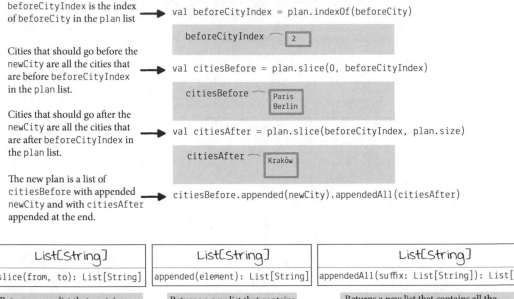

beforeCityIndex is the index
of beforeCity in the plan list

```
val beforeCityIndex = plan.indexOf(beforeCity)
```

beforeCityIndex ⌐ `2`

Cities that should go before the
newCity are all the cities that
are before beforeCityIndex
in the plan list.

```
val citiesBefore = plan.slice(0, beforeCityIndex)
```

citiesBefore ⌐ `Paris` `Berlin`

Cities that should go after the
newCity are all the cities that
are after beforeCityIndex in
the plan list.

```
val citiesAfter = plan.slice(beforeCityIndex, plan.size)
```

citiesAfter ⌐ `Kraków`

The new plan is a list of
citiesBefore with appended
newCity and with citiesAfter
appended at the end.

```
citiesBefore.appended(newCity).appendedAll(citiesAfter)
```

List[String]	List[String]	List[String]
slice(from, to): List[String]	appended(element): List[String]	appendedAll(suffix: List[String]): List[String]

Returns a new list that contains
some elements from this list: a slice
beginning at the from index and
ending before the to index.

Returns a new list that contains
all the elements from this list
with the element at the end.

Returns a new list that contains all the
elements from this list with all the elements
from the suffix list appended at the end.

```
val abcd = List("a", "b", "c", "d")
val bc = abcd.slice(1, 3)
```

```
val ab = List("a", "b")
val c = "c"
val abc = ab.appended(c)
```

```
val ab = List("a", "b")
val cd = List("c", "d")
val abcd = ab.appendedAll(cd)
```

Putting expressions into the function body

The hard part is already done! Now, we just need to copy these expressions
into compiling Scala code and write the function's signature:

```scala
def replan(plan: List[String],
           newCity: String,
           beforeCity: String): List[String] = {
  val beforeCityIndex = plan.indexOf(beforeCity)
  val citiesBefore = plan.slice(0, beforeCityIndex)
  val citiesAfter = plan.slice(beforeCityIndex, plan.size)
  citiesBefore.appended(newCity).appendedAll(citiesAfter)
}
```

And *voilà!* That's it—we have the working implementation, which doesn't
have any problems related to shared mutable state. We used the immutable
Scala List, and we can be sure that this function is pure; therefore, we
can trust that it will always behave in the same way!

Practicing immutable slicing and appending

It's time to **write some functions using the immutable List in Scala**:

Write the function called **firstTwo**, which gets a list and returns a new list that contains only the first two elements of the incoming list. This assertion should be true:

1

```
firstTwo(List("a", "b", "c")) == List("a", "b")
```

Write the function called **lastTwo**, which gets a list and returns a new list that contains only the last two elements of the incoming list. The assertion below should be true:

2

```
lastTwo(List("a", "b", "c")) == List("b", "c")
```

Write the function called **movedFirstTwoToTheEnd**, which gets a list and returns a new list with the first two elements of the incoming list moved to the end. The following assertion should be true:

3

```
movedFirstTwoToTheEnd(List("a", "b", "c")) == List("c", "a", "b")
```

Write the function called **insertedBeforeLast**, which gets a list and a new element. It returns a new list that has the element inserted before the last element of the incoming list. The assertion below should be satisfied:

4

```
insertedBeforeLast(List("a", "b"), "c") == List("a", "c", "b")
```

Answers

```
> def firstTwo(list: List[String]): List[String] =
    list.slice(0, 2)

  def lastTwo(list: List[String]): List[String] =
    list.slice(list.size - 2, list.size)

  def movedFirstTwoToTheEnd(list: List[String]): List[String] = {
    val firstTwo        = list.slice(0, 2)
    val withoutFirstTwo = list.slice(2, list.size)
    withoutFirstTwo.appendedAll(firstTwo)
  }

  def insertedBeforeLast(list: List[String], element: String): List[String] = {
    val last        = list.slice(list.size - 1, list.size)
    val withoutLast = list.slice(0, list.size - 1)
    withoutLast.appended(element).appendedAll(last)
  }
```

Note we can omit braces in Scala, and the compiler will not complain.

← We use appendedAll because last is a List that contains one element.

Summary

Let's summarize all the things we've learned about immutable values.

CODE: CH03_*
Explore this chapter's source code by looking at ch03_* files in the book's repository.

Mutability is dangerous

We started with a simple, imperative solution to a real-world problem. It turned out that the solution had some problems that were connected to operations on Java's List, which were changing the list given as the argument. We discovered that we need to pay special attention when using mutable collections. Just looking at the signature is not enough. We need to look very closely at the implementation to avoid getting burned by mutability.

Fighting mutability by using copies

We solved the problem by copying the incoming list and working only on the copied version inside the function. This way we made sure that the users of the function wouldn't be surprised.

What is shared mutable state?

Then, we tried to understand why mutability is such a big problem. We introduced shared mutable state, which is a variable that is shared between different entities in the codebase and can be mutated by them.

Fighting mutability by using immutable values

Finally, we introduced a more powerful technique to deal with shared mutable states: immutable values. If our functions take only immutable values and return immutable values, we can be sure nothing is unexpectedly mutated.

Using immutable APIs of String and List

At the end, we learned that Java's String is already using this approach because many of its methods return a new value of String. We learned that Scala has built-in support for immutable collections, and we played a bit with List's slice, append, and appendAll functions. We will spend the rest of the book learning about all kinds of immutable values.

> **Functional programming**
> is programming using *pure functions* that manipulate *immutable values*.

Functions | 4
as values

In this chapter

you will learn

- how to pass functions as arguments

- how to use the `sortBy` function

- how to use `map` and `filter` functions

- how to return functions from functions

- how to treat functions as values

- how to use the `foldLeft` function

- how to model immutable data using product types

66 *The most damaging phrase in the language is:*
'we've always done it this way!' **99**

—GRACE HOPPER

Implementing requirements as functions

We spent some time working with pure functions and immutable values. They make up the foundation of functional programming. This chapter focuses on showing how well these two concepts work together. We will discover how helpful it is to think about business requirements in terms of functions and how to treat pure functions as values.

Ranking words

We need to implement a functionality that ranks words in some word-based puzzle game.

> **Requirements for the word ranking**
> — The score of a given word is calculated by giving one point for each letter that is not an 'a'
> — For a given list of words, return a sorted list that starts with the highest-scoring word

Warning
Initial requirements may seem trivial, but be warned that we will be changing them and adding new requirements. This will allow us to check how well our code is prepared for such changes.

As promised we will try to implement both requirements as functions. The first requirement is pretty straight-forward, but the second one needs some more analysis to get it right. Let's start with some pseudocode first.

```
                        score
static int score(String word) {
    return word.replaceAll("a", "").length();
}
```

> Our task is to implement a function called `rankedWords` that satisfies the requirements. This is going to be our approach to all requirements in the book.

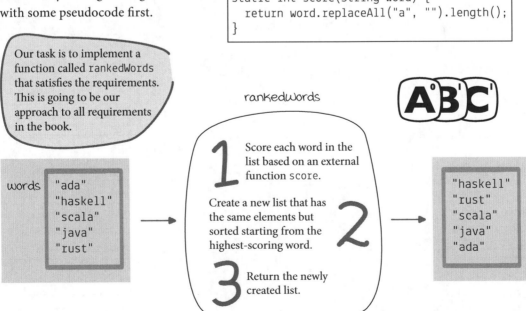

rankedWords

1 Score each word in the list based on an external function score.

2 Create a new list that has the same elements but sorted starting from the highest-scoring word.

3 Return the newly created list.

words
"ada"
"haskell"
"scala"
"java"
"rust"

"haskell"
"rust"
"scala"
"java"
"ada"

Impure functions and mutable values strike back

Our task is to write a function that, for a given list of words, returns a list of exactly the same words but sorted by their score (highest to lowest). We will try a few approaches to this problem and then decide which one is the best and why. Let's start with the very first implementation that comes to mind. We already have a function that returns a score for a given word:

```
static int score(String word) {
  return word.replaceAll("a", "").length();
}
```

rankedWords

1 Score each word in the list based on an external function score.

2 Create a new list that has the same elements but sorted starting from the highest-scoring word.

3 Return the newly created list.

Version #1: Using `Comparator` and `sort`

In Java, when we hear *sort* we usually think *comparator*. Let's follow this intuition and prepare a possible solution to the problem:

```
static Comparator<String> scoreComparator =
  new Comparator<String>() {
    public int compare(String w1, String w2) {
      return Integer.compare(score(w2), score(w1));
    }
  };
```

scoreComparator

compares two strings and prefers the one that has a higher score

Now, given a list of words, we can get the results by using the `sort` method that takes the `Comparator` we created:

```
static List<String> rankedWords(List<String> words) {
  words.sort(scoreComparator);
  return words;
}
```

This box means that the value defined in the text will be used and referenced later in the chapter.

Now, let's test the `rankedWords` function we've just created:

```
List<String> words =
    Arrays.asList("ada", "haskell", "scala", "java", "rust");
List<String> ranking = rankedWords(words);
System.out.println(ranking);
console output: [haskell, rust, scala, java, ada]
```

Note that the score function counts the letters that are different than 'a'. That's why "haskell" scored 6.

It worked! `haskell` is at the top of the ranking because its score is 6. There is one problem though. **We mutate the existing words list inside the function!** Note that the `sort` method returns void, making it obvious that it mutates the argument that we passed. This solution violates the rules of a pure function and invites all the problems we've discussed in previous chapters. We can do better and do it in Java!

Please forgive us if you experienced impure function flashbacks while reading the code that mutates existing values.

Using Java Streams to sort the list

Fortunately, Java enables us to use the `Comparator` we created in a way that doesn't violate the pure function rules: let's use Java Streams!

Version #2: Ranking the words using Streams

We have a function that returns a score for a given word and a `Comparator` that uses this function internally. Nothing needs to be changed there. We can safely use the Stream API and pass the `scoreComparator`.

> **Pure function**
> — It returns only a single value.
> — It calculates the return value based only on its arguments.
> — It doesn't mutate any existing values.

```java
static List<String> rankedWords(
  List<String> words
) {
    return words.stream()        ❶
                .sorted(scoreComparator)    ❷
                .collect(Collectors.toList());    ❸
}
```

❶ Returns a new `Stream`, which *produces* elements from the words list.

❷ Returns a new `Stream`, which *produces* elements from the previous `Stream` but sorts using the provided Comparator.

❸ Returns a new `List` by copying all elements from the previous `Stream`.

This is how the Stream API works. We are *chaining* the method calls. After calling `stream()` on a collection, we get a `Stream` object back. Most of the methods in the `Stream` class return a new `Stream`! And the most important thing: **nothing is mutated in this snippet**. Each method call returns a new immutable object, while `collect` returns a brand new `List`!

> **THIS IS BIG!**
> Some mainstream languages expose APIs that embrace immutability (e.g., Java Streams).

Now that we have a lot better code, let's check if it works as intended.

```java
List<String> words =
    Arrays.asList("ada", "haskell", "scala", "java", "rust");
List<String> ranking = rankedWords(words);
System.out.println(ranking);
```
console output: `[haskell, rust, scala, java, ada]`
```java
System.out.println(words);
```
console output: `[ada, haskell, scala, java, rust]`

ranking is a totally new list that holds the resulting ranked words list.

words list stayed the same. Big win!

Everything looks correct. We have a function that returns only a single value and doesn't mutate any existing values. However, it still uses an external value to compute its result. It uses `scoreComparator`, which is defined outside of the scope of the function. That means the `rankedWords` signature doesn't tell the whole story about what's going on inside. The Stream API helped, but we need more.

Remember when we discussed functions that lie? They lie when their signatures don't tell the whole story about their body.

Function signatures should tell the whole story

When we look at the signature of rankedWords, we may be asking ourselves, **how does this function know how to sort given words**? To answer this question a reader of our code would need to go into the implementation. However, ideally, we'd like to have an explanation in the parameter list, which is also expressed in the second rule of a pure function:

> The function calculates the return value based only on its arguments.

Version #3: Passing algorithms as arguments

In the next iteration of our solution, we need to be able to reason about what's going on inside the function just by looking at its signature. To do that, we need to expose the initially hidden dependency on the scoreComparator and require the Comparator to be passed as a second parameter.

Before

```
static List<String> rankedWords(List<String> words) {
  return
    words.stream()
        .sorted(scoreComparator)
        .collect(Collectors.toList());
}
```

✖ The function calculates the return value based only on its arguments.

After

```
static List<String> rankedWords(Comparator<String> comparator, List<String> words) {
  return
    words.stream()
        .sorted(comparator)
        .collect(Collectors.toList());
}
```

✔ The function calculates the return value based only on its arguments.

Now, the function is completely pure, and we can reason about what it's doing just by looking at its signature. Note that the additional parameter means that we need to modify the way we call the function.

```
List<String> words =
    Arrays.asList("ada", "haskell", "scala", "java", "rust");
List<String> ranking = rankedWords(scoreComparator, words);
System.out.println(ranking);
console output: [haskell, rust, scala, java, ada]
```

> scoreComparator
>
> compares two strings and prefers the one that has a higher score

The rules of a pure function may seem strict or unnecessary at first. However, applying these rules makes our code more readable, testable, and maintainable. And the more we think about these rules when we are programming, the more natural the whole process becomes.

Changing requirements

So far, we have tried to fulfill the initial requirements and adhere to the rules of a pure function. We have been trying to optimize the function toward better readability and maintainability. This is important because real-world codebases are more often read than written. It's also important when business requirements change, and we need to change some code. The easier it is to understand the current code, the easier it is to change it.

Version #4: Changing the ranking algorithm

Let's see how the rankedWords function will do under the new circumstances. Here are the original and additional requirements:

Original requirements	Additional requirements
— The score of a given word is calculated by giving one point for each letter that is not an 'a'. — For a given list of words, return a sorted list that starts with the highest-scoring word.	— A bonus score of 5 needs to be added to the score if the word contains a 'c'. — The old way of scoring (without the bonus) should still be supported in the code.

The scoring algorithm needs some updates. Fortunately, by following the functional approach, we ended up with a bunch of small functions, and that's why some of them won't need to change at all!

score

```
static int score(String word) {
  return word.replaceAll("a", "").length();
}
```

scoreWithBonus

```
static int scoreWithBonus(String word) {
  int base = score(word);
  if (word.contains("c")) return base + 5;
  else return base;
}
```

```
static Comparator<String> scoreComparator =
  new Comparator<String>() {
    public int compare(String w1, String w2) {
      return Integer.compare(score(w2), score(w1));
    }
  };
```

```
static Comparator<String> scoreWithBonusComparator =
  new Comparator<String>() {
    public int compare(String w1, String w2) {
      return Integer.compare(scoreWithBonus(w2),
                             scoreWithBonus(w1));
    }
  };
```

```
rankedWords(scoreComparator, words);
→ [haskell, rust, scala, java, ada]
```

```
rankedWords(scoreWithBonusComparator, words);
→ [scala, haskell, rust, java, ada]
```

We were able to implement the new requirement by providing a new version of Comparator. We reused exactly the same rankedWords function. That's good. We were able to do it because of the new function parameter we introduced previously. This solution works fine, but there seems to be too much duplication, especially between scoreComparator and scoreWithBonusComparator. Let's try to make it even better!

Since we are slowly moving toward the functional world, we will now stop using System.out.println to print results to the console and just use expressions and their values instead.

We just pass the code around!

Streams help our code become more functional by providing ways of doing operations on collections in an immutable way. But it's not the only functional thing that is going on here! The first parameter of the rankedWords function is a Comparator, but if we look closer, we can see that its only responsibility is to convey a behavior, just like a function!

> Java Streams are really great. We will use the ideas behind Java Streams to learn some fundamental concepts of FP.

Take a closer look at what is really going on in our rankedWords function. **By passing a Comparator instance, we pass the specific behavior—not an instance of some data.** We are passing the code responsible for ordering two words! Functions do it too.

```
List<String> rankedWords(Comparator<String> comparator,
                         List<String> words) {
   return words
         .stream()
         .sorted(comparator)
         .collect(Collectors.toList());
}
```

As we can see, the rankedWords function takes a Comparator, which really is just a piece of code responsible for sorting. The cool thing is we can represent this idea in Java and pass a function as Comparator.

```
Comparator<String> scoreComparator =
    (w1, w2) -> Integer.compare(score(w2), score(w1));
```

We can use this technique to cut a lot of code. Have a look:

> All these three code snippets are equivalent. They do exactly the same thing.

```
Comparator<String> scoreComparator =
   new Comparator<String>() {
      public int compare(String w1, String w2) {
         return Integer.compare(score(w2),
                                score(w1));
      }
   };
rankedWords(scoreComparator, words);
→ [haskell, rust, scala, java, ada]
```

```
Comparator<String> scoreComparator =
   (w1, w2) -> Integer.compare(score(w2), score(w1));

rankedWords(scoreComparator, words);
→ [haskell, rust, scala, java, ada]
```

```
rankedWords(
   (w1, w2) -> Integer.compare(score(w2), score(w1));
   words
);
→ [haskell, rust, scala, java, ada]
```

Thanks to Java's function syntax, we can provide (and swap, if requirements change!) a sorting algorithm in just one line of code.

Using Java's Function **values**

Let's investigate Java's Function type in more depth and try to use this
knowledge to make our solution even better. In Java, the Function type
represents a function that takes one parameter and returns one result.
For example, our scoreFunction, which takes a String and returns an
int, could be rewritten as an instance of a Function<String, Integer>.

```
Function<String, Integer> scoreFunction =
    w -> w.replaceAll("a", "").length();
```

← *scoreFunction is a reference to an object in memory that holds a function from String to Integer.*

We can now pass this scoreFunction thing around like a normal value.
We can say that **our function is stored as an immutable value!** We can
treat it in a way similar to any other reference (e.g., words)

> To call this function, we need to use the apply method.

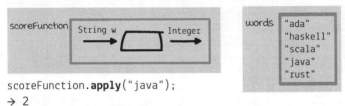

```
scoreFunction.apply("java");
→ 2
```

We can also create another reference to the same value and use it.

```
Function<String, Integer> f = scoreFunction;
f.apply("java");
→ 2
```

> **THIS IS BIG!**
> Functions *stored* as values are what FP is really about.

Note how we use the -> syntax in Java. It defines a function with no name. On the left, there are arguments, and on the right there is a function body.

---

using functions (static methods)

```
static int score(String word) {
  return word.replaceAll("a", "").length();
}
```

We call functions directly by providing the argument. Here, when we call score("java"), we get 2 as a result.

```
score("java");
→ 2
```

```
static boolean isHighScoringWord(String word) {
  return score(word) > 5;
}
```

```
isHighScoringWord("java");
→ false
```

using Function values

```
Function<String, Integer> scoreFunction =
    w -> w.replaceAll("a", "").length();
```

To create a Function value, we need to use the arrow syntax. This definition is equivalent to the one on the left.

```
scoreFunction.apply("java");
→ 2
```

We can call the functions stored as Function values by calling the apply method.

```
Function<String, Boolean> isHighScoringWordFunction =
    w -> scoreFunction.apply(w) > 5;
```

We can reuse Function values in a way similar to how we reuse functions.

```
isHighScoringWordFunction.apply("java");
→ false
```

Using the Function **syntax to deal with code duplication**

Let's try to use this newly acquired skill to get rid of the duplication we currently have in our code.

score
```static int score(String word) { return word.replaceAll("a", "").length(); }```

scoreWithBonus
```static int scoreWithBonus(String word) { int base = score(word); if (word.contains("c")) return base + 5; else return base; }```

```
static Comparator<String> scoreComparator =
    new Comparator<String>() {
      public int compare(String w1, String w2) {
        return Integer.compare(score(w2),
                               score(w1));
      }
    };

rankedWords(scoreComparator, words);
→ [haskell, rust, scala, java, ada]
```

```
static Comparator<String> scoreWithBonusComparator =
    new Comparator<String>() {
      public int compare(String w1, String w2) {
        return Integer.compare(scoreWithBonus(w2),
                               scoreWithBonus(w1));
      }
    };

rankedWords(scoreWithBonusComparator, words);
→   [scala, haskell, rust, java, ada]
```

scoreComparator and scoreWithBonusComparator are very similar—they differ only in calling different scoring functions. Let's see how functions shown above look when we create them using Java's arrow syntax (->). **These functions are equivalent but stored as values**:

```
Comparator<String> scoreComparator =
    (w1, w2) -> Integer.compare(
            score(w2),
            score(w1)
    );
rankedWords(scoreComparator, words);
→ [haskell, rust, scala, java, ada]
```
```
Comparator<String> scoreWithBonusComparator =
    (w1, w2) -> Integer.compare(
            scoreWithBonus(w2),
            scoreWithBonus(w1)
    );
rankedWords(scoreWithBonusComparator, words);
→ [scala, haskell, rust, java, ada]
```

Passing function values to a function (i.e., a static method in Java) that expects a Comparator looks nice and allows us to reuse big chunks of the code, even when business requirements change. Thanks to this feature, we were able to reuse the rankedWords function, which takes both the words parameter and the Comparator parameter. However, there are still some problems we need to address to make the code even better and more maintainable:

— The function we pass to rankedWords as a Comparator looks too complicated for what it does. We should be able to pass the desired sorting algorithm in a more concise and clean way.

— There is still some duplicated code shared between scoreComparator and scoreWithBonusComparator. The difference between them is only the scoring function used. We should be able to make this fact work to our advantage.

To be more precise, Comparator is equivalent to BiFunction, not Function. BiFunction is a type that defines a function with two parameters, while Function is a type for single-parameter functions. We will discuss it further later in the chapter.

Passing user-defined functions as arguments

We'd like our rankedWords function to take something smaller and simpler than the whole Comparator, which looks too complicated for what it does. Moreover, when we have two of them, the majority of the code is duplicated. **What we really want is to just specify the scoring behavior.** Maybe we could just pass the scoring behavior as an argument? Fortunately, we have already learned about the technique that is ideal for this job: the Function. We can pass the scoring behavior as a parameter!

Version #5: Passing the scoring function

We don't have to use Comparator as a parameter. The main functionality that we want to pass to the rankedWords function is *a way to calculate a score for a given word*. This is the only thing that has changed in our code because of the business requirements, and therefore, it should be the only customizable thing. **We achieve customization through parameters.**

Let's try to make the rankedWords function take another function as a parameter and use it to create the words' ranking. We are aiming to have a usage like the one on the right.

```
Function<String, Integer> scoreFunction =
    w -> score(w);
rankedWords(scoreFunction, words);
→ [haskell, rust, scala, java, ada]

Function<String, Integer> scoreWithBonusFunction =
    w -> scoreWithBonus(w);
rankedWords(scoreWithBonusFunction, words);
→ [scala, haskell, rust, java, ada]
```

To achieve this kind of API, we need to get a Function as a parameter and use it to create a Comparator, which is required by the sort method of the Stream class. Please note that we are able to figure out what this function does just by looking at its signature! **It's literally ranking the words using the wordScore scoring algorithm!**

```
static List<String> rankedWords(Function<String, Integer> wordScore,
                                List<String> words) {
  Comparator<String> wordComparator =
    (w1, w2) -> Integer.compare(
      wordScore.apply(w2),
      wordScore.apply(w1)
    );

  return words
    .stream()
    .sorted(wordComparator)
    .collect(Collectors.toList());
}
```

> We take a Function value as a parameter. It means that we allow the scoring behavior to be customizable. The Comparator is created internally using the scoring function provided inside the given wordScore value.

> We return a copy of the incoming list by using the immutable-friendly Java Stream API.

THIS IS BIG! Functions that take functions as parameters are ubiquitous in FP code.

Now our function can be used in a very concise and readable way.

```
rankedWords(w -> score(w), words);
rankedWords(w -> scoreWithBonus(w), words);
```

Note how the caller of the rankedWords function is responsible for providing the scoring algorithm.

Coffee break:
Functions as parameters

It's your turn to use the power of passing functions as parameters to other functions. We will need to add another requirement to the existing `rankedWords` function. But first, let's reiterate what we already have.

Requirement: Ranking words	**Requirement: Possibility of a bonus**
— The score of a given word is calculated by giving one point for each letter that is not an `'a'`.	— A bonus score of 5 needs to be added to the score if the word contains a `'c'`.
— For a given list of words, return a sorted list that starts with the highest-scoring word.	— An old way of scoring (without the bonus) should still be supported in the code.

```
static List<String> rankedWords(Function<String, Integer> wordScore,
                                List<String> words) {
  Comparator<String> wordComparator =
    (w1, w2) -> Integer.compare(
      wordScore.apply(w2),
      wordScore.apply(w1)
    );

  return words
    .stream()
    .sorted(wordComparator)
    .collect(Collectors.toList());

}
```

Exercise: Implement the new requirement

New requirement: Possibility of a penalty
— A penalty score of 7 needs to be subtracted from the score if the word contains an `'s'`.
— Old ways of scoring (with and without the bonus) should still be supported in the code.

Note that this is an additional requirement. All the previous requirements still need to be taken into account.

Your task is to implement a new version of the `rankedWords` function and provide some usage examples in three cases:

   — Ranking the words with just a score function (no bonus and no penalty)
   — Ranking the words with the score + bonus
   — Ranking the words with the score + bonus - penalty

Please think about both a new implementation (body) of `rankedWords` and its API (signature). What does the signature say? Is it self-documenting? How easy it is to figure out what's going on inside your new version?

Coffee break explained: Functions as parameters

Let's focus on the new requirement first. It looks like the rankedWords function doesn't need any change at all! That's because we have already "outsourced" the scoring algorithm to a Function that is passed as an argument.

> **New requirement: Possibility of a penalty**
> — A penalty score of 7 needs to be subtracted from the score if the word contains an 's'.
> — Old ways of scoring (with and without the bonus) should still be supported in the code.

So, we need to write a new function that covers all the addends: base score, bonus, and penalty:

```java
static int scoreWithBonusAndPenalty(String word) {
  int base = score(word);
  int bonus = word.contains("c") ? 5 : 0;
  int penalty = word.contains("s") ? 7 : 0;
  return base + bonus - penalty;
}
```

We use Java's conditional operator, which is an expression that produces a result (in our case, an int). In Java, if is a statement, and we can't use it here. We'll discuss expressions vs statements in chapter 5.

Now, we can just pass this function to rankedWords:

```java
rankedWords(w -> scoreWithBonusAndPenalty(w), words);
→ [java, ada, scala, haskell, rust]
```

The solution is to pass a different function to our unchanged rankedWords function.

We can do even better!

This part of the chapter is about passing functions, but the whole book is about functions and modeling using functions. That's why I can't resist showing you another solution that uses many small independent functions. Each requirement is implemented as a separate function, and all the functions are used when calling rankedWords, thanks to the flexibility of the arrow syntax.

```java
static int bonus(String word) {
  return word.contains("c") ? 5 : 0;
}

static int penalty(String word) {
  return word.contains("s") ? 7 : 0;
}

rankedWords(w -> score(w) + bonus(w) - penalty(w), words);
→ [java, ada, scala, haskell, rust]
```

Again, we just pass a different function to our unchanged rankedWords function, but this time we use arrow syntax to provide the algorithm inline. It's very clean and readable because each requirement has its own place in the code.

This exercise has many correct solutions, and we can't showcase every possible one. If your code looks different, but it returns correct results and you haven't changed anything in the rankedWords function, it's good!

Problems with reading functional Java

Our final solution is very functional in its nature. It respects immutability and pure function rules. And we've done it in Java, proving that it's a very versatile language that's able to express programs in non-object-oriented paradigms as well. That's great because we can learn functional concepts without jumping straight into a new language. Unfortunately, there are also some practical problems with using functional programming in Java: we need to write too much code and use mutable Lists.

Too much code to read

Opponents of writing fully functionally in Java say that this solution is somewhat bloated and contains a lot of *noise*. Let's have a look:

```
static List<String> rankedWords(Function<String, Integer> wordScore,
                                List<String> words) {
    Comparator<String> wordComparator =
        (w1, w2) -> Integer.compare(
            wordScore.apply(w2),
            wordScore.apply(w1)
        );

    return words
        .stream()
        .sorted(wordComparator)
        .collect(Collectors.toList());
}
```

The important bits are in bold. The rest seems to be just a "glue" code.

As we can see, this argument has some merit to it. When it comes to the codebase volume, the most important concern is the reader of the code—not the writer. **Code is read far more often than written. Therefore, we should always optimize our code for reading.** That means that if we are able to write clean, self-descriptive code using fewer characters, we should usually follow this path.

We still use mutable Lists

Our solution is a function—a pure one—but it still uses mutable Lists to get arguments and to return results. We make sure not to mutate the incoming List inside the function by using the Java Stream API, but the readers of our code don't know that by looking at the signature. They see Lists there, and they can't safely assume they are not mutated without looking at the implementation.

Passing functions in Scala

It's about time we move back to writing some Scala code. Let's fire up the REPL and code together! Over the course of the next few pages, we will first implement the rankedWords in Scala and then implement even more requirements using its special function syntax.

As a quick reminder, let's first define and use some small functions in Scala. Then, we'll try to pass one of them as an argument to a standard library function defined in Scala's List: sortBy. For now, please pay attention to how expressive the code is, and don't worry if you don't know how sortBy works internally—we'll dive into the details soon.

> ### Final reminder: Using code snippets from this book
>
> We have been doing a lot of Java in the book so far, and since we are now moving to the FP Scala code, it's a perfect place for the final reminder that > at the beginning is a sign that you should execute the Scala REPL in your terminal (by writing sbt console) and then follow the listing. Lines that contain **simplified REPL responses** are marked as →. REPL responses contain the results of the previously entered computation (expression).

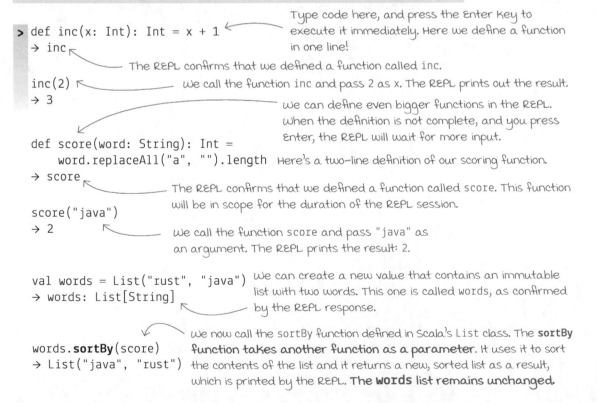

```
> def inc(x: Int): Int = x + 1
→ inc
```
Type code here, and press the Enter key to execute it immediately. Here we define a function in one line!

The REPL confirms that we defined a function called inc.

```
inc(2)
→ 3
```
We call the function inc and pass 2 as x. The REPL prints out the result.

We can define even bigger functions in the REPL. When the definition is not complete, and you press Enter, the REPL will wait for more input.

```
def score(word: String): Int =
    word.replaceAll("a", "").length
→ score
```
Here's a two-line definition of our scoring function.

The REPL confirms that we defined a function called score. This function will be in scope for the duration of the REPL session.

```
score("java")
→ 2
```
We call the function score and pass "java" as an argument. The REPL prints the result: 2.

```
val words = List("rust", "java")
→ words: List[String]
```
We can create a new value that contains an immutable list with two words. This one is called words, as confirmed by the REPL response.

```
words.sortBy(score)
→ List("java", "rust")
```
We now call the sortBy function defined in Scala's List class. The **sortBy** function takes another function as a parameter. It uses it to sort the contents of the list and it returns a new, sorted list as a result, which is printed by the REPL. **The words list remains unchanged.**

Deep dive into sortBy

Let's have a closer look at the sortBy function. We will try to intuitively understand what happens inside this function by looking at our previous REPL session from a different perspective:

1
```
def score(word: String): Int =
    word.replaceAll("a", "").length
```
We defined a function score that takes a String and returns an Int. There's nothing new here.

2
```
val words = List("rust", "java")
```
We defined a list words that holds multiple String values. Again, this isn't the first time we've done something like this.

3
```
val sortedWords = words.sortBy(score)
```
We defined a new list by calling the sortBy method on words. sortBy takes a function that takes a String and returns an Int, calls this function on each element of words, creates a new list and fills it with the elements from words but sorted usingthe corresponding Int value.

4
```
List("rust", "java").sortBy(score)
```
Note that we don't have to define words to execute sortBy. sortBy can be executed directly on List("rust", "java"), which is the same immutable list but used only here. The expression on the left returns exactly the same result.

As you see, we are able to sort the immutable List("rust", "java") by calling sortBy, which takes one parameter—a function. This function in turn takes a String and returns an Int. The sortBy function uses this function internally to sort the items in the list:

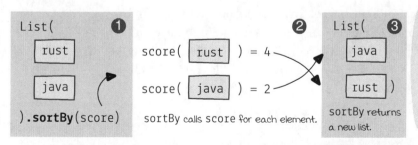

In Scala, integers have default ordering already defined. Here, sortBy implicitly *knows* to sort integers in ascending order. (It is achieved using the language feature called *implicits*.)

Q Wait, a function that takes a function that takes a String?

A Yes, I know it's a mouthful. This is one of the hardest things to learn in functional programming. It's also very rewarding! We will practice it a lot until it becomes second nature for you.

Signatures with function parameters in Scala

Given our freshly acquired knowledge about the sortBy function defined in immutable Scala Lists, let's try to rewrite the Java solution in Scala.

Here's the Java code we ended up with:

```java
static List<String> rankedWords(Function<String, Integer> wordScore,
                                List<String> words) {
  Comparator<String> wordComparator =
    (w1, w2) -> Integer.compare(
      wordScore.apply(w2),
      wordScore.apply(w1)
    );

  return words
    .stream()
    .sorted(wordComparator)
    .collect(Collectors.toList());
}
```

We concluded that it's a nice solution, because it doesn't mutate the incoming List and uses a Function object to parametrize the ranking algorithm. However, it's still a lot of code for such a small functionality, and Java's Lists are still mutable, so this solution may cause some problems for other teammates.

Now, let's write the rankedWords function in Scala, starting with its signature and then moving on to the implementation.

The signature

As you probably remember, when coding using pure functions, we need to make sure that their signatures are telling the whole truth about what they are doing inside. The signature of a pure function doesn't lie, and that's why **the reader of our code can just look at the signature and completely understand what's going on inside, without even looking at the implementation**. So, what does the signature of the rankedWords function look like in Scala compared to Java?

THIS IS BIG! Functions that don't lie are crucial for maintainable codebases.

wordScore is a function
that takes a String and returns an Int.

```scala
def rankedWords(wordScore: String => Int,
                words: List[String]): List[String]
```

words is an immutable
List of Strings.

The function returns a
new List of Strings.

In Scala, we use the double-arrow symbol (=>) to mark parameters that are functions (e.g., String => Int above). In Java, we had to write Function<String, Integer>to achieve a similar result.

Passing functions as arguments in Scala

We have the signature of the `rankedWords` function. Now, it's time to provide an implementation. Luckily, we already know how to sort lists in Scala. We'll use the `sortBy` function!

First attempt: Using `sortBy`

Here's our score function again:

```scala
def score(word: String): Int =
    word.replaceAll("a", "").length
```

> **Requirement: Ranking words**
> — The score of a given word is calculated by giving one point for each letter that is not an `'a'`.
> — For a given list of words, return a sorted list that starts with the highest-scoring word.

However, if we use it directly in `sortBy`, we will get an incorrect result.

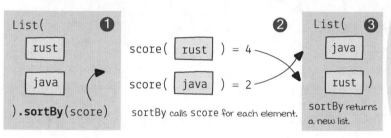

In Scala, integers have default implicit ordering already defined. It orders numbers in ascending order. That's why `sortBy` *knows* that the element with a lower score of 2 should be first.

`rust`'s score is higher than `java`'s (4 to 2), but `rust` is listed after `java` in the results. That's because `sortBy` sorts in ascending order by default. To counter that, we could use an old trick that makes the score negative.

```scala
def negativeScore(word: String): Int = -score(word)
```

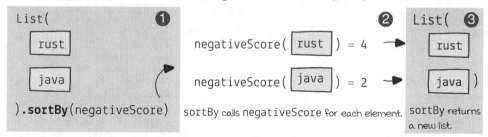

This works fine, and we can even use it inside our implementation:

```scala
def rankedWords(wordScore: String => Int,
                words: List[String]): List[String] = {
  def negativeScore(word: String): Int = -wordScore(word)
  words.sortBy(negativeScore)
}
```

This solves our business problem, but it feels hacky. **It's not the clean code we'd like to have in our projects.** We can do better than that, but before we try a new approach, let's practice what we've learned so far.

We can define functions anywhere in our code in Scala. Here we are defining the negativeScore function inside the rankedWords function. This internal function is available only inside the body of rankedWords.

Practicing function passing

It's time to **pass some functions in Scala**. Please use the Scala REPL.

Sort the list of `String`s by their length in *ascending* order.

> 1

```
input: List("scala", "rust", "ada")

expected output: List("ada", "rust", "scala")
```

Sort the list of `String`s provided below by number of the letter `'s'` inside these `String`s, in *ascending* order.

> 2

```
input: List("rust", "ada")    expected output: List("ada", "rust")
```

Sort the list of `Int`s provided below in *descending* order.

> 3

```
input: List(5, 1, 2, 4, 3)    expected output: List(5, 4, 3, 2, 1)
```

Similarly to the second one, sort the list of `String`s provided below by number of the letter `'s'` inside these `String`s but in *descending* order.

> 4

```
input: List("ada", "rust")    output: List("rust", "ada")
```

Answers

```
> def len(s: String): Int = s.length
  → len
  List("scala", "rust", "ada").sortBy(len)
  → List("ada", "rust", "scala")
```

Note that everything in FP is an expression, and REPL helps us remember that. Each line we input is evaluated, and we get a result. Here, the result is a confirmation that function len was defined. We will only show these "definition" responses in crucial listings, omitting them in the remaining ones.

> 1

```
  def numberOfS(s: String): Int =
    s.length - s.replaceAll("s", "").length
  → numberOfS
  List("rust", "ada").sortBy(numberOfS)
  → List("ada", "rust")
```

> 2

```
  def negative(i: Int): Int = -i
  → negative
  List(5, 1, 2, 4, 3).sortBy(negative)
  → List(5, 4, 3, 2, 1)
```

> 3

```
  def negativeNumberOfS(s: String): Int = -numberOfS(s)
  → negativeNumberOfS
  List("ada", "rust").sortBy(negativeNumberOfS)
  → List("rust", "ada")
```

> 4

Embracing declarative programming

We managed to implement the `rankedWords` in a few lines of Scala code, but we can do better. Let's have a look at the code we've written so far and make sure we understand why it's still not good enough.

By "hacky," we mean a "working solution developed using a trick." The trick here is the negative scoring system.

Ranking the words in a hacky way

```scala
def rankedWords(wordScore: String => Int,
                words: List[String]): List[String] = {
  def negativeScore(word: String): Int = -wordScore(word)
  words.sortBy(negativeScore)
}
```

Developer reads:

To calculate the score for a word, first make sure we can create a negative score, then use this negative score to sort the words.

These are just two lines of code, but a new developer who sees this code for the first time needs to think very carefully. They need to care about the score being negative, which is just an implementation detail of sorting in reverse order. It's a recipe for reversing the sorting order. And whenever we care about how something is achieved, instead of what needs to be achieved, we are making the code less readable.

Ranking the words declaratively

The declarative approach focuses on what needs to be done—not how. We can implement `rankedWords` by just stating what needs to be done. In this case we are saying we need the strings sorted by `wordScore` in a natural order (ascending) and reversed.

```scala
def rankedWords(wordScore: String => Int,
                words: List[String]): List[String] = {
  words.sortBy(wordScore).reverse
}
```

Developer reads:

The ranked words are sorted by score and reversed.

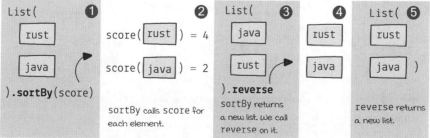

❶ List(
rust
java
).**sortBy**(score)

sortBy calls score for each element.

❷ score(rust) = 4
score(java) = 2

❸ List(
java
rust
).**reverse**

sortBy returns a new list. We call reverse on it.

❹ rust
java

reverse returns a new list.

❺ List(
rust
java)

Declarative code is usually more succinct and more comprehensible than imperative code. This approach makes the `rankedWords` function far more concise and readable.

Passing functions to custom-made functions

Our final version of rankedWords written in Scala is a pure function that uses immutable Lists and has a signature that tells the whole truth about its body. So far so good! What we have is this:

```scala
def rankedWords(wordScore: String => Int,
                words: List[String]): List[String] = {
  words.sortBy(wordScore).reverse
}
```

But how would we go about *using* this function? Exactly the same way as we did when we passed functions to the standard library's sortBy (i.e., by putting the name of the function as a parameter).

> ```scala
> def score(word: String): Int = word.replaceAll("a", "").length
> rankedWords(score, words)
> → List("haskell", "rust", "scala", "java", "ada")
> ```

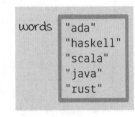

words   "ada"
        "haskell"
        "scala"
        "java"
        "rust"

Let's compare this solution to the Java version we previously came up with and try to recap and compare how all the requirements are fulfilled in both versions. Note that we'll add even more features soon.

Java

```java
List<String> rankedWords(
  Function<String, Integer> wordScore,
  List<String> words
) {
  Comparator<String> wordComparator =
    (w1, w2) -> Integer.compare(
      wordScore.apply(w2),
      wordScore.apply(w1)
    );

  return words.stream()
    .sorted(wordComparator)
    .collect(Collectors.toList());
}
```

Scala

```scala
def rankedWords(
  wordScore: String => Int,
  words: List[String]
): List[String] = {
  words.sortBy(wordScore).reverse
}
```

Requirement #1 Rank the words by the number of letters different than 'a'.

```java
static int score(String word) {
  return word.replaceAll("a", "").length();
}

rankedWords(w -> score(w), words);
→ [haskell, rust, scala, java, ada]
```

```scala
def score(word: String): Int =
  word.replaceAll("a", "").length

rankedWords(score, words)
→ List("haskell", "rust", "scala", "java", "ada")
```

Requirement #2 Additionally, if a word contains a letter 'c', it gets a bonus 5 points.

```java
static int scoreWithBonus(String word) {
  int base = score(word);
  if (word.contains("c"))
    return base + 5;
  else
    return base;
}

rankedWords(w -> scoreWithBonus(w), words);
→ [scala, haskell, rust, java, ada]
```

```scala
def scoreWithBonus(word: String): Int = {
  val base = score(word)
  if (word.contains("c")) base + 5 else base
}

rankedWords(scoreWithBonus, words)
→ List("scala", "haskell", "rust", "java", "ada")
```

Small functions and their responsibilities

Before we move on to implementing more features in our word-ranking code, let's stop for a bit and talk about *functional software design*. In this book we want to learn how to use pure functions as the go-to tools when designing and implementing new requirements. Each requirement in this book is implemented as a function—and this doesn't change even when we get to more advanced requirements later on!

Optimizing for readability

The main reason programmers are focusing on software design is to make it maintainable. For a piece of code to be maintainable, it needs to be easily understood by programmers on our team, so they can change it quickly and with certainty. That's why we focus on making the code readable. We apply the same general rules of good design in functional programming as in other programming paradigms. The difference is that we apply them on the function level. Therefore, **we focus on making our functions implement one small business requirement each.**

What's wrong with scoreWithBonus then?

Here's our scoreWithBonus function. What's the problem with it? It uses score inside but also adds some additional logic on top of it (calculating the bonus). That means it does more than just one thing.

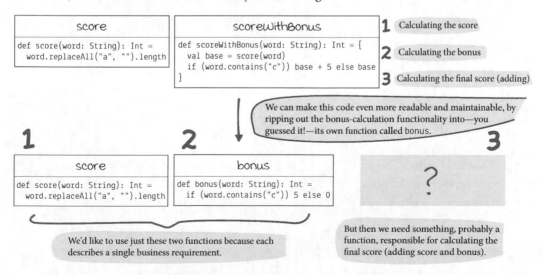

Passing functions inline

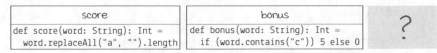

score	bonus	
`def score(word: String): Int =` `    word.replaceAll("a", "").length`	`def bonus(word: String): Int =` `    if (word.contains("c")) 5 else 0`	?

So how do we combine results of the `score` function and `bonus` function? We need a technique that is both effective and readable but **doesn't require a lot of ceremony**. We've already used this technique in Java: **anonymous functions**. They are usually pretty concise one-liners that don't need to be named because it's very obvious what they do.

> As a counter-example, creating a new named function with several lines of code, like `scoreWithBonus`, is a lot of ceremony.

We can define and pass a function to another function in one line of code inside a parameter list. Look at the code comparison below to see how to pass anonymous functions inline in both languages.

Requirement #1 Rank the words by the number of letters different than 'a'.

Java

```java
static int score(String word) {
  return word.replaceAll("a", "").length();
}

rankedWords(w -> score(w), words);
→ [haskell, rust, scala, java, ada]
```

Scala

```scala
def score(word: String): Int =
  word.replaceAll("a", "").length

rankedWords(score, words)
→ List("haskell", "rust", "scala", "java", "ada")
```

Requirement #2 Additionally, if a word contains a letter 'c', it gets a bonus 5 points.
Using a separate named function:

```java
static int scoreWithBonus(String word) {
  int base = score(word);
  if (word.contains("c"))
    return base + 5;
  else
    return base;
}

rankedWords(w -> scoreWithBonus(w), words);
→ [scala, haskell, rust, java, ada]
```

```scala
def scoreWithBonus(word: String): Int = {
  val base = score(word)
  if (word.contains("c")) base + 5 else base
}

rankedWords(scoreWithBonus, words)
→ List("scala", "haskell", "rust", "java", "ada")
```

> Recap of what we previously did

Requirement #2 Additionally, if a word contains a letter 'c', it gets a bonus 5 points.
Using an ananonymous function passed inline:

```java
static int bonus(String word) {
  return word.contains("c") ? 5 : 0;
}

rankedWords(w -> score(w) + bonus(w), words);
→ [scala, haskell, rust, java, ada]
```

```scala
def bonus(word: String): Int = {
  if (word.contains("c")) 5 else 0
}

rankedWords(w => score(w) + bonus(w), words)
→ List("scala", "haskell", "rust", "java", "ada")
```

> We define a new function that encodes the business requirement of a bonus. Then we use it together with the score function inside the anonymous function passed inline.

Note that we should pass only very small functions—simple, straightforward one-liners—as anonymous functions. Adding `score` and `bonus` is a perfect example. You can't read it wrong. And when you pass it as an argument, the code becomes more concise and readable.

Coffee break: Passing functions in Scala

It's your turn to use the power of passing functions as arguments to other functions. We have done this exercise before using Java. Now it's time to implement the new requirement using Scala and its built-in immutability. We will need to add another requirement to the existing rankedWords function. But first, let's reiterate what we have already done so far.

Requirement: Ranking words

— The score of a given word is calculated by giving one point for each letter that is not an 'a'.

— For a given list of words, return a sorted list that starts with the highest-scoring word.

```scala
def rankedWords(wordScore: String => Int,
                words: List[String]): List[String] = {
  words.sortBy(wordScore).reverse
}

def score(word: String): Int = word.replaceAll("a", "").length
```

This requirement was implemented using two pure functions.

Requirement: Possibility of a bonus

— A bonus score of 5 needs to be added to the score if the word contains a 'c'.

— An old way of scoring (without the bonus) should still be supported in the code.

```scala
def bonus(word: String): Int = if (word.contains("c")) 5 else 0
```

This requirement needed just one additional function.

Exercise: Implement the new requirement

Similarly to what you already coded in Java, you need to implement the penalty functionality. Before you start, as a hint, first try to show how rankedWords is meant to be used for the score and bonus scenario.

New requirement: Possibility of a penalty

— A penalty score of 7 needs to be subtracted from the score if the word contains an 's'.

— Old ways of scoring (with and without the bonus) should still be supported in the code.

Your tasks

— Show how to rank the words using the score function (no bonus and no penalty).

— Show how to rank the words using the score and bonus functions (no penalty).

— **Implement a new function that fulfills the new requirement**.

— Show how to rank the words with bonus and penalty requirements.

Coffee break explained: Passing functions in Scala

Let's go through all four tasks, one by one.

Using rankedWords with score

This is a warm-up task to make sure you remember how we create and pass *named functions* in Scala.

```
def score(word: String): Int =
  word.replaceAll("a", "").length
```

```
rankedWords(score, words)
→ List("haskell", "rust", "scala", "java", "ada")
```

> **Requirement: Ranking words**
> — The score of a given word is calculated by giving one point for each letter that is not an 'a'.
> — For a given list of words, return a sorted list that starts with the highest-scoring word.

If we have a named function that takes a String and returns an Int, we can pass it by stating its name.

Using rankedWords with score and bonus

In the second warm-up task, we need to add the results of two functions; therefore, we can't pass them by name. So we need to define a new *anonymous function* that does the addition and pass it using the function syntax (=>).

```
def bonus(word: String): Int = if (word.contains("c")) 5 else 0
```

```
rankedWords(w => score(w) + bonus(w), words)
→ List("scala", "haskell", "rust", "java", "ada")
```

> **Requirement: Possibility of a bonus**
> — A bonus score of 5 needs to be added to the score if the word contains a 'c'.
> — An old way of scoring (without the bonus) should still be supported in the code.

Here we need to define an anonymous function that takes a String (named w) and returns an Int. We provide its body inline.

Implementing the new requirement

Now it's time to do new things. In this book, we teach functional programming and functional software design. It should be pretty obvious by now that when we ask about implementing a new requirement, we expect a new function! Hence:

```
def penalty(word: String): Int =
  if (word.contains("s")) 7 else 0
```

> **New requirement: Possibility of a penalty**
> — A penalty score of 7 needs to be subtracted from the score if the word contains an 's'.
> — Old ways of scoring (with and without the bonus) should still be supported in the code.

It's yet another very simple function that implements the requirement directly. Are you bored? Well, maintainable code should be boring. That's something we all should aim for.

Using rankedWords with score, bonus, and penalty

Because of all those warmups, we now know how to use the new function to fulfill the new requirement. Here's a very readable anonymous function:

```
rankedWords(w => score(w) + bonus(w) - penalty(w), words)
→ List("java", "scala", "ada", "haskell", "rust"))
```

We define an anonymous function that takes a String (named w) and returns an Int.

What else can we achieve just by passing functions?

Q OK, I get it! We can sort things by passing a function as an argument. Is this the only thing this new function-passing technique is able to do?

A We have sorted many lists in this chapter, so many that someone may think that sorting is the only thing we can do by passing functions. But they would be mistaken! We will use functions as parameters to fulfill many requirements in this chapter and beyond! Furthermore, we won't be sorting anything in the foreseeable future—I promise.

The technique of passing functions as arguments is ubiquitous in functional programming. We will learn its other applications by implementing even more features inside our word-ranking system.

Let's see how a hypothetical conversation between a person requesting features and person implementing them could look in the case of the `rankedWords` function we have been working with.

As you can see, it's been pretty straightforward until now. We have been just passing functions to the `sortBy` function, but it won't do this time. Can we implement this new feature in the same concise and readable way? Yes, we can! We'll implement this and many more features next!

Applying a function to each element of a list

We now have a new requirement to implement.

> **New requirement: Get the scores**
> — We need to know the score of each word in the list of words.
> — The function responsible for ranking should still work the same (we cannot change any existing function).

As a reference: The solution in imperative Java

From now on we won't be solving problems in Java, but in some cases we will still provide for reference imperative solutions in Java, so you can quickly compare how they differ and draw conclusions for yourself.

```java
static List<Integer> wordScores(
  Function<String, Integer> wordScore,
  List<String> words
) {
  List<Integer> result = new ArrayList<>();
  for(String word : words) {
    result.add(wordScore.apply(word));
  }
  return result;
}
```

We create a new list that we will be filling with the resulting values.

We apply a given function for each element, using the for loop. The result of the function is added to the resulting list.

As you can see, the code above still has the same problems.

— It uses mutable collections (`ArrayList`).

— The code is not very concise. Intuitively, there is far too much code to read for such a small feature.

Spoiler alert! The list of problems will almost definitely be the same: mutable collections, impure functions, and/or too much code.

As a reference: The solution in Java using Streams

Of course, we can also write a somewhat better solution using Java Streams:

```java
static List<Integer> wordScores(
  Function<String, Integer> wordScore,
  List<String> words
) {
  return words.stream()
    .map(wordScore).collect(Collectors.toList());
}
```

Using stream() enables us to work on a copy of the incoming list. We use the Streams map to apply a function to each element. If you don't know map, keep reading.

Usually, we recommend Streams for these kinds of solutions because they don't mutate any existing values. However, we won't be providing reference Java examples using Streams. We will be providing generic, non-Streams versions of reference Java code because it's how it's done in other imperative languages and is easier to compare.

Applying a function to each element of a list using `map`

The new requirement can be quickly implemented using the `map` function, which is ubiquitous in functional programming. It's very similar to the `sortBy` function we have already met because it also takes just one parameter, and this parameter happens to be a function!

Let's look at the implementation of the new requirement using Scala and its built-in immutable `List` that has a `map` function.

```scala
def wordScores(wordScore: String => Int,
               words: List[String]): List[Int] = {
  words.map(wordScore)
}
```

Note how we change the List of Strings into a List of Ints without any hassle.

As you can see, it's very similar to the Java Streams version. What `map` does is **it takes each element of the list and applies the function to it, saving the result in a new list that is returned**. So, again, it doesn't mutate anything. The Scala `List` API supports immutability.

The signature

Let's dive deep into the code and see how it works underneath. As always, we start with the function signature to get a feeling of what's inside.

wordScore is a function
that takes a `String` and returns an `Int`.

```scala
def wordScores(wordScore: String => Int,
               words: List[String]): List[Int]
```

words is an immutable   The function returns a
List of Strings.   new List of Ints.

The body

The body of the function consists of just the call to `map`, which does all the heavy lifting. Assuming that `words` contain `"rust"` and `"java"` and the function passed as `wordScore` returns a number of letters different than `'a'`, here's what happens.

`map` is used instead of the for loop we needed in the imperative version.

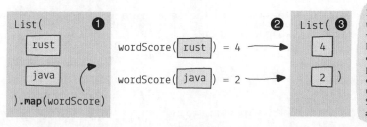

Note how we use the `wordScore` function without even knowing what it does! It's passed as a parameter so it could be anything until it takes a `String` and returns an `Int`.

Getting to know map

There are few things related to the map function that are always true. Let's discuss them now. map takes only one parameter, and this parameter is a function. If the List contains Strings, this function needs to take one String and return a value of the same or different type. The type of values returned by this function is exactly the type of elements the returned List contains. For example:

```
def wordScores(wordScore: String => Int,
               words: List[String]): List[Int] = {
    words.map(wordScore)
}
```

> Note how we change the List of Strings into a List of Ints by providing a function that take String and returns an Int.

map is called on words, which is a List[String]. That means the function that we pass to map needs to take an element of type String. Fortunately, wordScore takes Strings! The type of elements returned by wordScore is exactly the type of elements the List returned from map will contain. wordScore returns Ints; therefore, map returns a List[Int].

We will use many diagrams in this book for each generic function we meet. We will not use Strings and Ints in those diagrams. We will denote such things more generically: Lists will contain values of type A (i.e., List[A]), functions will take elements of type A and return elements of type B, and map will return List[B].

> In our case A is String and B is Int.

```
List[A].map(f: A => B): List[B]
```

Applies the function passed as f to each element of the original list of elements A, producing a new list with new elements of type B. Sizes of the incoming and resulting lists are the same. The ordering of elements is preserved.

> map preserves the ordering, which means that if an element was before another element in the original list, its mapped version will be before as well.

Using map **in practice**

Let's look at our solution once again and try to use it with the real scoring function to make sure we are headed in the right direction.

```
> val words = List("ada", "haskell", "scala", "java", "rust")
  wordScores(w => score(w) + bonus(w) - penalty(w), words)
  → List(1, -1, 1, 2, -3)
```

See? Passing functions is very effective. Now, it's your turn to do it.

> **score**
> gets a word and returns its score

> **bonus**
> gets a word and returns its bonus

> **penalty**
> gets a word and returns its penalty

Practicing map

It's time to **pass some functions to the map function**. Again, please use the Scala REPL to make sure using map becomes second nature for you:

Return lengths of the given Strings.

```
input: List("scala", "rust", "ada")   output: List(5, 4, 3)
```

1

Return the number of the letter 's' inside the given Strings.

```
input: List("rust", "ada")   output: List(1, 0)
```

2

Negate all the given Ints, and return them as a new List.

```
input: List(5, 1, 2, 4, 0)   output: List(-5, -1, -2, -4, 0)
```

3

Double all the given Ints, and return them as a new List.

```
input: List(5, 1, 2, 4, 0)   output: List(10, 2, 4, 8, 0)
```

4

Answers

```
> def len(s: String): Int = s.length
→ len
List("scala", "rust", "ada").map(len)
→ List(5, 4, 3)
```

1

```
def numberOfS(s: String): Int =
  s.length - s.replaceAll("s", "").length
→ numberOfS
List("rust", "ada").map(numberOfS)
→ List(1, 0)
```

2

```
def negative(i: Int): Int = -i
→ negative
List(5, 1, 2, 4, 0).map(negative)
→ List(-5, -1, -2, -4, 0)
```

3

```
def double(i: Int): Int = 2 * i
→ double
List(5, 1, 2, 4, 0).map(double)
→ List(10, 2, 4, 8, 0)
```

4

Learn once, use everywhere

When you look at the two functions we have created in this chapter, they have many things in common.

```
def rankedWords(wordScore: String => Int,
                words: List[String]): List[String] = {
  words.sortBy(wordScore).reverse
}


def wordScores(wordScore: String => Int,
               words: List[String]): List[Int] = {
  words.map(wordScore)
}
```

It's not a coincidence. The pattern of **defining a function that takes a function as parameter is very useful in many more contexts—not just for operations on collections**. For now, we are using collections as a first step to build an intuition for this pattern. When the intuition is built, you will see an opportunity to customize your functions with functional parameters almost everywhere, even beyond collections.

> **THIS IS BIG!**
> Functions that take functions as parameters are ubiquitous in FP code.

What else can we achieve by passing functions?

Now, let's go back to the hypothetical conversation between a person requesting features and a person implementing them casually by passing functions as parameters.

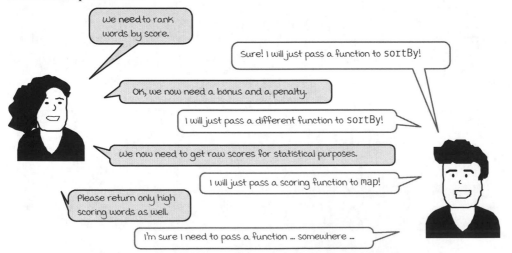

We have been passing functions to sortBy and map functions, and now we have yet another requirement! Can we implement this new feature in the same concise and readable way, passing a function to another function?

Returning parts of the list based on a condition

We now have a new requirement to implement.

> **New requirement: Return high-scoring words**
> — We need to return a list of words that have a score higher than 1 (i.e., high score).
> — Functionalities implemented so far should still work the same (we cannot change any existing function).

Quick exercise: The signature

We try to convey functional programming design principles in this book. That's why we always start designing new features from the function's signature. It's about time you try to figure out the signature yourself, directly from the requirements above. Please stop reading for a while, and try to answer this: **what would the signature of a function called highScoringWords look like in Scala?**

Answer in the discussion.

As a reference: The solution in imperative Java

Before we implement the functional solution, let's take a look at how an imperative Java solution would look and what kind of problems it would have.

```java
static List<String> highScoringWords(
  Function<String, Integer> wordScore,
  List<String> words
) {
  List<String> result = new ArrayList<>();
  for (String word : words) {
    if (wordScore.apply(word) > 1)
      result.add(word);
  }
  return result;
}
```

We create a new list that we will be filling with the resulting values.

We apply the function for each element using a for loop. The result of the function is added to the resulting list if the condition is satisfied.

Again, the code above has the same problems:

— It uses mutable collections (`ArrayList`).
— The code is not very concise. Intuitively, there is far too much code to read for such a small feature.

The list of problems contains the same, usual suspects.

The signature in Scala

In Scala (and other FP languages), we can use a `List` that is immutable.

```scala
def highScoringWords(wordScore: String => Int,
                     words: List[String]): List[String]
```

Returning parts of the list using `filter`

You have probably already guessed that the new requirement can be quickly implemented using a function from `List`. You are right! This function is called `filter`. It's very similar to the `sortBy` and `map` functions we have already met because it also takes just one parameter, and this parameter happens to be a function!

Let's look at the implementation of the new requirement using Scala and its built-in immutable `List` that has a `filter` function:

```scala
def highScoringWords(wordScore: String => Int,
                     words: List[String]): List[String] = {
  words.filter(word => wordScore(word) > 1)
}
```

We provide a condition for each element. If the condition is true, the element ends up in the resulting list.

What `filter` does is **take each element of the list and apply the provided condition to it, returning only elements that satisfy this condition**. Again, it doesn't mutate anything. The Scala `List` API supports immutability, so the returned list is a fresh list of elements that satisfied the condition we provided as a function to the `filter` function.

The signature

`wordScore` is a function that takes a `String` and returns an `Int`.

```scala
def highScoringWords(wordScore: String => Int,
                     words: List[String]): List[String]
```

`words` is an immutable List of Strings.

The function returns a new List of Strings.

The body

The body of the function consists of just the call to `filter`, which takes a function that returns a `Boolean`. Assuming that `words` contain `"rust"` and `"java"`, and the function passed as `wordScore` is our production function with bonuses and penalties, here's what happens.

`filter` is used instead of the for loop we needed in the imperative version.

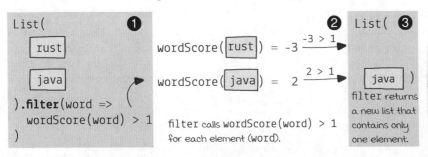

Again, note how we use the `wordScore` function without even knowing what it does! It's passed as a parameter so it could be anything until it takes a `String` and returns an `Int`.

Getting to know `filter`

`filter` takes only one parameter, and this parameter is a function. If the List contains `Strings`, this function needs to take one `String`. However, unlike `map`, this function must always return a `Boolean` value, which is used to decide whether a particular element should be included in the resulting list or not. The type of values returned by `filter` is exactly the same as the type of elements in the original List. For example:

```
def highScoringWords(wordScore: String => Int,
                     words: List[String]): List[String] = {
  words.filter(word => wordScore(word) > 1)  ⟵
}
```

filter takes one parameter that is a function. This function needs to take a String and return a Boolean.

`filter` is called on `words`, which is a `List[String]`. That means the function that we pass to `filter` needs to take an element of type `String`. `wordScore` takes `Strings`, but it returns `Ints`, so we need to create a new function out of it—a function that takes `Strings` and returns `Booleans`.

```
word => wordScore(word) > 1
```

We use double-arrow syntax to create an anonymous inline function, which returns `true` if the score of the given word is higher than 1 and `false` otherwise. You can think of the function passed to `filter` as a decision function. It decides what should be included in the result.

> `List[A].filter(f: A => Boolean): List[A]`
>
> **Applies the function passed as f to each element of the original list of elements A, producing a new list with all the elements of type A for which f returned `true`. Sizes of the incoming and resulting lists can be different. The ordering of elements is preserved.**
>
> `List(☐ ▨ ■).filter( ☐ => yes or no? )`
> `→ List(☐ ■)`

filter preserves the ordering, which means that if an element was before another element in the original list, it will be before it in the resulting list, assuming both are included.

Using `filter` in practice

Now that we got to know `filter` better, let's try to use our new function.

```
> val words = List("ada", "haskell", "scala", "java", "rust")
  highScoringWords(w => score(w) + bonus(w) - penalty(w), words)
  → List("java")
```

Only `java` has a total score higher than 1 (2, to be exact). We reused all the scoring functions again. The ability to pass functions saved the day.

score
`def score(word: String): Int =` `  word.replaceAll("a", "").length`

bonus
`def bonus(word: String): Int =` `  if (word.contains("c")) 5 else 0`

penalty
`def penalty(word: String): Int =` `  if (word.contains("s")) 7 else 0`

Practicing `filter`

It's time to **pass some functions to the `filter` function**. Again, please use the Scala REPL to make sure you really grok the `filter` function:

Return words that are shorter than five characters.

```
input: List("scala", "rust", "ada")    output: List("rust", "ada")
```

1

Return words that have more than two of the letter 's'.

```
input: List("rust", "ada")    output: List()
```

2

Return a new `List` with only odd numbers.

```
input: List(5, 1, 2, 4, 0)    output: List(5, 1)
```

3

Return a new `List` with all numbers larger than 4.

```
input: List(5, 1, 2, 4, 0)    output: List(5)
```

4

Answers

```
> def len(s: String): Int = s.length
→ len
List("scala", "rust", "ada").filter(word => len(word) < 5)
→ List("rust", "ada")
```

1

```
def numberOfS(s: String): Int =
    s.length - s.replaceAll("s", "").length
→ numberOfS
List("rust", "ada").filter(word => numberOfS(word) > 2)
→ List()
```

2

```
def odd(i: Int): Boolean = i % 2 == 1
→ odd
List(5, 1, 2, 4, 0).filter(odd)
→ List(5, 1)
```

Note that we can use the function by name only if it returns a Boolean. If not, we need to create an inline anonymous function.

3

```
def largerThan4(i: Int): Boolean = i > 4
→ largerThan4
List(5, 1, 2, 4, 0).filter(largerThan4)
→ List(5)
```

4

Our journey so far ...

Before we move on to the next topic, let's stop for a moment and think about what we've learned and what's still left to grasp. Generally, in this part of the book we have been learning about our fundamental tools: pure functions (chapter 2), immutable values (chapter 3), and how pure functions can be treated as immutable values (this chapter). These three things are all we need to be able to program in a functional way. However, there are multiple ways functions and values interact with each other, and that's why we need to look at different problems from different perspectives.

Learning to use
functions as values

The learning process in this chapter consists of three steps. We already completed the first one when we learned about a very specific technique. Now we are moving on to a more architectural topic but still heavily related to exploiting the fact that functions are just values.

Step 1 ✔

Passing functions as arguments
Functions are values that can be passed as arguments into other functions.

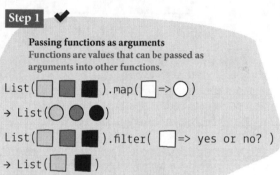

We **are here!** The next step is a big one! There is still plenty to learn in this chapter, so please have a look at what's ahead.

Step 2

Returning functions from functions
Functions are values that can be returned from other functions.

This part will focus more on functional design—how to create flexible APIs by treating functions as return values. We will be forced to use and learn about the functional way of implementing the *builder pattern*, *method chaining*, and *fluent interface* you may know from OOP. For example:

```
new HighScoringWords.Builder()
    .scoringFunction(w -> score(w))
    .highScoreBoundary(5)
    .words(Arrays.asList("java", "scala")
    .build();
```

We will introduce this tool by trying to solve a real requirement by returning functions from functions.

Step 3

Functions as values
Functions are values that can be passed and returned.

Finally, we will try to see how it all meshes together. We will learn about a standard library function that uses both techniques: passing as an argument and returning as a result. Then, we will see how well can we model data using immutable values and how nicely functions defined on those values can be passed together to create more advanced algorithms.

Let's move on to the second step then. There we will encounter yet another requirement that will test out our approach so heavily, we'll need to come up with a totally new way of doing things.

Don't repeat yourself?

Let's go back to our running example and see what happens when we add even more requirements. For now, we can return high-scoring words, and the **code looks very concise and readable**. ←

This is something we'd like to have all the time, even in the light of new and changing requirements.

The next requirement will really test our new approach out.

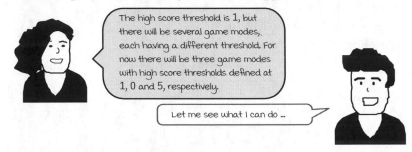

The high score threshold is 1, but there will be several game modes, each having a different threshold. For now there will be three game modes with high score thresholds defined at 1, 0 and 5, respectively.

Let me see what I can do ...

Let's assume that we need to return high-scoring words from a given list of words for three different cases:

— A high-scoring word is a word with a score higher than 1 (current implementation).
— A high-scoring word is a word with a score higher than 0.
— A high-scoring word is a word with a score higher than 5.

To implement the three cases above, **we need to repeat a lot of code**:

```
def highScoringWords(wordScore: String => Int,
                     words: List[String]): List[String] = {
  words.filter(word => wordScore(word) > 1)
}

def highScoringWords0(wordScore: String => Int,
                      words: List[String]): List[String] = {
  words.filter(word => wordScore(word) > 0)
}

def highScoringWords5(wordScore: String => Int,
                      words: List[String]): List[String] = {
  words.filter(word => wordScore(word) > 5)
}

val words = List("ada", "haskell", "scala", "java", "rust")
highScoringWords(w => score(w) + bonus(w) - penalty(w), words)
→ List("java")
highScoringWords0(w => score(w) + bonus(w) - penalty(w), words)
→ List("ada","scala","java")
highScoringWords5(w => score(w) + bonus(w) - penalty(w), words)
→ List()
```

The current version of the function has the high score boundary hardcoded as 1.

That's why we need to create two almost exact copies of this function with different names and high score thresholds of 0 and 5, respectively.

Additionally, we need to pass exactly the same scoring function to each of these almost-exact copies. That is a lot of repetition!

A lot of repetition! Let's see what tools we can use to counter it!

Is my API easy to use?

You probably think that the problem with high score boundaries can be solved by adding a third parameter to the highScoringWords function. Well, this is certainly a very sound approach, and it'd definitely solve some of the repetition in the code. However, over the next few pages you'll see that it's not enough. There is still going to be some nasty repetition there, and worse still, it's going to happen in the *client code*: the code that uses our function by using the API that we provided. **Note that in functional codebases, the API is usually the function signature.**

This book teaches functional programming. The main objective, however, is to teach how functional programming solves real-world software problems. Since codebases are read and analyzed more often than written, we need to focus on how our functions are used. The way we implement them is also important but secondary. **Our solution will be used by others, and we should keep that in mind at all times**.

Now you know why we focus so much on signatures!

Without thinking how our API is going to be used ...

```
                    highScoringWords

def highScoringWords(wordScore: String => Int,
                    words: List[String],
                    higherThan: Int): List[String] = {
  words.filter(word => wordScore(word) > higherThan)
}
```

I just added a new function parameter. Does it solve your problem?

Thanks, but it's hard to use, because I need to copy the scoring function everywhere:
```
highScoringWords(w => score(w) + bonus(w) - penalty(w), words, 1)
highScoringWords(w => score(w) + bonus(w) - penalty(w), words, 0)
highScoringWords(w => score(w) + bonus(w) - penalty(w), words, 5)
```

After thinking how our API is going to be used ...　　**SNEAK PEEK!**

After we conclude that adding a new parameter is not enough, we will learn about the new functional technique that will help us design a better API. **Note that the following code is a sneak peek.** Focus on the client code. Don't worry if you don't understand what's going on—we'll learn about it in the next part of the chapter.

```
                    highScoringWords

def highScoringWords(wordScore: String => Int,
                    words: List[String]
                    ): Int => List[String] = {
  higherThan => words.filter(word => wordScore(word) > higherThan)
}
```

I used the new technique I learned from GrokKing Functional Programming. Is the function easier to use now?

That's impressive! I now have very readable and concise code!
```
val wordsWithScoreHigherThan: Int => List[String] =
  highScoringWords(w => score(w) + bonus(w) - penalty(w), words)

wordsWithScoreHigherThan(1)     Scoring function doesn't change
wordsWithScoreHigherThan(0)     and it's defined just once. No
wordsWithScoreHigherThan(5)     more nasty repetition.
```

Adding a new parameter is not enough

When you saw the problem with different high score boundaries, hopefully your response was, "It's an easy fix: let's add a new parameter and be done with it!" Unfortunately, this is not enough. Let's see why.

As we can see, the new parameter helped because we don't have to define a new function for each high score threshold. However, some repetition is still there, and it cannot be fixed with a new parameter. We need something more—a technique that will enable us to specify only some parameters of a function and leave other ones for later. To sum it up:

```
def highScoringWords(wordScore: String => Int,
                     words: List[String]): List[String] = {
  words.filter(word => wordScore(word) > 1)
}
```

We need to parametrize the function and transform this value into an Int parameter.

```
def highScoringWords(wordScore: String => Int,
                     words: List[String],
                     higherThan: Int): List[String] = {
  words.filter(word => wordScore(word) > higherThan)
}
```

Now our highScoringWords function takes a scoring function, a list of Strings, and an Int. It still returns a list of Strings that are the high-scoring words. Both the scoring function and the Int parameter are used to construct an anonymous function that is passed inline to the filter function.

Now we can use this new highScoringWords function for all three (and more!) cases, without creating a new function for each case.

```
highScoringWords(w => score(w) + bonus(w) - penalty(w), words, 1)
→ List("java")

highScoringWords(w => score(w) + bonus(w) - penalty(w), words, 0)
→ List("ada", "scala", "java")

highScoringWords(w => score(w) + bonus(w) - penalty(w), words, 5)
→ List()
```

PROBLEM! We got rid of some repetitive code, but there is still a lot of it left! We still pass exactly the same scoring function each time we call highScoringWords.

```
def highScoringWords(wordScore: String => Int,
                     words: List[String],
                     higherThan: Int): List[String]
```

We'd like to provide wordScore and words in one place ...

... and the higherThan argument in another place to eliminate all the repetition.

Functions can return functions

To solve our problem without repeating ourselves, we need more than just a new parameter, we need a technique that will delay applying this new parameter. We can achieve this by having a function that will return a function. Let's modify highScoringWords function in this manner.

Remember that function signatures say a lot about what they do and how they should be used.

Signature

We start with the signature. Here, **we define our very first function that returns another function!**

The function takes two parameters!

Function returns a function that takes an Int and returns a List[String]

```
def highScoringWords(wordScore: String => Int,
                     words: List[String]): Int => List[String]
```

Body

How can we return a function from a body? We can use the same syntax we've been using to pass functions to sortBy, map, and filter.

```
def highScoringWords(wordScore: String => Int,
                     words: List[String]): Int => List[String] = {
  higherThan => words.filter(word => wordScore(word) > higherThan)
}
```

- Our return value is a function that takes higherThan as a parameter and returns a List[String].
- We use filter to create this new filtered list of Strings.
- We use higherThan inside the function passed to the filter function.

1 higherThan =>   ...

This is an inline definition of an anonymous function that takes one parameter named higherThan.

2 higherThan => words.filter(...   )

This is an inline definition of an anonymous function that takes one parameter named higherThan and returns a List[String] created by filtering a list defined as words.

3   ...   (word =>   ...   )

This is an inline definition of an anonymous function that takes one parameter named word.

4   ...   (word => wordScore(word) > higherThan)

This is an inline definition of an anonymous function that takes one parameter named word and returns a Boolean.

Using functions that can return functions

Returning a function from highScoringWords allows us to provide two parameters in one place of the code and the third parameter later in the code. Let's see how we can do it.

Our highScoringWords function takes a scoring function and a list of Strings. Then it returns a function that takes an Int and returns a List[String].

```
def highScoringWords(wordScore: String => Int,
                     words: List[String]): Int => List[String] = {
  higherThan => words.filter(word => wordScore(word) > higherThan)
}
```

1 highScoringWords(w => score(w) + bonus(w) - penalty(w), words)
→ Int => List[String]
When we call this function, we get another function back!

We were able to provide only first two arguments: the wordScore function and the words list.

2 val wordsWithScoreHigherThan: Int => List[String] =
  highScoringWords(w => score(w) + bonus(w) - penalty(w), words)
We can save the result of highScoringWords (ananonymous function) under a new name.

We now can store the result as a function that only needs one argument, an Int, to get the list of Strings.

3 Now, we can use this new wordsWithScoreHigherThan function for all three (and more!) cases without creating a new function for each case and without repeating the definition of the scoring function. This is possible because we already applied two arguments before. wordsWithScoreHigherThan already knows about words and the scoring function it operates on, it just needs the higherThan argument to return the end result. This is what we wanted!

```
wordsWithScoreHigherThan(1)
→ List("java")
```

PROBLEM SOLVED!

```
wordsWithScoreHigherThan(0)
→ List("ada", "scala", "java")
```

No repetition! We now know which piece of code is responsible for defining the scoring function and the high score threshold. No room for error here!

```
wordsWithScoreHigherThan(5)
→ List()
```

Not much code is needed now—and what's left is very concise. It may even feel like cheating! To get over this feeling, let's break down the most critical part and try to really understand what's going on.

This is a definition of a new immutable value.

It is a function that takes an Int and returns a List[String].

```
val wordsWithScoreHigherThan: Int => List[String] =
  highScoringWords(w => score(w) + bonus(w) - penalty(w), words)
```

This value is created by calling highScoringWord and getting its result, which is a function that takes an Int and returns a List[String]!

Even though we got the wordsWithScoreHigherThan function as a result from the highScoringWords function, we can treat it exactly as any other function. It needs an Int and will return a List[String] if we provide an Int:

```
wordsWithScoreHigherThan(1)
→ List("java")
```

Functions are values

Q So this all means we can return a function from a function and then store it as a val under whatever name we want? Just like we can return and store an Int, a String, or a List[String]?

A Yes! This is exactly what it means! Functions are treated like any other values in functional programming. We can pass them as arguments, return them as return results, and reference them through different names (using the val syntax).

> **THIS IS BIG!**
> Functions are treated exactly the same as other values in FP.

Functions passed as arguments are values

When you look at the parameter list of highScoringWords, it has two parameters. **Both are treated equally; both are just immutable values.**

```
def highScoringWords(wordScore: String => Int,
                     words: List[String]
                    ): Int => List[String] = {
  higherThan =>
    words.filter(word => wordScore(word) > higherThan)
}
```

> A value returned from highScoringWords is a function that can be used wherever a function that takes a Int and returns a List[String] is needed.

Functions returned from other functions are values

But wait, there is more! We were also able to return a function from a function and save it under a name of our choice and call it!

We are just passing values

We have been passing functions to sortBy, map, and filter functions. However, in Scala and other functional languages, there is no real difference between functions and other values. Before it becomes second nature for you, please treat functions like objects with behaviors. Just like you treat a Java Comparator object that holds a single function inside:

```
Comparator<String> scoreComparator =
  new Comparator<String>() {
    public int compare(String w1, String w2) {
      return Integer.compare(score(w2), score(w1));
    }
  };
```

The same intuition works in FP. Functions are just values; you can use them as arguments, you can create them, and you can return them from other functions. You can just pass them around like Strings.

> This is one of the hardest things for beginners in FP to learn. I assume that it may still be hard for you, even after reading this chapter. That's why I offer you an alternative mental model here, and I will make sure to go back to this topic from time to time.

Coffee break: Returning functions

During this coffee break session you will rewrite some of the functions you previously wrote. You should get a sense of using functions as real values. You'll also be returning functions from functions and using them in familiar built-in functions by passing them as arguments. Make sure to think about each requirement (and code it on your computer) before moving on to the answers.

Your task is to implement each of the four following requirements so that their design is good enough to accommodate required changes. That's why each exercise contains both an original requirement and its changed version. Make sure each solution uses a function that returns another function.

Return a new List with all numbers larger than 4.

```
input: List(5, 1, 2, 4, 0)    output: List(5)
```

Change: Now return a new List with all numbers larger than 1.

```
input: List(5, 1, 2, 4, 0)    output: List(5, 2, 4)
```

1 Hint: 4 and 1 need to be passed as arguments somewhere.

Return a new List that contains only numbers divisible by 5.

```
input: List(5, 1, 2, 4, 15)    output: List(5, 15)
```

Change: Now return a new List that contains only number divisible by 2.

```
input: List(5, 1, 2, 4, 15)    output: List(2, 4)
```

2 Hint: 5 and 2 need to be passed as arguments. maybe to a new function?

Return words that are shorter than four characters.

```
input: List("scala", "ada")    output: List("ada")
```

Change: Now return words that are shorter than seven characters.

```
input: List("scala", "ada")    output: List("scala", "ada")
```

3 Hint: 4 and 7 need to be passed as arguments to a function that returns a function.

Return words that have more than two of the letter 's' inside.

```
input: List("ru**s**t", "ada")    output: List()
```

Change: Now return words that have more than zero of the letter 's' inside.

```
input: List("ru**s**t", "ada")    output: List("rust")
```

4 Hint: You can reuse a function called numberOfS from previous pages, but that's not enough!

Coffee break explained: Returning functions

I hope you've had fun with this one! As always, there are multiple ways of solving these exercises. If you used functions that return functions and these functions took Ints as parameters, that's great! If you struggled, don't worry; the moment will come! The more time you've spent figuring this out, the closer to the revelation you are. Let's solve them together.

We will use the Scala REPL again. Please follow along, especially if you haven't managed to finish the exercise yourself.

Return a new List with all numbers larger than 4 (or 1).

```
> def largerThan(n: Int): Int => Boolean = i => i > n
→ largerThan
List(5, 1, 2, 4, 0).filter(largerThan(4))
→ List(5)
List(5, 1, 2, 4, 0).filter(largerThan(1))
→ List(5, 2, 4)
```

1

We defined a function largerThan, which takes an Int and returns a function that can be used inside filter.

Return a new List that contains only numbers divisible by 5 (or 2).

```
> def divisibleBy(n: Int): Int => Boolean = i => i % n == 0
→ divisibleBy
List(5, 1, 2, 4, 15).filter(divisibleBy(5))
→ List(5, 15)
List(5, 1, 2, 4, 15).filter(divisibleBy(2))
→ List(2, 4)
```

2

We defined a function divisibleBy, which takes an Int and returns a function that can be used inside filter. We then used this function to filter different numbers.

Return words that are shorter than four characters (or 7).

```
> def shorterThan(n: Int): String => Boolean = s => s.length < n
→ shorterThan
List("scala", "ada").filter(shorterThan(4))
→ List("ada")
List("scala", "ada").filter(shorterThan(7))
→ List("scala", "ada")
```

3

We defined a function shorterThan, which takes an Int and returns a function that can be used inside filter. We then used this function to filter different Strings.

Return words that have more than two of the letter 's' inside (or more than 0).

```
> def numberOfS(s: String): Int =
    s.length - s.replaceAll("s", "").length
→ numberOfS
def containsS(moreThan: Int): String => Boolean =
    s => numberOfS(s) > moreThan
→ containsS
List("rust", "ada").filter(containsS(2))
→ List()
List("rust", "ada").filter(containsS(0))
→ List("rust")
```

4

We defined a function containsS, which takes an Int and returns a function that can be used inside filter. Inside this new function, we reused function numberOfS, which we defined previously. We then used containsS to filter different Strings.

Designing functional APIs

We introduced a very important concept: functions are just values and can be returned from other functions. In our example we had a problem with our three-parameter function and transformed it into a two-parameter function that returns a one-parameter function. **The logic inside the function didn't change**—just the signatures—but it made our job a lot easier! Let's compare it in the classical before-and-after way.

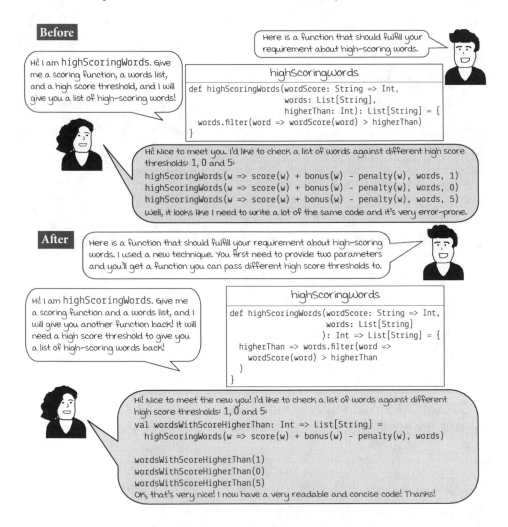

Before

Here is a function that should fulfill your requirement about high-scoring words.

Hi! I am highScoringWords. Give me a scoring function, a words list, and a high score threshold, and I will give you a list of high-scoring words!

highScoringWords

```
def highScoringWords(wordScore: String => Int,
                     words: List[String],
                     higherThan: Int): List[String] = {
  words.filter(word => wordScore(word) > higherThan)
}
```

Hi! Nice to meet you. I'd like to check a list of words against different high score thresholds: 1, 0 and 5:

```
highScoringWords(w => score(w) + bonus(w) - penalty(w), words, 1)
highScoringWords(w => score(w) + bonus(w) - penalty(w), words, 0)
highScoringWords(w => score(w) + bonus(w) - penalty(w), words, 5)
```

Well, it looks like I need to write a lot of the same code and it's very error-prone.

After

Here is a function that should fulfill your requirement about high-scoring words. I used a new technique. You first need to provide two parameters and you'll get a function you can pass different high score thresholds to.

Hi! I am highScoringWords. Give me a scoring function and a words list, and I will give you another function back! It will need a high score threshold to give you a list of high-scoring words back!

highScoringWords

```
def highScoringWords(wordScore: String => Int,
                     words: List[String]
                     ): Int => List[String] = {
  higherThan => words.filter(word =>
    wordScore(word) > higherThan
  )
}
```

Hi! Nice to meet the new you! I'd like to check a list of words against different high score thresholds: 1, 0 and 5:

```
val wordsWithScoreHigherThan: Int => List[String] =
  highScoringWords(w => score(w) + bonus(w) - penalty(w), words)

wordsWithScoreHigherThan(1)
wordsWithScoreHigherThan(0)
wordsWithScoreHigherThan(5)
```

OK, that's very nice! I now have a very readable and concise code! Thanks!

Note how all the information our client needs can be derived from signatures! By using this technique, we can make sure that clients know their options, and they can write readable, testable, and maintainable code. **It's the foundation of good software design.**

Iterative design of functional APIs

Functional programming gives us very versatile tools to design APIs. In this part of the book, we are learning about these tools. However, tools alone won't make us good programmers. We need to know how to use them in different contexts. That's what we'll learn later in the book, but in this chapter I've shown you one of the most universal ways of writing software and how it can be practiced using FP: **iterative design based on client feedback**. The design changes based on current assumptions. We are shaping our signatures based on the requirements and feedback from the client of our code. Changes are more than welcome.

And there are not many of them as well, which is a good thing! We have pure functions, immutable values, and functions as values, which we learn about in this chapter. We don't really need anything more!

We, as programmers, should not be surprised when requirements change or become more specific. This is exactly what happens in the next section of this chapter. Let's see how can we use the tools at our disposal—especially returning functions from functions—to deal with changing requirements.

I have been using highScoringWords function a lot lately, and I encountered a problem. When I want to check different lists of words against different high score thresholds, I need to repeat a lot of code. You can see it for yourself when you try to check the results of different word lists against different thresholds.

As we can see, our API is not as good as we thought. It's time to reproduce the problem by trying to use two different lists of words.

```
val words = List("ada", "haskell", "scala", "java", "rust")
val words2 = List("football", "f1", "hockey", "basketball")
```

Apart from the list of words we've been using so far, we define a new one to simulate how real players would play our word game (words2).

```
val wordsWithScoreHigherThan: Int => List[String] =
  highScoringWords(w => score(w) + bonus(w) - penalty(w), words)

val words2WithScoreHigherThan: Int => List[String] =
  highScoringWords(w => score(w) + bonus(w) - penalty(w), words2)
```

Here lies the biggest problem. We need to define a very similar-looking function for each list of words!

```
wordsWithScoreHigherThan(1)
→ List("java"))

wordsWithScoreHigherThan(0)
→ List("ada", "scala", "java")

wordsWithScoreHigherThan(5)
→ List()
```

We use the first function to get high scores for the first list of words. We need three results because there are three different thresholds; hence, we can't do better than three function calls.

```
words2WithScoreHigherThan(1)
→ List("football", "f1", "hockey")

words2WithScoreHigherThan(0)
→ List("football", "f1", "hockey", "basketball")

words2WithScoreHigherThan(5)
→ List("football", "hockey")
```

To add insult to injury, we need to use the second function to get high scores for the second list of words. Taking high score thresholds into account makes ourcode even more bloated with three additional function calls!

Returning functions from returned functions

When we look closely at the problem we encountered, we can spot some similarities to the problem we have solved previously by returning a function. Let's recap what we did.

If you feel dizzy reading such titles, don't worry: in the next few pages we will introduce a better way to define these things.

Before **The <u>three</u>-parameter function**

```
def highScoringWords(wordScore: String => Int,
                     words: List[String],
                     higherThan: Int): List[String]
```

We' wanted to provide wordScore and words in one place ...

... and the higherThan argument in another place to eliminate the repetition related to providing different higherThans.

After **The <u>two</u>-parameter function**

So we transformed the three-parameter function into a two-parameter function that returns a one-parameter function.

```
def highScoringWords(wordScore: String => Int, words: List[String]): Int => List[String]
```

This way we could provide the Int (higherThan argument) independently of wordScore and words. However, we still need to pass wordScore and words together, and this is what causes our current problem. We want to keep the same scoring algorithm and use different words and higherThan values. Fortunately, **this looks exactly like the previous problem, so we can use exactly the same tool to solve it.**

This technique has a name and is ubiquitous in functional programming. We will reveal its name very soon!

Before **The <u>two</u>-parameter function**

```
def highScoringWords(wordScore: String => Int
                     words: List[String]
                    ): Int => List[String]
```

Now we'd like provide wordScore in one place ...

... and the words argument in another place to eliminate the repetition related to providing different words.

After **The <u>one</u>-parameter function**

So what we need to do is to transform the two-parameter function that returns a one-parameter function into a one-parameter function that returns a one-parameter function that in turn returns another one-parameter function.

No, there is no mistake in the sentence on the left. We really need to do this.

```
def highScoringWords(wordScore: String => Int): Int => List[String] => List[String]
```

This function takes one parameter which is a function that takes a String and returns an Int.

This function returns a function that takes an Int and returns a function that takes a List[String] and returns a new List[String].

How to return functions from returned functions

We now know the signature of our new one-parameter function, and we expect it to solve our design problem: we don't like to provide the same argument over and over again. That's why we want to make sure each parameter is applied independently.

← Again, if you don't like reading such titles, don't worry: soon we will introduce a better way of discussing returning functions.

This function takes one parameter which is a function that takes a String and returns an Int.

This function returns a function that takes an Int and returns a function, which takes a List[String] and returns a new List[String].

```
def highScoringWords(wordScore: String => Int): Int => List[String] => List[String] = {
  higherThan => words => words.filter(word => wordScore(word) > higherThan)
}
```

- Our return value is a function that takes higherThan as a parameter and returns a function
- This returned function takes words as a parameter and returns a List[String].
- We use filter to create this new filtered list of Strings, just like before.
- We use higherThan and words inside the function we are passing to the filter function.

1 `higherThan =>` ⸻

This is an inline definition of an anonymous function that takes one parameter named higherThan.

2 `higherThan => words =>` ⸻

This is an inline definition of an anonymous function that takes one parameter named higherThan and returns another anonymous function that takes one parameter named words.

3 `higherThan => words => words.filter(` ⸻ `)`

This is an inline definition of an anonymous function that takes one parameter named higherThan and returns another anonymous function that takes one parameter named words and returns a List[String] created by filtering a list defined as words.

4 ⸻ `(word =>` ⸻ `)`

This is an inline definition of an anonymous function that takes one parameter named word.

5 ⸻ `(word => wordScore(word) > higherThan)`

This is an inline definition of an anonymous function that takes one parameter named word and returns a Boolean.

As you can see, we use exactly the same double-arrow syntax to define a function that returns a function that returns a function. Now, it's about time to test out our new implementation and see it in action.

Using the flexible API built with returned functions

Does transforming a three-parameter function into a function that takes just one parameter and returns a function really help solve our problems? Let's see how can we use the new version of `highScoringWords`.

> Hi! I am a new version of `highScoringWords`. For each given parameter, I return a new function. Give me a scoring function, and I will give you another function back! It will need a high score threshold and will return yet another function back. That function will need words and will return high-scoring words back.

> Here is a function that should fulfill all your requirements about high-scoring words. I used the same technique again. Now you first need to provide a scoring algorithm and then a high score threshold independently.

highScoringWords
``def highScoringWords(
wordScore: String => Int
): Int => List[String] => List[String] = {
higherThan => words => words.filter(word => wordScore(word) > higherThan)
}```

> Hi! Nice to meet the new you! I'd like to check a list of words against different high score thresholds of my choice. So first I need to provide a scoring function, then a high score threshold and only then the word lists I want to use. Let me try it out!

1 When I apply the first argument, the scoring function, I will get a function that still needs two arguments to return a result. I can provide them later. Good thing is that this function will "hold" the scoring algorithm and I won't have to repeat it later on.

```
val wordsWithScoreHigherThan: Int => List[String] => List[String] =
  highScoringWords(w => score(w) + bonus(w) - penalty(w))
```

2 Now I need to provide a high score threshold to get the next function. I can save it as a `val` if I know that I will have only one high score threshold. However, we already know that there will be different thresholds and different words lists, so we can apply both remaining arguments at once, without naming the "middle" function:

```
val words = List("ada", "haskell", "scala", "java", "rust")
val words2 = List("football", "f1", "hockey", "basketball")
```

```
wordsWithScoreHigherThan(1)(words)
→ List("java")

wordsWithScoreHigherThan(0)(words2)
→ List("football", "f1", "hockey", "basketball")

wordsWithScoreHigherThan(5)(words2)
→ List("football", "hockey")
```

Here we apply two arguments at once to the remaining two functions. There are still two function calls underneath: when we provide a high score threshold (`higherThan`), we get a function back. We don't save it as `val` and instead we call it immediately with the list of words of our choice. **This is only one of the ways we could use this function, but it fits perfectly to this specific case.**

Note that if we wanted to have full flexibility, we could still use the same `highScoringWords` function the way we used the three-parameter one, by providing each argument in a separate parameter list.

```
highScoringWords(w => score(w) + bonus(w) - penalty(w))(1)(words)
→ List("java")
```

It's up to the user of the function to choose which parameters should be fixed (by saving the function as a named `val`), and which should not (by applying arguments immediately after getting the function in the same line).

Using multiple parameter lists in functions

We now know that returning functions from other functions can be very beneficial for our codebases. The clients of our functions can write less code and still have lots of flexibility. They can write smaller, independent functions with single responsibilities. They are not forced to repeat themselves. However, there is still a slight problem with the syntax.

THIS IS BIG!
Returning functions is a foundation of designing flexible APIs.

Problem: Inconsistency with parameter naming

The problem is that we are not consistent with our function syntax, even inside one function. This works OK, but it may still cause some confusion for the reader. Let's look at the highScoringWords function as an example:

```scala
def highScoringWords(
  wordScore: String => Int
): Int => List[String] => List[String] = {
  higherThan =>
    words =>
      words.filter(word => wordScore(word) > higherThan)
}
```

There are really three parameter lists in this code snippet:

— wordScore: String => Int

— higherThan: Int

— words: List[String]

When I write "parameter list," I mean the part of the signature where we define the parameter names and their types.

However, we write them in a totally different way. The first one is written as a normal function parameter list, and the rest is written using the double-arrow syntax we have used for unnamed anonymous functions passed inline. **Fortunately, we can use a more consistent syntax!**

Note that the first parameter list includes a parameter, which is a function, while the second and third consist of primitive-type parameters.

Solution: Multiple parameter lists

In Scala and other functional languages, we can use a syntax that allows us to have multiple parameter lists. In our case, we want to have three.

```scala
def highScoringWords(wordScore: String => Int): Int => List[String] => List[String] = {
  higherThan =>
    words =>
      words.filter(word => wordScore(word) > higherThan)
}
```

Both highScoringWords definitions do the same thing. They take a function as a parameter and return a function that takes another parameter and returns a function. They just use a different syntax.

```scala
def highScoringWords(wordScore: String => Int)(higherThan: Int)(words: List[String]): List[String] = {
  words.filter(word => wordScore(word) > higherThan)
}
```

We have been currying!

We were able to use the same technique to solve the last two problems: we transformed a multiple-parameter function into a one-parameter function that returns another one-parameter function. This technique is called **currying**. This is what we've been doing to solve the last two problems with highScoringWords.

Currying is named after logician Haskell Curry—the same person who had a programming language named after him.

Currying

Transforming multiple-parameter functions into a series of one-parameter functions returned from each other is called *currying*. Currying enables us to create very versatile APIs. Client code can provide each parameter in different—and the most suitable!—part of the codebase. This helps with avoiding repetition and making the code more readable and maintainable because we don't have to overwhelm the reader with all different parameters at once.

```
def f(a: A, b: B, c: C): D
```
Uncurried multiple-parameter function that takes three parameters and returns a value of type D

```
def f(a: A): B => C => D
```
using "returning functions" syntax

Curried one-parameter function that takes one parameter and returns another one-parameter function which in turn returns a one-parameter function that returns a value of type D

```
def f(a: A)(b: B)(c: C): D
```
using "multiple parameter lists" syntax

Curried one-parameter function that takes one parameter and returns another one-parameter function which in turn returns a one-parameter function that returns a value of type D

This is exactly the same in terms of usage. The only difference is that in "returning functions" syntax we provide only types of the values, while "multiple parameter lists" include all value names.

So highScoringWords **became curried** when we transformed it into a one-parameter function that returns another function. It allowed us to provide each of three arguments independently of each other! We still needed to define which parameter went first, second, and so on. This order is very important and should be based on the requirements.

In the Haskell language, created by Haskell Curry, all functions are curried. That is, all functions in Haskell take just one argument.

1
Scoring algorithm

The scoring algorithm is used at the beginning of the game and is selected when game mode is chosen.

2
High score threshold

The high score threshold is chosen later in the flow of the program when the difficulty setting is chosen (that's why it's after scoring).

3
List of words

The list of words changes very dynamically each round of the game when a player provides new lists of words.

```
def highScoringWords(wordScore: String => Int)(higherThan: Int)(words: List[String]): List[String] = {
  words.filter(word => wordScore(word) > higherThan)
}
```

Practicing currying

Let's go back to the functions we wrote in the previous exercise. Please transform them into curried versions. This exercise should help you gain some muscle memory. Again, please use the Scala REPL to make sure you really grok it.

Your tasks

Return a new `List` with all numbers larger than 4 *(pass 4 as an argument)*.

1

```
input: List(5, 1, 2, 4, 0)    output: List(5)
```

Return a new `List` that contains numbers divisible by 5 *(pass 5 as an argument)*.

2

```
input: List(5, 1, 2, 4, 15)    output: List(5, 15)
```

Return words that are shorter than four characters *(pass 4 as an argument)*.

3

```
input: List("scala", "ada")    output: List("ada")
```

Return words that have more than two of the letter 's' inside *(pass 2 as an argument)*.

4

```
input: List("rust", "ada")    output: List()
```

Answers

1

```
> def largerThan(n: Int)(i: Int): Boolean = i > n
→ largerThan
List(5, 1, 2, 4, 0).filter(largerThan(4))
→ List(5)
```

2

```
def divisibleBy(n: Int)(i: Int): Boolean = i % n == 0
→ divisibleBy
List(5, 1, 2, 4, 15).filter(divisibleBy(5))
→ List(5, 15)
```

3

```
def shorterThan(n: Int)(s: String): Boolean = s.length < n
→ shorterThan
List("scala", "ada").filter(shorterThan(4))
→ List("ada")
def numberOfS(s: String): Int =
  s.length - s.replaceAll("s", "").length
→ numberOfS
```

4

```
def containsS(moreThan: Int)(s: String): Boolean =
  numberOfS(s) > moreThan
→ containsS
List("rust", "ada").filter(containsS(2))
→ List()
```

Programming by passing function values

Now let's go back to the hypothetical conversation between a person requesting features and a person implementing them casually by passing functions as parameters (*which are just values like* Ints *and* Lists, *right?*).

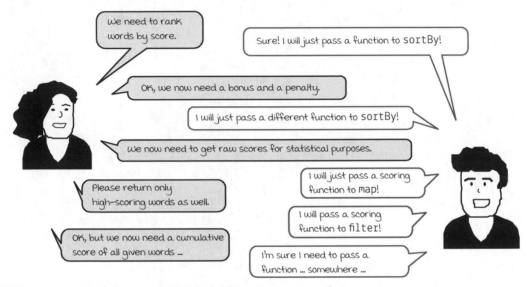

We've got yet another requirement! This time we need to return a cumulative score of all given words, and as always, we want to do it in a purely functional way: passing immutable values (including functions) into pure functions. This way we avoid lots of problems from the get-go!

Higher-order functions

Before we move on to replace another for loop with a one liner, let me highlight a very important thing: the technique of passing functions as parameters to other functions and returning functions from functions is universal in functional codebases. It's so universal that it has its own name: a function that takes or returns another function is called a **higher-order function**. sortBy, map, and filter are just examples from the standard library, but we will meet many more and even write some of our own!

The second very important thing is that we will use map, filter, and other higher-order functions not only on collections but other types as well. We learned them once and will use them everywhere.

Reducing many values into a single value

Let's have a closer look at our new requirement.

> **New requirement: Return cumulative score**
> — We need to return a cumulative score of words provided as an input list.
> — Functionalities implemented so far should still work the same (we cannot change any existing function).

Quick exercise: The signature

In functional programming the signature is a very important piece of information. That's why we always start designing new features from the function's signature. It's a very helpful tool that guides the thinking process and the implementation. That's why I include the following small exercise (again!). Before we move on, I kindly ask you to try to think about the new requirement and **figure out what the signature of a function implementing it would look like**.

Answer in the discussion.

As a reference: The solution in imperative Java

Before we implement the functional solution and uncover the mystery of the function signature, let's have a look at how the imperative Java solution would look and what kind of problems it has.

```
static int cumulativeScore(
  Function<String, Integer> wordScore,
  List<String> words
) {
  int result = 0;
  for (String word : words) {
    result += wordScore.apply(word);
  }
  return result;
}
```

We create a new mutable integer and initiate it with 0.

We apply a function for each element using a for loop. The result of the function is added to the mutable integer we created at the beginning.

The code above has problems we are all familiar with:

— It uses mutable collections (`List`).

— The code is not very concise. Intuitively, there is far too much code to read for such a small feature.

The signature in Scala

Here's how Scala version of the signature could look:

Remember that, though it's very similar to the Java version, it is using an immutable List instead!

```
def cumulativeScore(wordScore: String => Int,
                    words: List[String]): Int
```

Reducing many values into a single one using `foldLeft`

You've already seen how quickly we have been able to implement all the requirements so far. We used List's sortBy, map, and filter: functions that take other functions as parameters, use them internally, and return new, immutable values. This new requirement can also be implemented using the same technique. The function we introduce here is called foldLeft. Here's a possible implementation of the new requirement using Scala's immutable List that has the foldLeft function:

```
def cumulativeScore(wordScore: String => Int,
                    words: List[String]): Int = {
  words.foldLeft(0)((total, word) => total + wordScore(word))
}
```

We provide a function that is able to add the current element to the ongoing total, which starts at 0.

Yes, foldLeft is a little bit different than the previous ones, but the general rule stays the same. What it does is **it takes each element of the list, applies the provided function to it and an ongoing total, then passes it to the next element**. Again, it doesn't mutate anything.

The signature

wordScore is a function that takes a String and returns an Int.

```
def cumulativeScore(wordScore: String => Int,
                    words: List[String]): Int
```

words is an immutable List of Strings.

The function returns an Int.

The body

The body of the function consists of a lone call to foldLeft, which takes an Int and a function that takes two parameters and returns an Int.

Here we assume that we passed a wordScore function that includes bonus and penalties.

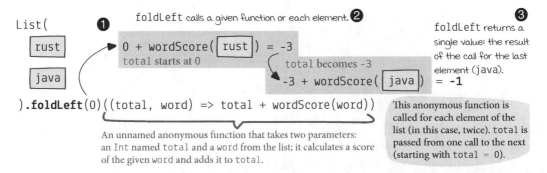

❶ foldLeft calls a given function or each element. ❷

```
List(
  rust
  java
).foldLeft(0)((total, word) => total + wordScore(word))
```

```
0 + wordScore( rust ) = -3
total starts at 0
                        total becomes -3
                        -3 + wordScore( java )
                                             = -1
```

❸ foldLeft returns a single value: the result of the call for the last element (java).

This anonymous function is called for each element of the list (in this case, twice). total is passed from one call to the next (starting with total = 0).

An unnamed anonymous function that takes two parameters: an Int named total and a word from the list; it calculates a score of the given word and adds it to total.

Getting to know `foldLeft`

`foldLeft` accumulates the value by going through all elements of the list and calling a provided function. The value it accumulates is called an *accumulator*. Its initial value is passed as a first parameter to `foldLeft`. In our case it was 0—our accumulator was an `Int` with initial value of 0:

```
words.foldLeft(0)
```

Assuming that `words` is a `List` of `Strings`, the above snippet returns a function that takes a two-parameter function that takes an `Int` and a `String` and returns an `Int` back:

```
words.foldLeft(0)((total, word) => total + wordScore(word))
```

← We use the double-arrow notation to create an inline anonymous function. This time, though, we create a two-parameter function—not a single-parameter one. As you can see, the syntax is always the same. We just provide the names of the arguments inside parentheses.

Internally, `foldLeft` calls the provided function for each element of the words list (passing it as a `word`) and **accumulates total based on the provided function**. For the first element, the function is called using the initial value of the accumulator (in our case: 0). The result of the function called for the last element becomes the result of the `foldLeft`.

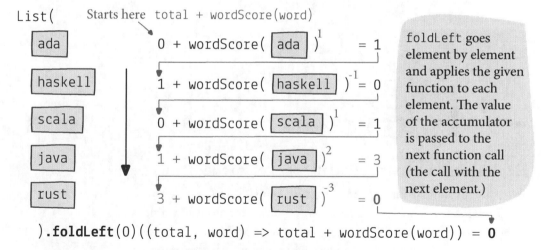

List(
Starts here total + wordScore(word)

ada		0 + wordScore(ada)^1	= 1
haskell		1 + wordScore(haskell)$^{-1}$	= 0
scala		0 + wordScore(scala)^1	= 1
java		1 + wordScore(java)^2	= 3
rust		3 + wordScore(rust)$^{-3}$	= 0

`foldLeft` goes element by element and applies the given function to each element. The value of the accumulator is passed to the next function call (the call with the next element.)

```
).foldLeft(0)((total, word) => total + wordScore(word)) = 0
```

```
List[A].foldLeft(z: B)(f: (B, A) => B): B
```

Accumulates a value of type **B** by applying the function passed as **f** to each element of the original list (which holds values of type **A**) and the current accumulator value, which starts at value **z**. Each parameter is on its own parameter list, so we can use currying. Only one value is returned.

```
List(☐ ▨ ▪).foldLeft(0)(☐ => incrementIfGrey)
```

→ 1

foldLeft **must-knows**

`foldLeft` may cause some issues, so let's go through some interesting things about this function before moving on to the `foldLeft` exercise. This should give you some much-needed perspective on what's going on.

Why is it called "left"?

When you look at the order of the calculations, they happen from left to right. `foldLeft` starts at the leftmost element and combines it with the initial value. Then, it proceeds to the next one.

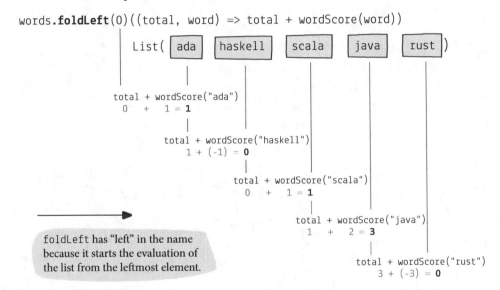

```
words.foldLeft(0)((total, word) => total + wordScore(word))
```

List(ada   haskell   scala   java   rust)

```
total + wordScore("ada")
  0  +    1 = 1
```

```
total + wordScore("haskell")
    1 + (-1) = 0
```

```
total + wordScore("scala")
    0  +   1 = 1
```

```
total + wordScore("java")
    1  +   2 = 3
```

```
total + wordScore("rust")
    3 + (-3) = 0
```

foldLeft has "left" in the name because it starts the evaluation of the list from the leftmost element.

Is it only used for calculating the sum of integers?

No, it's not just for calculating sums! `foldLeft` can be used anywhere you need to calculate one metric based on any number of values. Summing is just one of the classical examples, but you could (and will) calculate other things like minimum value, maximum value, a value closest to another value, etc. Moreover, we will also see `foldLeft` being used for non-collection types. We'll also see that the initial value may be a collection!

Something we'll visit later on is a real mind-boggler: if you pass an empty List as an initial value, then the result of foldLeft is a different List!

It's so similar to Java Streams reduce!

We mentioned earlier in this chapter that all of the functionalities could be implemented using Java Streams. They are better than imperative counterparts, but they still have some problems. If you knew Java Streams, this probably helped you a lot. On the other hand, if you didn't know Streams, it should be far easier for you now after reading this chapter.

That's the power of the functional approach. You can reuse the knowledge in multiple places!

Practicing `foldLeft`

It's time to write your own functions and pass them to `foldLeft`. Again, please use the Scala REPL to make sure you understand this subject.

Your tasks

Return a sum of all integers in the given list.

```
input: List(5, 1, 2, 4, 100)    output: 112
```

1

Return the total length of all the words in the given list.

```
input: List("scala", "rust", "ada")    output: 12
```

2

Return the number of the letter 's' found in all the words in the given list.

```
input: List("scala", "haskell", "rust", "ada")    output: 3
```

3

Return the maximum of all integers in the given list.

```
input: List(5, 1, 2, 4, 15)    output: 15
```

4

Answers

```
> List(5, 1, 2, 4, 100).foldLeft(0)((sum, i) => sum + i)
→ 112
```

1

```
def len(s: String): Int = s.length
→ len
List("scala", "rust", "ada")
  .foldLeft(0)((total, s) => total + len(s))
→ 12
```

2

```
def numberOfS(s: String): Int =
  s.length - s.replaceAll("s", "").length
→ numberOfS
List("scala", "haskell", "rust", "ada")
  .foldLeft(0)((total, str) => total + numberOfS(str))
→ 3
```

3

```
List(5, 1, 2, 4, 15)
  .foldLeft(Int.MinValue)((max, i) => if (i > max) i else max)
→ 15
```

4

The initial value needs to be a neutral value in the context of the operation. Here we can't use 0 because the list may contain a single negative value, and then 0 won't be the right answer.

We could also use `Math.max(max, i)` here.

Modeling immutable data

So far we've been using map, filter, and foldLeft on lists of String and Ints. This is usually enough for an introduction, but in real production applications we tend to use more complicated data models. Since this book is about practical and maintainable code that you can write and use on production, we need one more thing to be able to say that our functional toolkit is fully assembled.

Remember that map, filter, and foldLeft are functions that take functions as parameters. They and functions that return functions are called higher-order functions.

Coupling two pieces of information together

If String represents the whole entity, our higher-order functions work out of the box. But sometimes the entity consists of two or more pieces of information. For example, if we wanted to model a programming language with its name and the year of its first appearance, we'd be out of luck.

Functional languages provide a special language construct to define nonprimitive immutable values that can hold multiple values of different types. In FP, **it's called a product type,** and we encode it as a case class in Scala.

In Kotlin, we encode it as a data class. We will discuss why it's called a "product type" in chapter 7. For now, just assume that it's a type that represents a combination of other types in a fixed order.

In our example, we'd like to model a programming language that has a name and a year of its first appearance. That means we want to couple together two pieces of information: a String and an Int.

```scala
case class ProgrammingLanguage(name: String, year: Int)
```

And that's it! We have just defined a new type. How can we use it? Let's try it out together. Please follow along in your REPL session.

```scala
> case class ProgrammingLanguage(name: String, year: Int)
→ defined case class ProgrammingLanguage

val javalang  = ProgrammingLanguage("Java", 1995)
→ javalang: ProgrammingLanguage
val scalalang = ProgrammingLanguage("Scala", 2004)
→ scalalang: ProgrammingLanguage

javalang.name
→ Java
javalang.year
→ 1995
scalalang.name.length
→ 5
(scalalang.year + javalang.year) / 2
→ 1999
```

We create two values of type ProgrammingLanguage by stating its name and providing both values it consists of: a String and an Int. Note that we don't have to use a new keyword like in Java.

We can use the dot syntax to access internal "fields" of values. This line returns a String, "Java."

Because name returns a String, we can use it as any normal String (e.g., get its length).

Finally, because year returns an Int, we can use this integer as any other (e.g., to calculate an average first year of appearance for both languages, for what it's worth).

Using product types with higher-order functions

It turns out that product types are a perfect fit for modeling data. They also play nicely with higher-order functions.

Product types are immutable

The first great benefit is that product types are immutable. Once you create a value of a product type, it will stay the same until the end of the world (or program execution). That's why you can access all the fields in the `case class`, but you can't assign any other values to them.

```
> val javalang = ProgrammingLanguage("Java", 1995)
→ javalang: ProgrammingLanguage
javalang.year = 2021
→ error: reassignment to val
javalang.year
→ 1995
```

Getting the list of names with `map`

Product types and their immutability are used in higher-order functions to create more robust code and bigger pure functions. When you have a list of `ProgrammingLanguage` values and you want just a list of names back:

```
> val javalang   = ProgrammingLanguage("Java", 1995)
  val scalalang  = ProgrammingLanguage("Scala", 2004)

  val languages = List(javalang, scalalang)
→ List(ProgrammingLanguage("Java", 1995),
        ProgrammingLanguage("Scala", 2004))


  languages.map(lang => lang.name)
→ List("Java", "Scala")
```

map gets a function that takes a ProgrammingLanguage and returns a String.

Getting younger languages with `filter`

We can also use `filter` in a similar manner. We just provide a function that takes a `ProgrammingLanguage` and returns a `Boolean` that indicates our decision about whether or not to include this `ProgrammingLanguage` in the resulting list. Note that we get a `List` of `ProgrammingLanguages` back from the `filter` call:

```
> languages.filter(lang => lang.year > 2000)
→ List(ProgrammingLanguage("Scala", 2004))
```

filter gets a function that takes a ProgrammingLanguage and returns a Boolean. We write this function using the double-arrow syntax and pass it inline.

More concise syntax for inline functions

As we've just seen, product types and higher-order functions play very well together. They are the foundation for all functional applications—those used in production and those we will write in this book. They are so prevalent that Scala (and other languages as well) provides a special syntax for defining the inline functions that require a case-class typed value that is passed to `map`, `filter`, and others.

Using `map` and `filter` with the underscore syntax

Let's revisit the previous example in which we used `map` and `filter`. Note how repetitive we are when we try to quickly define and pass functions to `map` and `filter`:

```
val javalang   = ProgrammingLanguage("Java", 1995)
val scalalang  = ProgrammingLanguage("Scala", 2004)

val languages = List(javalang, scalalang)
→ List(ProgrammingLanguage("Java", 1995),
        ProgrammingLanguage("Scala", 2004))

languages.map(lang => lang.name)
→ List("Java", "Scala")

languages.filter(lang => lang.year > 2000)
→ List(ProgrammingLanguage("Scala", 2004))
```

We want to get the name, but most of the code is just naming the language lang and then using it to access the name field.

Same here. We want to get the year, but most of the code is just naming the language lang and then using it to access the year field.

What we can do is use **the underscore syntax**:

```
lang => lang.name              becomes   _.name
lang => lang.year > 2000  becomes   _.year > 2000
```

We don't really need to name the incoming parameter and can just say we are interested in only one of its fields. Here, the underscore is just a value of type `ProgrammingLanguage`, but it's not named explicitly.

Note that **the underscore syntax is just another way of defining a function!** We are still passing functions to `map` and `filter` but in a more concise way.

```
languages.map(_.name)
→ List("Java", "Scala")

languages.filter(_.year > 2000)
→ List(ProgrammingLanguage("Scala", 2004))
```

Remember that whenever you see a code snippet with >, make sure to follow along in your own REPL session. Have you followed the programming language snippets?

Summary

That's it! Now you know that functions are really important in functional programming (surprise!). Let's summarize all the things we learned.

Passing functions as parameters

We first learned about sorting and how it's achieved in Java. `sort` takes a `Comparator`, which is an object, but underneath it only contains an algorithm that compares two items. It turned out that this technique is prevalent in Scala and other functional languages, where we pass functions directly using the double-arrow syntax.

The `sortBy` function

Then, we sorted a given `List` in Scala by calling the `sortBy` function and providing a function as an argument. Nothing was mutated.

`map` and `filter` functions

We will be coming back to many of these functions throughout the book, so make sure you grokked them all!

Later in the chapter we used exactly the same technique to transform the `Lists` using the `map` and `filter` functions (and providing them a customization function as a parameter, of course!). Their usage is very similar to the Java Streams version, but in Scala and other FP languages, the `Lists` are immutable by default, making the code more robust and maintainable.

Returning functions from functions

Then, we learned that some functions can return functions. We can use this technique to *configure* a function based on incoming parameters. There is also a special syntax to define many parameter lists that makes the code more readable by making sure all the parameters and their types are inside the signature—it's called currying.

`foldLeft` function

Having learned all of the above, we were able to introduce and use the `foldLeft` function, which is able to reduce a list of values to a single value. Examples include summing, but other algorithms are also possible.

Modeling immutable data using product type

At the end we introduced product types as a way of coupling several pieces of information together. We learned that they play very well with higher-order functions because they are immutable.

> CODE: CH04_*
> Explore this chapter's source code by looking at ch04_* files in the book's repository.

Functions that take other functions as parameters are called higher-order functions.

`sortBy` is a higher-order function.

`map` and `filter` are higher-order functions.

Functions that take other functions as parameters and/or return functions are called higher-order functions.

`foldLeft` is a higher-order function, and it's curried. It has two parameter lists.

`case class` is a Scala implementation of the product type.

Part 2
Functional programs

We now have the foundation to start building real functional programs. In each of the following chapters we will use only immutable values and pure functions, including several higher-order functions.

In **chapter 5** we will introduce the most important higher-order function in FP: flatMap. It helps building sequential values (and programs) in a concise and readable way.

In **chapter 6** we will learn how to build sequential programs that may return errors and how to protect ourselves against different corner cases.

We will use **chapter 7** to properly introduce you to the world of functional design. We will model data and functions' parameters in a way that disallows many invalid (from a business perspective) instances and arguments.

Chapter 8 will teach you how to deal with an impure, external, side-effectful world in a safe and functional way. We will do a lot of IO actions (simulating external database or service calls), including many failing ones.

Knowing how to handle errors, model the data and behaviors, and how to use external IO actions will allow us to introduce streams and streaming systems in **chapter 9**. We will build streams of hundreds of thousands of items using the functional approach.

In **chapter 10** we will finally create some functional and safe concurrent programs. We will show how all the techniques from previous chapters are still applicable even in the presence of multiple threads.

Sequential programs | 5

In this chapter
you will learn

- how to deal with lists of lists using `flatten`

- how to write sequential programs using `flatMap`
  instead of `for` loops

- how to write sequential programs in a readable way
  using for comprehensions

- how to use conditions inside for comprehensions

- how to get to know more types that have `flatMap`

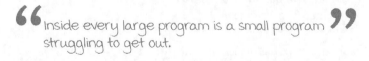

Inside every large program is a small program struggling to get out.

—TONY HOARE, "EFFICIENT PRODUCTION OF LARGE PROGRAMS"

Writing pipeline-based algorithms

One of the most popular patterns in modern programming languages is **pipelining**. We can write many computations as a sequence of operations—*a pipeline*—that together make a bigger, more involved operation. It's a different take on creating **sequential programs**.

In this chapter we will talk about sequential algorithms or sequential programs. A sequential program is a piece of code representing logic that takes a value, transforms it in a step-by-step manner (sequentially), and returns a final value.

Let's look at an example. We have a list of three interesting books:

```scala
case class Book(title: String, authors: List[String])

val books = List(
  Book("FP in Scala", List("Chiusano", "Bjarnason")),
  Book("The Hobbit", List("Tolkien")),
  Book("Modern Java in Action", List("Urma", "Fusco", "Mycroft"))
)
```

Our task is to count how many of them have the word "Scala" in the title. Having already met `map` and `filter` we can write the solution.

```scala
> books
  .map(_.title)
  .filter(_.contains("Scala"))
  .size
→ 1
```

Remember that this is equivalent to
```scala
books
  .map(book => book.title)
  .filter(title => title.contains("Scala"))
  .size
```

We have just created a pipeline! It consists of three *pipes*, and each of them has an input and an output. We can connect them together only if the output of one of them has the same type as the input of the next one. For example, the map pipe outputs a `List[String]`. Therefore, we can connect it to any pipe that takes a `List[String]` as the input. This way, we connected three pipes together and formed a **pipeline, which is an encoding of the algorithm** that solves our original problem. It's a step-by-step algorithm, or a sequential program, created using `map` and `filter`.

This is a very natural programming technique sometimes called chaining. If it feels natural to you already, you shouldn't have any problems grasping this chapter's content. If not, we will help you get there!

Composing larger programs from smaller pieces

Pipelines can be constructed from smaller pieces of code that are composable and reusable. Hence, we can divide a larger problem into smaller parts, solve each of them individually, then create a pipeline to solve the original problem.

This approach is called divide and conquer, and it has been a Holy Grail for generations of programmers. Functional programmers try to use this approach whenever possible.

Recommending book adaptations

Let's see what our first objective is. Again, we have a list of books:

```scala
case class Book(title: String, authors: List[String])
val books = List(
    Book("FP in Scala", List("Chiusano", "Bjarnason")),
    Book("The Hobbit", List("Tolkien"))
)
```

We also have a function that returns a list of book adaptations (Movies) for any given author (for now, just Tolkien is supported):

```scala
case class Movie(title: String)

def bookAdaptations(author: String): List[Movie] =
  if (author == "Tolkien")
    List(Movie("An Unexpected Journey"),
         Movie("The Desolation of Smaug"))
  else List.empty
```

bookAdaptations

a function that gets an author and returns a list of movies (adaptations of their books)

returns two movies if the author is `Tolkien` *and no movies otherwise*

Our task is to return a feed of movie recommendations based on books. The data shown above should result in a list of two feed items:

```scala
def recommendationFeed(books: List[Book]) = ???
recommendationFeed(books)
→ List("You may like An Unexpected Journey,
        because you liked Tolkien's The Hobbit",
       "You may like The Desolation of Smaug,
        because you liked Tolkien's The Hobbit")
```

"???" in Scala means that an "implementation is missing." It is used to leave some pieces out to be implemented later. This is part of the language. It compiles fine but fails at runtime.

The pseudocode that achieves the result above may look like

Step 1	For each book ⟶ extract its authors.
Step 2	For each author⟶ call the bookAdaptations function, returning movies.
Step 3	For each movie ⟶ construct a recommendation feed string.

In the first part of this chapter, we will encode this algorithm as a purely functional pipeline—a sequential program.

The imperative approach

Step 1 For each book ──▸ extract its authors.
Step 2 For each author ─▸ call the bookAdaptations function, returning movies.
Step 3 For each movie ──▸ construct a recommendation feed string.

The recommendation feed could be written as three nested for loops.

```
static List<String> recommendationFeed(List<Book> books) {
  List<String> result = new ArrayList<>();       ❶
  for (Book book : books)
    for (String author : book.authors)
      for (Movie movie : bookAdaptations(author)) {   ❷
        result.add(String.format(
   ❸      "You may like %s, because you liked %s's %s",
            movie.title, author, book.title));
      }
    return result;     ❶
}
```

> **bookAdaptations**
>
> a function that gets an author and returns a list of movies (adaptations of their books)
>
> returns two movies if the author is "Tolkien" and no movies otherwise

If you've programmed in Java or any other modern imperative programming language, you should feel pretty confident about this code. It first creates a mutable list and then iterates over three collections in nested for loops. In the for loop's body, new String elements are added to the mutable list. The last line returns this list as the result.

Problems with the imperative solution

There are three problems with the above solution.

❶ **We need to use and return a mutable** List

Reads and updates of the List are spread across the whole function—in the first line, the last line, and inside the for body. It is harder to reason about such code. The bigger the function is, the worse this problem gets. We already discussed it in chapter 3.

❷ **Each** for **adds another level of indentation**

The more nesting there is in the code, the harder it is to read it. Nested loops with local variables are indented to the right, so adding more conditions usually means the programmer needs to scroll more.

❸ **We use statements instead of expressions in the** for **body**

The whole nested for returns nothing, so we need to add side-effecting statements inside the body to solve the original problem. That's why we needed to use a mutable List. Additionally, usage of statements makes the code harder to test.

We will come back to the "expression vs. statement" problem later in this chapter.

flatten **and** flatMap

Step 1 For each book ⟶ extract its authors.
Step 2 For each author⟶ call the bookAdaptations function, returning movies.
Step 3 For each movie ⟶ construct a recommendation feed string.

Let's solve the problem using the functional paradigm, step by step. We start by extracting authors (Step 1 in the diagram above). Here's our list of two books:

> *Note that a book can have more than one author.*

```
case class Book(title: String, authors: List[String])
val books = List(
  Book("FP in Scala", List("Chiusano", "Bjarnason")),
  Book("The Hobbit", List("Tolkien"))
)
```

> **books**
> a list of two books:
> – "FP in Scala" by Chiusano, Bjarnason
> – "The Hobbit" by Tolkien

Now, we want to get a list of all authors of those books:

```
books.map(_.authors) // or: books.map(book => book.authors)
→ List(List("Chiusano", "Bjarnason"), List("Tolkien"))
```

Well, that's not really what we wanted. Instead of the promised "list of all authors," we got "list of lists of authors." When we look closely at the function we passed to the map function, it becomes clear what happened: book.authors is a List[String], so we mapped each element in the list to a new list, getting the list of lists. Mystery solved!

Fortunately, we can get rid of this unnecessary wrapping by using the flatten function, which, well, *flattens* the list of lists into a list.

```
List(                                    List(
    List( Chiusano   Bjarnason ),            Chiusano
    List( Tolkien )                          Bjarnason
).flatten                                    Tolkien )
```

> *flatten goes through the list of lists and takes all elements from the first list, then second, and so on …*

```
books.map(_.authors).flatten // or: books.map(book => book.authors).flatten
→ List("Chiusano", "Bjarnason", "Tolkien")
```

The scenario of mapping using a function that returns an instance of the type we are mapping over—followed by a flatten—is so common that all functional languages provide a function that does both steps at once. In Scala, **this function is called flatMap**. Armed with this knowledge, we can now get a list of all authors with even less code:

> *See the difference between map and flatMap?*

```
books.flatMap(_.authors) // or: books.flatMap(book => book.authors)
→ List("Chiusano", "Bjarnason", "Tolkien")
```

Practical use case of using more flatMaps

Step 1 For each book ──▶ extract its authors.
Step 2 For each author ─▶ call the bookAdaptations function, returning movies.
Step 3 For each movie ──▶ construct a recommendation feed string.

We have built the first part of our pipeline and now have a list of authors at our disposal. In the second step we need to convert this list into a list of movies—some of their books' adaptations. Fortunately, we have access to the bookAdaptations function we can use here.

```
val authors = List("Chiusano", "Bjarnason", "Tolkien")
authors.map(bookAdaptations)
→ List(List.empty,
       List.empty,
       List(Movie("An Unexpected Journey"),
            Movie("The Desolation of Smaug")))
```

> **bookAdaptations**
>
> a function that gets an author and returns a list of movies (adaptations of their books)
>
> returns two movies if the author is "Tolkien" and no movies otherwise

We got list of lists again, but we now know exactly what to do:

```
authors.map(bookAdaptations).flatten
→ List(Movie("An Unexpected Journey"),
       Movie("The Desolation of Smaug"))
```

And if we connect both steps of our pipeline (starting with the list of books, not authors), we will get

```
books
  .flatMap(_.authors) ❶
  .flatMap(bookAdaptations) ❷
→ List(Movie("An Unexpected Journey"),
       Movie("The Desolation of Smaug"))
```

> **books**
>
> a list of two books:
> - "FP in Scala" by Chiusano, Bjarnason
> - "The Hobbit" by Tolkien

List(FP in Scala Hobbit)

❶

List(Tolkien)

List(Chiusano   Bjarnason)

List(Chiusano   Bjarnason   Tolkien)

❷   List.empty List.empty   List(Unexpected Journey
                                   Desolation of Smaug)

List(Unexpected Journey Desolation of Smaug)

> First flatMap
> A given function is applied to both books, resulting in two lists, which are joined in sequence to produce a bigger list.
>
> Second flatMap
> A given function is applied to each element, producing three lists—two empty ones and one containing two movies. They are joined together to produce the final result.

`flatMap` **and changing the size of the list**

Let's see what really happened in the last example. We started out with two books, then

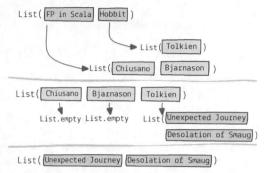

— the first `flatMap` returned a list of **three** authors and

— the second `flatMap` returned a list of **two** movies.

It is clear that `flatMap` not only can change the type of the list (e.g., from `Book` to `String`) but also can change the **size** of the resulting list, which isn't possible with `map`.

One question remains: where does a programmer make the decision about the size of the resulting list? To answer this question, let's focus on the second `flatMap` from the last example. Let's dissect it to separate calls of `map` and `flatten`:

```
> val authors = List("Chiusano", "Bjarnason", "Tolkien")

  val movieLists = authors.map(bookAdaptations)
  → List(List.empty,
         List.empty,
         List(Movie("An Unexpected Journey"),
              Movie("The Desolation of Smaug"))))
```

We see here that using `map` on a list of three elements results in a new list of exactly three elements. However, the elements of this list are lists, so we need to `flatten` them to get a meaningful result. Again, `flatten` goes through each list and extracts elements to a new resulting list. And because two of the resulting three lists are empty, the resulting list holds only the elements from the third list. That's why the third `flatMap` in the last example resulted in a list of two elements.

```
> movieLists.flatten
  → List(Movie("An Unexpected Journey"),
         Movie("The Desolation of Smaug"))
```

Quick exercise: How many elements will there be?

Tell how many elements the resulting lists will have:

```
List(1, 2, 3).flatMap(i => List(i, i + 10))
List(1, 2, 3).flatMap(i => List(i * 2))
List(1, 2, 3).flatMap(i =>
    if(i % 2 == 0) List(i) else List.empty)
```

Answers:
6, 3, 1

Coffee break:
Dealing with lists of lists

In this exercise we will work with the following Book definition:

```
> case class Book(title: String, authors: List[String])
```

Here's a function that takes a name of a friend and returns a list of their book recommendations:

```
> def recommendedBooks(friend: String): List[Book] = {
    val scala = List(
      Book("FP in Scala", List("Chiusano", "Bjarnason")),
      Book("Get Programming with Scala", List("Sfregola")))

    val fiction = List(
      Book("Harry Potter", List("Rowling")),
      Book("The Lord of the Rings", List("Tolkien")))

    if(friend == "Alice") scala
    else if(friend == "Bob") fiction
    else List.empty
  }
```

> recommendedBooks
>
> gets a friend name and returns a list of books they recommend:
> – Alice recommends "FP in Scala" and "Get Programming in Scala".
> – Bob recommends "Harry Potter" and "The Lord of the Rings".
> – Other friends don't recommend anything.

Assuming we have a list of friends, **compute the list of all books they recommend** (replace ??? with the actual code).

1

```
val friends = List("Alice", "Bob", "Charlie")
val recommendations = ???
→ List(Book(FP in Scala, List(Chiusano, Bjarnason)),
        Book(Get Programming with Scala, List(Sfregola)),
        Book(Harry Potter, List(Rowling)),
        Book(The Lord of the Rings, List(Tolkien)))
```

Having the list of all books recommended by our friends (created above), **compute a list of authors they recommend**.

2

```
val authors = ???
→ List(Chiusano, Bjarnason, Sfregola, Rowling, Tolkien)
```

Try to solve the second exercise using just one expression—starting with the friends list—by chaining functions together.

3

Quick reminder about function signatures in List[A]:

```
— def map(f: A => B): List[B]
— def flatten: List[B]  // A needs to be a List
— def flatMap(f: A => List[B]): List[B]
```

Coffee break explained: Dealing with lists of lists

1

We first look at functions and data at our disposal:

— friends: List[String]

— recommendedBooks: String => List[Book]

We have a List[String] and a function that takes a String and returns List[Book]. Our first idea is to use map.

```
val friends = List("Alice", "Bob", "Charlie")
val friendsBooks = friends.map(recommendedBooks)
→ List(
    List(
      Book("FP in Scala", List("Chiusano", "Bjarnason")),
      Book("Get Programming with Scala",List("Sfregola"))
    ),
    List(
      Book("Harry Potter", List("Rowling")),
      Book("The Lord of the Rings", List("Tolkien"))
    ),
    List()
  )
```

> recommendedBooks gets a friend name and returns a list of books they recommend:
> – Alice recommends "FP in Scala" and "Get Programming in Scala".
> – Bob recommends "Harry Potter" and "The Lord of the Rings".
> – Other friends don't recommend anything.

Oh, the dreaded list of lists! Fortunately, we know how to deal with it:

```
val recommendations = friendsBooks.flatten
→ List(Book(FP in Scala, List(Chiusano, Bjarnason)),
       Book(Get Programming with Scala, List(Sfregola)),
       Book(Harry Potter, List(Rowling)),
       Book(The Lord of the Rings, List(Tolkien)))
```

We solved the exercise using a map followed by a flatten. This combination reminds us that there is a shortcut called flatMap, which gives us the same result:

```
friends.flatMap(recommendedBooks)
```

For the second exercise, we already have a list of recommended books, so we need to just flatMap it with the _.authors function:

2

```
val authors = recommendations.flatMap(_.authors)
→ List(Chiusano, Bjarnason, Sfregola, Rowling, Tolkien)
```

We can write it in just one expression by chaining the flatMaps:

3

```
friends
  .flatMap(recommendedBooks)
  .flatMap(_.authors)
```

Chained `flatMaps` and `maps`

Step 1   For each book ⟶ extract its authors.

Step 2   For each author ⟶ call the `bookAdaptations` function, returning movies.

Step 3   For each movie ⟶ construct a recommendation feed string.

Let's go back to our running example. We are able to get movies. Now, we need to construct the final step of the pipeline: the generation of recommendation feed strings. Currently, our pipeline looks like this:

```
val books = List(
    Book("FP in Scala", List("Chiusano", "Bjarnason")),
    Book("The Hobbit", List("Tolkien")))
val movies = books
    .flatMap(_.authors)
    .flatMap(bookAdaptations)
→ List(Movie("An Unexpected Journey"),
        Movie("The Desolation of Smaug"))
```

> **bookAdaptations**
>
> a function that gets an author and returns a list of movies (adaptations of their books)
>
> returns two movies if the author is `"Tolkien"` and no movies otherwise

For each movie, we need to construct a string in the form of

"You may like $movieTitle *because you liked* $author's $bookTitle.*"*

The solution seems to be very straightforward. We just need to map each movie and construct a string, right?

```
movies.map(movie => s"You may like ${movie.title}, " +
                s"because you liked $author's ${book.title}")
```

What's the problem? We have access to neither author nor book inside the body of the mapping function! We can only create a string based on the movie, which only contains a `title`.

More formally, our `flatMaps` are **chained** one after another, and it means functions inside them have access only to a single element.

```
books
    .flatMap(book    => (       access to book      ))
    .flatMap(author  => (      access to author     ))
    .map    (movie   => (       access to movie     ))
```

First, we go through the list of books and transform the list into a list of authors. Only then the next `flatMap` is called. The consequence is that we can only use simple one-parameter functions as transformations.

If we wanted to write a third `flatMap` and pass `book` to it, we would be unable to do so because they are in different scopes due to chaining.

In Scala we can prefix any `String` literal with s to allow the compiler to interpolate values inside a given `String`. Only values wrapped in ${} or prefixed with $ are taken into account. For example, here ${movie.title} will be changed to a given movie's title during runtime. $author and ${book.title} will also be replaced by their values. It's similar to what we did in the Java version using `String.format`.

Nested flatMaps

Step 1 For each book ──→ extract its authors.
Step 2 For each author ──→ call the bookAdaptations function, returning movies.
Step 3 For each movie ──→ construct a recommendation feed string.

What we really need to implement the third step of our pipeline is to have access to all intermediate values—book, author, and movie—in one place. Hence, we need to keep them all in the same scope.

This is how we can pass a multi-line function to flatMap, map, filter, or any other higher-order function.

To achieve this we can use **nested** flatMaps. Each pipeline step should be defined inside the existing scope, so each intermediate value is accessible in all steps.

```
books.flatMap(book =>
  book.authors.flatMap(author =>
    bookAdaptations(author).map(movie =>
```

access to all values:
  – book
  – author
  – movie

We can create a single value based on all the intermediate values because they are now in scope.

```
    )
  )
)
```

Are we allowed to do this?

You may wonder whether the operation of switching from chained flatMaps to nested flatMaps is safe and warrants the same answer. Yes, it is safe. The answer will be exactly the same. Note that flatMap always returns a List, which, in turn, can be flatMapped. It doesn't matter whether we use a chained version or a nested one—as long as we are using flatMaps, we stay in the context of a List.

```
> List(1, 2, 3)
    .flatMap(a => List(a * 2))
    .flatMap(b => List(b, b + 10))
→ List(2, 12, 4, 14, 6, 16)

List(1, 2, 3)
  .flatMap(a =>
    List(a * 2).flatMap(b => List(b, b + 10))
  )
→ List(2, 12, 4, 14, 6, 16)
```

THIS IS BIG!
flatMap is the most important function in FP.

The flatMap function is very special. We wouldn't be able to transform chained maps into nested maps because map doesn't guarantee that it returns a List, no matter what function we pass. flatMap does.

Values that depend on other values

Step 1 For each book ──▶ extract its authors.
Step 2 For each author ─▶ call the bookAdaptations function, returning movies.
Step 3 For each movie ─▶ construct a recommendation feed string.

Now, let's see nested flatMaps in action and finally solve the original problem! We will create a recommendations feed: all the movies produced by our pipeline will need to be transformed into a human-readable string.

```
books
  .flatMap(book  =>         access to book         )
  .flatMap(author =>        access to author        )
  .map (movie   =>          access to movie         )
```

```
books.flatMap(book =>
  book.authors.flatMap(author =>
    bookAdaptations(author).map(movie =>
        access to all values:
        - book
        - author
        - movie
    )
  )
)
```

In the left code snippet, we can only return a String created from the values produced by the previous flatMap (i.e., we only have the movie value in the scope). To solve this, we need additional access to book and author—our String value needs to depend on three values in the scope. We need to transform the chained code into a **nested** flatMap.

```
> def recommendationFeed(books: List[Book]) = {
    books.flatMap(book =>
      book.authors.flatMap(author =>
        bookAdaptations(author).map(movie =>
          s"You may like ${movie.title}, " +
          s"because you liked $author's ${book.title}"
        )
      )
    )
  }

recommendationFeed(books)
→ List("You may like An Unexpected Journey,
        because you liked Tolkien's The Hobbit",
       "You may like The Desolation of Smaug,
        because you liked Tolkien's The Hobbit"))
```

bookAdaptations

a function that gets an author and returns a list of movies (adaptations of their books)

returns two movies if the author is "Tolkien" and no movies otherwise

books

a list of two books:
- "FP in Scala" by Chiusano, Bjarnason
- "The Hobbit" by Tolkien

This concludes the solution to the original problem. The recommendationFeed function is the functional programming version of the pipeline. It's better than the imperative one but still has some of its problems. One may argue that the nesting is very similar to the nesting of imperative for loops, and I'd agree with that completely! Fortunately, there is a solution for this problem as well.

Practicing nested `flatMaps`

Before we move on, let's make sure you are proficient with the nested `flatMaps`. Imagine you have defined the `Point` product type:

```
> case class Point(x: Int, y: Int)
```

Fill out the blanks to produce a list specified below:

```
List(   ???   ).flatMap(x =>
  List(   ???   ).map(y =>
    Point(x, y)
  )
)
→ List(Point(1,-2), Point(1,7))
```

As you can see, you need to fill two lists with numbers that would produce the desired resulting list. There are a few things worth remembering:

— We need to nest `flatMap` because we need access to both x and y to produce a single instance of `Point`.

— The last function is a `map` because the function we pass to it returns a `Point` value, not a `List`.

Again, read "???" as "missing implementation" in Scala. This code compiles fine but fails at runtime. It is used to leave some pieces out to be implemented later, especially when designing top-down. If they are part of an exercise, you need to replace them with real values to get a given answer.

Answer

The only possible way to produce this list is this:

```
> List(1).flatMap(x =>
  List(-2, 7).map(y =>
    Point(x, y)
  )
)
→ List(Point(1,-2), Point(1,7))
```

We wouldn't be able to create such a list using chained `flatMap` and `map` because the `Point` constructor needs both values in its scope.

Bonus exercises

Let's play more with the example above. The original snippet generates two points. How many points would be generated by the code above if we

— Changed `List(-2, 7)` to `List(-2, 7, 10)`?

— Changed `List(1)` to `List(1, 2)`?

— Changed both of the above at once?

— Changed `List(1)` to `List.empty[Int]`?

— Changed `List(-2, 7)` to `List.empty[Int]`?

Answers:
3, 4, 6, 0, 0

A better syntax for nested flatMaps

Our flatMaps became less readable when we started nesting them inside one another. We started nesting them because we wanted to have access to values from all chained lists, which is what we need in many pipeline-based sequential algorithms. Unfortunately, **nesting makes code less readable, especially when we add more levels of indentation**.

```
books.flatMap(book =>
  book.authors.flatMap(author =>
    bookAdaptations(author).map(movie =>
      s"You may like ${movie.title}, " +
      s"because you liked $author's ${book.title}"
    )
  )
)
```

flatMap nesting and its readability are not just a Scala issue. We may have the same problem when we use map, flatMap, and other functions in other languages.

So can we have our cake and eat it too? It turns out we can! Scala offers a special syntax that elegantly deals with nested flatMaps—the **for comprehension**. Let's see it in action right away! Have a look at the section below, and don't worry if you don't understand what's going on there. Focus on readability; we will dive into internals very soon.

Other languages have this feature too!
It's worth noting that the for comprehension is not just a Scala-specific mechanism. For example, in Haskell we have a do notation that achieves the same goal.

Getting started with for comprehensions

We haven't learned about for comprehensions yet, but before we do, let's first see how they can help us.

A for comprehension looks like this:

```
for {
  x <- xs
  y <- ys
} yield doSomething(x, y)
```

It reads like English: for each element x in xs and for each element y in ys, call the function doSomething(x, y). For example, if xs is a List(1, 2) and ys is a List(3, 4), then the for comprehension will end up calling doSomething four times:

```
doSomething(1, 3), doSomething(1, 4),
doSomething(2, 3), doSomething(2, 4).
```

The Scala compiler **transforms the for comprehension** above into the more familiar nested code, which does exactly the same thing:

```
xs.flatMap(x => ys.map(y => doSomething(x, y)))
```

Note that this is not a for loop! This is a totally different mechanism, which has a similar name and uses the same keyword. We don't use for loops in functional programming. We have a map for that!

For comprehensions to the rescue!

Step 1 For each `book` ──▶ extract its authors.
Step 2 For each `author` ──▶ call the `bookAdaptations` function, returning movies.
Step 3 For each `movie` ──▶ construct a recommendation feed string.

Now that we know how to mechanically transform nested `flatMap` calls into nicer, more readable for comprehension syntax, let's try to rewrite our original problematic example line by line to make it more readable.

```
                    for {
books.flatMap(book => ...
                        ➤ book <- books
book.authors.flatMap(author => ...
                        ➤ author <- book.authors
bookAdaptations(author).flatMap(movie => ...
                        ➤ movie <- bookAdaptations(author)
                    } yield s"You may like ${book.title}, " +
                            s"because you liked $author's ${book.title}"
```

Let's see the for comprehension version of the solution in isolation.

```
> for {
    book    <- books
    author  <- book.authors
    movie   <- bookAdaptations(author)
  } yield s"You may like ${movie.title}, " +
          s"because you liked $author's ${book.title}"
→ List("You may like An Unexpected Journey,
        because you liked Tolkien's The Hobbit",
        "You may like The Desolation of Smaug,
        because you liked Tolkien's The Hobbit"))
```

As you can see, the for comprehension version returns exactly the same answer as the imperative and nested `flatMap` solutions. But arguably, this code is far easier to read. Let's read it in plain English:

— *Extract each book from the books list.*

— *Then extract every author from each of the books above.*

— *Then, extract every movie from the book adaptations list (created by the* `bookAdaptations` *function) for each of the authors above.*

— *And for each such movie, produce a string value that is based on all the values extracted previously (i.e.,* book, author, *and* movie*).*

---

books

a list of two books:
- "FP in Scala" by Chiusano, Bjarnason
- "The Hobbit" by Tolkien

bookAdaptations

a function that gets an author and returns a list of movies (adaptations of their books)

returns two movies if author is "Tolkien", no movies otherwise

Coffee break:
flatMaps vs. for comprehensions

In this exercise we will work with the following definitions:

```
case class Point(x: Int, y: Int)

val xs = List(1)
val ys = List(-2, 7)
```

Previously, we used nested `flatMaps` to produce a list of points:

```
xs.flatMap(x =>
  ys.map(y =>
    Point(x, y)
  )
)
→ List(Point(1, -2), Point(1, 7))
```

Transform this code into a for comprehension:

```
for {
  ???
} yield ???
```

Now, imagine that we added a list of z coordinates and the 3D point:

2

```
case class Point3d(x: Int, y: Int, z: Int)

val xs = List(1)
val ys = List(-2, 7)
val zs = List(3, 4)
```

Create a for comprehension that will produce a list of all possible points
from the given coordinate lists:

```
for {
  ???
} yield ???
→ List(Point3d(1, -2, 3), Point3d(1, -2, 4),
       Point3d(1, 7, 3), Point3d(1, 7, 4))
```

Now, **try to create a nested flatMap version** of the 3D point generation
code above.

3

```
xs.flatMap(x =>
  ???
)
→ List(Point3d(1, -2, 3), Point3d(1, -2, 4),
       Point3d(1, 7, 3), Point3d(1, 7, 4))
```

Coffee break explained: `flatMaps` vs. for comprehensions

To solve the first exercise, we need to follow the mechanical transformation rules we defined earlier.

```
xs.flatMap(x => ...)          for {
                                x <- xs
                                ...
                              } yield ...
```

The code on the left can be transformed into the version on the right. We can follow the same technique with ys to get the final answer:

```
> for {
    x <- xs
    y <- ys
  } yield Point(x, y)
  → List(Point(1, -2), Point(1, 7))
```

The second exercise is a bit harder, but we can still solve it using the mechanical transformation approach:

```
> for {
    x <- xs
    y <- ys
    z <- zs
  } yield Point3d(x, y, z)
  → List(Point3d(1, -2, 3), Point3d(1, -2, 4),
         Point3d(1, 7, 3), Point3d(1, 7, 4))
```

As you can see, this looks very similar to the previous one. The additional list is just another line inside the for comprehension (no nesting!)

Now, let's solve the third exercise to be able to compare the for comprehension above with the nested `flatMap` version. We need to follow the mechanical transformation but in the reverse order.

```
> xs.flatMap(x =>
    ys.flatMap(y =>
      zs.map(z =>
        Point3d(x, y, z)
      )
    )
  )
  → List(Point3d(1, -2, 3), Point3d(1, -2, 4),
         Point3d(1, 7, 3), Point3d(1, 7, 4))
```

1

2

3

You can use both approaches (nesting or comprehensions), depending on what looks more readable and natural. In the remaining chapters we will be showing snippets of code that represent both styles.

Getting to know for comprehensions

Now, let's spend some time explaining inner workings of for comprehensions. We'll start by discussing some historical background.

For comprehensions are used as a *syntactic sugar* (i.e., they help write more comprehensible code, but they are not required to use). They are used as a replacement for three functions we have already met: `flatMap`, `map`, and `filter`.

In many languages this syntax is known as **list comprehensions**. Here is a sample of list comprehensions in a few languages for the expression equivalent to `list.filter(n => n < 10)`:

> **THIS IS BIG!**
> You will find a lot of for comprehensions in functional programs.

Python	`[n for n in list if n < 10]`
CoffeeScript	`for n in list when n < 10`
Clojure	`(for [n list :when (< n 10)] n)`
Haskell	`[n	n <- list, n < 10]`
C# (predicates)	`list.Where(n => n < 10)`
C# (queries)	`from n in list where n < 10 select n`
SQL	`select n from list where n < 10`

Notice how some languages use the keyword for. This is a very different for than the one used to construct simple loops in imperative programming.

Q Why is it called a list comprehension?

A This may seem like a really strange name, but it is actually a very good choice in naming. Comprehension is the ability to understand something. So list comprehension is the ability to understand lists.

Q Why do we use the name "for comprehension" in Scala?

A In Scala the name is for comprehension because we can use it for various other types—not just lists. In fact, as we will see in the next chapters, functional programmers use them mainly in types other than Lists.

And, again, as an example, Haskell also has its do notation that is used for the same purpose and works for more types than lists.

It's not the `for` you are looking for!

In Scala, a for comprehension is a first-class citizen of the language. Unfortunately for imperative programmers, it uses the keyword `for`.

Do not confuse the for expression in Scala with the traditional `for` statement in imperative programming. In imperative languages, we are accustomed to a `for` statement that simply loops over a collection using a counter or iterator.

In Scala, `for` is an **expression**. When used on a collection, it returns another collection with the transformed items. On the other hand, the imperative `for` is just a **statement** for constructing loops and returns nothing. That's why imperative `for` loops (statements) can't easily be used for immutable collections, which prefer expressions.

> ### Statements vs. expressions
>
> There is an important distinction between a statement and an expression. A **statement** is a language construct that needs to change the state of a program to be useful. In imperative languages, some examples of statements are `for`, `while`, and even `if`. Here's a Java snippet:
>
> ```java
> List<Integer> xs = Arrays.asList(1, 2, 3, 4, 5);
> List<Integer> result = new ArrayList<>();
>
> for (Integer x: xs) {
>   result.add(x * x);
> }
> ```
>
> An **expression,** on the other hand, doesn't operate on the global state, always returns something, and, when executed many times, it always returns the same result. If you want your expression to be useful, you need to use its result in your program.
>
> The above `for` statement can be transformed into a for expression in Scala (a for comprehension):
>
> ```scala
> val xs = List(1, 2, 3, 4, 5)
> val result = for {
>   x <- xs
> } yield x * x
> ```
>
> Remember! Functional programming is programming with expressions. Functional programmers don't use statements.

Everything you successfully evaluate in your REPL is a valid expression. A value name is an expression, a function name is an expression, and a function call is an expression, too!

THIS IS BIG! FP is programming with expressions, not statements.

Inside a for comprehension

It's time to finally define the generic shape of a for comprehension and
how it translates into flatMap and map calls.

```
for {
    enumerators
} yield output-expression
```

Enumerators are the lines of code looking like this: x <- xs. It means that
*every value from xs is enumerated, extracted as x, and passed to the next
enumerator or a yield expression.* We can have as many enumerators as
we want.

```
for {
    a <- as
    b <- bs
        .

        .

        .
    z <- zs
} yield function(a, b, ..., z)
```

All but the last enumerators
are translated into **flatMaps**.

The last enumerator is transformed into a **map**.

The expression after yield defines
the result of the whole for comprehension.

*We don't spend a lot of
time on syntax in this
book. However, the for
comprehension is so
prevalent and important
that we needed to make
an exception.*

What's the result type of a for comprehension?

If we can have many enumerators, what's the algorithm the compiler
uses to figure out the result type of the whole for comprehension? **The
resulting container type is defined by the enumerator type, and the
type of its elements is defined by the expression after yield.**

```
> for {
    a <- List[Int](1, 2)
    b <- List[Int](10, 100)
    c <- List[Double](0.5, 0.7)
    d <- List[Int](3)
} yield (a * b * c + d).toString + "km"
→ List("8.0km", "10.0km", "53.0km", "73.0km",
        "13.0km", "17.0km", "103.0km", "143.0km")
```

The container type of
the for expression is a
List.

*Even though this
comprehension goes
through different lists
(e.g., List[Int] and
List[Double]), the
whole expression yields a
List[String].*

In the code snippet above, the container type of the whole expression is
List (all enumerators are based on Lists). The type of its elements is the
type of the expression after yield (String here).

*Not only lists are
supported, though! We will
come back to this topic
later in the chapter.*

More sophisticated for comprehensions

Now, let's use techniques we've learned so far in a brand-new pipeline. We will try to use for comprehensions and see how to model more sophisticated algorithms using them.

Is the point inside a given circle?

We are given a list of points and a list of radiuses:

```
case class Point(x: Int, y: Int)

val points   = List(Point(5, 2), Point(1, 1))
val radiuses = List(2, 1)
```

Our task is to figure out which points are inside circles with given radiuses and centers in Point(0, 0). The function that does it for one specific pair of point and radius is defined as follows:

```
def isInside(point: Point, radius: Int): Boolean = {
  radius * radius >= point.x * point.x + point.y * point.y
}
```

Let's look at the example on the right. Imagine we call the `isInside` function with `radius = 1` and `Point(1, 1)`. In this case `isInside` returns `false` because `Point(1, 1)` is not inside a circle with radius 1. On the other hand, the same `Point(1, 1)` is inside a circle with radius 2. Thus, the `isInside` function returns `true`.

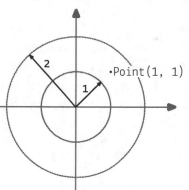

> **isInside**
>
> gets a point and a radius and returns a Boolean
>
> returns true if the given point is inside the circle with the given radius

This problem can be modeled as a pipeline. What we need to do is call the `isInside` function for each possible pair of point and radius. The pseudocode may look like this:

Step 1 Extract each possible `radius`.
Step 2 Extract each possible `point`.
Step 3 Call the `isInside(point, radius)` function, and return its result.

Yes! This is yet another **sequential program**! Let's use the techniques we have learned so far and write a for comprehension that quickly solves this problem.

Checking all combinations using a for comprehension

Step 1 Extract each possible `radius`.
Step 2 Extract each possible `point`.
Step 3 Call the `isInside(point, radius)` function, and return its result.

Again, here are lists of two points and two radiuses that we'll work with:

```
> val points  = List(Point(5, 2), Point(1, 1))
  val radiuses = List(2, 1)
```

We need to extract each radius as `r`, each point as `point`, and call the `isInside` function to get a result. We already know how to do that.

```
> for {
    r     <- radiuses
    point <- points
  } yield s"$point is within a radius of $r: " +
        isInside(point, r).toString
→ List("Point(5,2) is within a radius of 2: false",
       "Point(1,1) is within a radius of 2: true",
       "Point(5,2) is within a radius of 1: false",
       "Point(1,1) is within a radius of 1: false")
```

> **isInside**
>
> gets a point and a radius and returns a Boolean
>
> returns true if the given point is inside the circle with the given radius

We were able to produce the result using a two-step for comprehension. As you can see, the solution is very concise and readable, but there is a small problem. We are returning a string with the description of the result for each point–radius combination. It seems that we could do better by returning a list of points that satisfy the condition. In the case above only `Point(1,1)` is within the given radius.

Filtering inside a for comprehension

We already know how to filter collections, and we can easily reuse this approach inside for comprehensions. Here's how:

```
> for {
    r     <- radiuses
    point <- points.filter(p => isInside(p, r))
  } yield s"$point is within a radius of $r"
→ List("Point(1,1) is within a radius of 2")
```

There are two more approaches to perform filtering inside a for comprehension; one is mostly used with collections. The second one is more general and applicable beyond collection types, and it will serve as an introduction for more advanced usages of for comprehensions.

Filtering techniques

There are three basic techniques in Scala and functional programming that allow us to do filtering. We'll compare them by solving the same problem and getting the same results. Here are the values we'll use:

```
> val points   = List(Point(5, 2), Point(1, 1))
  val radiuses = List(2, 1)
```

Using `filter`

We already solved the problem using the `filter` function from `List`.

```
> for {
    r     <- radiuses
    point <- points.filter(p => isInside(p, r))
  } yield s"$point is within a radius of $r"
  → List("Point(1,1) is within a radius of 2")
```

> **isInside**
>
> gets a point and a radius and returns a Boolean
>
> returns true if the given point is inside the circle with the given radius

Using a guard expression (`if` in a for comprehension)

Some FP languages have a special syntax that can be used to filter collections in for comprehensions. In Scala, the `if` keyword can be a separate step inside a for comprehension. In our case, to ensure that only rs and points that satisfy the isInside(r, point) condition are yielded, we can

```
> for {
    r     <- radiuses
    point <- points
    if isInside(point, r)
  } yield s"$point is within a radius of $r"
  → List("Point(1,1) is within a radius of 2")
```

← We mention this approach briefly for the sake of completeness. We will be using the other two approaches in the rest of the book, as they are more universal.

Using a function passed to the `flatMap` function

We discussed how flatMap can change the size of a list, at the beginning of this chapter. Based on that, we can write a special function that we pass to flatMap (or in a for comprehension), which returns a list with one element if a condition is satisfied or an empty list otherwise.

← Remember that flatMaps are generated from for comprehensions by the compiler.

```
> def insideFilter(point: Point, r: Int): List[Point] =
    if(isInside(point, r)) List(point) else List.empty

  for {
    r       <- radiuses
    point   <- points
    inPoint <- insideFilter(point, r)
  } yield s"$inPoint is within a radius of $r"
  → List("Point(1,1) is within a radius of 2")
```

← This approach is overkill for this particular problem. However, as we shall see, it is a more universal technique that can be used beyond collection types. Stay tuned!

Coffee break: Filtering techniques

In this exercise we will try to use filtering techniques to protect ourselves against invalid data. Imagine that the list of radiuses contains some mathematically invalid values:

```
> val points    = List(Point(5, 2), Point(1, 1))
  val riskyRadiuses = List(-10, 0, 2)
```

What would happen if we ran our solution against those values? Let's look at the isInside function and our current solution:

```
> def isInside(point: Point, radius: Int): Boolean = {
    radius * radius >= point.x * point.x + point.y * point.y
  }

  for {
    r     <- riskyRadiuses
    point <- points.filter(p => isInside(p, r))
  } yield s"$point is within a radius of $r"
→ List("Point(5,2) is within a radius of -10",
        "Point(1,1) is within a radius of -10",
        "Point(1,1) is within a radius of 2")
```

The isInside function assumes that the radius we pass to it is nonnegative. If we pass negative values, it will return invalid results!

Let's filter invalid radiuses

In this coffee break section, you will try to filter invalid radiuses (all that are nonpositive) before running the isInside function. You will use all three different filtering techniques we learned about in the last section.

Your first task is to write a for comprehension that solves the problem and filters only the valid radiuses using the **filter function on List.**

1

Your second task is to solve exactly the same problem using the **guard expression** (if inside a for comprehension).

2

The third exercise is to solve the problem using a **function passed to the flatMap function**, using it as an enumerator in a for comprehension.

3

{ Note that the main reason for this coffee break is to get an intuition of how versatile flatMap is. It turns out mapping and flattening have plenty of useful applications! }

Coffee break explained: Filtering techniques

The first technique we need to use should be very familiar. We can use the filter function on riskyRadiuses to filter only nonnegative values.

1

```
> for {
    r       <- riskyRadiuses.filter(r => r > 0)
    point <- points.filter(p => isInside(p, r))
  } yield s"$point is within a radius of $r"
  → List("Point(1,1) is within a radius of 2")
```

The second exercise should be solved by adding an if guard expression inside the for comprehension.

2

```
> for {
    r <- riskyRadiuses
    if r > 0
    point <- points
    if isInside(point, r)
  } yield s"$point is within a radius of $r"
  → List("Point(1,1) is within a radius of 2")
```

The third exercise is the hardest one. We need to write another function, validateRadius, that takes a radius and returns it as a one-element List if it's valid or an empty List if it's not. This trick allows us to use it in flatMap or as another enumerator inside our for comprehension.

3

```
> def insideFilter(point: Point, radius: Int): List[Point] =
    if (isInside(point, radius)) List(point) else List.empty

  def validateRadius(radius: Int): List[Int] =
    if (radius > 0) List(radius) else List.empty

  for {
    r            <- riskyRadiuses
    validRadius <- validateRadius(r)
    point        <- points
    inPoint      <- insideFilter(point, validRadius)
  } yield s"$inPoint is within a radius of $r"
  → List("Point(1,1) is within a radius of 2")
```

As a bonus exercise, you can transform this for comprehension to raw flatMap/map calls. The answer can be found in the book's code repository.

You may feel that the last solution is a bit overcomplicated, but it has its benefits. **All the core logic is defined inside small functions, which are used to build a bigger algorithm inside the for comprehension.**

THIS IS BIG!
In FP, we build big programs from small functions.

Looking for a greater abstraction

So far we have learned how to deal with immutable values and collections, especially lists. We learned how to `map` things inside lists and how to `filter` them. In this chapter we've learned how to `flatMap` lists and how that helps us create pipeline-based algorithms. We focused on **creating small, reusable functions of our own**—and `map`, `filter`, and `flatMap` played a big role when we tried to connect them to build something bigger.

One may wonder, why are we so into lists? Is this really the most important thing in functional programming? Well, yes and no. Many things in programming can be modeled as lists. However, it's not the main reason we use lists here. It turns out that lists encompass many techniques of functional programming—and these techniques are used pretty much everywhere in functional codebases. Therefore, understanding lists is a stepping stone to understanding greater abstractions. We are learning an abstraction by following concrete examples, which usually are lists. When we learn how something works with lists, we can then move on and try to use it with something different. This is **abstraction** at work.

> **THIS IS BIG!**
> FP heavily relies on abstracting common features—you learn once and use them everywhere.

Let's see how this works when we try to learn `map`. Below are concrete examples of using `map` inside different types in Scala and Java:

```scala
val numbers = List(1, 2, 3, 4, 5)
numbers.map(_ * 2)
```

```java
List<Integer> numbers = Arrays.asList(1, 2, 3, 4, 5);
numbers.stream().map(n -> n * 2).collect(Collectors.toList());
```

Scala Collections

Java 8 Streams

Both snippets return a new list with all integers doubled.

Based on those two concrete examples, we can have a pretty good idea of how `map` would work for different types **in any language**. For example, what would the result of mapping over a tree be?

familyTree =

familyTree.map(node => node.birthyear) →

We are using an imaginary language that mixes text and graphics to show that it's possible to build an intuition for an abstraction based on concrete examples.

We expect that all the values in the tree will be changed using the function we provide—and that **the shape of the tree data structure will be preserved**. And this is exactly the abstraction behind `map`!

Comparing `map`, `foldLeft`, and `flatMap`

Before we move on to discuss more usages of the `flatMap` function in more types, let's use `List` one more time to compare the practicalities behind the three important functions: `map`, `foldLeft`, and `flatMap`.

`List[A].map(f: A => B): List[B]`

Applies the function passed as **f** to each element of the original list, producing a new list with modified elements. The shape of the data structure (**List**), its size, and its sequence of elements are preserved.

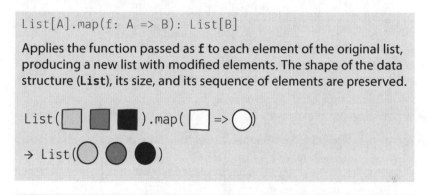

When we write "shape of the data structure," we mean the internal structure of elements (e.g., a list shape is different than a tree shape).

`List[A].foldLeft(z: B)(f: (B, A) => B): B`

Accumulates a value of type **B** by applying the function passed as **f** to each element (**A**) of the original list and the current accumulator value (**B**). The shape of the data structure (**List**) is lost as well as its size and sequence of elements. Only one value of type **B** is returned.

List(☐ ▨ ▩).foldLeft(0)(⬚ => incrementIfGrey)

→ 1

However, in some cases B can be another List!

`List[A].flatMap(f: A => List[B]): List[B]`

Applies the function passed as **f** to each element of the original list—producing multiple lists (one for each element), which are joined in the same order as the elements they originated from. The shape of the data structure (**List**) is preserved, but the size may be different—it can be an empty list or a list multiple times bigger than the original one.

List(☐ ▨ ▩).flatMap(⬚ => List(☐ ☐))

→ List(☐ ☐ ▨ ▨ ▩ ▩)

Remember how we used `flatMap` to filter out invalid values?

Using for comprehensions with Sets

The last part of this chapter will be focused on learning the abstraction behind flatMap and for comprehensions, which we'll use throughout the rest of the book. We have seen how to use them with lists. We need two more concrete examples to intuitively get the abstraction.

So, what are other types we can use for comprehensions with? Well, **all the types that have flatMap function defined for them**! And believe me, there are lots of them in the functional programming ecosystem! We will learn about many of them soon, but let's start with another collection type first: Set.

Using Set inside a for comprehension

There aren't many differences between List and Set as far as their usage inside for comprehensions is concerned. Have a look:

```
> for {
    greeting <- Set("Hello", "Hi there")
    name     <- Set("Alice", "Bob")
  } yield s"$greeting, $name!"
→ Set("Hello, Alice!", "Hello, Bob!",
      "Hi there, Alice!", "Hi there, Bob!")
```

As you see, in terms of mechanics, we are doing exactly the same thing. The choice of collection type, however, has a major impact on the values our for comprehension may return. Remember, Sets contain only unique values in an unspecified order, while Lists store all values in the order they were appended. We can see this difference in the example below:

```
> for {
    a <- List(1, 2)
    b <- List(2, 1)
  } yield a * b
→ List(2, 1, 4, 2)
```

```
> for {
    a <- Set(1, 2)
    b <- Set(2, 1)
  } yield a * b
→ Set(2, 1, 4)
```

In both cases there were four multiplication operations. Each result was added to the underlying collection, which means we had four additions. However, the collection itself defined how those additions were processed. Hence, the List stored four elements. In case of Set, two of those four elements had the same value (there are two 2s), so only three of them were stored.

Using for comprehensions with many types

One question still remains. Can we use more than one type inside a for comprehension? More concretely, can we use Lists and Sets in a single for comprehension? If so, what's the collection type returned from interpreting the whole for comprehension? Let's answer these questions by expanding on the previous example:

```
> for {
    a <- List(1, 2)
    b <- Set(2, 1)
} yield a * b
→ List(2, 1, 4, 2)
```

In this for comprehension we mixed List and Set but got List as a return type! So we now know that mixing is possible, but we don't quite get why List was chosen over Set. Let's figure it out by swapping the order of List and Set:

```
> for {
    a <- Set(1, 2)
    b <- List(2, 1)
} yield a * b
→ Set(2, 1, 4)
```

We are getting somewhere here! When we swapped the order and started with Set, the return collection was also a Set. When we started with List, the return collection was also a List. That's how it works.

We can mix enumerator types

Provided that the compiler can cast the collection type of enumerators inside the for comprehension, we can easily mix them inside one for comprehension. The Scala compiler can cast a List into a Set, and it can cast a Set into a List, so mixing those types inside for comprehensions is possible.

The first enumerator defines the return type

When we mix types inside a for comprehension, the collection type of the first enumerator is the type that will be returned by the for comprehension expression. So if we start with List, all the following enumerators need to be cast to Lists. If we start with Set, all the following enumerators will be cast to Sets. If it can't be done, the compiler will complain.

Practicing for comprehensions

It's time to make sure we are on the same page as far as for comprehension syntax is concerned. Please fill in the missing parts (???) of the code.

```
for {
  x <- List(1, 2, 3)
  y <- Set(1)
} yield x * y
→ List(   ???   )
```
1

```
for {
  x <- ???
  y <- List(1)
} yield x * y
→ Set(1, 2, 3)
```
2

```
for {
  x <- ???(1, 2, 3)
  y <- Set(1)
  z <- Set(   ???   )
} yield x * y * z
→ List(0, 0, 0)
```
3

Answers

— The first comprehension produces List(1, 2, 3).

— The second comprehension returns a Set, so the first enumerator should be a Set.

> ```
> for {
>   x <- Set(1, 2, 3)
>   y <- List(1)
> } yield x * y
> → Set(1, 2, 3)
> ```

— The third comprehension returns a List, so the first enumerator should be a List, and all the values are 0, so the yield expression (x * y * z) should always produce 0. Since both xs and ys are defined as nonzero, we need to put zero in zs.

> ```
> for {
>   x <- List(1, 2, 3)
>   y <- Set(1)
>   z <- Set(0)
> } yield x * y * z
> → List(0, 0, 0)
> ```

Defining for comprehensions ... again

We already defined for comprehensions formally earlier in this chapter. However, we've learned two new things since then: **guard expressions** and **mixing types**. Let's update the formal definition and include both of them inside the generic shape of the for comprehension.

```
for {
    a <- as The first enumerator defines the return type.
    b <- bs
        •          All but the last enumerators
                   are translated into flatMaps.
        •
                   Guard expressions
                   are translated into filters.
        •
    z <- zs The last enumerator is transformed into a map.
} yield function(a, b, ..., z)
```

The expression after yield defines
the result of the whole for comprehension.

An enumerator can be one of two things: a generator or a guard expression (filter). We can have as many enumerators as we want.

A **generator** is the line of code looking like this: x <- xs. It means that *every value from* xs *is enumerated, extracted as* x, *and passed to the next enumerator or* yield *expression*. Under the hood, it is transformed into a flatMap call or a map call if it's a **last generator** inside for.

A **guard expression** is the line of code that looks like this: if expression(x). It takes a value or values generated in previous steps and returns a Boolean value. Only the *values that satisfy the condition are passed to the next enumerator or* yield *expression*. Under the hood, it is transformed into a filter call. ←

A **first enumerator** is a generator that defines the collection return type of the whole for comprehension. All the other generators must generate values in the collection that can be transformed into this type.

A **yield expression** defines the type of the objects inside the collection.

This is a simplistic explanation. Scala transforms guard expression into withFilter calls, which are lazy counterparts of filter. This is not an important distinction because we won't use if guards in the book. Additionally, if you wonder what *lazy* means in this context, don't worry, we will discuss this later in the book.

Using for comprehensions with noncollection types

We've come a long way in learning about `flatMap`, pipelines, and sequential programs. We will use for comprehensions heavily in the rest of the book for many more types than `Lists` and `Sets`. This chapter's last example is also the first example of a for comprehension with a noncollection type.

Parsing historical events

Here's a product type that stores some information about an event:

```
case class Event(name: String, start: Int, end: Int)
```

`Event` has a `name`, `start` year, and `end` year. Obviously, there are some rules that `Event` needs to follow:

— `name` **should be a nonempty** `String`.
— `end` **year should be a reasonable number—say, less than 3,000.**
— `start` **should be less than or equal to** `end`.

We want to write a function that will take a raw `name`, `start`, and `end` year and return a valid `Event` if it's possible or an *empty* value if not.

This part of the chapter lays the foundation for the next chapter, where we'll focus on error handling. Generally, the whole chapter is fundamental, because we'll use for comprehensions and flatMaps in the remaining parts of the book. We'll use them for handling collections, handling errors, doing some input and output, and even streaming!

Ad hoc solution

Before we write a pipeline-based solution, let's get the ad hoc, straightforward solution out of our systems and discuss its problems.

```
> def parse(name: String, start: Int, end: Int): Event =
    if (name.size > 0 && end < 3000 & start <= end)
      Event(name, start, end)
    else
      null

  parse("Apollo Program", 1961, 1972)
  → Event("Apollo Program", 1961, 1972))
  parse("", 1939, 1945)
  → null
```

This solution works, but it's not a perfect one in terms of separation of concerns. All the **concerns are entangled in one line of code**—the `if` line. The three requirements we defined above should be treated separately in our code. It's not a big problem in this small example, but I'm sure you've seen and hated functions with lots of `if` clauses. Additionally, we'd like to **avoid using nulls**. Let's try to solve both problems!

Avoiding `nulls`: `Option` type

We will start by solving the problem of `nulls`. Why do we want to avoid them in the first place? Well, there are several reasons, and we will discuss some of them in this book. Here we'll just revisit one problem—a major one from a functional programming perspective. (More in chapter 6!)

Fun fact: Tony Hoare, the inventor of the null reference, called it his "one-billion dollar mistake."

`nulls` make our signatures lie

The main problem is that `nulls` make the signatures lie. Look at the solution proposed earlier:

```
def parse(name: String, start: Int, end: Int): Event
```

The signature says that the function returns an `Event` ... But it may, and does, also return a `null`! This is a very serious trust issue. If we can't say what the function does just by looking at its signature, we are no longer able to easily reason about our code. In functional programming, we want to build bigger programs from smaller ones, and to do that, **we need to have pure functions that don't lie about the things they can potentially return.**

Enter the `Option` type

To deal with this problem, many languages introduced an `Option` type. **It models a value that may or may not be there**. It has two subtypes: None and Some. If the value is not present, None is returned. If it's present, Some is returned with a concrete value inside.

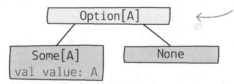

Other languages refer to this type differently. Haskell calls it Maybe and Java calls it Optional. However, the idea is the same in all of them. moreover, functional languages include some additional powers in these types (see the highlighted statement at the bottom of this page).

Armed with this type, we can rewrite our solution and make the signature of parse tell the truth and truth only:

```
def parse(name: String,
          start: Int, end: Int): Option[Event] = {
  if (name.size > 0 && end < 3000 & start <= end)
    Some(Event(name, start, end))
  else
    None
}
```

It seems like a small change, but on top of a better signature, `Option` gives us something more: **it has a `flatMap` function!** Let's use it!

Parsing as a pipeline

The second problem with the ad hoc solution based on the `if` expression was that all three requirements were entangled together in one line of code. Let's recall the requirements:

```
case class Event(name: String, start: Int, end: Int)
```
— name **should be a nonempty** String.
— end year **should be a reasonable number—say, less than 3,000.**
— start **should be less than or equal to** end.

We will explore error handling and parsing in more depth in the next chapter. Treat this section as a small introduction to what's possible.

Ideally, we should be able to model each of those requirements as a separate small function that can be maintained and changed individually without affecting others. Only then will we achieve true separation of concerns in our codebase.

Let's try to encode the requirements above as separate functions.

```
def validateName(name: String): Option[String] =
  if (name.size > 0) Some(name) else None

def validateEnd(end: Int): Option[Int] =
  if (end < 3000) Some(end) else None

def validateStart(start: Int, end: Int): Option[Int] =
  if (start <= end) Some(start) else None
```

Having these functions and knowing that `Option` has the `flatMap` function, we can now use them to easily filter out invalid data using plain, flat, `if`-less code that reads almost like English.

```
> def parse(name: String,
          start: Int, end: Int): Option[Event] =
    for {
      validName  <- validateName(name)
      validEnd   <- validateEnd(end)
      validStart <- validateStart(start, end)
    } yield Event(validName, validStart, validEnd)
```

No nulls!
No big if clauses!
Built from smaller functions that define real business logic!

```
parse("Apollo Program", 1961, 1972)
→ Some(Event("Apollo Program", 1961, 1972)))
parse("", 1939, 1945)
→ None
```

None is much better than null because it's a value of type Option[Event], and you can use it as such everywhere, without any worries.

The pipeline has three steps, and **if any of them fails (i.e., returns None), the whole for comprehension returns None**. This is exactly how we did it with lists; remember? We were able to filter out incorrect values by returning an empty `List`. **That's the feature of flatMap.**

Recall the section where we discussed how flatMap can change the size of its output compared to the input. It works for Option too!

Coffee break: Parsing with `Option`

In this exercise we will do something that is very common in the software engineering world: we will add a new requirement. Our pipeline-based design will allow us to do this change very efficiently without touching the code responsible for other requirements.

The new requirements states

— The event needs to take more than 10 years to be valid.

Your first task is to write a function that takes `start`, `end`, and a minimal length (`minLength`) of the event and returns `Some(length)` only if it's larger or equal to the minimal one. Here's the signature:

1

```
def validateLength(start: Int,
                   end: Int,
                   minLength: Int): Option[Int] = ???
```

Your second task is to use the function `validateLength` inside the for comprehension that we wrote earlier. It should be a part of a new function that parses raw data and returns an `Option[Event]`.

2

```
> def parseLongEvent(name: String,
                     start: Int, end: Int,
                     minLength: Int): Option[Event] = ???

parseLongEvent("Apollo Program", 1961, 1972, 10)
→ Some(Event("Apollo Program", 1961, 1972)))

parseLongEvent("World War II", 1939, 1945, 10)
→ None

parseLongEvent("", 1939, 1945, 10)
→ None

parseLongEvent("Apollo Program", 1972, 1961, 10)
→ None
```

Note that we've used more imperative names for our pure functions in this chapter, like `parse` and `validate`. As we discussed earlier in the book, experienced functional programmers prefer more declarative names: `eventFromRawData` or `validEventName`.

Make sure you reuse the functions responsible for the three remaining requirements. You shouldn't be concerned about their implementation, just their signatures.

```
def validateName(name: String): Option[String]
def validateEnd(end: Int): Option[Int]
def validateStart(start: Int, end: Int): Option[Int]
```

Coffee break explained:
Parsing with `Option`

We can approach writing `validateLength` in the same way we approached the other three functions.

```scala
def validateName(name: String): Option[String] =
  if (name.size > 0) Some(name) else None

def validateEnd(end: Int): Option[Int] =
  if (end < 3000) Some(end) else None

def validateStart(start: Int, end: Int): Option[Int] =
  if (start <= end) Some(start) else None
```

Based on the above, we just need an `if` expression, which returns `Some` if validation is successful and `None` otherwise.

1

```scala
def validateLength(start: Int,
                   end: Int,
                   minLength: Int): Option[Int] =
  if (end - start >= minLength) Some(end - start) else None
```

Your second task is to use the function `validateLength` inside the for comprehension we wrote earlier. It should be a part of a new function that parses raw data and returns an `Option[Event]`.

2

```scala
def parseLongEvent(name: String,
                   start: Int, end: Int,
                   minLength: Int): Option[Event] =
  for {
    validName   <- validateName(name)
    validEnd    <- validateEnd(end)
    validStart  <- validateStart(start, end)
    validLength <- validateLength(start, end, minLength)
  } yield Event(validName, validStart, validEnd)
```

Note how we used the fact that returning a None in one enumerator (a flatMap) makes the whole expression None. We did the same when we specifically returned an empty List.

Note that we just needed to define a new function and add another step inside the for comprehension. We didn't add anything to an existing if clause; we didn't change any existing code at all. This is nice because no existing requirements have changed! This hopefully shows the power of real separation of concerns and of functions that can easily be composed together.

Treat this small section about `Option` as a teaser of what is coming next in chapter 6. **We will need to add some error handling to our sequential programs.** We'll use `flatMap`, `Option`, and more!

Summary

In this chapter you learned five very important skills that will be very useful in the remaining chapters and your own programming encounters.

CODE: CH05_*

Explore this chapter's source code by looking at ch05_* files in the book's repository.

Deal with lists of lists using `flatten`

We first encountered the problematic List[List[String]] when we tried to process books that had several authors. We learned that Lists have the flatten function, which joins all the internal Lists in order into one big list and returns it as a List[String].

Write sequential programs using `flatMap` instead of `for` loops

Then, we introduced a function that is built on top of flatten and map: flatMap. It turned out that this function helps us build code that encodes functional pipeline-based algorithms—plain old sequential programs.

Write sequential programs in a readable way using for comprehensions

We still weren't convinced about the readability of flatMap-based code. It still had high levels of indentation. We learned that this could be solved using a for comprehension, which is very popular in the functional programming world. In Scala, a for comprehension is transformed into nested flatMap/map calls by the compiler.

Use conditions inside for comprehensions

We learned that there are three ways of doing filtering inside a for comprehension: using the filter function, using a guard expression (if inside a for comprehension), and using a function passed to the flatMap function. filter and guard expressions can only be used on specific types, like collections, while the last method is more generic and can be used on any type that has flatMap. We'll use it in the following chapters.

Get to know more types that have `flatMap`

In the last part of the chapter, we became familiar with more types that have a flatMap function: Set and Option. We learned how to use multiple types inside a for comprehension and how to build a parsing functionality as a sequential pipeline using a for comprehension and Option type.

Error handling | 6

In this chapter

you will learn

- how to handle all errors without `null`s and exceptions

- how to make sure all corner cases are handled

- how to indicate all the possible errors in the function signature

- how to compose bigger functionalities from smaller functions in the presence of different possible errors

- how to return user-friendly and descriptive errors

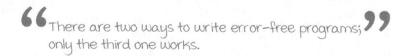

> There are two ways to write error-free programs; only the third one works.
>
> —Alan Perlis, "Epigrams on Programming"

Handling lots of different errors, gracefully

We can't write code that never fails. That's why we need to embrace all possible errors and make sure our code can handle them and recover from them gracefully. In this chapter we will discover how helpful it is to think about errors in terms of immutable values returned from pure functions. As always, we will learn based on a real-world example:

TV show–parsing engine

In this chapter we'll be dealing with popular TV shows. We'll start with simple requirements and then add more of them to make a full-blown TV show–parsing engine. There will be lots of corner cases to handle. We'll use them to learn how to use FP techniques to make sure all of them are covered gracefully without polluting the codebase.

We will work with raw values (i.e., values that are `Strings`). This will simulate real applications that get their data from the outside: a web service or a database. It may also simulate getting real user input. You will implement a few requirements yourself, but before you do, let's look at the trickiest one to understand how much you will learn.

What you will learn in this chapter

Here's a snippet of the example we will do later in this chapter. You will get a list of `Strings` that represent TV shows. Your function, called `parseShows`, **will need to parse all these `Strings`** and return the shows inside a nicely defined three-field `TvShow` value:

```
val rawShows = List("Breaking Bad (2008-2013)",
                    "The Wire (2002-2008)",
                    "Mad Men (2007-2015)")
```

We have a list of TV shows that are represented by raw strings that came from the outside world (a service or a database).

```
parseShows(rawShows)
→ List(TvShow("Breaking Bad", 2008, 2013),
       TvShow("The Wire", 2002, 2008),
       TvShow("Mad Men", 2007, 2015))
```

What if the raw show list contains two proper `Strings` and an invalid one?

What if the year is not inside brackets?

What if the year has an invalid format (2010-19)?

What if the end year is smaller than the start year (2010-2008)?

What if the user passes an empty `String`?

Is it even possible to handle them all?

Can we really handle all of these errors and still have great signatures, small implementations, immutable values, and pure functions? This chapter will resolve these doubts. But before we implement the real version of parseShows, which is prepared for all kinds of errors, we will need to recap some things about passing functions as parameters and returning functions (higher-order functions). Then, we will start learning about handling errors by looking at small functions and small errors. Next, we will build more functions by composing other small functions. This approach will work even when all of these functions fail.

Note how we are building on top of knowledge we gained in previous chapters. It's all about reusing the same blocks in more and more advanced scenarios.

The learning process in this chapter consists of five steps. We will learn how to indicate and handle errors in a functional way and see the benefits of this approach in comparison to exceptions.

Step 1

Recapping higher-order functions
Errors are handled using higher-order functions we learned about in chapter 4.

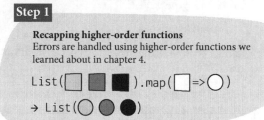

Step 2

Using Option to indicate an error
Indicating errors by returning immutable values from for comprehensions we learned about in chapter 5.

We will use these graphics during the course of the chapter to let you know how far along we are.

Step 3

Functional error handling vs. checked exceptions
Using the functional approach helps us indicate and handle errors in a much more readable and concise way than checked exceptions.

Step 4

Handling many errors at once
Defining higher-order functions that handle many errors using code that handles just a single error.

Step 5

Using Either to indicate descriptive errors
Indicating errors by returning immutable values that contain more information about what failed.

Apart from learning about functional error handling, you will get a chance to use almost all the things you've learned so far. Let's go!

Sort the list of TV shows by their running time

We will start with a warm-up exercise that will help us recap some things about higher-order functions we learned in chapter 4 and get acquainted with our new problem and its domain.

> **Requirement: Given a list of TV shows, sort it by running time**
> — We get a list of TV shows.
> — Each TV show has a name, the year it started airing, and the year it concluded.
> — We need to return a new list of TV shows, sorted by their running time, descending.

Quick exercise: The signature

Before we move on, we need you to design two things for us: a model of a TV show that we'll use and a signature of a pure function that will fulfill the requirement. This is how we usually start implementing requirements, both in this book and in real-world applications. That's why it's important not to skip this part. Please stop reading for a while and try to answer these questions:

1. What would a product type called TvShow look like?
2. What would a signature of a function called sortShows look like?

Answers in discussion.

> **Q** Didn't we implement a similar function before?
>
> **A** Yes, we did. It's repeated here on purpose. If it's easy for you, then great! The twist to this problem comes very soon, so please stay tuned.

The immutable model and the signature

Figuring out the model and a function signature is usually very hard, but if it's done right, we are rewarded with a straightforward implementation.

We'll use the following product type to model a TV show. TvShow should have a name, a year it started airing, and a year it ended. We just need to translate this sentence from English to Scala:

```scala
case class TvShow(title: String, start: Int, end: Int)
```

The signature of sortShows can also be translated directly from English to Scala:

```scala
def sortShows(shows: List[TvShow]): List[TvShow]
```

Note how this becomes a recurring theme in this book. We start implementing a requirement with two steps: a model (a product type) and a signature of a pure function.

That's how FP works: we program with pure functions, which manipulate immutable values.

Implementing the sorting requirement

We have the signature, so a big chunk of the requirement is already done. Now we need to provide an implementation that satisfies the signature.

> **Requirement: Given a list of TV shows, sort it by running time**
>
> — We get a list of TV shows.
> — Each TV show has a name, the year it started airing, and the year it concluded.
> — We need to return a new list of TV shows, sorted by their running time, descending.

To implement sortShows, we need to recall our old friends—functions that are defined for Lists—sortBy and reverse:

```
def sortShows(shows: List[TvShow]): List[TvShow] = {
  shows
    .sortBy(tvShow => tvShow.end - tvShow.start)
    .reverse
}
```

sortBy sorts in a natural order (from the smallest Int to the largest one), so to have a descending order, we need to reverse the List.

sortBy returns a new List that contains the same elements as the input List but sorted using a function provided as a parameter. Here, this anonymous function returns an Int: number of years a given show was running.

Using sortShows

Let's try to use the new sortShows function and make sure it works fine.

```
> val shows = List(TvShow("Breaking Bad", 2008, 2013),
                   TvShow("The Wire", 2002, 2008),
                   TvShow("Mad Men", 2007, 2015))
```

Mad Men ran for eight years, so it's at the top of the list.

```
sortShows(shows)
→ List(TvShow("Mad Men", 2007, 2015),
       TvShow("The Wire", 2002, 2008),
       TvShow("Breaking Bad", 2008, 2013))
```

It is the first time we take into consideration that no application works in isolation. Each application we create needs to communicate with the outside world. This communication usually happens using low-level primitives, like Strings.

The twist

OK, enough with warm-up exercises! Where is the catch? It turns out **we won't get the list of TV shows as a List[TvShow]**. We will get it as a List[String]! It's a pretty common scenario—we get data from the outside world: a database, a web service, or user input. So we usually need to deal with a raw String. In our case it's a List of Strings, each representing a single TV show and its details. Welcome to the real world!

Dealing with data coming from the outside world

So far we've been working with an ideal world scenario. We've always had object instances that contained only validly formatted data. We were operating on Books, Events, Points, ProgrammingLanguages—and now TvShows. It's been great but a little bit off. The real world is scarier than that. We need to operate on lower levels; we are getting raw inputs from the user; we are getting raw data from other services and even from our own database. There is always something that could go awry.

We are now going to start learning about these scary real-world scenarios based on parsing incoming data. We don't really get a List[TvShow], we get a List[String], and each of the Strings aims to represent a TV show, but it's our job to make sure each of these Strings really is a TV show. This operation is called **parsing**.

You most definitely know what parsing is. We mention it here explicitly because it occupies a special place in functional programming. For example, we have parser combinators, which are used to create more complicated parsers from basic ones using higher-order functions. It's the essence of FP.

> ### Parsing
>
> Parsing is an operation that transforms raw data, like String, into a domain model, usually represented by a product type (immutable value). We will use parsing to show how to deal with raw data coming from the outside world. This means that we will need to deal with all sorts of problematic scenarios.
>
> Note that **this chapter is not about parsing**. We just use parsing as an example of a potentially failing operation. All the techniques we use for parsing Strings can, and will, be used for other failing operations later in the book.

Here's the problem we now have to deal with:

```
val rawShows: List[String] = List(
  "Breaking Bad (2008-2013)",
  "The Wire (2002-2008)",
  "Mad Men (2007-2015)")

sortShows(rawShows)
→ compilation error: sortShows takes List[TvShow]
```

We now have a list of Strings, each potentially representing a TV show.

sortShows needs List[TvShow], so if we provide a List[String], it will protest loudly.

The natural question arises: do we now need to reimplement sortShows? It needs a new signature! It needs to take a List[String] and return a sorted List[TvShow], right? Well, **the answer is no!**

Functional design: Building from small blocks

The whole point of the functional design is to build bigger functionalities from small pieces: pure functions from smaller pure functions. Let's transfer this principle to our current example. We got the requirement about sorting, and we just implemented it.

```
def sortShows(shows: List[TvShow]): List[TvShow] = {
  shows
    .sortBy(tvShow => tvShow.end - tvShow.start)
    .reverse
}
```

It's a pure function that gets a List[TvShow] and returns a new list, sorted according to the requirements. The fact that the input type changes doesn't matter for this requirement; **it's a completely different requirement that should be implemented as a separate function!** This way we can focus on one thing at a time. We focused on sorting, and now it's time to focus on parsing the raw input.

The new requirement needs a new function. Let's think for a bit. We have a List[String], and we have function that needs a List[TvShow] as an input. That means that we need a new function that transforms a List[String] into a List[TvShow]. We'll then be able to compose both of those functions using a technique for sequential programs.

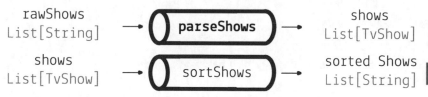

This way we don't have to change sortShows at all! It's small and does its job. That's the beauty of functional design. We do everything using small functions with single responsibilities. The composition is also a small function with one responsibility (merging two other ones).

```
def sortRawShows(rawShows: List[String]): List[TvShow] = {
  val tvShows = parseShows(rawShows)
  sortShows(tvShows)
}
```

The following pages will focus on implementing the parseShows function with error handling.

We will now move on to more advanced cases and leave sorting behind. Remember, however, that it still is there and can be used without modification.

Parsing Strings into immutable objects

Let's leave sorting behind for now. It's done, and we know it's working as intended. We know that it's been implemented using a pure function and immutable values, so it will be very easy to use it later.

Before we can use it, however, we need to make sure that we have a List[TvShow] that sortShows needs as an input. However, all we have now is a List[String]. Therefore, we need a function that takes a List[String] and returns a List[TvShow].

```
def parseShows(rawShows: List[String]): List[TvShow]
```

Before we try to implement it, let's try to list the requirements of parsing. You have probably guessed them already.

> **New requirement: Format of a raw TV show**
>
> Our application gets a List of raw TV shows. Each raw TV show is just a String that should have the following format:
>
>   TITLE (YEAR_START-YEAR_END)
>
> For example: In "The Wire (2002-2008)", TITLE is "The Wire", YEAR_START is 2002, and YEAR_END is 2008. The String "The Wire (2002-2008)" should, therefore, be transformed into an immutable value of TvShow("The Wire", 2002, 2008).

The format is TITLE (YEAR_START-YEAR_END). So our algorithm should do the following steps:

1. Find the occurrence of '(' and treat everything before it as a title (and trim all whitespaces).
2. Find the occurrence of '-' and treat everything between '(' and '-' as a starting year (it should be parsable to Int).
3. Find the occurrence of ')' and treat everything between '-' and ')' as an end year (it should be parsable to Int as well).

As you can see, there is a lot going on here. On top of that, we have a List[String], so we need to apply this algorithm to each String in this list. A lot can go wrong here, so our first reflex is to **split it up more!**

Parsing a `List` **is just parsing one element**

We have a `List[String]` and an idea for an algorithm that transforms one `String` into a `TvShow`.

Quick exercise

Before moving on, let's think for a bit. Do you remember what function defined on `List` we can use here to make our job easier?

Answer in discussion.

Before answering the question, let's approach it from the software architecture and design perspective. The first rule of functional design is to split a given requirement into small functions before implementing anything. We can do it by working with small, one-line implementations and signatures only, thus making it more about the design and less about the nitty-gritty details. In our case we want to parse an incoming `List[String]` into a `List[TvShow]`.

Parsing a `List` **by parsing each element separately**

A functional way of solving it is to extract the functionality of parsing just one `String` into a `TvShow` and then use it to parse the whole `List`. Sound familiar? It's our old friend, `map`!

```
def parseShows(rawShows: List[String]): List[TvShow] = {
  rawShows.map(parseShow)
}
```

> **Step 1**
>
> **Recapping higher-order functions**
> Errors are handled using higher-order functions we learned about in chapter 4.

As you can see, we are mapping each `String` element using a function called `parseShow`, which should return a `TvShow`. This function has not been written yet, but we already know what signature we need!

Now what's left to implement is a smaller function that takes care of parsing a single TV show:

```
def parseShow(rawShow: String): TvShow
```

Note the subtle difference between parseShows, which is implemented using a map, and a parseShow, which we haven't written yet, though we already know how we'll use it.

Now we can focus on implementing the smaller function (`parseShow`) because the bigger one is already done (`parseShows`)! After we implement the small function that parses one `String`, we will automatically gain the ability to parse the `List[String]` as well! This is the functional design at work! We have thought the functionality through, broken it down into smaller pieces, and reused some superpowers we learned about earlier. Let's implement the `parseShow` function!

Parsing a String into a TvShow

Let's try to implement the function that parses one String into a TvShow. Based on the requirements, given a well-formatted String TITLE (YEAR_START-YEAR_END), parseShow should first look for separator characters (brackets, dash) and then extract the information like this:

```scala
def parseShow(rawShow: String): TvShow = {
  val bracketOpen  = rawShow.indexOf('(')
  val bracketClose = rawShow.indexOf(')')
  val dash         = rawShow.indexOf('-')

  val name      = rawShow.substring(0, bracketOpen).trim
  val yearStart = Integer.parseInt(rawShow.substring(bracketOpen + 1, dash))
  val yearEnd   = Integer.parseInt(rawShow.substring(dash + 1, bracketClose))

  TvShow(name, yearStart, yearEnd)
}
```

We first need to find indices of the separator characters.

1

Finally, after we get three arguments, we can create and return a TVShow.

3

Then, we need to use these indices to extract three pieces of information based on the format from the requirement.

2

In Scala, we can use types and functions from Java. We've been using this feature as a learning tool in this book. Here we use Java's Integer.parseInt, which gets a String and returns an int value that the given String contains. If you wonder what happens if the String doesn't contain an int, that's good! We will address this very soon.

Let's try to use it and find out if it works correctly.

```
> parseShow("Breaking Bad (2008-2013)")
→ TvShow("Breaking Bad", 2008, 2013)
```

It does! Additionally, as promised, implementing the parseShow function should automatically give us the power to use parseShows, which was implemented using a map.

```scala
def parseShows(rawShows: List[String]): List[TvShow] = {
  rawShows.map(parseShow)
}
```

When we try to use it, everything works just fine! We get a list back!

```scala
val rawShows: List[String] = List(
  "Breaking Bad (2008-2013)",
  "The Wire (2002-2008)",
  "Mad Men (2007-2015)")
```

We have an input list of raw shows: three Strings that represent potential TV shows in a format we require.

```
> parseShows(rawShows)
→ List(TvShow("Breaking Bad", 2008, 2013),
       TvShow("The Wire", 2002, 2008),
       TvShow("Mad Men", 2007, 2015))
```

When we use the rawShows list as an input to our parseShows function, it maps each String using the parseShow (singular) function and returns a new list, with proper TvShow immutable values.

What about potential errors?

We now have our new `parseShow` and `parseShows` functions, and they produce correct results for our sample list of raw TV shows. So are we done already? The answer, unfortunately, is no; we are not done. As we mentioned earlier, the raw `Strings` are something coming from the outside world, a database, or user input. That means that we may, and most certainly will, not get all these `Strings` formatted as `TITLE (YEAR_START-YEAR_END)`. And what would happen then?

Let's see for ourselves. If we get an invalidly formatted raw show:

```
val invalidRawShow = "Breaking Bad, 2008-2013"

parseShow(invalidRawShow)
Exception in thread "main": String index out of range: -1
```

The years should be in brackets, but they are not! Note that this is only one of many ways it may fail. We will discuss it shortly.

Not only it does not return a `TvShow` back, it throws an exception and crashes the whole app, too. So our function breaks the promise it gave us with its signature:

```
def parseShow(rawShow: String): TvShow
```

If `parseShow` was a person, we could be tempted to ask it, "Dear `parseShow`. It seems you don't return a `TvShow` for any `String` we give you. **Why would you lie to us like that?"**

Pure functions should not throw exceptions

Our `parseShow` function throws an exception if a `String` we give is not properly formatted. This fact alone proves that the `parseShow` function is not pure—it doesn't always return a promised value (a `TvShow`). How can we solve it? Let's find out by looking at potential solutions.

In Java, we could use a `try...catch` and return `null` if something is thrown, although it's not a good practice.

```
try {
    return parseShow(invalidRawShow);
} catch(Exception e) {
    return null;
}
```

> **Pure function**
> - ☐ Returns a single value
> - ☑ uses only its arguments
> - ☑ Doesn't mutate existing values

We could also throw an exception and let the client worry about it. The problem remains the same: users of this function need to have two ways of handling it, one for proper values and one for exceptions/nulls. That means that there will be ifs and try...catches everywhere.

This approach makes sure that our application won't crash if TV shows can be parsed. But what's the cost of such a solution?

Is returning `null` a good idea?

There are two problems with functions that may return `null` in error cases. Both have an impact on users of our code:

- The function's return value does not contain any hint that it may fail (it promises to always return a `TvShow`, but it sometimes returns `null`).
- Users can't trust our functions, and they need to protect themselves against possible `null`s everywhere!

Let's put ourselves in our user's shoes. Let's try to use a function that returns `null` if the `String` is not formatted correctly. This means that the client code will probably look like this:

```
TvShow show = parseShow(invalidRawShow);
if(show != null) {
  // do more things with the show
}
```

← **Very bad ergonomics!**
Instead of focusing on business logic, a developer that uses our function needs to think about two different ways it may behave.

This is not a functional way! Signatures always indicate all of the possible return values. **A user always gets a value back!** The `parseShow` signature needs to change: for some `String`s there is no correct `TvShow`.

Option **to the rescue!**

The good news is that we can solve both of these problems by using the `Option` type we met in the previous chapter! A value with type `Option` can be one of two possible things: an existing value or a nonexisting value.

In the previous chapter we learned that `Option` can be used in sequential programs because it has the `flatMap` function. In this chapter we will use this knowledge and treat `Option` as a type that indicates successful and failed computations. Please recall the fact that returning a `None` in one enumerator flattens the whole for comprehension to `None`. The same happened when we `flatMapped` an empty `List`!

Quick reminder: How does `Option` work?

`Option[A]` has two concrete subtypes: `Some[A]` and `None`, meaning that if we want to create a value of type `Option[Int]` we need to choose whether it's an existing value (e.g., `Some(7)`) or not (`None`).

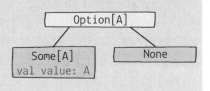

```
val existing: Option[Int] = Some(7)
val nonExisting: Option[Int] = None
```

There is no other way! To create a value of type `Option`, we need to choose `Some` or `None`. And the most profound thing is that both `Some` and `None` are values—they are both handled the same way.

How do we handle potential errors more gracefully?

Step 2
Using Option to indicate an error
Indicating errors by returning immutable values from for comprehensions we learned about in chapter 5.

Let's try to make the **parseShow** function more trustworthy by using the powers of the Option type. Our parseShow function will return an Option-typed value to let a user know whether the parsing succeeded or not.

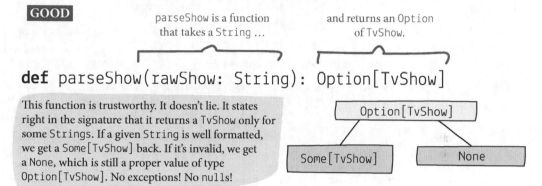

GOOD

parseShow is a function that takes a String ...

and returns an Option of TvShow.

```
def parseShow(rawShow: String): Option[TvShow]
```

This function is trustworthy. It doesn't lie. It states right in the signature that it returns a TvShow only for some Strings. If a given String is well formatted, we get a Some[TvShow] back. If it's invalid, we get a None, which is still a proper value of type Option[TvShow]. No exceptions! No nulls!

Option[TvShow]

Some[TvShow]   None

BAD

```
def parseShow(rawShow: String): TvShow
```

This function can't be trusted. It lies to us. It states right in the signature that it returns a TvShow for all Strings, but we know that's the case. It may throw an exception or return a null, and the signature doesn't mention these at all.

We now know that parseShow should return an Option[TvShow]. If you feel a little bit surprised by this, don't worry, as things should clarify very soon. You may also feel that **throwing a checked exception**, which is also visible in a signature, is perfectly fine. However, there are more reasons not to use exceptions than just language mechanics, and we will cover all of them soon. Before we do, let's focus on our new parseShow.

As you know, we want to design useful functions that are convenient and safe to use. That's why we always start from the perspective of its users. So, let's find out how Option-based parseShow would be used.

```
> parseShow("The Wire (2002-2008)")
→ Some(TvShow("The Wire", 2002, 2008))
  parseShow("The Wire aired from 2002 to 2008")
→ None
```

As you can see, when we provide a well-formatted String, we get the TvShow wrapped in Some. For an invalid String, we get None.

As a reminder, if your function throws a checked exception, it needs to indicate that in the signature by adding a throws clause. We will cover this soon, and we will compare this approach with the functional one.

No exceptions!

Implementing a function that returns an Option

We've talked a lot about signatures and how a user would use our parseShow function. By looking at the signature, our users know that the parseShow function gets a String and may return either Some(TvShow) if the String is formatted correctly or None if it isn't. Now it's time to try to implement parseShow. Before we do that, let's look again at the previous implementation that throws an exception if it gets an invalidly formatted String and compare it to the Option-based one.

> This is exactly what we want from pure functions. We expect they don't ever lie to us.

Before **Returning TvShow (or throwing an exception if something goes wrong)**

```
def parseShow(rawShow: String): TvShow = {
  val bracketOpen  = rawShow.indexOf('(')
  val bracketClose = rawShow.indexOf(')')
  val dash         = rawShow.indexOf('-')

  val name      = rawShow.substring(0, bracketOpen).trim
  val yearStart = Integer.parseInt(rawShow.substring(bracketOpen + 1, dash))
  val yearEnd   = Integer.parseInt(rawShow.substring(dash + 1, bracketClose))

  TvShow(name, yearStart, yearEnd)
}
```

> If rawShow doesn't contain at least one of these separator characters, we will get -1 as one of these values.

> Calling substring with -1 will inadvertently end up with a StringIndexOutOfBoundsException.

> We should probably define and throw our own exception here, but the code would get a lot messier, so let's leave it for now.

After **Returning Option[TvShow] (always!)**

```
def parseShow(rawShow: String): Option[TvShow] = {
  for {
    name      <- extractName(rawShow)
    yearStart <- extractYearStart(rawShow)
    yearEnd   <- extractYearEnd(rawShow)
  } yield TvShow(name, yearStart, yearEnd)
}
```

> We use a for comprehension to make sure everything is done in the context of Option, evaluated step by step in a sequential manner, like a pipeline. Each step is a function call. Each of these extract functions need to return an Option to satisfy the compiler. We will implement them next. Their signatures are:
> ```
> def extractName(rawShow: String): Option[String]
> def extractYearStart(rawShow: String): Option[Int]
> def extractYearEnd(rawShow: String): Option[Int]
> ```

> We yield a TvShow only if all three steps above return a Some. If any step returns None, the whole for comprehension will be None. Note that name is a String, and yearStart and yearEnd are Ints. The <- syntax inside a for comprehension makes sure that if the right-hand side is a Some(value), we get the bare value on the left-hand side.

> This function is totally safe. It will always return a value of type Option[TvShow], no matter what String we give it. That's a promise we get in the signature!

Let's imagine how such a function would be used. We expect that when we give a String that cannot be parsed, the whole function returns None instead of throwing an exception and crashing.

```
parseShow("Mad Men (-2015)")
→ None
```

However, it should return a TvShow wrapped in Some if the String is valid.

```
parseShow("Breaking Bad (2008-2013)")
→ Some(TvShow("Breaking Bad", 2008, 2013))
```

> Note that we still don't have a fully functional solution to the problem. We are just comparing the signatures and usages to obtain an intuition about how Option-based differs from exception-based.

`Option` **forces us to handle possible errors**

You probably wonder why we introduced small `extract` functions in the `Option`-based version and not in the exception-based version. The short answer is that in the `Option`-based version it really matters, while in the exception-based version it's just a matter of aesthetics. The longer answer requires us to discuss an important distinction between *being forced to handle an error* and *being able to handle an error*.

Option-based **Forces us to handle errors!**

```
def parseShow(rawShow: String): Option[TvShow] = {
  for {
    name      <- extractName(rawShow)
    yearStart <- extractYearStart(rawShow)
    yearEnd   <- extractYearEnd(rawShow)
  } yield TvShow(name, yearStart, yearEnd)
}
def extractName(rawShow: String): Option[String]
def extractYearStart(rawShow: String): Option[Int]
def extractYearEnd(rawShow: String): Option[Int]
```

This is our preferred version. These are all pure functions. They are letting us know, in their signatures, that they won't produce a TvShow for some Strings. **The most important thing, however, is that if we want to use them, we can't ignore the fact that they are returning Options!** What does it mean?

Let's assume you want to ignore the fact that extract functions return Options. You want to write something quickly in the same way you'd write an exception-based solution:

```
def parseShow(rawShow: String): Option[TvShow] = {
  val name      = extractName(rawShow)
  val yearStart = extractYearStart(rawShow)
  val yearEnd   = extractYearEnd(rawShow)

  TvShow(name, yearStart, yearEnd)
}
```

This version wouldn't compile, because extract functions return Options. And to create a TvShow you need a bare String and two Ints. Also, the function needs to return an Option, not a TvShow.

Exception-based Enables us to handle errors

```
def parseShow(rawShow: String): TvShow = {
  val name      = extractName(rawShow)
  val yearStart = extractYearStart(rawShow)
  val yearEnd   = extractYearEnd(rawShow)

  TvShow(name, yearStart, yearEnd)
}
def extractName(rawShow: String): [String]
def extractYearStart(rawShow: String): [Int]
def extractYearEnd(rawShow: String): [Int]
```

We don't want to use this version because these are not pure functions. Even worse, they look like ones! This is very bad for readability and maintainability. This version is very misleading because there is no mention of a possibility of a parsing error! You'd need to dive deep into the extract functions implementations to learn that they are not pure and may crash your application if you are not careful. Runtime exceptions can be thrown without including them in signatures, so there is nothing that stops us from just calling a function and assuming that it will return a proper value.

meet the functional compiler! From now on it will help us write better code by providing helpful compilation errors.

This version compiles even though there are unhandled exceptions that will crash the application!

The Option-based version is better exactly because it doesn't compile when we don't use for comprehensions (i.e., maps/flatMaps) to safely get values out of Options! In the Option-based solution, when we create small extract functions, we are forcing all its clients—functions that use this function—to handle possible errors (Nones). Whereas the exception-based solution merely enables us to handle errors and only if we really want to ... unless we use a checked exception, which we will discuss later in the chapter.

Building from small blocks

When we try to use an Option value, we are forced to handle the possibility of it being a None. There is no way around this! The same is true for other programming mechanics we will learn in later chapters. For now, we do just the error handling. When we want to write a function that returns a value only for some cases, we indicate it in the signature.

```
def extractName(rawShow: String): Option[String]
def extractYearStart(rawShow: String): Option[Int]
def extractYearEnd(rawShow: String): Option[Int]
```

We can tell exactly what's going on just by scanning the signature. Of course we don't know everything because the details of parsing each of the three fields are hidden inside three functions. The cool thing is that even though they are hidden, we can be sure there are no surprises there. These are just pure functions that return immutable values!

But there is more! By creating these small functions that return Options, we are setting the pace for everything else in the codebase! We are creating small blocks that can be used to build larger structures but only if the rules that we defined are satisfied! What rules, you might ask? Well, the rules included in the Option type, for example. As we have just discussed, when we return an Option, we are forcing our clients—users of our code—to handle the possibility of an error! They need to be aware that there is a possibility of None. This is the rule that we are enforcing!

> **THIS IS BIG!**
> Indicating an error in FP means returning an immutable value that represents an error.

When we use Option, we use None as a value that represents an error. We can use other types, too, which we'll soon see.

Functional design is building from small blocks

We have already discussed functional design on several occasions. The first rule of functional design is to break the functionality into small blocks of code, which, in our case, are always functions—pure functions. These blocks of code—functions—return immutable values that can be used together in a very specific way to compute another value, which represents a bigger thing. This idea of how well different, independent values can be used together to compute another value is called **composability**.

Let's look at our current example from the perspective of composability. In our case, we have three small functions: extractName, extractYearStart, and extractYearEnd. They all return Options, so we know that to use them, we'll need to handle both Some and None cases. We want to build a bigger function that is responsible for parsing a raw TV show, handling all the corner cases that are represented by Options encoded in extract functions. The for comprehension we used is one example of that; it composes three different values of Option to produce a single output value: an Option[TvShow].

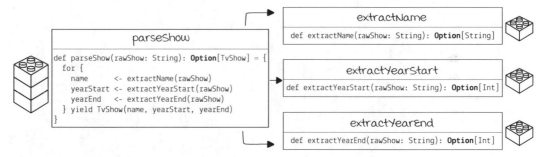

Breaking requirements into smaller blocks of code is a very natural approach in functional programming because it's much easier to achieve than in other paradigms. I know what you are thinking. "Why is this better than checked exceptions?!" Point taken. We will compare this approach to throwing checked exceptions in Java very soon. But before we do it, let's finish the Option-based parseShow by implementing the three small remaining extract functions, which contain details about extracting data from a raw string. I will show you how to implement the extractYearStart and ask you to do the two remaining as an exercise.

Writing a small, safe function that returns an Option

Now let's see how functional design works in practice. We created the parseShow function, which is built from smaller blocks. These blocks—smaller pure functions—are not implemented yet. We just know their signatures! We know that they need to return Options because there is a possibility that they won't be able to extract what we need.

We designed the code by creating four signatures (parseShow and three extract functions), and we implemented parseShow and got proof that these signatures make sense and can work well together. Now that we have the proof that these functions are useful, we can focus on each of these functions independently without assuming anything about the other ones! This is one of the most enjoyable things in functional programming; **the ability to focus on just one thing without worrying about disrupting others**. Let's implement extractYearStart.

> **THIS IS BIG!**
> In FP, you can focus on implementing one small function without worrying about others.

❶ We start with the signature. Our function takes a String and returns an Option[Int]:

```
def extractYearStart(rawShow: String): Option[Int] = {
  ???
}
```

❷ To get the start year, we need to find separator characters first: "TITLE (**START**-END)":

bracketOpen ⤴   ⤴ dash

```
def extractYearStart(rawShow: String): Option[Int] = {
  val bracketOpen = rawShow.indexOf('(')
  val dash        = rawShow.indexOf('-')
  ???
}
```

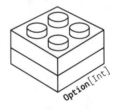

Option[Int]

You may worry about rawShow being null here. Here we only use FP concepts like Option in the whole codebase, so there's no need to worry about nulls. However, if you are integrating with some impure null-based codebases, you need to defensively check nulls and convert them into Options, for example.

❸ We know that String.substring can throw an exception, but we want to use Option instead. That's why we need to call String.substring only when we know it won't fail:

```
def extractYearStart(rawShow: String): Option[Int] = {
  val bracketOpen = rawShow.indexOf('(')
  val dash        = rawShow.indexOf('-')
  if (bracketOpen != -1 && dash > bracketOpen + 1)
    Some(rawShow.substring(bracketOpen + 1, dash))   Compilation error!
  else None                                          Option[String]
}
```

rawShow.indexOf returns -1 if a given character can't be found. We need to be sure that bracketOpen is different than -1. We also know that we want to extract a nonempty String that needs to exist between bracketOpen and dash. Thus, we also make sure that dash exists further in the rawShow than bracketOpen. If both conditions are met, we know we can safely call rawShow.substring and wrap the value in Some. If at least one of the conditions are not met, we return None without calling rawShow.substring and avoiding throwing an exception.
There is still a compilation error, though; we have Option[String] but need Option[Int]!

❹ Our signature says that we return an Option[Int], but our implementation returns an Option[String] instead. We need to transform the Option[String] into an Option[Int]:

```scala
def extractYearStart(rawShow: String): Option[Int] = {
  val bracketOpen = rawShow.indexOf('(')
  val dash        = rawShow.indexOf('-')
  val yearStrOpt  = if (bracketOpen != -1 && dash > bracketOpen + 1)
                       Some(rawShow.substring(bracketOpen + 1, dash))
                    else None
  yearStrOpt.map(yearStr => yearStr.toIntOption)
}
```

Compilation error! Option[Option[Int]]

`Option[String]` `Option[Option[Int]]` `String` `Option[Int]`

> yearStrOpt is a value of type Option[String], which means it can be either a Some[String] or a None. We want to transform the String into an Int, but only if yearStr is a Some[String], because we can't do anything with None. It turns out that this is a pattern we learned about in chapters 4 and 5: we need to use a map! If we map over None, the result is None, if we map over a Some, the result is Some with the value produced by the function we gave to map!

> Some(☐).map(☐ => ◯)   > None.map(☐ => ◯)

→ Some(◯)   → None

What function did we pass to map? In this case we passed the String.toIntOption—a Scala addition to Java String. It tries to parse an integer value from the given String. If it's possible, it returns an Option[Int]. If it's not, it returns a None! And it's already in the standard library!

> "1985".toIntOption   > "MCMLXXXV".toIntOption   > "".toIntOption

→ Some(1985)   → None   → None

The compiler is still not happy: we have Option[Option[Int]], but need Option[Int]!

❺ Our signature says that we return an Option[Int] but our implementation returns an Option[Option[Int]] instead. We need to transform the Option[Option[Int]] into an Option[Int]:

```scala
def extractYearStart(rawShow: String): Option[Int] = {
  val bracketOpen = rawShow.indexOf('(')
  val dash        = rawShow.indexOf('-')
  val yearStrOpt  = if (bracketOpen != -1 && dash > bracketOpen + 1)
                       Some(rawShow.substring(bracketOpen + 1, dash))
                    else None
  yearStrOpt.map(yearStr => yearStr.toIntOption).flatten
}
```

Now it compiles and works as intended!

❻ Wait! map and flatten? Doesn't it sound familiar? It's a flatMap!
And if it's a flatMap, then it's a for comprehension:

```scala
def extractYearStart(rawShow: String): Option[Int] = {
  val bracketOpen = rawShow.indexOf('(')
  val dash        = rawShow.indexOf('-')
  for {
    yearStr <- if (bracketOpen != -1 && dash > bracketOpen + 1)
                  Some(rawShow.substring(bracketOpen + 1, dash))
               else None
    year <- yearStr.toIntOption
  } yield year
}
```

Option[Int]

Our small, pure function is built from even smaller blocks! The first one safely gets a substring, and the second safely parses a String to an Int!

Functions, values, and expressions

Let's use this opportunity to quickly recap the difference between function applications, values, and expressions. In fact, we need to reiterate that there is no practical difference between them in FP. We will see this by using, as an example, the extractYearStart that we just wrote.

This is a pure function definition, which will be an expression after applying it to a rawShow! Moreover, this expression will always produce the same value for the same rawShow.

This is a pure function application, which is an expression! The indexOf('(') function will always produce the same value for the same rawShow.

This is a for expression that produces a value, which is always the same for the same rawShow.

```
def extractYearStart(rawShow: String): Option[Int] = {
  val bracketOpen = rawShow.indexOf('(')
  val dash        = rawShow.indexOf('-')
  for {
    yearStr <- if (bracketOpen != -1 && dash > bracketOpen +1)
                    Some(rawShow.substring(bracketOpen +1, dash))
                else None
    year <- yearStr.toIntOption
  } yield year
}
```

This is an if expression that produces a value, which is always the same for the same rawShow.

This is a pure function application which, is an expression as well. toIntOption function will always produce the same value for the same yearStr, which will always be the same for the same rawShow.

The extractYearStart can be used in expressions that produce values.

```
extractYearStart("Breaking Bad (2008-2013)")
→ Some(2008)
extractYearStart("Mad Men (-2015)")
→ None
extractYearStart("(2002- N/A ) The Wire")
→ Some(2002)
```

The extractYearStart function is applied to different String values. These are three expressions that produce values; each value is always the same for the same String. In fact, in FP, expressions and values they produce are interchangeable. It's the real definition of referential transparency we discussed earlier.

Recap: Statements vs. expressions

There is a distinction between a statement and an expression. A **statement** is a language construct that needs to change the state of a program in order to be useful. In Java, the following is unusable:

```
if (bracketOpen != -1 && dash > bracketOpen + 1)
  rawShow.substring(bracketOpen + 1, dash);
else null;
```

An **expression,** on the other hand, always returns something, and, when executed many times, it always returns the same result—a value. In fact, we can even say that **the following if expression is a value**:

```
val yearStrOpt = if (bracketOpen != -1 && dash > bracketOpen + 1)
                    Some(rawShow.substring(bracketOpen + 1, dash))
                 else None
```

THIS IS BIG!
FP is programming with expressions; functional programmers don't use statements.

Practicing safe functions that return Options

We designed our new parseShow function that gets three pieces of information and produces a TvShow, or it bubbles up any error that may have occurred, represented as None. We saw how to implement one of these three functions, extractYearStart.

The bubbling up works thanks to flatMap. We will do a quick recap after the exercise.

parseShow
| ```
def parseShow(rawShow: String): Option[TvShow] = {
  for {
    name      <- extractName(rawShow)
    yearStart <- extractYearStart(rawShow)
    yearEnd   <- extractYearEnd(rawShow)
  } yield TvShow(name, yearStart, yearEnd)
}
``` |

extractYearStart
| ```
def extractYearStart(rawShow: String): Option[Int] = {
  val bracketOpen = rawShow.indexOf('(')
  val dash        = rawShow.indexOf('-')
  for {
    yearStr <- if (bracketOpen != -1 && dash > bracketOpen + 1)
                 Some(rawShow.substring(bracketOpen + 1, dash))
               else None
    year <- yearStr.toIntOption
  } yield year
}
``` |

Your task is to implement the two missing functions. Each of them gets a rawShow String and returns an Option. The return value should be a Some in case a particular piece of information can be *extracted* from the raw TV show and None if it can't due to invalid formatting. More specifically, you need to implement the following two functions:

```
def extractName(rawShow: String): Option[String]
def extractYearEnd(rawShow: String): Option[Int]
```

Use the REPL to implement and test both functions. Make sure you test both correctly and incorrectly formatted Strings before looking below.

Answers

```
> def extractName(rawShow: String): Option[String] = {
    val bracketOpen = rawShow.indexOf('(')
    if (bracketOpen > 0)
      Some(rawShow.substring(0, bracketOpen).trim)
    else None
  }

  def extractYearEnd(rawShow: String): Option[Int] = {
    val dash         = rawShow.indexOf('-')
    val bracketClose = rawShow.indexOf(')')
    for {
      yearStr <- if (dash != -1 && bracketClose > dash + 1)
                   Some(rawShow.substring(dash + 1, bracketClose))
                 else None
      year <- yearStr.toIntOption
    } yield year
  }
```

1 We get the index of the bracket. If it's found, we return Some with the name inside. If not, we return None.

2 We get the index of the dash and closing bracket. If they are found, and the closing bracket is further in the String than the dash, we can safely call the substring function and pass the String to the next phase, which parses the integer.

How do errors propagate?

As you've seen, the functionality of parsing a raw TV show is implemented using four very small functions. All of them return an Option value, and since Option includes a flatMap function, it can be used inside for comprehensions. We are focusing on the happy path, but we can be sure that if anything goes wrong (i.e., any function returns a None value), the None value will be *bubbled up* to the topmost function and returned as a result of the whole computation, indicating that parsing was not successful. In short, we are discussing **short-circuiting**.

Short-circuiting is a programming concept that allows skipping evaluation of some expressions if a specific condition is met. Here, extractYearEnd won't be evaluated if extractName returns None.

You may wonder, how does it all work? Is it Scala-specific or Option-specific? It turns out it's neither. It is flatMap specific! We already learned about flatMap before, but this time we are in the context of error handling, and it needs to be reiterated. Let's see how it works.

```scala
def parseShow(rawShow: String): Option[TvShow] = {
  for {
    name      <- extractName(rawShow)
    yearStart <- extractYearStart(rawShow)
    yearEnd   <- extractYearEnd(rawShow)
  } yield TvShow(name, yearStart, yearEnd)
}
```

translates →

```scala
def parseShow(rawShow: String): Option[TvShow] = {
  extractName(rawShow).flatMap(name => {
    extractYearStart(rawShow).flatMap(yearStart => {
      extractYearEnd(rawShow).map(yearEnd => {
        TvShow(name, yearStart, yearEnd)
      }
    }
  }
}
```

As a reminder, the for comprehension code above does exactly the same thing as the flatMap-based code to the right. We will use for comprehensions in this book, but let's simulate the raw flatMaps one more time to make sure we know how errors propagate.

Both versions do the same thing! The flatMap-version is a translation from the for comprehension. It's worth knowing how this works to gain the intuition for error handling. ⚠️

Valid TV show   **Assuming we pass a valid String to parseShow, rawShow =** `Mad Men (2007-2015)`

If the rawShow is valid, then extractName(rawShow) returns Some("Mad Men"), extractYearStart(rawShow) returns Some(2007), and extractYearEnd(rawShow) returns Some(2015). Let's replace expressions with their values to gain more insight.

```scala
def parseShow(rawShow: String): Option[TvShow] = {
  for {
    name      <- Some( Mad Men )
    yearStart <- Some( 2007 )
    yearEnd   <- Some( 2015 )
  } yield TvShow( Mad Men , 2007 , 2015 )
}
```

The final result is Some(TvShow("Mad Men", 2007, 2015)).

translates to →

```scala
def parseShow(rawShow: String): Option[TvShow] = {
  Some( Mad Men ).flatMap(name =>
    Some( 2007 ).flatMap(yearStart =>
      Some( 2015 ).map(yearEnd =>
        TvShow( Mad Men , 2007 , 2015 )
      )
    )
  )
}
```

flatMap takes one function, which takes one parameter. This function can only be executed if the Option we are flatMapping is Some.

Invalid TV show   **Assuming we pass an <u>invalid</u> String to parseShow, rawShow =** `Mad Men (-2015)`

If the rawShow is "Mad Men (-2015)", then extractName(rawShow) returns Some("Mad Men"), extractYearStart(rawShow) returns **None**, and extractYearEnd(rawShow) returns Some(2015). Let's replace expressions with their values to gain more insight.

```scala
def parseShow(rawShow: String): Option[TvShow] = {
  for {
    name      <- Some( Mad Men )
    yearStart <- None
    yearEnd   <-    Won't be executed
  } yield          Won't be executed
}
```

The final result is None.

translates to →

```scala
def parseShow(rawShow: String): Option[TvShow] = {
  Some( Mad Men ).flatMap(name =>
    None.flatMap(yearStart =>
         Won't be executed
         Won't be executed
    )
  )
}
```

flatMap takes one function, which takes one parameter. This function can't be executed if the Option is None because there is no value to pass. The whole expression becomes None.

Values represent errors

Note that even though we talk about handling errors, we don't really throw or catch any exceptions. We operate only on values; parseShow is a pure function that gets a value and returns a value. flatMap is a pure function that gets an Option and a function and returns an Option. And because for comprehensions are just a syntactic sugar for flatMaps, the same applies to them; a for comprehension is an expression that produces a value.

> *flatMap gets two arguments: one is the Option we are calling flatMap on, and the second is the function that returns an Option.*

```
> def parseShow(rawShow: String): Option[TvShow] = {
    for {
      name      <- extractName(rawShow)
      yearStart <- extractYearStart(rawShow)
      yearEnd   <- extractYearEnd(rawShow)
    } yield TvShow(name, yearStart, yearEnd)
  }
```

An expression that produces a value of type Option.

Option[TvShow]

Some[TvShow]   None

If this value is Some we know that every thing went well, and we got a TvShow.   If this value is None we know that something went wrong—no TvShow for us!

Again, a very important thing is that the returned **Option type conveys information about a potential error**. And it does it by explicitly making it part of its signature! No surprises here—pure function for the win!

Quick exercise: Analyzing values

Before we move on and try to compare this technique with throwing and catching exceptions, we need to make sure you understand that all we've been doing here is calling pure functions that get and return immutable values and that even errors are represented by immutable values. So now **it's your turn to parse some TV shows**! In your head, execute the parseShow function shown above for the following three Strings, noting the return value:

— "Stranger Things (2016-)"
— "Scrubs (2001-2010)"
— "Chernobyl (2019)"

Values, values everywhere

This may be a paradigm shift for you. But, hopefully, you are getting the feel for the functional programming style. In the previous chapter we represented sequential programs as a sequence of pure function calls on immutable values. Now, we represent failures as values, but programs are still just sequences of pure function calls. It's surprising how powerful this idea really is and how much more we can do with it! Soon, you will acquire **error handling superpowers** by passing more descriptive values!

```
Answers:
None,
Some(TvShow(
    "Scrubs",
    2001,
    2010)),
None
```

Option, for comprehensions, and checked exceptions ...

OK, Option looks nice, but how exactly is it better than plain-old throws Exception in Java? Why should we prefer Option?

That's a great question, we will get our answer in the following pages. But before we move on, let's quickly gain some perspective on where we are in our journey to learn functional error handling!

 Step 1 ✔

Recapping higher-order functions
Errors are handled using higher-order functions we learned about in chapter 4.

We have recapped how to use higher-order functions like map and flatMap, then used this knowledge to handle our first error in a totally functional way—a for comprehension that works on Options.
Now the fun part begins.

 Step 2 ✔

Using Option to indicate an error
Indicating errors by returning immutable values from for comprehensions we learned about in chapter 5.

Step 3

Functional error handling vs. checked exceptions
Using a functional approach helps us indicate and handle errors in a much more readable and concise way than checked exceptions.

After we learn why functional error handling is better than using checked exceptions, we will try to make even more out of this new technique and handle multiple errors in this way:

Step 4

Handling many errors at once
Defining higher-order functions that handle many errors using code that handles just a single error.

Step 5

Using Either to indicate descriptive errors
Indicating errors by returning immutable values that contain more information about what failed.

Now, let's go back to our parseShow function and try to reimplement it in Java using checked exceptions. Will there be any difference? Is functional error handling really better? Let's find out by looking at some code!

What about checked exceptions?

So how exactly is the Option approach better than checked exceptions?
We will answer that by looking at some Java code that parses a raw TV
show String and uses exceptions to indicate problems. Note that we will
still want to use the same code structure with small units responsible
for extraction of name and years. The only difference is that instead of
Option we'll use Exception-based error handling.

We need to rewrite four functions: extractName, extractYearStart,
extractYearEnd, and, finally, parseShow. Here we will just show the
implementation of extractName and parseShow because the two
remaining extract functions look similar to extractName.

Functional

```scala
def extractName(rawShow: String): Option[String] = {
  val bracketOpen = rawShow.indexOf('(')
  if (bracketOpen > 0)
    Some(rawShow.substring(0, bracketOpen).trim)
  else None
}
```

Imperative

```java
public static String extractName(String rawShow) throws Exception {
  int bracketOpen = rawShow.indexOf('(');
  if(bracketOpen > 0)
    return rawShow.substring(0, bracketOpen).trim();
  else throw new Exception();
}
```

> To be equivalent, the Java version needs to explicitly throw a checked Exception when parsing is not possible.

```scala
def parseShow(rawShow: String): Option[TvShow] = {
  for {
    name      <- extractName(rawShow)
    yearStart <- extractYearStart(rawShow)
    yearEnd   <- extractYearEnd(rawShow)
  } yield TvShow(name, yearStart, yearEnd)
}
```

```java
public static TvShow parseShow(String rawShow) throws Exception {
  String name    = extractName(rawShow);
  int yearStart = extractYearStart(rawShow);
  int yearEnd   = extractYearEnd(rawShow);
  return new TvShow(name, yearStart, yearEnd);
}
```

> Note that probably the best approach would be to define a custom checked
> exception, but Exception should be sufficient for demonstration purposes.

Q Wait! It looks exactly the same! Why are we looking at Options when Exceptions can do exactly the same thing?

A That's true. Assuming that we use checked exceptions, the compiler makes sure that all the errors are either handled or present in the signature. However, when requirements get a little more complicated (and they always do!), our exception-based solution blows up while the functional one stays almost the same. Interested?

Let's add one small requirement to show how graceful the functional
error handling really is (as compared to the imperative type).

Conditional recovery

So far we haven't seen any practical difference between `Option`-based FP solutions and exception-based solutions. They looked and worked pretty much the same. No matter if we constrain ourselves to using only checked exceptions or `Option`s, we get exactly the same benefits:

1. Both signatures don't lie, they tell what they return, and they tell that they may fail without any result.
2. Both functions don't crash their whole applications, and they make sure all possible errors are handled somewhere else (by one of their clients).

A big difference appears when we try to implement branches that evaluate different code paths based on a possible error. Code that is executed in case of an error is called *recovery code*. The whole process is called **conditional recovery,** and you've probably dealt with many cases of it. Let's see an example by introducing yet another requirement.

If we have a branch in a function, it means there are at least two possible different code flows. If a branch is related to an error, one code flow is needed to handle this error.

> **New requirement: Some shows may have only one year**
>
> Some TV shows have just one season, and they are represented as a raw `String` in the following format: TITLE (YEAR). For example:
>
> ```
> val singleYearRawShow = "Chernobyl (2019)"
> ```
>
> For simplicity, let's assume that in this case, our function should return `Some(TvShow("Chernobyl", 2019, 2019))`. What matters here is that it should return a successfully parsed TV show for both cases: single-year shows and the ones that aired for multiple years.

Naturally, the current version of `parseShow` doesn't follow the expected format, and the function would return `None` (or an exception in the imperative version). What happens if we try to parse it using our `Option`-based `parseShow`?

```
parseShow("Chernobyl (2019)")
→ None
```

Similarly, the exception-based version throws an `Exception`:

```
parseShow("Chernobyl (2019)")
→ Exception in thread "main" Exception
```

We expected that. Our task is to add this new functionality—and keep the current functionalities intact—to both versions and then compare again. We'll start with the exception-based code. Take a moment to think about a possible solution before moving on.

Conditional recovery using the imperative style

The pseudocode of the logic we want to implement looks like this.

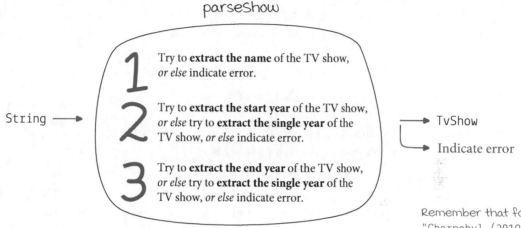

parseShow

1 Try to **extract the name** of the TV show, *or else* indicate error.

String →

2 Try to **extract the start year** of the TV show, *or else* try to **extract the single year** of the TV show, *or else* indicate error.

→ TvShow

→ Indicate error

3 Try to **extract the end year** of the TV show, *or else* try to **extract the single year** of the TV show, *or else* indicate error.

If we can't parse the start year, we need to recover this error by falling back to a single-year case. The same thing happens with the end year. ←

Remember that for "Chernobyl (2019)" we are falling back to single-year case for both start year and end year. Thus, we get a TvShow("Chernobyl", 2019, 2019).

To fall back to parsing a single year, we need to try parsing the start year first, and we need to know if it failed or not. The only way to do that in the exception-based code is using the `try...catch` syntax.

```
public static TvShow parseShow(String rawShow) throws Exception {
    String name = extractName(rawShow);
    Integer yearStart = null;
    try {
        yearStart = extractYearStart(rawShow);
    } catch(Exception e) {
        yearStart = extractSingleYear(rawShow);
    }
    Integer yearEnd = null;
    try {
        yearEnd = extractYearEnd(rawShow);
    } catch(Exception e) {
        yearEnd = extractSingleYear(rawShow);
    }
    return new TvShow(name, yearStart, yearEnd);
}
```

We need to first try to get the start year.

After we catch the Exception we know that the start year can't be parsed, and we can try to extract the single year.

We need to initialize yearStart and yearEnd to null, which makes the code even more unreadable.

Note we could optimize this code a bit in this case by not recalculating single year twice but the main conclusion would not change.

Note we still need to implement a new function, extractSingleYear. It will look very similar to other "extract" functions, so let's not focus on it here.

Well, this blew up, as promised! Compare the pseudocode with the code above and how much complication we needed to introduce to handle the conditional recovery for exception-based code.

Conditional recovery using the functional style

Step 3
Functional error handling vs. checked exceptions
Using a functional approach helps us indicate and handle errors in a much more readable and concise way than checked exceptions.

We've seen the imperative solution using exception-based code. It works, but it adds some complexity to the code, which in turn affects the maintainability. Remember that the code is read far more often than written, so to improve maintainability, we need to make the code as easy to read as possible. (That also means that we need to write boring code.)

I know that I repeat myself here, but it's really important. Boring code is good code. Writing boring code is hard. But it pays off!

OK, enough with this pep talk—let's see some code! If Java exception-based code is so complicated and not maintainable, how will the FP solution look? In FP, everything is an immutable value, so we don't really need any special syntax. **We just need a new pure function!**

Conveniently, `Option` already has a function named `orElse`.

extractYearStart returns a value of type Option, so we can call orElse on it and get another value of type Option back!

```
> def parseShow(rawShow: String): Option[TvShow] =
    for {
      name <- extractName(rawShow)
      yearStart <- extractYearStart(rawShow).orElse(extractSingleYear(rawShow))
      yearEnd <- extractYearEnd(rawShow).orElse(extractSingleYear(rawShow))
    } yield TvShow(name, yearStart, yearEnd)
```
Find the `extractSingleYear` implementation below.

No, that's not pseudocode. **It's a compiling piece of Scala code.** It correctly implements our requirement! `orElse` is just another function defined on `Option`, like `map`, `flatMap`, and others. **We will explain how `orElse` works very soon**. For now, just treat it as yet another pure function that helps us implement conditional error handling and recovery far better than exceptions.

THIS IS BIG!
In FP, there usually is a function for every problem in your code.

Does it really work as intended? Have a look for yourself.

```
> def extractSingleYear(rawShow: String): Option[Int] = {
    val dash        = rawShow.indexOf('-')
    val bracketOpen = rawShow.indexOf('(')
    val bracketClose = rawShow.indexOf(')')
    for {
      yearStr <- if (dash == -1 && bracketOpen != -1 && bracketClose > bracketOpen + 1)
                   Some(rawShow.substring(bracketOpen + 1, bracketClose))
                 else None
      year <- yearStr.toIntOption
    } yield year
  }

parseShow("Chernobyl (2019)")
→ Some("Chernobyl", 2019, 2019)
parseShow("Breaking Bad (2008-2013)")
→ Some("Breaking Bad", 2008, 2013)
parseShow("Mad Men (-2015)")
→ None
```

We need to finally implement the `extractSingleYear` function that handles the new requirement. Nothing interesting here, it's very similar to other examples.

Everything works like a charm! We were able to implement the new requirement without any big changes in our original function. It's because we didn't need a new syntax—just a new function.

Checked exceptions don't compose—Options do!

The main difference between checked exceptions and functional error handling is that checked exceptions don't compose, while functional handlers compose very well.

Functions and values compose well

When we say that something composes well, we mean that we are able to easily combine two small things to build a larger one. For example, when you have two small, independent pure functions that return an Option, you can compose them together into a bigger function that handles more cases by calling just one function (orElse):

```
extractYearStart(rawShow).orElse(extractSingleYear(rawShow))
```

That's how easy it is to compose extractYearStart and extractSingleYear functions into a bigger function.

> **THIS IS BIG!**
> Functions and values compose very well together— we use them to build big programs from smaller pieces.

Imperative code doesn't compose well

In the imperative approach, if you want to make a decision based on whether some particular piece of code failed or not, you need to explicitly catch the exception and execute follow-up code.

```
Integer yearStart = null;
try {
  yearStart = extractYearStart(rawShow);
} catch(Exception e) {
  yearStart = extractSingleYear(rawShow);
}
```

To compose two functions that can throw exceptions, we need to explicitly catch those exceptions and specify the exact steps the program needs to take to recover properly.

Exceptions can only be handled imperatively.

The amount of try..catches grows very quickly. It hit us when we tried to use just one level of branching! Imagine what would happen if you needed to make another decision based on another failure (e.g., what happens if the year is provided in the 2008-13 format?). We will explore such scenarios later in the chapter, but rest assured that functional programming has us covered. **We will use function composition to our advantage** not only in advanced error handling but also in side-effectful programming, multithreading, and testing later in the book!

How does `orElse` work?

We now know the benefits of the functional approach to error handling. In FP we create new immutable values based on immutable values by using pure functions. Using checked exceptions, we need to run the code, see if it fails, and run another piece of code based on that. Again, that's yet another example of our declarative programming versus imperative programming discussion. The declarative approach focuses on defining relationships between values, whereas imperative tries to implement step-by-step recipes for how the program should be executed by the computer.

It's probably getting repetitive by now. We've been talking about immutable values and pure functions since chapter 2. It's repetitive because this whole book is about pure functions and immutable values. We can do plenty of things with them!

`orElse` is a perfect example of a pure function that takes two immutable values and produces another immutable value. It's also a perfect example of defining relationships between values.

```
val seven: Option[Int] = Some(7)
val eight: Option[Int] = Some(8)
val none: Option[Int] = None
```

`seven.`**`orElse`**`(eight)`
→ Some(7)
    The first Option is Some, so return it.

`none.`**`orElse`**`(eight)`
→ Some(8)
    The first Option is None, so return the second one, no matter what it is.

`seven.`**`orElse`**`(none)`
→ Some(7)
    The first Option is Some, so return it.

`none.`**`orElse`**`(none)`
→ None
    The first Option is None, so return the second one, no matter what it is.

> **THIS IS BIG!**
> Handling errors in FP is taking an *error value* and returning a different value.

If this is `Some(value)`, `orElse` returns it ... ... but if it's not, the `alternative` is returned, no matter whether it's `Some` or `None`.

$$\text{Option[A].}\textbf{orElse}\text{(alternative: Option[A]): Option[A]}$$

In our case it's a relationship between values that represent a potential parsing problem. What `orElse` does in this case is **describe the error handling**!

```
val chernobyl = "Chernobyl (2019)"
extractYearStart(chernobyl)
→ None
extractSingleYear(chernobyl)
→ Some(2019)
extractYearStart(chernobyl).orElse(extractSingleYear(chernobyl))
→ Some(2019)
extractYearStart(chernobyl).orElse(extractSingleYear("not-a-year"))
→ None
```

The first Option is None, so return the second one, no matter what it is.

Practicing functional error handling

We designed our new parseShow function that gets three pieces of information and produces a TvShow. The three pieces of information are extracted using small functions that return Options to indicate a potential success or parsing problem. They are then composed into a bigger function that parses a String and returns an Option[TvShow]. It is able to handle some potential errors and recover from some of them using orElse. We already know how parseShow is implemented, but let's try to practice some different error-handling scenarios using the same set of small functions we've implemented so far.

```
def extractName(rawShow: String): Option[String]
def extractYearStart(rawShow: String): Option[Int]
def extractYearEnd(rawShow: String): Option[Int]

def extractSingleYear(rawShow: String): Option[Int]
```

If you don't have the previous REPL session open, it'd be beneficial to reimplement these three functions first.

We have just implemented this one after receiving the new "TITLE (YEAR)" requirement.

Your task is to implement the following scenarios by composing the aforementioned functions. Make sure to test different Strings: "A (1992-)", "B (2002)", "C (-2012)", "(2022)", "E (-)".

1. Extract a single year, and if it fails, extract an end year.
2. Extract a start year, and if it fails, extract an end year. If this fails as well, fall back to extracting a single year.
3. Extract a single year only if a name can be extracted.
4. In case a name exists, extract a start year, and if it fails, extract an end year. If this fails as well, fall back to extracting a single year.

Hint: This one doesn't need orElse! It needs a different function that we've already learned about earlier in the book.

Answers

```
def extractSingleYearOrYearEnd(rawShow: String): Option[Int] =
  extractSingleYear(rawShow).orElse(extractYearEnd(rawShow))

def extractAnyYear(rawShow: String): Option[Int] =
  extractYearStart(rawShow)
    .orElse(extractYearEnd(rawShow))
    .orElse(extractSingleYear(rawShow))

def extractSingleYearIfNameExists(rawShow: String): Option[Int] =
  extractName(rawShow).flatMap(name => extractSingleYear(rawShow))

def extractAnyYearIfNameExists(rawShow: String): Option[Int] =
  extractName(rawShow).flatMap(name => extractAnyYear(rawShow))
```

1 *This requirement is similar to what we've been doing with orElse.*

2 *More complicated cases can be implemented by sticking yet another orElse at the end.*

3 *The function passed to flatMap is executed only if Option is Some.*

4 *Functions compose well together! We use this superpower here!*

Functions compose, even in the presence of errors

I hope you already start seeing and appreciating the pattern. Throughout this book, we are learning how to think differently about problems we encounter. We learn that everything is just a value that we can take and return another one back. That's the essence of functional programming. We have already learned, in chapter 5, that we can represent sequential programs using values. Later in the book we will model full requirements as values (chapter 7) and even represent IO-based and concurrent programs as values! They will all use the same pattern: get an immutable value and create another one inside a pure function. `map`, `flatten`, `flatMap`, `filter`, `foldLeft`, and `orElse` are all examples of this pattern, and there are more yet to come.

In this chapter we learn that we can represent errors as values. `Option` is just a beginning; there are more ways of doing that. We have just discovered that using the functional approach is better because the small functions compose well together to form bigger functions, even in the presence of errors. The same cannot be said about exceptions.

 Step 3 ✔

Functional error handling vs. checked exceptions
Using a functional approach helps us indicate and handle errors in a much more readable and concise way than checked exceptions.

Now, it's time to level up our error-handling skills and start handling multiple errors at once. What do we mean by that? We've focused on parsing a single TV show and already dealt with multiple possible problems, such as missing name, missing year, and so on. The next problem, however, is exactly the same but multiplied by the amount of raw `Strings` in the incoming `List`. Remember that the original requirement was to parse a `List[String]` and give a `List[TvShow]` back:

```
def parseShows(rawShows: List[String]): List[TvShow]
```

We know it's not that straightforward because there are many corner cases. But how difficult could it be? Let's find out!

Next Step

Handling many errors at once
Defining higher-order functions that handle many errors using code that handles just a single error.

Compiler reminds us that errors need to be covered

We were able to parse one particular TV show functionally by creating a pure function that takes a String and returns an Option[TvShow]:

```
def parseShow(rawShow: String): Option[TvShow]
```

We now know it works well and is built from smaller, independent pure functions. However, please remember that, originally, we were tasked with a much bigger requirement—**we wanted to parse lists**.

> Note that we are using two similar function names. The function that parses one TV show is called parseShow, and the one that parses a list of TV shows is called parseShows.

> ## Original requirement recap: Parse a list of TV shows
>
> Our application gets a **list of raw TV shows**. Each raw TV show is just a String that should be in a specific format:
>
> ```
> TITLE (YEAR_START-YEAR_END) or TITLE (YEAR) (added later).
> ```
>
> For example:
>
> ```
> > val rawShows = List("The Wire (2002-2008)", "Chernobyl (2019)")
>   parseShows(rawShows)
>   → List(TvShow("The Wire", 2002, 2008), TvShow("Chernobyl", 2019, 2019))
> ```

We already implemented parseShows using map, but it was back in the days when we used the imperative parseShow version, which changed since then. However, the current version doesn't compile.

Before Returning TvShow or throwing an exception if something goes wrong

```
def parseShow(rawShow: String): TvShow
```

> Note again that we have two functions: parseShow, which parses one show and parseShows, which parses multiple shows. The names look similar, but they indicate exactly what happens inside.

```
def parseShows(rawShows: List[String]): List[TvShow] = {

  List(
    The Wire (2002-2008)    parseShow( The Wire (2002-2008) ) ────▶ TvShow(The Wire, 2002, 2008)

    Chernobyl (2019)        parseShow( Chernobyl (2019) ) ────▶ TvShow(Chernobyl, 2019, 2019)

  ).map(parseShow)                                          )
}
```

> It looks OK, but it may throw an exception and crash if an invalidly formatted String is provided!

Now Returning a Some[TvShow] or None if something goes wrong

```
def parseShow(rawShow: String): Option[TvShow]
```

Compilation error!

> **Compilation error!** We indicate that parseShows returns a List[TvShow], but after we changed the implementation of parseShow to use the Option type, the implementation of parseShows followed suit and started returning a List[Option[TvShow]]!

```
def parseShows(rawShows: List[String]): List[TvShow] = {

  List(
    The Wire (2002-2008)    parseShow( The Wire (2002-2008) ) ────▶ Some( TvShow(The Wire, 2002, 2008) )

    Chernobyl (2019)        parseShow( Chernobyl (2019) ) ────▶ Some( TvShow(Chernobyl, 2019, 2019) )

  ).map(parseShow)                                          )
}
```

Compilation errors are good for us!

The problem is subtle: the compiler does not like what it sees. parseShow
returns an Option[TvShow], so if we are mapping over a list of Strings,
we'll get a List[Option[TvShow]], not the List[TvShow] that is indicated
in the signature. This results in the compilation error!

> **Q** I hate compilation errors! Why can't things just work?
> Does functional programming mean that I will encounter
> more compilation errors?

> **A** Yes! Programming functionally usually means that
> we encounter more compilation errors. However, the
> benefit is that we will also get fewer runtime errors! We
> argue that handling compilation errors is less stressful
> than handling runtime errors. We'll see this in action in the
> remaining parts of this book.

THIS IS BIG!
In FP, we
prefer
compilation
errors over
runtime
crashes.

From this point on, we start treating our compiler as a friend, not a foe.
It will help us a lot by making sure we cover all our bases. Let's see what
exactly our new friend—the compiler—is telling us right now.

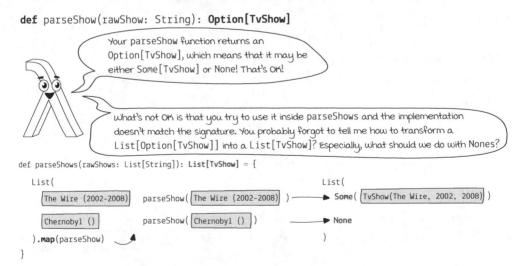

See? Nothing scary! Maybe the compiler is a bit passive-aggressive
sometimes, but let's assume it has only good intentions and just tries to
help us avoid runtime exceptions popping up in production.

Transforming a `List` of `Options` into a flat `List`

In functional programming, we work with values, and therefore, we can easily transform one value into another. We have just learned about `orElse` defined on `Options`. There had been many before (`map`, `flatten`, `flatMap`, `foldLeft`, `filter`, and `sortBy`), and there are still many more to come. The standard library gives us lots of built-in pure functions that take immutable values and return some new ones. Whenever you have a problem like "How do I transform X into Y?" you should first look at what's already at your disposal. **In this case you are looking for `toList`.**

Whenever you feel that a value you work with can be transformed into a `List` in a straightforward manner, you can probably do it by calling `toList` on it!

In our case, we are working with an `Option`, which can be either `None` or `Some`. Therefore, it can be transformed into a `List` without losing any information. That's why `Option` has a `toList` function built in. If you call it, you will get either an empty `List` (if the `Option` is `None`) or a one-element `List` (if it is `Some`).

```
> Some(7).toList
→ List(7)

None.toList
→ List()
```

If this is `Some(value)`, `toList` returns it as a one-element `List(value)` ... but if it's not (it's a `None`), `toList` returns an empty `List`.

`Option[A].`**`toList:`**` List[A]`

Now, we can use this information to modify our `parseShows` function and see what the compiler has to say this time.

```
def parseShows(rawShows: List[String]): List[TvShow] = {
  rawShows                // List( The Wire (2002-2008) , Chernobyl () )
    .map(parseShow)       // List(Some( TvShow(The Wire, 2002, 2008) ), None)
    .map(_.toList)        // List(List( TvShow(The Wire, 2002, 2008) ), List())
}
```

OK, so first you map a `List[String]`, using the `parseShow` function, and you get a `List[Option[TvShow]]`. Then, you map this list using the `toList` on each element, and you get a `List[List[TvShow]]`, but I expected a `List[TvShow]`!

Let the compiler be our guide ...

Our new friend—the compiler—tells us that we are not there yet. In the signature we want to promise that we return a List[TvShow], but our implementation returns a List[List[TvShow]]! Again, this is a problem of a familiar nature: "How do I transform X into Y?" How do we transform a List[List[TvShow]] into a List[TvShow]? There are many possible solutions, but we know one of them particularly well. **It is flatten.**

We used flatten in chapter 5 mostly in tandem with map (they both define the flatMap function). But it is a normal standalone function that can be used explicitly, like here!

flatten goes through each of the lists in this list and adds all their elements into the resulting list in the same order.

$$\text{List[List[A]]}.\textbf{flatten: } \text{List[A]}$$

List(List ▢ ▢), List(), List(■), List(▨)).flatten

→ List(▢ ▢ ■ ▨)

Using flatten should finally make the compiler happy. Let's see.

```
def parseShows(rawShows: List[String]): List[TvShow] = {
  rawShows                // List( The Wire (2002-2008) , Chernobyl () )
    .map(parseShow)       // List(Some( TvShow(The Wire, 2002, 2008) ), None)
    .map(_.toList)        // List(List( TvShow(The Wire, 2002, 2008) ), List())
    .flatten              // List( TvShow(The Wire, 2002, 2008) )
}
```

Yay! It compiles! parseShows returns a List[TvShow]!

We did it! The code compiles, and we are able to parse multiple shows without any exceptions and without crashing the application. We let the compiler guide us, and we ended up with a sequential program. However, please give this solution yet another thought. **Did we ignore something?** Were we allowed to ignore it?

? Can you replace the map/flatten combo with a flatMap call?

... but let's not trust the compiler too much!

We were able to implement the requirement: our function gets a list of Strings and returns a list of valid TV shows. We trusted the compiler to guide us in implementing the logic for handling lists of shows. **But we need to remember that the compiler works in a purely mechanical way!** It doesn't have the context of the feature we implement. That's our job! Anytime we let the compiler guide us, we need to control and verify that it's really what we want. Let's go back to our example. We have a sequential program.

```
rawShows                                                      shows
List[String] →  ( .map ) .map ) .flatten )  →  List[TvShow]
```

We met many sequential programs in chapter 5. At its core, the one we are dealing with right now is very similar to them. That's great, we are trying to tap into exactly the same intuition! From the mechanical perspective, error handling is very similar to sequential programs. We use many pure functions that transform immutable values, usually maps, flatMaps (or for comprehensions), filters, and so on. Let's keep that in mind and build our new error-handling intuition on top of that.

> To be more precise, all the techniques in functional programming are similar: it's always a bunch of pure functions that transform immutable values!

So what did we ignore while we were listening to the beautiful voice of the compiler and blindly following its guidance? Let's run the code:

```
val rawShows = List("Breaking Bad (2008-2013)",
                    "The Wire 2002 2008",
                    "Mad Men (2007-2015)")
parseShows(rawShows)
→ List(TvShow("Breaking Bad", 2008, 2013),
       TvShow("Mad Men", 2007, 2015))
```

What happened? We had a list of three raw shows, but one of them was using an invalid format. Good thing this didn't crash our app. One thing that may bother us, however, is that we got only two TvShow values back and **no information about the invalidly formatted String whatsoever!** By using toList and flatten, we made sure that all Nones were ignored without affecting the rest of the result. It may or may not be what you want, and **this is something that we, as developers, need to decide**. The compiler will not help us. Our current solution works in the *best-effort* mode—it returns only TV shows that are parsed correctly. Another approach would be to indicate a possible error within the parseShows signature! This is something we will implement next.

Coffee break:
Error-handling strategies

We've just implemented the *best-effort* error-handling strategy in the parseShows function. It's time to discuss more strategies. We'll implement the *all-or-nothing* error-handling strategy next. To do that, we'll need a little helper function, and I am asking you to implement it. **Your task is to implement the addOrResign function defined as**

All-or-nothing error-handling logic means that if we have a list of parsed shows, then we can add a new show to it but only if we can parse it. If we can't parse a new show (None), then we fail the whole thing by returning None.

```
def addOrResign(
    parsedShows: Option[List[TvShow]],
    newParsedShow: Option[TvShow]
): Option[List[TvShow]]
```

This looks like a head scratcher, so let's focus on the signature alone before implementing anything. Please have a look at this signature, and try to come up with the intention behind it. The best way to approach such dilemmas is to execute a function with some *random* arguments, and try to come up with a sensible answer in your head. In your opinion, **what should the result of the following executions be?**

1

```
addOrResign(Some(List.empty), Some(TvShow("Chernobyl", 2019, 2019)))
→ ???
addOrResign(Some(List(TvShow("Chernobyl", 2019, 2019))),
            Some(TvShow("The Wire", 2002, 2008)))
→ ???
addOrResign(Some(List(TvShow("Chernobyl", 2019, 2019))), None)
→ ???
addOrResign(None, Some(TvShow("Chernobyl", 2019, 2019)))
→ ???
addOrResign(None, None)
→ ???
```

If you managed to come up with some sensible results for the function executions above, the second part of this exercise should be a little bit easier. However, if not, fear not, and try to implement the function by satisfying the compiler. You get two Options as parameters, and you need to return one Option back. **You need to implement addOrResign by merging these two Options you get as parameters and return the result.** It can be challenging, so please take your time.

2

Hint

Maybe try to implement this function as a sequential program that has two steps, and if any of them fails, the whole program fails.

Don't look here if you haven't spent a good amount of time thinking about a solution.

Coffee break explained: Error-handling strategies

Let's try to answer the imaginary function executions first and try to come up with the intuition behind this function before trying to implement it, keeping in mind that we are implementing an *all-or-nothing* error-handling strategy. If any show can't be parsed, we return an error.

```
addOrResign(Some(List.empty), Some(TvShow("Chernobyl", 2019, 2019)))
→ Some(List(TvShow("Chernobyl", 2019, 2019)))
addOrResign(Some(List(TvShow("Chernobyl", 2019, 2019))),
        Some(TvShow("The Wire", 2002, 2008)))
→ Some(List(TvShow("Chernobyl", 2019, 2019),
        TvShow("The Wire", 2002, 2008)))
addOrResign(Some(List(TvShow("Chernobyl", 2019, 2019))), None)
→ None
addOrResign(None, Some(TvShow("Chernobyl", 2019, 2019)))
→ None
addOrResign(None, None)
→ None
```

We have an empty list of shows, and the new show has been parsed.

We have an existing list of shows, and the new show has been parsed. We expect to get a new list with two shows back.

We have an existing list of shows, and the new show couldn't be parsed. We get an error.

We don't have a list of shows, so a newly parsed show can't be added. We get an error.

We don't have a list of shows, and the new show couldn't be parsed. We get an error.

As you can see, `addOrResign` is responsible for adding a newly parsed show to the existing list of parsed shows, but only if this list *exists* (i.e., we haven't encountered any errors before). Even then, `addOrResign` resigns by returning None if a new show couldn't be parsed. We will use this function later in the chapter, but hopefully, you already have a sense for it. If not, you were probably able to follow the compiler and do the mechanical implementation that more or less satisfies the test cases above.

If at least one of the parameters is None, return None. If both are Some, append a new show to the existing list and return a Some of this newly created list. If for comprehensions and `flatMaps` rang a bell when you were implementing this exercise, your job became easy.

2

```
> def addOrResign(
    parsedShows: Option[List[TvShow]],
    newParsedShow: Option[TvShow]): Option[List[TvShow]] = {
    for {
      shows      <- parsedShows
      parsedShow <- newParsedShow
    } yield shows.appended(parsedShow)
  }
```

If parsedShows is Some, take the "inside" list, and save it as shows. If it's None, return None immediately.

If newParsedShow is Some, take the "inside" parsed show, and save it as parsedShow. If it's None, return None immediately.

Append the new show, and return the result in Some.

I hope you've enjoyed this exercise! It was meant to be challenging, as it required incorporating concepts we learned earlier in the book.

Two different error-handling strategies

Step 4

Handling many errors at once
Defining higher-order functions that handle many errors using code that handles just a single error.

There are two error-handling strategies that we've shown in this chapter based on the parseShows example, where we parse multiple Strings:

— Best-effort strategy

— All-or-nothing strategy

Note that there are many more possible strategies, which we won't focus on here. The important thing is that you will need to choose the best one for each particular business case. What we want to show here is that each of these is possible to implement using the functional approach, where we *only* use immutable values to create new immutable values. Let's see how these strategies can be implemented in parseShows.

Best-effort error handling

We've implemented parseShows using the best-effort strategy.

```
def parseShows(rawShows: List[String]): List[TvShow] = {
  rawShows            // List[String]
    .map(parseShow)  // List[Option[TvShow]]
    .map(_.toList)   // List[List[TvShow]]  // or: .flatMap(_.toList)
    .flatten         // List[TvShow]
}
```

Best-effort means that we try to parse every raw TV show from the incoming list, and we return only the ones that are valid, ignoring invalid ones.

It's a very concise implementation. It uses parseShow to do its job (which, in turn, uses smaller functions!), but if we started using it with real data, we'd quickly find out that getting a List that contains only some of the shows we wanted to parse may be frustrating.

```
> parseShows(List("Chernobyl [2019]", "Breaking Bad (2008-2013)"))
  → List(TvShow("Breaking Bad", 2008, 2013))
  parseShows(List("Chernobyl [2019]", "Breaking Bad"))
  → List()
```

We need to compare the size of the incoming list with the size of the result to know if something went wrong. And even then we don't know which item caused problems and why!

All-or-nothing error handling

We could implement parseShows using the all-or-nothing strategy. This needs to be encoded in the signature. How? By using Option again!

```
def parseShows(rawShows: List[String]): Option[List[TvShow]]
```

Our approach changes and the signature needs to change as well. We will implement this new parseShows version next, but I hope you have some idea of how to implement it because you have just done a majority of the work inside addOrResign you implemented in the last exercise!

All-or-nothing means that we try to parse every raw TV show from the incoming list, and we return the list of parsed shows only if all are valid.

All-or-nothing error-handling strategy

Let's reimplement parseShows using the *all-or-nothing* strategy. Before we do, let's revisit the signature, and try to understand it:

```
def parseShows(rawShows: List[String]): Option[List[TvShow]]
```

Note again that in the previous version, parseShows returned a List[TvShow], and if something failed, it was not returned on this list. This was the best-effort strategy.

The signature tells us that we can get one of two values:

— None if at least one raw TV show String was invalid (couldn't be parsed)
— Some[List[TvShow]] if everything went well and we parsed all shows

That's all we need. To check whether your intuition works correctly for this problem, let's do a quick exercise.

Quick exercise

Your task is to guess what the result of calling the all-or-nothing version of parseShows in the three cases below should be.

```
parseShows(List("Chernobyl (2019)", "Breaking Bad"))
parseShows(List("Chernobyl (2019)"))
parseShows(List())
```

Answers in discussion.

Implementing *all-or-nothing* strategy in parseShows

Functional programmers solve these kinds of quick exercises all the time. We first create a signature and then try to run it in our head by providing an input and thinking about the output. The quick exercise above probably caused you at least one headache. What should we return when we get an empty list as an input? Let's see:

If it sounds familiar to you, then you probably know about test-driven development. We first define the test by calling an unimplemented function and asserting its output. Then, we implement the function and rerun the test to check if it works. More about this is to come in chapter 12!

```
> parseShows(List("Chernobyl (2019)", "Breaking Bad"))
  → None
  parseShows(List("Chernobyl (2019)"))
  → Some(List(TvShow("Chernobyl", 2019, 2019)))
  parseShows(List())
  → Some(List())   ←
```

None means that at least one raw String was invalid. Some means that all raw Strings were valid and it returns parsed TV shows. That's why when we get an empty List, we return a successful Some of empty list back.

OK, let's try to implement this new version, at least as pseudocode.

```
def parseShows(rawShows: List[String]): Option[List[TvShow]] = {
  rawShows              // List( The Wire (2002-2008) , Chernobyl () )
    .map(parseShow)     // List(Some( TvShow(The Wire, 2002, 2008) ), None)
    .???                // None
}
```

❶ To implement this new parseShows version that uses the all-or-nothing error handling strategy, we need to parse each raw String element using the parseShow function (as we did previously).

All-or-nothing error handling can be done using a **higher-order function we already know**! Any ideas?

❷ Then, we need to go through the resulting List[Option[TvShow]] and somehow transform it into Option[List[TvShow]], which is our return value.

Folding a List of Options into an Option of a List

We will use our old friend foldLeft to accumulate the result by going through each Option[TvShow] on the List and returning Some[List[TvShow]] only if there are no Nones. Quick foldLeft recap follows.

List[A].foldLeft(z: B)(f: (B, A) => B): B

Accumulates a value of type B by applying the function passed as f to each element of the original list (A) and current accumulator value (B). The shape of the data structure (List) is lost as well as its size and sequence of elements. Only one value of type B is returned.

List(☐ ▦ ■).foldLeft(0)(⬚ => incrementIfGrey)

→ 1

We met foldLeft in chapter 4. Back then we suggested that you might also know this functionality as reduce. The intuition behind the name is that we fold a list into a single value.

What we need to do is start with the accumulator value of Some(List.empty) and then fold (or *reduce*) the list of Option[TvShow] values by *adding* successfully parsed TV shows to the list or *resigning* by making the accumulator None if there is None on the list.

```
def parseShows(rawShows: List[String]): Option[List[TvShow]] = {

  val initialResult: Option[List[TvShow]] = Some(List.empty)

  rawShows                    // List( The Wire (2002-2008) , Chernobyl () )

    .map(parseShow)           // List(Some( TvShow(The Wire, 2002, 2008) ), None)

    .foldLeft(initialResult)(addOrResign)    // None
}
```

Here, foldLeft requires a function that will be called for each element of the list. It takes the current accumulator of type Option[List[TvShow]] and the current element of type Option[TvShow] and returns a new accumulator of type Option[List[TvShow]]. Since we are implementing the all-or-nothing strategy, a new accumulator should become None if we encounter None on our list. You already implemented this function as addOrResign in the previous coffee break exercise.

```
def addOrResign(
    parsedShows: Option[List[TvShow]],
    newParsedShow: Option[TvShow]
): Option[List[TvShow]] = {
  for {
    shows      <- parsedShows
    parsedShow <- newParsedShow
  } yield shows.appended(parsedShow)
}
```

Let's zoom in and see just the last transformation in action. What happens when we foldLeft the List[Option[TvShow]]?

The accumulator starts as Some(List.empty) and is passed to addOrResign, which returns a new value of the accumulator, which is then passed to the next addOrResign call, and so on.

```
List(
  Some( The Wire ),     addOrResign(Some(List.empty), Some( The Wire )) = Some(List( The Wire ))

  None                  addOrResign(Some(List( The Wire )), None) = None

).foldLeft(Some(List.empty))(addOrResign)                           ➤ = None
```

We now know how to handle multiple possible errors!

We are almost there! Before we meet the last protagonist of the chapter, let's see what we've achieved. At the beginning of the chapter we were tasked with a requirement to parse raw TV shows. This alone took us on quite a journey:

1. We found out that we can implement the `parseShows` function using a `map` and a `parseShow`.

2. In `parseShow` we could therefore focus on parsing just one TV show, and we started with a straightforward approach by returning a `TvShow` directly from this function.

3. We found out that when a given `rawShow` `String` is invalidly formatted, we get an exception and crash the application.

4. We remembered that there is an `Option` type that models a value that may or may not be there.

5. We started using `Option[TvShow]` as a return type of `parseShow`, making it a pure function that doesn't lie (or throw!)

6. We were able to divide the functionality of `parseShow` into three separate small functions: `extractName`, `extractYearStart`, and `extractYearEnd`—all of which return an `Option` to signal parsing failure or success.

7. We found out that checked exceptions don't compose as well as `Option`, which has the `orElse` function.

8. We then moved on to parsing lists of `Strings` inside `parseShows`. The compiler made us decide what to do with `rawShow` `Strings` that had invalid formatting. First, we used `toList` and `flatten` to ignore errors and return a `List[TvShow]` without signaling that some shows were not parsed—the best-effort error-handling strategy.

9. We figured out that we can go even further and return an `Option[List[TvShow]]` from `parseShows` and use `foldLeft` to accumulate the result using a different strategy: all-or-nothing.

 Step 1

Recapping higher-order functions
Errors are handled using higher-order functions we learned about in chapter 4.

Step 2 ✔

Using Option to indicate an error
Indicating errors by returning immutable values from for comprehensions we learned about in chapter 5.

Step 3 ✔

Functional error handling vs. checked exceptions
Using a functional approach helps us indicate and handle errors in a much more readable and concise way than checked exceptions.

Step 4 ✔

Handling many errors at once
Defining higher-order functions that handle many errors using code that handles just a single error.

Now, it's time to wrap up the chapter and show you one last trick that will make sure you'll never miss exceptions again. **Descriptive errors!**

Coming up next ...

Using `Either` to indicate descriptive errors
Indicating errors by returning immutable values that contain more information about what failed.

How to know what failed

In the last part we implemented the all-or-nothing error-handling strategy inside the parseShows function. Let's assume this is what the business required from us. Now the function returns an Option if at least one of the raw TV shows can't be parsed.

```
> parseShows(List("Chernobyl (2019)", "Breaking Bad (2008-2013)"))
  → Some(List(TvShow("Chernobyl", 2019, 2019),
              TvShow("Breaking Bad", 2008, 2013)))
  parseShows(List("Chernobyl [2019]", "Breaking Bad (2008-2013)"))
  → None
  parseShows(List("Chernobyl (2019)", "Breaking Bad"))
  → None
```

As we can see, everything works correctly! We managed to implement a totally different logic for error handling by changing just a single function! We didn't have to change the function responsible for parsing one show (parseShow still returns Option[TvShow]). This showcases the power of modularity that FP promotes!

Let's disturb this idyllic view for a bit and look at the usage of the new version of parseShows from a more critical perspective. Look at the last two results in the code listing above. We get a None as a result—we know that something failed. However, **we don't know what!** There are multiple functions involved inside parseShows and the functions it uses—and each one returns an Option. Anything can "fail," and all we get is None. We can't have any idea why some of the rawShows have not been parsed. We could have used a wrong parenthesis, forgotten about years, used a dash in the wrong place, or a multitude of other problems. And all we get is None. This approach gets more problematic when we try to use Options as error indicators in more complex logic. In huge lists, where many things can go wrong, Option is not our best friend anymore.

> Q Isn't it worse than exceptions? When an exception is thrown, we know exactly where and why!
>
> A We know that exceptions give us more information than Option. However, as we already discussed, exception-based code is much less composable, and we need to write much more code whenever we want to conditionally or partially recover from errors.
>
> Q So you've been rambling about error handling using Options for like 40 pages, and now you tell me it's bad?
>
> A The Option type may not be the best choice, but all the things we used with Option can be immediately used for other, more descriptive types! It'll pay off!

We need to convey error details in the return value

If something fails, we want to know why! Option is good for handling errors and recovering from errors, but if something fails, all we get is None. So we need something that works like Option but, additionally, allows us to give and propagate specific information about errors.

Fortunately, Scala and other FP languages have us covered here as well. There is a type that can convey information about a particular error, and **it gives us all the functions we learned about when we handled errors using Option**. And by *all*, I mean just that. If you know how to handle errors using Option, you already know how to handle errors using this new type.

It's called Either

This new type is called Either, or, more specifically, Either[A, B]. Just like Option, it has two subtypes.

```
        Either[A, B]                          Option[A]

  Left[A]          Right[B]           None            Some[A]
  val value: A     val value: B                       val value: A
```

Why are they called Left and Right and not Success and Failure? We'll explain in chapter 12.

As you can see, these data types look pretty similar. Particularly, both Right and Some look identical, and it's not a coincidence. When dealing with possible error scenarios, these types are used to convey information about a successful case. The main difference is with the second subtype: None is just that—a single value. Left, however, can hold a value, just like Some and Right! So in Either, we can specify a value that will be present in the result for both successful (Right) and error (Left) cases. Let's see the comparison:

The type of value stored if an Either is Left (A) can be any type (primitive or product type). We will use String in this chapter, but generally a "description of an error" can be a more complex type.

```scala
def extractName(show: String): Either[String, String] = {
  val bracketOpen = show.indexOf('(')
  if (bracketOpen > 0)
    Right(show.substring(0, bracketOpen).trim)
  else
    Left(s"Can't extract name from $show")
}
```

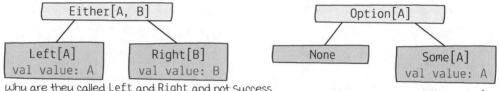

If you prefix your String with s, you will be able to print values inside this String using the $ prefix.

```scala
> extractName("(2022)")
→ Left("Can't extract name from (2022)")
```

```scala
def extractName(rawShow: String): Option[String] = {
  val bracketOpen = rawShow.indexOf('(')
  if (bracketOpen > 0)
    Some(rawShow.substring(0, bracketOpen).trim)
  else
    None
}
```

```scala
> extractName("(2019)")
→ None
```

Conveying error details using `Either`

Step 5
Using `Either` to indicate descriptive errors
Indicating errors by returning immutable values that contain more information about what failed.

If you still don't know why `Either` is such a big deal, the following paragraphs should clarify a lot! We will reiterate what we learned about functional error handling and how it gives us the very helpful skill of indicating descriptive errors. We'll see how changing the return type of `parseShows` from `Option` to `Either` helps us understand the error a lot quicker—and it does that using almost exactly the same code!

Traditionally, any time we introduce a new type or a function, we start with signatures and usages. `Either` won't be an exception! Before we start coding, let's compare the `Option`-based signature (which doesn't give us any hint about error details) with the `Either`-based one (which gives us a description of an error as a `String`).

Excuse the exception pun, but I hope it helps get the point across: using `Either` is the functional alternative to imperative exception-based error handling.

Before   **Returning `Some[TvShow]` (or `None` if something goes wrong)**

```
def parseShows(rawShows: List[String]): Option[List[TvShow]]
```

Now   **Returning `Right[List[TvShow]]` (or `Left[String]` if something goes wrong)**

```
def parseShows(rawShows: List[String]): Either[String, List[TvShow]]
```

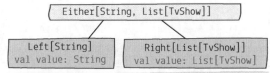

```
          Either[String, List[TvShow]]

   Left[String]              Right[List[TvShow]]
   val value: String         val value: List[TvShow]
```

`parseShows` returns an `Either[String, List[TvShow]]`, which we read as "either a `String` or a `List[TvShow]`." The signature tells us exactly that it will return one of two values. If we get a `String` (wrapped in a `Left`), we assume it contains a description of what went wrong with at least one of the raw shows we provided. Otherwise, it returns a `List[TvShow]` (wrapped in a `Right`).

Note again that `Either` has two subtypes: `Left(value: A)` and `Right(value: B)`. This is important because it means that both of them can be used whenever `Either[A, B]` is needed. We can therefore return any of them from a function that returns an `Either[A, B]`.

Now, let's test our intuition and see how this kind of function could be used in the real world. Again, there is no implementation yet, we just do a dry run of the signature to make sure we know what it should return:

This, again, is called test-driven development, or TDD! We first define the test by calling an unimplemented function and asserting its output. We'll cover TDD in chapter 12!

```
parseShows(List("The Wire (2002-2008)", "[2019]"))
→ Left("Can't extract name from [2019]")

parseShows(List("The Wire (-)", "Chernobyl (2019)"))
→ Left("Can't extract single year from The Wire (-)")

parseShows(List("The Wire (2002-2008)", "Chernobyl (2019)"))
→ Right(List(TvShow("The Wire", 2002, 2008),
             TvShow("Chernobyl", 2019, 2019)))
```

Left is a more helpful value than None because it holds a description!

Note that both `Left("Can't extract name from [2019]")` and `Right(List(TvShow(...))` are **just immutable values of type Either!**

Refactoring to Either

We'll spend the rest of this chapter refactoring parseShows and functions it depends on to use Either instead of Option. I promise that learning Either will not be as hard as learning Option because both types share many things in common. This means your existing experience with Option will come in handy. As we go, please note how a few changes in ← the code make such a big difference from the client-code perspective.

That's the power of pure functions that get and return immutable values!

How can we approach such a big change in the codebase? Let's go through each step of the refactoring, looking at the big picture of our current solution and seeing how it changes when we introduce Either.

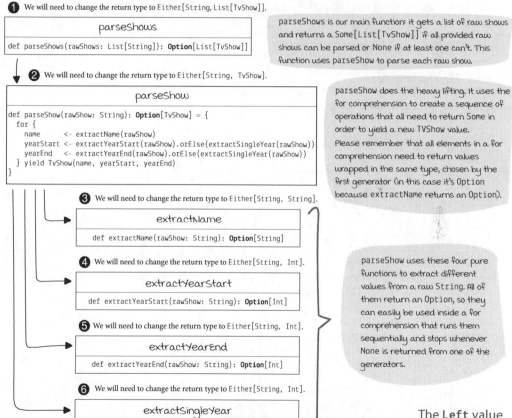

❶ We will need to change the return type to Either[String, List[TvShow]].

```
parseShows

def parseShows(rawShows: List[String]): Option[List[TvShow]]
```

parseShows is our main function: it gets a list of raw shows and returns a Some[List[TvShow]] if all provided raw shows can be parsed or None if at least one can't. This function uses parseShow to parse each raw show.

❷ We will need to change the return type to Either[String, TvShow].

```
parseShow

def parseShow(rawShow: String): Option[TvShow] = {
  for {
    name      <- extractName(rawShow)
    yearStart <- extractYearStart(rawShow).orElse(extractSingleYear(rawShow))
    yearEnd   <- extractYearEnd(rawShow).orElse(extractSingleYear(rawShow))
  } yield TvShow(name, yearStart, yearEnd)
}
```

parseShow does the heavy lifting. It uses the for comprehension to create a sequence of operations that all need to return Some in order to yield a new TVShow value.

Please remember that all elements in a for comprehension need to return values wrapped in the same type, chosen by the first generator (in this case it's Option because extractName returns an Option).

❸ We will need to change the return type to Either[String, String].

```
extractName

def extractName(rawShow: String): Option[String]
```

❹ We will need to change the return type to Either[String, Int].

```
extractYearStart

def extractYearStart(rawShow: String): Option[Int]
```

❺ We will need to change the return type to Either[String, Int].

```
extractYearEnd

def extractYearEnd(rawShow: String): Option[Int]
```

parseShow uses these four pure functions to extract different values from a raw String. All of them return an Option, so they can easily be used inside a for comprehension that runs them sequentially and stops whenever None is returned from one of the generators.

❻ We will need to change the return type to Either[String, Int].

```
extractSingleYear

def extractSingleYear(rawShow: String): Option[Int]
```

We have six refactoring steps. Each of the six functions that return an Option now will need to be rewritten to return an Either. We will approach these refactorings by starting from the smallest extract function and finishing with rewriting parseShow and parseShows.

*The **Left** value of **Either** can be parametrized with any other type, not just String. We will show an example of that in chapter 12.*

Returning an `Either` instead of an `Option`

We have six refactoring steps to do before wrapping up this chapter:

1 Change the return type of `parseShows` to `Either[String, List[TvShow]]`.

2 Change the return type of `parseShow` to `Either[String, TvShow]`.

3 Change the return type of `extractName` to `Either[String, String]`.

we will start from here! → **4** Change the return type of `extractYearStart` to `Either[String, Int]`.   *You will do these on your own!*

5 Change the return type of `extractYearEnd` to `Either[String, Int]`.

6 Change the return type of `extractSingleYear` to `Either[String, Int]`.

This will give us descriptive errors—we will know exactly what failed! We can split the workload almost equally between me and you—the reader. The plan is to show you how to refactor `extractYearStart` (number 4 on our list) and then let you refactor the three remaining `extract` functions as an exercise. I hope your existing experience with `Option`—plus seeing how **extractYearStart** will have been refactored—will be enough to refactor these three functions on your own. Let's start.

4a We start with the signature: our function takes a `String` and returns an `Either[String, Int]`:
```
def extractYearStart(rawShow: String): Either[String, Int] = {
  ???
}
```

```
                        Either[A, B]

          Left[A]                  Right[B]
          val value: A             val value: B
```

4b To get the start year, we need to find separator characters first: `"TITLE (`**`START`**`-END)"`:

bracketOpen ⌐   ⌐ dash
```
def extractYearStart(rawShow: String): Either[String, Int] = {
  val bracketOpen = rawShow.indexOf('(')
  val dash        = rawShow.indexOf('-')
  ???
}
```

4c We know that `String.substring` can throw an exception, but we want to use `Either` instead. That's why we need to call `String.substring` only when we know it won't fail:

```
def extractYearStart(rawShow: String): Either[String, Int] = {
  val bracketOpen = rawShow.indexOf('(')
  val dash        = rawShow.indexOf('-')
  if (bracketOpen != -1 && dash > bracketOpen + 1)
    Right(rawShow.substring(bracketOpen + 1, dash))
  else Left(s"Can't extract start year from $rawShow")
}
```
Compilation error!
Either[String, String]

> This looks almost identical to the `Option` version, doesn't it? There are two differences. First is that we wrap the value in `Right`, instead of `Some`. Second is that we return a more descriptive error message wrapped in a `Left`, instead of plain, nondescriptive `None` in the `Option` version. This assures us that if this function returns a `Left`, it will bubble up to the top. We will know what will have failed by looking at it: `"Can't extract start year from Chernobyl [2019]"`.
> **There is still a compilation error, though: we have an `Either[String, String]` but need an `Either[String, Int]`!** (Remember that the left type in `Either` is the type parameter of `Left`—`String` in our case—and the right type is the type parameter of `Right`, which should be an `Int`!

4d Our signature says that we return an Either[String, Int], but our implementation returns an Either[String, String] instead. We need to transform the right String into an Int.

```
def extractYearStart(rawShow: String): Either[String, Int] = {
  val bracketOpen  = rawShow.indexOf('(')
  val dash         = rawShow.indexOf('-')
  val yearStrEither = if (bracketOpen != -1 && dash > bracketOpen + 1)
        Either[String, String]         Right(rawShow.substring(bracketOpen + 1, dash))
                      else Left(s"Can't extract start year from $rawShow")
  yearStrEither.map(yearStr => yearStr.toIntOption)
}                                                      Compilation error!
         String                  Option[Int]          Either[String, Option[Int]]
```

yearStrEither is a value of type Either[String, String], which means it can be either a Left[String] or a Right[String]. If it's a Left[String], then we need to return it, because it is an error, and the String contains an error message. If it's a Right[String], however, we know that this is a substring that should contain the start year. So we want to transform this String into an Int but only if yearStrEither is a Right[String]. It turns out that this is a pattern we learned about earlier and already used in the Option-based version: we need to use the map! If we map over a Left, the result is the same Left. If we map over a Right, the result is Right with the value produced by the function we gave to map! It works exactly like in Option, where Some gets mapped and None doesn't.

```
> val e: Either[String, String] = Right("1985")   > val e: Either[String, String] = Left("Error")
  e.map(_.toIntOption)                               e.map(_.toIntOption)
  → Right(Some(1985))                                → Left("Error")
```

In this case we mapped using String.toIntOption again. As you remember, it tries to parse an integer value from a given String. If it's possible, it returns an Option[Int]. If it's not, it returns None! So we are mapping the right String of Either[String, String] using a function String => Option[Int], and that's why we get an Either[String, Option[Int]] back.

The compiler is not happy; it wanted Either[String, Int], not Either[String, Option[Int]]!

4e Our signature says that we return an Either[String, Int], but our implementation returns an Either[String, Option[Int]] instead. We need to transform the internal Option[Int] into an Int. However, we can't safely get the Int out of an Option[Int] because it may be None. What we can do is transform the Option[Int] into an Either[String, Int] by using a new pure function: **toRight**. This way, we will end up with Either[String, Either[String, Int]].

```
def extractYearStart(rawShow: String): Either[String, Int] = {
  val bracketOpen  = rawShow.indexOf('(')
  val dash         = rawShow.indexOf('-')
  val yearStrEither = if (bracketOpen != -1 && dash > bracketOpen + 1)
        Either[String, String]         Right(rawShow.substring(bracketOpen + 1, dash))
                      else Left(s"Can't extract start year from $rawShow")
  yearStrEither.map(yearStr =>
    yearStr  String

      .toIntOption   Option[Int]                      Either[String, Either[String, Int]]

      .toRight(s"Can't parse $yearStr")        Compilation error!
  )                                             Either[String, Either[String, Int]]
}             Either[String, Option[Int]]
```

yearStrEither is mapped using a function that takes a String and returns an Either[String, Int]. Remember that map is concerned only with the Right value—it maps only the successful value, not the error value. That's why the call to map changes only the right type, where, instead of the String, we get Either[String, Int]. This means that the expression creates a value of type Either[String, Either[String, Int]], which looks complicated but is very helpful, which we'll see in a moment. Inside the map function that transforms a String, we add the toRight function call. **This function converts an Option into an Either.** If the Option is Some, it returns the same value inside Right. If it's None, it returns the value we've provided—in our case a String—wrapped inside Left.

```
> Some(1985).toRight("Can't parse it")      > None.toRight("Can't parse it")
  → Right(1985)                               → Left("Can't parse it")
```

But our code doesn't compile; we want Either[String, Int], not Either[String, Either[String, Int]]!

4f Our signature says that we return an `Either[String, Int]`, but our implementation returns an
`Either[String, Either[String, Int]]` instead. We can flatten it to `Either[String, Int]`!

```
def extractYearStart(rawShow: String): Either[String, Int] = {
  val bracketOpen  = rawShow.indexOf('(')
  val dash         = rawShow.indexOf('-')
  val yearStrEither = if (bracketOpen != -1 && dash > bracketOpen + 1)
                        Right(rawShow.substring(bracketOpen + 1, dash))
                      else Left(s"Can't extract start year from $rawShow")
  yearStrEither.map(yearStr =>
    yearStr.toIntOption.toRight(s"Can't parse $yearStr")
  ).flatten
}
```

`Either[String, String]` (label on `yearStrEither` line)
`Either[String, Either[String, Int]]` (label on map call)
`Either[String, Int]` (label on `.flatten`)

> `yearStrEither` is a value of type `Either[String, String]`, which is transformed into an `Either[String, Either[String, Int]]` using a `map` call. Any time we have a nested type like this one, we can flatten it to get rid of one level of nesting. It works exactly like in `List` and `Option`:
>
> ```
> > List(List(1985)).flatten      > Some(Some(1985)).flatten      > Right(Right(1985)).flatten
>   → List(1985)                    → Some(1985)                    → Right(1985)
>
>   List(List()).flatten           Some(None).flatten              Right(Left("Error")).flatten
>   → List()                       → None                          → Left("Error")
> ```
>
> **Now it compiles!** Notice that the flattening part makes sure that if there is any error, it will be our result. Again, this is an example how `flatten` (and `flatMap`) propagates the first error ("short-circuiting").

4e Have you noticed that we used `map` and `flatten` again? That means we can simplify the whole thing into a `flatMap` call, like in `Option`. If we can use `flatMap`, we can also write it as a for comprehension, which should look very natural to you by now:

```
def extractYearStart(rawShow: String): Either[String, Int] = {
  val bracketOpen = rawShow.indexOf('(')
  val dash        = rawShow.indexOf('-')
  for {
    yearStr <- if (bracketOpen != -1 && dash > bracketOpen + 1)
                 Right(rawShow.substring(bracketOpen + 1, dash))
               else Left(s"Can't extract start year from $rawShow")
    year <- yearStr.toIntOption.toRight(s"Can't parse $yearStr")
  } yield year
}
```

> The for comprehension works in the context of `Either`, which is defined by the first generator. It creates a value of `Either[String, String]` and saves the right `String` as `yearStr` (or stops and returns the `Left[String]` if the expression returned it). Then, the second generator uses the value from the first expression, `yearStr`, and returns `Either[String, Int]`. Again, if this is `Left[String]`, it is immediately returned as a result of the whole for comprehension. If it's `Right[Int]`, then the right value, `Int`, is saved as `year`, which is `yield`ed as the result of the expression, inside `Either`.
>
> **Now we have a working code, which is safe and readable.** Based on the provided `String`, it returns `Either[String, Int]`, which means that it returns a `Right[Int]` if the function can extract a year from the `String`, or a `Left[String]` containing an error description otherwise.

Now, let's test how this function behaves in the real world.

```
> extractYearStart("The Wire (2002-2008)")
  → Right(2002)

  extractYearStart("The Wire (-2008)")
  → Left("Can't extract start year from The Wire (-2008)")

  extractYearStart("The Wire (oops-2008)")
  → Left("Can't parse oops")

  extractYearStart("The Wire (2002-)")
  → Right(2002)
```

Note that no matter what String we pass, we always get a value back! Some values are the years wrapped inside Rights, and some are error messages wrapped inside Lefts. But we always get something back!

Practicing safe functions that return Either

we'll do them → **1** Change the return type of parseShows to Either[String, List[TvShow]].

afterwards. → **2** Change the return type of parseShow to Either[String, TvShow].

3 Change the return type of extractName to Either[String, String].

we have just implemented → **4** ~~Change the return type of extractYearStart to Either[String, Int].~~

this! **5** Change the return type of extractYearEnd to Either[String, Int].

6 Change the return type of extractSingleYear to Either[String, Int].

You now need to code these!

Now it's your turn to code something. **Your task is to implement the three missing extract functions.** Each of them gets a rawShow String and returns an Either. Use the REPL to write and test all three functions.

Answers

```scala
def extractName(rawShow: String): Either[String, String] = {
  val bracketOpen = rawShow.indexOf('(')
  if (bracketOpen > 0)
    Right(rawShow.substring(0, bracketOpen).trim)
  else
    Left(s"Can't extract name from $rawShow")
}
```

3 We get the index of the bracket. If it's found, we return Right with the name inside. If not, we return Left with an error message inside.

```scala
def extractYearEnd(rawShow: String): Either[String, Int] = {
  val dash        = rawShow.indexOf('-')
  val bracketClose = rawShow.indexOf(')')
  for {
    yearStr <- if (dash != -1 && bracketClose > dash + 1)
                 Right(rawShow.substring(dash + 1, bracketClose))
               else Left(s"Can't extract end year from $rawShow")
    year <- yearStr.toIntOption.toRight(s"Can't parse $yearStr")
  } yield year
}
```

5 We get the index of the dash and closing bracket. If they are found and the closing bracket is further in the string than the dash, we can safely call the substring function and pass the string to the next phase, which parses the integer.

This line is repeated in three functions. maybe we should extract it into its own small function?

```scala
def extractSingleYear(rawShow: String): Either[String, Int] = {
  val dash        = rawShow.indexOf('-')
  val bracketOpen  = rawShow.indexOf('(')
  val bracketClose = rawShow.indexOf(')')
  for {
    yearStr <- if (dash == -1 && bracketOpen != -1 &&
                   bracketClose > bracketOpen + 1)
                 Right(rawShow.substring(bracketOpen + 1, bracketClose))
               else Left(s"Can't extract single year from $rawShow")
    year <- yearStr.toIntOption.toRight(s"Can't parse $yearStr")
  } yield year
}
```

6 We get the index of the dash and both opening and closing brackets. If there is no dash but brackets are found and the closing bracket is further in the String than the opening one, we can safely call the substring function and pass the String to the next phase.

What we learned about Option works with Either

Step 5
Using Either to indicate descriptive errors
Indicating errors by returning immutable values that contain more information about what failed.

Together we've completed four out of six refactoring steps. I hope that you've already noticed that we have almost exactly the same code using Either as we had when we used Option. The only difference is that instead of None, we use a Left value with a String that describes the problem. Now, it's time to use our new four functions to parse a single raw show.

2a We want to change the return type to Either[String, TvShow].

```
def parseShow(rawShow: String): Option[TvShow] = {        Compilation error!
  for {                                                    Either[String, TvShow]
    name     <- extractName(rawShow)
    yearStart <- extractYearStart(rawShow).orElse(extractSingleYear(rawShow))
    yearEnd   <- extractYearEnd(rawShow).orElse(extractSingleYear(rawShow))
  } yield TvShow(name, yearStart, yearEnd)
}
```

parseShow returns an Option, but extractName and other extract functions already return Either! That means that our for comprehension expression is already of type Either[String, TvShow]! But our signature still says that we return an Option[TvShow]. **This is a compilation error: our implementation returns Either[String, TvShow], but the signature promises Option[TvShow]!** To fix this compilation error, we need to adjust the signature to the implementation, and we are done! Yes, that means that Either-version of parseShow is identical to the Option version.

2b We need to change the return type in the signature to Either[String, TvShow]. No more changes are needed, because Either also has orElse.

```
def parseShow(rawShow: String): Either[String, TvShow] = {
  for {
    name     <- extractName(rawShow)
    yearStart <- extractYearStart(rawShow).orElse(extractSingleYear(rawShow))
    yearEnd   <- extractYearEnd(rawShow).orElse(extractSingleYear(rawShow))
  } yield TvShow(name, yearStart, yearEnd)
}
```

That's it! When we refactored extractName and other extract functions to use Either, we did all the heavy lifting! Thus, only the signature needed to be changed in parseShow. It also turned out that Either has an orElse function that works similarly to the Option one.

If this is Right(value),   ... but if it's not, the alternative is returned,
    orElse returns it ...   no matter whether it's Left or Right.

```
Either[A, B].orElse(alternative: Either[A, B]): Either[A, B]
```

```
parseShow("The Wire (-)")
→ Left("Can't extract single year from The Wire (-)")

parseShow("The Wire (oops)")
→ Left("Can't parse oops")

parseShow("(2002-2008)")
→ Left("Can't extract name from (2002-2008)")

parseShow("The Wire (2002-2008)")
→ Right(TvShow("The Wire", 2002, 2008))
```

Once we use Option/ Either, everything else gets "tainted" and bubbles up to client code! That's the way to make sure an error is explicitly handled.

Coffee break:
Error handling using Either

We now know that everything we learned about implementing error indication and handling using Option is useful when we use Either. This final exercise of the chapter will make sure that you understand functional error handling. **Your task is to refactor the parseShows:**

❶ Change the return type of parseShows to Either[String, List[TvShow]].

❷ ~~Change the return type of parseShow to Either[String, TvShow].~~

❸ ~~Change the return type of extractName to Either[String, String].~~

❹ ~~Change the return type of extractYearStart to Either[String, Int].~~

❺ ~~Change the return type of extractYearEnd to Either[String, Int].~~

❻ ~~Change the return type of extractSingleYear to Either[String, Int].~~

Your final quest!

Here's a reminder of how parseShows should work. It implements the all-or-nothing error-handling logic, which means that if at least one raw TV show can't be parsed, the error is returned (inside a Left!). Try to implement this function from scratch before going forward.

```
parseShows(List("The Wire (2002-2008)", "[2019]"))
→ Left("Can't extract name from [2019]")

parseShows(List("The Wire (-)", "Chernobyl (2019)"))
→ Left("Can't extract single year from The Wire (-)")

parseShows(List("The Wire (2002-2008)", "Chernobyl (2019)"))
→ Right(List(TvShow("The Wire", 2002, 2008),
           TvShow("Chernobyl", 2019, 2019)))
```

This is a harder version of this exercise, but you have all the knowledge to implement it. Use your time, and try to solve it. If you do, the rest of the book will be a lot easier!

Hint

If you spent a substantial amount of time trying to implement **parseShows** from scratch, and you can't figure it out, here's the Option-based version.

parseShows
| ```
def parseShows(rawShows: List[String]): Option[List[TvShow]] = {
  val initialResult: Option[List[TvShow]] = Some(List.empty)
  rawShows
    .map(parseShow)
    .foldLeft(initialResult)(addOrResign)
}
``` |

addOrResign
| ```
def addOrResign(
  parsedShows: Option[List[TvShow]],
  newParsedShow: Option[TvShow]
): Option[List[TvShow]] = {
  for {
    shows      <- parsedShows
    parsedShow <- newParsedShow
  } yield shows.appended(parsedShow)
}
``` |

parseShows uses the addOrResign helper function. Both use Option as a type that conveys information about an error. You need to make them work with Either instead.

Coffee break explained:
Error handling using `Either`

The final exercise of a chapter should be challenging, but I hope you've
enjoyed this ride! Let's do it together step by step:

1a We want to change the return type to `Either[String, List[TvShow]]`.

```
def parseShows(rawShows: List[String]): Option[List[TvShow]] = {
  val initialResult: Option[List[TvShow]] = Some(List.empty)
```

```
rawShows   List[TvShow]

  .map(parseShow)   List[Option[TvShow]]

  .foldLeft(initialResult)(addOrResign)
}           Option[List[TvShow]]
```

```
def addOrResign(
  parsedShows: Option[List[TvShow]],
  newParsedShow: Option[TvShow]
): Option[List[TvShow]] = {
  for {
    shows      <- parsedShows
    parsedShow <- newParsedShow
  } yield shows.appended(parsedShow)
}
```

1b Let's change the signature to `Either[String, List[TvShow]]` and see what the compiler has to say.

```
def parseShows(rawShows: List[String]): Either[String, List[TvShow]] = {
  val initialResult: Option[List[TvShow]] = Some(List.empty)
```

```
rawShows   List[TvShow]

  .map(parseShow)   List[Either[String, TvShow]]

  .foldLeft(initialResult)(addOrResign)
}           Option[List[TvShow]]

   Compilation error!
```

```
def addOrResign(
  parsedShows: Option[List[TvShow]],
  newParsedShow: Option[TvShow]
): Option[List[TvShow]] = {
  for {
    shows      <- parsedShows
    parsedShow <- newParsedShow
  } yield shows.appended(parsedShow)
}
```

> `parseShows` promises to return an `Either[String, List[TvShow]]`, but the implementation is not ready yet.
> We've already refactored `parseShow`, which now returns an `Either[String, TvShow]`. This means that mapping
> using `parseShow` creates a `List of Eithers`. We then proceed to folding this `List`, using a function that is able to
> fold `Options`, not `Eithers`. **This is a compilation error!** To fix this compilation error, we need to adjust both the
> `initialResult` and the `addOrResign` function.

1c Let's change the `initialResult` and `addOrResign` to use `Either` instead of the `Option` to make the compiler happy.

```
def parseShows(rawShows: List[String]): Either[String, List[TvShow]] = {
  val initialResult: Either[String, List[TvShow]] = Right(List.empty)
```

```
rawShows   List[TvShow]

  .map(parseShow)   List[Either[String, TvShow]]

  .foldLeft(initialResult)(addOrResign)
}           Either[String, List[TvShow]]
```

```
def addOrResign(
  parsedShows: Either[String, List[TvShow]],
  newParsedShow: Either[String, TvShow]
): Either[String, List[TvShow]] = {
  for {
    shows      <- parsedShows
    parsedShow <- newParsedShow
  } yield shows.appended(parsedShow)
}
```

> `parseShows` returns an `Either[String, List[TvShow]]` now! Mapping using the `parseShow` function creates a
> `List of Eithers`. We then proceed to fold this `List` using a function that is now able to handle `Eithers`. Note how
> both implementations are similar. But don't be misguided! The `Either`-based version provides us with much more
> detailed errors. We will always know exactly which TV show failed to parse and why. It's all done in the `extract`
> functions, though. Here, we have just provided a way to use `Either`-based `parseShow` with a `List` of TV shows.

Working with Option/Either

Before we finally wrap this chapter up, let's talk about the essence of functional error handling. Errors are encoded as immutable values. To handle errors, we write pure functions, which internally use map, flatten, flatMap, orElse, and toRight/toOption. All these functions are defined in both Option and Either types, **which look and behave similarly.** Let's summarize how we've worked with both of them in this chapter.

It's important to understand all these functions before moving on. Use the REPL, and follow the code to make sure you really grokked them all.

Working with Option

```
> val year: Option[Int] = Some(996)
  val noYear: Option[Int] = None
```

map
```
year.map(_ * 2)
→ Some(1992)
noYear.map(_ * 2)
→ None
```

flatten
```
Some(year).flatten
→ Some(996)
Some(noYear).flatten
→ None
```

flatMap
```
year.flatMap(y => Some(y * 2))
→ Some(1992)
noYear.flatMap(y => Some(y * 2))
→ None
year.flatMap(y => None)
→ None
noYear.flatMap(y => None)
→ None
```

orElse
```
year.orElse(Some(2020))
→ Some(996)
noYear.orElse(Some(2020))
→ Some(2020)
year.orElse(None)
→ Some(996)
noYear.orElse(None)
→ None
```

toRight
```
year.toRight("no year given")
→ Right(996)
noYear.toRight("no year given")
→ Left("no year given")
```

Working with Either

```
> val year: Either[String, Int] = Right(996)
  val noYear: Either[String, Int] = Left("no year")
```

map
```
year.map(_ * 2)
→ Right(1992)
noYear.map(_ * 2)
→ Left("no year")
```

flatten
```
Right(year).flatten
→ Right(996)
Right(noYear).flatten
→ Left("no year")
```

flatMap
```
year.flatMap(y => Right(y * 2))
→ Right(1992)
noYear.flatMap(y => Right(y * 2))
→ Left("no year")
year.flatMap(y => Left("can't progress"))
→ Left("can't progress")
noYear.flatMap(y => Left("can't progress"))
→ Left("no year")
```

orElse
```
year.orElse(Right(2020))
→ Right(996)
noYear.orElse(Right(2020))
→ Right(2020)
year.orElse(Left("can't recover"))
→ Right(996)
noYear.orElse(Left("can't recover"))
→ Left("can't recover")
```

toOption
```
year.toOption
→ Some(996)
noYear.toOption
→ None
```

Summary

In this chapter you've learned a lot about functional error handling. Additionally, you validated all the knowledge you gained in previous chapters. You are now a proficient user of immutable values and pure functions.

Handle errors without nulls and exceptions

We encountered the problematic substring calls that failed for some Strings. We learned that in FP all errors are just values, and we can use them instead of nulls and exceptions.

Make sure all corner cases are handled

We learned that using checked exceptions for error handling is not as composable as using Option or Either. When a function returns an exception, we needed to first catch it and then decide how to handle the error and recover from it. In Option and Either, we were able to use the orElse function that takes two immutable values that may be representing errors and returns one of them. This approach scales very well.

Indicate errors in the function signature

Our pure functions indicate when they may fail by exposing this information through their signatures. If a function returns an Option or Either, it's saying that for some arguments the result may not be generated.

Compose bigger functionalities from smaller functions in the presence of errors

We learned that we can divide the requirement into very small ones and implement a function for each of them with a custom error message that will be propagated if it's encountered. We built bigger functions (that handle lists) by composing them from these small functions. The compiler made us handle all possible errors along the way. Finally, we implemented the all-or-nothing error-handling strategy by using our old friend—foldLeft.

Return user-friendly and descriptive errors

On top of that, we learned that when we used Either we were able to provide very detailed error messages as Left[String].

CODE: CH06_*
Explore this chapter's source code by looking at ch06_* files in the book's repository.

Step 1

Recapping higher-order functions
Errors are handled using higher-order functions we learned about in chapter 4.

Step 2

Using Option to indicate an error
Indicating errors by returning immutable values from for comprehensions we learned about in chapter 5.

Step 3

Functional error handling vs. checked exceptions
Using a functional approach helps us indicate and handle errors in a much more readable and concise way than checked exceptions.

Step 4

Handling many errors at once
Defining higher-order functions that handle many errors using code that handles just a single error.

Step 5

Using Either to indicate descriptive errors
Indicating errors by returning immutable values that contain more information about what failed.

In this chapter
you will learn

- how to model your immutable data to minimize errors

- how to model your requirements as immutable data

- how to find problems in requirements using the compiler

- how to make sure your logic is always executed on valid data

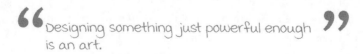

Designing something just powerful enough is an art.

—BARBARA LISKOV

Modeling data to minimize programmers' mistakes

In this chapter we will change the way we model data in our applications. We will use more types to minimize potential programmer mistakes. We will learn techniques that enhance the maintainability of our codebases. We will also make implementations smaller and less complicated! Too good to be true? Let's see this in action using an example.

we focus a lot on maintainability in this book. As a reminder, we say that a given codebase is maintainable if it's easy to change without introducing bugs.

Music artist catalogue

As always, we'll start with a potential real-world application. We will implement a music artist catalogue that will help us find artists by genres, their locations, or years they were active. There will be lots of corner cases to handle, and the main focus will be on data modeling. We will be modeling artists. Each artist will have a name, a main genre, and an origin. Seems easy, right? We just need to define a product type.

```
case class Artist(name: String, genre: String, origin: String)
```

What problems do you see with this definition of an artist?

There are many problems with this approach, but they all can be summarized like this: this data model makes the implementation based on it harder and more error-prone. The compiler allows many invalid instances like `Artist("", "", "")` or `Artist("Metallica", "U.S", "Heavy Metal")`, and it forces programmers to handle each of them in the code. (Do you see what the problem is with the latter value?) These kinds of mistakes are easy to make; they are not checked by the compiler, and they are pretty hard to debug in many cases. The funny thing is that **they all originate from using primitive types**, such as `Strings` and `Ints`, to model real-world, more complicated business entities and relations.

This is just a simplified version of the Artist definition we'll work with in this chapter. we will define the complete set of requirements soon.

So far we've used `Strings` or `Ints` to describe the data we used in our pure functions. In this chapter we can finally try to be better at data modeling. There are multiple problems we will list, explain, and propose a functional solution to. You will learn how to model data to make the implementation a lot easier, starting with modeling an artist using only what we've learned earlier (and primitive types). Then, we will discuss and analyze each possible mistake a programmer could make using this naive model. Solutions will come next. Let's go!

Some experience from the object-oriented world will come in handy as well!

Well-modeled data can't lie

So far in this book we've focused on implementing requirements using pure functions with signatures that tell readers what's going on inside. Pure functions don't lie, which makes reading code a breeze; readers don't need to go through each line of code to understand what it's doing. They just look at the signature and move on.

In this chapter we will show how we can apply exactly the same techniques to model our data! **In FP, we try to make our jobs easier by modeling data in a way that prevents representation of some invalid combinations!** That's the superpower behind functional design.

Enough introductions, let's code! We are faced with writing new software—a new function—that fulfills the following requirements.

> ### Requirements: Music artist catalogue
>
> 1. The function should be able to search through a list of music artists.
> 2. Each search should support a different combination of conditions: by genre, by origin (location), and by period in which they were active.
> 3. Each music artist has a name, genre, origin, year their career started, and a year they stopped performing (if they are not still active).

Note that of the three requirements above, the first two are **behavioral requirements**, while the last one is a **data requirement**. So far we've been focusing on behaviors (functions), and we modeled data requirements as simple types: `Strings`, `Ints`, and `Booleans`. We will start with this approach and quickly pivot to using safer functional programming techniques for both behaviors and data.

Good design makes an easy implementation

There will be five big general problems, and we will address each of them by introducing a functional programming technique that solves this particular problem and makes the model far **more bulletproof**. Being bulletproof means that only valid combinations of data from the business domain are possible in the implementation. This approach cuts a lot of *impossible* corner cases at the compilation level, so programmers don't need to worry about handling them. In the end our `Artist` definition will not only be bulletproof but also smaller, more readable, and far easier to work with. Interested?

> **THIS IS BIG!**
> In FP, we model data so that only valid business combinations are possible.

Quick exercise

Write your version of the `Artist` product type, which implements the third requirement above. Show your best design!

Answers in discussion.

Designing using what we know so far

(which is primitive types)

Notice that we use the terms data modeling and data design interchangeably in this book. They mean the same thing (i.e., how we transfer business entities into data structures).

I hope you've finished the quick exercise and written your own version of the `Artist` data model on a piece of paper so that you can compare and see how good your initial intuition was. We will start implementing the music artist catalogue data model using only the tools and techniques we have learned in previous chapters. The requirement for our data states the following:

> Each music artist has a name, genre, origin (location), year their career started, and a year they stopped performing (if they are not still active).

This looks like something we could model using a product type.

```
case class Artist(
    name: String,
    genre: String,
    origin: String,
    yearsActiveStart: Int,
    isActive: Boolean,
    yearsActiveEnd: Int
)
```

Name, genre, and origin location are modeled as raw `String`s.

Artists always have a year they started being active. We model that as a raw `Int`. If an artist is not active (`isActive=false`), `yearsActiveEnd` represents the year they stopped being active. However, some may be still active (`isActive=true`) and then `yearActiveEnd` should be 0.

Implementing behaviors that use the data

Now that we have modeled the data using a product type, we can implement the behavior—as a pure function—that uses this data. Let's start with the most important thing in FP: the function's signature.

> The function should be able to search through a list of music artists.

> Each search should support different combination of conditions: by genre, by origin, and by period in which they were active.

The incoming list of artists that contains all the artists we want to search through

```
def searchArtists(
    artists: List[Artist],
    genres: List[String],
    locations: List[String],
    searchByActiveYears: Boolean,
    activeAfter: Int,
    activeBefore: Int
): List[Artist]
```

These two `List`s represent two search conditions, and they work in a similar way. If a `List` is empty, we don't want to search using this condition. If it's not empty, we require that the resulting artists have the genres/locations specified in the list.

These three parameters together represent one search condition. If the Boolean flag is `false`, we don't trigger this condition. If it's `true`, we want to return only artists that were active within the `activeAfter-activeBefore` period (given in years as `Int`s).

The resulting list of artists that contains all the artists that satisfy given conditions

Using data modeled as primitive types

We used primitive types to model the data requirements. As you probably expect, this is far from ideal. However, it's still a very common practice, and many software architectures are built this way. You are probably aware of some limitations of this approach, but let's try to list them all.

We'll create a list of artists and search through them to get a feeling of how our primitive type–based model behaves in the real world. (Additionally, you will be tasked with implementing this raw version of searchArtists very soon, so it's a good idea to pay attention here.)

Here's a small list of all artists we are going to use in this chapter. The list has one active artist (as of date of publication) and two inactive ones.

```
val artists = List(
    Artist("Metallica", "Heavy Metal", "U.S.", 1981, true, 0),
    Artist("Led Zeppelin", "Hard Rock", "England", 1968, false, 1980),
    Artist("Bee Gees", "Pop", "England", 1958, false, 2003)
)
```

This is how we'd like to use our searchArtists function:

```
searchArtists(artists, List("Pop"), List("England"), true, 1950, 2022)
→ List(Artist("Bee Gees", "Pop", "England", 1958, false, 2003))


searchArtists(artists, List.empty, List("England"), true, 1950, 2022)
→ List(
    Artist("Led Zeppelin", "Hard Rock", "England", 1968, false, 1980),
    Artist("Bee Gees", "Pop", "England", 1958, false, 2003)
  )


searchArtists(artists, List.empty, List.empty, true, 1981, 2003)
→ List(
    Artist("Metallica", "Heavy Metal", "U.S.", 1981, true, 0),
    Artist("Bee Gees", "Pop", "England", 1958, false, 2003)
  )


searchArtists(artists, List.empty, List("U.S."), false, 0, 0)
→ List(Artist("Metallica", "Heavy Metal", "U.S.", 1981, true, 0))


searchArtists(artists, List.empty, List.empty, false, 2019, 2022)
→ List(
    Artist("Metallica", "Heavy Metal", "U.S.", 1981, true, 0),
    Artist("Led Zeppelin", "Hard Rock", "England", 1968, false, 1980),
    Artist("Bee Gees", "Pop", "England", 1958, false, 2003)
  )
```

Note that we don't say that this design is universally bad. It may have its benefits, like better performance. However, this book focuses on readability and maintainability in codebases. We argue that in this aspect primitive type–based modeling is not a good choice.

We still don't have an implementation of searchArtists, and you've probably already got accustomed to this approach. Remember: usage comes first, and implementation comes last.

Pop artists from England active between 1950–2022.

Artists from England active between 1950–2022. An empty list means we don't care about genre.

Artists active between 1981–2003. Empty lists mean we don't care about genre and location.

Artists from the United States with all other conditions disabled.

All conditions disabled. Note that years we provided don't matter because the flag is false.

Coffee break: The pain of primitive types

There are several serious problems with the approach we have just presented. It looks and works correctly, but it's very error-prone, and we will show all the places where programmers like us can make a mistake. That's what this exercise is for. You will have a go and try to implement the searchArtists function yourself. Can you get it right on your first try? Second? We will learn how to model data so that implementing behaviors such as searchArtists is a breeze. Let's feel the pain first, though!

Your task is to implement `searchArtists` as a pure function that has the signature we've discussed above.

The incoming list of artists that contains all the artists we want to search through

```
def searchArtists(
    artists: List[Artist],
    genres: List[String],
    locations: List[String],
    searchByActiveYears: Boolean,
    activeAfter: Int,
    activeBefore: Int
): List[Artist]
```

These two `List`s represent two search conditions, and they work in a similar way. If a `List` is empty, we don't want to search using this condition. If it's not empty, we require that the resulting artists have the genres/locations specified in the list.

These three parameters together represent one search condition. If the Boolean flag is `false`, we don't trigger this condition. If it's `true`, we want to return only artists that were active within the `activeAfter-activeBefore` period (given in years as Ints).

The resulting list of artists that contains all the artists that satisfy given conditions

Here are the use cases you should test against to make sure you have covered all bases:

— Search for pop artists from England active between 1950 and 2022:

```
searchArtists(artists, List("Pop"), List("England"), true, 1950, 2022)
```

— Search for artists from England active between 1950 and 2022:

```
searchArtists(artists, List.empty, List("England"), true, 1950, 2022)
```

— Search for artists active between 1950 and 1979:

```
searchArtists(artists, List.empty, List.empty, true, 1950, 1979)
```

— Search for artists active between 1981 and 1984:

```
searchArtists(artists, List.empty, List.empty, true, 1981, 1984)
```

— Search for heavy-metal artists active between 2019 and 2022:

```
searchArtists(artists, List("Heavy Metal"), List.empty, true, 2019, 2022)
```

— Search for artists from the U.S. active between 1950 and 1959:

```
searchArtists(artists, List.empty, List("U.S."), true, 1950, 1959)
```

— Search for artists without any conditions:

```
searchArtists(artists, List.empty, List.empty, false, 2019, 2022)
```

It's not a mistake, but including years here feels misleading, doesn't it?

List of artists to test with

Use these three artists in tests:
- Metallica, Heavy Metal, U.S., 1981–now,
- Led Zeppelin, Hard Rock, England, 1968–1980
- Bee Gees, Pop, England, 1958–2003

Coffee break explained: The pain of primitive types

I hope you've had some fun implementing the searchArtists function. As always has been the case in this book, there are different possible correct solutions. Make sure all the test cases listed in the task description are satisfied! Here's one possible (and annotated) solution:

```
def searchArtists(artists: List[Artist], genres: List[String],
                  locations: List[String], searchByActiveYears: Boolean,
                  activeAfter: Int, activeBefore: Int
): List[Artist] =
  artists.filter(artist =>
    (genres.isEmpty || genres.contains(artist.genre)) &&
    (locations.isEmpty || locations.contains(artist.origin)) &&
    (!searchByActiveYears || (
      (artist.isActive || artist.yearsActiveEnd >= activeAfter) &&
      (artist.yearsActiveStart <= activeBefore)))
  )
```

we need to use the filter higher-order function that takes a function, which is executed against each artist and returns true if it should be included in the output list.

If genres is not empty, we check whether the artist has a genre from the list. The same story is true with locations.

If the searchByActiveYears is true, we check whether the artist was active in the specified period. If an artist is still active, we only check the start year. Otherwise, we check both start and end years.

Did you enjoy all the nasty **nested ifs**? Let's see how they work:

```
searchArtists(artists, List("Pop"), List("England"), true, 1950, 2022)
→ List(Artist("Bee Gees", "Pop", "England", 1958, false, 2003))

searchArtists(artists, List.empty, List("England"), true, 1950, 2022)
→ List(Artist("Led Zeppelin", ...), Artist("Bee Gees", ...))

searchArtists(artists, List.empty, List.empty, true, 1950, 1979)
→ List(Artist("Led Zeppelin", ...), Artist("Bee Gees", ...))

searchArtists(artists, List.empty, List.empty, true, 1981, 2003)
→ List(Artist("Metallica", ...), Artist("Bee Gees", ...))

searchArtists(artists, List("Heavy Metal"), List.empty, true, 2019, 2022)
→ List(Artist("Metallica", "Heavy Metal", "U.S.", 1981, true, 0))

searchArtists(artists, List.empty, List("U.S."), true, 1950, 1959)
→ List()

searchArtists(artists, List.empty, List.empty, false, 2019, 2022)
→ List(Artist("Metallica", ...), Artist("Led Zeppelin", ...),
       Artist("Bee Gees", ...))
```

They work fine! The main outcome of this exercise, however, is this nagging feeling that it shouldn't be that hard. We should be able to implement these kinds of features without thinking much about the internals, right? What if I told you that **the way we modeled the Artist is the reason why implementing searchArtists was so difficult**? Now that you've felt the pain of implementing this function, let's see how the functional approach to modeling data could have made the job easier.

Problems with the primitive type approach to modeling

We now know that implementing behaviors (like the `searchArtists` function) based on primitive type data models is possible but error-prone. Let's cut to the chase and list three of the most important problems that we'll address and present a functional solution to in this chapter.

Primitive type–based model   Our current version that works, but is error-prone:

```
case class Artist(name: String, genre: String, origin: String,
                  yearsActiveStart: Int, isActive: Boolean, yearsActiveEnd: Int)
```

Problem 1

Programmers need to be careful about the order of parameters.
Answer this without looking at the product type definition: is the code below a valid representation of an artist?

```
Artist("Metallica", "U.S.", "Heavy Metal", 1981, true, 0)
```
→ compiles! (unfortunately)

It surely is for the compiler because it compiles fine! **However, it's not a valid value** because the parameters of `genre` and `origin` have been misplaced. There is no geographical `Heavy Metal` location, although I'm pretty sure some people would love it!

Problem 2

Programmers need to know the additional meaning of parameter combinations.
What about this? Is this a valid artist?

```
Artist("Metallica", "Heavy Metal", "U.S.",  1981, false, 2022)
```
→ compiles! (but it's not valid)

We agreed that to model an active artist, we should set `isActive` to `true`. If `isActive` is `true`, then the `yearsActiveEnd` parameter doesn't matter and should be set to 0. These parameters are interconnected, which means that we can represent lots of different combinations, but many of them will not be valid in terms of our domain.

Problem 3

Programmers need to ensure that some parameters have a finite set of values.
Is this a valid representation of an artist?

```
Artist("Metallica", "Master of Puppets", "U.S.",  1981, true, 0)
```
→ compiles! (again, compiler hasn't helped)

We put the name of the album as a genre, and the compiler gladly accepted it. But we know that there is a finite number of possible genres to choose from. If we are making a music-based software, we can safely narrow down the genres we support. `String` doesn't help us there at all. It can hold many more values than there are music genres.

Using primitive types makes our jobs harder!

But there's more! We also have similar problems with our behavior (the searchArtists pure function)! When you look closer, you can see that it also uses primitive types as parameters. Similar problems arise.

Primitive type-based model Our current error-prone version of function parameters:

```
def searchArtists(artists: List[Artist], genres: List[String],
                  locations: List[String], searchByActiveYears: Boolean,
                  activeAfter: Int, activeBefore: Int): List[Artist]
```

Problem 4

Programmers need to come up with, understand, and convey additional meanings to primitive types.

What does genres: List[String] mean in the searchArtists signature? If it's empty, it means we shouldn't search using the genre criteria. If it's not empty, it means that this is a required criterium: returned artists should have at least one of the genres on the list. See how much explanation is needed? It's an explanation that is not conveyed by just writing genres: List[String] because it's just a list of Strings that happens to be named genres.

Problem 5

Programmers need to remember that some parameters only make sense when used together.

The activeAfter and activeBefore parameters can only be used together. They both implement the requirement of "filtering artists that were active in the given period." Additionally, they are only applicable when searchByActiveYears is true. So as you can see, there is a lot of semantic bundling of different parameters, which, again, is not directly explainable by looking at the function signatures and product type definitions.

We've just seen how using primitive types in models and functions caused a lot of silly mistakes. We were able to represent combinations that are not valid regarding the business domain, but they were OK for the compiler. So, on top of real valid combinations that represent the logic our users want, we need to additionally understand and take care of **all the invalid combinations that are representable only because we modeled our data using primitives**. More work for us! We can, and will, do better. We will address all five problems by reusing some techniques we already know and learning two very important new ones. Additionally, we will build on things we learned in the previous chapters where we used the compiler to find and report many of these mistakes. The remaining parts of this chapter tackle all five problems, one problem at a time.

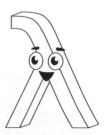

Newtypes protect against misplaced parameters

Let's start with the simplest new technique, which is used widely in functional programming. Let's tackle the first problem.

Current model Our current version that works but is error-prone:

```
case class Artist(name: String, genre: String, origin: String,
                  yearsActiveStart: Int, isActive: Boolean, yearsActiveEnd: Int)
```

Problem 1

Programmers need to be careful about the order of parameters.
The `String` parameters (e.g., `genre` and `origin`) can be misplaced.

Let's look at the above definition again. We see three `String` parameters, which means all of them can be misplaced, and the compiler won't complain. So all of the following invalid combinations are possible (i.e., compilable):

```
> Artist("Metallica", "U.S.", "Heavy Metal", 1981, true, 0)
  Artist("U.S.", "Metallica", "Heavy Metal", 1981, true, 0)
  Artist("U.S.", "Heavy Metal", "Metallica", 1981, true, 0)
```

If you want to define the Location type in the REPL, make sure to put it inside an object definition.

```
object model {
  ...
}
```

then use

```
import model._
```

Introducing newtypes

There is a very straightforward technique that can protect us from these kinds of mistakes, making our lives a lot easier in the process. It's called **newtype**, also known as a *zero-cost wrapper*. Instead of using primitive types like `String`, we *wrap it* in a named type.

We use Scala's `opaque` type to state that `Location` internally is just a `String`. The compiler will treat it as a different type outside of the scope `Location` was defined in.

```
opaque type Location = String

object Location {
  def apply(value: String): Location = value
  extension(a: Location) def name: String = a
}
```

We use apply to allow creating a `Location` out of any `String`. `apply` is a special function that is called when someone calls `Location(...)`.

We add the `name` function to any `Location` value by using the `extension` keyword. It returns the underlying `String` value. Note that we can treat a `String` `a` as a `Location` only in this scope.

Now we can use `Location` as a separate type (`String` will not do!):

```
val us: Location = Location("U.S.")
val wontCompile: Location = "U.S."
→ compilation error!
```

You could achieve exactly the same result by creating a case class Location(name: String). However, newtypes are zero-cost wrappers, which means they are just Strings in the runtime.

The compiler understands a `String` is not a `Location`. Let's use it!

Using newtypes in data models

We can now use the Location newtype we have just created to update our
Artist model.

Updated model   We are now using the Location newtype.

```
case class Artist(name: String, genre: String, origin: Location,
                  yearsActiveStart: Int, isActive: Boolean, yearsActiveEnd: Int)
```

That means that now the compiler has our back when we mistakenly try
to misplace the parameters.

```
> Artist("Metallica", Location("U.S."), "Heavy Metal", 1981, true, 0)
  → compilation error!
  Artist(Location("U.S."), "Metallica", "Heavy Metal", 1981, true, 0)
  → compilation error!
  Artist(Location("U.S."), "Heavy Metal", "Metallica", 1981, true, 0)
  → compilation error!
```

Pure win! There is only one place that Location fits in, but in the runtime
it will still behave like a bare String! We can't get it wrong. This is a very
small and subtle change, but it provides us with an **additional layer of
safety without any performance costs**.

The newtype pattern is
ubiquitous in functional
programming. You can
encode it in many
languages, including
Haskell, Rust, and
Kotlin. In some of them,
however, it involves a bit
of boilerplate code.

In terms of usage, there is not much difference. Instead of
artist.origin, which was a bare String, we now need to use
artist.origin.name inside the Boolean expression in searchArtists.

```
def searchArtists(artists: List[Artist], genres: List[String],
                  locations: List[String], searchByActiveYears: Boolean,
                  activeAfter: Int, activeBefore: Int
): List[Artist] =
  artists.filter(artist =>
    (genres.isEmpty || genres.contains(artist.genre)) &&
    (locations.isEmpty || locations.contains(artist.origin.name)) &&
    (!searchByActiveYears || (
      (artist.isActive || artist.yearsActiveEnd >= activeAfter) &&
      (artist.yearsActiveStart <= activeBefore)))
  )
```

Note that we focus
on data modeling
in this part of the
chapter. That's why
the searchArtists
signature will still use
primitive types. We will
fix it when we get to
behavior modeling.

The only change
needed after
introducing the
Location newtype
is here. We need
to extract the
raw String for
comparison.

Problem 1   Solved by the newtype.

Programmers need to be careful about the order of parameters.
The String parameters (e.g., genre and origin) can be misplaced.

Practicing newtypes

It's time to use newtypes in the rest of our Artist definition.

Exercise   *Replace primitive types with more newtypes.*

```
case class Artist(name: String, genre: String, origin: Location,
                  yearsActiveStart: Int, isActive: Boolean, yearsActiveEnd: Int)
```

Let's leave the name as a String for now. There shouldn't be any more Strings (besides the name) in the definition after you finish this exercise. Note also that there are also two Ints, which we can misplace. Please use newtypes there as well. **Your task is to introduce three newtypes and use them in Artist and searchArtists.** These are: Genre (String), YearsActiveStart (Int), and YearsActiveEnd (Int).

Answers

We will bundle all types from our model inside the model module.

We create three newtypes that "wrap" primitive values in the compile time (remember that in runtime they are still behaving like primitive values). We start with Genre, which internally is just a String, but the compiler won't allow us to use Strings as Genres.

```
> object model {
    opaque type Genre = String
    object Genre {
      def apply(value: String): Genre = value
      extension(a: Genre) def name: String = a
    }

    opaque type YearsActiveStart = Int
    object YearsActiveStart {
      def apply(value: Int): YearsActiveStart = value
      extension(a: YearsActiveStart) def value: Int = a
    }

    opaque type YearsActiveEnd = Int
    object YearsActiveEnd {
      def apply(value: Int): YearsActiveEnd = value
      extension(a: YearsActiveEnd) def value: Int = a
    }

    case class Artist(name: String, genre: Genre, origin: Location,
                      yearsActiveStart: YearsActiveStart,
                      isActive: Boolean, yearsActiveEnd: YearsActiveEnd)
}
import model._

artists.filter(artist =>
  (genres.isEmpty || genres.contains(artist.genre.name)) &&
  (locations.isEmpty || locations.contains(artist.origin.name)) &&
  (!searchByActiveYears || (
    (artist.isActive || artist.yearsActiveEnd.value >= activeAfter) &&
    (artist.yearsActiveStart.value <= activeBefore)))
  )
```

We "add" two functions to all our newtypes. The apply function allows us to create a newtype value (like YearsActiveStart) from a primitive value (Int).

The value extension function allows us to extract primitive values from the newtype wrapper values (see below).

Functions that want to use our data model will need to import everything from the model module.

We need to change the implementation of the searchArtists function and "unwrap" newtype-based values at the call site inside (using extension functions we defined on each of them).

There is nothing magical about the newtype. It's a tool that allows the compiler to help us. It also improves the readability!

Making sure only valid data combinations are possible

There is an even better technique we can use to model genre and active years, so let's revert your changes and leave only the Location newtype. The second technique is a little bit more complex than newtypes but as ubiquitous. Let's look at the definition again.

Current model   Our current model uses the Location newtype.

```
case class Artist(name: String, genre: String, origin: Location,
                  yearsActiveStart: Int, isActive: Boolean, yearsActiveEnd: Int)
```

Note that so far we only introduced a Location newtype. A genre and active years can also be modeled as newtypes (which you've shown in the previous exercise), but we are going to use a more fitting technique now.

We see three parameters that are used to describe the active years requirement: yearsActiveStart, isActive, and yearsActiveEnd. Note how isActive and yearsActiveEnd are interconnected. Whenever you see more than one parameter describing a single logical business entity inside your data class, you can be sure that it will cause headaches.

```
Artist("Metallica", "Heavy Metal", Location("U.S."),
       1981, true, 2022)
```

2022 doesn't matter here because isActive = true. It can be misleading!

```
Artist("Led Zeppelin", "Hard Rock", Location("England"),
       1968, true, 1980)
```

1980 is the real year that Led Zeppelin stopped being active, but again, it doesn't matter because isActive = true. The programmer may not see it right away!

Modeling complex entities

Our problem is that we have three parameters that, together, make up a single business entity. We want to model a period of time, which may be open-ended; it always has a start, but it might not have an end. We will show you the best functional way to approach such a problem in a bit, but let's first start with modeling the end part. Do we already know any type that can be used to represent something that may or may not be there?

Using Option to describe our data

We've used the Option type as a return type of our pure functions (behaviors). But this simple type is so versatile that it can do even more! It models a potentially missing value, so it fits well in the active years requirement. See? We learned one thing a few chapters earlier, and now we can use it in more scenarios—and the fact is that functional programmers really use the Option type all the time. That's why we introduced it so early in the book.

Modeling possibility of absence in your data

Any time you see more than one value representing a single logical business entity, make sure to stop and think how to model it better. As an example, we now have two parameters that together make up a single entity. This is a **very common pattern in programming in general: a Boolean flag plus a parameter that is only applicable if the Boolean flag is true**. I am sure you recognize this pattern. We will show you two ways of approaching this pattern using functional programming techniques: the Option type and *algebraic data types*. First up is the Option type.

Current model　A version that uses primitive types to represent active years.

```
case class Artist(name: String, genre: String, origin: Location,
            yearsActiveStart: Int, isActive: Boolean, yearsActiveEnd: Int)
```

These two parameters represent a single logical entity: the time an artist stopped being active. They are interconnected logically, but our code doesn't ensure this because each of these two parameters can be set to any value, independently.

Updated model　A version that uses the Option type instead.

```
case class Artist(name: String, genre: String, origin: Location,
            yearsActiveStart: Int, yearsActiveEnd: Option[Int])
```

We replaced two parameters that always needed to be written and interpreted together with a single parameter that models the potential absence of a value (in this case the value is an end year in a period of time).

Let's see our problematic example to make sure it really helped our case.

```
Artist("Metallica", "Heavy Metal", Location("U.S."),
      1981, None)
```
↖　None means there is no end year because the artist is still active. We can't put any year as an end year!

```
Artist("Led Zeppelin", "Hard Rock", Location("England"),
      1968, Some(1980))
```
↖　1980 is the real year Led Zeppelin stopped being active, so to define it we need to pass Some, which means the artist has an end year and, therefore, is not active anymore.

Now, it's not possible to make any mistake because we have only one parameter that models the whole logical entity of the *end year*. The Option type models a value that may not be there. It's exactly what we needed here. The end year may not be there only if the artist is still active!

Changes in the model force changes in the logic

We changed our `Artist` data model substantially (there is one parameter less!), so it should be obvious that we need to change the behavior—the logic implemented as a function—that uses this data model. Let's see how the new definition of the `Artist` model is going to be used by the `searchArtists` function, which implements the main requirement.

```
def searchArtists(artists: List[Artist], genres: List[String],
                  locations: List[String], searchByActiveYears: Boolean,
                  activeAfter: Int, activeBefore: Int
): List[Artist] =
  artists.filter(artist =>
    (genres.isEmpty || genres.contains(artist.genre)) &&
    (locations.isEmpty || locations.contains(artist.origin.name)) &&
    (!searchByActiveYears || (
      (artist.isActive || artist.yearsActiveEnd >= activeAfter) &&
      (artist.yearsActiveStart <= activeBefore)))
  )
```

Oh no! I can't compile it because artist doesn't have the isActive field! Also, how can I compare Option to Int?

We got a compilation error! As we can see, using an `Option` is not that straightforward as using primitive types. We know how to compare `Strings` and `Ints` with each other and how `Booleans` can be used as conditions. As we've shown in the `searchArtists` case, once we get the conditions right it's very rewarding. But we've also shown that modeling data using only primitive types is not the best way to create maintainable software. That's why we've introduced—and plan to introduce even more—techniques that make our models more robust. The cost of these refactorings is that we also need to make amendments in our logic. They are not straightforward, but—surprise, surprise they make the logic more robust as well! Let's see!

In our case, we now have an `Option` value inside our model. This value represents an end year of an artist's active period. It may or may not be there, depending on whether a given artist stopped performing. That makes sense, but now how do we check whether an artist was active in the specified `activeAfter` and `activeBefore` period?

```
case class Artist(name: String, genre: String, origin: Location,
                  yearsActiveStart: Int, yearsActiveEnd: Option[Int])
```

We need to compare these two values inside an artist with the specified `activeAfter` and `activeBefore` parameters that are part of the search logic. Note that we can't just compare an `Int` with an `Option[Int]` because these are different types!

Using data modeled as Options **in your logic**

Again, the problem we face now is that we need to somehow implement the logic of checking whether an artist was active between given activeAfter and activeBefore years. Specifically, how can we check that artist.yearsActiveEnd >= activeAfter, knowing that artist.yearsActiveEnd is an Option[Int]?

> You may be tempted to use the yearsActiveEnd == Some(year) condition or the yearsActiveEnd == None condition, and while it's possible, it's not a preferred approach in FP.

```
artist.yearsActiveEnd: Option[Int]
activeAfter: Int
```

How can we compare these two values? So far, we've had an Int-Int comparison, which was triggered only when isActive wasn't true:

```
(artist.isActive || artist.yearsActiveEnd >= activeAfter)
```

Now we got rid of isActive and modeled yearsActiveEnd as an Option. What should we do? It turns out that **Option has even more *hidden* goodies than we dared to imagine**. And by goodies I obviously mean higher-order functions: functions that take functions as arguments (or return functions)! We will meet more of them soon! First, let's recap what we know.

> **THIS IS BIG!**
> In FP, each type has many higher-order functions.

Higher-order functions for Option

```
> val year: Option[Int] = Some(996)
  val noYear: Option[Int] = None
```

map
year.map(_ * 2) → Some(1992) noYear.map(_ * 2) → None

flatMap
year.flatMap(y => Some(y * 2)) → Some(1992) noYear.flatMap(y => Some(y * 2)) → None year.flatMap(y => None) → None noYear.flatMap(y => None) → None

filter
year.filter(_ < 2020) → Some(996) noYear.filter(_ < 2020) → None year.filter(_ > 2020) → None noYear.filter(_ > 2020) → None

And some new ones: **forall** **exists** !

The first one is called forall. We can write our condition for the active years requirement as follows:

```
artist.yearsActiveEnd.forall(_ >= activeAfter)
```

> Remember that _ >= activeAfter is a shorthand for:
> ```
> activeEnd =>
>   activeEnd >= activeAfter
> ```
> It's a function that takes one parameter and returns a Boolean.

forall returns true if the element inside the given Option (if the Option is Some) satisfies the condition passed as an anonymous function or if there is no element inside the Option (i.e., it is None).

Higher-order functions for the win!

forall is a higher-order function defined on Option. It takes one function as a parameter, just like map, flatMap, and filter.

> Option[A].forall(f: A => Boolean): Boolean
>
> **Applies the function passed as f to the element held by this Option. Returns true if this Option is empty (None) or the given function f returns true when applied to this Option's value.**

Intuitively, we say, "If this represents a value, check if it satisfies the given condition, and if there is no value, ignore the condition."

```
def searchArtists(artists: List[Artist], genres: List[String],
                  locations: List[String], searchByActiveYears: Boolean,
                  activeAfter: Int, activeBefore: Int
): List[Artist] =
  artists.filter(artist =>
    (genres.isEmpty || genres.contains(artist.genre)) &&
    (locations.isEmpty || locations.contains(artist.origin.name)) &&
    (!searchByActiveYears || (
      (artist.yearsActiveEnd.forall(_ >= activeAfter)) &&
      (artist.yearsActiveStart <= activeBefore)))

  )
```

We removed one parameter from the model and removed one additional condition inside our logic. Now, our model is more robust, and our logic is a little bit simpler to comprehend.

Learning about many higher-order functions is a functional programmer's bread and butter. In this book we just scratch the surface of what's at your disposal. What I want you to take away, however, is how useful they are and how you can apply them for many different requirements. Remember: The signature, documentation, and examples are your allies! Let's see some usage example of forall, compared with filter and a totally new one: exists. **Can you learn about exists just by looking at its signature and examples?**

```
> val year: Option[Int] = Some(996)
  val noYear: Option[Int] = None
```

forall	**exists**	**filter**
year.forall(_ < 2020) → true	year.exists(_ < 2020) → true	year.filter(_ < 2020) → Some(996)
noYear.forall(_ < 2020) → true	noYear.exists(_ < 2020) → false	noYear.filter(_ < 2020) → None
year.forall(_ > 2020) → false	year.exists(_ > 2020) → false	year.filter(_ > 2020) → None
noYear.forall(_ > 2020) → true	noYear.exists(_ > 2020) → false	noYear.filter(_ > 2020) → None

There is probably a higher-order function for that!

The lesson from all of this is that whenever you work with an immutable FP type like Option, List, or Either and you have a problem implementing logic around it, you should remember that there probably is a higher-order function for your use case. (And if there's not, what keeps you from implementing it? You will probably need it again!)

THIS IS BIG!
There is a higher-order function available for all the common use cases!

We have just met forall and, hopefully, exists. It turns out that these functions are not only available for Options but can also be found in Either, List, and many more types! Again, the power of FP is that you learn one thing for one type, and you can almost immediately apply it in many different scenarios. forall is just one example, but if you are curious about more examples, look no further. Remember contains, which we used on Strings and Lists? Do you think it's available in Option as well? If it was, what do you think its behavior would be?

Yes, Option does have the contains function defined. You will soon find out how to use it. Note that contains is not really a higher-order function because it doesn't take a function nor return a function. However, it is an example of a function defined on more than one immutable type, which is also known universally by all developers. This example is intended as an intuition for you if you still struggle with the idea of usefulness of higher-order functions.

Q If there is a higher-order function for all common cases, doesn't it mean that there are lots of them?

A There are definitely plenty of them, yes. However, note that usually they can be used in many situations, and when you learn about a new higher-order function using one type, you already know how it works on lots of other types. For example, you know how forall works for Option. That means you already know how forall works on Either, List, and even the types you haven't learned about yet! The same thing applies to exists, map, flatMap, flatten, filter, foldLeft, orElse, and others. You learn once and use it everywhere. As a bonus, this knowledge doesn't expire, and it carries over to other functional languages! How cool is that?

Coffee break: forall/exists/contains

It's time to take a small break from the `Artist` data model and practice your intuition when it comes to implementing behaviors using three functions—`forall`, `exists`, and `contains`—on two types: `Option` and `List`. I know that we've only talked about `Option.forall` and `List.contains`. That means that you will need to, as a part of this exercise, figure out `List.forall`, `Option.exists`, `List.exists`, and `Option.contains` on your own!

User search functionality

Assume there is an unchangeable data model already at your disposal:

```
> case class User(name: String, city: Option[String],
                  favoriteArtists: List[String])
```

The user of our system has a name, potentially a city, and has a list of favorite artists (provided as `Strings` to make this exercise more self-contained—I hope you will let it slide and not turn your nose up at the fact that we still use primitive types instead of newtypes here).

Here's a list of users we will use in this exercise:

```
> val users = List(
    User("Alice", Some("Melbourne"), List("Bee Gees")),
    User("Bob", Some("Lagos"), List("Bee Gees")),
    User("Eve", Some("Tokyo"), List.empty),
    User("Mallory", None, List("Metallica", "Bee Gees")),
    User("Trent", Some("Buenos Aires"), List("Led Zeppelin"))
  )
```

Your task is to implement six functions that take a list of users and return a list of users that satisfy a given condition. Each function implements one condition to make things a little bit easier:

— f1: users that haven't specified their city or live in Melbourne
— f2: users that live in Lagos
— f3: users that like Bee Gees
— f4: users that live in cities that start with the letter T
— f5: users that only like artists that have a name longer than eight characters (or no favorite artists at all)
— f6: users that like some artists whose names start with an M

Make sure to test your solution before looking at the next page!

Hint: All the implementations should be very concise, so if you feel like a condition needs a lot of implementation, take a break, go for a walk, and come back to think again. Remember that we want to show differences between three functions defined on two types.

Coffee break explained: forall/exists/contains

I hope you've had some fun with this one, and you were able to figure at least some of the six functions on your own! Here are the six solutions that are the standard way of implementing such requirements in FP.

— f1: **users that haven't specified their city or live in Melbourne**

```
> def f1(users: List[User]): List[User] =
    users.filter(_.city.forall(_ == "Melbourne"))
f1(users).map(_.name)
→ List("Alice", "Mallory")
```

We are mapping the return lists with a function that leaves only the name so that the output is cleaner.

— f2: **users that live in Lagos**

```
def f2(users: List[User]): List[User] =
    users.filter(_.city.contains("Lagos"))
f2(users).map(_.name)
→ List("Bob")
```

— f3: **users that like Bee Gees**

```
def f3(users: List[User]): List[User] =
    users.filter(_.favoriteArtists.contains("Bee Gees"))
f3(users).map(_.name)
→ List("Alice", "Bob", "Mallory")
```

— f4: **users that live in cities that start with the letter T**

```
def f4(users: List[User]): List[User] =
    users.filter(_.city.exists(_.startsWith("T")))
f4(users).map(_.name)
→ List("Eve")
```

— f5: **users that only like artists that have a name longer than eight characters (or no favorite artists at all)**

```
def f5(users: List[User]): List[User] =
    users.filter(_.favoriteArtists.forall(_.length > 8))
f5(users).map(_.name)
→ List("Eve", "Trent")
```

— f6: **users that like some artists whose names start with an M**

```
def f6(users: List[User]): List[User] =
    users.filter(_.favoriteArtists.exists(_.startsWith("M")))
f6(users).map(_.name)
→ List("Mallory"))
```

1 Option has a forall function that takes a condition. If the Option is None or if the value inside Some satisfies the condition, true is returned.

2 Option has a contains function that takes a value of internal Option's type. In this case it's a String. contains returns true if this Option's String equals the given one.

3 List has a contains function as well! It takes a value of internal List's type (String) and returns true if this list contains the given String.

4 Option has an exists function. It takes a function that is a condition. It returns true if this Option is Some and its value satisfies the given condition.

5 List has a forall function. It takes a function that is a condition. It returns true if this List is empty or when all its values satisfy the given condition.

6 List has the exists function. It takes a function that is a condition. It returns true if this List contains at least one element that satisfies the given condition.

Coupling a concept inside a single product type

Did we solve our problem with Option and its overpowered ally forall?

Problem 2 *Can be solved by the* Option *type but only in some cases*

> **Programmers need to know the additional meaning of parameter combinations.**
> A Boolean flag and an Int parameter (e.g., isActive and activeYearsEnd) are interconnected.

We solved it but not entirely. There is one more detail related to this problem that we haven't addressed so far. Notice how we are talking about *parameter combinations*. Both yearsActiveStart and yearsActiveEnd represent a single concept: the period of time an artist was or still is active. Whenever you come to this kind of conclusion, it's a great indicator that you need to create **yet another product type**.

```
case class PeriodInYears(start: Int, end: Option[Int])
```

See? Now both parameters are coupled together in a single entity that represents a period of time in years. The end is still represented as an Option that conveys that it's possible this value is absent (None), which in turn makes such an instance of Period open-ended. Now, we can use this newly defined Period inside our Artist definition.

Current model *A version that uses yet another product type to define the active years.*
```
case class Artist(name: String, genre: String, origin: Location, yearsActive: PeriodInYears)
```

Isn't it better? The definition is getting more and more robust, while becoming smaller and easier to comprehend. What's not to like about it? Now, let's see how it is going to be used. Look how descriptive this is and how we lowered the risk of making a programmer's mistake:

```
val artists = List(
  Artist("Metallica", "Heavy Metal", Location("U.S."), PeriodInYears(1981, None)),
  Artist("Led Zeppelin", "Hard Rock", Location("England"), PeriodInYears(1968, Some(1980))),
  Artist("Bee Gees", "Pop", Location("England"), PeriodInYears(1958, Some(2003)))
)

def searchArtists(...): List[Artist] =
  ...
  (artist.yearsActive.end.forall(_ >= activeAfter) &&
  (artist.yearsActive.start <= activeBefore)))
```
Only a small change is needed in the searchArtists function. There is an additional access level to both the end and start values. Nothing complicated.

We are going in the right direction! But let's not rest on our laurels!

Problem 2 *Solved by the product type with a primitive type and an* Option.

> **Programmers need to know the additional meaning of parameter combinations.**
> Several parameters (e.g., a Boolean flag and two Ints) represent one business entity.

Modeling finite possibilities

I hope you've been enjoying the techniques we've introduced so far. They are simple but very useful and universally acclaimed by functional programmers. The next technique is the main part of this chapter and the reason many people prefer functional domain design over other approaches. Let's have a look at the next problem.

> **Problem 3**
>
> **Programmers need to ensure that some parameters have a finite set of values.**
> Some entities in the domain have a finite set of possible values (e.g., music genre).

Here are some manifestations of the problem:

```
- Artist("Metallica", "Heavy Meta", Location("U.S."),
      PeriodInYears(1981, None))
- Artist("Led Zeppelin", "", Location("England"),
      PeriodInYears(1968, None))
- Artist("Pop", "Bee Gees", Location("England"),
      PeriodInYears(1958, Some(2003))).
```

"Heavy meta" is not a possible value, but it compiles!

"" is not a possible value, but it compiles!

"Bee Gees" is not a possible value, but it compiles! (Recap: This one could be solved by a newtype definition we did as an exercise.)

All the above are accepted by the compiler without any issues. And who could blame the compiler? It's our fault that we modeled the Artist in a way that these instances are possible. The good news is that we can solve this problem using one of the most powerful tools in functional programming: **a type that can only take a finite set of values**. In FP that's a job for a **sum type**. In Scala, it's encoded as an **enum**:

We will explain the name of the sum type very soon. Let's first use it in practice!

```
> enum MusicGenre {
    case HeavyMetal
    case Pop
    case HardRock
  }
```

We defined four types here: MusicGenre and its three possible values—HeavyMetal, Pop, and HardRock.

We have just defined a sum type called MusicGenre. Before we use it inside our Artist definition, let's use it in a REPL session.

```
> import MusicGenre._
  val genre: MusicGenre = Pop
  → Pop
  val x: MusicGenre = HeavyMeta
  → compilation error!
  val y: MusicGenre = "HeavyMeta"
  → compilation error!
```

Now I can help you!

A sum type allows us to delegate even more work to the compiler.

Using sum types

The sum type makes sure that its value is always legal; it comes from a set defined by us, up front, and unchangeable in the runtime. This is checked and assured by one of our most trusted allies: the compiler. There is no way our application will compile with a wrong value of MusicGenre: we can't use a String (so, again, it can't be misplaced), and we can't misspell the genre. Hence, we get even broader protection than we did with a newtype.

> **Q** Isn't it just a plain enum?
>
> **A** The example we've shown looks and serves a similar purpose as enum. However, enum in Scala is much more powerful than in Java. The sum type is not just a wrapper around a value, it's more than that. Sum types together with product types can model much more complex concepts, which we'll see very soon.

Again, remember that we've used a lot of product types in this book, and a more in-depth explanation of both product types and sum types is just around the corner.

Our Artist definition has become a lot more polished now:

```scala
case class Artist(name: String, genre: MusicGenre,
                  origin: Location, yearsActive: PeriodInYears)
```

Just by looking at the definition, we can see what's going on and what's necessary. Remember that so far we've been just defining data models using types: newtypes, **product types**, and **sum types**. Here's how this new definition can be used to define real values of artists:

```scala
val artists = List(
  Artist("Metallica", HeavyMetal, Location("U.S."), PeriodInYears(1981, None)),
  Artist("Led Zeppelin", HardRock, Location("England"), PeriodInYears(1968, Some(1980))),
  Artist("Bee Gees", Pop, Location("England"), PeriodInYears(1958, Some(2003)))
)
```

Look, no quotes needed! Music genres are not Strings anymore!

Only a small signature change is needed in the searchArtists function. We need to pass a List of MusicGenre values, not Strings. The implementation doesn't need to change.

```scala
def searchArtists(artists: List[Artist], genres: List[MusicGenre], locations: List[String],
                  searchByActiveYears: Boolean, activeAfter: Int, activeBefore: Int): List[Artist]
```

Look's good, right? Plus, notice how it's getting harder and harder to make a mistake. These techniques ensure that our code is both safe and very readable. All these techniques we've learned about, when used together, make up very maintainable code. We are giving the compiler a lot more information now, and it's using it to help us!

Problem 3 ✔ Solved by the sum type

Programmers need to ensure that some parameters have a finite set of values.
Some entities in the domain have a finite set of possible values (e.g., music genre).

Even better modeling with sum types

Our MusicGenre type looks better than String, but you are probably still not convinced. Why are we glorifying this idea so much? Again, it looks like an enum with better type safety but still an enum!

What if I told you that we can use sum types—these *glorified* enums—to improve our Artist model even more? Specifically, we can use them to enhance the active years model. We will improve the readability (and maintainability) of the model by making it even more specific than it is right now. That's the place where we leave the plain old enums analogy far behind. Here's our current model.

Current model A version that uses a sum type, a newtype, and a product type.

```
case class Artist(name: String, genre: MusicGenre, origin: Location, yearsActive: PeriodInYears)
```

What do we want to improve, you may ask? Looking at this type, there are no real issues we could pinpoint, or are there? Let's focus on the PeriodInYears type that represents the active years requirement:

```
case class PeriodInYears(start: Int, end: Option[Int])
```

We wanted to model a period of time, in years, when a given artist was active. There are two options: the artist may still be active, and then the period is open-ended (end = None), or the artist is no longer active, and then we have a fixed period of time (end = Some(endYear)).

Did you notice what we just wrote? There are **two options**. They are exclusive—they can't be used together for the same Artist—and they are the only possible values. That's exactly the same case we had when we modeled finite possibilities. We need to **use a sum type again**!

```
enum YearsActive {
  case StillActive(since: Int)
  case ActiveBetween(start: Int, end: Int)
}
```

See? We defined two possible values for our YearsActive type: StillActive and ActiveBetween. They explain—in business terms—what they mean. Note how we use product types as possible values and compare to what we did in MusicGenre when we used singletons:

```
enum MusicGenre {
  case HeavyMetal
  case Pop
  case HardRock
}
```

ActiveBetween is a product type that bundles two values together. MusicGenre didn't have such cases.

THIS IS BIG!
Sum type + product type combo gives us modeling superpowers.

Using the sum type + product type combo

Notice how we made sure to encode even more business context into the type itself. Now we don't have to guess or possess any insider knowledge to know what this means. Compare this to the old version to really appreciate how such small changes make such a big difference from the readability aspect. (Did I mention that programmers read the code far more often than they write it? Let's give them less guesswork and more love!)

Before Using a product type + `Option`

```
case class PeriodInYears(start: Int, end: Option[Int])

Artist("Metallica", HeavyMetal, Location("U.S."), PeriodInYears(1981, None))
Artist("Led Zeppelin", HardRock, Location("England"), PeriodInYears(1968, Some(1980)))
```

After Using a sum type + product types

```
enum YearsActive {
  case StillActive(since: Int)
  case ActiveBetween(start: Int, end: Int)
}
```

> Naming is always hard. We could also use `ActiveSince` instead of `StillActive`. Additionally, we can always explicitly repeat the name of the parameter for readability.

```
Artist("Metallica", HeavyMetal, Location("U.S."), StillActive(since = 1981))
Artist("Led Zeppelin", HardRock, Location("England"), ActiveBetween(1968, 1980))
```

Here's what our model looks like after modeling genre and yearsActive using sum + product types and origin using a newtype:

```
enum MusicGenre {
  case HeavyMetal
  case Pop
  case HardRock
}
opaque type Location = String
object Location {
  def apply(value: String): Location = value
  extension(a: Location) def name: String = a
}
enum YearsActive {
  case StillActive(since: Int)
  case ActiveBetween(start: Int, end: Int)
}
case class Artist(name: String, genre: MusicGenre,
                  origin: Location, yearsActive: YearsActive)
```

> Note that we can use only very specific values to create artists, and many constraints are ensured by our old friend: the compiler.

> In FP there are some more advanced techniques that are out of the scope of this book, such as type-level programming and dependent types, that allow us to model even more complicated constraints, but the ideas of newtypes, product types, and sum types are still the foundation and main tool in the FP programmer toolbox.

It's a very bulletproof model—it's both readable and maintainable.

Product types + sum types = algebraic data types (ADTs)

You may be surprised to know that you've just learned one of the most influential and useful concepts in the functional domain design: **algebraic data types**. In Scala, case class and enum are used together to implement this concept, which is also available in many other functional languages. What are they and what's algebraic about them? Let's learn by recapping what we've done so far in the data modeling department.

First, earlier in this book we introduced the product type, but in this chapter we started to use it more intently. At its core, it bundles together other types, which, together, can be treated as one type with a name. So any time you have a requirement where two business concepts together make up a bigger business concept, you will want to use the product type, just like we did with PeriodInYears:

```scala
case class PeriodInYears(start: Int, end: Option[Int])
```

Secondly, we learned that we can implement a finite set of possible values using a sum type with singleton objects:

```scala
enum MusicGenre {
  case HeavyMetal
  case Pop
  case HardRock
}
```

Moreover, we learned that there are sum types that have product types as cases with each child having a different set of fields:

```scala
enum YearsActive {
  case StillActive(since: Int)
  case ActiveBetween(start: Int, end: Int)
}
```

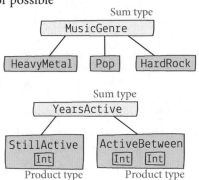

So what's algebraic about them? When you look at MusicGenre or YearsActive, you can see that they model something that may only be one of many things at once: the first thing, the second thing, or the third thing, and so on. All these possible options together form a **sum type**. On the other hand, when you look at a PeriodInYears or other product types we've used, you can see that they model an opposite idea: something that **is** one or more things **at once**: the first thing, the second thing, and the third thing <u>at once</u>. So it's a *product* of smaller things—hence, a **product type** name. We will use algebraic data types (ADTs) a lot!

In set theory, which is related to programming and type theory, types can be treated as sets of values. Many names in FP come from the math background.

Using ADT-based models in behaviors (functions)

Now, we know two out of five of our modeling problems were solved using an ADT. The last new thing we are going to learn in this chapter is how to use ADT values in our pure functions. Let's go back to our running example. We want to search for artists, but the Artist model changed, and yearsActive is now an ADT, so we can't directly compare it to activeAfter and activeBefore like we did with primitive values. We also can't use Option.forall anymore because we got rid of the Option and modeled the potential absence of a value in a better business-related context.

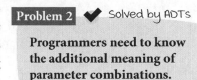

Problem 2 ✔ Solved by ADTs

Programmers need to know the additional meaning of parameter combinations.

Problem 3 ✔ Solved by ADTs

Programmers need to ensure that some parameters have a finite set of values.

```scala
> def searchArtists(artists: List[Artist], genres: List[MusicGenre],
                    locations: List[Location], searchByActiveYears: Boolean,
                    activeAfter: Int, activeBefore: Int
  ): List[Artist] =
    artists.filter(artist =>
      (genres.isEmpty || genres.contains(artist.genre)) &&
      (locations.isEmpty || locations.contains(artist.origin)) &&
      (!searchByActiveYears || ???)
    )
```

↖ How can we check whether artist.yearsActive was between activeAfter and activeBefore?

Remember how we approached such problems before? Whenever you have more complicated logic that misses some part of a functionality, you can just extract a function that has a well-defined signature and a descriptive name. Then, you can focus on implementing the smaller function. This clears your head from the unnecessary burden and helps you get the job done quicker. What we need here is a function that returns true if an artist was active in a given period of time.

```scala
> def wasArtistActive(
    artist: Artist, yearStart: Int, yearEnd: Int
  ): Boolean =

    ???
```

← Remember that ??? is part of the Scala language. It compiles but throws an exception in the runtime. It helps with designing functions and leaving some implementation for later. In our case, the missing part is something new we want to introduce.

Before we show you the new technique that deals with ADTs, we can call this new function from searchArtists and leave it for now:

```scala
(!searchByActiveYears ||
    wasArtistActive(artist, activeAfter, activeBefore))
```

It's about time we learn how to *destructure* ADTs.

Destructuring ADTs using pattern matching

In the pure `wasArtistActive` function we need to make a decision based on an artist that has `yearsActive`. `YearsActive` is an ADT with two cases: `StillActive` and `ActiveBetween`. Depending on whether `artist.yearsActive` is `StillActive` or `ActiveBetween`, we have different values to work with (the former has just one `Int` named `since`, and the latter has two `Int`s named `start` and `end`). It all proves that we need (and want) to have a slightly different logic for each case.

```
enum YearsActive {
  case StillActive(since: Int)
  case ActiveBetween(start: Int, end: Int)
}
```

```
          YearsActive

StillActive          ActiveBetween
  since                start  end
```

And this is exactly what we are going to do. **Enter pattern matching!**

1 We start with the `match` keyword; we match on `artist.yearsActive`, which is a value of `YearsActive`:

```
def wasArtistActive(artist: Artist, yearStart: Int, yearEnd: Int): Boolean =
  artist.yearsActive match
    ???
```

2 The compiler requires us to handle all cases. `YearsActive` has two cases (because it's a sum type with two cases):

```
def wasArtistActive(artist: Artist, yearStart: Int, yearEnd: Int): Boolean =
  artist.yearsActive match {
    case StillActive(since)         => since <= yearEnd
    case ActiveBetween(start, end)  => start <= yearEnd && end >= yearStart
  }
```

If it's `StillActive`, destructure it into an `Int` named `since`. Then return `since <= yearEnd`.

If `yearsActive` is `ActiveBetween`, destructure it into two `Int`s: `start` and `end`. Then, return the value calculated by the expression to the right of `=>`.

The pattern matching expression destructures a concrete value of a sum type into one of its product type cases, extracts internal values, and calculates the result using the expression provided to the right of the `=>` operator. This becomes the result of the whole pattern matching expression.

We know, and the compiler knows too, that `YearsActive` has two possible values. So any time we want to destructure a `YearsActive` value, the compiler makes sure we destructure fully (i.e., we don't miss any case). That's a huge help. Any time we add a new case to our sum type (new `case` to an `enum`), the compiler will pinpoint each place that doesn't handle this new case. We will see it in action very soon when we'll add a new requirement to our artist search engine. Stay tuned.

I've got your back!

Duplication and DRY

Q What about the duplication in this pattern match:

```
artist.yearsActive match {
    case StillActive(since) =>
      since <= yearEnd
    case ActiveBetween(start, end) =>
      start <= yearEnd && end >= yearStart
  }
```

Shouldn't we try to create an abstraction to remove the duplication of since/start <= yearEnd?

A In this book we embrace code maintainability and readability. That means that we accept duplication if it helps to understand the underlying decision process better. When we destructured the YearsActive value, we showed the reader that there are two cases, and they slightly differ. We are directly showing that if an artist is still active, we just care about the end of the search period. There is nothing to mentally decode here.

Compare our current solution with the first version we wrote:

```
def searchArtists(artists: List[Artist], genres: List[String],
                  locations: List[String], searchByActiveYears: Boolean,
                  activeAfter: Int, activeBefore: Int
): List[Artist] =
  artists.filter(artist =>
    (genres.isEmpty || genres.contains(artist.genre)) &&
    (locations.isEmpty || locations.contains(artist.origin)) &&
    (!searchByActiveYears || (
      (artist.isActive || artist.yearsActiveEnd >= activeAfter) &&
      (artist.yearsActiveStart <= activeBefore)))
  )
```

How easy would it be to implement a new requirement that allows us to search by the length of activity period? Or if the artist could have more than one active period?

Sure enough, it doesn't have any duplication. How easy was it to read it? Do you remember how hard it was to write it and get it right? When we model data using ADTs and use pattern matching in our functions, we are dividing our workload into small steps and can focus on each of them separately. Later on, the reader can follow our thought process. This makes the code a lot more readable. I am not arguing for duplication here; I am arguing for code maintainability. **Sometimes we don't need to worry about the DRY principle,** especially when the two duplicated code snippets are independent at their core, and only share a similar structure, usually by accident. It's better to leave them be, duplicated, each evolving in its own direction.

We mentioned DRY (don't repeat yourself) in the first part of the book. As a recap, it is a well-known principle in software development, which aims at reducing the duplication of code by creating abstractions that enhance code sharing between two or more entities. As with other software principles, we should not treat it dogmatically.

Practicing pattern matching

Pattern matching, just like ADTs, is universally used in functional programming. That's why it's important to train your muscle memory. **Your task is to implement a function that gets an artist and the current year and returns the number of years this artist was active.**

Current model A version that uses a newtype and two ADTs

```
case class Artist(name: String, genre: MusicGenre, origin: Location, yearsActive: YearsActive)

enum YearsActive {
  case StillActive(since: Int)
  case ActiveBetween(start: Int, end: Int)
}
```

Remember that YearsActive has two options. That means that your pattern matching expression needs to consider both of them.

Before peeking, make sure your function passes the following tests:

```
def activeLength(artist: Artist, currentYear: Int): Int = ??? // TODO

activeLength(
  Artist("Metallica", HeavyMetal, Location("U.S."), StillActive(1981)),
  2022
)
→ 41
```

metallica have been active for 41 years, as of 2022!

```
activeLength(
  Artist("Led Zeppelin", HardRock, Location("England"),
       ActiveBetween(1968, 1980)),
  2022
)
→ 12
```

Led Zeppelin were active for 12 years.

```
activeLength(
  Artist("Bee Gees", Pop, Location("England"),
       ActiveBetween(1958, 2003)),
  2022)
→ 45
```

Bee Gees were active for 45 years!

Bonus questions: Why do we need to pass the current year? Why can't we just get the current year inside the function?

Answers

The answer to the coding question can be found on the right. The bonus questions have deeper answers. The short answer is that if we don't pass a

```
def activeLength(artist: Artist, currentYear: Int): Int =
  artist.yearsActive match {
    case StillActive(since) => currentYear - since
    case ActiveBetween(start, end) => end - start
  }
```

year as an argument, the function is no longer pure! Getting the current year is a side-effectful action, which we'll address in chapter 8.

Newtypes, ADTs, and pattern matching in the wild

Q This book is about functional programming, but it feels like newtypes, ADTs, and pattern matching are very Scala-specific. Are they?

A They are not Scala-specific! As we mentioned in the first chapter, Scala is used here only as a teaching tool. Newtypes, ADTs, and pattern matching are all available in other languages, so it's beneficial that you understand these concepts and practice them. Plus, as a side effect, you're learning some Scala!

moreover, these tools are being added to traditionally imperative languages. Pattern matching, for example, has been added to both Java and Python.

To prove this point, let's go through some examples of newtypes, ADTs, and pattern matching in other languages: **F#** and **Haskell**.

F# (You don't have to understand this code, it's just to show you these tools are reusable in many functional languages.)

MusicGenre is a sum type.

```fsharp
type MusicGenre = HeavyMetal | Pop | HardRock
type YearsActive = StillActive of int | ActiveBetween of int * int
type Location = struct
    val value:string
    new(value) = { value = value }
end

type Artist = {Name:string; Genre:MusicGenre;
               Origin:Location; Active: YearsActive}

let metallica = {Name="Metallica"; Genre=HeavyMetal;
                 Origin=Location "U.S."; Active=StillActive 1981}


let totalActive = match metallica.Active with
| StillActive since -> 2022 - since
| ActiveBetween (activeStart, activeEnd) -> activeEnd - activeStart
```

We can use a struct with one field (with some performance cost) instead of newtype.

YearsActive is a sum type that consists of two product types.

Artist is a product type.

This is an example of how we can create a value of an Artist in F#.

Since YearsActive is a sum type, we can destructure it using a pattern matching expression.

Haskell

```haskell
data MusicGenre = HeavyMetal | Pop | HardRock
data YearsActive = StillActive Int | ActiveBetween Int Int
newtype Location = Location { value :: String }
data Artist = Artist { name :: String, genre :: MusicGenre,
                       origin :: Location, yearsActive :: YearsActive }

let metallica = Artist "Metallica" HeavyMetal
                (Location "U.S.") (StillActive 1981)
let totalActive = case yearsActive metallica of
                    StillActive since -> 2022 - since
                    ActiveBetween start end -> end - start
```

A very similar code can be written in Haskell. As you can see, these concepts really are universal! Once you learn them in Scala, you will be able to apply this knowledge quickly in other languages. Learning the syntax will be the only obstacle.

What about inheritance?

Q Isn't the ADT concept just glorified inheritance? We can define two or three subtypes of an interface or an abstract class and achieve a similar result, right? Or is there more to it?

A The similarity between ADTs and the inheritance concept from OOP may be striking, but it quickly becomes clear that they are very different. There are two major and defining differences between these concepts:

1. ADTs don't contain behaviors, while in OOP data (mutable fields) and behaviors (methods that mutate those fields) are bundled together in an object. In FP, data and behaviors are separate entities. Data is modeled using immutable values (like ADTs or raw values), and behaviors are independent pure functions.

2. When we define a sum type, we must provide all possible values of this type, and the compiler always checks whether we handle all cases in functions that destructure this sum type.

And remember that we have pattern matching at our disposal that allows us to easily destructure ADTs, which is not possible to do with imperative objects.

In FP there is a very powerful distinction between behaviors and data. Behaviors are functions; data are immutable values. Functions use values, which may be functions, but never ever does a value contain a set of functions that mutates it like we do in OOP. In FP, we first model the data to convey the business requirements and constraints in a readable and maintainable way, enforced as much as possible by the compiler. We do it by defining our ADTs and other immutable types. **This is the data part**. Then, we move to the **behavior part** and create pure functions that use these immutable, possibly ADT-based values. These pure functions implement choices and logic. That's the process we undertook in the Artist example.

Now, it's time to move on to the behavior part of this chapter. You've learned everything you need to create safe, readable, and maintainable data models in your applications. Newtypes and ADTs will get you very far, I promise. But to be good at design, you need to design things and a lot of them. **Practice is the key here.** So before we move on to modeling behaviors (pure functions), let's do a design exercise!

THIS IS BIG!
In FP, behaviors are separated from the data model.

The remaining part of this chapter contains two design exercises that should give you a lot of perspective on these somewhat simple, yet powerful, tools and techniques. Please approach them diligently.

Coffee break: Functional data design

It's about time you design something of your own from scratch, using the ideas we've discovered in this chapter: newtypes and ADTs. This chapter is very musical at its core. Remember that, just like a melody defines a catchy song, we need a great design to have a catchy data model. Since we've just modeled a music artist, now **your task is to model a playlist**.

1

Requirements

1. Playlist has a name, a kind, and a list of songs.
2. There are three kinds of playlists: curated by a user, based on a particular artist, and based on a specific set of genres.
3. A song has an artist and a name.
4. A user has a name.
5. An artist has a name.
6. There are only three music genres: use your three favorite genres.

Your answer should be a `Playlist` type that models the above requirements in a readable way. The majority of work in this exercise is weighing different choices and naming things. I encourage you to prototype it yourself and experiment with the model by trying to create different values, business-wise. Looking at type definitions gives a lot of perspective. Remember that newtypes, ADTs, and the compiler are your friends. Keep a wary eye on the problems we want to avoid.

Here are few examples of playlists to test:

— A playlist named "This is Foo Fighters," which is a playlist based on a particular artist (Foo Fighters) with two songs: "Breakout" and "Learn To Fly."

— A playlist named "Deep Focus," which is a playlist based on two genres (funk and house) and has three songs: "One More Time" by Daft Punk and "Hey Boy Hey Girl" by The Chemical Brothers.

— A playlist named "<Your Name>'s playlist," which is a user-based playlist.

Your second task is to use the `Playlist` model you'll have created inside a new function called `gatherSongs`, which should have the following signature:

2

Hint: This may be a little bit harder than usual. The return type is a List[Song], so the filter function won't cut it! Still, you've already learned everything to solve this one!

```
def gatherSongs(playlists: List[Playlist], artist: Artist,
                genre: MusicGenre): List[Song]
```

It should return some songs from given `playlists`, namely, songs performed by the `artist` from user-based playlists plus all songs from artist-based playlists plus all songs from `genre`-based playlists.

Coffee break explained: Functional data design

There are multiple ways to model the Playlist. The most important point of this exercise is to create as readable and as bulletproof a design as possible, using ADTs and newtypes. Here's one of the possible solutions:

```
object model {
  opaque type User = String
  object User {
    def apply(name: String): User = name
  }

  opaque type Artist = String
  object Artist {
    def apply(name: String): Artist = name
  }

  case class Song(artist: Artist, title: String)

  enum MusicGenre {
    case House
    case Funk
    case HipHop
  }

  enum PlaylistKind {
    case CuratedByUser(user: User)
    case BasedOnArtist(artist: Artist)
    case BasedOnGenres(genres: Set[MusicGenre])
  }

  case class Playlist(name: String, kind: PlaylistKind, songs: List[Song])
}

import model._, model.MusicGenre._, model.PlaylistKind._

val fooFighters = Artist("Foo Fighters")
val playlist1 = Playlist("This is Foo Fighters",
  BasedOnArtist(fooFighters),
  List(Song(fooFighters, "Breakout"), Song(fooFighters, "Learn To Fly"))
)

val playlist2 = Playlist("Deep Focus",
  BasedOnGenres(Set(House, Funk)),
  List(Song(Artist("Daft Punk"), "One More Time"),
      Song(Artist("The Chemical Brothers"), "Hey Boy Hey Girl"))
)

val playlist3 = Playlist("My Playlist",
  CuratedByUser(User("Michał Płachta")),
  List(Song(fooFighters, "My Hero"),
      Song(Artist("Iron Maiden"), "The Trooper"))
)

def gatherSongs(playlists: List[Playlist], artist: Artist, genre: MusicGenre): List[Song] =
  playlists.foldLeft(List.empty[Song])((songs, playlist) =>
    val matchingSongs = playlist.kind match {
      case CuratedByUser(user)           => playlist.songs.filter(_.artist == artist)
      case BasedOnArtist(playlistArtist) => if (playlistArtist == artist) playlist.songs
                                            else List.empty
      case BasedOnGenres(genres)         => if (genres.contains(genre)) playlist.songs
                                            else List.empty
    }
    songs.appendedAll(matchingSongs)
  )
```

To make sure Strings are not misplaced anywhere, we define newtypes for User and Artist.

Song is a normal product type bundling an Artist and a String.

MusicGenre is a simple sum type with case objects. It makes sure we only support a finite set of genres (three in this case).

PlaylistKind is a full-blown ADT. It's a sum type that contains three product types: one for each requirement.

Playlist is a product type with three parameters, which are all of a different type.

Here we create three playlists for testing purposes.

We need to use foldLeft to gather all filtered songs inside the aggregator, which is a list of Songs.

The new aggregator value is created here.

Modeling behaviors

Let's go back to our original problem: searching through music artists. We solved three problems with our data using a newtype and ADTs.

Problem 1 ✔ Solved by newtypes.
Programmers need to be careful about the order of parameters.

Problem 2 ✔ Solved by ADTs.
Programmers need to know an additional meaning of parameter combinations.

Problem 3 ✔ Solved by ADTs.
Programmers need to ensure that some parameters have a finite set of values.

But we are still not done! When we look back at our requirements, we can see that we haven't focused on a big part of them. Specifically:

> Each search **should support a different combination** of conditions: by genre, by origin, and by period they were active in.

We focused on the Artist data model and moved from using primitive types to a bulletproof functional model. The compiler joined our efforts and now has got our backs. However, we ignored our search logic—the behavior that uses this data model. We just encoded behaviors as parameters of the searchArtists function and switched to using MusicGenre and Location along the way, but nothing more changed. Now, we face problems similar to the ones we've already solved when modeling data.

Primitive type–based behavior Function parameters are still problematic.

```
def searchArtists(artists: List[Artist], genres: List[MusicGenre],
                  locations: List[Location], searchByActiveYears: Boolean,
                  activeAfter: Int, activeBefore: Int): List[Artist]
```

Problem 4

Programmers need to come up with, understand, and convey additional meanings to parameter types.

What does genres: List[MusicGenre] mean in the searchArtists signature? If it's empty, it means we shouldn't search using the genre criteria. If it's not empty, it means this is a required criterium: returned artists should have at least one of the genres on the list. See how much explanation is needed? It's an explanation that is not conveyed by just writing genres: List[MusicGenre] because it's just a list of MusicGenre that is not very descriptive in the context of searching for artists.

Problem 5

Programmers need to remember that some parameters only make sense when used together.

The activeAfter and activeBefore parameters can only be used together. They both implement the requirement to "filter artists that were active in the given period." Additionally, they are only applicable when searchByActiveYears is true. So as you can see, there is a lot of semantic bundling of different parameters, which, again, is not directly explainable by looking at the function signatures and product type definitions.

Modeling behaviors as data

The good news is that we can reuse what we learned about data modeling and apply exactly the same techniques to behavior modeling. The key is to start **treating requirements as data**. Thus, a search condition from requirements can be one of three things: a search by genre, a search by origin, or a search by activity period. We can directly translate the previous sentence from English to Scala by creating a sum type:

```
enum SearchCondition {
  case SearchByGenre(genres: List[MusicGenre])
  case SearchByOrigin(locations: List[Location])
  case SearchByActiveYears(start: Int, end: Int)
}
```

Surprised? But how are we going to use this new SearchCondition type? Is it really better than the previous version? We needed to support different combinations of conditions, meaning that some searches may just use one condition and not others. How can we model this? Well, a list seems like a perfect fit! Have a look:

```
def searchArtists(artists: List[Artist],
                  requiredConditions: List[SearchCondition]): List[Artist] =
  artists.filter(artist => ???)
```

A bit cleaner and more readable, don't you think?

```
searchArtists(artists, List(
  SearchByGenre(List(Pop)),
  SearchByOrigin(List(Location("England"))),
  SearchByActiveYears(1950, 2022))
)
→ List(Artist("Bee Gees", Pop, Location("England"), ActiveBetween(1958, 2003)))
```

If we want to use just some conditions, we need to include only them on the list:

```
searchArtists(artists, List(SearchByActiveYears(1950, 2022)))    One condition
searchArtists(artists, List(SearchByGenre(List(Pop)),
                            SearchByOrigin(List(Location("England")))))    Two conditions
searchArtists(artists, List.empty)    No conditions
```

It's impossible to misplace any parameters, there are no hidden handling cases for empty lists, all parameter combinations are encoded inside product types that are correctly named, and the function has fewer parameters. **Win–win–win!** Notice how we used verbs in type names. This is a common pattern that indicates that we model behaviors as data. From the client side, we can see how much more readable and understandable this new API is. Fewer mistakes are possible, and all the necessary meanings are conveyed. Surely, there must be a catch, right?

> **THIS IS BIG!**
> In FP, some behaviors can be modeled as data.

Implementing functions with ADT-based parameters

There is no catch, really. These tools are really that good. However, it's important to understand that the hardest part of both data and behavior modeling remains the same: it's your job as a programmer to understand business requirements and encode them as newtypes and ADTs. Now, let's see how to refactor searchArtists to this new, safer API.

1 As always, we start with the signature. We see that we get a List[Artist], and we need to return List[Artist]. It's filtering!

```
def searchArtists(artists: List[Artist],
                  requiredConditions: List[SearchCondition]): List[Artist] =
  artists.filter(artist => ???)
```

> We need to return a Boolean true if all conditions in requiredConditions are satisfied by a given artist and false if at least one of them isn't.

2 We can use forall! It will go through each of the conditions, and apply the function we pass as an argument.

```
def searchArtists(artists: List[Artist],
                  requiredConditions: List[SearchCondition]): List[Artist] =
  artists.filter(artist =>
    requiredConditions.forall(condition => ???)
  )
```

> How can we check whether this Artist satisfies a SearchCondition, which is an ADT?

3 If a value is an ADT, we can always use a pattern match to provide an expression for each condition.

```
def searchArtists(artists: List[Artist],
                  requiredConditions: List[SearchCondition]): List[Artist] =
  artists.filter(artist =>
    requiredConditions.forall(condition =>

      condition match {
        case SearchByGenre(genres)         => genres.contains(artist.genre)
        case SearchByOrigin(locations)     => locations.contains(artist.origin)
        case SearchByActiveYears(start, end) => wasArtistActive(artist, start, end)
      }
    )
  )
```

> We need to destructure the condition and provide a behavior for each possibility.

> Remember that the compiler will make sure that we've handled all the possible conditions!

That's it! A safe, readable, and maintainable version of searchArtists created by using ADTs to encode behavior requirements. Now, we have **two parameters instead of seven, no primitive types, no nested if conditions, no Boolean flags—only the code that's really needed.** Additionally, we've used the power of two higher-order functions: filter and forall. To handle the ADT parameter inside the function passed to forall, we used the pattern-matching syntax.

I hope you are not tired of ADTs because we will use even more of them in the following chapters. We will also pay more attention to modeling from now on. That's what the final exercise prepares you for!

Problem 4 ✔

Solved by ADTs.

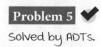

Problem 5 ✔

Solved by ADTs.

Coffee break:
Design and maintainability

We've shown how to design the Artist data model and searchArtists behavior so that they implement given requirements in a safe (i.e., minimizing programmer's mistake risk) and readable way. We argued that designing this way also improves the maintainability of a codebase. And since maintainability of a given piece of software is defined as the ease of making amendments (fixes or new requirements), now it's time to put our money where our mouth is and find out how easy would it be to build some new features into our existing solution.

New requirements

— *Change in the model*—Support the fact that some artists take breaks. For example, the Bee Gees were active from 1958 to 2003 and then from 2009 to 2012.

— *New search condition*—The searchArtists functions should handle the new search condition: return artists that have been (or were) active for a given number of years (in total).

Your task in this final exercise of the chapter is to use all the tools, techniques, and superpowers we've learned to modify the Artist model and searchArtists behavior. They should accommodate the new changes, defined as requirements above. Here are the current signatures of the Artist model and the searchArtists function:

```
case class Artist(name: String, genre: MusicGenre,
                  origin: Location, yearsActive: YearsActive)
def searchArtists(
  artists: List[Artist],
  requiredConditions: List[SearchCondition]
): List[Artist]
```

Do you think these signatures need to change to accommodate the new requirements or not?

Tips and Hints

Make sure to work this problem out yourself before looking at the answer. Modeling is hard, but getting it right is very rewarding. Here are some hints if you've gotten stuck:

1. Write down all the possibilities directly from requirements, and see if they may form a sum type. This will be your starting point.

2. Test your model first by creating instances. Notice how easy it is to create new values and how much the compiler helps.

3. Then, test your model by using it in a function. If it's hard, remodel, refactor, and start over.

As always, running sbt console from the book's code repository is your friend!

Coffee break explained: Design and maintainability

Congratulations! This was the hardest exercise in the book, and I am sure you learned a lot while trying to finish it. As with other design exercises, there are multiple good ways to solve it. Here's one of the possible designs:

```scala
case class PeriodInYears(start: Int, end: Int)

enum YearsActive {
  case StillActive(since: Int, previousPeriods: List[PeriodInYears])
  case ActiveInPast(periods: List[PeriodInYears])
}
```

We can define a closed-ended PeriodInYears (without an Option) instead of using a pair of Ints to make the code even more readable.

Both active and inactive artists can have previous periods of inactivity.

```scala
case class Artist(name: String, genre: MusicGenre,
                  origin: Location, yearsActive: YearsActive)

enum SearchCondition {
  case SearchByGenre(genres: List[MusicGenre])
  case SearchByOrigin(locations: List[Location])
  case SearchByActiveYears(period: PeriodInYears)
  case SearchByActiveLength(howLong: Int, until: Int)
}

import SearchCondition._, YearsActive._
```

SearchedCondition sum type now needs a fourth case.

The new helper function will check if checkedPeriod overlaps with given periods.

```scala
def periodOverlapsWithPeriods(checkedPeriod: PeriodInYears,
                              periods: List[PeriodInYears]): Boolean =
  periods.exists(p =>
    p.start <= checkedPeriod.end && p.end >= checkedPeriod.start
  )

def wasArtistActive(artist: Artist, searchedPeriod: PeriodInYears): Boolean =
  artist.yearsActive match {
    case StillActive(since, previousPeriods) =>
      since <= searchedPeriod.end || periodOverlapsWithPeriods(searchedPeriod, previousPeriods)
    case ActiveInPast(periods) =>
      periodOverlapsWithPeriods(searchedPeriod, periods)
  }

def activeLength(artist: Artist, currentYear: Int): Int = {
  val periods = artist.yearsActive match {
    case StillActive(since, previousPeriods) =>
      previousPeriods.appended(PeriodInYears(since, currentYear))
    case ActiveInPast(periods) =>
      periods
  }
  periods.map(p => p.end - p.start).foldLeft(0)((x, y) => x + y)
}
```

The new version of the YearsActive sum type requires us to reimplement wasArtistActive. We also start using PeriodInYears instead of raw Ints.

> After defining the model and small helper functions, the only change needed inside searchArtists is the new condition pattern match case. Implementing a new requirement wasn't that painful after all!

```scala
def searchArtists(artists: List[Artist],
                  requiredConditions: List[SearchCondition]): List[Artist] =
  artists.filter(artist =>
    requiredConditions.forall(condition =>
      condition match {
        case SearchByGenre(genres)          => genres.contains(artist.genre)
        case SearchByOrigin(locations)      => locations.contains(artist.origin)
        case SearchByActiveYears(period)    => wasArtistActive(artist, period)
        case SearchByActiveLength(howLong, until) => activeLength(artist, until) >= howLong
      }
    )
  )
```

We use the activeLength function in the final condition. It returns a total number of active years for a given artist, even in the presence of multiple activity periods.

Summary

In this chapter we learned about newtypes and **ADTs** (which are **sum types** implemented in Scala as enums and/or **product types** implemented as case classes). We learned about **pattern matching,** which helps us handle ADTs in our pure functions (behaviors). We approached the problem of code duplication and compared ADTs to object-oriented inheritance. We also learned a handful of new higher-order functions that are very versatile. They are defined on Options, Lists, and many more types. But most importantly, we learned how to use all of these techniques as design tools.

ADT stands for algebraic data type.

> **CODE:**
> CH07_*
> Explore this chapter's source code by looking at ch07_* files in the book's repository.

Model our immutable data to minimize errors

We learned that the fewer primitive types we use, the fewer problems we may encounter later on. It's always good to wrap a type in a newtype or use a more business-oriented ADT. That's how we minimize potential mistakes.

Model our requirements as immutable data

We found out that we can use ADTs as parameters to our functions and make both the signatures and implementations a lot safer and more readable.

Also, we used the Option type as a part of the model, which is a totally different context than what we've seen previously. Remember that so far we've used Option as a return type that hinted a function may not return or compute a value.

Find problems in requirements using the compiler

We upgraded our friendship with the compiler to the next level. It helped us a lot when we started using newtypes and ADTs instead of primitive types.

Make sure our logic is always executed on valid data

We addressed a concern similar to the one from the previous chapter. But we didn't really need full-blown runtime-error handling like the one introduced there, which used Either. We didn't need it because we modeled the requirements in such a great detail—using types—that it was impossible to even instantiate many incorrect values. This so-called compile-level *error handling* is far superior to the runtime version, though it is not always possible.

ADTs and Either can be used for similar purposes, as we'll see in chapter 12.

These techniques are ubiquitous in FP. They are simple and very powerful, just like pure functions, immutable values, and higher-order functions. That's why we spent so much time practicing different approaches to software design and showing the advantages of functional domain design. Now, we are going to reap the benefits of all this hard design work because, as it turns out, ADTs are going to stay with us for a long time. (Well, they've been with us since the beginning in the form of List, Option, and Either—yes, these are ADTs too—but let's not get ahead of ourselves!) Next stop: IO!

We will come back to this topic later in chapter 12.

In this chapter
you will learn

- how to use values to represent side-effectful programs

- how to use data from unsafe sources

- how to safely store data outside your program

- how to indicate your code does have side effects

- how to separate pure and impure code

“ *... we have to keep it crisp, disentangled,* ”
*and simple if we refuse to be crushed by
the complexities of our own making ...*

—EDSGER DIJKSTRA, "THE NEXT FORTY YEARS"

Talking to the outside world

In this chapter we'll finally address the elephant in the room.

> **Q** I now see how pure functions and trustworthy signatures can help me write better, more maintainable software. But let's be honest. We will always need to get something from the outside—be it an API call or fetching things from a database. Additionally, almost every application in the world has a state that needs to be persisted somewhere. So isn't this pure function concept a bit limited?
>
> **A** We can talk with the outside and still use pure function goodies! The intuition here is exactly the same as with error handling (chapter 6) and modeling requirements as types (chapter 7). We represent everything as values of descriptive types!

Remember that if we write a function that may fail, we don't throw exceptions. Instead, we indicate that it may fail by returning a value of a specific type (e.g., `Either`). Analogically, when we want to have a function that takes only a specific combination of arguments, we indicate that in the signature by taking a specific type that models this assumption.

We will show how you can apply exactly the same approach to generate and handle side effects! Remember that a side effect is anything that makes the function impure. Code that does IO actions is side-effectful and makes functions impure. Let's see an example of this kind of function. The following code needs to **persist a given meeting**:

```
void createMeeting(List<String> attendees, MeetingTime time)
```

As we discussed in chapter 2, such a function is not pure. More importantly, it lies in its signature by stating that it returns nothing (void in Java). This technique is pretty popular in imperative languages. If a function doesn't return anything, it probably does something underneath that's important. To understand what it is—saving something in the database or just updating an internal `ArrayList`—a programmer needs to dive into an implementation.

Pure functions don't lie, which assures that reading code is a breeze because readers don't need to go through each line of the implementation to understand what it's doing on a higher level. We will show how to do these things in the spirit of functional programming by wrapping the `createMeeting` call in a pure function!

IO and side effects
We will use "IO" and "side effects" interchangeably in this chapter and the remaining pages of the book. It usually doesn't matter what makes a function impure. What matters is that we need to handle it and assume the worst-case scenario, which is usually some kind of IO.

Pure function
- [ ] Returns a single value
- [ ] Uses only its arguments
- [ ] Doesn't mutate existing value

Integrating with an external API

Let's backtrack a bit and introduce the requirements for this chapter's application. Our task is to create a simple meeting scheduler.

> **Requirements: Meeting scheduler**
>
> 1. For given two attendees and a meeting length, your function should be able to find a common free slot.
> 2. Your function should persist the meeting in the given slot in all attendees' calendars.
> 3. Your function should use impure functions that talk with the outside world: `calendarEntriesApiCall` and `createMeetingApiCall` without modifying them. (Assume they are provided by an external client library.)

`calendarEntriesApiCall` and `createMeetingApiCall` functions do some IO actions. In this case these side-effectful IO actions are talking with some kind of **calendar API**. Let's assume that these functions are provided by an external client library. It means **we can't change them but we are obliged to use them** to implement the functionality properly because the calendar API holds the state of all people's calendars.

> Remember that by IO actions we mean actions that need to fetch data from or persist data outside of our program. These actions are often called side effects.

Calendar API calls

To make things simpler, we will not use a real API (yet!), but something that only simulates it, exposing a similar behavior—one that we could expect from a real-world API. We will use a `MeetingTime` product type as our data model. It is supported by simulated API calls that may not always succeed and may return different results each time they are called. This simulates accessing unknown data residing outside of our program.

> We will introduce more problematic versions of "client library" functions soon. Plus, we will use a real API in chapters 11 and 12!

```
case class MeetingTime(startHour: Int, endHour: Int)
```

> The simulated API client library functions are implemented imperatively in Java. We don't control them and can't change them. Here, we provide impure "wrappers" we can use in our codebase.

```
def calendarEntriesApiCall(name: String): List[MeetingTime] = {

  static List<MeetingTime> calendarEntriesApiCall(String name) {
    Random rand = new Random();
    if (rand.nextFloat() < 0.25)
      throw new RuntimeException("Connection error");    25% chance
    if (name.equals("Alice"))
      return List.of(new MeetingTime(8, 10),
                     new MeetingTime(11, 12));
    else if (name.equals("Bob"))
      return List.of(new MeetingTime(9, 10));
    else
      return List.of(new MeetingTime(rand.nextInt(5) + 8,
                                     rand.nextInt(4) + 13));
  }
}
```

```
def createMeetingApiCall(
  names: List[String],
  meetingTime: MeetingTime
): Unit = {

  static void createMeetingApiCall(
    List<String> names,
    MeetingTime meetingTime) {                 25% chance
    Random rand = new Random();
    if(rand.nextFloat() < 0.25)
      throw new RuntimeException("⚡");
    System.out.printf("SIDE-EFFECT");
  }
}
```

For anyone who is neither Alice nor Bob, a successful API call returns a random meeting starting between 8:00 and 12:00 and ending between 13:00 and 16:00. We mark such impure side-effectful functionalities with the lightning icon.

Properties of a side-effectful IO action

Our task is to create a meeting-scheduling function. It needs to be a pure function, too! That means it needs to have a signature that doesn't lie. We also need it to use the two provided *impure* functions that are external to our code but do some crucial IO actions that our functionality will depend on: calendarEntriesApiCall and createMeetingApiCall. We wrapped them as impure Scala functions.

The Unit type in Scala is equivalent to void in Java and other languages. If a function returns Unit, that means it does some impure things inside.

```
def calendarEntriesApiCall(name: String): List[MeetingTime]
def createMeetingApiCall(names: List[String],
                         meetingTime: MeetingTime): Unit
```

Again, we have to use both of them, and we can't change them. Moreover, we may not even know how they are implemented inside (which is often the case when client libraries are provided as binaries). Also, we shouldn't really care what's inside them. The important bit is that they can't be trusted. That's the *outside world* for us. We should assume all the worst possible things about them! These functions may (and will) behave indeterministically.

We showed a simulated implementation that sometimes fails and returns random results for the sake of completeness. We won't show it anymore and will focus on how FP handles such functions.

How IO actions may (mis)behave

In this chapter we will use an example of an API call, which represents an IO action. It's a pragmatic approach, since everything may be represented as an API call (even a database call). Integrating with external APIs is a common programming activity, including pure FP codebases, so it's important our logic is able to **gracefully handle all the corner cases.**

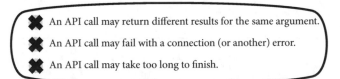

- ✖ An API call may return different results for the same argument.
- ✖ An API call may fail with a connection (or another) error.
- ✖ An API call may take too long to finish.

We will handle all three scenarios in this book, but this chapter focuses mainly on the first two, which are exposed by the two "client library" *ApiCall functions we need to integrate with. These two impure functions that are provided as a part of the task **return random results and throw random exceptions**. They are written in Java as a convention but also to make sure we understand they are not part of our codebase. Remember that we can't change them to make them more functional. But we'll need to handle all their impurity in our pure functions!

Scala can use imperative code

It's worth noting that we can use Java functions in Scala, since they are both JVM languages. This is a pretty common scenario, since a lot of client libraries are written in Java, and they are imperative. You will be able to use all of them in your FP applications, including the big real-world app in chapter 11.

Imperative solution to side-effecting IO code

Before we start introducing purely functional IO concepts, let's set the stage and see how the meeting scheduler we are required to implement in this chapter would look like in **imperative Java**. We will use the provided API client library functions directly. Note that this solution includes many of the drawbacks we've already covered in previous chapters. We will address them all (as a recap), while refactoring this imperative, impure schedule function to a pure version, written in Scala.

> I appreciate that modern Java is more functional, but I explicitly chose to use a more classical, imperative approach in our Java programs to compare these approaches. You will be able to apply many functional techniques from this book in your Java (and Kotlin!) programs as well.

```java
static MeetingTime schedule(String person1, String person2,
                            int lengthHours) {
```

❶ We first need to get all the current calendar entries for both attendees by calling an external API (i.e., the calendarEntriesApiCall function that simulates a potentially misbehaving calendar API).

```java
  List<MeetingTime> person1Entries = calendarEntriesApiCall(person1);
  List<MeetingTime> person2Entries = calendarEntriesApiCall(person2);

  List<MeetingTime> scheduledMeetings = new ArrayList<>();
  scheduledMeetings.addAll(person1Entries);
  scheduledMeetings.addAll(person2Entries);
```

❷ We create a list of all already scheduled meeting times.

```java
  List<MeetingTime> slots = new ArrayList<>();
  for (int startHour = 8; startHour < 16 - lengthHours + 1; startHour++) {
    slots.add(new MeetingTime(startHour, startHour + lengthHours));
  }
```

❸ We generate all possible slots in the working hours (8-16) of a given length (lengthHours).

```java
  List<MeetingTime> possibleMeetings = new ArrayList<>();
  for (var slot : slots) {
    var meetingPossible = true;
    for (var meeting : scheduledMeetings) {
      if (slot.endHour > meeting.startHour
          && meeting.endHour > slot.startHour) {
        meetingPossible = false;
        break;
      }
    }
    if (meetingPossible) {
      possibleMeetings.add(slot);
    }
  }
```

❹ Now, we can create a list of all slots that are not overlapping with already scheduled meeting times by going through each possible slot and checking whether it overlaps with any existing meeting. If not, we add it to the resulting possibleMeetings list.

❺ Finally, if there are any possibleMeetings, we can get the first one, call an external API to persist this meeting, and return it. If we haven't found any matching slot, we can't persist anything, so we return null.

```java
  if (!possibleMeetings.isEmpty()) {
    createMeetingApiCall(List.of(person1, person2),
                         possibleMeetings.get(0));
    return possibleMeetings.get(0);
  } else return null;
}
```

MeetingTime is a class with two fields (startHour and endHour), equals, hashCode, and toString. It can be defined as a Java record type (see the book's code repository).

Problems with the imperative approach to IO

There are many problems with the imperative solution even though it works correctly (kind of):

```
schedule("Alice", "Bob", 1)
→ MeetingTime[startHour=10, endHour=11]
```
1-hour meeting

```
schedule("Alice", "Bob", 2)
→ MeetingTime[startHour=12, endHour=14]
```
2-hour meeting

```
schedule("Alice", "Bob", 5)
→ null
```
5-hour meeting can't be scheduled.

```
schedule("Alice", "Charlie", 2)
→ MeetingTime[startHour=14, endHour=16]
```

calendarEntriesApiCall

calls a calendar API. Our simulated version:
- Returns two meetings for Alice: 8-10, 11-12
- Returns one meeting for Bob: 9-10,
- Returns one meeting for anyone else:
  • Randomly starting between 8 and 12 and ending between 12 and 16.
  • It may also fail (25% chance), so you need to be lucky (or persistent) to get these results.

However, as we've discussed many times in this book, **code is read far more often than written**, so we should always optimize for readability. This is the only way to ensure that the code is maintainable (i.e., it can be updated or changed by many future programmers with a highest-possible level of certainty). Here are the problems we can think of, based on what we know so far.

Note that an API call for "Charlie" may return different values each time it's called (it's impure) so you may get different results when you call schedule for "Charlie" (even null).

Imperative solution works for happy-path scenarios.

```
static MeetingTime schedule(String person1, String person2, int lengthHours)
```

Problem 1

The function has at least two responsibilities.
It calls external APIs, plus it finds a free slot, all done inside one function.

Problem 2

If any of the three external API calls fails, the whole function fails.
If there is any problem in the API call (network error, server error, etc.), the whole function fails with an exception, which may be confusing to the user. For now, our simulated API client library fails only sometimes, but that shouldn't be a consolation, because it heavily affects the imperative implementation of the schedule function we just wrote. We shouldn't have assumed API calls would always succeed.

Problem 3

The signature lies.
The signature states that the function returns a MeetingTime, however, if an API call fails, it will throw an exception instead of returning a MeetingTime. Additionally, it will return null if no slot is available. (We already know how to model a thing that may not exist, and we will use this knowledge in the functional version of the schedule function. Do you remember what options are at our disposal?)

Can we really do better using FP?

Q Isn't this a wild-goose chase? The majority of real-world applications will need to do IO, handle connection errors, and many more impure things. I don't think we can do significantly better than the Java code you showed.

A Yes, we can do better. We don't have to live with IO-based code spread all over our codebase. This would make our lives miserable. We will solve all three aforementioned problems by pushing the impurity out of most of our functions. This is the functional way.

> **THIS IS BIG!**
> In FP, we push the impurity out of most of our functions.

At the end of the chapter **you will be able to write and understand** the functional solution to the problem that looks like this:

```
def schedule(attendees: List[String],
             lengthHours: Int): IO[Option[MeetingTime]] = {
  for {
    existingMeetings <- scheduledMeetings(attendees)
    possibleMeeting = possibleMeetings(scheduledMeetings,
                               8, 16, lengthHours).headOption
    _ <- possibleMeeting match {
      case Some(meeting) => createMeeting(attendees, meeting)
      case None => IO.unit
    }
  } yield possibleMeeting
}
```

SNEAK PEEK

We are yet to cover how the IO type works, but note how rich the signature is and what it says about the function.

Additionally, note that this implementation is more versatile because it is able to schedule meetings for more than two people.

Our journey has already begun. We will address all three problems in this chapter by introducing functional programming alternatives and rewriting the schedule function to Scala, using these new concepts. Additionally, as promised, you will have a chance to recap the material from the previous chapters and see how all these functional pieces fall into place.

See how many familiar techniques are used in the snippet above!

Problem 1

The function has at least two responsibilities.

In this chapter, we will learn how to solve each of these problems using FP, problem by problem.

Problem 2

If any of the three external API calls fails, the whole function fails. →

Problem 3

The signature lies.

Doing IO vs. using IO's result

IO is an abbreviation for input/output. Hence, we have two types of IO.

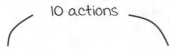

IO actions

Input actions

These include all actions that need to go outside our program and fetch something (e.g., read a value from a database, do an API call, or get some input from a user). It also includes reading a shared memory address, which is mutable.

Output actions

These include all actions that need to store something for later use (e.g., to a database or an API or outputting to a GUI). They also include writing to a shared memory address, which is mutable, and many other cases.

The purpose of making this distinction is to help us think about IO from a different perspective. Some actions can be categorized as both input and output, which we'll see later in the chapter.

> ## Unsafe code
>
> The main property of both types of IO actions is that they execute unsafe code, which is code that may behave differently, depending on many factors. That's why reading from and writing to a shared mutable memory address is treated as unsafe and belongs to the side-effectful IO actions category. Remember that pure functions should always behave exactly the same, no matter where and when we use them.

Both actions are already represented in our API client library functions. `calendarEntriesApiCall` is an **input action** that reads a value from a potentially unsafe location, while `createMeetingApiCall` is an **output action** that writes a value to a potentially unsafe location.

Naturally, we'll first focus on using IO to fetch data (i.e., input actions). Let's dive into the beginning of the `schedule` function:

```
List<MeetingTime> person1Entries = calendarEntriesApiCall(person1);
List<MeetingTime> person2Entries = calendarEntriesApiCall(person2);
```

Note we are still analyzing the imperative Java version we wrote a few pages ago.

The first line of the function is what you'd see in lots of codebases. It's bad because it does two things:

— Involves some IO action underneath (an API call, most likely over a network)
— Provides the result of the IO action (`List<MeetingTime>`)

Note that **what really matters for us is the result, not the action itself**. We want a `List` of `MeetingTime` values to be able to produce a potential slot for a meeting. But the fact that this value is fetched from the outside world has important consequences: it can fail (connection error), take too long, or simply have a different format than what we expect and fail with a deserialization error of some kind. To sum it up: we execute a reading IO action just to get a value, but we are drawn into some hairy corner cases in the process. And we need to handle them all!

In other words, reading IO actions focuses on the value they produce, while writing IO actions focuses on the side effect itself.

Handling IO imperatively

Even though we just care about a value produced by an IO action, we are forced to think about all the consequences of it being an IO action. Imperatively, in Java you'd need to do something like this:

Problem 1

The function has at least two responsibilities.

```java
List<MeetingTime> person1Entries = null;
try {
  person1Entries = calendarEntriesApiCall(person1);
} catch(Exception e) {
  // retry:
  person1Entries = calendarEntriesApiCall(person1);
}
```

Plus, similar code for person2Entries as well! This would probably be encapsulated in its own function/object, but it wouldn't help with the problem we are trying to solve now.

Of course, it's just a single possible solution to a much more complicated problem of detecting and dealing with failures. Basically, in such scenarios we try to have a **recovery mechanism** in case of a failure. Here we used a **retry strategy** with one retry. But there are many more options: more retries, using a cached value, using a default value (fallback), or retrying after some backoff period, to name a few. Recovery mechanisms are a huge topic, deserving their own book. What matters here is this: **should we really care about a recovery strategy inside the schedule function?**

We should not! The more retries and try-catches, the less obvious the whole business logic is. The fact that we use IO in the schedule function should merely be a small detail because the most important thing is finding the free slot for a new meeting and storing it in the API. Did you see any mention of a retry strategy in the business requirements?

Entangled concerns

This mix of different responsibilities and levels of abstraction is called *entangled concerns*. The more concerns we entangle in one function, the more difficult the function will be to change, update, and maintain. ⟶

Note that we don't say that the concern of retrying a potentially failing operation is not important. It is! What we say is that it can't be entangled in the business logic code (i.e., it can't distract the reader of the code from business concerns). Sure enough, if our schedule function consists of lots of try-catches or other failure-handling mechanisms, it can't be very readable—and, therefore, not very maintainable.

Let's disentangle the fact of getting and using a value in our business-related code from the fact that we need a reading IO to fetch it.

In Edsger Dijkstra's words quoted at the beginning of this chapter: we will be "crushed by the complexities of our own making."

Note that in the schedule function, we entangled the act of using a List<MeetingTime> with the fact that we needed an unsafe IO action to get it.

Computations as IO values

Fortunately, functional programming has got our backs. Just like using the Either type to handle errors and the Option type to handle things that are possibly absent, we can use the IO type to disentangle the act of getting and using a value from an IO action that we need to execute to fetch that value. Let's first see IO in action, and then we will dig deeper to build some intuition around it. That should be pretty easy because IO is very similar to Either, Option, and List—**it even has many functions that you already know!**

> **THIS IS BIG!**
> In FP, we just pass immutable values around!

First things first. IO[A] is a value, just like Option[A] is a value and Either[A, B] is a value. FP is all about functions and immutable values.

The functional IO type in Scala is part of the cats-effect library. To use IO, you need to import cats.effect.IO first. You already have it in scope if you use the sbt console from the book's repository.

How does IO work?

IO[A] has several concrete subtypes, but we'll introduce just two of them here for the sake of simplicity: Pure[A] and Delay[A].

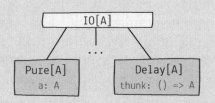

If we want to create a value of type IO[Int], we need to decide whether it's a value that we already know, or we need to run unsafe, side-effectful code to get it.

If we know the value, we can use an IO.pure constructor that will just wrap this value and return IO[A] (which, internally, is a Pure[A]):

```
val existingInt: IO[Int] = IO.pure(6)
```

If we need to call an unsafe function getIntUnsafely(), which is an impure function that may throw exceptions, then we need to use the IO.delay constructor that will **wrap the potentially unsafe call without executing it** (using a mechanism similar to *closures*):

```
val intFromUnsafePlace: IO[Int] =
  IO.delay(getIntUnsafely())
```

No matter which constructor we choose (pure or delay), we get back an IO[Int] value. It's a value that represents a *potentially* unsafe computation (like a side-effectful IO action) that, if successful, produces an Int value. Note the usage of the word *represents* in the previous statement. **IO[Int] value is just a representation of a computation** that will provide an Int value. We will need to somehow *execute* or *interpret* this IO[Int] to get the resulting Int value.

The difference between IO.pure and IO.delay is that the former is an example of eager evaluation, while the latter is an example of lazy evaluation. We will discuss this in more depth later in the chapter.

What's important now is that we use the power of lazy evaluation to not call unsafe code and delegate this responsibility to some other entity in a different place.

IO **values**

It's very important to remember that IO[Int], or IO[MeetingTime], is just an immutable value like any other immutable value.

> **What is IO?**
> IO[A] is a **value** that represents a potentially side-effectful IO action (or another unsafe operation) that, if successful, produces a value of type A.

Q So how exactly does IO help us? And what about the requirement that we need to use the impure calendarEntriesApiCall function, which is provided externally and potentially unsafe? Surely, we can't change its signature because we can't change it at all!

A We won't change the calendarEntriesApiCall function. Usually, when you are provided with some external library that integrates with an outside-world system, you can't easily change anything there. So calendarEntriesApiCall stays untouched! What we'll do, however, is wrap this external, impure, side-effectful function within a function that returns an IO value!

In our example we have an unsafe function that acts as a client library function with the following unchangeable signature:

```
def calendarEntriesApiCall(name: String): List[MeetingTime]
```

Compare both signatures. There is a fundamental difference, which we will dig into later on.

Since this is an IO action that we use to fetch a value, and we don't want to be responsible for executing it; we can put it inside an IO[List[MeetingTime]] value using the IO.delay constructor:

```
import ch08_SchedulingMeetings.calendarEntriesApiCall

def calendarEntries(name: String): IO[List[MeetingTime]] = {
  IO.delay(calendarEntriesApiCall(name))
}
```

If you want to follow along in your REPL, please import the impure API client library functions from the ch08_SchedulingmeetingS module, as shown in the code snippet.

And that's it! We used calendarEntriesApiCall as required. Our new function returns IO[List[MeetingTime]], which is a pure value that represents an IO action, which, once successfully executed, will provide a List[MeetingTime]. What's cool about the calendarEntries function is that **it will never fail**, no matter how many exceptions calendarEntriesApiCall throws! So how exactly does it work, and what exactly have we achieved by doing so? Next, we'll play with the IO type a bit, using a smaller example, so you get more intuition about it.

Values don't throw exceptions, and pure functions don't throw exceptions as well!

IO **values in the wild**

IO.delay takes a block of code and doesn't execute it, but it returns a value that *represents* this passed block of code and the value it will produce when executed. Before we use (and execute) IO in our meeting scheduler, let's see a smaller example first. Assume we have an impure Java function that prints a line and then returns a random number between 1 and 6.

```
def castTheDieImpure(): Int = {

    static int castTheDieImpure() {
        System.out.println("The die is cast");
        Random rand = new Random();
        return rand.nextInt(6) + 1;
    }
}
```

We wrapped this impure function without any modifcation so that it's usable in our project.

After executing this function, we surprisingly get two results back.

```
>   import ch08_CastingDie.castTheDieImpure
    castTheDieImpure()
→   console output: The die is cast
→   3
```

To follow along, import this function into an sbt console REPL session.

→ 3   What happened here? We call a function and get more than advertised in the signature?

In fact, you get just one result—an Int, but the function itself prints an additional line, which we can treat as a side effect because it does more than advertised in the signature (which promises to just return an Int!). Additionally, when you run it the second time, there is a chance you will get a different result! It's not a pure function, so as FP programmers, we need to treat it as a potential threat to code maintainability—**it's an unsafe code that we need to wrap in an IO!**

Functional programmers treat all impure functions with the same level of scrutiny as IO actions.

Let's wrap the impure function call inside an IO using IO.delay.

```
>   def castTheDie(): IO[Int] = IO.delay(castTheDieImpure())
→   def castTheDie(): IO[Int]
    castTheDie()
→   IO[Int]
```

And what? **Nothing happened!** IO.delay took a block of code (a call to castTheDieImpure()) and didn't execute it. It returned a value that *represented* the passed block of code without executing it. No matter how many times we execute castTheDie(), it will always return the same IO[Int] value, just like List(1, 2, 3) will always return the same List[Int] value. No side effects are executed, no printlns, and no random numbers returned. castTheDie() returns a value that can later be interpreted (*executed*) and may eventually provide an Int value by calling the castTheDieImpure() function lazily *stored* inside. This allows us to **focus on using a generated Int value without running the code that generates it**. We will show how to *run* and *use* an IO next.

Remember that we can use the Java code from Scala, because they are both JVM languages. We are going to use this convention in the remaining part of the book. Java code represents imperative solutions, which usually are impure functions. In Scala, we will use them the FP way without any modifcations. Hopefully, this approach aligns with your future experience.

THIS IS BIG!
In FP, we treat impure functions as unsafe code.

Problem 1

The function has at least two responsibilities.

In other words, the responsibility for running the unsafe code is delegated.

Pushing the impurity out

We split the responsibilities of using a value produced by an IO action and running this IO action. Let's first see how we run an IO value.

Running IO values

IO[A] can be run by executing a special function called **unsafeRunSync()**.

```
> val dieCast: IO[Int] = castTheDie()
→ dieCast: IO[Int]
  import cats.effect.unsafe.implicits.global
  dieCast.unsafeRunSync()
→ console output: The die is cast
→ 3
```

We need to insert this import statement before running an IO value. It provides an access to thread pools, which will be used to execute delayed computations and side effects. We will discuss threads and concurrency in chapter 10. (BTW, the book's sbt console session imports it automatically.)

See? We can run it, and we get exactly the same behavior as running castTheDieImpure() previously (a printed line and a random Int value). However, in FP, we call unsafeRunSync in a different place, usually only once, at the end of our program, which only contains a small amount of impure code! A different entity is responsible for running it.

The main benefit of using IO is that it's just a value, so it belongs to the pure world. We want to have as much code as possible in the pure world to use all the superpowers we've learned in this book to our advantage. All the impure functions—random generators, printing lines, API calls, and database fetches—belong to the impure world.

THIS IS BIG!
In FP, we push the impurity out of most of our functions.

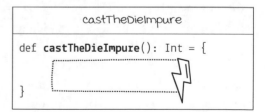

Pure world	**Impure world**

castTheDie
| ```
def castTheDie(): IO[Int] = {
  IO.delay(castTheDieImpure())
}
``` |

castTheDieImpure
| ```
def castTheDieImpure(): Int = {

}
``` |

We pushed the responsibility for executing the unsafe code to the caller of the castTheDie function. The caller resides in the impure world. We can safely write the rest of the business logic on the pure side of the world, using only IO values.

main application process
| ```
val dieCast: IO[Int] = castTheDie()
dieCast.unsafeRunSync()
``` |

Now, let's see how we can work solely with IO values that represent side-effectful IO actions **without running them**! IO values, just like Lists, Options, and Eithers, can be transformed using pure functions. What's more, these are the functions that you are already familiar with! Let's feel the real power of the pure side of the world!
```

Using values fetched from two IO actions

Enough theory! It's time to connect all the dots and use the power of functional programming to our advantage. We will first conclude the smaller *casting the die* example and then we'll ask you to implement a similar solution in the meeting scheduler!

Imagine that you'd like to cast the die twice and return a sum of both results. It looks trivial using the impure version:

```
castTheDieImpure() + castTheDieImpure()
→ console output: The die is cast
→ console output: The die is cast
→ 9
```

Easy, right? We get two printed lines and the final result of the function, which, in this case, was 9. Now, remember that IO actions are usually connected to a higher risk of something not going according to the plan. We could say there is a chance that a die falls off the table.

```
def castTheDieImpure(): Int = {

    static int castTheDieImpure() {
        Random rand = new Random();
        if (rand.nextBoolean())
            throw new RuntimeException("Die fell off");
        return rand.nextInt(6) + 1;
    }

}
    import ch08_CastingDie.WithFailures.castTheDieImpure
```

Problem 1

The function has at least two responsibilities.

When a function returns an Int, its client can assume it will return an Int when called.

When a function returns an IO[Int] it indicates that it returns a value, which can later be executed, but it may contain some unsafe code and may fail. It will return an Int only if it succeeds.

Does castTheDieImpure() + castTheDieImpure() still look good in your opinion? If you didn't know what's inside the castTheDieImpure function and just relied on its signature, which promises to always return an int, you'd be in **big trouble**. Codebases in real projects are usually large, and you don't have enough time to closely investigate each and every line of an implementation, do you?

That's where IO type comes in. We don't want to think about try-catches in this particular place of our codebase, we just want to indicate the logic behind our program, which is *getting two numbers out of somewhere and summing them*. Wouldn't it be nice to say just this and get back a value that represents this and only this with no strings attached?

```
def castTheDie(): IO[Int] = IO.delay(castTheDieImpure())
→ def castTheDie(): IO[Int]

castTheDie() + castTheDie()
→ compilation error!
```

This fails at compile time, because IO[Int] doesn't define an addition operation. You can't simply add two values that represent potentially unsafe computations!

Combining two IO values into a single IO value

Q we can't simply add two IO values together? So how is it possible to combine them into one? Why does it need to be so hard?

```
castTheDie() + castTheDie()
→ compilation error!
```

A It can't be added because an IO[Int] value represents more than just an Int value. It also represents a potentially side-effectful and unsafe action that needs to be executed later on because it may fail. Isn't it helpful? As you see, it's a pretty rich value, and we will use this fact to our advantage.

Let's combine those IOs. Fortunately, we've already tackled a very similar problem: getting two numbers, and if they both exist, summing them.

```
val aOption: Option[Int] = Some(2)
val bOption: Option[Int] = Some(4)
aOption + bOption
→ compilation error!
```

This fails at compile time, because Option[Int] doesn't define an addition operation. You can't simply add two potentially absent values!

Do you remember what we used to combine two or more Option values? The answer is that we used our old friend, flatMap, which is used inside a for comprehension.

```
val result: Option[Int] =
  for {
    a <- aOption
    b <- bOption
  } yield a + b
```

This whole for expression produces a value of type Option[Int]. In this case it's Some(6), but it would produce None if either aOption or bOption was None.

It turns out IO has `flatMap` as well!

```
def castTheDieTwice(): IO[Int] = {
  for {
    firstCast <- castTheDie()
    secondCast <- castTheDie()
  } yield firstCast + secondCast
}
```

This whole for expression produces a value of type IO[Int]. It describes a program to be executed in a different place.

We created a new function that returns an IO[Int]—a description of a program that, when executed later, will produce an Int, which will be a result of throwing the die twice. And since IO is just a pure value, there is no chance an exception is thrown here because we've not run it yet.

I hope it's not a surprise for you, since we've been flatMapping and using for comprehensions since their introduction in chapter 5. flatMap is everywhere in functional programs.

And since castTheDieTwice belongs to the pure world, we won't run this value here. It will be delegated to the client of this function.

Practicing creating and combining IO values

The casting dies setup we have just described is very similar to a feature in the meeting scheduler app we've been working on in this chapter. We need to get calendar entries for two attendees and then *merge* these two lists together to get a list of all scheduled meetings for both of them.

Given an impure side-effectful function that is potentially unsafe and returns a list of meetings for a given attendee:

```
def calendarEntriesApiCall(name: String): List[MeetingTime]
> import ch08_SchedulingMeetings.calendarEntriesApiCall
```

write a pure calendarEntries function that uses this function but returns only a value that describes what will happen once executed.

1

Remember to import both impure functions into your book's sbt console REPL session.

Given an impure side-effectful function that is potentially unsafe and saves a given meeting for future use:

```
def createMeetingApiCall(names: List[String], meetingTime: MeetingTime): Unit
> import ch08_SchedulingMeetings.createMeetingApiCall
```

write a pure function that uses this API call function but returns only a value that describes what will happen once executed.

2

Your final task is to **write a pure function that returns a description of a program that gets calendar entries for person1 and person2** and returns a single list of all their meetings. It should use calendarEntries inside (implemented above). Here's the signature of this function:

3

```
def scheduledMeetings(person1: String, person2: String): IO[List[MeetingTime]]
```

Answer

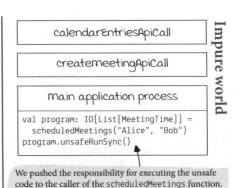

Pure world

```
def calendarEntries(name: String): IO[List[MeetingTime]] = {
  IO.delay(calendarEntriesApiCall(name))
}
```
1
  This function describes an input action (reads a value).

```
def createMeeting(names: List[String],
                  meeting: MeetingTime): IO[Unit] = {
  IO.delay(createMeetingApiCall(names, meeting))
}
```
2
  IO[Unit] means that it's an output action (writes a value).

```
def scheduledMeetings(person1: String,
  person2: String): IO[List[MeetingTime]] = {
    for {
      person1Entries <- calendarEntries(person1)
      person2Entries <- calendarEntries(person2)
    } yield person1Entries.appendedAll(person2Entries)
}
```
3
  Did you remember how to append two immutable lists?

Impure world

| calendarEntriesApiCall |
| createmeetingApiCall |
| main application process |

```
val program: IO[List[MeetingTime]] =
  scheduledMeetings("Alice", "Bob")
program.unsafeRunSync()
```

We pushed the responsibility for executing the unsafe code to the caller of the scheduledMeetings function. Note that, even though we have three functions that return IO, we only call unsafeRunSync once, at the end!

Disentangling concerns by working with values only

Problem 1

The function has at least two responsibilities.

We now have three functions that return an IO value. calendarEntries and createMeeting are simple wrappers around their impure counterparts (API calls). scheduledMeetings is a function that uses calendarEntries to return all meetings scheduled in the person1 and person2 calendars.

There is a small, but very important, distinction between imperative calendarEntriesApiCall(String name) and its functional *wrapper*: calendarEntries(name: String). The imperative one **does two things**:

— Returns a List[MeetingTime] for a given person
— Executes an IO action responsible for getting the List[MeetingTime]

The functional version doesn't execute any IO action—its sole responsibility is to indicate that it will return a List[MeetingTime] and that somebody else will need to execute it (using unsafeRunSync()). Therefore, one of the responsibilities is delegated to the client of calendarEntries or any other function that uses calendarEntries internally and returns an IO value as well.

```
> val scheduledMeetingsProgram = scheduledMeetings("Alice", "Bob")
→ IO[List[MeetingTime]]
```

Nothing happened, we just got a description of a program as a value.

Meanwhile, somewhere in the impure world, in the main process:

```
> scheduledMeetingsProgram.unsafeRunSync()
→ List(MeetingTime(8, 10), MeetingTime(11, 12), MeetingTime(9, 10))
```

We executed IO actions that the given IO value describes and got some results. Remember that, since we are doing unsafe actions and haven't discussed failure handling yet, this line can also result in an exception. Try again if that happens.

Note how we used this new scheduledMeetings function that returns a description of a program (an IO value). Internally, this function uses a different description of a program (IO values returned by calendarEntries). No IO actions were executed when we called calendarEntries, and no IO actions were executed when we called scheduledMeetings. We just worked with IO values and got the scheduledMeetingsProgram value as the final version of the program. Then, finally, we just executed it. **It was the only impure line in the whole application**. The rest of the application is still purely functional because we only work with functions that operate on values.

This is how functional programs are designed. We will discuss it in more detail later in the chapter and again in chapter 11.

The essence of FP is writing functions that transform input values into new output values. We've been doing it since chapter 1. We've been working with Lists, Strings, Sets, Options, Eithers, and, now, with IOs, which are immutable values, just like the rest.

The IO **type is viral**

One other very important consequence of using IO is that if we want to use a function that returns an IO inside a function we write, we are forced to return an IO value from that function as well! For example, when we developed the scheduledMeetings function, we knew that we needed to call calendarEntries for both person1 and person2—otherwise, we wouldn't be able to implement this requirement:

```
def scheduledMeetings(person1: String,
                      person2: String): IO[List[MeetingTime]] = {
  for {
    person1Entries <- calendarEntries(person1)
    person2Entries <- calendarEntries(person2)
  } yield person1Entries.appendedAll(person2Entries)
}
```

Notice that the return type is IO[List[MeetingTime]], which is forced on us exactly because we use calendarEntries internally. There is no way around this. To do any computation on a value that is produced by an IO action (i.e., wrapped as an IO value), we need to produce a new IO value as well. (Using unsafeRunSync or other unsafe functions is forbidden, as they are not pure.) **The IO type is viral**; once your function returns an IO, all other functions that use it will need to return an IO as well. It spreads, which has three important consequences.

> **THIS IS BIG!** When we use a function that returns an IO, we are forced to return an IO as well.

Use IO **in as few places as possible**

We'd like to give as much freedom to users of our functions as possible. Returning an IO is constraining because it makes them return an IO as well. Hence, we need to use IO sparsely. This chapter introduces IO, so we use it heavily, but, as we implement more things, notice how we try to extract most of the logic into pure non-IO functions.

IO **acts as a tag for potentially failing cases**

The good thing about IO being viral is that there is no way around it. That means it can help a lot in terms of identifying functionalities that need some special care—all functions that return IOs are functions that describe programs that may fail when executed. The IO type is therefore a highly visible tag in your codebase.

We will deal with failures and recovery strategies after solving the next exercise.

Nobody can hide unsafe side-effectful code

That all means that if your function doesn't return an IO, we and all our teammates can be sure that it doesn't create any unsafe side effects.

Coffee break: Working with values

To get you into the spirit of working with values (and recap some of the material from previous chapters), you are going to write the next major part of our meeting-scheduling app!

Your first task is to write the `possibleMeetings` function:

```scala
def possibleMeetings(existingMeetings: List[MeetingTime],
                     startHour: Int, endHour: Int,
                     lengthHours: Int): List[MeetingTime]
```

1

It should return all the `MeetingTime`s, starting at `startHour` or later, ending at `endHour` or earlier, lasting `lengthHours` hours, and not overlapping with any `existingMeetings`. You already know everything to write such a function, but you may need to look through the `List` API docs to find a very handy function that creates lists containing a range of `Int`s.

Documentation and API docs can be found at https://scala-lang. org/api/3.x/.

Using the function implemented in the previous step, **implement the schedule function**, which finds a free slot and, if found, returns the created meeting in `Some`, or `None` otherwise:

2

```scala
def schedule(person1: String, person2: String, lengthHours: Int): IO[Option[MeetingTime]]
```

Note the return type: `IO[Option[...]]`! Use the fact that we are allowed to schedule meetings only inside working hours (8–16). Use the `scheduledMeetings` function you implemented earlier. You don't have to persist the meeting using the API call yet. We'll do that later, but as a bonus, try to think about how that might look.

```
scheduledmeetings

def scheduledMeetings(person1: String,
  person2: String): IO[List[MeetingTime]] = {
    for {
    person1Entries <- calendarEntries(person1)
    person2Entries <- calendarEntries(person2)
  } yield person1Entries.appendedAll(person2Entries)
}
```

Tips and hints

Remember that in FP we work with values and declaratively transform them into new values.

Try working on your own first, and don't look at the hints or the answer before you have something:

1. The `List` class API has a `range` function that may help you generate a `List` of all possible starting hours. This may be used as a base for further transformations (e.g., to create a list of all possible `MeetingTime` slots [remember `map`, `filter`, and `forall`?]).
2. It may be beneficial to go through the `List` API again and find out how to return an `Option` of the first element of the `List`.

Coffee break explained: Working with values

I hope you've put a lot of effort into solving this exercise. Remember that you learn the most in the long run when the learning process doesn't feel easy! So don't worry if you didn't get it right on your first try. Have a look at the following solution, and find places where you struggled.

```
def meetingsOverlap(meeting1: MeetingTime, meeting2: MeetingTime): Boolean = {
  meeting1.endHour > meeting2.startHour && meeting2.endHour > meeting1.startHour
}
```

We first create a helper pure function that will tell us whether two meeting times overlap.

```
def possibleMeetings(
    existingMeetings: List[MeetingTime],
    startHour: Int,
    endHour: Int,
    lengthHours: Int
): List[MeetingTime] = {
  val slots = List
    .range(startHour, endHour - lengthHours + 1)
    .map(startHour => MeetingTime(startHour, startHour + lengthHours))

  slots.filter(slot =>
    existingMeetings.forall(meeting => !meetingsOverlap(meeting, slot))
  )
}
```

We use List.range to create a List[Int], starting at startHour, and ending at the last possible start of a meeting of lengthHours. **We now have a list of all possible starting hours.**

Then, we map this List[Int] of all possible starting hours to a List[MeetingTime].

Finally, given all possible slots, we filter out all slots that overlap with existing meetings, and voilà—we get a list of all possible meetings back!

```
def schedule(person1: String, person2: String, lengthHours: Int): IO[Option[MeetingTime]] = {
  for {
    existingMeetings <- scheduledMeetings(person1, person2)
    meetings          = possibleMeetings(existingMeetings, 8, 16, lengthHours)
  } yield meetings.headOption
}
```

We need to use values produced by unsafe IO actions—we know that because scheduledMeetings tells us this by having IO in its signature. So, just like working with values in the context of List or working with values in the context of Option, we use the flatMap power of the IO type inside a for comprehension to *extract* and work on a value that will eventually be produced by scheduledMeetings.

possibleMeetings returns a List, so meetings is a List[MeetingTime]. We use headOption to take only the first element of this list (it will be None if the list is empty and Some otherwise).

possibleMeetings is a function that produces a value we want to use directly (it's not contained in IO), so we use the equals sign. It works just like an assignment to a val, but we omit the val keyword when we are inside a for comprehension.

Congratulations! This exercise is one of the milestone exercises in the book. If you feel comfortable with your solution, it means you've mastered topics covered in chapters 5, 6, and 7. This will help a lot with the next topic we are going to cover, which is failure handling!

Toward functional IO

Introducing IO solved the first of our problems: now the function describes a program that will execute some IO actions, but the responsibility for executing them is delegated to a different place in the application, chosen by its client. Somebody needs to call unsafeRunSync() eventually, but **it's not a concern of the schedule function anymore.** schedule provides an IO value, and nothing happens until it's *run* (or *interpreted*).

```
> val program = schedule("Alice", "Bob", 1)
→ IO[Option[MeetingTime]]
program.unsafeRunSync()
→ Some(MeetingTime(10, 11))
```

If you are unlucky, you may need to run it multiple times before getting this answer. We'll discuss it shortly.

The important thing is that we created a value that represents a rather complex program. We used many values that represent smaller programs and mapped and flatMapped them together. This is one of the key takeaways, not only of this chapter but of the whole book. At its core, **functional programming is about transforming immutable values using pure functions.**

> **THIS IS BIG!**
> FP is about transforming immutable values using pure functions, even when handling IO.

Current solution

```
def calendarEntries(name: String): IO[List[MeetingTime]]
```
This function returns a description of a side-effectful IO action that, when executed, will return a list of MeetingTimes.

```
def createMeeting(names: List[String], meeting: MeetingTime): IO[Unit]
```
This function returns a description of a side-effectful IO action that, when executed, will not return anything (hence IO[Unit]).

Both functions are just wrappers around potentially unsafe, side-effectful IO actions defined in our unchangeable client library. We used IO.delay to make sure they are lazily evaluated later.

```
def scheduledMeetings(person1: String, person2: String): IO[List[MeetingTime]]
```
This function returns a description of a side-effectful IO action that, when executed, will return a list of MeetingTimes for two attendees.

```
def schedule(person1: String, person2: String, lengthHours: Int): IO[Option[MeetingTime]]
```
This function returns a description of a side-effectful IO action that, when executed, will return a possible MeetingTime. It is built using smaller descriptions (IO values), but no action is executed in this function. It's all just a combination of descriptions.

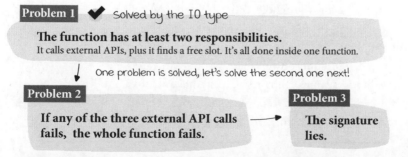

Problem 1 ✔ Solved by the IO type

The function has at least two responsibilities.
It calls external APIs, plus it finds a free slot. It's all done inside one function.

↓ One problem is solved, let's solve the second one next!

Problem 2

If any of the three external API calls fails, the whole function fails. →

Problem 3

The signature lies.

What about IO failures?

Now, let's address the second problem we found at the beginning. We have already encountered it several times, but let's recall what we are really facing here. The provided `calendarEntriesApiCall` function may fail (in our case—throw exceptions). We delegated the responsibility of running IO actions, but they still fail when they are run. That's not good!

```
def calendarEntriesApiCall(name: String): List[MeetingTime] = {

  static List<MeetingTime> calendarEntriesApiCall(String name) {
    Random rand = new Random();
    if (rand.nextFloat() < 0.25)
      throw new RuntimeException("Connection error");
    if (name.equals("Alice"))
      return List.of(new MeetingTime(8, 10), new MeetingTime(11, 12));
    else if (name.equals("Bob"))
      return List.of(new MeetingTime(9, 10));
    else
      return List.of(new MeetingTime(rand.nextInt(5) + 8, rand.nextInt(4) + 13));
  }
}
```

25% chance

Note that this function is impure and unsafe because it doesn't always return a result (sometimes it fails), and when it does, it's not always the same for the same argument.

In the imperative solution, we tried to write a simple recovery strategy with one retry. Obviously, some more sophisticated strategies are available, but the point here is

Problem 2

If any of the three external API calls fails, the whole function fails
If there is any problem in the API call (network error, server error, etc.), the whole function fails with an exception, which may be confusing to the user. From the business logic perspective, we cannot assume anything about any API calls.

that their implementations should not entangle with the business logic too much. We don't want to have a dozen lines of recovery code entangled with a single line of business logic! It's a different responsibility.

```
List<MeetingTime> person1Entries = null;
try {
  person1Entries = calendarEntriesApiCall(person1);
} catch(Exception e) {
  person1Entries = calendarEntriesApiCall(person1);
}
```

Earlier in the chapter we implemented a simple recovery mechanism that retries the same call once if it fails. The same needs to be written for other API calls as well!

In imperative programming we program *recipes*: step-by-step guides for the processor to execute. That's why recovery code is often intertwined between business logic lines, making the whole thing unreadable and unmaintainable in the long run. In FP, we use **declarative style**— describing what we want and delegating the responsibility to execute our wishes. That gives us many design superpowers because we can build programs using compatible blocks (values). Surprisingly, we have already covered a function that we'll use to build recovery strategies. **Quick question:** do you remember how we transformed an `Option` value that might have potentially been `None`?

Answer:
`Option.orElse`

Running a program described by IO may fail!

Since our IO actions may sometimes fail (as is the case with the majority of side-effectful IO calls), programs that are based on them may fail as well! Wrapping unsafe calls as an IO value guards us from immediate failures. We decoupled the description of a program (IO value) from its execution (calling unsafeRunSync()), so we won't get any failures as long as we stay in the context of IO. Thus, calling these functions is guaranteed to be safe and won't ever fail—they just return values!

> These functions will never fail!

```
def calendarEntries(name: String): IO[List[MeetingTime]]
def createMeeting(names: List[String], meeting: MeetingTime): IO[Unit]
def scheduledMeetings(person1: String, person2: String): IO[List[MeetingTime]]
def schedule(person1: String, person2: String, lengthHours: Int): IO[Option[MeetingTime]]
```

However, that doesn't mean we are completely safe. If the underlying IO actions randomly fail (as is the case with our unchangeable calendarEntriesApiCall, which has a failure rate at around 25%), our programs may fail when descriptions (IO values) get executed. If you've been following along in your REPL, you've probably seen it already.

```
val program = schedule("Alice", "Bob", 1)
→ IO[Option[MeetingTime]]

program.unsafeRunSync()
→ Exception in thread "main": Connection error
```

Note that the program described by the IO value returned by the schedule function may contain several unsafe API calls. They all need to succeed for the whole execution to succeed.

However, *sometimes* the underlying actions may all succeed, so we should eventually get lucky if we try again and again.

```
program.unsafeRunSync()            Not this time!
→ Exception in thread "main": Connection error

program.unsafeRunSync()
→ Some(MeetingTime(10, 11))
```

Since program is just an immutable value, we can reuse it and run it as many times as we want. This time it worked, and we got a result!

So it's clear that if an IO action is unsafe and may fail, so can the program described by the IO value that calls this action. This can happen only after an IO value is run using unsafeRunSync(), not earlier (again, because earlier it's just a value). Even though we disentangled the execution from the description, we still need to *declare* what happens in case of a failure. We still need a way to describe a recovery mechanism, like a single retry. Fortunately, **we can encode a recovery mechanism inside an IO value too!** And this can be a very sophisticated recovery mechanism, too! We will use a familiar function to do it.

Remember `orElse`?

IO type gives us the ability to describe what should be used if something fails, just like Option and Either give us the ability to describe what should be used if they are None or Left. Just like Option and Either have orElse, **IO has it too!**

The main difficulty of grasping IO is changing the mental model from *running IO code* to *having a value that describes IO-based code*. Once you grok it, everything becomes easier because you are able to tap into intuitions that have already been built. With failure handling, the intuition is that IO is really similar to Option and Either, among others. When you need to recover from something that doesn't belong to your program's happy path, you use orElse, which creates a new value. Let's see this for ourselves.

> The IO type is part of the cats-effect library. To use IO, you need to import cats.effect.IO first. To use orElse, which is a generic function, you need to import cats.implicits._ as well. Again, everything is already imported for you if you use sbt console from the book's repository.

Option.orElse

```
val year: Option[Int] = Some(996)
val noYear: Option[Int] = None

year.orElse(Some(2020))
→ Some(996)
noYear.orElse(Some(2020))
→ Some(2020)
year.orElse(None)
→ Some(996)
noYear.orElse(None)
→ None
```

Either.orElse

```
val year: Either[String, Int] = Right(996)
val noYear: Either[String, Int] = Left("no year")

year.orElse(Right(2020))
→ Right(996)
noYear.orElse(Right(2020))
→ Right(2020)
year.orElse(Left("can't recover"))
→ Right(996)
noYear.orElse(Left("can't recover"))
→ Left("can't recover")
```

IO.orElse

Look for similarities in outputs. Some and Right values are similar to successful IO value executions. None and Left values are similar to failed IO value executions!

```
val year: IO[Int] = IO.delay(996)
val noYear: IO[Int] = IO.delay(throw new Exception("no year"))

val program1 = year.orElse(IO.delay(2020))
→ IO[Int]
val program2 = noYear.orElse(IO.delay(2020))
→ IO[Int]
val program3 = year.orElse(IO.delay(throw new Exception("can't recover")))
→ IO[Int]
val program4 = noYear.orElse(IO.delay(throw new Exception("can't recover")))
→ IO[Int]

program1.unsafeRunSync()
→ 996
program2.unsafeRunSync()
→ 2020
program3.unsafeRunSync()
→ 996
program4.unsafeRunSync()
→ Exception in thread "main": can't recover
```

noYear is a description of a program that, if successful, will return an Int. However, we see that it will always fail when we run it! So how can we recover?

Up until this point we have only created IO values, so both year and noYear are values. program1, 2, 3, and 4 are also just values. Some of these values, however, incorporate a simple failure recovery strategy! We can see it by running programs described by these values using unsafeRunSync().

The exception message is from the IO value passed to orElse. Running noYear failed, so the one from orElse was used and failed as well.

Lazy and eager evaluation

The behavior of IO.orElse is very similar to what we had with both Either and Option. orElse gets another IO value that is used only if the original one is *not successful*. Option's unsuccessful case is None, Either's is Left, and IO's is a side-effectful IO action that fails (throws an exception) after it's executed.

Here's yet another way to look at how orElse works:

```
val p = IO.delay( ⚡ ).orElse(IO.pure(■))
→ IO[ ⬚ ]
p.unsafeRunSync()
→ ■
```

orElse needs an IO value as its parameter, just like Option.orElse needs an Option and Either.orElse needs an Either. Did you notice how, this time, we used IO.pure to produce an IO that always succeeds with a hardcoded value?

```
val alwaysSucceeds: IO[Int] = IO.pure(42)
```

As the name suggests, the code we pass to IO.delay is not evaluated (it's *delayed*) until we call unsafeRunSync() on this IO or another IO value that uses this IO. On the other hand, IO.pure **evaluates** the given code (in this case 42) **immediately** and saves it inside an IO value. This is a great example of the difference between lazy and eager evaluation.

> The code we pass to IO.delay is "stored" in a similar way closures are stored for later use. In case of IO, they are only executed once someone calls unsafeRunSync().

Lazy evaluation

Lazy evaluation of an expression is a delayed evaluation—it's not evaluated until it's really needed somewhere.

Function bodies are lazily evaluated. The code you write inside a function is not executed until the function is called.
Code passed to IO.delay is also lazily evaluated. The following will always succeed (both value creation and unsafeRunSync() call.)

```
val program = IO.pure(2022).orElse(
  IO.delay(throw new Exception())
)
→ IO[Int]   This will never get executed!
program.unsafeRunSync()
→ 2022
```

Eager evaluation

Eager evaluation of an expression is an immediate evaluation—the code is executed (evaluated) in the same place it's defined, immediately.

Value definitions are eagerly evaluated. The code you write on the right side of the equals sign is executed rightaway.
Code passed to IO.pure is also eagerly evaluated. The following will fail at the value creation because the code is eagerly evaluated and always throws an exception.

```
val program = IO.pure(2022).orElse(
  IO.pure(throw new Exception())
)
→ Exception thrown
```

The exception is evaluated eagerly—we didn't even call unsafeRunSync because we had no value to call it on!

The same techniques are used in IO types from other functional languages!

Implementing recovery strategies using `IO.orElse`

Let's first implement the *single retry* strategy we implemented imperatively using try-catches but this time using IO and its `orElse` function. It should be pretty straightforward knowing what we know.

```
calendarEntries("Alice").orElse(calendarEntries("Alice"))
```

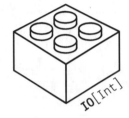

calendarEntries("Alice") returns an IO value that describes a program, which, when executed, will try to call the external API and return a list of calendar entries (MeetingTimes).

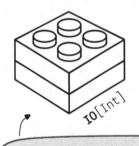

`orElse` returns another IO value that describes a program, which, when executed, will try to execute the program described by the original IO, and only if that one fails, it will try to execute the program described by the IO value passed to `orElse` as an argument (which happens to be yet another call to `calendarEntries("Alice")`).

This IO value describes a program that implements the *single retry* recovery strategy!

And that's it! The good news is that once you get accustomed to IO being just a value, it becomes very easy to implement many—supposedly complex—strategies, involving not only retries but also fallbacks, backoffs, and cached values, some of which we'll see later in the chapter. `orElse` works as one may expect, having had only some exposure to `Either` and `Option`. That's a big win too, you must agree.

One more important thing to discuss is that `orElse` returns IO, which means **we can chain orElse calls as many times as we want** to create bigger, more complicated IO values from smaller ones. We'll use this a lot, but before we do, let's make sure we are on the same page.

Quick exercise

Write down an expression that creates an IO value that describes a program that will retry `calendarEntries` two times.

Answer:
```
calendarEntries(...)
.orElse(
calendarEntries(...)
).orElse(
calendarEntries(...)
)
```

Implementing fallbacks using orElse and pure

> **Problem 2**
>
> **If any of the three external API calls fails, the whole function fails.**

Let's use the power of orElse chaining with lazy and eager evaluation of IO constructors (IO.delay and IO.pure, respectively) to create a more complicated recovery strategy encoded as a *single* IO value. We can use IO.pure as a last call in our orElse chain because we know it will always succeed. We know it will always succeed because the expression we pass to IO.pure is evaluated eagerly. When we use a value created using IO.pure as an argument to the last orElse call in the chain, we get ourselves an IO value that, when executed, **will never fail**. That's how we can implement yet another recovery strategy that first does a retry, and if it fails again, it uses a **safe fallback value**.

```
calendarEntries("Alice")
  .orElse(calendarEntries("Alice"))
  .orElse(IO.pure(List.empty))
```

An IO value that describes the following behavior: call the side-effectful IO action, and return results if it's successful. If it fails, retry max one time. If the retry fails, return an IO value that will always succeed and return an empty list.

> **Q** Is it OK to just return an empty list if the call to an external API fails two times in a row?
>
> **A** It depends! Note that right now we are just discussing tools that we can use to implement different failure recovery strategies. However, it's very important to understand how these strategies may affect business logic. Returning an empty list may or may not be OK in a given business context. We will continue discussing this trade-off when we cover functional architecture in more depth later in the chapter.

we'll discuss it soon in the "Functional architecture" section.

To sum it up, all of the following are values that describe different programs that have different failure recovery behaviors.

```
calendarEntries("Alice")
  .orElse(calendarEntries("Alice"))
```

An IO value that describes the following behavior: call the side-effectful IO action, and return results if it's successful. If it fails, retry max one time.

```
calendarEntries("Alice")
  .orElse(IO.pure(List.empty))
```

An IO value that describes the following behavior: call the side-effectful IO action, and return results if it's successful. If it fails, return an IO value that will always succeed and return an empty list.

```
calendarEntries("Alice")
  .orElse(calendarEntries("Alice"))
  .orElse(calendarEntries("Alice"))
  .orElse(IO.pure(List.empty))
```

An IO value that describes the following behavior: call the side-effectful IO action, and return results if it's successful. If it fails, retry max two times. If all retries fail, return an IO value that will always succeed and return an empty list.

Practicing failure recovery in `IO` values

It's time you try writing some code on your own. Here are two functions that return an `int` in Java and are not pure functions.

```
def castTheDie(): Int = {
  static int castTheDieImpure() {
    Random rand = new Random();
    if (rand.nextBoolean())
      throw new RuntimeException("Die fell off");
    return rand.nextInt(6) + 1;
  }
}
            import ch08_CardGame.castTheDie
```

```
def drawAPointCard(): Int = {
  static int drawAPointCard() {
    Random rand = new Random();
    if (rand.nextBoolean())
      throw new RuntimeException("No cards");
    return rand.nextInt(14) + 1;
  }
}
            import ch08_CardGame.drawAPointCard
```

Your task is to create three different IO values that describe the following programs:

1. Cast the die, and if it fails to produce a result, return 0.
2. Draw a card, and if it fails, cast the die.
3. Cast the die, and if it fails—retry once. If it fails again, return 0.
4. Cast the die, and draw a card, using a fallback of 0 for each of them. Return the sum of both.
5. Draw a card, and cast the die twice. Return the sum of all three or 0 if any of them fails.

> *Hint: Remember that everything in FP is an expression that produces a value.*

> These are impure and unsafe functions that may throw exceptions. They are written in Java as a convention we use in the book. We are wrapping them in Scala functions that you can conveniently import into your REPL session.

Answers

```
IO.delay(castTheDie()).orElse(IO.pure(0))
```
1

```
IO.delay(drawAPointCard()).orElse(IO.delay(castTheDie()))
```
2

```
IO.delay(castTheDie())
  .orElse(IO.delay(castTheDie()))
  .orElse(IO.pure(0))
```
3

```
for {
  die <- IO.delay(castTheDie()).orElse(IO.pure(0))
  card <- IO.delay(drawAPointCard()).orElse(IO.pure(0))
} yield die + card
```
4

```
(for {
  card <- IO.delay(drawAPointCard())
  die1 <- IO.delay(castTheDie())
  die2 <- IO.delay(castTheDie())
} yield card + die1 + die2).orElse(IO.pure(0))
```
5

> This for expression produces an IO value as well. We can therefore use orElse on the whole value and have a wider fallback.

Where should we handle potential failures?

Do you remember the multiple try-catches we needed to handle potential failures in the imperative code? Now compare this to the following IO-based different possible versions that use a single retry and a default value in case anything (including retries) fails. Whatever we choose, there is not much overhead because we operate on values, and we can implement failure handling on any level we need and want.

Yes, it's still not a perfect solution, but it shows failure-handling logic. We will build an even safer version soon, using the same concepts!

1 The first option is to implement failure handling in `calendarEntries`. Then, we don't need to change `schedule` at all:

```
def calendarEntries(name: String): IO[List[MeetingTime]] = {
  IO.delay(calendarEntriesApiCall(name))
    .orElse(IO.delay(calendarEntriesApiCall(name)))
    .orElse(IO.pure(List.empty))
}
```

2 The second option is to implement failure handling at the level of the `scheduledMeetings` helper function:

```
def scheduledMeetings(person1: String,
                      person2: String): IO[List[MeetingTime]] = {
  for {
    person1Entries <- calendarEntries(person1)
                        .orElse(calendarEntries(person1))
                        .orElse(IO.pure(List.empty))
    person2Entries <- calendarEntries(person2)
                        .orElse(calendarEntries(person2))
                        .orElse(IO.pure(List.empty))
  } yield person1Entries.appendedAll(person2Entries)
}
```

3 The third option is to implement failure handling at the level of the `schedule` function:

```
def schedule(person1: String, person2: String,
             lengthHours: Int): IO[Option[MeetingTime]] = {
  for {
    existingMeetings <- scheduledMeetings(person1, person2)
      .orElse(scheduledMeetings(person1, person2))
      .orElse(IO.pure(List.empty))
    meetings = possibleMeetings(existingMeetings, 8, 16, lengthHours)
  } yield meetings.headOption
}
```

You can use any of the three approaches above or mix them up! The final decision depends on many factors, including business logic context and general architecture of handling failures. The key takeaway is that you have lots of possibilities by using IO values alone. We will choose the third one for now.

Toward functional IO with failure handling

Introducing IO has already solved two of the three problems we encountered in the imperative solution earlier in the chapter. We now have code that is able to handle failures by describing complicated recovery strategies without impeding the business logic flow (that, in turn, has a major impact on readability and maintainability). We compared the functional way to the imperative Java version, where the business logic got lost inside many lines of try-catches and related mechanisms.

```scala
def schedule(person1: String, person2: String,
            lengthHours: Int): IO[Option[MeetingTime]] = {
  for {
    existingMeetings <- scheduledMeetings(person1, person2)
      .orElse(scheduledMeetings(person1, person2))
      .orElse(IO.pure(List.empty))
    meetings = possibleMeetings(existingMeetings, 8, 16, lengthHours)
  } yield meetings.headOption
}
```

Remember that our solution still doesn't persist any meetings—it doesn't call one of the required `createMeetingApiCall` functions—when it finds a free slot. We will deal with that at the end of the chapter.

This problem will also be solved as an IO value, but since this is an output action, we need to discuss some caveats around it.

We can, however, transform a failure into an error, explicitly, by transforming one value into another, of course. We'll show that in the last part of the book.

Failure vs. errors

Have you noticed that we've been discussing failures—not errors—in this chapter? When we say *failure*, we usually mean a problem that presents itself when running some unsafe, side-effectful code: connection dropped, server unexpectedly failed, and so on. We use *error* to indicate some business-level errors, such as *user provided wrong password* or *provided* `String` *cannot be parsed*. In chapter 6 we discussed error handling—there were no failures there!

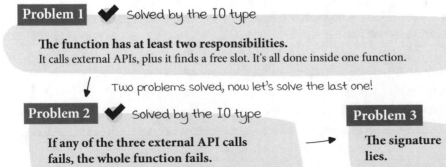

Problem 1 ✔ Solved by the IO type

The function has at least two responsibilities.
It calls external APIs, plus it finds a free slot. It's all done inside one function.

Two problems solved, now let's solve the last one!

Problem 2 ✔ Solved by the IO type

If any of the three external API calls fails, the whole function fails.

Problem 3

The signature lies.

Pure functions don't lie, even in the unsafe world!

Problem 3

The signature lies.

The third problem with the initial imperative solution we wrote was related to the old notion that we've been exercising since the beginning of the book. Compare the following two function signatures. The first signature is the imperative version, while the second is the functional IO-based version we've been tuning for a while. Which difference is the most obvious one?

Imperative `static MeetingTime schedule(String person1, String person2, int lengthHours)`

Functional `def schedule(person1: String, person2: String, lengthHours: Int): IO[Option[MeetingTime]]`

The signatures look similar; they both take three parameters, but they return a different thing: the imperative version returns a `MeetingTime`, while the functional version returns an `IO[Option[MeetingTime]]`. Which one lies, and which one tells the truth?

If a signature tells the truth, our job becomes much easier! We don't have to analyze all implementations to understand what can happen when we call a function. Additionally, the compiler has an easier job helping us out!

That was a leading question, wasn't it? We already know that the imperative `schedule` won't always return a `MeetingTime`, although it promises in the signature that it will! There are two ways in which it won't deliver on its promise:

1. There is a connection error retrieving calendar entries for a person, then the function throws an exception instead of returning a `MeetingTime`.

2. There is no common slot for a meeting of length `lengthHours` to be scheduled for both attendees, then the function returns `null`, which is not exactly a `MeetingTime` it promises us.

Now, compare this to the functional signature, which doesn't lie and always, no matter what, returns an `IO[Option[MeetingTime]]`. It tells us that this function **returns a value that describes a program that**

- Does some IO actions, which may potentially be side-effectful and fail for many reasons, including that they are dependent on the outside world (IO).

- When it's executed (later in the program) and succeeds, it will return an `Option[MeetingTime]`, which means that we need to take into consideration a possibility of `MeetingTime` not being there. Note that the signature forces us to handle this possibility by returning an `Option[MeetingTime]`.

If there were more than one possibility of business-related problems (not just a lack of a common slot), we might use `Either[String, MeetingTime]` to further describe such a possibility.

Functional architecture

Our software needs to do unsafe IO actions. But we also want to have as many pure functions as possible! We've been pondering the idea of a functional architecture since the beginning of the book. Since we've just learned about IO values, we can fully discuss how all pure and impure functions may work with each other inside a single software solution.

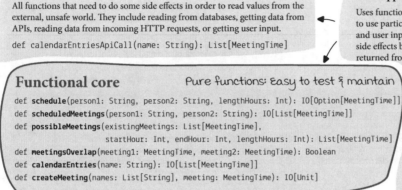

Input actions

All functions that need to do some side effects in order to read values from the external, unsafe world. They include reading from databases, getting data from APIs, reading data from incoming HTTP requests, or getting user input.

```
def calendarEntriesApiCall(name: String): List[MeetingTime]
```

Main application process

Uses functional core and "configures" it to use particular external world code and user input/output code. Executes all side effects by running all the IO values returned from the functional core.

```
val program: IO[Int] =
  ...
    ...
program.unsafeRunSync()
```

Functional core   Pure functions: Easy to test & maintain

```
def schedule(person1: String, person2: String, lengthHours: Int): IO[Option[MeetingTime]]
def scheduledMeetings(person1: String, person2: String): IO[List[MeetingTime]]
def possibleMeetings(existingMeetings: List[MeetingTime],
                     startHour: Int, endHour: Int, lengthHours: Int): List[MeetingTime]
def meetingsOverlap(meeting1: MeetingTime, meeting2: MeetingTime): Boolean
def calendarEntries(name: String): IO[List[MeetingTime]]
def createMeeting(names: List[String], meeting: MeetingTime): IO[Unit]
```

We will discuss output actions in depth soon!

Output actions

All functions that need to do some side effects to write values to the external, unsafe world.

The black arrows in the diagram indicate a *knows about* relation. That means all the functions inside the *functional core* can't directly access functions from the outside.

Q How is it possible to achieve? The calendarEntries function returns an IO and needs to call the calendarEntriesApiCall inside it, so it clearly knows about it! What's going on?

A So far we've defined calendarEntries and createMeeting as functions that directly call impure functions (wrapping them in IO.delay). However, we may use a different strategy and **pass these functions as parameters**! Then, the functional core knows only about their signatures, while the implementation is provided from the outside! We can say that we "configure" functions inside the functional core. We'll cover it next.

This is a very common pattern in FP. We extract all the possible business-related logic into pure functions that don't lie, bundle them together as a functional core, test them separately, then use them in the main process. This way the concerns are becoming more and more disentangled. **That is the foundation of the functional architecture.**

THIS IS BIG!
We push the impurity out of the functional core, so it's easier to test and maintain.

Using IO to store data

So far we've focused mostly on input actions—side-effectful actions that read values from the outside world. The schedule function implementation is still missing one final piece, which I'll ask you to do in the next exercise. Before this happens, we need to show how to handle output actions (i.e., side-effectful actions that write [or store, persist] values for later use). Fortunately, it doesn't differ much from what we've learned about input actions. Let's write a function, that returns a *description* of a program, that:

1. Gets a first name from the outside world
2. Gets a second name from the outside world
3. Finds a two-hour meeting slot for both names
4. Shows an Option[MeetingTime] when executed
5. Doesn't return any value

Note that we don't specify how the input is provided to the program. This is an important piece. We are leaving this decision to the client of our function.

We obviously can use the unfinished schedule function to find and return a potential meeting, but the most important things are the first three requirements. Let's do a step-by-step implementation of this function, which we'll call schedulingProgram. Treat this also as an example of a simple functional architecture that we've just discussed.

We'll cover the functional core idea in more depth in the last chapters of the book. Here, we'll just show how we can pass functions as parameters to "configure" a program.

❶ We start with the signature. Based on the requirements above, we can write:

```scala
def schedulingProgram(
  getName: IO[String],
  showMeeting: Option[MeetingTime] => IO[Unit]
): IO[Unit] = {

}
```

Our program needs to be able to get names from the outside world. That means it needs a description of a program that gets a String: IO[String].

This function returns a program that, when executed, doesn't return anything (Unit). Remember that Scala's version of the type void is Unit (you may think of it as a singleton type that only has one value). When a function returns an IO[Unit], we can assume that it exists only to describe some side effects. We may assume that this is an IO-heavy program (and lack of any result means we expect some kind of output action to happen—in this case we expect that it will *show* a meeting when executed). This function describes an **output action**.

Our program needs to be able to show a potential meeting. That means it needs a function that gets an Option[MeetingTime] and returns a description of a program that somehow shows it without doing anything more. Therefore, we expect that the client of the schedulingProgram function will provide a function Option[MeetingTime] => IO[Unit].

❷ We will work in the context of IO and order all actions sequentially; we'll need to use for comprehensions (flatMap):

```scala
def schedulingProgram(
  getName: IO[String],
  showMeeting: Option[MeetingTime] => IO[Unit]
): IO[Unit] = {
  for {

  } yield ()
}
```

We will now implement all the sequential operations inside this for comprehension.

We are yielding (), which is the only value of type Unit. This is a common expression when describing side-effectful output actions.

3 The first two steps of the program is to get two names from the outside world:

```
def schedulingProgram(
  getName: IO[String],
  showMeeting: Option[MeetingTime] => IO[Unit]
): IO[Unit] = {
  for {
    name1 <- getName
    name2 <- getName
  } yield ()
}
```

This is an expression that produces an IO[Unit] value that consists of two smaller programs (getName programs). When executed, this will execute the getName program twice and, if successful, will provide two String values: name1 and name2.

IO[Unit]

4 Then, the next step is to call the schedule function, which takes two Strings and the lengthHours integer:

```
def schedulingProgram(
  getName: IO[String],
  showMeeting: Option[MeetingTime] => IO[Unit]
): IO[Unit] = {
  for {
    name1 <- getName
    name2 <- getName
    possibleMeeting <- schedule(name1, name2, 2)
  } yield ()
}
```

The schedule returns an IO[Option[MeetingTime]], and since we are using flatMap (<- in the for comprehension), we extract Option[MeetingTime] and save it as possibleMeeting value.

Remember how flatMap works? Essentially, each step is done sequentially, assuming all the previous steps succeeded. A failure is defined differently, depending on the type we are working with. For List it's List.empty, for Option it's None, for Either it's Left, and for IO–a description of a program that fails when executed.

5 The last step is to show the meeting using a description of a program that is passed as a parameter:

```
def schedulingProgram(
  getName: IO[String],
  showMeeting: Option[MeetingTime] => IO[Unit]
): IO[Unit] = {
  for {
    name1            <- getName
    name2            <- getName
    possibleMeeting <- schedule(name1, name2, 2)
    _                <- showMeeting(possibleMeeting)
  } yield ()
}
```

showMeeting is a function that returns an IO[Unit]. That means that we call it only to make sure its side effects are executed as a part of this program. We know that it will always return a value of type Unit (which has only one value: ()), so we save it as _ which in Scala means *an unnamed value*.

6 We now have a full implementation of the new program. The client can choose where and how this program gets names and how it outputs them. Let's assume that we want to use these two imported functions:

```
def consolePrint(message: String): Unit   import ch08_SchedulingMeetings.consolePrint

def consoleGet(): String                  import ch08_SchedulingMeetings.consoleGet
```

These two impure, imperative functions use console to get and print Strings. We want to use them as both input and output actions of the scheduling program above. Is it possible? **How would you approach that?**

7 Now, we are far outside the functional core. We want to use the new `schedulingProgram` function and configure it to use `console` as both user input and output. (Configuring is just a fancier name for passing arguments to a function!) Note that the `schedulingProgram` function doesn't know anything about impure functions it calls. This is a concern of its client. It could configure it to use HTTP or a GUI, or even something different like stubbed values in tests (using `IO.pure`, for example!). `schedulingProgram` knows only as much as it should.

```
def consolePrint(message: String): Unit    Prints a given message to the console output

def consoleGet(): String    Gets a single line from the console input
```

> We use the two impure, imperative functions that use `console` and wrap them in `IO.delay`. The first parameter is an `IO` value we create directly. The second is a function, so we pass an anonymous function as an argument.

```
schedulingProgram(
  IO.delay(consoleGet()),
  meeting => IO.delay(consolePrint(meeting.toString))
).unsafeRunSync()
```

> We call `schedulingProgram` with these arguments, and we get an `IO[Unit]` value back, which is a `console`-based scheduling app. We then run it using `unsafeRunSync()`. What we get is a program execution that waits for two names to be read from the console and then prints a `Some` or `None` value, depending on what names were given and what `calendarEntriesApiCall` returned (or an empty list if it failed two times).

That's all! We've written another small function that is very versatile. It returns an `IO[Unit]`, so we know it's heavy on side effects, and its main responsibility will be to output something important in a way that is required by the user. It could be a console application, like we showed, or something totally different. It doesn't really matter as far as the `schedulingProgram` implementation is concerned. The function, through its signature, requires its clients to choose the IO actions implementation themselves. We could say that concerns are disentangled: the `schedulingProgram` concern is the sequence of operations (get two names, run scheduling program, and show the result), while the concern of its client (and probably the main application process) is to choose the interface. One way to look at this is that `schedulingProgram` represents an **essential concern**, while the rest is an **accidental concern**.

FP provides tools that allow you to disentangle concerns in your specific application. However, the most difficult job still lies in your hands: deciding what are essential concerns (directly related to your business domain) in your application and what are accidental ones. In the `schedule` function we've implemented, you may say that the retry logic is not an essential concern: the crucial thing is that we get a value. And that may be true. However, if we add a fallback value, doesn't it impact the business logic at least a little bit? It probably does, so it may be essential after all. There are no universal answers to this question, and I won't try to provide one. What's important is that concerns are visible in the code, preferably in pure function signatures. You should aim to put as many essential concerns as possible inside pure functions, and they should be the core of your application—the **functional core**.

Remember, you need to provide a configuration of thread pools that will be used to execute an IO (done automatically in our REPL). It's also done outside of the functional core!

THIS IS BIG!
In FP, we strive to put as many essential concerns as possible inside pure functions.

For more information about this I recommend reading the "Out of the Tar Pit" paper (Moseley & Marks, 2006.)

Coffee break:
Using IO to store data

There is still one thing that we haven't solved yet in our original problem. Here's the schedule function we've implemented so far:

```
def schedule(person1: String, person2: String,
             lengthHours: Int): IO[Option[MeetingTime]] = {
  for {
    existingMeetings <- scheduledMeetings(person1, person2)
      .orElse(scheduledMeetings(person1, person2))
      .orElse(IO.pure(List.empty))
    meetings = possibleMeetings(existingMeetings, 8, 16, lengthHours)
  } yield meetings.headOption
}
```

And here are the requirements we were tasked to implement at the beginning of this chapter.

> ### Requirements: Meeting scheduler
>
> 1. For given two attendees and a meeting length, your function should be able to find a common free slot.
> 2. Your function should persist the meeting in the given slot in all attendees' calendars.
> 3. Your function should use impure functions that talk with the outside world, **calendarEntriesApiCall** and **createMeetingApiCall** without modifying them. (Assume they are provided by some external client library.)

See? We've implemented the first requirement and part of the third one! You now need to add the functionality to persist a potential meeting using the provided side-effectful createMeetingApiCall function without changing it.

```
def createMeetingApiCall(names: List[String],
                         meetingTime: MeetingTime): Unit = {
  static void createMeetingApiCall(
    List<String> names,
    MeetingTime meetingTime) {
    Random rand = new Random();
    if(rand.nextFloat() < 0.25) throw new RuntimeException("🍪");
    System.out.printf("SIDE-EFFECT");
  }
}
  import ch08_SchedulingMeetings.createMeetingApiCall
```

> We already created a function that should be used in this case, but we haven't used it yet. It's called createMeeting, and it returns an IO[Unit] value. It describes a program that, when executed, will call the impure API function that stores the given meeting for given names (see left). You should be able to quickly recreate it in this exercise if it's not already in your REPL.

Your task is to change the schedule function above, so it returns a program that not only finds and returns a potential meeting but also stores it for later, using the provided output action. **As a bonus exercise,** think about a recovery strategy for a createMeeting call. Please take your time, and try to solve it before looking at the answer.

Hint: Remember that Unit has only one value: (). You can use IO.pure(()) as an IO[Unit] value. Also, check out the IO.unit function.

Coffee break explained:
Using IO to store data

One of the possible solutions can be written using only the things we've
learned so far, including pattern matching!

```scala
def schedule(person1: String, person2: String, lengthHours: Int): IO[Option[MeetingTime]] = {
  for {
    existingMeetings <- scheduledMeetings(person1, person2)
                        .orElse(scheduledMeetings(person1, person2))
                        .orElse(IO.pure(List.empty))
    meetings = possibleMeetings(existingMeetings, 8, 16, lengthHours)
```

> First, we need to create another value, meetings, which is a list returned by
> possibleMeetings. Remember that possibleMeetings returns a List[MeetingTime] (not
> wrapped in an IO because it doesn't do any IO!), so we need the = operator. We use headOption
> on this list to return the first meeting wrapped in Some, or None if the list is empty.

```scala
    possibleMeeting = meetings.headOption
    _ <- possibleMeeting match {
        case Some(meeting) => createMeeting(List(person1, person2), meeting)
        case None          => IO.unit // same as IO.pure(())
    }
  } yield possibleMeeting
```

} value of
type
IO[Unit]

> Then we pattern match on possibleMeeting, which is an Option[MeetingTime]. Note that the whole
> pattern matching expression needs to be an IO value (because we are in the for comprehension that works
> on IO values, plus we use the <- operator). Both cases should return values of the same type—in our case,
> it's an IO[Unit]. If a meeting is found (case Some(meeting)), the expression becomes an IO[Unit] value
> created by calling the createMeeting function. If no meetings are found (case None), the expression
> becomes an IO.unit value, which is a pure IO[Unit] value (evaluated eagerly). It will always succeed and
> won't do any side effects when executed. This way the whole pattern matching expression has type
> IO[Unit] and compiles fine. It will also do the right thing when executed: it will call the
> createMeetingApiCall function only when a meeting is found.

Bonus exercise

> Note that the solution above provides a program that may fail if a call to createMeetingApiCall fails.
> But since createMeeting returns an IO value, we can use exactly the same approach (i.e., IO.orElse)
> to produce values that describe programs with some recovery strategies built in. For example:

```scala
case Some(meeting) => createMeeting(List(person1, person2), meeting)
                      .orElse(createMeeting(List(person1, person2), meeting)
                      .orElse(IO.unit)
```

> However, **output actions may change data stored externally**, so retrying them may not be the most
> safe approach, especially if these operations are not *idempotent* (i.e., can't be applied multiple times
> without changing the final result).

And it's solved! We've managed to write a function that implements all
requirements. Note how few lines were needed to implement this logic.
It contains the step-by-step flow and calls external APIs with simple
recovery strategies and safe fallbacks. It also says a lot about itself in its
signature. That's the power of functional programming!

Treating everything as values

At this point you should be very competent treating IO-based code as values. We've shown a real problem and its functional solution that takes advantage of all the tools and ideas we learned in previous chapters.

> Q OK, treating IO as values looks very useful, but I still feel this is too good to be true. There are multiple more IO-based problems that surely can't be addressed using this approach, can they?
>
> A You are in for a treat! We will spend the rest of the book showing even more advanced examples solved using the tools we've introduced here. We will play around with retries and executing an unknown number of programs before we wrap up this chapter. Then, we will talk about data streams and message-based systems. We are going to represent them as IO values as well. In chapter 10 we will address problems related to asynchronous and multithreaded computing. We will use IO values there, too!

Phil Karlton's wise saying is, "There are only two hard things in computer science: cache invalidation and naming things." We'll deal with caching later in the book. Here, we just present a sneak peek.

Caching and using cached values in case of a failure

Let's show how we can use IO in three more scenarios related to the meeting scheduler example. The first one is **caching**. Our current solution would definitely benefit from using a cache for scheduled meetings, so we can get a cached value when an API call fails. Generally, this is a topic we will discuss in depth later because there are multiple additional problems we need to consider, such as removing stale values from the cache, updating values in the cache, making sure the caches are consistent, and many others. Here, we will briefly show how could it be implemented using the IO type. **The whole solution is just three more functions**:

> calendarEntries
>
> Wrapper around impure API call. Returns a description of a program that returns a list of meetings for a given name.

```scala
def cachedCalendarEntries(name: String): IO[List[MeetingTime]]
def updateCachedEntries(name: String,
                        newEntries: List[MeetingTime]): IO[Unit]

def calendarEntriesWithCache(name: String): IO[List[MeetingTime]] = {
  val getEntriesAndUpdateCache: IO[List[MeetingTime]] = for {
    currentEntries <- calendarEntries(name)
    _              <- updateCachedEntries(name, currentEntries)
  } yield currentEntries
  cachedCalendarEntries(name).orElse(getEntriesAndUpdateCache)
}
```

We don't show the implementation but you will be able to code it after reading chapter 10. Note that these two functions need to use the same mutable data store. It can be an in-memory variable or an API like Redis or memcached.

Treating retries as values

The second small improvement we can make to the meeting scheduler is a more universal approach to retries. So far we've been retrying once and then falling back to an empty list:

```
scheduledMeetings(person1, person2)
  .orElse(scheduledMeetings(person1, person2))
  .orElse(IO.pure(List.empty))
```

But what if wanted to use 3 retries, or 7, or 10? Would we need to write orElse(scheduledMeetings(person1, person2)) 10 times? That would work, but it wouldn't be a very handy or readable solution. Moreover, the number of retries is usually passed from an environmental variable or a configuration file (i.e., from the *outside*). So we can't really use this approach. We need to retry a given, unknown, number of times. We need **configurable retry strategies**.

```
def retry[A](action: IO[A], maxRetries: Int): IO[A]
```

> Note that the retry function doesn't care what A type is because it is not going to work with its values at all. It will only work with the IO value and the Int value. So A can be a List, an Int, a String, a Unit, or even another IO. Anything.

This new retry function is generic with regard to the type, just like a List[A] is. It takes a value named action, which has type IO[A]—a description of an action that produces a value of type A and a maximum number of retries when this action fails (the maxRetries parameter). Note that the function returns another description of a program that, when executed successfully, returns a value of type A. Before we implement it, let's see how can we would use it.

```
retry(scheduledMeetings(person1, person2), 10)
  .orElse(IO.pure(List.empty))
```

> scheduledMeetings(person1, person2) is the IO value that represents a program we want to retry. If it fails, it is going to be retried a maximum of 10 times. If all retries fail, we will return an empty list using orElse.

So how can we implement the retry function? You already know every tool and mechanism we need to do it. But it still may not be clear to you how to approach this problem. **The key here is to start thinking in terms of values**. We need to think about a list of programs in exactly the same way we thought about a list of possible meeting slots.

> **THIS IS BIG!** Functional programmers treat everything as values.

❶ Let's start simple. If we wanted to retry maximum once, we'd need the following:

```
def retry[A](action: IO[A], maxRetries: Int): IO[A] = {
  action.orElse(action)
}
```

> We will approach this implementation gradually and use the help of our old friend: the compiler.

> Our first approach to writing the retry function is to ignore the maxRetries parameter and use a fixed number of retries: in this case we use orElse once, so if the action fails, this function will retry a maximum of one time.

❷   Generally, if we wanted to retry a fixed number of times, we'd need a fixed amount of orElses:

```
def retry[A](action: IO[A], maxRetries: Int): IO[A] = {
  action.orElse(action).orElse(action).orElse(action)
}
```

> Here, we use orElse three times, so that means a program described by the action value, in case it fails three times in a row, will be retried three times. This is the outcome we want when we pass maxRetries = 3.

❸   Now, let's switch the mindset to the value-based one. We know that if we want to retry a maximum of one time, we need a value produced by calling orElse once. When we want to retry a maximum of three times, we need a value produced by calling orElse three times. Therefore, to implement the real version of retry, we need a value produced by calling orElse maxRetries times. We can achieve this by creating a list of maxRetries elements first.

```
def retry[A](action: IO[A], maxRetries: Int): IO[A] = {
  List.range(0, maxRetries)
}
```
Note that this doesn't compile yet, because types don't match.

> List.range creates an incremental list of integers, starting with the value provided as the first argument and ending with an integer one smaller than the one provided as the second argument. So, for maxRetries = 3 we'd get the List(0, 1, 2).

❹   Now we have a list with the exact amount of retries we need. But we don't need integers, we need actions themselves. Enter map:

```
def retry[A](action: IO[A], maxRetries: Int): IO[A] = {
  List.range(0, maxRetries)
    .map(_ => action)
}
```

> _ => action is a function that takes an integer and returns an IO value. We use underscore _ to let the compiler know we don't need the int value, so we leave it unnamed.

> We map the list of integers with a function that changes each integer to the same action value. So, for maxRetries = 3 we'd get the List(action, action, action), which is a List[IO[A]].

❺   The last step is to somehow transform the list of IO values into a single IO value that will become the result of the retry function. Remember how we transformed a list of integers into one integer? We used foldLeft, which will work here as well!

```
def retry[A](action: IO[A], maxRetries: Int): IO[A] = {
  List.range(0, maxRetries)
    .map(_ => action)
    .foldLeft(action)((program, retryAction) => {
      program.orElse(retryAction)
    })
}
```
Yay! It compiles now!

> We fold the list of IO values by starting with program = action and then going through each element of the list (named retryAction) and appending it to the program using orElse. We end up with a value that describes the program passed as action, which is retried using orElse a maximum of maxRetries times.

Treating an unknown number of API calls as values

The third and final improvement we will make to the meeting scheduler is support for any number of attendees. The current version supports only one-on-one meetings between person1 and person2:

```
def schedule(person1: String, person2: String,
             lengthHours: Int): IO[Option[MeetingTime]]
```

Instead, we'd like to have a more generic and useful version:

```
def scheduledMeetings(attendees: List[String]): IO[List[MeetingTime]]
```

We can approach this problem with the same mindset we approach the retry function implementation.

1 We already have a list of names, so we can start with mapping each of those names to a program that fetches this particular attendee's meetings.

```
def scheduledMeetings(attendees: List[String]): IO[List[MeetingTime]] = {
  attendees
    .map(attendee => retry(calendarEntries(attendee), 10))
}
```

Again, note that this doesn't compile yet because types don't match. However, the compilation error is helpful because it pushes us in the right direction.

We map each of the attendees to a calendarEntries call, which will be retried a maximum of 10 times. We end up with a List[IO[List[MeetingTime]]], but the type of the returned value should be an IO[List[MeetingTime]].

Attendees: List(Alice , Bob) List of strings

After map: List(IO(List[🕐]),IO(List[🕐])) List of IOs

IO describing a program that fetches a list of Alice's meetings

IO describing a program that fetches a list of Bob's meetings

2 Since we have a list of IOs, we can use foldLeft again to fold this list into an IO value. This would be a little harder than with retry, because we'd need to use a flatMap inside the function passed to foldLeft. Generally, foldLeft is a very universal function, like map and flatMap, so it can be used in many different cases. However, we also have more specific functions that provide us with some folding logic out of the box. **Here, we can use the new sequence function:**

```
def scheduledMeetings(attendees: List[String]): IO[List[MeetingTime]] = {
  attendees
    .map(attendee => retry(calendarEntries(attendee), 10))
    .sequence
}
```

We sequence a List[IO[List[MeetingTime]]] into an IO[List[List[MeetingTime]]]. What sequence does is fold all IOs from a given list into a single IO that holds a list of their resulting values. We say that the List of multiple IOs is sequenced into a single IO, which runs all IOs and returns their results in a single List.

After map: List(**IO**(List[🕐]),**IO**(List[🕐])) List of IOs

After sequence: **IO**(List(List[🕐] , List[🕐])) IO of list of lists

We are very close to solving this function. We have a single IO that will call the API for each attendee and then return a list of results—one result per attendee. And since each result is another List, we end up with a List of Lists. We don't really need such a detailed result—we only need a list of *all* meetings for all attendees. That's why it's safe to just flatten the list of lists into a list of all elements from all lists. Remember that the list of lists is inside an IO—we still operate only on values describing side-effectful programs—so we need to flatten inside the second map call.

```
def scheduledMeetings(attendees: List[String]): IO[List[MeetingTime]] = {
  attendees
    .map(attendee => retry(calendarEntries(attendee), 10))
    .sequence
    .map(_.flatten)
}
```

Note that the first map operates on a List, while the second one operates on an IO returned by the sequence call.

It compiles now!

Inside the second map call we have a function that takes a List[List[MeetingTime]] and returns a List[MeetingTime]. That means that after map we have IO[List[MeetingTime]], which is exactly what the signature requires.

After sequence: IO(List(List[ ],List[ ]))   IO of list of lists

A list of Alice's meetings   A list of Bob's meetings

After and map: (+ flatten)   IO(List[ ])   IO of list

A list of Alice's and Bob's meetings

We now have the final version of the scheduledMeetings function, which we can use in the **final version** of the meeting scheduler that handles more than two attendees.

THIS IS BIG!
In FP, we "solve" a signature by providing the function body.

```
def schedule(attendees: List[String],
             lengthHours: Int): IO[Option[MeetingTime]] = {
  for {
    existingMeetings <- scheduledMeetings(attendees)
    possibleMeeting  = possibleMeetings(
                           existingMeetings, 8, 16, lengthHours
                       ).headOption
    _ <- possibleMeeting match {
           case Some(meeting) => createMeeting(attendees, meeting)
           case None          => IO.unit
         }
  } yield possibleMeeting
}
```

sequence and other functions don't work on Lists of IOs only. They work on Lists of other types we've met. For example, you can also sequence a List of Options into an Option of a List!

sequence, traverse, flatTraverse, **and more!**

The sequence function we've just met is just one of the possibilities to solve the problem of transforming a List of IOs into an IO of a List. The combination of map followed by sequence is so popular that there is another function that performs these two actions: traverse. Moreover, the combination of *traversing* followed by *flattening* is also a popular one; we use flatTraverse to do that. **You can have a look at all scheduledMeetings implementations using foldLeft, traverse, and flatTraverse in the book's source code.**

Practicing functional signature intuitions

We've learned a lot of new functions in this chapter. Many of them are variations of functions we met in previous chapters, but there are a few new ones as well. Before we move on to tackle streams of infinite IO values, let's see how well your *functional intuition* works. **Your task is to fill in the blank implementations of the following 40 function signatures.** You will need to use only functions that we've met so far. Hint: All the missing implementations are one-liners!

Example We are given the following two signatures:

```
def ex1[A, B](x: List[A], y: A): List[A]      = x.appended(y)
def ex2[A, B](x: List[A], f: A => B): List[B] = x.map(f)
```

Solution We provide implementations:

You can use your computer to check if your implementation solves the signature (i.e. *compiles*). Here, ex1 takes a list and an element and returns a list. One of the possible implementations is to append the element to the list. The second function, ex2, takes a list and a function from A to B and returns a list of Bs. That looks very familiar, because it's a map in disguise, and that's the correct answer.

```
def f01[A, B](x: IO[A], f: A => B): IO[B]

def f02[A](x: IO[IO[A]]): IO[A]

def f03[A, B](x: IO[A], f: A => IO[B]): IO[B]

def f04[A](x: A): IO[A]

def f05[A](impureAction: () => A): IO[A]

def f06[A](x: IO[A], alternative: IO[A]): IO[A]

def f07[A](x: List[IO[A]]): IO[List[A]]

def f08[A](x: Option[IO[A]]): IO[Option[A]]

def f09[A, B](x: List[A], y: List[A]): List[A]

def f10[A](x: List[A], f: A => Boolean): List[A]

def f11[A](x: List[A], zero: A, f: (A, A) => A): A

def f12[A](x: List[List[A]]): List[A]

def f13[A, B](x: List[A], f: A => List[B]): List[B]

def f14[A](x: List[A], f: A => Boolean): Boolean

def f15[A, B](x: Set[A], f: A => B): Set[B]

def f16[A](x: Set[A], f: A => Boolean): Set[A]

def f17[A](x: Set[A], zero: A, f: (A, A) => A): A

def f18[A](x: Set[Set[A]]): Set[A]

def f19[A, B](x: Set[A], f: A => Set[B]): Set[B]

def f20[A](x: Set[A], f: A => Boolean): Boolean
```

```
def f21[A, B](x: Option[A], f: A => B): Option[B]

def f22[A](x: Option[A], f: A => Boolean): Option[A]

def f23[A](x: Option[A], zero: A, f: (A, A) => A): A

def f24[A](x: Option[Option[A]]): Option[A]

def f25[A, B](x: Option[A], f: A => Option[B]): Option[B]

def f26[A](x: Option[A], f: A => Boolean): Boolean

def f27(x: String): Option[Int]

def f28[A](x: Option[A], alternative: Option[A]): Option[A]

def f29[A, B](x: Option[A], y: B): Either[B, A]

def f30[A, B](x: Option[A], y: B): Either[A, B]

def f31[A](x: List[Option[A]]): Option[List[A]]

def f32[A, B, C](x: Either[A, B], f: B => C): Either[A, C]

def f33[A, B, C](x: Either[A, B], zero: C, f: (C, B) => C): C

def f34[A, B](x: Either[A, Either[A, B]]): Either[A, B]

def f35[A, B, C](x: Either[A, B], f: B => Either[A, C]): Either[A, C]

def f36[A, B](x: Either[A, B], f: B => Boolean): Boolean

def f37[A, B](x: Either[A, B], alternative: Either[A, B]): Either[A, B]

def f38[A, B](x: Either[A, B]): Option[B]

def f39[A, B](x: List[Either[A, B]]): Either[A, List[B]]

def f40[A, B](x: Either[A, List[B]]): List[Either[A, B]]
```

Answers

(1) x.map(f) (2) x.flatten (3) x.flatMap(f) (4) IO.pure(x) (5) IO.delay(impureAction())
(6) x.orElse(alternative) (7) x.sequence (8) x.sequence (9) x.appendedAll(y) or prependedAll
(10) x.filter(f) (11) x.foldLeft(zero)(f) (12) x.flatten (13) x.flatMap(f) (14) x.forall(f) or exists
(15) x.map(f) (16) x.filter(f) (17) x.foldLeft(zero)(f) (18) x.flatten (19) x.flatMap(f)
(20) x.forall(f) or exists (21) x.map(f) (22) x.filter(f) (23) x.foldLeft(zero)(f) (24) x.flatten
(25) x.flatMap(f) (26) x.forall(f) or exists (27) x.toIntOption (28) x.orElse(alternative)
(29) x.toRight(y) (30) x.toLeft(y) (31) x.sequence (32) x.map(f) (33) x.foldLeft(zero)(f)
(34) x.flatten (35) x.flatMap(f) (36) x.forall(f) or exists (37) x.orElse(alternative)
(38) x.toOption (39) x.sequence (40) x.sequence

Summary

I hope you've enjoyed the ride and appreciate the versatility of pure functions operating on (IO) values. In this chapter we used a lot of things we had learned in previous chapters and took advantage of them to produce a real-world application that really does something that's visible for an end user.

Use values to represent side-effectful programs

We learned that side-effectful programs can be described using the IO type. We learned that it has two constructors: IO.delay, which takes a block of code (a closure) that is lazily evaluated only when the IO value is executed, and IO.pure, which produces a value immediately (eagerly evaluated). This IO value will always succeed and return the given argument when executed.

Use data from unsafe sources

We used this newfound power to call an external API that returns meetings for a given attendee. However, we learned that these kinds of calls are unsafe, meaning they may not behave exactly the same way each time they are called. One time they succeed, another time they fail with an exception. We learned that we can build values that describe recovery strategies like retries and fallbacks by using the IO.orElse function. We also noticed that intuition obtained using Option and Either helped a lot when working with IO.

Safely store data outside your program

We used the same approach to store data outside our program. The API that stores a meeting was called inside IO.delay, which delegated the responsibility of executing the side effect to its clients of our function. To do that, they need to call unsafeRunSync() in a different place of our codebase.

Indicate your code does side effects

The signatures of our functions indicate what they do. If a function returns a List[MeetingTime], we know it doesn't do any side effects because it's just a pure function that returns a list. However, if a function returns an IO[Option[MeetingTime]], we know it may execute some unsafe side-effectful, IO-heavy code when executed. It's all in the signature!

Separate pure and impure code

Finally, we learned about the **functional core** concept. We bundle all pure functions together and delegate the impurity to the clients, so they can configure them to use specific IO actions (like console, HTTP, or APIs).

CODE:
CH08_*
Explore this chapter's source code by looking at ch08_* files in the book's repository.

Note that we only talked about synchronous programs. We will use many of these concepts when we write multi-threaded applications.

We also discussed that retries and fallbacks may be relevant to the business logic, especially when we try to retry output actions.

If functions don't lie in their signatures, they become friendlier to developers; they are easier to test, maintain and refactor.

We also learned about essential and accidental concerns and that we should strive to put as many essential concerns as possible in the functional core.

In this chapter

you will learn

- how to declaratively design complicated program flows

- how to use recursion and laziness to defer some decisions

- how to handle IO-based streams of data

- how to create and handle infinite stream of values

- how to isolate time-dependent functionalities

> **"** Thinking is not the ability to manipulate language; it's the ability to manipulate concepts. **"**
>
> —LESLIE LAMPORT

To infinity and beyond

We have just learned how to read and write data using IO. In this chapter we will still use IO to represent our side-effectful programs as values, but our data will become much bigger—possibly infinite.

You have probably heard about data streams and streaming infrastructures. They have been very popular in recent years. The word *streams*, however, has become very overloaded and can mean different things to different people. Generally, streams were conceived to deal with incoming data that needs to be processed but doesn't fit in the memory. However, we tend to use it in other cases, too—it has become a way to architect the control flow in many applications. Hence, it's one of the possible software architecture choices and a very powerful one, too!

We will reuse a lot of knowledge about IO and its laziness. We will use sequence and orElse in this chapter, too! They really are ubiquitous in FP.

During the course of this chapter, we will show how functional programmers deal with streams of data in both use cases: as an architectural pattern and as a way to process big data. We will introduce the Stream type, which represents a description of streaming operations that, when executed, **emit from zero to an infinite number of values**. We will also put this Stream type in perspective of some of the existing stream-like solutions you may be familiar with, such as Java 8 streams, Java 9 reactive streams, functional reactive programming, or *MapReduce* systems.

We can also say that such a stream is unbounded. We will stick with using the infinity term in this chapter, though.

The learning process in this chapter consists of three steps. We will learn how to handle possibly infinite streams of data the functional way, starting with a version that uses only the IO type and ending with purely functional streams.

Step 1

Using only IO
We will try to implement the first version of this chapter's problem solution, using IO alone as a recap. This version will serve as a basis for comparing with other approaches.

On the side *To catch some breath, we will introduce two immutable data structures that are very important in FP: Map and tuple.*

Step 2

Using IO with recursion
We will try to address the need for an unknown amount of API calls by introducing and using recursion.

On the side *We will show and use a different approach to functional design: bottom-up. We will start with small functions and work our way up.*

Step 3

Using IO with Streams
In the last step we will show how to make API calls at a fixed rate and use sliding windows on possibly infinite amounts of incoming data. We will use the functional approach to a streaming architectural pattern and compare it to other versions of this pattern.

On the side *We will discuss separation of concerns and inversion of control.*

Dealing with an unknown number of values

We will try to *rediscover* the stream-based approach by implementing an online currency exchange that has the following requirements.

> **Requirements: Online currency exchange**
>
> 1. The user can request an exchange of a given amount of money from one currency to another currency.
> 2. A requested exchange should be performed only when the exchange rate between the given pair of currencies is **trending**, which means that each of the last n rates is higher than the previous one—for example, `0.81, 0.82, 0.85` is a trend, while `0.81, 0.80, 0.85` is not (for n=3).
> 3. We are given the API call function (`exchangeTable`) that fetches only the current exchange rates table from a given currency to all other supported currencies.

We will first try to implement the currency exchange using IO directly, recapping what we learned in the previous chapter. This won't be an easy task because the second requirement is a tricky one. We will need to call the external API many times until we get a trend. Hence, the **number of API calls that we need to make is initially unknown!** This is a new thing for us, but it's pretty common in real-world cases. We will figure it out in this chapter.

Example

A user wants to exchange 1000 USD to EUR, but only when the USD-EUR rate is trending (i.e., the last three exchange rates from USD to EUR are increasing).

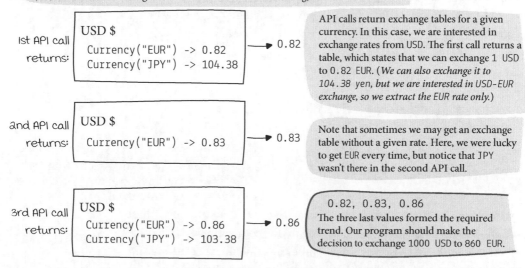

1st API call returns:
```
USD $
   Currency("EUR") -> 0.82
   Currency("JPY") -> 104.38
```
→ 0.82

API calls return exchange tables for a given currency. In this case, we are interested in exchange rates from USD. The first call returns a table, which states that we can exchange 1 USD to 0.82 EUR. (*We can also exchange it to 104.38 yen, but we are interested in USD-EUR exchange, so we extract the EUR rate only.*)

2nd API call returns:
```
USD $
   Currency("EUR") -> 0.83
```
→ 0.83

Note that sometimes we may get an exchange table without a given rate. Here, we were lucky to get EUR every time, but notice that JPY wasn't there in the second API call.

3rd API call returns:
```
USD $
   Currency("EUR") -> 0.86
   Currency("JPY") -> 103.38
```
→ 0.86

`0.82, 0.83, 0.86`
The three last values formed the required trend. Our program should make the decision to exchange 1000 USD to 860 EUR.

Dealing with external impure API calls (again)

To get current exchange rates for a currency of our choice, we will need to call an impure, external, side-effectful API. For demonstration purposes, we will use a simulated version, but as was the case in chapter 8, remember that in real-world applications this would have to be an HTTP client library that makes calls to a server that holds and updates current rates. Of course, all the caveats discussed earlier apply here as well. A call may randomly fail, take too long, or return some unexpected values.

Or it could be a different protocol, but this doesn't matter until we get raw Strings and numbers back. We don't care about the internal communication protocol.

```
def exchangeRatesTableApiCall(currency: String): Map[String, BigDecimal] = {

  static Map<String, BigDecimal> exchangeRatesTableApiCall(String currency) {
    Random rand = new Random();
    if (rand.nextFloat() < 0.25) throw new RuntimeException("Connection error");
    var result = new HashMap<String, BigDecimal>();
    if(currency.equals("USD")) {
      result.put("EUR", BigDecimal.valueOf(0.81 + (rand.nextGaussian() / 100)).setScale(2, RoundingMode.FLOOR));
      result.put("JPY", BigDecimal.valueOf(103.25 + (rand.nextGaussian())).setScale(2, RoundingMode.FLOOR));
      return result;
    }
    throw new RuntimeException("Rate not available");
  }

}    import ch09_CurrencyExchange.exchangeRatesTableApiCall
```

The implementation of this function is not important here, so please do not try to remember what it really does inside. The thing that we need to remember is its interface because this is something we are going to use throughout this chapter. So exchangeRatesTableApiCall takes a String, which is a name of the currency we want to exchange, and returns a Map of all available currencies we can exchange to. Each entry in this Map is a pair of String and BigDecimal—a name of a currency we can exchange to and the rate we can use to do it. Let's see this in action.

We haven't introduced a functional immutable Map yet, but we will do it very soon. For now, just assume that it works like a Java HashMap or a Python dictionary.

```
> import ch09_CurrencyExchange.exchangeRatesTableApiCall
  exchangeRatesTableApiCall("USD")
  → Map("JPY" -> 104.54, "EUR" -> 0.81)

  exchangeRatesTableApiCall("USD")
  → Exception in thread "main": Connection error

  exchangeRatesTableApiCall("USD")
  → Map(JPY -> 102.97, EUR -> 0.79)
```

We got a Map that contains two entries. It means we can exchange 1 USD for 104.54 JPY or for 0.81 EUR.

We got another Map back on our third call, with different rates!

Here, we got an exception, which is expected when we use impure code. Your REPL session might look different, and you may get way more connection errors (or none if you are lucky).

Again, imagine that there is an external server that provides these exchange tables for us. We need to prepare for connection errors, other errors, dynamically changing rates, and even some unexpected missing rates (what if our third call returned a Map with only a JPY rate?).

The functional approach to the design

We know what we need to do and what tools we have at our disposal. Since we are FP programmers now, there are two design choices that we may blindly assume from the get-go. First is that we will use a newtype (see chapter 7) to represent a currency, instead of using a raw `String`:

```
object model {
  opaque type Currency = String
  object Currency {
    def apply(name: String): Currency = name
    extension (currency: Currency) def name: String = currency
  }
}
import model._
```

Second is that the external data will be available as an input IO action—an `exchangeTable` function that returns an IO value:

```
def exchangeTable(from: Currency): IO[Map[Currency, BigDecimal]]
```

It should return a description of a program that does some side effects and returns a `Map[Currency, BigDecimal]`. It needs to use the `exchangeRatesTableApiCall` impure function internally, but it needs to be wrapped using a function we met in chapter 8. **What was its name?**

We could also introduce a special type, or even multiple types, to wrap the BigDecimal type, which represents both rates and money. Can you come up with some suggestions?

Answer:
`IO.delay`

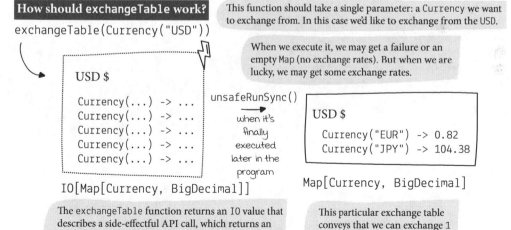

How should exchangeTable work?

```
exchangeTable(Currency("USD"))
```

This function should take a single parameter: a `Currency` we want to exchange from. In this case we'd like to exchange from the USD.

When we execute it, we may get a failure or an empty `Map` (no exchange rates). But when we are lucky, we may get some exchange rates.

```
USD $

Currency(...) -> ...
Currency(...) -> ...
Currency(...) -> ...
Currency(...) -> ...
Currency(...) -> ...
```

`IO[Map[Currency, BigDecimal]]`

`unsafeRunSync()`

when it's finally executed later in the program

```
USD $

Currency("EUR") -> 0.82
Currency("JPY") -> 104.38
```

`Map[Currency, BigDecimal]`

The `exchangeTable` function returns an IO value that describes a side-effectful API call, which returns an exchange table for a given currency to other currencies. We don't know the rates because it's just a description of a program. No API call has been executed yet.

This particular exchange table conveys that we can exchange 1 USD into 0.82 EUR or 104.38 JPY. Other currencies are not currently available.

We now have the `Currency` model and a function that returns an IO. However, we can't implement this `exchangeTable` function yet because the API call it uses internally returns a **Map[String, BigDecimal]**, not a **Map[Currency, BigDecimal]**. We need to learn some new stuff first!

That's why we haven't shown its implementation yet. Calling `IO.delay` is not enough in this case!

Immutable maps

Let's dig into immutable maps. In Scala, we usually use the Map type. Treat this section as a break from all the IO-based code that we will need to come back to very soon. Since our API is returning a map-like structure, we have a great opportunity to learn about immutable maps in practice. It should be pretty straightforward now because at this point you have a pretty good intuition about immutable data structures. You've seen lots of them already!

> **Q** I thought this chapter would be about streams, not maps!
>
> **A** It is about streams! We will use the Map type not only to solve this chapter's task (online currency exchange) but also as a foundation to learn about more advanced stream operations. Additionally, the Map type is ubiquitous in programming, so it's a good idea to get acquainted. Stay tuned!

Map is immutable in Scala and other FP languages. Having immutable collections as a part of the standard library is one of the definitive FP language traits.

Map is an **immutable type that contains key-value pairings** (or mappings). It is parametrized using two types: one is the type of keys, and the second is the type of values. So a Map[Currency, BigDecimal] is a data structure that holds key-value mappings, where keys are Currency, and values are BigDecimal (we use BigDecimal because we work with money).

```
> val noRates: Map[Currency, BigDecimal] = Map.empty
  val usdRates: Map[Currency, BigDecimal] =
    Map(Currency("EUR") -> BigDecimal(0.82))
  val eurRates: Map[Currency, BigDecimal] = Map(
    Currency("USD") -> BigDecimal(1.22),
    Currency("JPY") -> BigDecimal(126.34)
  )
```

We use -> notation to represent a single key-value mapping. Note that we use => in functions.

1 EUR can be exchanged to 1.22 USD.

1 EUR can be exchanged to 126.34 JPY.

Obviously, just like with Lists and Sets, when you **add** a new key-value pair to a Map, you create a new Map value, leaving the original untouched.

```
> val updatedUsdRates = usdRates.updated(Currency("JPY"), BigDecimal(103.91))
  usdRates
→ Map(Currency(EUR) -> 0.82)
  updatedUsdRates
→ Map(Currency(EUR) -> 0.82, Currency(JPY) -> 103.91)
```

usdRates hasn't changed. It's still the same as above when we created it.

updatedUsdRates is a new Map value that holds two key-value pairs.

Note that we append something to a List using appended, and we update mappings in a Map using updated. Intuitively, to **remove** a mapping under a key, we use removed, and to **get** a value stored under a specific key, we use get. And that's all! That's how learning a new immutable data structure looks when you already have experience with other ones.

Think for a minute about the type Map.get returns. What if we want to get a value from a nonexisting key?

Practicing immutable maps

When learning a new immutable data structure, it's best to give a quick intro
and then go straight into coding. We've just gone through some Map operations,
and now it's time to write some code and learn the remaining ones. **Your first
six tasks are to create the following values** (replace ??? with actual code that
will produce the described values):

```
val m1: Map[String, String] = ???
m1
→ Map("key" -> "value")

val m2: Map[String, String] = ???
m2
→ Map("key" -> "value", "key2" -> "value2")

val m3: Map[String, String] = ???
m3
→ Map("key" -> "value", "key2" -> "another2")

val m4: Map[String, String] = ???
m4
→ Map("key2" -> "another2")

val valueFromM3: Option[String] = ???
valueFromM3
→ Some("value")

val valueFromM4: Option[String] = ???
valueFromM4
→ None
```

1 A map that contains a single pair: "key" -> "value"

2 A map that updates m1 and stores "value2" under "key2"

3 A map that updates m2 and stores "another2" under "key2"

4 A map that updates m2 and removes the "key"

5 A String value stored under "key" in m3

6 A String value stored under "key" in m4 (which doesn't have this key)

The last task is to write down the results of the five expressions below:

```
val usdRates = Map(Currency("EUR") -> BigDecimal(0.82))
usdRates.updated(Currency("EUR"), BigDecimal(0.83))
usdRates.removed(Currency("EUR"))
usdRates.removed(Currency("JPY"))
usdRates.get(Currency("EUR"))
usdRates.get(Currency("JPY"))
```

7 Five values created from the original usdRates map

Answers

1. val **m1**: Map[String, String] = Map("key" -> "value")
2. val **m2**: Map[String, String] = m1.updated("key2", "value2")
3. val **m3**: Map[String, String] = m2.updated("key2", "another2")
4. val **m4**: Map[String, String] = m3.removed("key")
5. val **valueFromM3**: Option[String] = m3.get("key")
6. val **valueFromM4**: Option[String] = m4.get("key")

7a. Map(Currency(EUR) -> 0.83)
7b. Map.empty
7c. Map(Currency(EUR) -> 0.82)
7d. Some(BigDecimal(0.82))
7e. None

Notice that Map.get returns an Option.
This should not come as a surprise. The
consistency of functional programming APIs
is much higher than imperative ones. That's
why knowing the Option type may be enough
to guess what Map.get returns. It returns an
Option because a value under any given key
may or may not be in the map.

How many IO calls should we make?

Now that we know how Map works, we can go back to our example. All we
have at our disposal is the function that makes an unsafe API call for a
currency and returns a Map back. What should our next step be?

> We will go back to the
> problem of wrapping this
> API call in an IO-based
> function soon.

Let's think about the task description in more detail. Remember that
a single API request provides a single exchange rate. This introduces a big
problem when we think in terms of one of the requirements.

> A requested exchange should be performed only when the exchange
> rate between the given pair of currencies is *trending*, which means that
> each of the last n rates is higher than the previous one—for example,
> 0.81, 0.82, 0.85 is a trend, while 0.81, 0.80, 0.85 is not (for n=3).

Let's assume n=3 for now to simplify the thinking process. The requirement
says that we need to make decisions based on several currency rates.
However, we don't know whether a trend will happen after the first three
API calls, or we'll need to make a hundred of them. **It's also possible that
we'll never find a trend at all!** In other words, we may imagine that, in
some circumstances, we may need to wait for a long time until a currency
rate changes in our favor. We need to be prepared to make a very large,
possibly infinite, number of IO calls.

Top-down vs. bottom-up design

We don't really know how to approach this problem. So far, we've been
making a fixed number of IO calls, and it has worked fine. Here, we'll
need something more. We can approach such a problem in two ways.
The first is to start at the *top* of our program, and the second is to start
from the *bottom*. FP allows us to use either approach. Up until now we
prioritized the top-down approach. We usually started with a signature
of a highest-level function that would be used by our clients and then
worked our way down, implementing smaller and smaller functions. If
we chose this approach again, we'd need to start with

```
def exchangeIfTrending(amount: BigDecimal,
                  from: Currency, to: Currency): IO[BigDecimal]
```

> This function returns a
> description of a program,
> which, when executed
> successfully, continuously
> checks exchange rates
> from the "from" currency
> to the "to" currency, and
> if they are trending, it
> exchanges the amount
> using the last rate. It
> doesn't finish successfully
> (or at all) otherwise.

In fact, the signature above is exactly what we'll end up with at the end of
this chapter. However, right now there are too many unresolved problems
related to a possibly infinite number IO calls. We just wouldn't know
where to start. Thus, **we'll use the bottom-up approach instead!**

The bottom-up design

Even though the top-down approach is usually better—it enables us to focus on our client needs instead of technical obstacles—there are some cases in which we can't use it. Then, we need to fall back to using the bottom-up design, meaning we start solving smaller and easier problems first and build our way up to getting a fully working solution. This will also allow us to catch some breath before we tackle the difficult problem of a potentially infinite number of IO calls. Let's use the bottom-up design. What are the **small problems** that need to be solved and we can tackle right away?

As you can see, the top-down approach is about starting with a signature and implementing it. The bottom-up approach is looking for small problems and starting with them.

1 Checking if rates are trending

We know we need a function that decides whether a given sequence of rates is trending or not. That means we need a function with the following signature:

```
def trending(rates: List[BigDecimal]): Boolean
```

Here are some calls that explain how `trending` should work:

```
trending(List.empty)
→ false
trending(List(BigDecimal(1), BigDecimal(2),
             BigDecimal(3), BigDecimal(8)))
→ true
trending(List(BigDecimal(1), BigDecimal(4),
             BigDecimal(3), BigDecimal(8)))
→ false
```

2 Extracting a single currency from a table

We know that we'll need to deal with exchange tables for a single given currency—represented by a `Map[Currency, BigDecimal]`. When we make three successful API calls, we'll have three maps. For example:

```
val usdExchangeTables = List(
  Map(Currency("EUR") -> BigDecimal(0.88)),
  Map(Currency("EUR") -> BigDecimal(0.89), Currency("JPY") -> BigDecimal(114.62)),
  Map(Currency("JPY") -> BigDecimal(114))
)
```

We will have a list of multiple maps at hand, but we will only need a single exchange rate from each of them. In this case we need to extract the EUR rate from each map. Hence, a function called `extractSingleCurrencyRate` will come in handy:

```
usdExchangeTables.map(extractSingleCurrencyRate(Currency("EUR")))
→ List(Some(BigDecimal(0.88)), Some(BigDecimal(0.89)), None)
```

This function will need to return an Option because we can't be sure that all maps include a given currency. What would the result be if we used JPY instead?

Advanced list operations

We identified two small functionalities that we will most likely need in the final solution. We do not care about connections between them yet. We will just implement them in isolation and then look for the next challenges, going *up* in the solution blueprint.

Hence the "bottom-up" name.

Let's implement the `trending` function first. We will do it by introducing two new `List` functions, **drop** and **zip**, and a related new type: **the tuple**. Both *dropping* and *zipping* can be used for many collection types you already know, and we will use them in streams later in the chapter. Nevertheless, these are pretty powerful and worth having in your functional programmer toolbox (alongside all the others we have already met in this book—dozens of them, so far).

A naive trending implementation, assuming that the list always contains three elements may look like this:

```
def naiveTrending(rates: List[BigDecimal]): Boolean = {
  rates(0) < rates(1) && rates(1) < rates(2)
}
```

It's usually a bad sign when you implement a function that relies too much on a given list size and specific indices.

If you don't like this solution, welcome to the club. **It's a very bad solution!** We can't assume that any given list will always contain three elements. So the function above is not a pure function. It doesn't return a `Boolean` for all possible `List`s. It will fail for lists smaller than three elements and will not produce correct results for larger lists. We need something different, something better and more bulletproof—a real, pure function. Let's try implementing `trending` step by step:

❶ Traditionally, let's start with the signature and try to think about what should happen when a given list is small:

```
def trending(rates: List[BigDecimal]): Boolean = {
  rates.size > 1 && ...
}
```

If the list is empty or contains just a single element, there is no way that it forms a trend, so return `false`.

❷ Usually, when we want to get a Boolean based on a condition applied to all elements of a list, we need to use `forall`. Will it work here? Let's try:

```
def trending(rates: List[BigDecimal]): Boolean = {
  rates.size > 1 &&
  rates.forall(rate => rate > ???)
}
```

This won't work, because we need to somehow check whether each element is larger than the *previous one* in the list, so the function we pass to `forall` needs access to the current and the previous element at once to make an informed decision.

Introducing tuples

Is there a way out of this? Could we use the elegant `forall` function and still be able to safely implement the `trending` function without worrying about list indices and sizes? Yes, but we'll need a *tuple*!

Before we introduce it properly, let's talk about our use case. We failed to implement the `trending` function because a single element of the input list contained only a single rate. We could have used `foldLeft` to solve that, but there is another solution that may be a better fit. We need to make sure **a single element in the list contains all the information we need to make a decision**. In our case, a given list forms a trend if each rate is larger than the previous one. So for each rate, we also need access to the previous one. **We need a list of pairs**.

> Did you try to implement the trending function using foldLeft? foldLeft is a versatile tool, and you will find yourself reaching for it on many occasions. It's good to practice using it whenever you can.

```
> val rates = List(BigDecimal(0.81), BigDecimal(0.82), BigDecimal(0.83))

  val ratePairs: List[(BigDecimal, BigDecimal)] = List(
    (BigDecimal(0.81), BigDecimal(0.82)),
    (BigDecimal(0.82), BigDecimal(0.83))
  )
```

Given a sequence of three rates …

… we'd like to be able to convert it to this list of two pairs.

Note that to define a tuple we use an additional set of braces: `(a, b)`.

Tuples

`(A, B)` is a two-tuple—a product type that consists of two values: the first is of type A, and the second is of type B. For example, `(String, Int)` is a tuple, `(String, Boolean)` is a tuple, and even `(String, List[String])` is a tuple. Generally, the tuple is an implementation of the product type, just like the `case class`—the only difference is that tuples don't have names, and the values they hold are not named as well. We also can use tuples with the same type (i.e., `(A, A)`). For example `(BigDecimal, BigDecimal)` is a tuple of two BigDecimals. `(BigDecimal(0.81), BigDecimal(0.82))` is a value of this type. `List[(BigDecimal, BigDecimal)]` is a list of tuples.

> There are also tuples that can hold a different number of values: for example, (A, B, C) is a three-tuple (triplet). (String, Int, Boolean) is one of its possible types. One of its possible values is ("a", 6, true). In this chapter, we'll use two-tuples only, sometimes called pairs or just tuples.

So `ratePairs` above is a list of tuples. Each tuple in this list consists of two values, each of the `BigDecimal` type. They are unnamed, but we will use the mechanism we learned about in chapter 7 to **destructure them into individual values**. They are product types after all, so we could achieve exactly the same result by creating a named tuple instead:

> Remember which mechanism that was? If not, we'll refresh you very soon.

```
> case class RatePair(previousRate: BigDecimal, rate: BigDecimal)
```

> This is analogical to a tuple (BigDecimal, BigDecimal).

Both of the following can more or less do the same job:

```
  val tuple: (BigDecimal, BigDecimal) = (BigDecimal(2), BigDecimal(1))
  val caseClass: RatePair = RatePair(BigDecimal(2), BigDecimal(1))
```

> However, they carry a different amount of information!

Zipping and dropping

We can create a list of tuples by **zipping** two lists together. For example:

```
val ints: List[Int]      = List(1, 2, 3)
val strings: List[String] = List("a", "b", "c")
ints.zip(strings)
→ List((1, "a"), (2, "b"), (3, "c"))
```

Given two Lists: a list of Ints and a list of Strings …

… using zip we can create a single list of (Int, String) tuples that contain corresponding elements from both lists.

In our case we could **zip** rates with itself:

```
val rates = List(BigDecimal(0.81), BigDecimal(0.82), BigDecimal(0.83))
rates.zip(rates)
→ List(
  (BigDecimal(0.81), BigDecimal(0.81)),
  (BigDecimal(0.82), BigDecimal(0.82)),
  (BigDecimal(0.83), BigDecimal(0.83))
)
```

But it's not exactly what we wanted. Here we just zipped two identical lists with each other. It's good to know that it's possible, and useful in some cases. This one is not one of them, though. We want to have a list of (BigDecimal, BigDecimal) tuples that contain the previous and the current rate. We need to **drop** the first element of the second list to be able to have pairs of neighboring rates. rates.drop(1) returns a new list with one element less than the original rates list. Practically, it drops n elements from the beginning of the list.

dropRight, on the other hand, drops from the end.

List(A B C).**drop**(1)

→ List(B C)

```
rates
→ List(BigDecimal(0.81), BigDecimal(0.82), BigDecimal(0.83))
rates.drop(1)
→ List(BigDecimal(0.82), BigDecimal(0.83))
rates.zip(rates.drop(1))
→ List(
  (BigDecimal(0.81), BigDecimal(0.82)),
  (BigDecimal(0.82), BigDecimal(0.83))
)
```

There are also alternatives like zipWithNext and zipWithPrevious that we could use here.

When we zip a three-element list with a two-element list, we get a new two-element list back because only two tuples can be safely created (the third element of the bigger list is ignored). There are more versions of the zip function in different libraries and APIs that cover more zipping outcomes (just like there are several versions of joins in relational databases). We will learn one more version later, when we will need to zip two infinite streams of values. But first, let's implement trending.

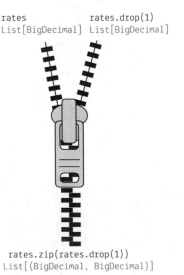

rates   rates.drop(1)
List[BigDecimal]   List[BigDecimal]

rates.zip(rates.drop(1))
List[(BigDecimal, BigDecimal)]

Pattern matching on tuples

Let's go back to implementing trending. We tried to use forall as the most natural way of checking if a condition holds for all elements in a list. We now have more tools in our inventory: drop and zip. Let's try again.

Note we are in the bottom-up design mode. We start with small functions and then use them in IO-based ones.

1 Traditionally, we start with the signature and try to think about what should happen when a given list is small:

```
def trending(rates: List[BigDecimal]): Boolean = {
  rates.size > 1 && ...
}
```

If the list is empty or contains just a single element, there is no way that it forms a trend, so return false.

2 Usually, when we want to get a Boolean based on a condition applied to all elements of a list, we need to use forall. Will it work here? Let's try:

```
def trending(rates: List[BigDecimal]): Boolean = {
  rates.size > 1 &&
  rates.forall(rate => rate > ???)
}
```

This won't work, because we need to somehow check whether each element is larger than the *previous one* in the list, so the function we pass to forall needs access to the current and the previous element at once to make an informed decision.

This is where we left off before meeting zip and drop.

3 Now we know what to do to implement trending using forall. We need to operate on a different list—one that holds tuples of BigDecimals: (previousRate, rate).

```
def trending(rates: List[BigDecimal]): Boolean = {
  rates.size > 1 &&
  rates.zip(rates.drop(1))
}
```

We zip the rates list with the same list that doesn't have the first element. This way, the first rate is zipped with the second rate, the second is zipped with the third, and so on. This way we get a list of tuples, each of them having both a previous rate and rate.

4 Finally, we can use forall, which returns true if all the elements in the list return true when applied to the function we pass as an argument. We can access and easily name both values in the tuple by destructuring it using a familiar pattern-matching mechanism.

```
def trending(rates: List[BigDecimal]): Boolean = {
  rates.size > 1 &&
  rates.zip(rates.drop(1))
    .forall(ratePair => ratePair match {
      case (previousRate, rate) => rate > previousRate
    })
}
```

Note how naming both values in the tuple improves readability.

ratePair is a tuple. A tuple represents a product type, just like the case class we have been using so far. We can destructure a tuple using the match-case syntax. This is a tuple of two values, so we name both values in the tuple and return true if the second value is bigger than the first one.

That's it! We coded the pure trending function that supports all list sizes.

Coffee break:
Working with maps and tuples

Now, it's your turn to play around with maps and tuples. **Your task is to implement the second small function in our bottom-up design journey**. Afterwards, we will have all the information and implementations to finally start working with infinite IO-based streams of values. Here's the signature of the function you need to implement:

```
def extractSingleCurrencyRate(currencyToExtract: Currency)
            (table: Map[Currency, BigDecimal]): Option[BigDecimal]
```

This is a curried function—it has two lists of parameters. It's a pretty common choice in FP when you plan to use a function with map. Here's how we imagine it may be used:

```
val usdExchangeTables = List(
  Map(Currency("EUR") -> BigDecimal(0.88)),
  Map(Currency("EUR") -> BigDecimal(0.89), Currency("JPY") -> BigDecimal(114.62)),
  Map(Currency("JPY") -> BigDecimal(114))
)

usdExchangeTables.map(extractSingleCurrencyRate(Currency("EUR")))
→ List(Some(BigDecimal(0.88)), Some(BigDecimal(0.89)), None)
```

Note how we pass a function from a Map to Option[BigDecimal]. This function is created by calling extractSingleCurrencyRate(Currency("EUR"))— note that only the first parameter list was used. This approach heavily improves readability; we map all the USD exchange tables we got (represented as Maps) with a function that extracts a rate to EUR from a given exchange table. Your implementation needs to use both parameters: the map representing an exchange table (table) and the currency we want to extract (currencyToExtract). If a given currency rate is present in the exchange table, return it as Some. Otherwise, return None.

Please make sure your implementation satisfies the use case defined above before proceeding. It'd be a good idea to come up with some additional tests, too. What if we want to extract yen (JPY)? Or BTC?

Hints

1. All functions you know from **Lists**, like **map** or **filter**, work on **Maps** too. However, remember they operate on key-value tuples.
2. **Map** has a **values** function that returns an **Iterable**, which has many functions similar to **List**, including **headOption**.

Note that we don't have any special exercise for the drop and zip functions. At this point you should be able to learn new pure functions in a breeze. If any of them cause problems, the chapter's source code in the book repository is your friend.

Here are few exchange tables for USD. You may interpret this as a list of three API call results. Note that one of the results doesn't contain an exchange rate to EUR.

Additionally, note how using the ubiquitous map function helped us frame the problem differently: instead of extracting an EUR rate from all exchange tables, we can focus on a single exchange table.

The use case presented above is like a test: you need to call a function with an input and expect a specific output.

Coffee break explained: Working with maps and tuples

The function can be solved in multiple different ways, but there is one way that is the most reasonable. If you got it, congratulations! However, if you did it differently, don't worry. Generally, if you tested your implementation against the test cases proposed in the task description, you can be pretty sure that your solution is correct. Here, we will show two possible approaches to solving this exercise. One of them uses filter and treats the Map as a list of tuples, while the second uses Map.get directly. The latter is superior, because the **function we asked to implement is in fact Map.get in disguise**. No matter which version is closer to your implementation, make sure you understand why these implementations are doing the same thing.

A situation when you first define a signature and then it turns out there is already a function that does exactly what you need is pretty common in FP.

Version 1 This is worse than the second one, but it shows how to do operations on tuples using pattern matching.

```
> def extractSingleCurrencyRate(currencyToExtract: Currency)
        (table: Map[Currency, BigDecimal]): Option[BigDecimal] = {
    table
      .filter(kv =>
        kv match {
          case (currency, rate) => currency == currencyToExtract
        }
      )
      .values
      .headOption
  }
```

Scala allows us to write this function in a more concise way, but we use only the basic syntax in this book. See Appendix A for details.

Map has the filter function defined as well. filter gets a tuple and needs to return a Boolean value that indicates whether this particular entry should be filtered. The function we pass to filter uses the pattern-matching syntax to destructure a tuple into two named values.

After calling filter we get a Map back that contains only filtered entries. Then, we call the values function that returns a list of values, in our case BigDecimals. We know that there will be a maximum of one entry (we filtered a single key), so we call headOption to get the first (and only) element of this list wrapped in Some, or None if it's empty.

Version 2 Did you notice that we asked you to implement Map.get?

```
> def extractSingleCurrencyRate(currencyToExtract: Currency)
        (table: Map[Currency, BigDecimal]): Option[BigDecimal] = {
    table.get(currencyToExtract)
  }
```

Map.get gets a key and returns an Option. If the provided key has a corresponding value inside the map, this value (wrapped in Some) is returned. Otherwise, None is returned.

We first defined a function that we need and then it turned out that a simple Map.get call implements it. We can now get rid of this function and use Map.get directly or we can leave the function as is because it explains more in terms of domain language.

Functional jigsaw puzzle

We just implemented two new functions based only on requirements.

```
def trending(rates: List[BigDecimal]): Boolean
def extractSingleCurrencyRate(currencyToExtract: Currency)(table: Map[Currency, BigDecimal]): Option[BigDecimal]
```

We also learned everything to finally wrap our impure API call in IO.

```
> def exchangeTable(from: Currency): IO[Map[Currency, BigDecimal]] = {
    IO.delay(exchangeRatesTableApiCall(from.name)).map(table =>
      table.map(kv =>
        kv match {
          case (currencyName, rate) => (Currency(currencyName), rate)
        }
      )
    )
  }
```

> An API call returns a Map[String, BigDecimal], so on top of wrapping it in
> IO.delay, we also need to transform its potential result using IO.map. We pass a
> function that transforms a Map[String, BigDecimal] into our domain model–
> based Map[Currency, BigDecimal] using pattern matching on Maps.

Since we are building bottom-up, we need to make a decision now:

1. **Are these functions enough to start building something bigger?**
2. **Are we still missing another independent small function?**

In this case we have all we need, so we can continue with #1. So how
exactly can we use these three functions?

Working with small functions means you need to look at their
signatures and find out which functions' inputs are compatible
with others' outputs. It's like solving a *jigsaw puzzle*—only some
pieces fit together. Let's take a look.

extractSingleCurrencyRate takes a Map[Currency, BigDecimal],
and exchangeTable returns a Map[Currency, BigDecimal], wrapped in
IO. Thus, we can fit these pieces together using a map call:

exchangeTable(Currency("USD")).map(**extractSingleCurrencyRate**(Currency("EUR")))

Similarly, we see that the trending function takes a List[BigDecimal],
while we only have an Option[BigDecimal] on our hands (returned
from extractSingleCurrencyRate). We also know that trending will
need lists of multiple elements to be able to detect a trend at all. Thus,
we need to fetch more BigDecimal-typed exchange rates before calling
trending. For simplicity, let's assume we only want to detect trends of
size three (for now):

```
> for {
    table1 <- exchangeTable(from)
    table2 <- exchangeTable(from)
    table3 <- exchangeTable(from)
    lastTables = List(table1, table2, table3)
  } yield lastTables.flatMap(extractSingleCurrencyRate(to))
```

from and to are Currencies. We are looking for a trend in rates between from and to.

Note that this flatMap works on a List and flattens internal Options by implicitly treating them as Lists of 0 or 1 element.

It turns out that this is an implementation of a very useful function!

Following types in a bottom-up design

Just by following types and analyzing the requirements, we ended up with a function that returns a description of a program, which, when executed successfully, will return a `List` of up to three last exchange rates of currencies: `from` and `to`. We will name this function `lastRates`. Remember that API calls and many other side-effectful functions are not safe, so we need to implement some recovery strategies. Here, we'll reuse the `retry` function from chapter 8 (with `maxRetries = 10`).

```
import ch08_SchedulingMeetings.retry
def lastRates(from: Currency, to: Currency): IO[List[BigDecimal]] = {
  for {
    table1      <- retry(exchangeTable(from), 10)
    table2      <- retry(exchangeTable(from), 10)
    table3      <- retry(exchangeTable(from), 10)
    lastTables = List(table1, table2, table3)
  } yield lastTables.flatMap(extractSingleCurrencyRate(to))
}
```

Note that generators in the for comprehension are flatMapping IOs, while flatMap in the yield expression works on a List.

Our newly discovered `lastRates` function takes a currency we'd like to convert `from` and the currency we'd like to convert `to`, and it returns a description of a program that, when executed, will return a list of exchange rates between these currencies. And that's exactly the `List[BigDecimal]` we need for `trending`!

That all means we can finally take the last step up and implement the last high-level function that exchanges money if rates are trending.

```
def exchangeIfTrending(
  amount: BigDecimal, from: Currency, to: Currency
): IO[Option[BigDecimal]] = {
  lastRates(from, to).map(rates =>
    if (trending(rates)) Some(amount * rates.last) else None
  )
}
```

We are returning the amount that can be exchanged using a rate, which is trending. In the real world, we'd probably need to persist it using an additional output action.

> trending
>
> A function that takes a `List[BigDecimal]` and returns a Boolean; it is true if the given rates list contains a trend.

We are done! `exchangeIfTrending` implements this chapter's requirements. We have a function that describes a program that will check last rates and exchange the given amount using the most recent rate, but only if the rates between the given currency pair have been *trending*. If not, it will return None. Obviously, you could plug in another IO value that describes an output action, which stores the resulting exchanged amount somewhere, transactionally. However, for simplicity, we'll skip this part and focus on other aspects instead.

After calling exchangeIfTrending, we could call flatMap and pass some other function that describes a program that stores the resulting exchange transaction externally.

Prototyping and dead ends

The functional jigsaw puzzle we just solved was not a particularly demanding one, but I hope it has shown that the bottom-up design is a perfectly fine approach, especially when working with pure functions and their signatures. We started small and have been *pushing upward* and learning quite a bit about a possible solution space and requirements along the way. **We have been prototyping.**

However, let's remember that we made some critical assumptions, such as fixing the number of rates that are taken into consideration in trend computation (we only take three for now). Some details were hardcoded and allowed us to focus on more important, higher-level aspects. However, the time has come to revisit them and decide whether this particular prototype is worth expanding into the final product.

It must be highlighted that most of the time **prototypes turn out to be dead ends**. And this is, unfortunately, true in our case as well. Let's recall the main requirement we were tasked to implement:

> A requested exchange should be performed only when the exchange rate between the given pair of currencies is **_trending_**, which means that each of the last n rates is higher than the previous one—for example, `0.81, 0.82, 0.85` is a trend, while `0.81, 0.80, 0.85` is not (for n=3).

There are several very important unknowns in our current prototype that disqualify it from being the final solution. Right now our prototype tries only the first three rates, checks whether they are trending, and exchanges a given amount if they are trending (which we signal by returning a Some that contains an amount of exchanged money in the new currency). However, if the first three rates are not trending, our function returns None and calls it a day.

We want something more useful: an app (a function) that will wait for a trend to happen and only then conclude with a successful exchange. In other words, the problem with the current implementation is that we fetch three rates and make a single decision. Instead, we'd like to fetch potentially thousands of rates and only make a decision when we stumble upon a trending sequence. Additionally, we'd like to be able to configure our function to use arbitrary sizes of trending sequences. We've used n=3 so far, but n=20 should definitely be possible as well without any additional hassle. How can we do this? We need to enter the world of possibly infinite IO calls we mentioned earlier in the chapter.

The first version of exchangeIfTrending function uses only the concepts we've learned previously.

Recursive functions

Step 2

Using IO with recursion

The problem we are facing right now is a very common one. We want to make multiple calls to an external API, but we don't know how many will suffice because it depends on the values this API produces—which we'll know only in the future! In other words, we'd like to be able to call exchangeIfTrending until it returns a Some. Hence:

```
lastRates(from, to).map(rates =>
  if (trending(rates)) Some(amount * rates.last) else None
)
```

If we end up in this case, we know that we don't have a trend, so we'd like to try again instead of returning None.

This is a job for **recursion**. We talk about recursion when something is defined in terms of itself. We will talk about **recursive functions** and **recursive values**. Let's start with recursive functions.

THIS IS BIG! In FP, we solve a lot of problems using recursion.

A function is recursive if it's used inside its own implementation (i.e., it's defined, at least partially, in terms of itself). If this sounds cryptic, let's try to apply this to our example. In our case we'd like exchangeIfTrending to try again in case no trend was found for the first three API calls. And how can we try again? By providing exactly the same program—that is, calling changeIfTrending internally!

```
def exchangeIfTrending(
  amount: BigDecimal, from: Currency, to: Currency
): IO[Option[BigDecimal]] = {
  lastRates(from, to).map(rates =>
    if (trending(rates)) Some(amount * rates.last)
    else exchangeIfTrending(amount, from, to)
  )
}
```
Compilation error!

We replaced the None with a call to the function we are defining. However, the compiler complains that exchangeIfTrending returns an IO in the else clause, while it expected an Option (previously, we had None there, and remember that the if-else expression needs to provide a value of the same type in both cases).

That means we need a flatMap (on IO) or a for comprehension. Additionally, we can't get rid of the IO from the signature, which makes us promote (*lift*) the if clause expression into an IO value and move it into the for comprehension (it's going to be flatMapped now, not mapped):

```
> def exchangeIfTrending(
    amount: BigDecimal, from: Currency, to: Currency
  ): IO[Option[BigDecimal]] = {
    for {
      rates  <- lastRates(from, to)
      result <- if (trending(rates)) IO.pure(Some(amount * rates.last))
                else exchangeIfTrending(amount, from, to)
    } yield result
  }
```

Both clauses are IO now; the compiler is happy.

Here is the recursive function call.

Remember how flatMap/map can be rewritten to a for comprehension like we did in chapter 5?

The result is an Option[BigDecimal], and because it's yielded from a for comprehension that works on IO values, the signature of the whole function is maintained. It's IO[Option[BigDecimal]]. **We have just defined a recursive function!**

Infinity and laziness

When you look closely at our recursive function, you will notice that if we never get rates that are trending, the function describes a program that will end up calling itself again and again without returning. So it's possible that when we `unsafeRunSync`, the `IO` value returned by this function, our application will keep working infinitely.

*Remember that we use `unsafeRunSync` to execute the program described by the given IO value. It's done **outside** of the functional core of the application.*

But again, since we are working with `IO`, this potentially infinite execution won't happen after calling the `exchangeIfTrending` function. The function call will just return an `IO` value that describes a program that may not finish at all, depending on external world values—in this case, exchange rates returned by API calls. So even though we described a possibly infinite program, we are on the safe side, while we keep working with `IO` values. This is possible because, as discussed previously, `IO` takes advantage of laziness (lazy evaluation). The code we pass to `IO.delay` is not executed, it's just saved for later execution.

If it sounds simple and repetitive to you, consider another example. We implemented the recursive function by calling itself inside the `flatMap` call and making use of its internal laziness. However, had we used recursion to directly create the value itself, without making any lazy calls, **we won't get any value back**. For example, calling the following function crashes or freezes the program:

```
def exchangeCrash(
  amount: BigDecimal, from: Currency, to: Currency
): IO[Option[BigDecimal]] = {
  exchangeCrash(amount, from, to)
}

exchangeCrash(BigDecimal(100), Currency("USD"), Currency("EUR"))
→ Exception in thread "main" java.lang.StackOverflowError
```

Note that we didn't even call unsafeRunSync. This failed before even returning an IO value! As you can see, we need to be very careful when using recursion. It worked fine when we used flatMap, but it didn't work when it called itself directly.

But we can still create a function that returns a program which, when executed, will never stop—it will go infinitely, unconditionally.

Additionally, did you notice that when you defined exchangeCrash, the compiler warned you?

```
def exchangeInfinitely(
  amount: BigDecimal, from: Currency, to: Currency
): IO[Option[BigDecimal]] = {
  for {
    rates  <- lastRates(from, to)
    result <- exchangeInfinitely(amount, from, to)
  } yield result
}

exchangeInfinitely(BigDecimal(100), Currency("USD"), Currency("EUR"))
→ IO
```

We use IO.flatMap. The recursive call will not happen until we get rates some time in the future. Note that we don't even use the rates value anywhere. Nevertheless, it will work fine—that is, it will not crash and return an IO value.

We properly got an IO value, which describes a program that will never finish. Note that we did not call unsafeRunSync again. We used the power of lazy evaluation to create an infinite program.

Recursive function structure

We were able to use flatMap and its lazy evaluation to create a recursive function that returns an IO value describing a potentially infinite program. There are, of course, more caveats and details—we are just scratching the surface here—but this insight alone should allow us to go very far. Remember that with great power comes great responsibility. Let's learn about these caveats first and then move on to functional streams, which use all these recursion techniques underneath but hide many details, so we can focus on solving business problems.

Infinity, laziness, and recursion go hand in hand in a lot of functional programs. This popular combination allows us to use descriptive expressions instead of imperative recipes.

We established that recursion is very important for functional programmers. However, building a proper recursive function may not be an easy task, especially when we start working with possibly infinite executions. The most important thing to remember is that we need to have a **base case** (i.e., a place in the function where it doesn't call itself). This will be the exit point of a recursive function call. This is the place that allows us to at least believe that it may be executed and return a result. Without a base case all bets are off. In our recursive function the base case is when we confirm that given rates are trending and the whole function returns an Option[BigDecimal].

> **THIS IS BIG!**
> Lazy evaluation, recursion, and potential infinite executions have a lot in common.

```
def exchangeIfTrending(
  amount: BigDecimal, from: Currency, to: Currency
): IO[Option[BigDecimal]] = {
  for {
    rates  <- lastRates(from, to)
    result <- if (trending(rates)) IO.pure(Some(amount * rates.last))
              else exchangeIfTrending(amount, from, to)
  } yield result
}
```

The recursion base case is here. When this if returns true, we don't recursively call the function itself. We return the eagerly evaluated value wrapped in IO.

Again, this function returns an IO, which, when executed, will return an Option[BigDecimal], fail, or never finish. We discussed failure handling earlier and all of these techniques still apply whenever you work with unsafe side-effectful code. Let's put failures aside for now and focus on the difference between getting a successful value and getting no result at all (meaning that the program, when executed, never finishes).

Quick question: Look closer at the function above. It returns an IO of Option. Is it possible that executing this program returns None? How?

The answer is on the next page (it's "no").

Dealing with an absence in the future (using recursion)

The `exchangeIfTrending` function claims that it returns an `IO[Option[BigDecimal]]`. When you look at the implementation, it all looks OK—if rates are `trending`, we will get an exchanged amount of money wrapped in `Some`. However, on closer inspection, there is no way executing an `IO` returned from this function can return `None`. Whenever we don't have a trend, we recursively call the same function, and then it can, again, return a `Some` or call itself one more time. And so on ...

Again, when we get trending rates, we return a pure value with no additional recursive calls. This is the recursion base case.

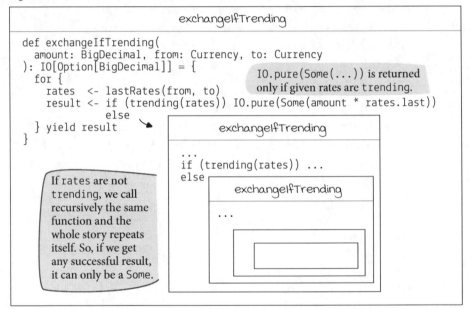

```scala
def exchangeIfTrending(
    amount: BigDecimal, from: Currency, to: Currency
): IO[Option[BigDecimal]] = {
  for {
    rates  <- lastRates(from, to)
    result <- if (trending(rates)) IO.pure(Some(amount * rates.last))
              else
  } yield result
}
```

IO.pure(Some(...)) is returned only if given rates are trending.

exchangeIfTrending
```
...
if (trending(rates)) ...
else
```
exchangeIfTrending
```
...
```

If rates are not trending, we call recursively the same function and the whole story repeats itself. So, if we get any successful result, it can only be a Some.

To sum it up, the program described by `exchangeIfTrending` can only return a `Some`, fail, or never finish at all. `Option` stayed in the signature unnecessarily when we rewrote the function from the version that didn't try to make an exchange until it succeeded, but it just fetched three exchange tables and made a decision. That's why we needed to indicate that the decision might have been negative (by returning `None`). Now, **we can model a possible absence of a trend with possibly infinite recursive calls instead of an `Option`.**

In other words, if there is no trend, the program doesn't return, but it continues to search for it, indefinitely.

```scala
> def exchangeIfTrending(amount: BigDecimal, from: Currency, to: Currency): IO[BigDecimal] = {
    for {
      rates  <- lastRates(from, to)
      result <- if (trending(rates)) IO.pure(amount * rates.last)
                else exchangeIfTrending(amount, from, to)
    } yield result
  }
```

The only two changes we need are the signature and the if clause. Note that we don't need to change the else clause because it already returns IO[BigDecimal].

Usefulness of infinite recursive calls

Q We just replaced a function that returns a program, which always returns something with a function that returns a program, which may not finish at all. Doesn't it mean that, from the user's perspective, such a program freezes (or *hangs*)? How's that better?

A It's better in a few areas. The most important one is separation of concerns. The function's responsibility is to create a program that will exchange a given amount of money when a rate is trending. That's all. It doesn't care about how many times it should try before giving up or how much time the user is able to wait for a result. These are different concerns! We only have a value that describes a possibly infinite program, and we know it will try to do its part. We can further transform this IO value into another IO value, which describes a program that times out after 60 seconds, 10 minutes, or trying 100 times. What's important is that these are different concerns, which we are still able to implement. Functional programming allows us to easily separate them from the business logic, which just tries to fulfill the user's exchange request. We are able to play with independent, but compatible, blocks.

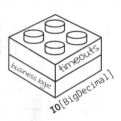

We will use this new recursion superpower to fix even more problems and get a cleaner overall design. Our next prototype is going to be a lot better! Let's start by fixing the `lastRates` function.

```
for {
  table1 <- exchangeTable(from)
  table2 <- exchangeTable(from)
  table3 <- exchangeTable(from)
  lastTables = List(table1, table2, table3)
} yield lastTables.flatMap(extractSingleCurrencyRate(to))
```

BTW, transforming an IO value into an IO value that has a timeout built in is as simple as calling the IO.timeout function! We'll discuss this more in chapter 11.

Remember that extractSingleCurrencyRate returns an Option[BigDecimal] because sometimes the API may not return a Map that contains the currency we are interested in.

`lastTables` is a `List[Map[Currency, BigDecimal]]`. When we `flatMap` with a function that returns an `Option`, `Options` are converted to zero- or one-element `Lists`. `Nones` are converted to empty `Lists`, and we end up with a `List` of `BigDecimals` that may be smaller than three elements—even empty! So we may not be checking for trends of size three at all! We will fix this issue very soon, but first we need your help.

For example, if lastTables contains two empty maps and a map with a single "to" currency key, we will yield a List with a single rate back, not three!

Coffee break:
Recursion and infinity

Now, it's your turn to practice recursion, laziness, and dealing with infinity. This is an exercise that will move us toward a better solution to this chapter's problem—the implementation you provide here will be used in the final, stream-based solution!

We'd like `lastRates` to always return a fixed amount of last rates, but before we are able to implement that, we will need you to implement a smaller helper function. **Your task is to implement a completely new function, `currencyRate`**, which will always return the latest rate between currencies:

```
def currencyRate(from: Currency, to: Currency): IO[BigDecimal]
```

Note that this function doesn't return IO[Option[BigDecimal]]. That means it should try to get an exchange table until it gets what it needs.

Functions at your disposal

You will need to use three functions to make it happen—the ones you already know (and should have in your REPL session already):

```
def exchangeTable(from: Currency): IO[Map[Currency, BigDecimal]]
```

This function returns a value describing an API call that returns an exchange table for a given (`from`) currency. Next:

```
def extractSingleCurrencyRate(currencyToExtract: Currency)
                (table: Map[Currency, BigDecimal]): Option[BigDecimal]
```

This function extracts a rate of a single currency (`currencyToExtract`) from a given exchange table (note there may not be anything to extract; hence, the `Option`). Finally:

```
def retry[A](action: IO[A], maxRetries: Int): IO[A]
```

`retry` wraps a potentially failing API call and retries it a given number of times before giving up. Let's retry a maximum of 10 times for now.

Remember to use the power of recursion and laziness. Moreover, we accept that your function may return an IO value, which, when executed, may never finish (this will happen where the `from` currency is never found in any of the exchange tables returned by API calls represented by the `exchangeTable` function).

As a bonus exercise, you may want to try to reimplement `retry` using recursion.

Coffee break explained:
Recursion and infinity

❶ Here's the signature of the function we need to implement. It will return a program description:

```
def currencyRate(from: Currency, to: Currency): IO[BigDecimal] = {
  for {

  } yield ???
}
```

We will need to return an IO, so it's safe to assume we will need a for comprehension. Let's start with that.

❷ We need an exchange rate between `from` and `to` currencies. An exchange table for `from` will come in handy:

```
def currencyRate(from: Currency, to: Currency): IO[BigDecimal] = {
  for {
    table <- exchangeTable(from)
  } yield ???
}
```

`table` is a `Map[Currency, BigDecimal]`.

We started building an IO value that describes a program. Its first step is to fetch an exchange table for the `from` currency using an API call.

❸ Since `exchangeTable` describes a raw single API call, we need some protection:

```
def currencyRate(from: Currency, to: Currency): IO[BigDecimal] = {
  for {
    table <- retry(exchangeTable(from), 10)
  } yield ???
}
```

`table` is still a `Map[Currency, BigDecimal]`.

❹ Now we need to extract a single rate using `extractSingleCurrencyRate`:

```
def currencyRate(from: Currency, to: Currency): IO[BigDecimal] = {
  for {
    table <- retry(exchangeTable(from), 10)
    rate  <- extractSingleCurrencyRate(to)(table)
  } yield ???
}
```

Compilation error!

`extractSingleCurrencyRate` returns an `Option[BigDecimal]`, not an IO value that the `flatMap` inside this for comprehension expects.

❺ We need the pattern matching to transform the `Option` into an `IO[BigDecimal]`, which is then yielded:

```
def currencyRate(from: Currency, to: Currency): IO[BigDecimal] = {
  for {
    table <- retry(exchangeTable(from), 10)
    rate  <- extractSingleCurrencyRate(to)(table) match {
               case Some(value) => IO.pure(value)
               case None        => currencyRate(from, to)
             }
  } yield rate
}
```

This is the **recursion base case.** When we have a rate, we return it.

When the rate of the `to` currency is not found in the `from`'s exchange table (i.e., we got None), we just try again using a **recursive call** to itself.

Creating different IO programs using recursion

So far, we've been getting rid of Option from the signatures in favor of a potentially infinite execution. We previously used Option, which was meant to indicate that no rate satisfied the *trending condition*:

```
def exchangeIfTrending(
    amount: BigDecimal, from: Currency, to: Currency
): IO[Option[BigDecimal]]
```

The new version of the function tries to exchange the given amount, until it succeeds, so we can drop the Option altogether:

```
def exchangeIfTrending(
    amount: BigDecimal, from: Currency, to: Currency
): IO[BigDecimal]
```

We used the same approach to implement currencyRate. It tries to find the rate until it succeeds:

```
def currencyRate(from: Currency, to: Currency): IO[BigDecimal]
```

Just for the sake of completeness, let's mention that we could also implement it differently with an Option inside. This implementation would probably try once and return Some if successful or None if not:

```
def currencyRate(from: Currency, to: Currency): IO[Option[BigDecimal]
```

As we discussed earlier, we won't be having any *frozen* or *unresponsive* programs. We are talking about IO values that represent infinitely running programs. But nobody has run them yet! We can still compose them with other IO values and change the final behavior.

A second way we can use recursion in real-world IO-based programs is to make sure another program—like an API call—is executed exactly n times and the results of all calls are available as a List of n elements. This may sound familiar to you, since we previously used List.range, map, and sequence to solve such issues. Here, we will briefly present a recursion-based alternative, so you are aware of both approaches.

To show this using an example, we will try to parametrize lastRates, so trends can be calculated based on lists of a specified number of rates. We've used n=3 so far, but we need to give our users the ability to specify a different number as a function parameter. We can use the new currencyRate function that returns IO[BigDecimal] (without Option) and already uses retry, exchangeTable, and extractSingleCurrencyRate internally.

1

We used recursion to create values that describe programs that may run infinitely when executed.

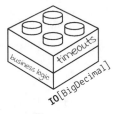

IO[BigDecimal]

2

We can also use recursion to create values that describe programs making an arbitrary number of calls.

Recursion is useful in non-IO contexts as well, e.g., List is a recursive data structure: it is defined as its first element (head) plus another List (tail).

Using recursion to make an arbitrary number of calls

Let's see how to use recursion to make as many API calls as needed to get exactly n last rates of a given currency pair (from-to). Here's the current version of lastRates:

```
def lastRates(from: Currency, to: Currency): IO[List[BigDecimal]] = {
  for {
    table1    <- retry(exchangeTable(from), 10)
    table2    <- retry(exchangeTable(from), 10)
    table3    <- retry(exchangeTable(from), 10)
    lastTables = List(table1, table2, table3)
  } yield lastTables.flatMap(extractSingleCurrencyRate(to))
}
```

> currencyRate
>
> Wrapper around the impure API call. Returns a description of a program that returns a rate at which you can convert from one currency to another. It may not finish if getting the rate is impossible.

Let's add a new parameter and try to reimplement the function, using the new currencyRate we've just implemented:

```
def lastRates(from: Currency, to: Currency, n: Int): IO[List[BigDecimal]]
```

There are two ways we can implement this function:

Using sequence   We used this approach in chapter 8, and it's still a viable option.

```
> def lastRates(from: Currency, to: Currency, n: Int): IO[List[BigDecimal]] = {
    List.range(0, n).map(_ => currencyRate(from, to)).sequence
  }
```
We create a List of n IOs and then sequence it to create an IO of an n-element List.

Using recursion   Just for the sake of completeness, we can achieve exactly the same result using recursion.

```
> def lastRates(from: Currency, to: Currency, n: Int): IO[List[BigDecimal]] = {
    if (n < 1) {
      IO.pure(List.empty)
    } else {
      for {
        currencyRate   <- currencyRate(from, to)
        remainingRates <- if (n == 1) IO.pure(List.empty)
                          else lastRates(from, to, n - 1)
      } yield remainingRates.prepended(currencyRate)
    }
  }
```

These are **recursion base cases**. As you can see, we can have more than one.

We call lastRates recursively whenever n is larger than 2. Note that calling currencyRate is the first step of this function, and as you probably remember, it will return a single rate (or fail or continue indefinitely). Hence, we can be sure that when we reach the second step of the for comprehension, we already have one currencyRate. Now, we need to make a decision: do we need more rates or not? **If so, we recursively call lastRates but with a smaller n.** This is how we can be sure the function converges to the base case.

No matter which version we choose, we get a List[BigDecimal] that is n elements long. The program may run infinitely though.

Problems with the recursive version

Now we have the `lastRates` function that takes the additional `n` parameter. We also know that it will return a list of last `n` rates and will try to get it until it succeeds. We can use the new version of `lastRates` to update our solution to this chapter's problem.

```
def exchangeIfTrending(
  amount: BigDecimal, from: Currency, to: Currency
): IO[BigDecimal] = {
  for {
    rates  <- lastRates(from, to, 3)
    result <- if (trending(rates)) IO.pure(amount * rates.last)
              else exchangeIfTrending(amount, from, to)
  } yield result
}
```

We can now be sure that rates is going to be a n-element list.

An IO value that this function returns describes a program that will return a result, fail, or will continue executing indefinitely.

Here's how we'd use it:

```
exchangeIfTrending(BigDecimal(1000), Currency("USD"), Currency("EUR"))
→ IO
```

We got an IO value back, which you can try to unsafeRunSync()! You should get back an amount in euros.

We got a value describing a program that, when executed, will try to exchange 1,000 USD to EUR but only when there is a trend of three increasing rates from USD to EUR.

However, when you look closer at what's happening inside, the function doesn't work very well performance-wise, especially when you take into account how expensive API calls usually are:

Processing data in isolated batches is a very popular paradigm, but it has its disadvantages. One of them is that sometimes valuable information is lost in the process of splitting data.

- It always fetches three (or **n**) rates first, then it makes a decision, and if it's not successful, it fetches three again. Hence, even though six rates were fetched in total, only the first triplet and the second triplet are analyzed, ignoring potential trends in between. For example, if a first analyzed batch is [0.77, 0.79, 0.78] and the next batch is [0.80, 0.81, 0.75], the current version would not find a trend of [0.78, 0.80, 0.81], which exists in the middle. We need to analyze *sliding windows* of rates to make the most of the API calls we have already made (and paid for).
- It runs as quickly as possible, so it may fetch **n** rates even in milliseconds. Practically, there is little chance that the rates change in such a small time frame. We need to make calls at a *fixed rate*.

Remember that we don't want to just solve these problems. We want to solve them in a readable and maintainable way with separation of concerns in mind.

Solving the issues above would be possible to achieve using the FP tools we already know (IO and recursion) or imperatively. However, it'd take a substantial amount of time to get right, for many programmers. There are lots of corner cases to handle. **We need a different approach!**

Introducing data streams

There is a better approach to implement sliding windows, delays, and fixed rates. This approach is especially useful when we work with an unspecified amount of data, in our case data fetched from API calls. We have shown the classical approach to handle such problems, using recursion. We also briefly touched on the subject of separation of concerns; we want isolated modules that handle different aspects of the functionality:

- One function should be responsible for fetching (e.g., last n rates or a single exchange rate between a given currency pair).
- Another function should be responsible for aspects like timeouts, delays between calls, and retries.

All these characteristics, together with a possibly infinite execution, usually hint at a usage of a different architectural approach: **streams**.

As we will soon find out, using streams helps us invert the control and, therefore, isolate even more pieces of functionality without sacrificing any performance metrics. So far, the exchangeIfTrending function has been making API calls explicitly, adding the business logic on top of API results. With streams we will invert this dependency and use **a lazily evaluated infinite stream of IO-based API calls,** which will be defined elsewhere. We will break this long definition down for you on the following pages.

> Having unspecified amounts of data means that our function may need to fetch and process 1, 10, hundreds of thousands, or infinite data entities before making a decision. This is something we need to accept and deal with separately.

> We will use this knowledge to implement a far superior, bulletproof, and readable solution to this chapter's original problem.

The learning process in this chapter consists of three steps. We started with using only the IO type, then we used recursion to make an indefinite number of API calls. It's time for purely functional streams.

Step 1 ✔

Using only IO
We will try to implement the first version of this chapter's problem solution, using IO alone as a recap. This version will serve as a basis for comparing with other approaches.

On the side To catch some breath we will introduce two immutable data structures that are very important in FP: Map and tuple. ✔

Step 2 ✔

Using IO with recursion
We will try to address the need for an unknown amount of API calls by introducing and using recursion.

On the side
We will show and use a different approach to functional design: bottom-up. We will start with small functions and work our way up. ✔

Step 3

Using IO with Streams
In the last step we will show how to make API calls at a fixed rate and use sliding windows on possibly infinite amounts of incoming data. We will use the functional approach to a streaming architectural pattern and compare it to other versions of this pattern.

On the side
We will discuss separation of concerns and inversion of control.

Streams in imperative languages

Before we meet the functional Stream type, let's first talk about something you may be more familiar with: Java's Stream type. Java's Stream has been around for some time now. It's Java's way of copying and introducing some of the functional concepts into the language. Let's take a look.

Note that we discuss Java's Stream here only to establish some common context. We are not going to use it in this book.

```
Stream<Integer> numbers = Stream.of(1, 2, 3);
```
We define a finite stream of numbers. This stream emits (or generates) three values.

```
static Stream<Integer> oddNumbers(Stream<Integer> numbers) {
  return numbers.filter(n -> n % 2 != 0);
}
```
Then, we define a pure function that takes one Stream and returns another, internally filtering only numbers that are odd.

```
Stream<Integer> oddNumbers = oddNumbers(numbers);
```
We can then call this function and get another Stream back.

```
List<Integer> result = oddNumbers.collect(Collectors.toList());
```
The result is [1, 3].

First of all, there is no mutability involved while we work just on the Stream type. Secondly, nothing is really computed until somebody wants to transform the Stream *value* into something different, such as a List (using collect) or a number (using count). In Java, we say that filter, map, and other *functional* stream operations—pure functions that take Streams and return Streams—are **intermediate operations**, while the functions that take us out of the Stream world (like collect) are **terminal operations**.

All this may be treated as yet another proof that functional programming ideas are slowly making their way into many mainstream languages.

Java's Stream vs. IO

I think it's pretty easy to see a small, but important, resemblance between Stream and IO types. They both describe something without executing anything. A Stream value stores all the operations for a given stream, and they are executed only after using a terminal operation. An IO value stores all the side-effectful operations, which are executed only after using unsafeRunSync. The Stream type provides functions that return new immutable Stream values (think filter, map, and others). The IO type provides functions that return new immutable IO values.

Sometimes you may see that instead of terminal operations, some say that a stream has a consumer. We will expand on this soon.

This comparison may be—and definitely is—a little too far-fetched, but it's important to understand these similarities and where they are coming from. They are both implementations of immutability and lazy evaluation we've been talking a lot about in this book.

Unfortunately, Java doesn't allow us to reuse a Stream value. Once we use a Stream value, we can't do it again. So it's not really immutable, it just acts as immutable.

Values on demand

Some of you may have encountered another approach to explain how Java's Stream type works: it's *generating* (or *emitting*) values on demand. Some people say that such streams are *cold*—they need a consumer to even start generating values. However, **it's just another way of explaining lazy evaluation**. It's also just another way of allowing us to create an infinite stream of values. When we use lazy evaluation, we can, without any hesitation, create streams that are able to generate any number of values. In practice, however, they only generate values that are really needed at the client side—**on demand**. Here's an infinite stream of values in Java:

```
Stream<Integer> infiniteNumbers = Stream.iterate(0, i -> i + 1);
Stream<Integer> infiniteOddNumbers = oddNumbers(infiniteNumbers);
```

We define an infinite stream of numbers and then we call oddNumbers that return another infinite Stream back. We manipulate values, and nothing else happens.

The following line, if uncommented, would try to collect all the elements from an infinite stream to a list, which would freeze the program:

```
// infiniteOddNumbers.collect(Collectors.toList());

Stream<Integer> limitedStream = infiniteOddNumbers.limit(3);
```

Instead we can state how many elements from the infinite stream we'd like to use (e.g., three).

```
List<Integer> limitedResult =
  limitedStream.collect(Collectors.toList());
```

We now have a finite stream on our hands, and we can safely collect. The limitedResult is [1, 3, 5].

Java Streams are not the only place where an imperative language implements such a mechanic. For example, in Python, we have a notion of **generators**. The code above could be written in Python as follows:

```
def infinite_numbers():
    x=0
    while(True):
        x=x+1
        yield x

def odd_numbers(numbers):
    return filter(lambda i: i%2 != 0, numbers)

infinite_odd_numbers = odd_numbers(infinite_numbers())
limited_result = itertools.islice(infinite_odd_numbers, 3)
```

This Python function returns a generator that returns numbers infinitely.

This Python function takes a generator and returns another one using filter.

PYTHON CODE A small snippet that shows these techniques are ubiquitous!

We use both functions and take only three elements from the infinite stream. At the end we get [1, 3, 5] back.

Similar approaches can be found in Reactive Streams (JDK 9), RxJava, Kotlin's Flow, and more. **They all have two things in common**.

Separation of concerns	Inversion of control
The place where we take a finite number of elements (limit) doesn't know anything about how the stream was created. It doesn't know how many elements it can have and how many transformations were needed—and vice versa, the stream just generates elements and doesn't care about how they will be used.	The oddNumbers function is able to generate odd numbers without knowing how to generate **all** numbers. It doesn't have to call or generate anything. It gets all it needs as a parameter in the form of a Stream and just uses it. The user of this function has control now.

Stream processing, producers, and consumers

We now know that the streaming paradigm has been implemented in many languages. It has a lot of advantages because it uses the power of lazy evaluation and helps **decouple our modules**—especially when we deal with lots of incoming data that we need to process.

When you decouple modules, you make them more independent of each other. Both separation of concerns and inversion of control represent an approach to decoupling.

Let's get our definitions straight before we move on. **Stream processing** means transformations of values representing infinite streams of values. When we do stream processing, we focus on operations on data first. However, the data needs to be stored somewhere—it needs to have a source. The output of the stream processing should also be used in one way or another. That's why discussing stream processing inevitably brings up the topic of the **producer/consumer** pattern.

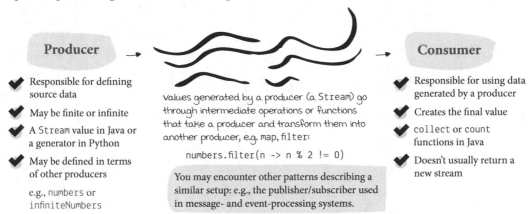

Producer

- Responsible for defining source data
- May be finite or infinite
- A Stream value in Java or a generator in Python
- May be defined in terms of other producers

  e.g., numbers or infiniteNumbers

values generated by a producer (a Stream) go through intermediate operations or functions that take a producer and transform them into another producer, e.g. map, filter:

```
numbers.filter(n -> n % 2 != 0)
```

You may encounter other patterns describing a similar setup: e.g., the publisher/subscriber used in message- and event-processing systems.

Consumer

- Responsible for using data generated by a producer
- Creates the final value
- collect or count functions in Java
- Doesn't usually return a new stream

We have just scratched the surface by talking about imperative streams. All of the streams we met so far have been operating on values generated locally in memory. However, the **streaming paradigm scales very well**. You can have streams operating on data coming from external APIs—as you will soon see—or any other external sources. There are lots of stream processing solutions out there, and they usually focus on different characteristics. But you can be sure that the general paradigm is the same. We want to separate different concerns by decoupling the source of the data, its processing, and its clients into isolated entities. On the producer side, we don't know how many values the consumer will need, so we might just create lazily evaluated, potentially infinite streams of elements. On the consumer side, we don't know anything about the source of data, but we are able to process it independently.

The paradigm fits well when we program for more than a single machine. We'll discuss multithreading in chapter 10. What's important right now is that all the tools we learn here will apply there as well.

Streams and IO

As we mentioned earlier, we have only used streams of **values generated locally, in-memory**. We did it to show the idea and its general applications. However, our software usually is not that simple. We need to get data from the outside world and store it somewhere as well. Our current problem requires us to use an external API. Now that we understand the stream processing paradigm, we could envision the **external API as a producer**, which will produce exchange tables for a given currency as values.

However, it's not that easy to implement at first sight. We've been trying to solve this problem functionally, using the IO type and some recursion. Additionally, we have used many other FP types and techniques extensively—they solve smaller parts of the problem, and they do it very well. The question remains: is it possible to use IO and other good bits of the existing solution inside a stream-based approach?

> **Q** But do we really need IO in streams? Can't we execute side-effectful impure functions directly? We could use something like Java's `Stream.generate` that takes a function and emits as many elements as needed (calling the provided function for each of them). What's wrong with that?
>
> **A** Unfortunately, although it is indeed possible, this approach is flawed in the same way normal impure functions are flawed.

Imperative approaches tend to suffer from one very important flaw: **they don't isolate side effects from pure functions**. Their APIs tend to treat both impure and pure producers as equals. For example:

```
Stream<Integer> randomNumbers = Stream.generate(new Random()::nextInt);

List<Integer> randomResult =
    oddNumbers(randomNumbers).limit(3).collect(Collectors.toList());

Stream<Map<String, BigDecimal>> usdRates =
    Stream.generate(() -> exchangeRatesTableApiCall("USD"));
usdRates.limit(100).collect(Collectors.toList());
```

We already know now that purity needs to be isolated if we want to have more maintainable and testable codebases. Imperative stream versions won't be enough. We need something that will let us use all the superpowers we learned about: IO and other immutable data types, pure functions, and lazy evaluation. **We need functional Streams!**

Note again that, although we talk about an external API being a producer, it won't matter to its consumers, or clients of this data stream. A different function will be responsible for using exchange tables, but it won't know where it will have originated from.

`Stream.generate` takes a Java function and uses it each time an element is requested. You may think of this as an infinite stream!

randomResult is most definitely different each time we run it. In my case it was [1816734507, 1516189193, 1552970581].

Here's our API call function that may throw connection errors. Calling it 100 times almost guarantees getting an exception back.

The functional Stream

It's time to meet the functional Stream type, which is a purely functional implementation of the stream processing idea. Since streaming is a very popular paradigm, many languages usually have more than one stream library available—each of them focusing on slightly different aspects. In this book we will show the IO-based approach, which, in Scala, is available using the fs2 library. Note that this is a very different thing from Java's Stream type we have discussed so far, although the general idea of having a producer, consumer, and a bunch of operators in the middle is exactly the same. The main difference is that the functional Stream embraces the inherent immutability and purity of FP. But the real deal maker is that we can reuse—and enjoy—a lot of functions and ideas we already know from using other functional types, including a seamless integration with IO values. In fact, a Stream value is analogical to IO because it only describes the stream processing program, just like an IO value describes a potentially side-effectful program.

> Note that the library choice is secondary, though. We want to show how functional programming libraries can work together and how the same ideas of immutable values and pure functions are used in different contexts. You learn a functional idea once, and you can apply it everywhere.

Just like with other functional solutions, there are multiple different ways to spawn a Stream value. Showing them all is outside of the scope of this book, as this is not meant to be a comprehensive introduction to any particular library. It's an introduction to a specific, functional mindset. Having that in mind, let's create some Stream values.

> You need to import fs2._ if you are not using the book's sbt console REPL.

> Both numbers and oddNumbers are streams of pure values, created and maintained in memory. It's a use case very similar to what we saw with imperative streams. No IO yet!

```
val numbers = Stream(1, 2, 3)
val oddNumbers = numbers.filter(_ % 2 != 0)
oddNumbers.toList
→ List(1, 3)
numbers.toList
→ List(1, 2, 3)
oddNumbers.map(_ + 17).take(1).toList
→ List(18)
```

> toList goes through each element emitted by the stream and returns all of them as a list.

> We add 17 to each value emitted by oddNumbers and then take the first one (18).

No surprise here. We get exactly what we expect at this point: full immutability (numbers and oddNumbers can be reused any number of times) and a set of well-named and defined functions (filter, map, take, toList and more). A Stream is just a value. That means that if we need a stream with side effects (like API calls), we can define a lazily evaluated stream using recursion and encode it as a Stream of IO values just like the Stream of raw integers above. Additionally, we can convert a Stream value into an IO value and treat it just like any other IO value. So **functional Streams are just values**—even the most complicated ones!

> You can reuse a single stream value many times because it's immutable.

Streams in FP are values

We've been working with immutable values, and streams are no exception. The Stream type takes two type parameters—they both explain a lot about what happens inside.

Stream[F, O] has two type parameters: F is the effect type, and O is type of the output elements.

Stream[F, O]

A value of type Stream[F, O] **describes** a stream-based computation.

For example:

Stream[Pure, Int]

A value of this type **describes** a stream-based computation that produces integers **without any side effects**.

Stream[IO, String]

A value of this type **describes** a stream-based computation that produces Strings **with possible side effects** described as IO values.

Note **how much information is packed into a single type definition**. When you see a function that returns a Stream[Pure, String], you can be sure that it returns an immutable value that describes a stream-based computation, which, **when executed**, will produce zero or more String values **in memory**. On the other hand, when a function returns a Stream[IO, BigDecimal], you can be sure that it returns an immutable value that describes a stream-based computation which, **when executed**, will produce zero or more BigDecimal values potentially using and executing side effects under the hood. That means that all strategies and techniques related to side effects apply here as well.

Q But what does it mean to "execute" a Stream value? I understand that we can "execute" an IO value that describes a program, using unsafeRunSync. Does Stream has unsafeRunSync as well?

A Not directly. Note that Stream describes a lazy producer of values. It won't execute anything until there is a consumer that requests at least one element from this stream. unsafeRunSync is only needed when a Stream value describes a side-effectful computation (has IO as the first type parameter). But even then nothing happens if there is no consumer for any stream:

```
val numbers = Stream(1, 2, 3)
val oddNumbers = numbers.filter(_ % 2 != 0)
```

The function we passed to filter won't be executed until there is a consumer that requests at least one element. Here's one possible consumer: oddNumbers.toList.

Again, remember that we are just discussing a single stream library here. You might use this particular one soon, but it's not what this book prepares you for. Focus instead on how all the FP mechanisms can work so well together. Immutable values, pure functions, laziness, and trustworthy signatures for the win!

Here we show an example of a pure stream because we haven't shown an IO-based one yet. What matters is the concept, which is the same in both types.

Streams are recursive values

Before we move on to the IO-handling streams for good, let's play more
with streams of primitive values and learn how to handle them using the
familiar FP techniques.

Here's how you can append a stream at the end of another stream:

```
val stream1 = Stream(1, 2, 3)
val stream2 = Stream(4, 5, 6)
val stream3 = stream1.append(stream2)
stream3.toList
→ List(1, 2, 3, 4, 5, 6)
```

We don't consume anything from any of the three
streams until `stream3.toList` is called. Only then the
`stream3` definition is used and only then values from
`stream1` and `stream2` are used, indirectly.

Again, streams are just values, so you can append a stream to itself:

```
val stream4 = stream1.append(stream1)
stream4.toList
→ List(1, 2, 3, 1, 2, 3)
```

Here we create a stream that produces fewer values than another one:

```
val stream5 = stream4.take(4)
stream5.toList
→ List(1, 2, 3, 1)
```

Note that `stream5` is yet another stream. We haven't
consumed any elements at this point. It's just a producer that
produces a maximum of four elements.

As you probably expect, functional streams take laziness very seriously—
append is lazy! Hence, in order to create an infinite `Stream`, we can use
the **append + recursion combo** without any hesitation.

```
def numbers(): Stream[Pure, Int] = {
  Stream(1, 2, 3).append(numbers())
}

val infinite123s = numbers()

infinite123s.take(8).toList
→ List(1, 2, 3, 1, 2, 3, 1, 2)
```

`numbers` is a function that returns a value, which
represents a stream-based computation that
produces integers without any side effects.

We append a stream described by calling the `numbers`
function at the end of `Stream(1, 2, 3)`. **This is a
recursive call!** Nothing blows up, because append
doesn't eagerly evaluate what's passed. It makes the
recursive calls only when a consumer demands values,
not earlier—it's lazily evaluated.

`numbers` is a recursive function that
produces a **recursive value**. When we
take eight elements, `numbers` is called
three times.

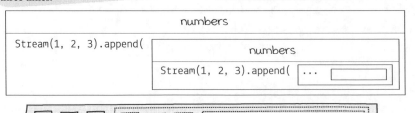

If a consumer
requests more than
three elements,
`numbers` are called
recursively.

This is a recursively defined `Stream[Pure, Int]` value.

Primitive operations and combinators

The Stream type has a lot of functions defined inside. Remember that this is a standard functional API, so a majority of functions take Stream values and return new Stream values. We divide them into primitive operations and combinators. Their differences lay in their internal implementations. Primitives are functions that are implemented without using any other API functions. append, which we met earlier, is a primitive. Combinators are functions that are defined in terms of other API functions (primitives or other combinators). That means that we, as developers, can **choose from a variety of different options when implementing a particular functionality**, as we'll soon see. Having many options means we can pick the one that best fits in terms of readability.

It's useful to understand the difference between primitive operations and combinators, because this idea comes up in many functional APIs. This way we can build a common vocabulary with other developers. We have used combinators on IO, for example.

For example, we have just implemented an infinite stream using append and recursion. It turns out that we can use the repeat function to achieve the same result (repeat calls append and itself recursively, but it's hidden from us). Therefore, we can write

So, repeat is a combinator because it's defined in terms of append.

```
> val numbers = Stream(1, 2, 3).repeat
  numbers.take(8).toList
  → List(1, 2, 3, 1, 2, 3, 1, 2)
```

An infinite stream of
1, 2, 3, 1, 2, 3, 1, 2, 3, ...

No matter what stream solution your team chooses for your next project, it's usually a very good idea to **go through its API and documentation** and see how all functions, especially combinators, are implemented internally. This will give you a lot of insight into how this particular API should be used and what its strengths are.

We will use a small subset of primitive operations and combinators in this book, but if you are able to master them, you will be able to use any of the remaining ones with some help from the API documentation. It's also worth mentioning that the majority of functions in this particular stream library are useful for both pure and IO-based streams.

Quick exercise

Let's make sure we are on the same page with regards to pure streams before we tackle IO. What do the following expressions return?

1. `Stream(1).repeat.take(3).toList`
2. `Stream(1).append(Stream(0, 1).repeat).take(4).toList`
3. `Stream(2).map(_ * 13).repeat.take(1).toList`
4. `Stream(13).filter(_ % 2 != 0).repeat.take(2).toList`

Answers:
List(1, 1, 1),
List(1, 0, 1, 0),
List(26),
List(13, 13).

Streams of IO-based values

You now probably agree that functional streams of primitive values are pretty useful, right? Hold your breath—their real superpower comes from their integration with the IO type. All we learned about IO and handling side effects is going to be used in side-effectful streams as well!

The whole idea in one sentence goes like this: **we can have streams of IO values that will be automatically executed, on demand, when someone else consumes elements from the stream**. But until someone does, we just operate on immutable values. Let's break down this idea to really grok what it means in practice. We will explain it, starting from the impure side-effectful Java function that casts the die.

```
def castTheDieImpure(): Int = {
  static int castTheDieImpure() {
    System.out.println("The die is cast");
    Random rand = new Random();
    return rand.nextInt(6) + 1;
  }
}
```

We come back to the "cast the die" example just for a moment. It's self-contained and understandable. It also shows the difference between raw IOs and streams. We will use what we learn here to write the final version of the rate exchange program.

```
> import ch08_CastingDie.castTheDieImpure
  def castTheDie(): IO[Int] = IO.delay(castTheDieImpure())
```

As a recap: we first need to create a function that "delays" the execution of side effects.

Previously, we just called such a function as many times as we wanted, inside a for comprehension because the requirements allowed us to do so (e.g., "cast the die *twice*"). But let's imagine we have a situation similar to the currency exchange case—that is, we don't know up front how many times we need to call this particular IO value to get what we want. An example would be a requirement to cast the die until we get a six! It could be at our first try or never at all. Hence, it's a small representation of a bigger problem we are facing in the currency exchange case. Let's learn how the functional Stream can help us here.

We need to do that to be able to write pure functions and take advantage of their benefits. "Delayed" side-effectful actions will be executed outside the functional core when we call unsafeRunSync.

```
> val dieCast: Stream[IO, Int] = Stream.eval(castTheDie())
  val oneDieCastProgram: IO[List[Int]] = dieCast.compile.toList
```

By calling .compile.toList on the dieCast stream, we transform it to another value: IO[List[Int]]. This is exactly the same IO that we learned about in chapter 8. We know how to deal with that!

dieCast is a Stream of a single IO value. eval takes an IO value and "evaluates" it (i.e., executes the given IO value and emits the Int produced by this IO action but only when a consumer requests it later on!).

We, therefore, got a description of a program that, when executed successfully, will produce a List[Int]. And since we know that dieCast is a one-element stream (eval takes an IO and returns a Stream value that produces just a single value based on this IO, when requested), we should get a one-element list back. Let's manually execute the IO value.

```
> oneDieCastProgram.unsafeRunSync()
  → console output: The die is cast
  → List(4)
```

"The die is cast" is written to the console because it's a side effect, not the result of the function, which, in this case, was List(4). (Yours may differ, since it's random.)

Infinite streams of IO-based values

The functions we have just met, `eval` and `compile`, are very important when dealing with IO-based streams. Here are their summaries.

eval	compile.toList
`Stream.eval` creates a new `Stream` value that, when used by a consumer, will produce one `Int` value, based on the result of a side-effecting program described by an `IO` value passed as the single parameter: Stream.**eval**(IO(1-6?)) → Stream[IO, Int]	A `Stream` value can be compiled to an IO value describing a side-effectful stream-processing program by calling the `compile` function. There are a few options we can compile a stream to, and we will use more of them later. The first one, `compile.toList`, makes sure that the underlying stream is processed, all its elements are consumed, and added to a `List` that is then returned as a result of the whole execution: val s = Stream.**eval**(IO(1-6?)) s.**compile.toList** → IO[List[Int]]

We will use them a lot in the remaining part of the chapter. Additionally, we will use functions we met when we dealt with pure streams. For example, we already know that we can transform any `Stream` value into an infinite stream that repeats the original one recursively by using the `repeat` combinator. It turns out that `repeat` works for IO-based streams as well. Hence:

```
val infiniteDieCasts: Stream[IO, Int] = Stream.eval(castTheDie()).repeat
val infiniteDieCastsProgram: IO[List[Int]] = infiniteDieCasts.compile.toList
```

So far, so good. We have two immutable values: a `Stream` and an `IO`. `compile.toList` transforms a `Stream` into an `IO` that, when executed successfully, will result in a list of all `Int`s produced by the stream. But are we really able to fit an infinite number of integers in a `List`?

> **THIS IS BIG!**
> Types tell a lot about the internals in both IO and streaming programs.

```
infiniteDieCastsProgram.unsafeRunSync()    ← This program will continue
→ console output: The die is cast              running indefinitely!
→ console output: The die is cast          (Do not run it if you want
→ console output: The die is cast          to keep your REPL session
...                                        intact.)
```

No! When we execute this value, it just writes to the console, which means the IO action has been executed. The program itself never finishes. It just overflows the console with lots of "The die is cast" messages that won't stop appearing until we quit the application. We will never get a `List[Int]` back because there is no limit to how many elements the stream produces. But that doesn't mean this program is useless. **The side-effectful actions are being executed**. That's useful!

Executing for side effects

In fact, programs that are running until manual termination are pretty common. We are running them only for the side effects they are making. We don't care what they produce at the end. We can even encode this in the type: IO[Unit] is exactly the type we expect when we have a value describing a program that is executed only for its side effects. We have already used this type when we used an API call that stores data for a future use. There are lots of other cases where we may be interested only in side effects: user interfaces, handling server endpoints, and socket connections. In our current die-casting scenario, our only side effect is the single log line we print each time we cast the die. However, we used compile.toList even though the stream is infinite, and there's no way it will ever return a list. Streams have us covered for this opportunity as well. Let's use **compile.drain** instead, which does exactly what we need. It "drains" the stream and returns Unit when it finishes.

```
val infiniteDieCasts: Stream[IO, Int] = Stream.eval(castTheDie()).repeat
val infiniteDieCastsProgram: IO[Unit] = infiniteDieCasts.compile.drain
```

```
infiniteDieCastsProgram.unsafeRunSync()
→ console output: The die is cast
→ console output: The die is cast
→ console output: The die is cast
...
```

This program will continue running indefinitely! (Do not run it if you want to keep your REPL session intact.)

We get exactly the same infinitely running program, but the IO value doesn't have any illusions about returning a list in the near future. Now, it's IO[Unit], thanks to the drain usage. This return type means we'll run this IO value purely for the side effects it describes. In chapter 10, we'll make this concept even better by returning IO[Nothing]. Stay tuned!

Infinite streams are useful, but whenever we want to get some values back—not just side effects—we need to transform them into finite streams by using Stream functions. One of them is take, which will work for IO-based streams exactly like it did for pure ones.

```
val firstThreeCasts: IO[List[Int]] = infiniteDieCasts.take(3).compile.toList
firstThreeCasts.unsafeRunSync()
→ console output: The die is cast
→ console output: The die is cast
→ console output: The die is cast
→ List(6, 2, 6)
```

Note that filter operates on Ints that will be returned by executing IO values in the future. In this sense, it works like flatMap inside the for comprehension. We can define functions that operate on values that are not yet available.

We can use filter to filter only values that are interesting to us. In this case, we wanted to throw the die until we get a 6:

```
val six: IO[List[Int]] = infiniteDieCasts.filter(_ == 6).take(1).compile.toList
six.unsafeRunSync()
→ console output: The die is cast
→ console output: The die is cast
→ console output: The die is cast
→ console output: The die is cast
→ List(6)
```

As you see, in this case, four IO calls were enough to get the first 6. Your mileage may vary!

Practicing stream operations

It's your turn to feel the power of functional stream processing. In this exercise you are going to use the infiniteDieCasts stream value:

```
val infiniteDieCasts: Stream[IO, Int] = Stream.eval(castTheDie()).repeat
```

Your task is to create the following IO values. Each of them should internally use numbers (and side effects) produced by infiniteDieCasts and do the following:

1. Filter odd numbers, and return the first three such casts.
2. Return the first five die casts, but make sure all 6 values are doubled (so a [1, 2, 3, 6, 4] becomes [1, 2, 3, 12, 4]).
3. Return the sum of the first three casts.
4. Cast the die until there is a 5 and then cast it two more times, returning three last results back (a 5 and two more).
5. Make sure the die is cast 100 times, and values are discarded.
6. Return the first three casts unchanged and the next three casts tripled (six in total).

Remember that each subtask should be represented by an IO value, not the Stream value; that means that you need to compile the Stream and transform it into a properly typed IO value that can be immediately executed.

If the above exercises were too easy, here's one that uses a combinator we haven't introduced, but a very useful one: scan. It behaves exactly like foldLeft, but it works on Streams and returns a Stream that additionally emits an accumulator value each time the internal aggregation function is called.

7. Cast the die until there are two 6s in a row.

> You can also use scan to solve #3 above!

Answers

```
1. infiniteDieCasts.filter(_ % 2 != 0).take(3).compile.toList
2. infiniteDieCasts.take(5).map(x => if (x == 6) 12 else x).compile.toList
3. infiniteDieCasts.take(3).compile.toList.map(_.sum)
4. infiniteDieCasts.filter(_ == 5).take(1)
     .append(infiniteDieCasts.take(2)).compile.toList
5. infiniteDieCasts.take(100).compile.drain
6. infiniteDieCasts.take(3)
     .append(infiniteDieCasts.take(3).map(_ * 3)).compile.toList
7. infiniteDieCasts
     .scan(0)((sixesInRow, current) => if (current == 6) sixesInRow + 1 else 0)
     .filter(_ == 2).take(1).compile.toList
```

> How hard would it be if we needed to return all casts in #4—not just the last three?

Using streams to our advantage

Now we know enough to tackle the chapter's original problem. We designed the whole functionality bottom-up, and we succeeded, although the for comprehension–based function wasn't as good as we wanted. The good thing is that we don't have to start over. We used the functional approach and created a few small functions that have single, isolated responsibilities. We can reuse them in our new prototype without any changes!

```
def trending(rates: List[BigDecimal]): Boolean
def extractSingleCurrencyRate(currencyToExtract: Currency)
              (table: Map[Currency, BigDecimal]): Option[BigDecimal]
```

Remember that we also have the API call, which was given to us from outside. We, as functional programmers usually do, wrapped it in IO, so we can reason about it with clarity—in a referentially transparent way:

```
def exchangeTable(from: Currency): IO[Map[Currency, BigDecimal]]
```

We used all three functions, IO, and recursion to create a working version of exchangeIfTrending. However, we encountered two very serious problems when we tried to use it:

1. It always fetches three (or n) rates first, then makes a decision, and if it is not successful, fetches another three again. Hence, even though six rates were fetched in total, only the first triplet and the second triplet are analyzed, ignoring potential trends in between. For example, if a first analyzed batch is [0.77, 0.79, 0.78] and the next batch is [0.80, 0.81, 0.75], the current version would not find a trend of [0.78, 0.80, 0.81], which exists in the middle. We need to analyze *sliding windows* of rates to make the most of the API calls we have already made (and paid for).

2. It runs as quickly as possible, so it may fetch n rates even in milliseconds. Practically, there is little chance that the rates change in such a small time frame. We need to make calls at a *fixed rate*.

We need to introduce a delay between consequent API queries.

I hope you see where this is going. **We can solve both problems using functional streams!** The first problem seems pretty straightforward, and we will start with it. The second looks scarier, but I promise that it's not that bad! We are going to learn a few more stream combinators and end up with a very small and clear solution to the rate exchange problem. The trick is changing the mindset (and the architecture) to a stream-based one. We need a different view on API calls—instead of making them, we need to **consume** a stream of them.

Pay attention to all the new combinators we will introduce!

Infinite stream of API calls

Let's create an infinite stream of rates from one currency to another. This will help us solve our issues by separating the concern of making individual API calls from the concern of detecting trends and making decisions based on them. This single change opens the door to a whole new world of design possibilities—it's that powerful! As we go, please note that we don't need to change any of the small functions we developed at the beginning.

It's yet more evidence that the design based on small, independent functions saves us a lot of time.

1 We need a stream of rates between a pair of currencies. We can easily come up with a signature:

```
def rates(from: Currency, to: Currency): Stream[IO, BigDecimal] = {

}
```

This function returns a value representing a side-effectful stream of `BigDecimal`s, which are exchange rates between `from-to` currencies.

2 Let's start by creating an infinite stream of exchange tables of the `from` currency:

```
def rates(from: Currency, to: Currency): Stream[IO, BigDecimal] = {
  Stream
    .eval(exchangeTable(from))
    .repeat
}
```
Compilation error!

This is a stream of `Map[Currency, BigDecimal]`.

We use the `Stream.eval` function to create a single-element stream that uses the provided IO action to produce a single `BigDecimal`. Then, we `repeat` this stream infinitely.

3 Since we now have a stream of maps and need a stream of `BigDecimal`s, we must somehow extract a single `BigDecimal` rate from the map of all possible exchanges. Fortunately, we already have a function for that:

```
def rates(from: Currency, to: Currency): Stream[IO, BigDecimal] = {
  Stream
    .eval(exchangeTable(from))
    .repeat
    .map(extractSingleCurrencyRate(to))
}
```

This is a stream of `Option[BigDecimal]`.
Compilation error!

We map each value in the stream (each `Map[Currency, BigDecimal]` representing all `from` currency rates) using a function that extracts a single rate (for `to` currency).

4 We need to filter out Nones and leave only values that were wrapped in Some. This can be achieved in a few different ways—one of them involves pattern matching—but, fortunately, there is a combinator that does that for us: **unNone**.

```
def rates(from: Currency, to: Currency): Stream[IO, BigDecimal] = {
  Stream
    .eval(exchangeTable(from))
    .repeat
    .map(extractSingleCurrencyRate(to))
    .unNone
}
```

unNone takes a stream of `Option[A]` values and returns a stream of As, filtering out Nones along the way.

Now we have an infinite stream of rates between `from` and `to` currencies.

Handling IO failures in streams

Q What about failures? IO actions may randomly fail, right? Side-effectful streams need to run underlying IO actions to produce an element. So what happens if evaluating one of the IO values fails?

A Then, the whole stream fails too! But don't worry. We can use retry strategies we learned about in chapter 8, such as the `retry` function. Additionally, it turns out that Stream has **orElse** too!

How exactly does `orElse` work for streams? We have some experience in FP, and thanks to that we can get a sense of how this "new" functionality works by comparing it to what we already know.

Remember that IO has the orElse function, too!

Option.orElse

```
val year: Option[Int] = Some(996)
val noYear: Option[Int] = None

year.orElse(Some(2020))
→ Some(996)
noYear.orElse(Some(2020))
→ Some(2020)
year.orElse(None)
→ Some(996)
noYear.orElse(None)
→ None
```

Either.orElse

```
val year: Either[String, Int] = Right(996)
val noYear: Either[String, Int] = Left("no year")

year.orElse(Right(2020))
→ Right(996)
noYear.orElse(Right(2020))
→ Right(2020)
year.orElse(Left("can't recover"))
→ Right(996)
noYear.orElse(Left("can't recover"))
→ Left("can't recover")
```

Stream.orElse

Look for similarities in outputs. Some and Right values are similar to successful Stream value executions. None and Left values are similar to failed Stream value executions!

```
val year: Stream[IO, Int] = Stream.eval(IO.pure(996))
val noYear: Stream[IO, Int] = Stream.raiseError[IO](new Exception("no year"))

val stream1 = year.orElse(Stream.eval(IO.delay(2020)))
→ Stream[IO, Int]
val stream2 = noYear.orElse(Stream.eval(IO.delay(2020)))
→ Stream[IO, Int]
val stream3 = year.orElse(Stream.raiseError[IO](new Exception("can't recover")))
→ Stream[IO, Int]
val stream4 = noYear.orElse(Stream.raiseError[IO](new Exception("can't recover")))
→ Stream[IO, Int]

stream1.compile.toList.unsafeRunSync()
→ 996
stream2.compile.toList.unsafeRunSync()
→ 2020
stream3.compile.toList.unsafeRunSync()
→ 996
stream4.compile.toList.unsafeRunSync()
→ Exception in thread "main": can't recover
```

noYear is a stream that will always fail when we run it! So how can we recover?

Up until this point we have only created Stream values, so both year and noYear are values. stream1, 2, 3 and 4 are also just values. Some of these values, however, incorporate simple failure recovery strategies! We can see it by compiling streams and running their IO programs using unsafeRunSync().

Separated concerns

We know how orElse works. Now we need to provide a Stream value that will be run in case the original stream fails. What value should we provide? Let's assume that we want to just start over. Therefore, **we can recursively call the same function again!** This way we get an infinite failure-free stream of BigDecimals, which are exchange rates from a given currency (from) to another (to).

```
> def rates(from: Currency, to: Currency): Stream[IO, BigDecimal] = {
    Stream
      .eval(exchangeTable(from))
      .repeat
      .map(extractSingleCurrencyRate(to))
      .unNone
      .orElse(rates(from, to))
  }
```

If anything goes wrong with this stream, do not fail. Instead, recover with the given fallback stream (which is exactly the same one).

A great thing about streams, especially when we start filtering emitted elements, is that from the perspective of the stream's consumer it doesn't matter how many times an IO has been executed (or how many different IO actions have been used). The consumer has a function (rates) that returns a Stream[IO, BigDecimal]. When it wants just the three first rates between a from-to currency pair, it just says so.

```
> val firstThreeRates = rates(Currency("USD"), Currency("EUR")).take(3).compile.toList
→ IO[List[BigDecimal]]
```

But when executed, internally, the stream may call the exchangeTable API dozens of times for various reasons (e.g., a Map may not contain the to currency, or the API call fails or takes too long to complete). The producer needs to worry about these things (and handle them) by coding these concerns inside the rates function that returns a Stream. But the users (consumers) of this Stream don't need to care about such small implementation details (at least for them). They may focus on higher-level functionalities like checking trends and making decisions based on them. **There are lots of concerns on both sides**, but using the Stream type, we can draw a very visible boundary between them.

> **THIS IS BIG!**
> Streams help to separate concerns in your application.

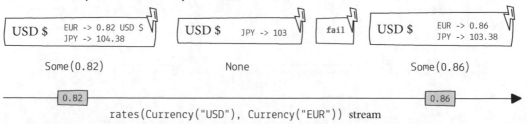

Sliding windows

We implemented the `rates` stream. Now we can take off our "rates producer" hat and put on the "rates consumer" one. We need to implement a new version of the `exchangeIfTrending` function using the `rates` stream that encapsulates all the nitty-gritty details regarding API calls and IO. We must solve the main problem as efficiently as possible, and that means we'll need **sliding windows** (the `sliding` combinator).

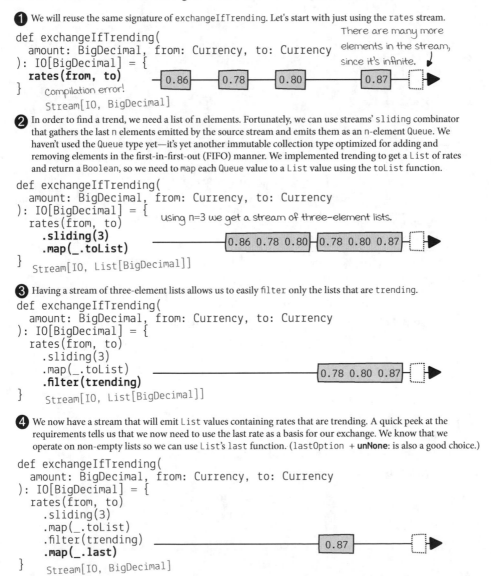

❶ We will reuse the same signature of `exchangeIfTrending`. Let's start with just using the `rates` stream.

```
def exchangeIfTrending(
  amount: BigDecimal, from: Currency, to: Currency
): IO[BigDecimal] = {
  rates(from, to)
}
```

There are many more elements in the stream, since it's infinite.

Compilation error!
`Stream[IO, BigDecimal]`

❷ In order to find a trend, we need a list of n elements. Fortunately, we can use streams' `sliding` combinator that gathers the last n elements emitted by the source stream and emits them as an n-element `Queue`. We haven't used the `Queue` type yet—it's yet another immutable collection type optimized for adding and removing elements in the first-in-first-out (FIFO) manner. We implemented `trending` to get a `List` of rates and return a `Boolean`, so we need to `map` each `Queue` value to a `List` value using the `toList` function.

```
def exchangeIfTrending(
  amount: BigDecimal, from: Currency, to: Currency
): IO[BigDecimal] = {
  rates(from, to)
    .sliding(3)
    .map(_.toList)
}
```

using n=3 we get a stream of three-element lists.

`Stream[IO, List[BigDecimal]]`

❸ Having a stream of three-element lists allows us to easily `filter` only the lists that are `trending`.

```
def exchangeIfTrending(
  amount: BigDecimal, from: Currency, to: Currency
): IO[BigDecimal] = {
  rates(from, to)
    .sliding(3)
    .map(_.toList)
    .filter(trending)
}
```

`Stream[IO, List[BigDecimal]]`

❹ We now have a stream that will emit `List` values containing rates that are trending. A quick peek at the requirements tells us that we now need to use the last rate as a basis for our exchange. We know that we operate on non-empty lists so we can use `List`'s `last` function. (`lastOption` + **unNone**: is also a good choice.)

```
def exchangeIfTrending(
  amount: BigDecimal, from: Currency, to: Currency
): IO[BigDecimal] = {
  rates(from, to)
    .sliding(3)
    .map(_.toList)
    .filter(trending)
    .map(_.last)
}
```

`Stream[IO, BigDecimal]`

⑤ We don't really need multiple trending rates. One is enough! Hence, we can just create a stream that emits a single element: **take(1)**. (There is also a **head** combinator that does exactly the same thing.) That's all we need so we compile the stream, but this time we use **lastOrError**, which returns an IO value that takes the last element a stream produced before it finishes (or an IO failure if this stream finishes without emitting anything, which won't happen in our case because the rates stream is infinite).

```
def exchangeIfTrending(
  amount: BigDecimal, from: Currency, to: Currency
): IO[BigDecimal] = {
  rates(from, to)
    .sliding(3)
    .map(_.toList)
    .filter(trending)
    .map(_.last)
    .take(1)
    .compile
    .lastOrError
}
```

> The function returns an IO value that describes a program that will do an unknown number of API calls and produce a BigDecimal value representing a trending rate. **It uses stream processing internally, but it's hidden from clients of this function.** They see and use only a single IO value.

It compiles now!

⑥ The requirements say we need to exchange the given amount. This is something we already know how to handle using the standard IO-based approach. Here, let's just return the total amount we'd exchange:

```
def exchangeIfTrending(
  amount: BigDecimal, from: Currency, to: Currency
): IO[BigDecimal] = {
  rates(from, to)
    .sliding(3)
    .map(_.toList)
    .filter(trending)
    .map(_.last)
    .take(1)
    .compile
    .lastOrError
    .map(_ * amount)
}
```

And that's it! We now have a working solution, based on streams. Note how we represented the streams graphically. This is a pretty common approach in both FP and stream processing paradigms. Here's the full diagram that shows all the intermediate stream values.

Remember that each stream is represented by an immutable Stream value!

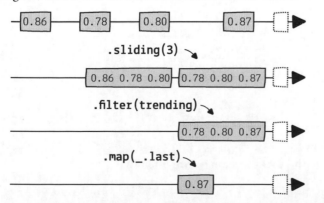

> Note that each function returns a new immutable value. Nothing is changed or modified. We can reuse each of these values any number of times.

Waiting between IO calls

The last problem we want to address is that we make subsequent IO calls as quickly as possible, usually in milliseconds. This is OK for demonstration purposes, but in real life you'd quickly drain API call quotas without getting any real value out of them. It's more practical to wait between API calls, cache them, or introduce some additional mechanisms. Let's focus on waiting between calls for now. How can we achieve a fixed one-second delay between subsequent API calls using the stream processing paradigm? A quick search in the documentation results in the Stream.fixedRate function.

> If you are not using the book's sbt console REPL, import scala.concurrent .duration._ and java.util .concurrent._

> The Stream.metered combinator would work as well.

```
> val delay: FiniteDuration  = FiniteDuration(1, TimeUnit.SECONDS)
  val ticks: Stream[IO, Unit] = Stream.fixedRate[IO](delay)
```

> FiniteDuration is just a product type that is used to represent duration in the Scala standard library. Here we define a value representing duration of one second.

ticks is a Stream value that represents a stream that emits Unit values (()) every 1 second, once executed. The great thing about this stream is that it won't block the running thread, while waiting to produce another value. IO-based programs, when executed, play fair and don't use threads from your thread pools when they don't need them. Additionally, remember that we operate on immutable values—delay and ticks above are just values—and we'll only start caring about thread pools when we go outside the functional core, later on.

> We are inside the functional core, where we only have pure functions and no unsafeRunSync calls.

Now that we have a stream of ticks that is time dependent, we can compose them with rates by **zipping** them.

> When we execute it we can be sure that it will work at least three seconds. To execute it, you will need to import a default thread pool configuration: import cats.effect.unsafe. implicits.global.

```
> val firstThreeRates: IO[List[(BigDecimal, Unit)]] =
    rates(Currency("USD"), Currency("EUR"))
      .zip(ticks).take(3).compile.toList
  firstThreeRates.unsafeRunSync()
→ List((0.80,()), (0.79,()), (0.82,()))
```
A list of tuples (BigDecimal, ()).

When we **zip** two streams, we need to wait for an element from both streams to produce an element of the combined stream. This way, the rate of emitting values in the combined stream is the rate of the slower input stream. If API calls are quick, then the slower one is ticks. This may be counterintuitive at first, but since all functional streams are lazy, this approach ensures that **we don't make API calls** (defined inside the rates stream) **more often than once a second!**

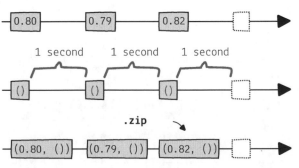

> There are more corner cases here, but the general approach to solving them remains the same.

Zipping streams

Step 3 ✔
Using IO
with
`Streams`

Note that when we `zip` two streams together, we get a stream of tuples back. Each tuple has an element from both streams, and its type is derived from the types of the elements emitted by each of the zipped streams. However, we sometimes don't care about both elements because we use `zip` to slow down one stream using another stream like we did with `ticks`. For these occasions we have special versions of `zip`: `zipLeft`, which zips two streams but produces elements from the "left" stream, and `zipRight`, which zips two streams and produces elements from the "right" one.

```
> val firstThreeRates: IO[List[BigDecimal]] =
    rates(Currency("USD"), Currency("EUR"))
      .zipLeft(ticks).take(3).compile.toList
  firstThreeRates.unsafeRunSync()
  → List(0.85, 0.71, 0.72)
```

When we execute it we can still be sure that it will work at least three seconds.

A list of BigDecimals, because we used `zipLeft` (rates are on the "left" of the `.zipLeft` call).

Now, we can create the final version of the `exchangeIfTrending` function, which behaves correctly and with a lot better performance.

```
def exchangeIfTrending(
  amount: BigDecimal, from: Currency, to: Currency
): IO[BigDecimal] = {
  rates(from, to)
    .zipLeft(ticks)
    .sliding(3)
    .map(_.toList)
    .filter(trending)
    .map(_.last)
    .take(1)
    .compile
    .lastOrError
    .map(_ * amount)
}
```

```
┌──────┐      ┌──────┐      ┌──────┐      ┌┄┄┄┐
│ 0.78 │──────│ 0.80 │──────│ 0.87 │──────│   │────▶
└──────┘      └──────┘      └──────┘      └┄┄┄┘

        1 second    1 second    1 second
         ⌒⌒⌒⌒        ⌒⌒⌒⌒        ⌒⌒⌒⌒
┌──┐      ┌──┐      ┌──┐      ┌┄┄┐
│()│──────│()│──────│()│──────│  │────▶
└──┘      └──┘      └──┘      └┄┄┘

                  .zipLeft ↘
┌──────┐      ┌──────┐      ┌──────┐      ┌┄┄┄┐
│ 0.78 │──────│ 0.80 │──────│ 0.87 │──────│   │────▶
└──────┘      └──────┘      └──────┘      └┄┄┄┘

                  .sliding(3) ↘
                        ┌────────────────┐ ┌┄┄┐
────────────────────────│ 0.78 0.80 0.87 │─│  │▶
                        └────────────────┘ └┄┄┘

              .filter(trending) ↘
                        ┌────────────────┐ ┌┄┄┐
────────────────────────│ 0.78 0.80 0.87 │─│  │▶
                        └────────────────┘ └┄┄┘

            .map(_.last) ↘
                          ┌──────┐        ┌┄┄┐
──────────────────────────│ 0.87 │────────│  │▶
                          └──────┘        └┄┄┘
```

And that's a wrap! We have a function that returns an IO value that describes a program that will make unknown number of API calls at a fixed rate of a maximum one call per second and will produce a given amount in the new currency only if the rates are trending.

The **IO** value we return is still just a value and can be used in a bigger program as a normal building block. The fact that it uses a stream-based approach internally is just another implementation detail. Clients of this function get an IO value, and that's what matters to them.

Benefits of using the stream-based approach

We have shown just a small fraction of possible stream functions to give you an intuition of what's possible. Whenever you have a new problem, it's usually **a good idea to explore the API of the functional type you are working with**. Chances are high that there is a helpful and well-tested function already available (like `sliding` and `zipLeft`).

There are several benefits of using the stream-based approach that are so compelling that many mainstream imperative technologies have included it in their APIs:

— *Definition of a stream is separated from its use site*—That means the definition may be infinite, and it will be up to the call site to define how many elements it really needs.

— *Nothing is done until it's really needed*—All operations are lazily evaluated.

— *The high-level API enables us to focus on the business domain instead of implementation details*—It's another example of essential versus accidental complexity.

— *More separated concerns*—Functions we pass as parameters to `Stream` combinators don't know they are used inside a stream.

— *Composability*—Developers can analyze a larger functionality by understanding smaller, independent pieces first and then understanding connections between them.

— *Encapsulating asynchronous boundaries*—Another implementation detail (an accidental concern) is that we may be running many streams concurrently, potentially on different computers (nodes), and joining results together using a larger stream. This approach may encapsulate all the details of crossing boundaries between nodes and synchronizing their results.

> There are multiple examples of providing higher-level APIs and hiding details like paging, buffering, chunking, batching, and distributing workloads. Encapsulating implementation details is especially popular in big data paradigms like MapReduce.

Synchronous vs. asynchronous

So far in the book we've been doing synchronous, sequential computations (i.e., computations that don't need more than one thread). In the last example, with the `ticks` stream, we have gently entered a new realm of multiple threads: asynchronous and non-blocking computations. It turns out that both `IO` and `Stream` values are useful in multi-threaded, asynchronous environments as well! That's something we are going to explore in the next chapter.

> **THIS IS BIG!**
> Many languages and libraries try to use the power of FP by including stream-like lazy APIs.

Many existing technologies expose APIs that try to tap into these benefits. You may have came across some terms like FRP (functional reactive programming), reactive programming, or reactive APIs. Such a "reactive" API usually mean that it includes combinators that operate lazily. **That's the power of FP sneaking into the mainstream!**

Summary

Stream-based architectures are very popular in many scenarios. You can use much of what you learned here in the following use cases:

CODE: CH09_*
Explore this
chapter's
source code
by looking at
ch09_* files
in the book's
repository.

— Streams are popular in UI programming (e.g., you get a stream of user clicks and can make some decision based on them similarly to our currency stream).

— Streams are used in distributed computing, where we may have producers and consumers that produce and consume elements at vastly different paces on different nodes. This is where reactive streams help a lot—this was implemented as part of reactive streams initiative and included in Java 9 (see the `Flow` class).

> many message-based systems choose reactive APIs by default.

— The stream approach is very popular when dealing with big data (i.e., sets of data that can't fit into the memory of a single computing node). This is a very broad definition, but it includes geographic data, paging infinite news and social feeds, and processing very big files and storing them (e.g., Hadoop/Spark).

No matter your use case, you can use well-known stream functions in all of the above, using a streaming library of your choice. Some function names will be different, but your intuition will help you find the right one! The following sections discuss the skills we've learned in this chapter.

Declaratively design complicated program flows

We learned to define program flows that include API calls using stream functions like `map`, `filter`, `append`, `eval`, `take`, `orElse`, `sliding`, `zip`, `zipLeft`, `repeat`, and `unNone`. We also learned how to use immutable Maps and tuples—they both are ubiquitous in FP.

> When you iterate over Maps, you iterate over a list of tuples. When you zip lists, you get a list of tuples. When you zip streams, you get a stream of tuples.

Use recursion and laziness to defer some decisions

We saw how recursion helps us start over in many places. We used it to make IO calls until we got what we needed to recover from a failure.

Handle IO-based streams of data

Streams of integers and streams of IO-based integers are very different, but we still managed to apply the same techniques and a similar API to handle all of them.

> We also learned how streams in general help us separate the concerns and invert the control by moving the API call responsibility to a different place.

Create and handle infinite stream of values

The inherent stream functions' laziness helped us create infinite streams.

Isolate time-dependent functionalities

We discussed a stream of Unit values produced every 1 second. We *zipped* it with the API calls stream to produce a stream that emits values at a fixed rate. We gently entered the multi-threaded environment by doing so. Now it's time to do a deep dive into the concurrent world.

Concurrent programs | 10

In this chapter
you will learn

- how to declaratively design concurrent program flows

- how to use lightweight virtual threads (fibers)

- how to safely store and access data from different
  threads

- how to process a stream of events asynchronously

> *We know the past but cannot control it. We control the future but cannot know it.*
>
> —Claude Shannon

Threads, threads everywhere

So far in the book we've been focusing on sequential programs: each program consisted of a sequence of expressions that were evaluated one by one using a single execution thread, usually connected to a single core.

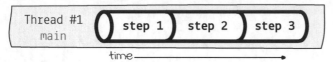

We won't be focusing on cores (or CPUs) in this chapter. We will focus on having multiple threads. Note that multiple threads can still run on a single core. The operating system switches between different threads to make sure everyone gets a chance to progress.

This mode of operation is very useful in practice. It's far easier to understand a program when it's sequential. It's easier to debug, and it's easier to make changes. However, we've witnessed some great improvements in the hardware area over the last decade, and right now the majority of consumer hardware is armed with multiple cores. The software needed to follow suit, and that's how multithreaded programming became the way to develop modern applications. Our programs need to do many things at once to deliver results for our users faster. They need to use many threads to preprocess data in the background or split computations into multiple parallel chunks. When we implement concurrent programs, they usually look like this.

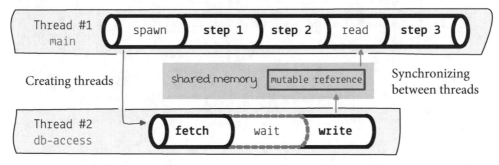

Entering the multithreaded world means that we no longer can debug and understand our applications with the level of confidence we had with single-threaded sequential ones. The mainstream, imperative approach doesn't help here, either. Having to deal with shared mutable states accessed by multiple threads, which additionally need to synchronize with each other, avoiding deadlocks and race conditions, turns out to be very hard to get right. On top of this, we still need to deal with all the problems we had in the sequential world, such as error handling and IO actions. **Concurrency adds another layer of complexity.** Does FP have some things that can help? Let's see and compare them with all the most popular imperative approaches to concurrency as we go.

We deal with a race condition when a result depends on the sequence or timing of other uncontrollable events, such as which thread finishes first.

Declarative concurrency

Functional programming has some ideas about how to handle concurrency differently. The main assumption still holds: immutable values and pure functions are always the same, no matter whether they are used and accessed by a single thread or multiple threads. It turns out these FP ideas make the concurrent programs easier to write! They take away the whole category of complexity problems related to shared mutable state and impure functions.

> **THIS IS BIG!**
> Writing concurrent programs is much easier when we can only deal with immutable values and pure functions.

An additional benefit is that we will still develop programs that consist of sequences of expressions executed on different threads. Hence, **everything we have learned so far will be applicable to multithreaded environments as well**! The only difference is that our pure functions will be evaluated concurrently. The rest remains the same: they will be evaluated as a part of programs defined using familiar IO values. Our **concurrent programs will still be defined declaratively** as lazily evaluated values!

Remember that in FP we want to be as declarative as possible (i.e., focus on what, not how).

In this chapter we will show just a single approach to functional concurrency. It's very practical and can be used in several functional languages besides Scala. Note, however, that this area is still undergoing rapid, dynamic development, so make sure to focus mostly on how pure functions, immutable values, and multiple threads can be used together to create user-friendly, responsive apps that are easy to read, change, and maintain. At the end of this chapter we will also point out some additional approaches that use these concepts in a different way (in Scala and other languages).

We will develop an application that gathers tourist "check-ins" in cities around the world and provides an up-to-date ranking of cities.

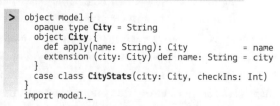

> **Requirements: City rankings**
> 1. The program needs to process a stream of check-ins from people around the world (a `Stream[IO, City]` value will be provided).
> 2. The program should allow getting the current top three cities' ranking (ranked by check-ins), while the check-ins are still being processed.

Let's start with some basic modeling. The model of a City is just a *newtype*. Additionally, we will need a product type that keeps a current check-ins counter for a given City.

```
object model {
  opaque type City = String
  object City {
    def apply(name: String): City      = name
    extension (city: City) def name: String = city
  }
  case class CityStats(city: City, checkIns: Int)
}
import model._
```

Sequential vs. concurrent

Before we move on to the full-blown multithreaded application, we'd like to show you that requirements for the check-ins ranking application, even though they scream *multithreading*, can be implemented on a single thread, using the sequential approach and functional techniques you already know! This will also help us make sure we understand what needs to be done in general and why we may still need concurrency (and multiple threads) to develop this application as required. Moreover, this is old but proven advice: start simple and iterate from there. Let's start simple.

The learning process in this chapter consists of three steps. We will recap what we learned about sequential programs and use that to learn about batching. Then we will start running things in parallel. Finally we will add some asynchronicity and end up with a full-blown multithreaded application that has some state.

Step 1

Sequential IOs
We will implement the first version of this chapter's problem solution using a sequential program described as an IO value, which is evaluated using a single thread.

Step 2

IOs with fibers
We will start using multiple threads (and potentially multiple cores) by learning about fibers. We will also need to store the current state safely, in a FP manner.

Step 3

Concurrent IOs and asynchronous access
In the last step we will show how to create a program that returns a handle to all running resources (including fibers and states) asynchronously in a user-friendly and readable manner.

When constrained to the sequential, single-threaded approach we need to interleave implementations for both requirements.

This process is called **batching**. We gather a batch of n items, process them, update the progress in some way (still sequentially), and then we proceed to do the same for the next batch of n items. Sometimes we may use a different way of batching (e.g., time-based), but the idea remains the same. By updating the ranking (which is a measure of progress from the user perspective) after each batch we give a feeling of *live* updates (users may get a feeling that things are happening at the same time), and it's fine in some scenarios. However, there is a hidden trade-off there, which we'll discuss in further detail after you implement this version.

Updating the ranking step may be an output IO action, like storing in a database, printing to the console, storing using an API call, or showing on an UI.

Coffee break: Sequential thinking

Requirements: City rankings
1. The program needs to process a stream of check-ins from people around the world (a `Stream[IO, City]` value will be provided).
2. The program should allow getting the current top three cities' ranking (ranked by check-ins), while the check-ins are still being processed.

Your first task is going to be a mix of some functional design, IO, and stream handling, which will all serve well to recap the material from the last few chapters and prepare you to handle concurrency issues.

Implement a function that processes each check-in one-by-one and produces a current ranking after processing each check-in element:

```
def processCheckIns(checkIns: Stream[IO, City]): IO[Unit]
```

To make things simpler, we are going to simulate "updating the ranking" as just printing the current version of a ranking on the console using `println`. Here's a stream that you can use to test your solution.

```
> val checkIns: Stream[IO, City] =
    Stream(
      City("Sydney"),
      City("Sydney"),
      City("Cape Town"),
      City("Singapore"),
      City("Cape Town"),
      City("Sydney")
    ).covary[IO]
```

You are free to come up with a design of your own. If you are stuck, remember that you can start with a small function first (e.g., function that gets a Map of check-ins and returns a List of the top three cities).

covary transforms a Stream of pure values into a stream of IO-based values, so we don't have to wrap them in IO.pure manually. checkIns is a Stream of six programs that will return cities when executed. The programs will be evaluated in the given order.

In a sense, it's going to be a batching algorithm with a batch size of n = 1. We will show how to use bigger batches after the exercise, but you are free to explore the APIs and think about the solution on your own.

Calling the **processCheckIns** function should return a program, which, once executed, prints seven ranking updates (including the first, empty ranking) to the console and returns a Unit value, ().

```
processCheckIns(checkIns).unsafeRunSync()
List()
List(CityStats(City(Sydney),1))
List(CityStats(City(Sydney),2))
List(CityStats(City(Sydney),2), CityStats(City(Cape Town),1))
List(CityStats(City(Sydney),2), CityStats(City(Singapore),1), CityStats(City(Cape Town),1))
List(CityStats(City(Cape Town),2), CityStats(City(Sydney),2), CityStats(City(Singapore),1))
List(CityStats(City(Sydney),3), CityStats(City(Cape Town),2), CityStats(City(Singapore),1))
→ ()
```

We "unsafeRunSync" this value here for testing purposes. Normally, we operate solely on IO values and "unsafeRunSync" only once outside of the functional core.

If you have problems coming up with a solution, have a look at `scan`, `foreach`, the Map type, and its `updated` function (or `updatedWith`?).

Go through the Stream API to find them.

Coffee break explained: Sequential thinking

There are many ways you could have approached this problem. The following is one of them. When confronted with a blank page, it's always hard to figure out where to start. Fortunately, our business requirements are pretty clear: each city has an integer indicating the current number of check-ins, and we need to return a ranking of the top three cities back.

```
> def topCities(cityCheckIns: Map[City, Int]): List[CityStats] = {
    cityCheckIns.toList
      .map(_ match {
        case (city, checkIns) => CityStats(city, checkIns)
      })
      .sortBy(_.checkIns)
      .reverse
      .take(3)
  }
```

> City
>
> a newtype (zero-cost wrapper) around a String value

> CityStats
>
> a product type of two types: City and Int (check-ins number)

We transform the Map into a List of tuples, then transform each tuple to a CityStats value, sort by check-ins, reverse to get the descending order, and take the maximum of the three first elements.

Another thing we need to do is to look at what's given to us and what options it provides. In our case, we have a Stream[IO, City]—a stream of City values, each indicating a single check-in. We know streams have many combinators, and going through a stream and accumulating values is a pretty common use case. And indeed, we can use scan to accumulate check-ins as a Map[City, Int]!

```
> checkIns.scan(Map.empty[City, Int])((cityCheckIns, city) => {
    val newCheckIns = cityCheckIns.get(city) match {
      case None          => 1
      case Some(checkIns) => checkIns + 1
    }
    cityCheckIns.updated(city, newCheckIns)
  })
```

This code does its job, but Map has an updatedWith function that takes both a key and a function from Option to Option, which we can use to make this code more concise. See the final solution (below) where we used the updatedWith function that behaves the same way.

Since scan emits a value of our accumulator each time it's computed, we now have a stream of Maps, which we can map using the topCities function we wrote and then show (println) the ranking to the user.

```
> def processCheckIns(checkIns: Stream[IO, City]): IO[Unit] = {
    checkIns
      .scan(Map.empty[City, Int])((cityCheckIns, city) =>
        cityCheckIns.updatedWith(city)(_.map(_ + 1).orElse(Some(1)))
      )
      .map(topCities)
      .foreach(IO.println)
      .compile.drain
  }
```

After the map function we have a Stream of List[City], which is what our users are interested in. We can then use the foreach function that takes an IO value describing a program that needs to be executed for each element of the stream. We pass a function, which is a more convenient way of writing this:
foreach(ranking => IO.delay(println(ranking)))

The need for batching

The first version of the check-ins processing app looks good, but unfortunately, it does not scale. The more cities in the accumulator Map, the longer the sorting process takes; therefore, more and more computation power will go into sorting. And since we only use one thread, the more time a single piece of functionality takes, the less time the other ones will get. In our case, more check-ins (cities) will make the accumulator large. So far, we used small streams to test our implementation. Let's notch it up a bit. Try to run your function on a stream of hundreds of thousands check-ins.

You can write big numbers like that in Scala, so they are more readable. Underscores are ignored by the compiler.

Our large stream of check-ins This is a stream of 600,003 (600_003) cities which we will use in the chapter to show how concurrency helps create responsive programs even in the presence of large datasets.

```
> val checkIns: Stream[IO, City] =
    Stream(City("Sydney"), City("Dublin"), City("Cape Town"), City("Lima"), City("Singapore"))
      .repeatN(100_000)
      .append(Stream.range(0, 100_000).map(i => City(s"City $i")))
      .append(Stream(City("Sydney"), City("Sydney"), City("Lima")))
      .covary[IO]
```

A stream of five cities: Sydney, Dublin, Cape Town, Lima, and Singapore is repeated 100_000 times, resulting in a stream of 500_000 elements. Then we append another 100_000 randomly named cities. Finally we append a small stream of three cities to make sure we know what the top of the ranking should look like.

```
> processCheckIns(checkIns).unsafeRunSync()
... // a long, long time (several minutes)
```

Quick exercise

Since we are waiting for your program to finish running, can you tell us what the final TOP3 ranking should be? This will test your streaming knowledge because you need to decode both the big checkIns stream above and the current sequential implementation. Additionally, it should make you feel better when you get the correct answer before the computer (how often does that happen?).

If the number of check-ins is large, say several hundred thousand, then these two elements will be executed several hundred thousand times!

Additionally, updating the ranking means calling the topCities function which needs to sort all the entries in the accumulator. The bigger the accumulator, the longer it takes to sort. Hence we are setting ourselves up for a very disappointing performance, especially in the light of a large amount of unique check-ins.

Our implementation does not scale! We need some **real batching**, not n = 1, but something bigger—let's say n = 100_000.

Answer:
See next page.

Batching implementation

To make our implementation more scalable, we will need yet another stream combinator, namely, chunkN. It takes a number n and transforms n elements into a single collection-like element, which is then emitted.

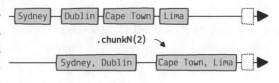

That's how we can quickly replace computing the ranking 600_000 times (once for each check-in) to computing it only six times (once for every 100_000 check-ins):

```
def processCheckIns(checkIns: Stream[IO, City]): IO[Unit] = {
  checkIns
    .scan(Map.empty[City, Int])((cityCheckIns, city) =>
      cityCheckIns.updatedWith(city)(_.map(_ + 1).orElse(Some(1)))
    )
    .chunkN(100_000)
    .map(_.last)
    .unNone
    .map(topCities)
    .foreach(IO.println)
    .compile.drain
}
```

Each check-in is processed and produces an accumulator Map, as was the case before. However, in this version, we batch (chunk) the accumulators into batches of 100_000 elements and then take only the last accumulator from a batch to compute the ranking. The ranking is still presented using a println.

Now you can check whether you got it right and taunt your computer if you did.

Now, it will finish processing pretty quickly, printing the final ranking in the process (the last one from seven printed lines).

```
List(CityStats(City(Sydney),100002), CityStats(City(Lima),100001), CityStats(City(Singapore),100000))
```

Batching trade-offs

We won't be focusing on batching in this chapter, but please remember that it's always a possibility and may prove to be better for some cases. Sometimes, if you can get away with writing a sequential solution to a business problem, it will end up being a simpler one as well. However, there are always some trade-offs to consider. In our case:

- The bigger the batch size in this sequential example, the lower the frequency of ranking updates (users get an update only every n check-ins). It may be OK for some cases but will definitely not be for others.

- There are some corner cases that need to be handled. For example, what happens when there are 590_000 check-ins and then 5 minutes of silence? 90_000 check-ins will sit there, not processed, waiting for the remaining 10_000 to be able to compute a new ranking. Therefore, you'd need to add some additional time-based constraints, which is totally doable but adds complexity nonetheless. Again, this may or may not be OK in a given case.

The concurrent world

The context has been set. We have implemented the requirements for a check-in processor in a sequential way, using batching to make it good enough in terms of performance and scalability. But that's as long as we can possibly go constrained to a single thread. When we allow ourselves to use more than one thread, a brand new world of opportunities emerges. We no longer need to decide how much computation time each functionality needs. We can give each of the two functionalities its own thread, and if our program gets assigned two CPUs, they will do their work simultaneously. In the case where we had many threads at our disposal, we could use n threads to process batches of check-ins in parallel and a single thread that updates the ranking.

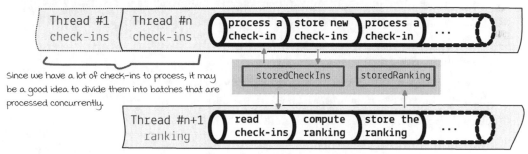

Since we have a lot of check-ins to process, it may be a good idea to divide them into batches that are processed concurrently.

This, in turn, exposes us to a problem of **shared mutable state** because the ranking functionality needs access to the current checkIns Map, which is updated by the check-in processing functionality. So all execution threads will need to access the same memory address, which additionally changes over time. This is the *concurrent* shared mutable state in action, and we will try to deal with it using functional programming techniques.

Note that the amount of threads we want to create is strictly dependent on the amount of CPU resources we have at our disposal. When you have two CPUs for the whole application, creating one hundred threads to process check-ins may not be a good idea. There are lots of variables that play a role here, so the best advice in such cases is this: benchmark your implementation and optimize based on results. To make things simpler **we will use two threads**—one for check-ins and one for ranking—throughout the rest of the chapter, but it's going to be implemented in a way that makes it safe even when there are more threads.

Using multiple threads is faster because the ranking is being updated continuously in a separate thread in parallel with the check-ins' processing threads. However, this improvement comes at a cost! (More on that soon.)

Using two threads doesn't really expose us to the shared mutable state problem because each variable is mutated by a single thread. However, we will increase the number of check-in threads at the end of the chapter to prove that the FP solution works fine in such cases as well.

The concurrent state

Let's first give some background on how we deal with threads and concurrent state in some imperative languages, based on Java.

```java
var cityCheckIns = new HashMap<String, Integer>();
Runnable task = () -> {
  for(int i = 0; i < 1000; i++) {
    var cityName = i % 2 == 0 ? "Cairo" : "Auckland";
    cityCheckIns.compute(cityName,
            (city, checkIns) -> checkIns != null ? checkIns + 1 : 1);
  }
};
new Thread(task).start();
new Thread(task).start();
```

We create a mutable HashMap that models our concurrent state. Then, we create a Runnable that adds 500 check-ins to each Cairo and Auckland.

Then, we start two threads that use the same Runnable, so we expect that both Cairo and Auckland will have 1000 check-ins each in the HashMap once they finish processing. But they won't. What will be the result, in your opinion?

(Answer at the bottom.)

We will use the setup above to introduce the imperative approaches to solving our concurrent state problem. We will use a combo of diagrams and small Java snippets when necessary, but we won't show a full-blown imperatives solution in the book.

Fully working examples are available in the book's companion source code.

More generally, we will discuss **synchronization primitives**. These are tools implemented in operating systems, languages, and libraries that help us synchronize the execution of multiple threads. This usually means one of the two following things:

— *Synchronizing the access to a common resource*—For example, a file, socket, in-memory variable, database connection

Also known as the critical section problem

— *Synchronizing (or coordinating) the execution order of multiple threads*—For example, making sure a thread starts executing only after another thread produced something or waiting for something to happen before launching a set of threads

Also known as the thread signaling/thread interaction problem

There are many various primitives used in the industry, and we can't cover them all here. We will just briefly identify the most common approaches and then show how some of them are very useful in composition with FP concepts.

Have you ever used a Semaphore or a CountDownLatch?

Q Is it even possible to be able to mutate a value in memory and still write pure functions?

A Yes! Note that even though we explicitly started using immutable values at the beginning of the book, we have still been able to write so many different applications, and they all have been modeling data that changes over time. We have tools that use similar approaches in the concurrent world as well, but before we introduce them, let's see what are the most popular solutions to the concurrent state in modern languages.

Answer: much fewer than 1000 check-ins. There is also a chance that one of the threads throws an exception.

Imperative concurrency

When you manually create two threads that modify the same mutable variable, you will most likely end up with nondeterministic behavior. Each thread needs to read the current value, compute something, and then store the updated value. In the meantime, the other thread could have written an updated value, which would now be overwritten. That's why we got fewer than 1,000 check-ins in the previous example.

All the imperative concurrency examples we will show in this section are written in Java.

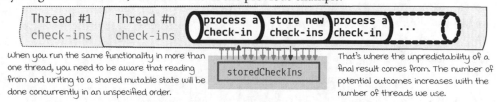

When you run the same functionality in more than one thread, you need to be aware that reading from and writing to a shared mutable state will be done concurrently in an unspecified order.

That's where the unpredictability of a final result comes from. The number of potential outcomes increases with the number of threads we use.

Some implementations, including the one we showed, may additionally *sometimes* cause a ConcurrentModificationException. This will pop up from time to time, nondeterministically, depending on how operations from both threads are ordered. Therefore, in a nutshell, just creating more than one thread and not caring about the concurrent access problem guarantees we will encounter random behavior or random failure—all bets are off. We need to guard the access to a common resource, which in this case is a mutable in-memory variable. Let's see which synchronization primitives are the most popular.

Monitors and locks

Monitors are synchronization primitives that control the access to a given resource by making sure only a single thread uses it at a time. They also keep track of all other threads that want to use (or acquire) the resource and notify them once it becomes available. They use

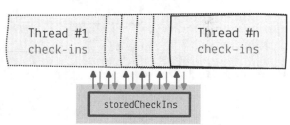

locks (*mutexes*) internally. In its most basic form, a monitor works like this:

```
var cityCheckIns = new HashMap<String, Integer>();
Runnable task = () -> {
  for(int i = 0; i < 1000; i++) {
    var cityName = i % 2 == 0 ? "Cairo" : "Auckland";
    synchronized (cityCheckIns) {
      cityCheckIns.compute(cityName,
        (city, checkIns) -> checkIns != null ? checkIns + 1 : 1);
    }
  }
};
```

When we enter the synchronized block, no other thread can enter it, and it waits until we exit. This means that all read-write sequences done by the compute function are ordered.

There are lots of other options that could help us achieve this result. For example, in Java you also have a Lock interface. We treat all such options as similar, imperative mechanisms because you need to explicitly provide lock and unlock statements to use them.

The actor model

In the actor model, we use actors as primary concurrency units, instead of using threads directly. Actors **encapsulate** state, and the only way we can interact with an actor and its state is by **sending and receiving asynchronous messages**. These messages are buffered in an inbox and processed by the actor instance one by one, making sure only a single thread has access to

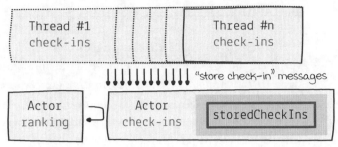

The ranking actor is responsible for computing the ranking. It gets the current check-ins by sending the "get check-ins" message and waiting for a reply from the check-ins actor, which encapsulates the Map.

its state at a given time. Actors can create more actors—forming actor hierarchies—which help in dealing with potential failures. Here's the example implemented using the actor model in Java (and the Akka library):

We show this implementation in Java because it belongs to the imperative world. More in the book's code repository.

```
class CheckInsActor extends AbstractActor {
  private Map<String, Integer> cityCheckIns = new HashMap<>();

  public Receive createReceive() {
    return receiveBuilder()
      .match(StoreCheckIn.class, message -> {
        cityCheckIns.compute(message.cityName,
            (city, checkIns) -> checkIns != null ? checkIns + 1 : 1);
      }).match(GetCurrentCheckIns.class, message -> {
        getSender().tell(new HashMap<>(cityCheckIns), null);
      }).build();
  }
}
```

The receive method is called sequentially for each incoming message. Here we expect two kinds of messages, represented by two classes: StoreCheckIn and GetCurrentCheckIns.

tell sends a message to an actor.

You can't create the CheckInsActor class using a new statement. You can create it using a special function that returns an ActorRef, which only enables you to send messages. The state is safely stored inside the actor.

Thread-safe data structures

Using the actor model to safely modify a HashMap may seem like overkill because we also can use mutable data structures that can be accessed (both reading and writing) by multiple threads at once without damaging the consistency of the data it holds: "thread-safe" data structures. One example is Java's ConcurrentHashMap:

Additional synchronization layer

storedCheckIns

Note that, while thread-safe data structures work very well, they are specialized and can't easily be used in many scenarios. Actors are much more versatile.

```
var cityCheckIns = new ConcurrentHashMap<String, Integer>();
Runnable task = () -> {
  for(int i = 0; i < 1000; i++) {
    var cityName = i % 2 == 0 ? "Cairo" : "Auckland";
    cityCheckIns.compute(cityName,
          (city, checkIns) -> checkIns != null ? checkIns + 1 : 1);
  }
}
```

Atomic references

We won't be using any of the imperative synchronization primitives in our functional programs because they are all based on mutability and providing "recipes." Using them would mean that we couldn't write pure functions, and we'd lose all the benefits that come with them: trustworthy signatures, readability, and risk-free refactoring.

We could use these mechanisms in functional programs by wrapping them in some IOs. This is always a possibility if you really need to use some impure code in your applications. However, there are better options we'd like to introduce.

There is a far better option that we will use and which is already available in many mainstream languages, including Java. **An atomic reference** is a very practical mechanism that makes use of the **compare-and-set** (or *compare-and-swap*, or *CAS*) operation. This operation behaves deterministically in a multithreaded environment without needing to use locks, even internally, as is the case with thread-safe data structures (some people describe such mechanics as *"lock-free"*).

```
var cityCheckIns = new AtomicReference<>(new HashMap<String, Integer>());
Runnable task = () -> {
  for(int i = 0; i < 1000; i++) {
    var cityName = i % 2 == 0 ? "Cairo" : "Auckland";

    var updated = false;
    while(!updated) {
      var currentCheckIns = cityCheckIns.get();
      var newCheckIns = new HashMap<>(currentCheckIns);

      newCheckIns.compute(cityName, (city, checkIns) -> checkIns != null ? checkIns + 1 : 1);
      updated = cityCheckIns.compareAndSet(currentCheckIns, newCheckIns);
    }
  }
};
```

AtomicReference provides the compareAndSet function that takes two values: the first is what we think is the current value stored inside the atomic reference, and the second is the value we'd like to store there. The function returns true if the value was successfully replaced and false if the current value we provided is not valid (it was changed by some other thread in the meantime).

If compareAndSet returns false, we need to repeat the whole process of getting the current value and updating it. Note that we are required to use a copy of the HashMap, because compareAndSet uses reference equality. We used the copying technique earlier in the book, just before introducing immutable values, which are a perfect fit for AtomicReference and compareAndSet!

This operation is very versatile and can be used to implement other synchronization primitives. Additionally, if you are familiar with database locks, this is exactly the technique that is used to implement *optimistic locking* (all updates are accepted when your application proves that it knows the most up-to-date version of given data). It turns out that this technique is very universal and readable. It **perfectly suits the functional programming paradigm**, even in Java, which has a functional alternative to the compareAndSet + imperative loop technique used above, called **updateAndGet**, which takes a function.

THIS IS BIG! In FP, programmers tend to use atomic references a lot when creating concurrent programs.

```
cityCheckIns.updateAndGet(oldCheckIns -> {
  var newCheckIns = new HashMap<>(oldCheckIns);
  newCheckIns.compute(cityName,
            (city, checkIns) -> checkIns != null ? checkIns + 1 : 1);
  return newCheckIns;
});
```

This code can safely replace the body of the for loop above.

Introducing Ref

We have just discussed some approaches to both the concurrent access problem and thread coordination. We will now show functional tools that enable us to use many threads and solve the concurrent access problem.

To write concurrent programs, you don't need to create locks, wait for them, or notify other threads when you are finished. You also don't need to settle for mutable data structures. In FP, we model everything as immutable values. We will now show a **functional atomic reference** that will allow us to safely store a changing value using just pure functions and IO values.

Ref[IO, A] is an immutable value that represents an asynchronous concurrent mutable (and thus, side-effectful) reference to an immutable value of type A (essentially, a wrapper around an AtomicReference).

Note how similar this description is to the way we described the Stream[IO, A] type, which is an immutable value that represents a stream of side-effectfully generated values of type A and how similar it is to IO[A], which is an immutable value representing a side-effectful program that, when executed, will produce an A value.

> We will talk about synchronous versus asynchronous computation more later in the chapter, but for now it means that the thread that updates the reference doesn't actively wait nor block.

> Remember how we used Java's AtomicReference? It required us to use immutable values. We used copies, but real immutable values are far easier to use!

Concurrency primitives trade-offs

All of the primitives we describe in this chapter can help us write correct multithreaded applications. Without them, all bets are off and we **can be sure** that the data will quickly become inconsistent. Making sure all changes to our data are consistent is not free though. It comes at a cost, which needs to be properly managed. Debugging possible deadlocks, livelocks, and contention problems will become the bread and butter for a programmer of a multithreaded application.

Performance is usually heavily affected. For example, we use more CPU cycles when using *compare-and-swap operations* to update highly contended memory address. Sometimes we make users wait for the up-to-date results longer. All of these concerns are usually not essential from the business perspective, unless they visibly affect the user experience. However, returning correct results is always an essential concern. We don't want any race conditions or indeterministic outputs, but we still want all the pure function benefits (for the same arguments, you always get the same result!) and easier maintenance. We need to design applications that are responsive enough and return correct results.

> We discuss low-level programmer-centric tools in this chapter, but remember you have also some user-facing concepts at your disposal. For example, eventual consistency means that the ranking users get is a correct one but may be from the past, and they will eventually get the current one when they repeat the process. This is a valid approach to some problems!

Updating Ref **values**

Ref[IO, A] is a value representing a concurrently accessible mutable reference. I know it's a mouthful, but let's appreciate how consistent it is with all the previous concepts we discussed. We use immutable values to represent everything and make it simple to write programs using pure functions. What kind of pure functions can we use with Ref? There are many built-in options, but we will focus on a single one, which is a functional alternative to the compare-and-swap (CAS) operation. Ref[IO, A] provides an update function that has the following signature:

```
def update(f: A => A): IO[Unit]
```

Do you see the CAS operation there? We just need to provide a function from A to A and we are done! This is how we mutate a reference to the concurrently accessible value of type A. We won't need anything else. The function we pass will get the current A and will need to return the new A back. The Ref type internals take care of everything, including a possibility of value A being changed by another thread. If the value A changes in the meantime, our function f will be called again with the changed value A. Note how this behavior is consistent with how other CAS implementations, including AtomicReference we discussed earlier, work. Most importantly, **the update function returns an IO value back**, which means that **we just get a description of a side-effectful program that changes the reference to a different immutable value**. Nothing is executed until somebody, outside of the functional core, executes this IO value (which most likely is as a part of a bigger IO value).

For example, say we have a value of type Ref[IO, Int], which represents a concurrently mutable reference to an integer, which is 0 at the beginning, and we run two threads.

> Thread #2
> ```
> ref.update(_ + 2).unsafeRunSync
> ```
> Thread #1
> ```
> ref.update(_ + 1).unsafeRunSync
> ```

The mutable reference will always have value 3 when both threads conclude. That's how we mutate using only pure functions and immutable values. It doesn't look bad so far, does it? If it all feels too easy for you, let's see if you can correctly answer the following question.

Quick exercise

Assume that the expression Ref.of[IO,Int](0) creates the concurrently accessible mutable reference to an Int value that is initially 0. What, in your opinion, should be the type of this expression?

THIS IS BIG!
We model concurrently accessible shared mutable states as immutable values.

→ 1. We will learn how to create Ref values very soon. Focus on the usage for now.

2. We will learn how to create threads as a part of programs described by IO values later in the chapter. Until then, let's use unsafeRunSync to prove the properties of Ref values.

Answer:
IO[Ref[IO, Int]]

Using Ref **values**

Not only updating a concurrently accessible mutable reference to an immutable value is side-effectful. **Creating** such a value is side-effectful too! This fact is represented in the Ref.of function signature:

```
def of(a: A): IO[Ref[IO, A]]
```

Ref.of returns a description of a program, which, when executed, will return an immutable Ref value that represents a concurrently mutable reference. **Updating** this mutable reference is described as another IO value (returned by the update function we have just discussed).

    A very similar story can be told when it comes to **getting** the value held by the concurrent reference. Ref[IO, A] has a get function that returns ... an IO[A] of course!

```
def get: IO[A]
```

We have dealt with so many side-effectful programs in the last two chapters that we can now repurpose the lightning symbol to represent the IO value that describes an unsafe program, which needs to be executed later in the codebase. Earlier, we marked only bare unsafe code this way.

More generally, Ref[F, A] has two type parameters: F is the "effect" type (we use IO in the book) and A is the type of the stored element.

Ref[IO, A]

A value of type Ref[IO, A] **describes** a concurrently accessible mutable reference that refers to an immutable value of type A.

To create a value, you call

```
Ref.of[IO, A](initialValue: A)
```

The Ref.of function returns a Ref[IO, A] **wrapped in an IO**. You can get or update the A value stored inside, getting another IO back:

```
ref.get   ref.update(f: A => A)
```

    A   ()   We only provide a pure function from A to A, and the internals take care of the rest.

Combining all of this knowledge allows us to create a simple program, which, while still single-threaded—we still don't know how to create threads in FP—shows how the Ref API behaves in the wild. We are going to introduce multithreaded programs very soon, and we'll take full advantage of Ref then. For now, the following example doesn't really provide any benefit over using an Int directly; it's just an API demonstration.

```
> val example: IO[Int] = for {
    counter <- Ref.of[IO, Int](0)
    _       <- counter.update(_ + 3)
    result  <- counter.get
  } yield result

  example.unsafeRunSync()
  → 3
```

We use all three functions: Ref.of, update and get. Remember that each of them returns an IO value, and that is why we can safely flatMap them all in a single for comprehension.

This example is not spectacular, but all these three functions and Ref will come in handy once we start using them in multiple threads. Note that all update operations are guaranteed to be executed safely (i.e., they will never overwrite any updates coming from other threads).

If you don't use the book's sbt console, import cats.effect._.

Making it all concurrent

We know how Refs work and how they embrace the compare-and-swap mechanism without making programmers think too much about all the possible execution orders in the concurrent environment—it's much more declarative than the imperative solutions presented earlier. Starting a new thread is done in a similar spirit. You don't have to create any Thread objects. **You just need to declaratively state which things should run in parallel**. In a sense, a concurrent application is just a bunch of small, sequential, side-effectful programs running in parallel. And if you think about it long enough, you'll notice that we already have a value that describes a sequential, side-effectful program: an IO. Intuitively, we should have an option to execute a list of IOs using multiple threads, right? And we do! Let's see this in action. Here's a *sequential* program.

```
> val exampleSequential: IO[Int] = for {
    counter <- Ref.of[IO, Int](0)
    _        <- List(counter.update(_ + 2),
                     counter.update(_ + 3),
                     counter.update(_ + 4)).sequence
    result  <- counter.get
  } yield result

  exampleSequential.unsafeRunSync()
  → 9
```

Remember that update returns an IO value, so we have a List of three IO values. As you remember, calling sequence on such a List returns a single IO value that, when executed, will execute all the IO values from the original List and return their results as a List.

The sequence function, which is defined on a List of IO values, executes them in a sequence, just like the for comprehension (flatMaps) executes IO values sequentially. However, note that none of the three IO values—three different Ref updates—depends on each other, so they don't need to be executed one by one (sequentially). On the other hand, the creation of the counter Ref value needs to happen before any counter.update programs because they all use (or depend on) the counter value. Hence, we still need to use flatMap in this case, but we can safely run the three counter.update programs in parallel. And it's not hard at all—we can do so using the **parSequence** function.

THIS IS BIG!
In FP, a multi-threaded program can be modeled as an immutable list of sequential programs.

```
> val exampleConcurrent: IO[Int] = for {
    counter <- Ref.of[IO, Int](0)
    _        <- List(counter.update(_ + 2),
                     counter.update(_ + 3),
                     counter.update(_ + 4)).parSequence
    result  <- counter.get
  } yield result

  exampleConcurrent.unsafeRunSync()
  → 9
```

parSequence has the same API: it takes a List of IO values and returns an IO value describing a program that, when executed, will execute all the IO programs and return their results in a List. However, unlike sequence, parSequence doesn't run the IOs sequentially; it runs them in parallel, each in its own "thread"!

parSequence **in action**

The programs we tried to run in parallel are very small, and therefore, we can't really see any difference in the running time between sequence and parSequence. Let's change that and introduce some latency to our IO programs. Let's use IO.sleep that has the following signature:

```
def sleep(delay: FiniteDuration): IO[Unit]
```

This function returns an IO value that describes a program that, when executed, sleeps for a given time and returns. This is the purely functional equivalent of Thread.sleep. It doesn't block any threads.

We say it's asynchronous and non-blocking, meaning that it doesn't block any threads while waiting. The threads can therefore be used by other pieces of functionality.

Again, when we use flatMap, we get a sequential program, so to have an IO value describing a program that first sleeps for one second and then updates the Ref value adding 3, we can just write

```
IO.sleep(FiniteDuration(1, TimeUnit.SECONDS))
  .flatMap(_ => counter.update(_ + 3))
```

A two-step for comprehension would work here as well.

We can use sleep to update our previous example and have three counter updates, but two of them executing after waiting for one second.

```
for {
  counter  <- Ref.of[IO, Int](0)
  program1 = counter.update(_ + 2)
  program2 = IO.sleep(FiniteDuration(1, TimeUnit.SECONDS)).flatMap(_ => counter.update(_ + 3))
  program3 = IO.sleep(FiniteDuration(1, TimeUnit.SECONDS)).flatMap(_ => counter.update(_ + 4))

  _        <- List(program1, program2, program3)._____
  result   <- counter.get
} yield result
```

Remember that we can define values inside the for comprehension without flatMapping them by using = instead of <-, so program1, 2, and 3 are all IO values.

sequence

parSequence

How long (in seconds) will both versions be running when executed? In most scenarios, the sequence-based program will run for at least two seconds because all three programs are running one by one. The parSequence-based version **will run for at least one second**. In this version the three programs described by the three IO values are executed in parallel, safely updating the concurrent mutable reference (counter). During its execution, the IO value created using parSequence waits for all three "threads" to finish their work before returning a value (a list of program results) or an error in case at least one IO failed. If everything goes well, we get 9 as a result—**no race conditions, no surprises**.

Handling errors in programs described by IO values works exactly the same as in sequential ones. We learned all the techniques previously.

We were able to create an IO value describing a concurrent program that always returns the value we expect. And since it's a concurrent program described by a single IO value, we can use it in any place we used other IO values previously. It's a seamless integration with all the other programs. But how does concurrent IO work internally?

Threads and fibers

Notice that when we write "threads" (in quotes) we don't really mean the threads you are accustomed to from imperative languages. Classically, a Thread object, which is an operating system's native thread under the hood, incurs a large overhead—allocating and deallocating threads are heavyweight operations due to underlying operating system native calls. That's why many modern applications use **thread pools**—preallocated sets of worker threads that execute submitted logic.

However, both solutions—manually creating OS-level threads and using thread pools—suffer from a more pressing issue. They are pretty low-level, and they require a lot of code to cover all the corner cases. When using these approaches, programmers need to write and maintain code, which is not usually related to an essential business concern. Creating and managing concurrent threads of execution should be a more straightforward endeavor. From the business logic perspective, we'd ideally want to just say "run this in parallel"—it should be as simple as that. Handling corner cases, thread pools, and scheduling things to run in parallel are not simple tasks, and more importantly, they shouldn't clutter the logic of our application! Hence, there is a big trade-off between simplicity, correctness, and efficiency in writing concurrent programs.

Many modern programming languages and libraries, including Scala, use a more lightweight concept for threads: **fibers** (or *green threads*). This is an efficient concurrency mechanism, which is not connected directly with OS-level threading and, therefore, is much more usable, light, and worry-free. Conceptually, they are used for exactly the same thing: to run things in parallel.

Fibers are sometimes called logical threads because they are just objects representing computations, while the real work is still done on real threads, which are now a more low-level concept. Many fibers can be executed on a single thread. We still use thread pools, but they are **completely separated from the application perspective**. You don't need any thread pools to create an IO value. You need a thread pool only when you want to execute it. This idea improves maintainability and helps us focus on the logic—not accidental concerns.

Fibers have made their way into imperative languages, too. Java will introduce them as a part of Project Loom. They are called virtual threads there, but the underlying principles are very similar.

THIS IS BIG! In functional programs we work with fibers instead of OS-level threads.

Note that there is a difference between concurrency and parallelism. When you run two pieces of logic concurrently, it means that they may start and make progress in the same time period. Even a single CPU core can run them concurrently. When you run two pieces of logic in parallel, you need at least two cores to run them exactly at the same time, simultaneously—one alongside the other.

We have already used import cats.effect .unsafe.implicits .global in chapter 9. That's where thread pools are configured. You can always provide your own configuration.

Practicing concurrent IOs

It's time we check your understanding of fibers and concurrent states. Let's go back to a familiar example where we use an IO value:

```
def castTheDie(): IO[Int]   import ch10_CastingDieConcurrently.castTheDie
```

Your task is to define the following IO values:

1. Wait one second, then cast two dies concurrently, wait for both of them, and return their sum.

2. Cast two dies concurrently, store each result in a concurrently accessible reference that holds a `List`, and, finally, return it as a result.

3. Cast three dies concurrently, store each result in a concurrently accessible reference that holds a `List`, and, finally, return it as a result.

4. Cast 100 dies concurrently, store the total number of 6s in a concurrently accessible reference, and return its value as a result.

5. Cast one hundred dies concurrently, waiting one second before each of them, and return their sum (without using a concurrent reference).

Hint: You already know how to create lists of many programs. List.range will work here, but try using List.fill instead!

Program #5, when executed, should run for a little bit more than one second.

Answers

1
```
for {
  _      <- IO.sleep(1.second)
  result <- List(castTheDie(), castTheDie()).parSequence
} yield result.sum
```

> After importing `scala.concurrent.duration._`, you can easily transform any `Int` into `FiniteDuration` by using many built-in functions: `second`, `seconds`, `milliseconds` and more.

2
```
for {
  storedCasts <- Ref.of[IO, List[Int]](List.empty)
  singleCast   = castTheDie()
                   .flatMap(result => storedCasts.update(_.appended(result)))
  _           <- List(singleCast, singleCast).parSequence
  casts       <- storedCasts.get
} yield casts
```

3
```
for {
  storedCasts <- Ref.of[IO, List[Int]](List.empty)
  singleCast   = castTheDie()
                   .flatMap(result => storedCasts.update(_.appended(result)))
  _           <- List.fill(3)(singleCast).parSequence
  casts       <- storedCasts.get
} yield casts
```

> You can use `List.fill` to create a list of many elements instead of using `List.range(...).map(...)`.

4
```
for {
  storedCasts <- Ref.of[IO, Int](0)
  singleCast   = castTheDie().flatMap(result =>
                   if (result == 6) storedCasts.update(_ + 1) else IO.unit)
  _           <- List.fill(100)(singleCast).parSequence
  casts       <- storedCasts.get
} yield casts
```

5
```
List.fill(100)(IO.sleep(1.second).flatMap(_ => castTheDie())).parSequence.map(_.sum)
```

Modeling concurrency

Let's go back to our initial plan for creating the check-ins processor.

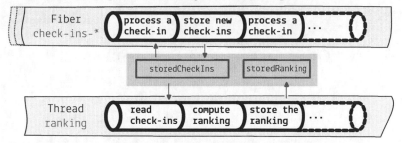

This diagram has been useful to model our thread-based world. However, knowing how fibers, parSequence, and Ref work, we can now model this application in a **functional way: using just values** and their relationships!

Modeling concurrently accessible references

We need two concurrent references: one for storing check-ins (**storedCheckIns**) and a second for storing the current ranking (**storedRanking**). This will ensure that getting the current ranking is a really fast operation because we will just read from memory instead of calculating the ranking on each read. This is a common optimization.

Modeling sequential and concurrent programs

We need at least two different sequential programs: **checkInsProgram**, which, when executed, will drain the input stream of check-ins, storing each of them safely in the storedCheckIns reference; and **rankingProgram** which, when executed, will infinitely read the current check-ins, calculate the ranking, and safely store it inside storedRanking. Both of them are IO values. We also know that the final solution needs to run both programs concurrently, and we can model that as another IO value.

> You create fibers indirectly by transforming a list of IO values using parSequence. Hence, the whole program will just be an IO value that, when executed, will run "fibered" IO values concurrently.

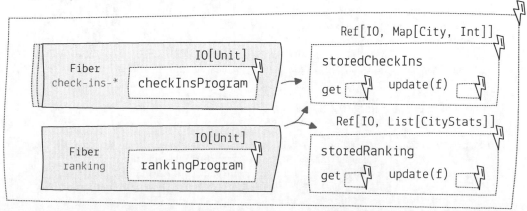

Coding using Refs and fibers

Our previous version was a sequential program that looked like this:

Step 2

IOs with fibers

```
def processCheckIns(checkIns: Stream[IO, City]): IO[Unit] = {
  checkIns
    .scan(Map.empty[City, Int])((cityCheckIns, city) =>
      cityCheckIns.updatedWith(city)(_.map(_ + 1).orElse(Some(1)))
    )
    .map(topCities)
    .foreach(IO.println)
    .compile.drain
}
```

We also wrote a better, batching version that used the chunkN stream combinator, but it had its disadvantages as well. The ranking wasn't updating as often as we wanted.

We can, therefore, rewrite processCheckIns to a concurrent application. We will show how to implement it but then will leave a very tiny but important detail for you to implement, so pay attention because this is the place where all of what we've learned comes together.

❶ Let's delete the current implementation and start over. The for comprehension represents a sequential program. The first step will be to create both concurrent references:

```
def processCheckIns(checkIns: Stream[IO, City]): IO[Unit] = {
  for {
    storedCheckIns <- Ref.of[IO, Map[City, Int]](Map.empty)
    storedRanking  <- Ref.of[IO, List[CityStats]](List.empty)
  } yield ()
}
```

❷ We need two programs: one for updating the ranking infinitely and the second to store the check-ins that appear in the incoming stream. Let's start with the ranking one:

```
def processCheckIns(checkIns: Stream[IO, City]): IO[Unit] = {
  for {
    storedCheckIns <- Ref.of[IO, Map[City, Int]](Map.empty)
    storedRanking  <- Ref.of[IO, List[CityStats]](List.empty)
    rankingProgram = updateRanking(storedCheckIns, storedRanking)
  } yield ()
}
```

> We first define the rankingProgram IO value by calling the updateRanking function, which will be implemented later. We now focus on finishing the processCheckIns function. This is yet another example of the top-down approach to design, where we focus on the client side first. When we get the processCheckIns function right, we will be able to move "down" and fill all the unimplemented signatures.

```
def updateRanking(
    storedCheckIns: Ref[IO, Map[City, Int]],
    storedRanking: Ref[IO, List[CityStats]]
): IO[Unit] = ???
```

> We will need this kind of function. It will need to read current checkins, calculate the ranking and store it in storedRanking. Then it will need to repeat the process again and again. It will need to happen concurrently with other functionalities. We will implement it soon.

❸ The second program is the one that stores check-ins in the concurrently accessible reference. We already know how to transform a Stream value into an IO value. We need to run a program for each element in the stream. We'll call it storeCheckIn and use it inside processCheckIns:

```
def processCheckIns(checkIns: Stream[IO, City]): IO[Unit] = {
  for {
    storedCheckIns  <- Ref.of[IO, Map[City, Int]](Map.empty)
    storedRanking   <- Ref.of[IO, List[CityStats]](List.empty)
    rankingProgram  = updateRanking(storedCheckIns, storedRanking)
    checkInsProgram =
      checkIns.evalMap(storeCheckIn(storedCheckIns)).compile.drain
  } yield ()
}
```

> compile.drain transforms the stream into an IO[Unit] value.

> This evalMap combinator is an alias for writing checkIns.flatMap(checkIn => Stream.eval(storeCheckIn(checkIn))). It maps each city element with the provided function and evaluates it. This is useful when you want to run an side-effectful program for each element in your stream. In our case, we need side effects because we are updating concurrently accessible references.

```
def storeCheckIn(
  storedCheckIns: Ref[IO, Map[City, Int]]
)(city: City): IO[Unit] = {
  storedCheckIns.update(_.updatedWith(city)(_ match {
    case None          => Some(1)
    case Some(checkIns) => Some(checkIns + 1)
  }))
}
```

> This function has two parameter lists. It's curried to allow for more convenient usage in the processCheckIns function.

> storedCheckIn is a Ref value, which has the update function. Remember that the update function, in this case, takes a Map[City, Int] and returns a new Map[City, Int]. It needs to return a new Map that has an updated check-ins value for a given city. We could use the Map.updated function we learned previously, but using updatedWith is much more concise. It takes a function that takes an element which is an Option (None meaning that there is no value under the given city key), and returns a new Option. Returning None means we want to remove the value, but we always return Some in our pattern matching expression: Some(1) when the value was not there before and Some(checkIns + 1) if it was.

❹ Finally, we need to run both programs concurrently. That means we need parSequence:

```
def processCheckIns(checkIns: Stream[IO, City]): IO[Unit] = {
  for {
    storedCheckIns  <- Ref.of[IO, Map[City, Int]](Map.empty)
    storedRanking   <- Ref.of[IO, List[CityStats]](List.empty)
    rankingProgram  = updateRanking(storedCheckIns, storedRanking)
    checkInsProgram = checkIns.evalMap(storeCheckIn(storedCheckIns)).compile.drain
                    <- List(rankingProgram, checkInsProgram).parSequence
  } yield ()
}
```

Note we only use a two fibers: rankingProgram and checkInsProgram. In reality we'd probably have many fibers processing batches of check-ins, which can be implemented very similarly to what we just showed by adding more IO values to the List. Nothing else would need to change because this implementation is already safe, despite being concurrent.

This function works, but there are still two unresolved issues with it:

- The **updateRanking** function needs an implementation.
- When we execute the IO value returned by **processCheckIns**, it will run without any feedback! We haven't provided any way to output a current ranking for the users—not even a simple println.

IOs that run infinitely

Let's first implement the function that infinitely updates the ranking. We
can do it using recursion, as we did in the previous chapter.

> ```
> def updateRanking(
>   storedCheckIns: Ref[IO, Map[City, Int]],
>   storedRanking: Ref[IO, List[CityStats]]
> ): IO[Unit] = {
>   for {
>     newRanking <- storedCheckIns.get.map(topCities)
>     _          <- storedRanking.set(newRanking)
>     _          <- updateRanking(storedCheckIns, storedRanking)
>   } yield ()
> }
> ```

> **topCities**
>
> a function we
> implemented
> earlier that takes
> a Map[City, Int]
> and returns a
> List[CityStats],
> which is a TOP3
> ranking

This will work fine. However, note that the IO[Unit] return type doesn't
convey a very important aspect of this function: it will never complete.
Fortunately, there is a way to fix that. **Meet the Nothing type.**

> ```
> def updateRanking(
>   storedCheckIns: Ref[IO, Map[City, Int]],
>   storedRanking: Ref[IO, List[CityStats]]
> ): IO[Nothing] = {
>   for {
>     newRanking <- storedCheckIns.get.map(topCities)
>     _          <- storedRanking.set(newRanking)
>     result     <- updateRanking(storedCheckIns, storedRanking)
>   } yield result
> }
> ```

Nothing is a type that doesn't have
any values. You can't create any
values of type Nothing. However, by
using recursion, we can still create
a compiling function that returns
IO[Nothing].

result has the Nothing type here. Note that it will never be any value,
because it's defined using an infinite recursion.

We can also use the **foreverM** function to achieve the same result.

> ```
> def updateRanking(
>   storedCheckIns: Ref[IO, Map[City, Int]],
>   storedRanking: Ref[IO, List[CityStats]]
> ): IO[Nothing] = {
>   (for {
>     newRanking <- storedCheckIns.get.map(topCities)
>     _          <- storedRanking.set(newRanking)
>   } yield ()).foreverM
> }
> ```

foreverM transforms a given IO[A] and returns an
IO[Nothing], which is a description of a program
created by repeating the given IO indefinitely (so it
won't ever return, hence, Nothing). We didn't need
to use it before because we had only one thread
to work with, and executing such an IO value
synchronously on a single thread will take "forever."
(Note that for streams we use repeat to achieve a
similar result.)

> ```
> def updateRanking(
>   storedCheckIns: Ref[IO, Map[City, Int]],
>   storedRanking: Ref[IO, List[CityStats]]
> ): IO[Nothing] = {
>   storedCheckIns.get
>     .map(topCities)
>     .flatMap(storedRanking.set)
>     .foreverM
> }
> ```

The last alternative we want to show is for people who
prefer using flatMap/map sequences instead of for
comprehensions. Again, this may be good for some teams
and not for others.

IO[Nothing] means that the program, when executed, will
not return or will fail. The Nothing type is called a "bottom
type" in other FP languages.

Coffee break: Concurrent thinking

We now have a program that has some pieces that run concurrently. However, we still need one more thing: the implementation of the second requirement.

> ### Requirements: City rankings
>
> 1. The program needs to process a stream of check-ins from people around the world (a `Stream[IO, City]` value will be provided).
> 2. The program should allow getting the current top three cities' ranking (ranked by check-ins), while the check-ins are still being processed.

Our users need to be able to see the current version of the ranking. We will spend the rest of the chapter implementing the most convenient—asynchronous—way of doing so, but before we do that, let's practice what we learned so far by writing a more basic version.

Here's the current version of `processCheckIns` function:

```
def processCheckIns(checkIns: Stream[IO, City]): IO[Unit] = {
  for {
    storedCheckIns  <- Ref.of[IO, Map[City, Int]](Map.empty)
    storedRanking   <- Ref.of[IO, List[CityStats]](List.empty)
    rankingProgram  = updateRanking(storedCheckIns, storedRanking)
    checkInsProgram = checkIns.evalMap(storeCheckIn(storedCheckIns))
                              .compile.drain
    _               <- List(rankingProgram, checkInsProgram).parSequence
  } yield ()
}
```

Update this function to a version that works exactly the same but additionally **prints the current ranking every one second**.

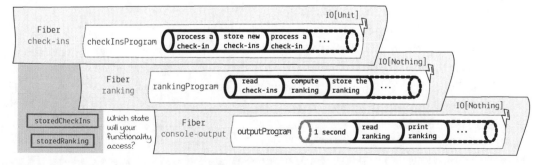

`outputProgram` needs to run concurrently with others. It should first wait one second, then read the current ranking, print it, and repeat the process, starting with waiting.

Coffee break explained: Concurrent thinking

There are many ways you could have approached this exercise. There are a few points that needed to be considered—no matter what your final solution looks like.

A correct solution should include a new IO value in the List we are calling the parSequence function on. That means that there is going to be another IO program running concurrently when the whole function is executed. Secondly, a correct solution should make sure that printing the ranking happens every one second and repeats indefinitely.

Here's one possible version of the processCheckIns function that takes into consideration both aspects:

```
def processCheckIns(checkIns: Stream[IO, City]): IO[Unit] = {
  for {
    storedCheckIns  <- Ref.of[IO, Map[City, Int]](Map.empty)
    storedRanking   <- Ref.of[IO, List[CityStats]](List.empty)
    rankingProgram  = updateRanking(storedCheckIns, storedRanking)
    checkInsProgram =
        checkIns.evalMap(storeCheckIn(storedCheckIns)).compile.drain
    outputProgram   =
        IO.sleep(1.second)
          .flatMap(_ => storedRanking.get)
          .flatMap(IO.println)
          .foreverM
    _ <- List(
      rankingProgram,
      checkInsProgram,
      outputProgram).parSequence
  } yield ()
}
```

We need to create a new IO value that describes a program that first sleeps for one second, then gets a current value of the ranking, then prints it to the console, and finally repeats the process from the start forever.

We then include this value in a List of IOs, which we then parSequence into an IO of Lists, running all the programs concurrently on a thread pool provided later in the program, outside of the functional core.

This is just one possibility. We could refactor the whole outputProgram implementation to another function like we did with the rankingProgram. We could also use recursion instead of foreverM or use a for comprehension instead of flatMaps. All of these solutions would be valid. The important thing is that running the IO returned by this function should never finish, **printing** the ranking every second.

Remember that you need to provide a thread pool that will be used to run your fibers on. This is required when you want to call the unsafeRunSync. You don't have to do it in the book's sbt console.

```
> import cats.effect.unsafe.implicits.global
  processCheckIns(checkIns).unsafeRunSync()
  → console output: List(CityStats(City(Sydney),100002), ...)
    ...
```

The need for asynchronicity

We now have solutions for two major parts of the puzzle:

- The ability to process check-ins
- The ability to keep the ranking updated

We are almost there. There is still one problem, though. The access to the ranking is not the most user-friendly approach. Printing to the console may be a good idea for development when we debug and check if everything goes according to the plan, but it's not a production-ready solution. We can do better.

Let's talk briefly about the API we currently expose and why it's no longer enough:

```
def processCheckIns(checkIns: Stream[IO, City]): IO[Unit]
```

When you run a program like that, it spawns some threads that process all incoming check-ins and update the ranking. You expect that it won't finish any time soon. And indeed, our current solution runs forever, printing the ranking every second. But the requirements say that we want to be able to access the current ranking at any given moment—no matter how many check-ins have already been processed—not every second, as we encoded in the current version.

Yes, the program we implemented is concurrent; it uses many fibers, but it doesn't give its users any choice regarding the way rankings are "consumed." We encoded the outputProgram inside the processCheckIns function, but it's encapsulated, and the behavior is not customizable at all. Additionally, this function shouldn't be responsible for both producing and consuming the data. We could invert the control by returning a Stream or by adding an additional parameter(s) to the processCheckIns function (e.g., outputAction, which takes a ranking and returns an IO value that describes a program that consumes a ranking). These would all be welcome adjustments, but we can do even better: completely isolate the processing of check-ins and generating the ranking by using the current ranking in whatever way someone needs. We need to start the threads **asynchronously**.

However, we'd probably need to expose the 1.second as a parameter as well, so exposing everything as a parameter may not be a good solution, either.

Step 2 ✔	Step 3
IOs with fibers	**Concurrent IOs and asynchronous access**
We will start using multiple threads (and potentially multiple cores) by learning about fiers. We will also need to store the current states afely in an FP manner.	In the last step we will show how to create a program that returns a handle to all running resources (including fibers and states) asynchronously in a user-friendly and readable manner.

Preparing for asynchronous access

Synchronous vs. asynchronous

Even though our current program is concurrent, we use it in a **synchronous** way. That is, we execute the program and must **wait for it to complete**. Only when we receive a result of our program can we proceed with executing the next ones. We say that the **caller thread blocks** while waiting for a result. If the program takes a long time to complete, the caller thread is blocked for a long time. In the case of processCheckIns, running the IO value is never going to finish, so we end up blocking the caller thread (main in this case).

On the other hand, **asynchronous** communication happens when the caller thread initiates a program and doesn't wait for it to finish but instead proceeds with the next ones. If it cares about the results provided by such a program, it will need to have a way to get them by providing a callback or using some kind of "handle" that has access to them. No matter which way is used, we say that the caller thread accesses the results asynchronously.

That all sounds good for our case, so we'd like to replace the current, synchronous solution with an asynchronous one.

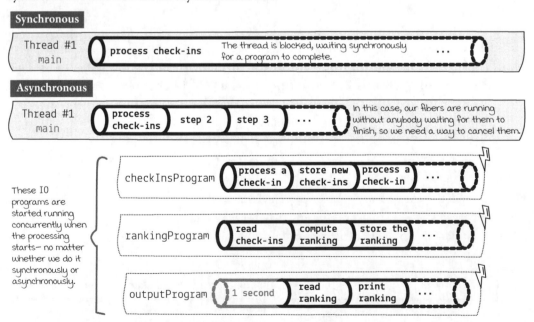

Designing functional asynchronous programs

We need a function that returns a program, which, when executed, spawns all the threads, connects them together using concurrent references, and returns immediately, giving back a handle that allows us to access the current ranking any time.

Since we model everything as immutable values, we can also model such an asynchronous handle as an immutable value. We will call it ProcessingCheckIns:

```
> case class ProcessingCheckIns(
    currentRanking: IO[List[CityStats]],
    stop: IO[Unit]
  )
```

This product type can now become part of the return type:

```
def processCheckIns(checkIns: Stream[IO, City]): IO[ProcessingCheckIns]
```

Before we implement the new version, let's see how a function with such an API could be use to allow asynchronous access:

```
for {
  processing <- processCheckIns(checkIns)
  ranking    <- processing.currentRanking
  _          <- IO.println(ranking)
  _          <- IO.sleep(1.second)

  ... // more things here

  newRanking <- processing.currentRanking
  _          <- processing.stop
} yield newRanking
```

There are some built-in solutions for a problem like that in FP libraries (e.g., the Resource type), and we will cover them in the last part of the book. For now, the important aspect to focus on here is the mindset. This example shows how immutable and purely functional thinking can be used to elegantly solve a very imperative-looking problem like the one in this chapter.

This IO value, when executed, runs processing and ranking fibers concurrently and returns immediately. Then, it prints the current ranking; sleeps for one second; does "more things"; and then gets an up-to-date version of the ranking, stops the processing, and yields a ranking.

This is an example of a program that our clients could write. They first need to call the processCheckIns function, which spawns all the fibers and immediately returns the ProcessingCheckIns value that holds two IO values: one that returns the current ranking and one that stops all the fibers. That means that the client is now responsible for executing both of them at their convenience. They could get the newest ranking every second, every minute, or 100 times an hour. It doesn't matter from the perspective of the processCheckIns developer. By using asynchronous communication, we are able to decouple producing ranking from its consumption. Only one question remains: how difficult is implementing such a solution?

Managing fibers manually

Fortunately, the IO type has a function that allows us to execute a given IO value in a fiber and returns a handle to this fiber without waiting for it to finish.

```
def start[A]: IO[FiberIO[A]]
```
The function start is defined for IO values.

Don't be misled by the imperative name of the start function. The signature tells a declarative story: this function returns a description of a program, which, when executed, will start a new fiber and immediately return a handle to this thread represented by an immutable FiberIO[A] value. You are able to do several things with this handle, but the most important one is the cancel function.

```
def cancel: IO[Unit]
```
The cancel function is defined for FiberIO[A] values (i.e., handles returned by the program described by IO.start).

The handle has a cancel function that returns an IO[Unit]—a program, which, when executed, cancels the underlying fiber.

Quick exercise

Let's see if we've got this right. What does the following program do? How long will it run?

```
for {
  fiber <- IO.sleep(300.millis)
             .flatMap(_ => IO.println("hello")).foreverM.start
  _     <- IO.sleep(1.second)
  _     <- fiber.cancel
  _     <- IO.sleep(1.second)
} yield ()
```

> ### Starting fibers manually considered low-level
>
> Note that using the parSequence function we discussed earlier (and other functions with similar semantics) is considered a better choice for creating concurrent IOs than functions like start and cancel. The main difference is that when you start a fiber manually (using start), you become completely responsible for making sure it stops and nothing leaks, while parSequence (and other declarative functions) take care of those things for you, even when something fails.
>
> You should use parSequence or its "siblings" (see the book's companion source code for more information) whenever you can and treat IO.start, FiberIO.cancel and other less declarative options as a last resort. Remember to double-check whether they really finish when you no longer need them (even when something fails).

Answer
The IO value above starts a fiber which prints "hello" every 300 milliseconds infinitely and returns a handle to it. After one second the fiber is canceled, which means that, most likely, the program will print "hello" three times and should take around two seconds.

Coding functional asynchronous programs

Let's use the recently met `start` and `cancel` functions to model the final version of the `processCheckIns` that has the following signature:

```
def processCheckIns(checkIns: Stream[IO, City]): IO[ProcessingCheckIns]
```

This API means that the program returns a handle (immutable value of `ProcessingCheckIns`) that allows the user to get the current ranking any number of times at any given moment. No strings attached. It also allows the user to explicitly stop all the underlying fibers once they don't need the ranking anymore.

```
case class ProcessingCheckIns(
  currentRanking: IO[List[CityStats]],
  stop: IO[Unit]
)
```

This parent fiber will be "waiting" for both child fibers to "finish." They will probably not finish (as designed), but it's not important here. Having access to the parent fiber means we only need to cancel this one. We don't have to cancel its "children" individually.

The changes we need to apply to the existing `processCheckIns` function are not extensive. We need to run yet another fiber that will be the "parent" of the two fibers responsible for storing check-ins and updating the ranking. No thread will be wasted in the process because fibers don't use any threads when they are not doing anything.

```
def processCheckIns(
  checkIns: Stream[IO, City]
): IO[ProcessingCheckIns] = {
  for {
    storedCheckIns  <- Ref.of[IO, Map[City, Int]](Map.empty)
    storedRanking   <- Ref.of[IO, List[CityStats]](List.empty)
    rankingProgram  = updateRanking(storedCheckIns, storedRanking)
    checkInsProgram = checkIns.evalMap(storeCheckIn(storedCheckIns))
                        .compile.drain
    fiber           <- List(rankingProgram,
                          checkInsProgram).parSequence.start
  } yield ProcessingCheckIns(storedRanking.get, fiber.cancel)
}
```

Note that we no longer need any `outputProgram` because now the client is responsible for reading and using the ranking.

We can return the `storedRanking.get` IO value as a way to quickly read the current ranking and `fiber.cancel` as a way to cancel the fiber that waits for both parSequenced programs—`rankingProgram` and `checkInsProgram`—to finish.

That's a wrap! The solution above is all we need to implement the requirements in a concise, safe, and readable manner. The best thing is that we used only pure functions and immutable values to do that!

Step 3 ✔

Concurrent IOs and asynchronous access
In the last step we will show how to create a program that returns a handle to all running resources (including fibers and states) asynchronously in a user-friendly and readable manner.

Summary

We showed some basic functional concurrent concepts that are available in many FP languages. The main objective was to show you how all the ideas, concepts, and mental models we learned from sequential programs are still applicable here. Hopefully, it gives you a good intuition about how more advanced types and mechanism can be used to solve even more complicated concurrency problems. The following sections cover what we've learned this chapter.

> **CODE:** CH10_*
> Explore this chapter's source code by looking at ch10_* files in the book's repository.

Declaratively design concurrent program flows

We used parSequence to transform a List of IO values into an IO of a List. This function is similar to sequence, but it runs the programs described by IO values **concurrently**—not sequentially. We compared this approach to some more traditional and imperative concurrency models like monitors, locks, actors, and thread-safe data structures.

> There are other functions that run IOs concurrently. For example, have a look at parTraverse.

Use lightweight virtual threads (fibers)

parSequence and other functions are taking advantage of the fibers' mechanism that is also available in many other languages. A fiber is a higher-level concept than a Thread object. Unlike Threads, fibers are not mapped to operating system threads. That means they are very lightweight, and you can create many of them.

Safely store and access data from different threads

The Ref[IO, A] value represents a mutable reference that can be accessed and changed by many threads at once. It uses the well-known compare-and-swap operation, which is also available in Java's AtomicReference (and similar types). It provides a very straightforward way to update this reference. Programmers need to provide a pure function that takes a current value and returns the new one.

> If you want to use more concurrent goodies in Scala, go to the cats-effect library documentation, and dive right in!

Process stream of events asynchronously

Finally, we implemented an asynchronous communication model by using the low-level IO.start and FiberIO.cancel functions.

As a final note, remember that concurrency is hard! Whenever possible, err on the side of sequential execution. Use concurrency and multiple threads only when needed. When you mostly stick to using parSequence, you are covered because it's a concept that gives you a lot without any big trade-offs. We will discuss some additional concurrency concepts in chapter 12, but the main underlying idea will stay the same.

Part 3
Applied functional programming

You have learned everything you need to know to easily write real-world applications using functional programming! As proof, in this part we will implement such a real-world application that uses Wikidata as a data source. We will apply all the techniques we learned earlier in the book and show that they can be used to create readable and maintainable code.

In **chapter 11** we will introduce requirements for an application that generates a very peculiar travel guide. We will need to create an immutable-based data model and use proper types in signatures, including IO to integrate with Wikidata, use caching and multiple threads to make the application fast. We will wrap all of these concerns in pure functions and additionally show how we can reuse our object-oriented design intuitions in the functional world. As has been the case in the first 10 chapters, we will still keep maintainability, readability, and testability in mind.

In **chapter 12** we will show how to test the application we developed in chapter 11 and how easy it is to maintain, even in the presence of big requirement changes. We will also show how we can use tests to discover unknown bugs and test-driven development to implement new business features.

Designing functional programs | **11**

In this chapter

you will learn

- how to design real-world functional applications

- how to model more complicated requirements as types

- how to integrate with real data-source APIs using IO

- how to avoid resource leaks

- how to cache query results to speed up execution

> ❝*What I cannot create, I do not understand.*❞
>
> —RICHARD FEYNMAN

Make it work, make it right, make it fast

It's time to put all the knowledge you've gained to a good use and implement something tangible! We will use all the functional tools and techniques we learned to follow some very old programming advice: first make the solution work, then make it work correctly, and, only then, think about making it fast. Following are the requirements, which, understandably, are a bit more involved than what we were used to.

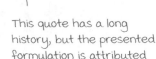

This quote has a long history, but the presented formulation is attributed to Kent Beck.

Requirements: Pop culture travel guide

1. The application should take a single `String` value: a search term for the tourist attraction that the user wants to visit and needs a travel guide for.

2. The application needs to search for a given attraction, its description (if it exists), and its geographical location. It should prefer locations with larger populations.

3. The application should use a location to do as follows:
   — Find artists originating from this location, sorted by the number of social media followers
   — Find movies that take place in this location, sorted by the box office earnings

4. For a given tourist attraction, artists and movies form its "pop culture travel guide" that should be returned to the user. If there are more possible guides, the application needs to return the one with the highest *score*, which is calculated as follows:
   — 30 points for a description
   — 10 points for each artist or movie (max. 40 points)
   — 1 point for each 100,000 followers (all artists combined; max. 15 points)
   — 1 point for each $10,000,000 in box office earnings (all movies combined; max. 15 points)

5. We will add support for more pop culture subjects in the future (e.g., video games).

There is a lot to unpack here. A simple usage example is in order:

```
travelGuideProgram("Bridge of Sighs").unsafeRunSync()
→ Bridge of Sighs is a bridge over a canal in Venice. Before visiting,
  you may want to listen to Talco and watch some movies that take place
  in Venice: "Spider-Man: Far from Home" and "Casino Royale."
```

Here, we show a String result, but in reality we will return a nice immutable value containing all the information that can be used to create such a String.

Yes, this is exactly what the application we are going to develop in this chapter will be able to do! And not just for "Bridge of Sighs" but for **any other tourist attraction described in Wikipedia**! This chapter is going to be mostly a code walk-through, but I strongly advise you to take your time and think about each problem we encounter before moving on to the solution. We will mark these problems in a specific way.

Let's think about it first. What immutable values can you use to model the requirements above? Look for nouns, their properties, and how they will need to be used.

Modeling using immutable values

When requirements are provided in such a clear way, modeling using immutable values (product and sum types, or ADTs) is very straight-forward and is usually a very good first step in designing a new program.

Algebraic data types

ADTs were introduced in chapter 7.

Let's see how we can transform requirements into types in this case.

Look for subjects in requirements　Model subjects as custom ADTs, built-in ADTs (like `Options`), or primitives:

"...a search term for the **tourist attraction** that the user wants to visit..."
```
case class Attraction(name: String, ...)
```

"...and its **geographical location**..."
```
case class Location(name: String, ...)
```

"...find **artists** originating from this location..."
```
case class Artist(name: String, ...)
```

"...find **movies** that take place in this location..."
```
case class Movie(name: String, ...)
```

"...sorted by number of social media **followers**..."
```
followers: Int
```

Requirements hint that the description may not exist, so we model is as an `Option` value.

"...search for a given attraction, its **description** (if it exists)"
```
description: Option[String]
```

"...locations with larger **populations**..."
```
population: Int
```

"We will add support for more **pop culture subjects**..."
```
enum PopCultureSubject
```

"...pop culture **travel guide** that should be returned to the user..."
```
case class TravelGuide(...)
```

Look for properties of subjects in requirements　Model properties as fields in product types.

"...attraction, **its description** (if it exists), and its geographical **location**..."
```
case class Attraction(name: String, description: Option[String], location: Location)
```

```
enum PopCultureSubject {
```
"...artists **sorted by** number of social media **followers**..."
```
  case Artist(name: String, followers: Int)
```
"...movies **sorted by** the box **office** earnings..."
```
  case Movie(name: String, boxOffice: Int)
}
```

Since we know more pop culture subjects will need to be supported later on, we can model both an artist and a movie as instances of the PopCultureSubject sum type and use a list of such values as a guide's property.

"...for a given tourist attraction, artists and movies **form** its pop culture travel guide..."

"...add support **for more pop culture subjects** in the future (e.g. video games)..."
```
case class TravelGuide(attraction: Attraction, subjects: List[PopCultureSubject])
```
"...locations **with** larger populations..."
```
case class Location(..., name: String, population: Int)
```

Look for subject usages　Model usages as identification fields in product types.

```
case class Location(id: LocationId, name: String, population: Int)
```

"The application should **use** a location to find..."
```
opaque type LocationId = String
```

We don't want to accidentally mix this very important `id` with some other `String` values so it's better to use a specific **newtype** for that.

Requirements state that the location is needed to find pop culture subjects, such as movies or artists. That's how we know we will need to uniquely identify locations by some `id` value.

Business domain modeling and FP

Requirements as types

modeling requirements as types was discussed in detail in chapter 7.

Modeling business domain concepts directly in the code may look familiar to those of you who at least once in their career were responsible for software architecture and needed to use concepts like *domain-driven design* (DDD). This and other architecture design techniques are compatible with functional programming as long as you constrain yourself to use only pure functions and immutable values.

As you see, we will additionally use this chapter to recap a lot of material from previous chapters. If you have trouble remembering how to approach some problems, please use provided bookmarks to schedule some additional chapter re-readings.

The model design activity may seem a bit chaotic at first, but remember that there usually is some process you can follow and well-known techniques you can take advantage of. In the end, whether you follow DDD or another technique is up to you and your team.

Once we are comfortable with the initial model, we can move on to designing the rest of the application. Remember that nothing is set in stone, so we may be forced to return to the model design phase when new requirements surface (we'll see an example of that in chapter 12).

```
object model {
  opaque type LocationId = String
  object LocationId {
   def apply(value: String): LocationId       = value
   extension (a: LocationId) def value: String = a
  }

  case class Location(id: LocationId, name: String, population: Int)
  case class Attraction(name: String, description: Option[String], location: Location)

  enum PopCultureSubject {
    case Artist(name: String, followers: Int)
    case Movie(name: String, boxOffice: Int)
  }

  case class TravelGuide(attraction: Attraction, subjects: List[PopCultureSubject])
}
import model._, model.PopCultureSubject._
```

This is the model we ended up with after following the requirements-based design process on the previous page.

Finally, note that we chose to use the same model for the whole application in all the layers. In bigger applications, however, it's usually smarter to represent each concept depending on the context it appears in (again, see DDD and the concept of a *bounded context*). In our case, we could say that an Artist model is only viable in the context of calculating the score of a guide because this is where we need followers. We will use this class in other contexts as well, but we can imagine that for the final user presentation (e.g., in a UI) we might want a simpler artist model:

If you choose to follow such design advice, you are able to separate concerns better but at the cost of implementing additional mapping functions between Artist and ArtistToListenTo.

```
case class ArtistToListenTo(name: String)
```

Data access modeling

We can apply a very similar process to modeling the data access layer. Let's look at our requirements and find IO-related functionalities. These will need to return our model values wrapped in an IO because we know some unsafe side-effectful actions will need to happen—data resides outside of our application, so reaching out to fetch it means there are some additional risks involved.

> **Input/Output actions**
>
> IO actions and separation of concerns were heavily discussed in chapter 8.

Look for **data access actions** ...and model them as pure function signatures.

*"...find **artists** originating from this location..."*

```
def findArtistsFromLocation(locationId: LocationId, limit: Int): IO[List[Artist]]
```

*"...find **movies** that take place in this location..."*

```
def findMoviesAboutLocation(locationId: LocationId, limit: Int): IO[List[Movie]]
```

*"The application needs to **search** for a given attraction..."*

```
def findAttractions(name: String, ordering: AttractionOrdering, limit: Int): IO[List[Attraction]]
```

Look for **data access properties** ...and model them as types.

*"It should **prefer locations** with larger populations...."*

```
enum AttractionOrdering {
  case ByName
  case ByLocationPopulation
}

import AttractionOrdering._
```

> The requirements don't directly state that we will need different ordering options (we will need just the population-based ordering), but we use this example to show again how to use ADTs to make data access functions less error-prone and very readable.

Separation of concerns

We ended up with three function signatures that represent the data access layer. Note that we don't need to assume anything about where the data will come from. We may assume it's going to be Wikidata, but we won't encode this assumption in the code just yet. Similarly, we won't choose any client library that talks with Wikidata, nor will we make any final decision about the query format. It's usually wise to delay such decisions until the very last possible moment. That's why having just function signatures is enough for now.

Coding to the interface

We can implement the business side of our program using only the data access functions defined above without having their implementations. We will of course need to encode the way to access the data and transform it to our domain model values eventually. But in the spirit of delaying as many decisions as possible, we will do it later in the chapter. You may recognize this technique from object-oriented programming as *coding to the interface*. It's a useful technique in FP as well. Signatures are our interfaces and function bodies are our implementations.

> **THIS IS BIG!**
> Many OO design principles can be used with pure functions and immutable values (FP).

A bag of functions

When we have a bunch of functions that are usually used together or their implementations share many common expressions, we may be tempted to bundle them inside a bigger type: a **bag of functions**.

```
case class DataAccess(
  findAttractions: (String, AttractionOrdering, Int) => IO[List[Attraction]],
  findArtistsFromLocation: (LocationId, Int) => IO[List[Artist]],
  findMoviesAboutLocation: (LocationId, Int) => IO[List[Movie]]
)
```

A value of type `DataAccess` will provide three pure functions. And since in FP languages functions are just values, `DataAccess` can be encoded as a product type. This is perfectly fine and usable, but some people find it hard to operate on product types that are just functions. They may find the lack of function parameter names misleading, too. That's why we may implement the bag-of-functions pattern using an alternative approach akin to an interface from OOP.

> We use the trait keyword in Scala to define an interface. Other languages may offer other encodings of the bag-of-functions pattern.

```
trait DataAccess {
  def findAttractions(name: String, ordering: AttractionOrdering,
                      limit: Int): IO[List[Attraction]]
  def findArtistsFromLocation(locationId: LocationId, limit: Int): IO[List[Artist]]
  def findMoviesAboutLocation(locationId: LocationId, limit: Int): IO[List[Movie]]
}
```

As you see, these are the same three functions bundled together, but we use normal function signatures with parameter names instead of function types. You may treat the `DataAccess` type as a "signature" for a value. It's a blueprint for a value, just like a signature is a blueprint for a function body, and an interface in OOP is a blueprint for its implementation. All these intuitions are valid. Most importantly, these three functions are pure functions, and any implementation of `DataAccess` must not have any internal state—it's **just a bag of pure functions related to each other**.

No matter which version (a product type or an interface) you choose, the benefits are the same. By using this pattern you will be able to:

— *Pass a single value to a function* that needs data access functionalities instead of passing three individual function values; this benefit is more important when we have many different functions that require data access. In such a case all these bloated signatures would look very repetitive and make the code look messier.

— *Implement all the functions at once,* using some common expressions.

There is at least one disadvantage, too. It's hard to find a good "common shared identity" for many functions. It's not as bad here—we have three functions that share the "data access" identity. But this identity would not work in bigger programs because it would include a lot of functions.

We won't provide bodies for DataAccess functions just yet!
We will first show how we can use a bare, unimplemented bag of functions (trait) in a business logic function. Separation of concerns FTW!

We will show both benefits during the following implementation steps.

Again, we just show what's at our disposal. The final decision is always yours to make.

Business logic as a pure function

We have just finished the modeling phase! We have all the types we need to finally start implementing the core functionality. Yes, our data access layer is not yet implemented, but this doesn't mean we can't implement the required business behavior. We will implement it as a pure function. As we wrote in the introduction, we are following the old advice by first aiming to make the whole thing work in at least one basic case. This has a very important consequence: we can quickly check which assumptions are correct and which need more thought. Our first approach is the simplest possible version that *works*: a function that returns an IO value describing a program that returns a single travel guide. We won't implement some of the requirements just yet—namely, the ones that define the scoring algorithm. Hence, we will try to return the first possible travel guide. Only then will we try to "make it right" by implementing the remaining requirements, including scoring and sorting possible guides.

We will focus on implementing the data access layer after implementing the first version of the main behavior. We are following the top-down design again! We think about the top-level function, its clients, and the interface before anything else.

1 Let's start with the signature. We know that the user input is the name of the attraction, and the function needs to return a program which, when executed, will return a travel guide:

```
def travelGuide(attractionName: String): IO[Option[TravelGuide]] = {
  ???
}
```

2 We first need to find attractions with a given name. That's why we require a DataAccess parameter. This is a value that contains three data access functions, but we'll use just one of them now:

```
def travelGuide(data: DataAccess, attractionName: String): IO[Option[TravelGuide]] = {
  for {
    attractions <- data.findAttractions(attractionName, ByLocationPopulation, 1)
  } yield ???
}
```

We call findAttractions to get an IO value describing a program that will try to find a tourist attraction that contains a given attractionName. We'd like to get a single attraction that resides in a geographic location with the largest population (order ByLocationPopulation and limit 1).

3 If we find any attraction, we look for artists and movies. Otherwise, we return None:

```
def travelGuide(data: DataAccess, attractionName: String): IO[Option[TravelGuide]] = {
  for {
    attractions <- data.findAttractions(attractionName, ByLocationPopulation, 1)
    guide <- attractions.headOption match {
               case None => IO.pure(None)
               case Some(attraction) =>
                 for {
                   artists <- data.findArtistsFromLocation(attraction.location.id, 2)
                   movies  <- data.findMoviesAboutLocation(attraction.location.id, 2)
                 } yield Some(TravelGuide(attraction, artists.appendedAll(movies)))
               }
  } yield guide
}
```

We use pattern matching and provide two different IO values depending on whether we got Some or None.

We get a maximum of two artists and two movies connected with a given location. To simplify the example, we don't directly state how to order them—they will be sorted internally by followers and box office. However, the approach we showed in findAttractions would work here as well.

Separating the real data access concern

We now have a function that implements some business requirements, but we don't have a way to call it because we have no DataAccess value.

```
def travelGuide(
   data: DataAccess, attractionName: String
): IO[Option[TravelGuide]]
```

We reached the point of the implementation process at which we can no longer delay choosing and implementing the real data access API. There are many data sources we could use here, including some custom SQL or NoSQL databases. **The main concern here is that the data access layer details don't leak to other layers**. The travelGuide function uses a DataAccess value that exposes everything travelGuide will ever need to know without any internal details.

Again, DataAccess contains three values that are pure functions. travelGuide doesn't have any idea how these functions are implemented.

```
trait DataAccess {
   def findAttractions(name: String, ordering: AttractionOrdering,
                       limit: Int): IO[List[Attraction]]
   def findArtistsFromLocation(locationId: LocationId, limit: Int): IO[List[Artist]]
   def findMoviesAboutLocation(locationId: LocationId, limit: Int): IO[List[Movie]]
}
```

To call travelGuide, we first need to create such a DataAccess value. We need to implement these three functions: each of them needs to return an IO value describing a program that fetches data from somewhere. Note that we may also use IO.pure with a hardcoded value there (like we did in previous chapters), but we promised you before that this chapter was going to be different: we want to show a real-world integration. We will use **Wikidata**, which is a collaboratively edited, multilingual, knowledge graph and a common source of open data that projects such as Wikipedia use.

This Wikidata description was taken from Wikipedia.

SPARQL query language

Wikidata allows us to query the data it exposes using the SPARQL query language. We won't go into SPARQL details in this book—we will use just three queries as examples (attractions, artists, and movies). They won't be optimized for production usage, and you don't really need to understand them. Focus on the way we treat them: as some internal implementation detail which should not leak outside the DataAccess internals. The same principle would apply for SQL queries if we used MySQL as a data access layer or N1QL queries if we used Couchbase. **This concern is separated**.

Note that DataAccess is so generic that it allows us to provide implementations for a variety of data access solutions, including MySQL, Couchbase, and many more.

Integrating with APIs using imperative libraries and IO

We need to create a value that implements the DataAccess "interface" (i.e., provides three pure functions with very specific signatures). We want to implement them so that they return IO values describing programs that connect to Wikidata and query data using SPARQL. Let's approach them one by one. The first function to implement is findAttractions:

```
def findAttractions(name: String, ordering: AttractionOrdering,
                    limit: Int): IO[List[Attraction]]
```

We need to solve three problems before implementing it:

1. What SPARQL query will implement it?
2. How can we connect to and query the Wikidata API?
3. How can we transform the raw response to the `List[Attraction]` value?

1. Creating the SPARQL query

Let's start with the query itself. We want to find tourist attractions that contain the given name and can be ordered by name or population. Wikidata offers a service where we can test our queries live. Let's go to **Wikidata Query Service** and try to implement such a query.

Please read the following pages without trying to repeat only the code marked with ">". There are some big Wikidata queries ahead. You will be able to import final implementations into your REPL with a single command (if you use the book's code repository).

Since the SPARQL queries we use are pretty big, we won't show their complete versions in the book. Please refer to the book's companion source code if you want to learn more.

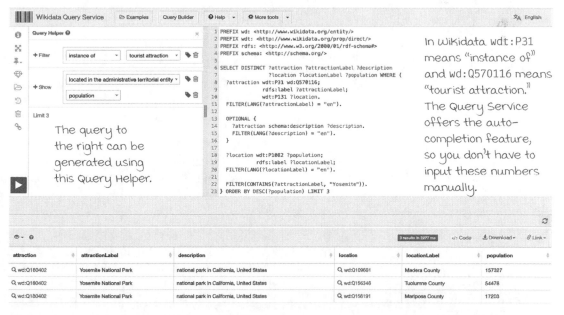

In Wikidata wdt:P31 means "instance of" and wd:Q570116 means "tourist attraction." The Query Service offers the auto-completion feature, so you don't have to input these numbers manually.

The query to the right can be generated using this Query Helper.

(You can visit this page by going to https://query.wikidata.org. There are examples that'll get you started.)

2. Connecting to and querying the Wikidata service

Now that we know what query we want to use, we need a way to send this query to the Wikidata server:

— We need the address of the server.

— We need to understand the preferred format of request and response.

There are multiple ways we could approach this task. The address of the server is pretty straightforward. We are going to use the https://query.wikidata.org/sparql endpoint. In terms of format we could try to implement both the networking and query formatting ourselves or use an existing library. There are multiple choices, and you probably think that if we want to follow the functional way, our choices are very limited. Truth being told, there are some options out there that expose more functional APIs than others—they use immutable values and pure functions and expose IO values. You already know how to use such APIs. What you may not know is that **your choice is not really limited to them!** If there is a popular, well-established client library that you'd like to use, but its nature is imperative, you can still incorporate it in your functional program! This is what we are going to show in this chapter. The imperative, Java-based client library for connecting and querying the Wikidata server is **Apache Jena**—"a free and open source Java framework for building Semantic Web and Linked Data applications." Here's a simple query written in **imperative Java**:

> **THIS IS BIG!**
> IO enables you to use well-established imperative client libraries in your functional programs!

We are showing imperative Java here because that's what you usually see in documentation or tutorials introducing the library you want to use.

```
String query = "PREFIX wd: <http://www.wikidata.org/entity/>\n" +
               "PREFIX wdt: <http://www.wikidata.org/prop/direct/>\n" +
               "PREFIX rdfs: <http://www.w3.org/2000/01/rdf-schema#>\n" +
               "SELECT DISTINCT ?attraction ?label WHERE {\n" +
               "  ?attraction wdt:P31 wd:Q570116;\n" +
               "              rdfs:label ?label.\n" +
               "  FILTER(LANG(?label) = \"en\").\n" +
               "} LIMIT 3";
```

A query that finds three tourist attractions (you can input this query into Wikidata Query Service and see results for yourself)!

```
RDFConnection connection = RDFConnectionRemote.create()
  .destination("https://query.wikidata.org/")
  .queryEndpoint("sparql")
  .build();
```

We create a connection to the Wikidata server. RDFConnection, QueryExecution, and QuerySolution are Apache Jena types.

```
QueryExecution execution = connection.query(QueryFactory.create(query));
Iterator<QuerySolution> solutions = execution.execSelect();

// TODO: parse and use solutions
```

Here, we get results as an Iterator, which only enables you to lazily process one item at a time. This is the place we need to use this data in our application (see the next page for details).

```
execution.close();
connection.close();
```

We need to close both a query execution context and the connection, because they are holding some side-effectful resources as their state. In Java, the best approach would be to use the try-with-resources clause.

3. Extracting and parsing the query results

The last problem we need to solve is how to extract the results from Apache Jena's Iterator<QuerySolution> into something usable. Let's focus on extracting the Strings first because we already know how to work with them in the functional context.

```
String query = ... + "SELECT DISTINCT ?attraction ?label WHERE {\n" + ...;
RDFConnection connection = ...;
QueryExecution execution = ...;
Iterator<QuerySolution> solutions = execution.execSelect();

solutions.forEachRemaining(solution -> {
  String id = solution.getResource("attraction").getLocalName();
  String label = solution.getLiteral("label").getString();
  System.out.printf("Got attraction %s (id = %s)%n", label, id);
});

execution.close();
connection.close();
```

Here, we get results as an Iterator. Then, we print an attraction id and label for each "row." Note that both attraction and label were part of the SELECT clause in our SPARQL query.

When we run this piece of code, we should see exactly three tourist attractions printed to the console—and since we haven't provided any ordering mechanism, there will be some differences in which attractions are returned. In one of my executions I got the following:

```
Got attraction Cappadocia (id = Q217265)
Got attraction Great Geysir (id = Q216846)
Got attraction Yellowstone National Park (id = Q351)
```

Note that all the samples we show, including imperative Java examples, can be found in the book's companion source code. They are packaged in executable classes.

This is all we need to understand how to query Wikidata using the imperative Apache Jena library. There is a lot of side-effectful, **unsafe code that can't be used directly in pure functions**. Even the getResource and getLiteral calls above **can produce exceptions**! So until we have our hands on immutable values, like Strings, we need to wrap the imperative library code in IO values to be able to safely use it in our functional programs. Additionally, we have a new problem of resource handling (opening and closing connections, even in the presence of a failure), which we'll also need to handle using IO to be on the safe side.

We will use the library directly in our functional codebase by wrapping its functionalities directly in IO. We will show you how to do it and allow to import it directly into your REPL for further use.

This is just an example, but note that all three problems we described—creating a query, connection to a server, and parsing a response—apply to many other existing use cases, for example, database queries. The point here is that you can use existing well-known imperative libraries, but you need to wrap the unsafe code as IO values yourself. They need to describe side-effectful programs, which, when executed, produce immutable values. Next, we'll show how to do it.

Following the design

Now that we know how to query Wikidata, we can now go back to our functional program and try to integrate our findings into it. The design so far has been done in three steps: we created the data model using provided requirements, then we sketched the signatures of three pure functions that we want to use as input actions (and bundled them together as a `DataAccess` type), and finally, we drafted the first version of the business logic as the `travelGuide` function.

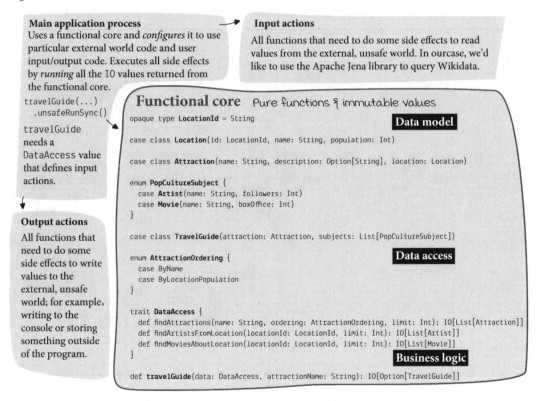

Main application process
Uses a functional core and *configures* it to use particular external world code and user input/output code. Executes all side effects by *running* all the IO values returned from the functional core.

```
travelGuide(...)
  .unsafeRunSync()
```

`travelGuide` needs a `DataAccess` value that defines input actions.

Output actions
All functions that need to do some side effects to write values to the external, unsafe world; for example, writing to the console or storing something outside of the program.

Input actions
All functions that need to do some side effects to read values from the external, unsafe world. In ourcase, we'd like to use the Apache Jena library to query Wikidata.

```scala
Functional core   Pure functions & immutable values
opaque type LocationId = String                      Data model

case class Location(id: LocationId, name: String, population: Int)

case class Attraction(name: String, description: Option[String], location: Location)

enum PopCultureSubject {
  case Artist(name: String, followers: Int)
  case Movie(name: String, boxOffice: Int)
}

case class TravelGuide(attraction: Attraction, subjects: List[PopCultureSubject])

enum AttractionOrdering {                             Data access
  case ByName
  case ByLocationPopulation
}

trait DataAccess {
  def findAttractions(name: String, ordering: AttractionOrdering, limit: Int): IO[List[Attraction]]
  def findArtistsFromLocation(locationId: LocationId, limit: Int): IO[List[Artist]]
  def findMoviesAboutLocation(locationId: LocationId, limit: Int): IO[List[Movie]]
}                                                    Business logic

def travelGuide(data: DataAccess, attractionName: String): IO[Option[TravelGuide]]
```

We also learned how to use Apache Jena to query Wikidata. The next step should be pretty obvious: **we need to implement the three functions defined inside DataAccess, so they use Apache Jena internally**. Note how we first defined `DataAccess` and chose the library just now! We made this decision as late as possible. However, the main objective is still not achieved: we still need to make the whole thing work.

> Let's think about it first. How would you approach implementing the `findAttractions` function using Apache Jena? How do we make sure the functional core doesn't know anything about what library is used internally to query data?

Implementing input actions as IO values

Let's try to implement findAttractions using Apache Jena and the Wikidata server. This example should also show you what kinds of problems you are going to encounter when trying to write an IO-heavy functional application.

As always, we can approach this problem from the top (starting with the signature) or from the bottom (figuring out smaller pieces before using them in the final function implementation). Since we have already defined the three smaller problems, it would be wise to solve them individually. That's why the bottom-up approach is what we'll use here.

Connecting to the server

Creating Apache Jena's RDFConnection value is side-effectful and unsafe. That's why we need to wrap it inside an IO value:

```
> val getConnection: IO[RDFConnection] = IO.delay(
    RDFConnectionRemote.create
      .destination("https://query.wikidata.org/")
      .queryEndpoint("sparql")
      .build
  )
```

Creating the query and executing it

A query is just a String value, so we don't need anything more here. We also need to support an AttractionOrdering argument. We can "transform" it into a String value using pattern matching and then use the resulting String value inside the query final value.

```
val orderBy = ordering match {
  case ByName               => "?attractionLabel"
  case ByLocationPopulation => "DESC(?population)"
}

val query = s"""... SELECT DISTINCT ?attraction ?attractionLabel
  ?description ?location ?locationLabel ?population WHERE {
  ...
  } ORDER BY $orderBy LIMIT $limit"""
```

```
> def execQuery(getConnection: IO[RDFConnection],
               query: String): IO[List[QuerySolution]] = {
    getConnection.flatMap(c => IO.delay(
      asScala(c.query(QueryFactory.create(query)).execSelect()).toList
    ))
  }
```

We flatMap the getConnection value with a function that uses this connection and returns another IO value that describes how the connection is used to send the query to the server and return an Iterator back, which is transformed into an immutable value using asScala.

You need to import org.apache.jena.query._ and org.apache.jena.rdfconnection._ to use the library types. The book's sbt console session imports them automatically.

RDFConnection is the type coming from the external library. It's imperative and potentially side-effectful, so we wrap it in an IO. The same will happen with other library types (e.g., QueryFactory and QueryFactory below).

many languages have advanced features that allow you to create more complicated String values. The features we use here are string interpolation (embedding a smaller String value inside a bigger one using a name) and multi-line string values. In Scala, string interpolation is achieved using the s prefix and $name, while multi-line strings are defined using triple quotes.

Parsing the results

If our query is successful, we will get a List of QuerySolutions back. These are not immutable values, so we need to be very careful when dealing with them. The best way is to wrap every usage of a QuerySolution in IO.delay. This way we will get a description back, which we can pass around and handle functionally. Note that the signature helps to understand what is going on inside. You need to pass a QuerySolution, and you will get a description of a program that produces our immutable Attraction when executed successfully. Let's first recap how the model looks.

> Note that even though the List is immutable, its elements are imperative mutable types, which we still need to handle before calling it a day.

```
opaque type LocationId = String
case class Location(id: LocationId, name: String, population: Long)
case class Attraction(name: String, description: Option[String], location: Location)
```

And here's how we can safely produce an IO[Attraction] from an existing impure QuerySolution.

```
def parseAttraction(s: QuerySolution): IO[Attraction] = {
  IO.delay(
    Attraction(
      name = s.getLiteral("attractionLabel").getString,
      description =
        if (s.contains("description"))
          Some(s.getLiteral("description").getString)
        else None,
      location = Location(
        id = LocationId(s.getResource("location").getLocalName),
        name = s.getLiteral("locationLabel").getString,
        population = s.getLiteral("population").getInt
      )
    )
  )
}
```

> Note how we use named parameters here to make the code more readable. This code creates the Attraction value using some unsafe calls to the provided QuerySolution (named s). The unsafe calls that can throw exceptions are highlighted. Note that QuerySolution is specific to the Apache Jena library. You need to be aware which calls are unsafe when integrating with another one. Such calls should be wrapped in IO.

The gray area between the functional core and impure code

The function above is not a pure function even though it uses IO. It's not pure because it operates on values that are not immutable. We need to be very careful when writing and using it. It should be separated from other, especially functional modules (no pure function can directly use parseAttraction) and used privately inside a function with a wider IO context without being exposed anywhere. This extra care we need to take is the cost of using imperative client libraries.

You won't have such problems if you choose functional libraries to fetch data from databases and other APIs. They expose pure functions only, which you've already learned to use. There are also languages, like Haskell, that only offer purely functional libraries.

Functional core

Design principles of integrating pure and impure code in a program were discussed in chapter 8.

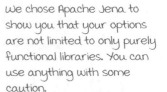

We chose Apache Jena to show you that your options are not limited to only purely functional libraries. You can use anything with some caution.

Separating the library IO from other concerns

Let's put it all together in a single implementation of our input actions defined in the DataAccess type. We have defined one value and two helper functions that we will be able to reuse. Here are their signatures:

```
val getConnection: IO[RDFConnection]
def execQuery(getConnection: IO[RDFConnection], query: String): IO[List[QuerySolution]]
def parseAttraction(s: QuerySolution): IO[Attraction]

def findAttractions(name: String, ordering: AttractionOrdering,
                    limit: Int): IO[List[Attraction]] = {
  val orderBy = ordering match {
    case ByName              => "?attractionLabel"
    case ByLocationPopulation => "DESC(?population)"
  }

  val query = s"""... SELECT DISTINCT ?attraction ?attractionLabel
    ?description ?location ?locationLabel ?population WHERE {
    ...
    } ORDER BY $orderBy LIMIT $limit"""

  for {
    solutions   <- execQuery(getConnection, query)
    attractions <- solutions.traverse(parseAttraction) // or map(parseAttraction).sequence
  } yield attractions
}
```

We could implement the other two functions defined in the DataAccess type in a similar manner. However, there are several problems with this approach, and since we are trying to get something to work, we will just focus on the most critical one now. The getConnection value describes a program that creates a connection when executed. That means we will create a connection every time we want to query the server! Additionally, we don't have any chance to close connections. That's something that needs to be addressed right away because it affects a lot of places, and it couldn't possibly be used in any real-world program. But there is a design trick we can use here—namely, **making it someone else's problem**, which may just be a specific case of making decisions as late as possible. Instead of figuring out how to handle closeable resources functionally (there is a very clean solution to this problem, which we will show later), we can just require something different to be passed to our function. We have a very powerful functional technique at our disposal: **passing functions as parameters!**

> **Functions as parameters**
>
> We discussed passing functions, (which are just values) as parameters and currying in chapter 4.

It's still a helpful trick, even if by "someone else" we mean "us in the future."

Currying and inversion of control

Whenever you need to deal with a problem of too many responsibilities or too complex flows that are not directly related to the main responsibility of the function you implement, it means it's a more of an accidental concern. The best course of action is to introduce a new parameter and "outsource" this particular concern to the user of your function.

In our case, we tried to implement a function that gets some input parameters and returns an IO[List[Attraction]] program that queries the real Wikidata server.

> **THIS IS BIG!** "Outsourcing" a concern by requiring a new parameter is a very common design practice in FP.

```
val getConnection: IO[RDFConnection]
```

getConnection is just a value that creates and returns a new connection every time it's executed.

```
def findAttractions(name: String, ordering: AttractionOrdering,
                    limit: Int): IO[List[Attraction]] = {
  ...
  for {
    solutions   <- execQuery(getConnection, query)
    attractions <- solutions.traverse(parseAttraction)
  } yield attractions
}
```

We open a new connection every time this program is executed. Additionally, we are required to close this connection, which we forgot to do here. If a design requires us to remember to do something not strictly related to the business logic, it means it's not a good design.

Passing a connection

The first idea would be to pass the connection as a parameter.

```
def findAttractions(connection: RDFConnection)
                   (name: String, ordering: AttractionOrdering,
                    limit: Int): IO[List[Attraction]]
```

> **Inversion of control**
>
> We discussed inversion of control in a slightly different context in chapter 9.

We provide it in a separate parameter list (we say that the function is curried) because this parameter is not related to the essential concern. We use currying to be able to "configure" functions by providing only some parameters (like connection) to get a fully working version and pass it to modules that don't want to know anything about a connection. Here's how it could look in action:

The caller of findAttractions needs to provide a connection to get a "configured" function that will be able to query attractions.

```
findAttractions(connection)
  → (String, AttractionOrdering, Int) => IO[List[Attraction]]
```

However, as discussed earlier, RDFConnection is not an immutable value, and we should refrain from using it directly whenever we can. Passing an IO[RDFConnection] is not ideal as well because we are not able to reuse a single connection in many queries. IO is just a description of a program that creates a new connection, so executing it will always create a new connection. That's not a sustainable solution.

That means that the caller of findAttractions needs to worry about creating and closing connections, not us.

Functions as values

It may feel like we are going round in circles thinking about all the problems with passing and handling connections. This feeling should trigger an urge to outsource even more. Let's think about what we really need in findAttractions and other API input (data access) functions.

Passing a "querying behavior"

We don't need a connection. We need a way to execute a query. We have a query String and want a List of QuerySolutions that we know how to parse. Does that sound familiar to you? We have just defined a function we need. And there is no mention about any connection-specific things, too!

```
def findAttractions(execQuery: String => IO[List[QuerySolution]])
                   (name: String, ordering: AttractionOrdering,
                    limit: Int): IO[List[Attraction]]
```

Now, we can just expect the querying behavior from the caller. This means that the caller now has more responsibilities, and that was the whole point of this refactoring. We pushed the responsibility upwards. There will be a module somewhere in our program that will be more competent in handling connections and creating proper String => IO[List[QuerySolution]] functions to pass downwards.

Proper implementations of all DataAccess functions can be found in the book's repository. The implementations are all similar to what we showed with findAttractions.

Configuring a bag of functions

There is one outstanding issue. We have already defined the DataAccess type and stated exactly which three functions need to be implemented.

```
trait DataAccess {
  def findAttractions(name: String, ordering: AttractionOrdering,
                      limit: Int): IO[List[Attraction]]
  def findArtistsFromLocation(locationId: LocationId, limit: Int): IO[List[Artist]]
  def findMoviesAboutLocation(locationId: LocationId, limit: Int): IO[List[Movie]]
}
```

There is no place for any additional parameter. These signatures don't assume anything about the internal querying mechanism, and since they are used inside the functional core, we need to keep it this way. We need a different function that returns a specific DataAccess implementation!

You can create a DataAccess value by using the new keyword and providing all required implementations.

```
def getSparqlDataAccess(execQuery: String => IO[List[QuerySolution]]): DataAccess =
  new DataAccess {
    def findAttractions(name: String,
                        ordering: AttractionOrdering, limit: Int): IO[List[Attraction]] = ⚡
    def findArtistsFromLocation(locationId: LocationId, limit: Int): IO[List[Artist]] = ⚡
    def findMoviesAboutLocation(locationId: LocationId, limit: Int): IO[List[Movie]] = ⚡
  } // import ch11_WikidataDataAccess.getSparqlDataAccess
```

Connecting the dots

We now have all the building blocks we need to run a first, fully working version of the travel guide application! Try it yourself!

If you haven't followed along, run sbt console now, and execute code marked with ">" from this page only.

Functional core   *Pure functions & immutable values*

Data model

```
opaque type LocationId = String

case class Location(id: LocationId, name: String, population: Int)
case class Attraction(name: String, description: Option[String], location: Location)

enum PopCultureSubject {
  case Artist(name: String, followers: Int)
  case Movie(name: String, boxOffice: Int)
}

case class TravelGuide(attraction: Attraction, subjects: List[PopCultureSubject])

enum AttractionOrdering {
  case ByName
  case ByLocationPopulation
}
```

Data access

```
trait DataAccess {
  def findAttractions(name: String, ordering: AttractionOrdering, limit: Int): IO[List[Attraction]]
  def findArtistsFromLocation(locationId: LocationId, limit: Int): IO[List[Artist]]
  def findMoviesAboutLocation(locationId: LocationId, limit: Int): IO[List[Movie]]
}
```

Business logic

```
def travelGuide(data: DataAccess, attractionName: String): IO[Option[TravelGuide]]
```

```
> import ch11_TravelGuide._, model._, PopCultureSubject._
  import AttractionOrdering._
  import Version1.travelGuide
```

Input actions   *Input actions know about things in the functional core, but the functional core doesn't know anything about them.*

```
def getSparqlDataAccess(execQuery: String => IO[List[QuerySolution]]): DataAccess
```

```
> import ch11_WikidataDataAccess.getSparqlDataAccess
```

```
def execQuery(connection: RDFConnection)(query: String): IO[List[QuerySolution]] =
  IO.blocking(asScala(connection.query(QueryFactory.create(query)).execSelect()).toList)
```

This is a new version of execQuery that allows us to reuse a single connection.
IO.blocking does the same thing as IO.delay, but the delayed action is executed on a thread pool that is better suited for blocking operations, like external API queries.

This arrow means that one module knows about the other and can use its public functions and types. The main process is thin but knows about everybody else.

Main application process

```
> val connection = RDFConnectionRemote.create
    .destination("https://query.wikidata.org/")
    .queryEndpoint("sparql")
    .build
→ RDFConnectionRemote
  val wikidata = getSparqlDataAccess(execQuery(connection))
  travelGuide(wikidata, "Yosemite").unsafeRunSync()
→ Some(TravelGuide(Attraction(Yosemite National Park, ...)))
  connection.close()
```

And that's it! Running this code will query the Wikidata server and return a travel guide for Yosemite! Make sure to execute the code snippets and see the guide yourself.

We made it work

We pushed the design as much as we could to get a working version. It's
time to focus on making sure all the requirements are met.

Requirements: Pop culture travel guide

1. The application should take a single **String** value: a search term for the tourist
   attraction that the user wants to visit and needs a travel guide for.

2. The application needs to search for a given attraction, its description (if it exists), and
   its geographical location. It should prefer locations with larger populations.

3. The application should use a location to do as follows:

   — Find artists originating from this location, sorted by the number of social media followers

   — Find movies that take place in this location, sorted by the box office earnings

4. For a given tourist attraction, artists and movies form its "pop culture travel guide"
   that should be returned to the user. If there are more possible guides, the application
   needs to return the one with the highest *score*, which is calculated as follows:

   — 30 points for a description

   — 10 points for each artist or movie (max. 40 points)

   — 1 point for each 100,000 followers (all artists combined; max. 15 points)

   — 1 point for each $10,000,000 in box office earnings (all movies combined; max. 15 points)

5. We will add support for more pop culture subjects in the future (e.g., video games).

Since we already designed the blueprint of the application and separated
the data access concern and its internals, we can safely focus on our
business logic and iteratively make it better.

Version 1   The first version of travelGuide we implemented earlier

```
def travelGuide(data: DataAccess, attractionName: String): IO[Option[TravelGuide]] = {
  for {
    attractions <- data.findAttractions(attractionName, ByLocationPopulation, 1)
    guide <- attractions.headOption match {
             case None => IO.pure(None)
             case Some(attraction) =>
               for {
                 artists <- data.findArtistsFromLocation(attraction.location.id, 2)
                 movies <- data.findMoviesAboutLocation(attraction.location.id, 2)
               } yield Some(TravelGuide(attraction, artists.appendedAll(movies)))
           }
  } yield guide
}
```

In the current version of travelGuide, we just look at a single attraction returned
by the findAttractions program. However, as we see above, there may be more
attractions and we need to look at more than one, score them using the provided
algorithm, and return the one with the highest score.

Let's think about it first. What would be the next step, in your opinion? What
change do we need to introduce? Is there a need for a new pure function?

Making it right

The natural next step is to query more attractions, apply the scoring algorithm to them, and return the one with the highest score.

1 The scoring algorithm defined in the requirements can easily be implemented as a pure function. It should get a TravelGuide and return its score:

```scala
def guideScore(guide: TravelGuide): Int = {
  val descriptionScore = guide.attraction.description.map(_ => 30).getOrElse(0)
  val quantityScore = Math.min(40, guide.subjects.size * 10)
  val totalFollowers = guide.subjects
    .map(_ match {
      case Artist(_, followers) => followers
      case _                    => 0
    })
    .sum
  val totalBoxOffice = guide.subjects
    .map(_ match {
      case Movie(_, boxOffice) => boxOffice
      case _                   => 0
    })
    .sum
  val followersScore = Math.min(15, totalFollowers / 100_000)
  val boxOfficeScore = Math.min(15, totalBoxOffice / 10_000_000)
  descriptionScore + quantityScore + followersScore + boxOfficeScore
}
```

> We count 30 points if there is a description and 0 if there's not. Then, we add 10 points for each pop culture subject (max 40).

> We use pattern matching to destructure subjects and calculate the sum of followers. Then we use the same technique to sum the box office.

2 Now we can change the travelGuide function to use the guideScore function internally:

```scala
def travelGuide(data: DataAccess, attractionName: String): IO[Option[TravelGuide]] = {
  for {
    attractions <- data.findAttractions(attractionName, ByLocationPopulation, 3)
    guides <- attractions
                .map(attraction =>
                  for {
                    artists <- data.findArtistsFromLocation(attraction.location.id, 2)
                    movies <- data.findMoviesAboutLocation(attraction.location.id, 2)
                  } yield TravelGuide(attraction, artists.appendedAll(movies))
                )
                .sequence
  } yield guides.sortBy(guideScore).reverse.headOption
}
```

> We map each attraction to an IO value describing a program that fetches artists and movies for the attraction's location. We use sequence to transform a List[IO[TravelGuide] into an IO[List[TravelGuide]] and sort the internal list using the guideScore function. We return a guide with the highest score, if there is any, or None otherwise.

We now have a better version that returns the best guide!

Quick exercise

Assuming we execute this new version of the travelGuide function with the Wikidata DataAccess and provide an attractionName for which there are at least three attractions in Wikidata, how many Wikidata server queries will there be in total?

Answer:
maximum seven
queries in total.

Resource leaks

The current version of the `travelGuide` function will make seven data queries if there are at least three attractions with a given name. When you try to run it for `"Yosemite"`, you can get various results. That's because we have accidentally introduced a bug into our application: **a resource leak!**

This leak is not present in the functional core because we only have immutable values and pure functions there. The usual suspect for such things is code outside of the functional core—usually, the impure code that connects all the modules together (i.e., the main process).

```
def execQuery(connection: RDFConnection)(query: String): IO[List[QuerySolution]] =
  IO.blocking(
    asScala(connection.query(QueryFactory.create(query)).execSelect()).toList
  )
```

> Here, the `connection.query` call returns a `QueryExecution` object that is responsible for executing the query and getting results on demand. **It needs to be closed explicitly to release its resources**. We don't do it here, and that's where the resource leak comes from.

```
val connection: RDFConnection = RDFConnectionRemote.create
  .destination("https://query.wikidata.org/")
  .queryEndpoint("sparql")
  .build
→ RDFConnectionRemote
```

```
val wikidata = getSparqlDataAccess(execQuery(connection))
travelGuide(wikidata, "Yosemite")).unsafeRunSync()
```

`connection.close()` ◀

Please restart your REPL session now and use the following imports:

> You already executed this snippet in your REPL session a few pages ago, and you most likely got a proper guide back. However, you will probably not be able to run it again here in the same session because of the internal resource leak.

```
import ch11_TravelGuide._, model._, PopCultureSubject._, AttractionOrdering._, Version2.travelGuide
import ch11_WikidataDataAccess.getSparqlDataAccess
```

Such things may happen in other cases as well. For example, if you implement a web client and forget to read the whole HTTP response, you may end up with a similar leak, depending on the library you use. You need to understand what resources your programs need to acquire no matter what programming paradigm your team prefers.

When you deal with impure, stateful values (objects) that additionally acquire and consume some resources, such as filesystem or network connections, you need to be very careful and always release those resources when you no longer need them. That's usually very hard to achieve in the presence of several possible program flows and error cases. That's why many languages introduce special syntax that deals with resource handling and provides ways to always release them. Java has `try-with-resources`, and some FP languages have the `Resource` type. Before we learn about it, let's figure out the problem using only `IO`.

It is a problem related to our library, but you can encounter it in many other libraries that come with their own connection pool tools or other resource management tools. It's a universal problem, and we will provide a universal FP solution.

Handling resources

We are able to handle releasable resources using the knowledge we've gained so far (i.e., using the IO type alone).

```
> def createExecution(connection: RDFConnection, query: String): IO[QueryExecution] =
    IO.blocking(connection.query(QueryFactory.create(query)))

  def closeExecution(execution: QueryExecution): IO[Unit] =
    IO.blocking(execution.close())

  def execQuery(connection: RDFConnection)(query: String): IO[List[QuerySolution]] = {
    for {
      execution <- createExecution(connection, query)
      solutions <- IO.blocking(asScala(execution.execSelect()).toList)
      _         <- closeExecution(execution)
    } yield solutions
  }
```

As a reminder, IO.blocking does the same thing as IO.delay and has the same API. The difference is that the delayed action is executed on a thread pool that is better suited for blocking operations.

We are running the closeExecution program after we get solutions. However, if a query fails we are still not covered. We may need to use orElse for that.

It may work, but it doesn't feel very declarative. It also is prone to human error: we already learned the hard way that it's very easy to forget to release something. We'd like to use more of the functional programming power here. Fortunately, there is something more declarative and more descriptive—something that always releases the resource no matter what happens. Meet the Resource type!

If you don't use the book's sbt console, please import cats .effect.Resource.

More generally, Resource[F, A] has two type parameters: F is the effect type (we use IO in the book), and A is a type of value that represents a resource that can be acquired and released.

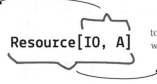

A value of type Resource[IO, A] **describes** a value of type A that needs to be acquired before using it and released when it is no longer needed (whether after successful execution or on error).

To create a Resource value, you call Resource.make, which takes an IO value and a function.

Resource.make(acquire: IO[A])(release: A => IO[Unit])

The acquire function takes an IO[A], which describes a program that acquires an A value.

The release function takes an A value and returns a program that needs to be executed when A is no longer needed.

```
acquire   A        release   A => ()
```

For example, since QueryExecution is something that needs to be acquired and released, **we can represent this fact as a Resource value**:

```
def execQuery(connection: RDFConnection)(query: String): IO[List[QuerySolution]] = {
  val executionResource: Resource[IO, QueryExecution] =
    Resource.make(createExecution(connection, query))(closeExecution)
  ???
}
```

Note: We reused functions defined at the beginning of this page and passed them as the acquire and release functions.

We now have a Resource[IO, QueryExecution] value, but what's next?

Using a Resource **value**

How does the Resource value help? Let's write a different version of the execQuery function and see what it gives us.

```
> def execQuery(connection: RDFConnection)(query: String): IO[List[QuerySolution]] = {
    val executionResource: Resource[IO, QueryExecution] =
      Resource.make(createExecution(connection, query))(closeExecution)
    executionResource.use(execution => IO.blocking(asScala(execution.execSelect()).toList))
  }
```

Not much changed at first sight. But this function is a lot safer than anything we've written before! A Resource value has a **use** function defined on it, which takes another function from a value representing the acquired resource to a program that needs to be executed. Note that the function will be called internally after the resource is acquired (using the function we provided when we created this Resource value). If anything goes wrong (a failure), the resource will be released. If the program provided in use finishes successfully, the resource will also be released (using the function we provided when we created this Resource value). **This way we can focus on using the resource without worrying about acquiring and releasing it!** And the best news is that it's all modeled as immutable values!

resource.use(f: A => IO[B])

The use function takes a function that takes an A and returns an IO[A], which describes a program that needs to be executed after acquiring the resource represented by an A value and before releasing it.

f   A => B

Both RDFConnection and QueryExecution implement the AutoCloseable interface, so we could use Resource .fromAutoCloseable instead of make.

Now, we can model the connection as Resource, too:

```
> val connectionResource: Resource[IO, RDFConnection] = Resource.make(
    IO.blocking(
      RDFConnectionRemote.create
        .destination("https://query.wikidata.org/")
        .queryEndpoint("sparql")
        .build
    ))(connection => IO.blocking(connection.close()))

  val program: IO[Option[TravelGuide]] =
    connectionResource.use(connection => {
      val wikidata = getSparqlDataAccess(execQuery(connection))
      travelGuide(wikidata, "Yellowstone")
    })

  program.unsafeRunSync()
  → Some(TravelGuide(
        Attraction(Yellowstone National Park, Some(first national park in the world...),
                   Location(LocationId(Q1214), Wyoming, 586107)),
        List(Movie(The Hateful Eight, 155760117), Movie(Heaven's Gate, 3484331))
  ))
```

Nothing will leak in this implementation—even in the presence of connection failures, parsing failures, or query issues. The only option to use a connection is to call the use function that takes another function. The connection cannot be used outside the scope of this function. Moreover, when the returned IO program finishes, the connection is already released.

As always, nothing is acquired until somebody executes IO.

You can execute it as many times as you want. No leaks! This is the power of functional IO.

We made it right

It turned out our initial design was quite good. We needed to fix some issues regarding missing requirements (sorting travel guides) and resource handling. We learned about the Resource type along the way.

> **THIS IS BIG!**
> We model releasable resources as values.

Functional core   Pure functions and immutable values

Data model

LocationId   Location   Attraction   PopCultureSubject
      Artist   Movie   TravelGuide

Data access

```
trait DataAccess {
  def findAttractions(name: String, ordering: AttractionOrdering, limit: Int): IO[List[Attraction]]
  def findArtistsFromLocation(locationId: LocationId, limit: Int): IO[List[Artist]]
  def findMoviesAboutLocation(locationId: LocationId, limit: Int): IO[List[Movie]]
}
```

Business logic

```
def travelGuide(data: DataAccess, attractionName: String): IO[Option[TravelGuide]] =
  for {
    attractions <- data.findAttractions(attractionName, ByLocationPopulation, 3)
    guides <- attractions
                .map(attraction =>
                  for {
                    artists <- data.findArtistsFromLocation(attraction.location.id, 2)
                    movies <- data.findMoviesAboutLocation(attraction.location.id, 2)
                  } yield TravelGuide(attraction, artists.appendedAll(movies))
                )
                .sequence
  } yield guides.sortBy(guideScore).reverse.headOption
```

Input actions

```
def getSparqlDataAccess(execQuery: String => IO[List[QuerySolution]]): DataAccess = [...][...][...]

def execQuery(connection: RDFConnection)(query: String): IO[List[QuerySolution]] = {
  val executionResource: Resource[IO, QueryExecution] =
    Resource.make(createExecution(connection, query))(closeExecution)

  executionResource.use(execution => IO.blocking(asScala(execution.execSelect()).toList))
}

val connectionResource: Resource[IO, RDFConnection] = Resource.make(
  IO.blocking(
    RDFConnectionRemote.create
      .destination("https://query.wikidata.org/")
      .queryEndpoint("sparql")
      .build
  )
)(connection => IO.blocking(connection.close()))
```

Main application process

```
connectionResource.use(connection => {
  val wikidata =
    getSparqlDataAccess(execQuery(connection))
  travelGuide(wikidata, "Yosemite")
}).unsafeRunSync()
```

One more thing! Resource has map and flatMap functions! That means we can make the main application process even better.

> *See the book's source code for more about Resource!*

```
val dataAccessResource: Resource[IO, DataAccess] =
  connectionResource.map(connection => getSparqlDataAccess(execQuery(connection)))

dataAccessResource.use(dataAccess => travelGuide(dataAccess, "Yosemite")).unsafeRunSync()
```

Coffee break: Make it fast

The current implementation of travelGuide makes several queries to choose and return the best possible guide. However, all of these queries are done sequentially. Taking into account that each of them may take even one second, that's not going to be a very fast application.

```
def travelGuide(data: DataAccess, attractionName: String): IO[Option[TravelGuide]] = {
  for {
    attractions <- data.findAttractions(attractionName, ByLocationPopulation, 3)
    guides <- attractions
                .map(attraction =>
                  for {
                    artists <- data.findArtistsFromLocation(attraction.location.id, 2)
                    movies  <- data.findMoviesAboutLocation(attraction.location.id, 2)
                  } yield TravelGuide(attraction, artists.appendedAll(movies))
                )
                .sequence
  } yield guides.sortBy(guideScore).reverse.headOption
}
```

Your task is to refactor the function so it uses concurrency as much as possible. Specifically, queries for each attraction are independent of each other and can be run in parallel. Similarly, finding artists and movies for a given attraction are two independent queries and can be run in parallel, too.

When you think about the solution, please note that the change from a sequential to a multithreaded application is completely contained within one pure function that returns an immutable value. That's the power of functional programming and functional design!

1

Your second task is to look at the current design and solution from the bird's-eye perspective. What are other things we could do to make it faster? How often does the same query return a different answer? Maybe we could reuse that fact to make the following program faster?

2

The second task is harder than the first, but you already have all the knowledge and tools at your disposal to solve it!

```
connectionResource.use(connection => {
  val dataAccess = getSparqlDataAccess(execQuery(connection))
  for {
    result1 <- travelGuide(dataAccess, "Yellowstone")
    result2 <- travelGuide(dataAccess, "Yellowstone")
    result3 <- travelGuide(dataAccess, "Yellowstone")
  } yield result1.toList.appendedAll(result2).appendedAll(result3)
})
```

Remember Ref values from chapter 10? maybe you could use them to cache query results?

Hints

— We use sequence in the current version. Do you remember **parSequence**?

— We may need caching to make it even faster when more guides are searched for.

Coffee break explained: Make it fast

Making concurrent queries is just a matter of replacing sequence and flatMap calls with parSequence. Since fetching artists and movies is independent, we don't really need to do them in sequence. That's why we need to replace the for comprehension with a List.

1

```
def travelGuide(data: DataAccess, attractionName: String): IO[Option[TravelGuide]] = {
  for {
    attractions <- data.findAttractions(attractionName, ByLocationPopulation, 3)
    guides <- attractions
                .map(attraction =>
                  List(
                    data.findArtistsFromLocation(attraction.location.id, 2),
                    data.findMoviesAboutLocation(attraction.location.id, 2)
                  ).parSequence
                  .map(_.flatten)
                  .map(popCultureSubjects => TravelGuide(attraction, popCultureSubjects))
                ).parSequence
  } yield guides.sortBy(guideScore).reverse.headOption
}
```

We map each attraction to a program. Programs for all attractions are run concurrently (the second parSequence). Inside each attraction's program there are two other programs that are run concurrently (the first parSequence): one for artists and one for movies. Since the first program's result is a List[Artist], and the second's is a List[Movie], we end up with a List of two Lists, and the resulting type is List[List[PopCultureSubject]] (because Movie and Artist are both PopCultureSubjects).We flatten them and use them, name the resulting list popCultureSubjects, and put it inside a new TravelGuide.

We can make it even faster by noticing that our queries usually return the same results (locations of artists or movies don't change very often), so we can heavily cache them. It turns out that our design and its separated concerns allow us to introduce cache by passing a different function to getSparqlDataAccess! (Yes, that's all we need!)

2

```
def cachedExecQuery(connection: RDFConnection, cache: Ref[IO, Map[String, List[QuerySolution]]])(
    query: String
): IO[List[QuerySolution]] = {
  for {
    cachedQueries <- cache.get
    solutions <- cachedQueries.get(query) match {
      case Some(cachedSolutions) => IO.pure(cachedSolutions)
      case None =>
        for {
          realSolutions <- execQuery(connection)(query)
          _ <- cache.update(_.updated(query, realSolutions))
        } yield realSolutions
    }
  } yield solutions
}
```

Our function first gets a program that, when executed, will read the current value of the cache and then will get query results for the given query. If they are not present, we fire up the old execQuery function, store the solutions in cache, and return them.

Summary

In this chapter we used multiple tools and techniques from earlier parts to create a real-world application that fetches data from Wikidata.

Design real-world functional applications

We used the *functional core* design concept, which contains only pure functions and immutable values that are used by external modules like the main application process, which "configures" pure functions with specific input and output actions.

Model more complicated requirements as types

The design process started with requirements. We transformed them into a data model and pushed toward a working solution in the spirit of "make it work, make it right, make it fast."

Integrate with real data-source APIs using IO

We modeled the data access layer as a bag of three pure functions, which we called DataAccess. Only after implementing the first version of the business logic (the travelGuide function) did we start wondering about the specifics of the service that would become our data provider. We chose Wikidata, which is a free service exposing a SPARQL endpoint.

We used SPARQL for queries, but the techniques we showed can also be used in other places, such as SQL servers and queries.

We used the Apache Jena library to connect and query the Wikidata server. We showed that, even though it's an imperative library, we have tools at our disposal to integrate with it without changing any of the pure functions and immutable values we had already put in place.

Avoid resource leaks

Internally, the data access layer implemented using the imperative Apache Jena library keeps its own connection pool and query execution contexts. These are stateful resources that need to be acquired (e.g., creating a connection to a server) and released when no longer needed, even in the presence of errors. Not releasing such resources leads to resource leaks. We learned that we can easily manage such cases without any headaches using Resource values, which describe releasable resources.

There are more cases of resources we can manage using a Resource value. You can model your application's internal resources in this way as well!

Cache query results to speed up the execution

Finally, we tried to make the application fast. We used some concurrency and implemented a query results cache by changing just a single small dependency, which proved that the design is very robust.

There's more! Have a look at the source code in the book repository to see some additional improvements, including IO timeout support!

In this chapter
you will learn

- how to test pure functions by providing examples

- how to test pure functions by providing properties

- how to test side effects without using any mocking libraries

- how to develop new functionalities in a test-driven way

66 Beware of bugs in the above code; I have 99
only proved it correct, not tried it.

—DONALD KNUTH

Do you have tests for that?

This last chapter of the book is devoted to one of the most important software engineering activities: **testing**. Tests are one of the major methods of writing maintainable software. They can be used to make sure the program behaves according to the requirements, it doesn't have bugs we discovered earlier, and that it integrates with external APIs, services, or databases properly.

Having an application that consists mostly of pure functions that operate on immutable values makes writing tests a very enjoyable endeavor. The tests in this chapter are small and readable, and they cover a lot of production code.

On top of all that, we can also use tests to document the application: to help clarify the responsibilities and inner working to other team members. This is the best kind of documentation because it can't get outdated as easily as normal text-based documentation usually does—assuming that the test itself is easy to understand. That all makes tests a very important element of well-developed, readable, and maintainable software.

Testing by providing examples
We will add quick tests by providing examples and asserting the correct outcomes.

Does the program behave according to the requirements?

Does it have bugs?

Does it integrate correctly with its external dependencies?

Testing integration
We will show how to test integration with an external dependency, including running the real server and side effects.

Testing by defining properties
We will define some properties and let the testing library explore possible inputs.

Tests as documentation
All our tests will be small and easy to understand. They will help others quickly grasp the requirements and implementation details.

We have dropped a few testing techniques and hints earlier in the book, but now it's time to bring all we learned together and show how easy our testing job becomes once we choose the functional paradigm. We will first try to add tests to the existing pop culture travel guide application from the previous chapter. We will show you how to approach writing tests for our existing pure functions, including the IO-based ones. Unsurprisingly, we will discover some not-so-obvious bugs in our original implementations!

Did you catch any bugs in the previous chapter? If not, don't worry. Tests have got your back, too!

We will then show you how easy it is to use tests as a documentation of features that are not yet implemented and use them to guide the implementation process. We will write tests first, then fill the implementation, following a very popular test-driven development practice. This will become a very important tool in your functional testing inventory. We will also learn some new pure functions and recap material from previous chapters along the way. Let's start!

Tests are just functions

The main takeaway from this chapter is that we don't introduce any new concepts that are useful only in the testing code. **We reuse exactly the same mechanisms**: pure functions and immutable values. We don't need any mocking libraries because what we learned previously is enough to write any kind of tests!

The only additional tool we will need is the testing framework itself: we will run our tests using the scalatest library. One of the most basic options is calling the provided test function.

testName is a String that describes the test.   testFun is a function that doesn't take any arguments and returns a value of Assertion.

```
def test(testName: String)(testFun: => Assertion): Unit
```

After calling this function, we don't care about what it returns because the execution itself is delegated to the test runner provided by scalatest.

The signature above is a simplified version of what's available in scalatest, but it's enough to **get accustomed to functional testing**. We don't want to go into scalatest library details. We will use it only to showcase functional programming testing techniques, which are also possible to achieve (and very popular) in other functional languages.

So what can we do with the test function? We can call it inside a testing class, passing the two required parameters: a String (testName) and a parameterless function (testFun), like this:

```
import org.scalatest.funsuite.AnyFunSuite
class ch12_BasicTest extends AnyFunSuite {
  test("2 times 2 should always be 4")({
    assert(2 * 2 == 4)
  })
}
```

scalatest requires us to define all the function calls inside a class that extends from one of the built-in traits. In this case we use AnyFunSuite.

We call the test function with the test case name and with a parameterless function (a block of code that will be executed lazily by the testing framework) that returns an Assertion. Here, we use a helper assert function that takes a Boolean condition and returns an Assertion value.

When we execute such a test in the terminal, we will get the following answer:

```
> sbt test
ch12_BasicTest:
- 2 times 2 should always be 4
Run completed in 95 milliseconds.
Total number of tests run: 1
All tests passed.
```

In this chapter we will work from the IDE and terminal—not the REPL.

Now that you know how all this works, let's see some real test cases!

You can find all the code we discuss in this chapter in the src/test/scala directory in the books' companion code repository. Open the ch12_BasicTest file and try to write tests there! You should also remove other test files if you want to run only your tests!

scalatest is the most popular Scala testing tool, and it provides a lot of different options and testing flavors. Here, we just focus on the most basic ones that are available in other tools and languages.

Look at the book's source code to see all the tests in action. Call sbt test and see the output of more than twenty tests we are going to implement in this chapter!

Choosing functions to test

The most convenient functions to test are pure functions that use simple types. Our testing adventure should start with trying to write tests for pure functions that don't take or return IO values. There are two main reasons for choosing this particular strategy:

- Such non-**IO** functions usually represent an important business logic. We can be pretty sure that they are part of the functional core.
- Tests for such functions are very easy to write.

Looks like a win-win, right? We are writing tests for the most important functionality, and at the same time, these tests are the easiest to write. If we have a small, pure function that takes some immutable values and returns an immutable value back, the only job—and sometimes a very difficult one—is choosing the right immutable values. That's when we are doing **testing by providing examples**. Usually, the better the requirements and the more the design of our application resembles those requirements, the easier the job of choosing the right examples becomes.

> Yes, I know IOs are also immutable values! Testing functions that take and return them are also quite easy to write, but we'd like to focus on such tests separately, later in the chapter.

One of the pure functions that doesn't use IO values is guideScore. Sure enough, it's one of the most important functions in the travel guide application. Here it is, along with the requirements:

> We wrote and discussed this function in chapter 11.

```
def guideScore(guide: TravelGuide): Int = {
  val descriptionScore =
    guide.attraction.description.map(_ => 30).getOrElse(0)
  val quantityScore = Math.min(40, guide.subjects.size * 10)

  val totalFollowers = guide.subjects
    .map(_ match {
      case Artist(_, followers) => followers
      case _                    => 0
    }).sum
  val totalBoxOffice = guide.subjects
    .map(_ match {
      case Movie(_, boxOffice) => boxOffice
      case _                   => 0
    }).sum

  val followersScore = Math.min(15, totalFollowers / 100_000)
  val boxOfficeScore = Math.min(15, totalBoxOffice / 10_000_000)
  descriptionScore + quantityScore + followersScore + boxOfficeScore
}
```

> The guide *score* consists of
>
> — 30 points for a description
> — 10 points for each artist or movie (max. 40 points)
> — 1 point for each 100,000 followers (all artists combined; max. 15 points)
> — 1 point for each $10,000,000 in box office earnings (all movies combined; max. 15 points)

Let's think about it first. How would you approach making sure that this implementation satisfies the requirements?

Testing by providing examples

The guideScore function can easily be tested by providing examples (input parameters), calling the function and asserting on its output. Pure functions always return the same outputs for the same inputs, so there shouldn't be any nondeterminism or flakiness in such a test.

The difficult job here, however, is to come up with the right examples and right assertions. It's very important to double-check—probably on a piece of paper or maybe in the code comment—that the asserted output is correct. Remember, **your test is your last resort**. It needs to be correct!

The best approach is to look at the function's signature:

```
def guideScore(guide: TravelGuide): Int
```

We can immediately see that we need to come up with an example—a TravelGuide value—call the function passing that value, and then assert on an Int value we get back. That's all we need.

```
test("score of a guide with a description, 0 artists, and 2 popular movies should be 65") {
  val guide = TravelGuide(
    Attraction(
      "Yellowstone National Park",
      Some("first national park in the world"),
      Location(LocationId("Q1214"), "Wyoming", 586107)
    ),
    List(Movie("The Hateful Eight", 155760117), Movie("Heaven's Gate", 3484331))
  )

  // 30 (description) + 0 (0 artists) + 20 (2 movies) + 15 (159 million box office)
  assert(guideScore(guide) == 65)
}
```

Here, the guide value is the **example** we generated and provided. We then use it, referring to the requirements, to **manually calculate** what the result should be. Finally, we call the function and **assert** that the return value is correct. Our test suite consists of one test. Let's run it.

```
> sbt test
ch12_TravelGuideTest:
- score of a guide with a description, 0 artists,
  and 2 popular movies should be 65
All tests passed.
```

Great news! Our implementation is not that bad—it works correctly in at least one case. Let's generate more examples in the same spirit.

Important: Open ch12_TravelGuideTest in your editor and remove all the test functions from there if you want to code along.

In Scala, we can omit the round brackets if we pass a function as a parameter. Here, it is passed using only curly brackets.

THIS IS BIG! FP tests are just calling functions and asserting on their outputs.

Practicing testing by example

It's your turn to write some tests and provide more examples that cover more combinations. Remember that the most important activity is to make sure your example is valid and the expected value you use in the assertion is correct according to the requirements. Here is the function-under-test signature:

```
def guideScore(guide: TravelGuide): Int
```

Your task is to create a TravelGuide value, calculate manually the correct answer and write the following two tests:

1. Score of a guide with no description, 0 artists, and 0 movies should be ...
2. Score of a guide with no description, 0 artists, and 2 movies with no box office earnings should be ...

Remember to finish both sentences, providing the manually calculated expected value!

Answers

```
test("score of a guide with no description, 0 artists, and 0 movies should be 0") {
  val guide = TravelGuide(
    Attraction(
      "Yellowstone National Park",
      None,
      Location(LocationId("Q1214"), "Wyoming", 586107)
    ),
    List.empty
  )

  // 0 (description) + 0 (0 artists) + 0 (0 movies)
  assert(guideScore(guide) == 0)
}
```

> The guide *score* consists of
>
> — 30 points for a description
> — 10 points for each artist or movie (max. 40 points)
> — 1 point for each 100,000 followers (all artists combined; max. 15 points)
> — 1 point for each $10,000,000 in box office earnings (all movies combined; max. 15 points)

```
test("score of a guide with no description, 0 artists,
    and 2 movies with no box office earnings should be 20") {
  val guide = TravelGuide(
    Attraction(
      "Yellowstone National Park",
      None,
      Location(LocationId("Q1214"), "Wyoming", 586107)
    ),
    List(Movie("The Hateful Eight", 0), Movie("Heaven's Gate", 0))
  )

  // 0 (description) + 0 (0 artists) + 20 (2 movies) + 0 (0 million box office)
  assert(guideScore(guide) == 20)
}
```

Generating good examples

I hope you appreciate how concise and understandable the tests are when we fully embrace the functional programming paradigm. Note that this characteristic—**great testability**—comes with every pure function—no matter what language and testing library you choose.

Testing in FP

Testing in FP is testing pure functions by providing parameters and asserting on expected output values.

We now have three test cases that cover quite different scenarios. Let's execute the whole test suite.

```
> sbt test
ch12_TravelGuideTest:
- score of a guide with a description, 0 artists,
  and 2 popular movies should be 65
- score of a guide with no description, 0 artists,
  and 0 movies should be 0
- score of a guide with no description, 0 artists, and 2 movies
  with no box office earnings should be 20
All tests passed.
```

As you've just seen, we wrote three tests by providing three examples, and it looks like the function works correctly! However, while writing tests for pure functions is pretty straightforward, generating examples and **looking for potential corner cases can be very challenging**. This and the fact that we are the authors of the implementation (which makes the function ultimately bug-free, right?) tempts us to consider guideScore as a properly implemented function. Many programmers would agree that this is enough and safely move on, even though many various different examples are still missing.

Now, the worst thing is that—spoiler alert!—guideScore has at least one bug, which we haven't found yet—neither in the previous chapter, where we implemented it nor here after writing a few example-based test cases. Can you spot it? Can you think of any examples that would expose this or another bug? If not, don't worry. Testing is such a popular and powerful programming practice, specifically because finding bugs just by looking at the implementation is hard. And again, it's even harder if you are the author of the implementation!

Some programmers would find the problem with the implementation quickly, and some would not. We can't leave that much to chance! Too much is at stake. That's why we need more techniques that help maximize the chance of finding the right examples and, as a consequence, the majority of bugs in our pure functions. FP gives us such techniques!

As a word of caution, remember to always double-check that you are testing the right thing. If you write some tests and they pass immediately, try changing the implementation of the function-under-test randomly and see whether tests start failing.

There are programmers who excel at finding bugs just by looking at the implementation; however, they too are using tests to confirm and prove what they found!

Generating properties

If you think that the function you implemented is correct and you can't come up with any examples that prove otherwise, it's best to add a few **property-based tests for your pure function**—especially if it belongs to the functional core and represents an essential concern.

What are those mysterious properties? They are more general descriptions of your function's desired behavior. They require you to stop thinking about specific examples and focus on more high-level properties instead. This change of focus helps you look at the functionality from a different perspective, enhancing your chances of finding bugs. Let's see this in practice and ask ourselves this: **what are high-level requirement-like constraints of the guide scoring functionality?**

> **Separation of concerns**
>
> Separation of concerns was heavily discussed in chapter 8.

 ① The guide score should not depend on its attraction's name and description strings.

If an attraction has a description and its travel guide has two movies, the score of the guide will always be the same, **no matter what** the name and the description strings contain.

what are some high-level constraints of the guide-scoring functionality?

Here we define three high-level constraints. The next step is going to be a big one, so make sure you understand each of these constraints by validating them with the requirements below.

③ The guide score should always be between 20 and 50 if there is an artist and a movie but no description.

If an attraction has no description, and its travel guide has a single artist and a single movie, its score will always be between 20 and 50 (inclusive), **no matter how much** the movie earned and how many followers the artist has.

② The guide score should always be between 30 and 70 if it has a description and some bad movies.

If an attraction has a description, and its travel guide has no artists and some movies with $0 box office earnings, its score will always be between 30 and 70 (inclusive), **no matter how many** movies there are.

The guide *score* consists of

— 30 points for a description

— 10 points for each artist or movie (max. 40 points)

— 1 point for each 100,000 followers (all artists combined; max. 15 points)

— 1 point for each $10,000,000 in box office earnings (all movies combined; max. 15 points)

We came up with three properties. The process of generating them is similar to generating specific examples: you look at the requirements and try to figure out how some values should impact (or not) the end result. For example, given all other values are the same, how much does the different number of movies affect the output value? You need to encode that in the test code. That's where property-based tests come in.

Property-based testing

Generating properties is the hardest part of defining the property-based test. Once we have them, we can very conveniently transform them into test code. Let's see the first property-based test in action.

We use the scalacheck library (it's already installed if you use the book's sbt console) to write property-based tests.

```
import org.scalacheck._, Arbitrary._, org.scalatestplus.scalacheck._
test("guide score should not depend on its attraction's name and description strings") {
  forAll((name: String, description: String) => {
    val guide = TravelGuide(
      Attraction(
        name,
        Some(description),
        Location(LocationId("Q1214"), "Wyoming", 586107)
      ),
      List(Movie("The Hateful Eight", 155760117), Movie("Heaven's Gate", 3484331))
    )

    // 30 (description) + 0 (0 artists) + 20 (2 movies) + 15 (159 million box office)
    assert(guideScore(guide) == 65)
  })
}
```

It looks pretty similar to what we previously had, right? The only difference is this new forAll helper function that takes a function, which—in this case—takes two String values and generates an Assertion. It turns out this function internally generates the two String values for us and calls our function multiple times with different Strings! So the test above is executed many times with a different name and a different description! When we run this test, we get a familiar message:

The behavior of the forAll and test functions are fully configurable. You can, for example, set the number of successfully executed assertions that are required to mark the whole test as successful. We will use default values in this book, which should be enough in most cases.

```
> sbt test
...
- guide score should not depend on its
  attraction's name and description strings
All tests passed.
```

We get a successful execution, but internally, the testing framework executed the function we passed to forAll multiple times and confirmed that no matter what String values are passed as name and description, the guide score will always be 65. Isn't it nice? We, as humans, came up with general properties of the system and delegated the hard work of generating examples to the computer.

> ## Property-based testing
> Property-based testing is testing applications by providing high-level requirement-like constraints and letting the testing framework generate and run the example-based test cases.

Testing by providing properties

Before implementing the remaining three property-based tests, let's look at them from yet another perspective. If we look closely, these properties can be treated as examples but with some additional "wiggle points."

	Attraction's name	Attraction's description	Number of movies	Total box office	Number of artists	Total followers
Property ❶	**Random**	**Random**	2	$159m	0	0
Property ❷	Yellowstone National Park	First national park in the world	**Random**	$0m	0	0
Property ❸			1	**Random**	1	**Random**

These are exactly the same properties we listed earlier but now in a tabular form. Looking at this, we can quickly understand that the assertions also need to be more relaxed. Most of the time we are looking at asserting on ranges of possible output values, not specific ones. We asserted on the exact guide score for property #1 because the value of the attraction's name and description shouldn't have any impact on the score. For the remaining two properties we need ranges. Let's implement one of them.

We will write more properties in this chapter (you will too!). However, we will only show details, tables, and descriptions of the creation process for the first three properties. Explanations of properties in this table can be found in the "Generating properties" section two pages back.

```scala
test("guide score should always be between 30 and 70
    if it has a description and some bad movies") {
  forAll((amountOfMovies: Byte) => {
    val guide = TravelGuide(
      Attraction(
        "Yellowstone National Park",
        Some("first national park in the world"),
        Location(LocationId("Q1214"), "Wyoming", 586107)
      ),
      if (amountOfMovies > 0) List.fill(amountOfMovies)(Movie("Random Movie", 0))
      else List.empty
    )

    val score = guideScore(guide)

    // min. 30 (description) and no more than 70 (upper limit with no artists and 0 box office)
    assert(score >= 30 && score <= 70)
  })
}
```

The second test makes sure that the functionality behaves correctly for any number of movies. The framework automatically picks different values of the expected type. In this case, it's Byte, which may represent negative values; thus, we should make sure to not use them in the test.

There is a better way of achieving that, which we'll show very soon.

Delegating the work by passing functions

Q So we are just giving a function to the forAll function, and when the test runner runs the test, forAll automatically generates different parameters and then calls our function using them?

A Yes! Note we can pass any function we want. In the first test we passed a two-parameter function that took String values. Then, we passed a function with a single Byte parameter. The values were generated automatically based on the types, so, in a sense, we delegated some work by passing a function.

Now, let's try to implement the third property-based test, passing a different function to the **forAll** function. We can do that by looking at the description and its tabular version.

❸

The guide score should always be between 20 and 50 if there is an artist and a movie but no description.

If an attraction has no description, and its travel guide has a single artist and a single movie, its score will always be between 20 and 50 (inclusive), **no matter how much** the movie earned and how many followers the artist has.

Attraction's name	Attraction's description	Number of movies	Total box office	Number of artists	Total followers
Fixed	Fixed	1	**Random**	1	**Random**

```
test("guide score should always be between 20 and 50
     if there is an artist and a movie but no description") {
  forAll((followers: Int, boxOffice: Int) => {
    val guide = TravelGuide(
      Attraction(
        "Yellowstone National Park",
        None,
        Location(LocationId("Q1214"), "Wyoming", 586107)
      ),
      List(Artist("Chris LeDoux", followers), Movie("The Hateful Eight", boxOffice))
    )

    val score = guideScore(guide)

    // the score needs to be at least: 20 = 0 (no description) + 10 (1 artist) + 10 (10 movie)
    // but maximum of 50 in a case when there are lots of followers and high box office earnings
    assert(score >= 20 && score <= 50)
  })
}
```

This time we pass a function that takes two Ints. That means the test runner will run it with different Int values. The assertion below needs to hold for any combination.

Understanding failures of property-based tests

We have written three example-based tests and three property-based tests. Let's run the whole test suite and see what happens.

```
> sbt test
  ch12_TravelGuideTest:
    - score of a guide with a description, 0 artists,
      and 2 popular movies should be 65
    - score of a guide with no description, 0 artists,
      and 0 movies should be 0
    - score of a guide with no description, 0 artists,
      and 2 movies with no box office earnings should be 20
    - guide score should not depend on its a
      attraction's name and description strings
    - guide score should always be between 30 and 70
      if it has a description and some bad movies
    - guide score should always be between 20 and 50
      if there is an artist and a movie but no description *** FAILED ***

    TestFailedException was thrown during property evaluation.
      Message: 19 was not greater than or equal to 20
      Occurred when passed generated values (
        arg0 = 0, // 63 shrinks
        arg1 = -11438470 // 39 shrinks
      )

  Run completed in 1 second, 55 milliseconds.
  Tests: succeeded 5, failed 1
  *** 1 TEST FAILED ***
```

Three example-based tests passed.

Two property-based tests passed.

> The last property-based test failed! The test executor gives us a lot of helpful details. It turns out that it generated 0 followers and -11438470 box office. The guide score was 19 while we were asserting that no matter what, it will be equal to or larger than 20.

What are shrinks?

As you can see, the error message we got is pretty detailed and understandable, except for two pieces of information: 63 and 39 **shrinks**. Let's try to understand them. Here's how the process looks from the start:

1. The test runner randomly chooses some parameters and executes our test multiple times with different combinations of parameters.

2. If all the generated combinations succeed, the test runner stops and reports test success.

3. Otherwise, when it encounters an error case, it is usually an "unreadable" combination like -1103249821 and 1567253213. It could report them, but it likes us humans and wants to be nicer.

4. The test runner tries to simplify the error-case parameters. It "guesses" a simpler parameter value (e.g., closer to 0) that may still fail and runs the test again. If the test still fails, the test runner has just performed a single shrink. This process continues until it cannot find a simpler value that still fails the test.

So, in our example, 63 shrinks indicates that the test runner tried 63 times to simplify the first parameter, and it decided that "0" is the simplest one that still causes the failure.

Wrong test or a bug?

The test runner executed our property-based test and found a failing combination of parameters, simplified them (shrinking), and reported them. Now it's our turn to interpret this result.

Adding tests after the implementation carries more risk than adding them before the implementation. We always need to double-check whether we test the right thing—for example, by changing the implementation detail that should fail the test. We will explore adding tests before the implementation (test-driven development) at the end of this chapter.

The problem of making sure we test the right thing is present in the example-based tests, but it's even more visible in the property-based ones because of the sheer number of different combinations. However, in both cases, when we write a new test and it fails, we first need to determine where the problem lies: **is it the test that is wrong, or did we just find a bug in the implementation?** Then, we'll act accordingly.

The property-based test we wrote fails with the following exception:

```
TestFailedException was thrown during property evaluation.
    Message: 19 was not greater than or equal to 20
    Occurred when passed generated values (
      arg0 = 0, // 63 shrinks
      arg1 = -11438470 // 39 shrinks
    )
```

arg0 is the first argument of the function we passed to forAll (followers), and arg1 is the second one (boxOffice). Here, based on the business case we have at hand, we can safely assume that the test is wrong. While 0 followers seems like a perfectly fine value, –11 million box office earnings is probably not something we need to support. If it was, then it'd be an implementation bug, and we'd need to change the implementation to support negative box office earnings. Let's assume that, for our case, we only want to support and test nonnegative box office earnings. That means we need to make sure our property-based test generates only nonnegative boxOffice values. And while we are at it, the same should apply to followers. **We need to change the test**.

Previously, we showed a snippet that partially solved such an issue:

```
if (amountOfMovies > 0) List.fill(...) else List.empty
```

amountOfMovies was a generated Byte value. When the test runner generated a negative Byte, we just replaced it with 0. However, this is not a perfect solution, and we can do a lot better.

> **THIS IS BIG!**
> Property-based tests help us look at our functions more critically.

We use "nonnegative" numbers because 0 is a completely acceptable box office score, contrary to what Hollywood executives say.

That doesn't mean our function is bug-free, though! No celebration yet. There is still a bug hiding there, waiting to be discovered. We will catch it with one of the next property-based tests we will write.

Custom generators

Using an `if` expression in the test case to cut out half of the possibly generated values (e.g., all `Int` values smaller than 0) and replacing it with a constant value makes the test runner unaware of what's going on inside. It may execute a lot of test cases with different negative values, but internally, it will always be the same test. What a waste!

Q How, exactly, does the `forAll` function choose the parameters?

A Let's look at what's going on internally when we pass a function with a single `Byte` parameter to `forAll`. The `forAll` function may call our test case (a function) against the following values: -34, -5, 29, 57, 0, -128, -59, 1, 127, -7. Every time you execute such a test, you may get a different set of values with a different number of entries, depending on the results. What's important here is that "corner case" values have higher chances of being picked (e.g., 0, the largest possible value [127 for Byte], the smallest one [-128], and so on) and they are given extra weights in the generation process. Again, every execution is different, but if you include such a test in your continuous integration (CI) environment, your functions will get a lot of exposure to different parameter values!

Going back to our original problem with negative values: if we replace all the negative values in the test with zeros, we will "get rid" of around half of our tests. This happens because all the generated negative values become zeros when we pass them to our pure function—and since it's a pure function, we know we will always get the same result. Why do we bother calling it over and over again? We need to use the underlying resources more thoughtfully and pass as many different parameters on each execution as possible. We want to constrain the set of possible generated values. We want to customize how the parameters are generated. We need **custom generators**. To be able to generate only nonnegative integers, we need the following :

```
val nonNegativeInt: Gen[Int] = Gen.chooseNum(0, Int.MaxValue)
```

`nonNegativeInt` is an **immutable value describing a process of generating Int values**. Again, note that it only describes the process, but this should no longer be a surprise for you because everything in functional programming is designed using this mindset.

THIS IS BIG!
In FP, even generating random test values can be described by a single immutable value.

chooseNum is a built-in pure function that creates Gen values. It's one of many such helper functions. You can discover and explore them by going to the scalacheck library documentation.

Using custom generators

Using a custom Gen value is very straightforward because there is a special, curried version of the forAll function. It takes generators on its first parameter list, leaving the second parameter list to the function that executes our test case. Hence, not much changes in the new version.

nonNegativeInt is just an immutable value, and it can be reused by many tests, so let's define it in the outer scope.

```scala
val nonNegativeInt: Gen[Int] = Gen.chooseNum(0, Int.MaxValue)
```

```scala
forAll(nonNegativeInt, nonNegativeInt)((followers: Int, boxOffice: Int) => {
  val guide = TravelGuide(
    Attraction("Yellowstone National Park", None,
               Location(LocationId("Q1214"), "Wyoming", 586107)),
    List(Artist("Chris LeDoux", followers), Movie("The Hateful Eight", boxOffice))
  )
  val score = guideScore(guide)
  assert(score >= 20 && score <= 50)
})
```

A cool thing about Gen values is that they can easily be reused and composed together. We can build more complicated, bigger generators from smaller ones. We already know how to do it because **Gen has the flatMap function defined on itself**! Since we have a lot of intuition about using flatMaps—it's our bread and butter now—we should be able to figure out how to compose smaller generators into a bigger one.

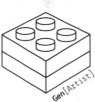

Gen[Artist]

```scala
val randomArtist: Gen[Artist] = for {
  name      <- Gen.identifier
  followers <- nonNegativeInt
} yield Artist(name, followers)
```

Here, we create a custom generator of Artist values, which is built from two smaller generators. identifier is a built-in one that generates alphanumeric strings, and nonNegativeInt is the one we created earlier. It's building big things from smaller ones all over again!

```scala
test("guide score should always be between 10 and 25 if there is just a single artist") {
  forAll(randomArtist)((artist: Artist) => {
    val guide = TravelGuide(
      Attraction("Yellowstone National Park", None,
                 Location(LocationId("Q1214"), "Wyoming", 586107)),
      List(artist)
    )
    val score = guideScore(guide)

    // no description (0), just a single artist (10) with random number of followers (0-15)
    assert(score >= 10 && score <= 25)
  })
}
```

Our new property-based test gets randomly generated artists, which have random alphanumerical names and nonnegative followers.

We have just fixed one test and written a new one. Let's run them.

```
> sbt test
...
All tests passed.
```

Testing more complicated scenarios in a readable way

Building generators is a great way to write many good and readable property-based tests—and do it quickly. The fact that we can easily combine smaller generators into bigger, more complicated ones means that we are able to test more sophisticated properties without sacrificing the readability. For example, let's write a generator of lists of Artists.

```
val randomArtists: Gen[List[Artist]] = for {
  numberOfArtists <- Gen.chooseNum(0, 100)
  artists         <- Gen.listOfN(numberOfArtists, randomArtist)
} yield artists
```

We first generate a number of elements in the output list.

Then, we use another built-in helper function that generates a list of numberOfArtists elements, and each element is a value generated by the randomArtist generator we implemented earlier.

See? We have just created a Gen[List[Artist]] value that describes the process of generating random lists of a maximum of 100 Artist values (each with an alphanumeric name and nonnegative followers). It's still just an immutable value created using the flatMap function. The randomArtists generator uses the randomArtist generator, which, in turn, uses the nonNegativeInt generator. randomArtists could easily be reused to create even more complicated generators (e.g., Gen[List[PopCultureSubject]]), which we'll ask you to implement yourself very soon. This process of creating more generators and properties should continue until we find a bug or exhaust our possibilities of writing new, good test cases.

> **Sequential programs**
>
> flatMap as a way of sequentially building bigger values from smaller ones was introduced in chapter 5, and we've used it in every chapter since.

Having a new randomArtists generator, we can now create a few more **property-based tests that are still very concise and readable**. Let's see one of them.

```
test("guide score should always be between 0 and 55 if there is no description and no movies") {
  forAll(randomArtists)((artists: List[Artist]) => {
    val guide = TravelGuide(
      Attraction("Yellowstone National Park", None,
                 Location(LocationId("Q1214"), "Wyoming", 586107)),
        artists
    )

    // 40 points if 4 artists or more + 15 if 1_500_000 followers or more
    val score = guideScore(guide)
    assert(score >= 0 && score <= 55)
  })
}
```

Nothing unusual, right? However, it turns out this test finally finds a bug!

Finding and fixing bugs in the implementation

When we run our new test, we get the following test failure:

```
- guide score should always be between 0 and 55
  if there is no description and no movies *** FAILED ***
TestFailedException was thrown during property evaluation.
  Message: -19196 was not greater than or equal to 0
  Occurred when passed generated values (
    arg0 = List(Artist(1,225818040), Artist(q,2147483647)) // 6 shrinks
  )
```

Remember that your failure details may be different, but you should get a failure when running this test!

Note that the test runner performed six shrinks. That means that it first encountered a failure for a much more complicated list of artists, but it then worked its way through to simplify it, and it got us a perfectly small and self-contained failing example. Isn't it helpful?

It's exactly what we needed! A real implementation bug—not a test problem. How can we know it's an implementation bug just by looking at the failure message? Because the test runner provided us with a small, concise example of a list, which, when included in the travel guide, caused the `guideScore` function to return a negative score! Negative scores weren't part of any of the requirements we listed earlier! The score should always be 0–100.

The two generated artists look OK, too. Yes, they are called "1" and "q," so they are not your usual celebrity names. But they have these big, 2-billion+ followings, which is not impossible, even now. I'd like to think they are some big artists from the future, maybe even extraterrestrial ones? Their names wouldn't look so strange then, would they?

All jokes aside—the implementation problem we found is a pretty common and dangerous one: **integer overflow**. This problem appears when an arithmetic operation creates a value that is outside of the given type's range. In the case of Scala's Int, the range is from `-2147483648` to `2147483647`. When we add two 2-billion+ values, we get a negative value.

Note that in some cases you may need to work with larger numbers and will hit the Long-overflow problem. You can generate this problem by using Gen[Long] instead of Gen[Int] in the tests. You'd need to use the BigInt type to solve this safely. One of the possible solutions can be found in the book's companion code.

Fixing this problem is very straightforward. Inside the `guideScore` function, we need to use a type with a wider range, such as Long, to perform the internal additions.

```
val totalFollowers: Long = guide.subjects
  .map(_ match {
    case Artist(_, followers) => followers.toLong
    case _                    => 0
  }).sum
```

Here, we use the .toLong function to transform the followers Int to a Long value. This way adding two 2-billion+ values will not overflow.

We need to do the same for `totalBoxOffice` and then transform Longs back to Ints when we deal with small scores.

```
val followersScore = Math.min(15, totalFollowers / 100_000).toInt
```

We can safely use .toInt here because we know it can't be bigger than 15.

Coffee break: Property-based tests

It's time you develop our final property-based test. We'd like to check how the guideScore function behaves when it gets guides with different lists of PopCultureSubjects (Artists or Movies). Hopefully it's going to be successful and we will finally be able to move on!

Your task is to

1. Write new properties that will allow generating lists of random **PopCultureSubject** values
2. Write the new test that ensures that **guideScore** will always return a score of 0 to 70 if it gets a guide with pop culture subjects only (without a description, which is "worth" 30 points).

> When in doubt, remember that all we need is immutable values and pure functions. We use exactly the same ideas but applied to generating values for testing purposes.

This new test can be described using the tabular view we introduced earlier:

Attraction's name	Attraction's description	Number of movies	Total box office	Number of artists	Total followers
Fixed	Fixed	**0-100**	**Random**	**0-100**	**Random**

As you can see, the generator should be able to generate different combinations of random movies and artists. Here are the generators that we have already implemented. They may be used as an inspiration (and maybe even more?).

```
val nonNegativeInt: Gen[Int] = Gen.chooseNum(0, Int.MaxValue)

val randomArtist: Gen[Artist] = for {
  name      <- Gen.identifier
  followers <- nonNegativeInt
} yield Artist(name, followers)

val randomArtists: Gen[List[Artist]] = for {
  numberOfArtists <- Gen.chooseNum(0, 100)
  artists         <- Gen.listOfN(numberOfArtists, randomArtist)
} yield artists
```

> You will probably need to use Gen.identifier, Gen.chooseNum, and Gen.listOfN in your generators, too!

Hints

— Make sure to reuse the generators above in your new generators.

— The main generator should be a value of type Gen[List[PopCultureSubject]].

— When you have a List[Movie] and you append all the elements from the List[Artist] to it, the compiler will be able to infer the resulting type automatically. It's going to be List[PopCultureSubject].

Coffee break explained: Property-based tests

As with many other property-based tests, the most difficult work is to come up with the property itself, taking into consideration all domain-related caveats. Once that's done, the rest of the process becomes easier. We first need to develop the generators.

```
val randomMovie: Gen[Movie] = for {
  name       <- Gen.identifier
  boxOffice <- nonNegativeInt
} yield Movie(name, boxOffice)
```

A randomMovie generator uses the built-in Gen.identifier generator to generate a random alphanumerical name and our own nonNegativeInt to generate the boxOffice value.

```
val randomMovies: Gen[List[Movie]] = for {
  numberOfMovies <- Gen.chooseNum(0, 100)
  movies         <- Gen.listOfN(numberOfMovies, randomMovie)
} yield movies
```

We can use the randomMovie generator to generate a list of 0 to 100 random movies.

```
val randomPopCultureSubjects: Gen[List[PopCultureSubject]] = for {
  movies  <- randomMovies
  artists <- randomArtists
} yield movies.appendedAll(artists)
```

Then, we can build the final generator by using the new randomMovies generator and randomArtists we implemented earlier. We use appendedAll and get the list of pop culture subjects back.

Once we have generators, we can write this very small, readable, and concise test case:

```
test("guide score should always be between 0 and 70
      if it only contains pop culture subjects") {
  forAll(randomPopCultureSubjects)((popCultureSubjects: List[PopCultureSubject]) => {
    val guide = TravelGuide(
      Attraction("Yellowstone National Park", None,
                 Location(LocationId("Q1214"), "Wyoming", 586107)),
      popCultureSubjects
    )

    // min. 0 if the list of pop culture subjects is empty (there is never any description)
    // max. 70 if there are more than four subjects with big followings
    val score = guideScore(guide)
    assert(score >= 0 && score <= 70)
  })
}
```

We pass the generator to forAll and use the generated value directly.

THIS IS BIG!
We use exactly the same techniques in tests as in production code.

When we run it, the test runner will generate a lot of lists and make sure that no matter how big or small a list is or how big or small the followers and boxOffice values are, the guideScore will always be between 0 and 70. Additionally, all of this is achieved using **standard functional tools, which makes the tests easy to read and comprehend.**

Properties and examples

As you can see, property-based tests can be pretty helpful and not very hard to write. This is, however, dependent on the application design: the more small, pure functions you have in your codebase, the better this form of tests will serve you. Remember that it's usually hard for us humans to assume a function doesn't behave correctly after writing a couple of passing example-based tests. When we can't come up with any examples, it's usually a good strategy to turn to property-based tests, just to be sure.

> **Q** What about unit tests, integration tests, and the testing pyramid? Can we use this categorization in functional program tests as well?
>
> **A** All the intuitions you have developed while testing imperative programs will definitely help you write better tests for your functional programs. However, there is an important difference that we need to highlight now to get this out of the way. Functional tests are about testing that a function returns an expected output value once we pass it a given set of parameters. That can mean that all functional tests are just unit tests, and we need to cover integration and end-to-end tests in an imperative way. However, as you shall see, the reality is that if we approach the design of the whole program in a functional way, we can cover a huge majority of functionalities (and code) just by writing those functional "unit" tests! And that's great news, taking into account that writing unit tests is much easier than writing other types of tests: they are usually smaller, faster, and more stable.

The next section of this chapter does exactly that. **We will write integration tests using examples and properties.**

Testing by providing examples
We added quick tests by providing examples and asserting the correct outcomes.

Does the program behave according to the requirements?

Does it have bugs?

Does it integrate correctly with its external dependencies?

Testing integration
We will show how to test integration with an external dependency, including running the real server and side effects.

Testing by defining properties
We defined some properties and let the testing library explore possible inputs.

Tests as documentation
All our tests will be small and easy to understand. They will help others quickly grasp the requirements and implementation details.

Requirements coverage

Let's get one important issue out of the way. We should not write tests for the sake of writing tests. The ultimate goal is to **ensure that our implementation works correctly according to the requirements**. Tests are one way of achieving that—and the most popular one for sure, but we need to always remember that they are just a means to an end. Moreover, there are other ways of ensuring the code implements the requirements correctly, especially when we start using functional programming.

We have focused on testing `guideScore` using example-based and property-based tests, but there are more requirements that need to be covered, and it's always a good idea to plan our testing strategy based on requirements. Here's a summary of how confident we can be that each requirement is implemented correctly.

Requirements: Pop culture travel guide

1. The application should take a single **String** value: a search term for the tourist attraction that the user wants to visit and needs a travel guide for.

2. The application needs to search for a given attraction, its description (if it exists), and its geographical location. It should prefer locations with larger populations.

3. The application should use a location to
   - Find artists originating from this location, sorted by the number of social media followers
   - Find movies that take place in this location, sorted by the box office earnings

4. For a given tourist attraction, artists and movies form its "pop culture travel guide" that should be returned to the user. If there are more possible guides, the application needs to return the one with the highest *score*, which is calculated as follows:
   - 30 points for a description
   - 10 points for each artist or movie (max. 40 points)
   - 1 point for each 100,000 followers (all artists combined; max. 15 points)
   - 1 point for each $10,000,000 in box office earnings (all movies combined; max. 15 points)

5. We will add support for more pop culture subjects in the future (e.g., video games).

Requirement #1 is already covered because we encoded it as a function signature.

The only requirements we still need to test are #2 and #3, and that's where we will focus our attention next.

We have covered requirement #4 by testing a single pure function, using examples and properties. That's why we can be sure that this does what's required.

Requirement #5 is also covered because we encoded it as a type. This is yet another functional technique we can use, together with function signatures and different forms of tests. Note that there are different functional programmers that prefer one style over others. For example, type-level programming tries to put as many requirements in the types as possible and not write too many tests. We will not cover this in the book, but it's important to understand different preferences.

Testing side-effectful requirements

The remaining requirements need some sort of external service to be implemented. In our case, we need a SPARQL endpoint that feeds our application with data. Parts of these requirements are already covered by types, but a majority of them aren't. That's why we still need tests for them.

Remember that what we discuss here can be easily reused in other contexts such as SQL databases. The problems and solutions we show in the book would look very similar.

Side-effectful requirements

This requirement is partially covered by types. We modeled Attraction *exactly after this.*

The application needs to search for a given attraction, its description (if it exists), and its geographical location. **It should prefer locations with larger populations.**

The application should prefer locations to
— Find artists originating from this location, sorted by the number of social media followers
— Find movies that take place in this location, sorted by the box office earnings

We are entering one of the most difficult territories: **testing side-effectful requirements** (i.e., requirements that need external data sources and read/write IO actions). If your application needs an external service of any kind to do its job, you are going to face integration problems. These include low-level things, such as proper request formats, parsing responses, API limits, performance; and high-level ones like synchronizing business data requirements with the way data is represented in the external service and transforming it correctly. And that's just the tip of the iceberg because we also need to keep security issues, version upgrades, schema evolution, and more in mind. These problems can be verified using **integration testing** strategies.

To cover these requirements, we will need two different kinds of tests: one for covering the request/response side (whether our read/write IO actions integrate correctly with the external data source) and one for covering the usage side (whether the data from responses is used correctly). Fortunately, the functional design paradigm we have embraced will help us write both kinds of tests without changing anything in the production code and without any need for specialized mocking libraries. Functional tools, the fact that everything is an immutable value, and your preexisting intuitions from testing imperative programs would be enough to write concise and helpful tests.

Imperative programming embraced mocking and mocking libraries to write tests that focus on a single aspect of an integration. To achieve that, one needs to imitate other aspects or fix them. This is where mocks and stubs are helpful.

Identifying the right test for the job

Identifying requirements for a particular type of test is not a trivial task, and it gets substantially harder when we deal with side-effectful functionalities. The best approach is to ask a question about responsibilities: "Is this particular requirement handled mostly by the application or the external service itself?"

> The application needs to search for a given attraction, its description (if it exists), and its geographical location. **It should prefer locations with larger populations.**

This is an **external service concern**, because our application only **specifies** how the date in the response should be ordered—the ordering itself needs to be handled by the service. The same applies to SQL queries: we don't usually want to query all the rows of a table and then sort them—that would be wasteful and not always possible. That's why "how to sort the results" and "prefer locations with larger populations" are both mostly the external service's internal concerns, and we don't need to test them directly.

There is no point in stubbing a response that is already sorted and claim that we tested it. If our functionality depends completely on a concern that is internal to the external service, we can only test it properly by using the real service. Otherwise, if we deal with a concern internal to our application, we can "imitate" the external service by using mocks or **stubs** (simple versions of the external service that always return the same responses).

To stub or not to stub?

We can use this information to identify the two different types of tests we need to write to verify side-effectful functionalities against requirements:

- *Service data usage tests*—How the application uses data after it's fetched or prepares data before it's stored, including the way it's transformed from and to business values (the external service data can be stubbed here because it's not the concern we test).
- *Service integration tests*—Whether the application formats requests and fetches responses from the real service correctly (the data can't be stubbed—we need to use the real service to test it).

Note that both types of tests test only our application's concerns. The first tests high-level ones, while the second tests more low-level ones, including proper API message formatting.

Data usage tests

Let's start by adding tests that make sure the application we've written uses the external data according to the requirements. Remember that it's always a good idea to try to infer test cases directly from the requirements.

As discussed earlier, sorting is a concern of the data source (external service) itself, and we will test it separately later.

The application should use a location to
— **Find artists originating from this location,** sorted by number of social media followers
— **Find movies that take place in this location,** sorted by the box office earnings

```
test("travel guide should include artists originating
from the attraction's location") { ... }

test("travel guide should include movies set in
the attraction's location") { ... }
```

As you can see, we are able to produce test cases based only on the requirements without touching or analyzing the production code! The only assumption here is that artists and movies need to be fetched from the external data source and used in the application (i.e., included in the travel guide returned by the application's main function). Note that we don't discuss anything about the requests, servers, APIs, or even the response's format. In these tests we want to make sure our application uses the external data according to the requirements. We will make sure the data is correctly fetched and parsed using a different form of tests with real servers running in the background!

Let's write our first test that "assumes" there is a specific location and artist available in the external data source.

1 Let's start with the test "scaffold." Let's describe what we'd like the test to look like from a birds-eye perspective. We will use a given–when–then template and write comments.

```
test("travel guide should include artists originating from the attraction's location") {
  // given an external data source with an attraction named "Tower Bridge"
  // at a location that brought us "Queen"
  ...

  // when we want to get a travel guide for this attraction
  ...
  // then we get a travel guide with "Queen"
  ...
}
```

Note that the **given** section will be the one that prepares the data that we will then "stub" in the **when** section, which will execute the *function under test*. Finally, the **then** section will contain the assertion.

Using such a template helps to understand what we'd like to test in detail without writing any code. Note that scalatest and other test libraries have a better way of writing a given–when–then template, but we decided to keep tests in this book as simple as possible and leave all possible improvements and decorations to you and your team.

2 Next, let's fill the given section, which should contain all the data we'd like to have available for our test. It's up to us to pick the right examples: some real ones may give test readers some additional context. Here, we want our stubbed external service to have information about Tower Bridge in London and be able to return a single artist ("Queen") originating from London.

```
test("travel guide should include artists originating from the attraction's location") {
  // given an external data source with an attraction named "Tower Bridge"
  // at a location that brought us "Queen"
  val attractionName = "Tower Bridge"
  val london         = Location(LocationId("Q84"), "London", 8_908_081)
  val queen          = Artist("Queen", 2_050_559)
  val dataAccess     = new DataAccess {
    def findAttractions(name: String,
                        ordering: AttractionOrdering, limit: Int): IO[List[Attraction]] =
      IO.pure(List(Attraction(attractionName, None, london)))

    def findArtistsFromLocation(locationId: LocationId, limit: Int): IO[List[Artist]] =
      if (locationId == london.id) IO.pure(List(queen)) else IO.pure(List.empty)

    def findMoviesAboutLocation(locationId: LocationId, limit: Int): IO[List[Movie]] =
      IO.pure(List.empty)
  }
```

> The dataAccess value contains three functions that represent our stubbed external service. It always returns a single attraction, never return any movies, and returns "Queen" only if somebody wants to fetch artists from London.

```
  // when we want to get a travel guide for this attraction
  ...

  // then we get a travel guide with "Queen"
  ...
}
```

3 Note that our job is very straightforward now. We have a single dataAccess value that contains three pure functions (which are also values!) that return specific, hardcoded information without any failures (this is how we "stubbed" the external service). We now need to call the function under test (travelGuide) and see whether it correctly read the data and included it in the resulting guide.

```
test("travel guide should include artists originating from the attraction's location") {
  // given an external data source with an attraction named "Tower Bridge"
  // at a location that brought us "Queen"
  val attractionName = "Tower Bridge"
  val london     = Location(LocationId("Q84"), "London", 8_908_081)
  val queen      = Artist("Queen", 2_050_559)
  val dataAccess = new DataAccess {
    def findAttractions(name: String,
                        ordering: AttractionOrdering, limit: Int): IO[List[Attraction]] =
      IO.pure(List(Attraction(attractionName, None, london)))

    def findArtistsFromLocation(locationId: LocationId, limit: Int): IO[List[Artist]] =
      if (locationId == london.id) IO.pure(List(queen)) else IO.pure(List.empty)

    def findMoviesAboutLocation(locationId: LocationId, limit: Int): IO[List[Movie]] =
      IO.pure(List.empty)
  }
```

> We pass the dataAccess value representing the stubbed external service to the travelGuide function. Then, we unsafeRunSync the IO value to "run" the program.

```
  // when we want to get a travel guide for this attraction
  val guide: Option[TravelGuide] = travelGuide(dataAccess, attractionName).unsafeRunSync()

  // then we get a travel guide with "Queen"
  assert(guide.exists(_.subjects == List(queen)))
}
```

> Finally, in the then section, we assert that the resulting travel guide contains the artist, which confirms that the function read and used the value from an external service correctly.

And that's all! We have just tested travelGuide and confirmed that it **uses the data from the external service properly**! The test is small, concise, and there is no magic in it: just values and functions.

Such tests are even more powerful when we have more external services.

Practicing stubbing external services using IO

To practice what we learned, let's try to write a similar test that confirms that our implementation correctly uses movie-related data coming from an external service. You will be testing the travelGuide function:

```
def travelGuide(
    data: DataAccess,
    attractionName: String
): IO[Option[TravelGuide]]
```

Your task is to create the test of "travel guide should include movies set in the attraction's location" that uses the following template:

> **Given** an external data source with an attraction named *"Golden Gate Bridge"* at a location where *"Inside Out"* was taking place,
>
> **when** we want to get a travel guide for this attraction,
>
> **then** we get a travel guide that includes the *"Inside Out"* movie.

"Inside Out" (box office 857611174) was taking place in San Francisco (population 883963), which has id "Q62" in Wikidata (all these may not be important, but you need to put some values there, and it's usually better to use values that improve comprehension and act as documentation, which we'll discuss later).

Answer

```
test("travel guide should include movies set in the attraction's location") {
  // given an external data source with an attraction named "Golden Gate Bridge"
  // at a location where "Inside Out" was taking place in
  val attractionName = "Golden Gate Bridge"
  val sanFrancisco   = Location(LocationId("Q62"), "San Francisco", 883_963)
  val insideOut      = Movie("Inside Out", 857_611_174)
  val dataAccess = new DataAccess {
    def findAttractions(name: String,
                        ordering: AttractionOrdering, limit: Int): IO[List[Attraction]] =
      IO.pure(List(Attraction(attractionName, None, sanFrancisco)))

    def findArtistsFromLocation(locationId: LocationId, limit: Int): IO[List[Artist]] =
      IO.pure(List.empty)

    def findMoviesAboutLocation(locationId: LocationId, limit: Int): IO[List[Movie]] =
      if (locationId == sanFrancisco.id) IO.pure(List(insideOut)) else IO.pure(List.empty)
  }

  // when we want to get a travel guide for this attraction
  val guide: Option[TravelGuide] = travelGuide(dataAccess, attractionName).unsafeRunSync()

  // then we get a travel guide that includes the "Inside Out" movie
  assert(guide.exists(_.subjects == List(insideOut)))
}
```

Testing and design

In the last two tests we made use of the fact that `travelGuide` takes a `DataAccess` value as a parameter. This way we could pass a `DataAccess` value that had hardcoded responses. (We wrote that this was a "stubbed" external service, but we don't really do anything out of the ordinary here. It's still just a value holding references to three pure functions—nothing more).

> **Q** What if I need to stub something that is not exposed as a function parameter?
>
> **A** That is a very good question that doesn't have a definitive answer. However, just asking such question should make us aware that there might be a problem in the design of the application. If we generated test cases directly from requirements and our code didn't support providing some of the things we wanted to "stub" (assume they are always the same), it would usually mean that there are some entangled concerns that we need to separate. In FP, it usually means exposing something as a parameter: either a pure function or a different immutable value. That's how merely thinking about tests may improve the overall design.

A well-designed function exposes only the right amount of parameters that represent essential concerns. Tests help us find this balance. Moreover, remember that the function itself should be responsible for doing a single thing only. All that is usually difficult to pull off, but designing immutable values and writing pure functions with tests for them iteratively helps a lot in making it happen.

> **Q** OK, another question. Why do we treat functions that use IO values differently? They are just values like everything else, right? And the tests look like normal example-based tests we wrote earlier.
>
> **A** They look the same because they use the same FP tooling! However, the rule of thumb is that the majority of our code should consist of pure functions that don't take or return IO values because they mean that there is going to be some external, impure world involved, and that's important for testing. We need to verify a lot more about such functions: how they use the data from the external source is just one of them.

We can use this technique in many more testing scenarios, including "semi-end-to-end" tests, which we will briefly discuss later.

Note that we will design using TDD later in the chapter.

Separation of concerns

Separation of concerns was heavily discussed in chapter 8.

If you additionally feel that our IO-based tests had too much duplicated code, especially in the test setup phase, don't worry because we will address these concerns later.

Service integration tests

The second aspect we need to test to make sure our application works correctly in the presence of side effects is its integration with the real service that is used in production. In our case, we need to make sure the application integrates correctly with real SPARQL endpoints. There are several different approaches we can use here, and they are usually paradigm-agnostic, meaning that in these tests it doesn't matter whether we use imperative or functional programming that much. However, FP does give us a little bit more flexibility, as we will show later in the chapter, even in this case.

Again, remember that the same rules apply to SQL integration or any other external service or data source, for that matter.

Testing low-level integration with external APIs

The important thing here is that we want to test only the integration with a SPARQL endpoint, and that means we don't really need to write any business-related tests, which are covered by the tests where we stubbed the IO values (data usage tests). We are going to test on a lower level now. We only need to "prove" that all three `DataAccess` functions used in production are correctly integrating with a real SPARQL endpoint—no matter how they are later used by the `travelGuide` and other functions. Different aspects of the application may need different testing approaches, and we need to choose carefully. Here, we will use a *Fuseki SPARQL server* that is part of the Apache Jena library we've used so far (see the `FusekiServer` type in Jena's documentation). It exposes real SPARQL endpoints.

Depending on the external service you use and would like to test against, you need to find a server that is as close to the original as possible. Sometimes you can get exactly the same server, to the version, by using Docker. For example, the `testcontainers` library uses Docker to provide those real servers in a test-friendly manner.

Remember that we'd like to avoid using an internet connection in tests because of query limits, network problems, state-related issues, and so on! Such tests are usually very flaky and not very useful. The best way to achieve great tests is to test each case in isolation, preferably using it's own fresh server instance.

```
val model  = RDFDataMgr.loadModel(getClass.getResource("testdata.ttl").toString)
val ds     = DatasetFactory.create(model)
val server = FusekiServer.create.add("/test", ds).build
server.start()
```

The server starts serving data from the `testdata.ttl` file (see `src/test/resources`) we prepared. This data includes an attraction in Venice, some US national parks, their locations, artists from those locations, and movies taking place in those locations. We downloaded this data from Wikidata, using a script available in the book's repository.

Note that this data is stable and won't change between tests!

Let's think about it first. The snippet above uses imperative programming. Do you know any technique we could use here to make it functional?

Local servers as Resources in integration tests

The library we use to read from the Wikidata SPARQL server and to run a local server instance is an imperative Java library. There are many caveats when using this library—one of the most important caveats is a possible resource leak we learned about earlier. This problem applies to our test server as well. When we call start, we trigger a lot of side effects like running a server, opening a port, and waiting for incoming connections. These are all finite resources. Multiply that by the number of tests we'd like to run, each one having its own instance, and you get the idea. We need to clean up all the resources when we no longer need them, even when a test fails! That's why we need the Resource type again.

> **Handling resources**
>
> Resource leaks were handled using Resource in chapter 11.

```
def localSparqlServer: Resource[IO, FusekiServer] = {
  val start: IO[FusekiServer] = IO.blocking {
    val model = RDFDataMgr.loadModel(
      getClass.getResource("testdata.ttl").toString
    )
    val ds = DatasetFactory.create(model)
    val server = FusekiServer.create.add("/test", ds).build
    server.start()
    server
  }

  Resource.make(start)(server => IO.blocking(server.stop()))
}
```

Apache Jena's local SPARQL server implementation

An IO value that describes a program that starts a server and returns a handle to it (FusekiServer)

An IO value that describes a program that needs to be executed when the resource is no longer needed (regardless of anything else)

We now have a value representing a closeable resource that we can use without worrying about potential resource leaks. As you remember, Resource has the **flatMap** function defined, which allows us to compose different small Resource values into more powerful ones. Let's create a Resource that represents an existing connection to the local server.

```
val testServerConnection: Resource[IO, RDFConnection] =
  for {
    localServer <- localSparqlServer
    connection  <- connectionResource(localServer.serverURL(), "test")
  } yield connection
```

connectionResource was a value we developed in the previous chapter. It represented a connection to the real server. We needed to parametrize it with a URL and endpoint name to be able to use a different server. Note that it's production code that becomes part of our test suite!

It is another value representing a closeable resource. When it's used, it returns an IO value describing a program that creates a local server and opens a connection to it (another finite resource). Both the connection and the server are closed automatically, even after failure.

Writing isolated integration tests

We now have a single value, testServerConnection, that we can reuse in all our integration tests. It's going to create and close a server and a connection for us! Note that, once again, we've reused a technique we learned previously when writing production code. This time we used it in tests. I hope you appreciate how versatile these tools are and how learning one of them applies to more than a single scenario.

Enough introductions! Let's see our first real integration test now.

```
test("data access layer should fetch attractions from a real SPARQL server") {
  val result: List[Attraction] = testServerConnection
    .use(connection => {
      // given a real external data source with attractions in Venice
      val dataAccess = getSparqlDataAccess(execQuery(connection))

      // when we use it to find attractions named "Bridge of Sighs"
      dataAccess.findAttractions("Bridge of Sighs", ByLocationPopulation, 5)
    })
    .unsafeRunSync()

  // then we get a list of results with Bridge of Sighs in it
  assert(result.exists(_.name == "Bridge of Sighs") && result.size <= 5)
}
```

And that's all! This small test creates a server that opens a local port, and creates a connection to it using production code:

— connectionResource is production code that is reused internally by testServerConnection.

— getSparqlDataAccess is production code used to create a DataAccess value that executes real SPARQL queries.

Then, it calls the findAttractions function, which returns an IO value describing a side-effectful execution of a SPARQL query on our local server that was populated by some test data, including an attraction in Venice. That's why we can assert that at least "Bridge of Sighs" is returned from the server. Finally, the connection is safely disposed of and the server is closed, releasing all the resources.

This happens because we used the Resource value, which disposes of the connection automatically after the function we pass to the use function finished its execution.

That means we have just written a small, **isolated integration test**. It doesn't depend on any preexisting setup, and it cleans up after itself. It focuses on testing only the small "data layer" represented by one of the three DataAccess functions without any additional context that we tested in previous tests. In this and the following tests, we only want to know whether SPARQL queries are correct and the input and output values are properly transformed to and from our data model values.

Integration with a service is a single responsibility

If writing integration tests is so easy, why don't we add more of them? There are lots of details to focus on from the integration perspective: Does `DataAccess` pass the ordering parameters correctly? Does it conform to the provided results-set limit? Does it return proper artists and movies? We have already tested a simple attractions fetching, and here's an example of how we would approach testing the ordering.

```
test("data access layer should fetch attractions sorted by location population") {
  val locations: List[Location] = testServerConnection
    .use(connection => {
      // given a real external data source with national parks in the US
      val dataAccess = getSparqlDataAccess(execQuery(connection))

      // when we use it to find three locations of the attraction named "Yellowstone"
      dataAccess.findAttractions("Yellowstone", ByLocationPopulation, 3)
    })
    .unsafeRunSync()        Our test data includes three locations for the Yellowstone
    .map(_.location)        National Park: Wyoming, Montana, and Idaho.

  // then we get a list of three locations sorted properly by their population
  assert(locations.size == 3 && locations == locations.sortBy(_.population).reverse)
}
```

We should test every useful combination of parameters, each combination in its own test. This should not be problematic because our **data access implementation is business agnostic**. It only knows about the SPARQL data service, the queries, and the immutable values it takes and returns. It's a small layer consisting of single-responsibility functions. We can test them in isolation to ensure that when used in a bigger program, they will do what's required. We don't test the integration from the perspective of `travelGuide` or any other function. **DataAccess has a single responsibility**, which is integration with an external SPARQL endpoint!

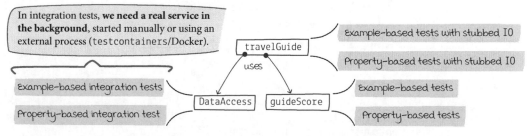

Yes, you see it right! We can also write property-based integration tests. We will show one very soon, but first, let's confirm we are on the same page regarding example-based integration tests.

Coffee break:
Writing integration tests

We now know how to write isolated integration tests that use real services. In this exercise, we will develop three more such integration tests that verify our DataAccess component.

Your task is to write the following three tests:

```
test("data access layer should fetch attractions sorted by name") {
  // given a real external data source with national parks in the US
  // when we use it to find five attractions named "National Park"
  // then we get a list of five attractions sorted properly by their name
}
```

```
test("data access layer should fetch artists from a real SPARQL
      server") {
  // given a real external data source with attractions in Venice
  // when we use it to find an artist from Venice
  // then we get a list of a single artist named "Talco"
}
```

```
test("data access layer should fetch movies from a real SPARQL server") {
  // given a real external data source with attractions in Venice
  // when we use it to find max two movies set in Venice
  // then we get a list of a two movies:
  // "Spider-Man: Far from Home" and "Casino Royale"
}
```

We provided the templates for you. Not much more code is needed. Remember that our integration tests are very concise!

Remember that you have the testServerConnection value at your disposal:

```
val testServerConnection: Resource[IO, RDFConnection]
```

It describes a server that loads the testdata.ttl file from test resources. It includes all the data you need, such as attractions, movies, artists from Venice, and two US national parks. All the information you need is included in the given-when-then templates above. One more thing that you will need is the following value that represents Wikidata identifier for Venice. You can use it directly in the two last tests:

```
val veniceId: LocationId = LocationId("Q641")
```

Remember that you can explore the Wikidata database yourself at https://query.wikidata. org. You can download any entities and put them in the testdata.ttl file, using the script provided in the book's companion source code.

Hints

— Use the map function to assert only on artist and movie names.

— Remember that we also provide limit parameters in each test. They are included in the given–when–then templates.

— Remember to run the IO values to execute the side effects!

Coffee break explained:
Writing integration tests

Writing integration tests is not that exciting anymore, is it? After creating the testServerConnection value, we could safely reuse it and test different aspects of our application's data layer. And that's how it's supposed to be! Integration tests (and tests in general) should not be exciting; they should be boring, both when reading and when writing them.

getSparqlDataAccess is the function we test. It returns the implementation of DataAccess functions that perform real SPARQL queries on production. (Of course, we don't use a production database here. The connection we pass is the local test instance.)

```
test("data access layer should fetch attractions sorted by name") {
  val attractions: List[Attraction] = testServerConnection
    .use(connection => {
      // given a real external data source with national parks in the US
      val dataAccess = getSparqlDataAccess(execQuery(connection))
      // when we use it to find five attractions named "National Park"
      dataAccess.findAttractions("National Park", ByName, 5)
    })
    .unsafeRunSync()
    // then we get a list of five attractions sorted properly by their name
    assert(attractions.size == 5 &&
      attractions.map(_.name) == attractions.sortBy(_.name).map(_.name))
}
```

We use sortBy to verify the order without assuming anything about specific values.

```
test("data access layer should fetch artists from a real SPARQL server") {
  val artists: List[Artist] = testServerConnection
    .use(connection => {
      // given a real external data source with attractions in Venice
      val dataAccess = getSparqlDataAccess(execQuery(connection))
      // when we use it to find an artist from Venice
      dataAccess.findArtistsFromLocation(veniceId, 1)
    })
    .unsafeRunSync()
    // then we get a list of a single artist named "Talco"
    assert(artists.map(_.name) == List("Talco"))
}
```

When we set the limit to 1, we expect only a single artist, always.

If you feel that there is too much duplication between tests, maybe a good idea would be to introduce a reusable Resource[IO, DataAccess] value.

```
test("data access layer should fetch movies from a real SPARQL server") {
  val movies: List[Movie] = testServerConnection
    .use(connection => {
      // given a real external data source with attractions in Venice
      val dataAccess = getSparqlDataAccess(execQuery(connection))
      // when we use it to find max two movies set in Venice
      dataAccess.findMoviesAboutLocation(veniceId, 2)
    })
    .unsafeRunSync()
    // then we get a list of a two movies: "Spider-Man: Far from Home" and "Casino Royale"
    assert(movies.map(_.name) == List("Spider-Man: Far from Home", "Casino Royale"))
}
```

We could also add more cases—for example, testing whether the box office is returned correctly.

Integration tests take more time

The integration tests we have written are pretty small and understandable. They test the real integration with a real server! Have you tried introducing a bug into one of the queries in the production code? If not, go do it now because our new integration tests should fail when somebody does something like that!

There is a drawback to using too many of such isolated integration tests. **They may slow down our testing pipeline considerably**. If we use real servers, we need to wait more to start the process, open ports, wait and handle incoming connections, and so on. It's far more work than just calling a function and asserting on its result. We need to think about that when designing our test suites.

Starting and stopping a server takes time, so it may sometimes be tempting to use a single instance for all tests. This, however, comes with another trade-off. Your tests are no longer isolated, and you need to ensure the isolation through a different mechanism (e.g., by creating randomly named tables in an SQL database). This is especially important if your tests change data in the external service. This discussion is about a more general topic, which is software testing disconnected from any specific paradigm, but rest assured that functional programming gives you all the tools you need to implement any of the known testing strategies. For example, you could use a `Resource` value once and add all the integration tests there. This would be a preferred solution in our case because in this application, we only have input actions (we only read from the external service/data source).

Concurrent IOs

Concurrent IO programs were discussed in chapter 10.

Another approach would be to use a concurrent execution of integration tests. This would require using a `parSequence` on our IOs. Since we are dealing with opening ports, which are a shared resource, we need to make sure our server-starting implementation is able to look for an available port (resources like CPU or memory play a role, too).

Functional core

Design principles of integrating pure and impure code in a program were discussed in chapter 8.

As you can see, there are some very important decisions we need to make, especially when writing integration tests. All the tools we've used in the production code can be reused in testing, which is very reassuring. Fortunately, we only need to test single-responsibility `DataAccess` functions this way because we extracted as much functionality as possible into pure non-IO functions—their tests are always quick!

Property-based integration tests

Q Are we still using pure functional programming in these integration tests? I noticed that we need to call unsafeRunSync in each of them, which definitely is not pure, because it executes the side effects encoded in a given IO value.

A The integration tests we have written are not completely pure because they can't be. We are testing the side-effectful functionalities. However, note that the majority of the tests are still pure functions. The impurity is introduced when we call unsafeRunSync directly. If calling this impure function is not OK for you or your team, you could create a helper test function, which takes an IO[Assertion] and runs it internally. Then, all your tests would just be IOs and completely pure, and the impure calls would be hidden, just like in the production application when we call unsafeRunSync once, outside of the functional core.

You can also go all in and create tests using for comprehensions: using Ref for local servers and parSequence to run tests concurrently.

The great thing about having everything modeled as pure functions and immutable values is that we can use any tool that works with pure functions and immutable values! In the case of testing, we can use property-based tests even for testing functionalities that require side effects!

For example, here is a test that checks whether our implementation of the SPARQL client uses the limit parameter properly. No matter how big or small the limit parameter is, we should always get maximum limit results.

```
test("data access layer should accept and relay limit values to a real SPARQL server") {
  forAll(nonNegativeInt)((limit: Int) => {
    val movies: List[Movie] = testServerConnection
      .use(connection => {
        val dataAccess = getSparqlDataAccess(execQuery(connection))
        dataAccess.findMoviesAboutLocation(veniceId, limit)
      })
      .unsafeRunSync()

    assert(movies.size <= limit)
  })
}
```

Note that each tests creates and stops a SPARQL server. This can happen dozens of times in a property-based test!

This test shows that we can use property-based checks in integration tests as well. This test would fail with an internal SPARQL server error if we used a default generator (that generates negative integers) because negative limits are not supported. That's why we use the custom nonNegativeInt generator.

This tests makes sure the limit parameter is relayed properly. This test may take some time, but we get a lot of confidence back.

Choosing the right testing approach

We can choose the testing tool, depending on how confident we are about an implementation. There are quite a few options to choose from, so let's do a quick recap.

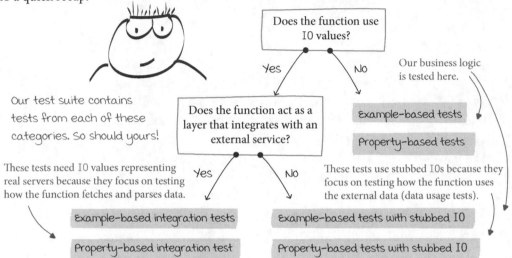

Additionally, remember what your function–under–test is. For example, when we wanted to test the logic inside the travelGuide function, we didn't want to test whether an external data source sorts results properly. That seems obvious in hindsight, but it's often the main reason behind bloated and not very useful test suites.

We need to be aware of all the options and choose the right tool that ensures the software is tested and documented in an understandable way. We need to keep tests small and useful. We also need to make sure the tests cover all the requirements.

It's important to understand that there are some different approaches out there, even in the FP world. For example, type-level programming (not covered in the book) tries to put as many things in the types as possible.

Test-driven development

So far we have been adding tests only to existing functions. Before we wrap up this chapter (and the book!), I'd like to show you that all these techniques can be used for **test-driven development** (i.e., adding new features by writing a failing test first and only then implementing it properly). Let's see an example of that—here's a new big requirement.

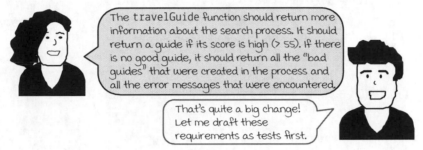

Let's try to approach this problem as we did with previous ones: by trying to figure out how to model this new requirement. What we have so far is a function with the following signature:

```
def travelGuide(data: DataAccess, attractionName: String): IO[Option[TravelGuide]]
```

Now, the new requirement says that we should return only a guide that has a score higher than 55. That's still possible using the signature above (returning Some when there is a good guide with a high score and None otherwise). However, in case we can't find a good guide, we need to return a search report that shows what guides were generated and considered and what kinds of problems we have encountered.

What problems can there be?

Aren't we using pure functions? What kinds of problems can we expect? Note that we use a lot of IO actions in our current implementation. Some of those actions may fail with a network error or timeout. Currently, the whole IO program will fail if something like that happens. However, when we analyze this closely, we are able to recover from such situations. If there are three locations that we need artists and movies for and fetching one of them fails, we still have the remaining two locations that may produce a good guide.

That's why we need a new signature that models both scenarios.

```
case class SearchReport(badGuides: List[TravelGuide], problems: List[String])
def travelGuide(dataAccess: DataAccess,
          attractionName: String): IO[Either[SearchReport, TravelGuide]]
```

Writing a test for a feature that doesn't exist

Changing the signature of the travelGuide function means we first need to adjust the current implementation to the new signature. That shouldn't be too difficult because we can change Some(guide) to Right(guide) and None to Left(SearchReport(List.empty, List.empty)) without changing anything else (they are semantically the same). The same should be done for tests. That should make the code compile again, but it doesn't really implement any new feature—specifically, we don't return bad guides or any problems (the lists are always empty). That's the cue for our first failing test. Let's employ the TDD approach and write a test for one of the new functionalities.

> **Using Either**
>
> Option, Either, and error handling were discussed in chapter 6. We mentioned there that Either can be used in more scenarios, and here's an example of that.

Since we are testing a function that uses IO values, but is not acting as the direct integration layer, we will use tests with stubbed IO values (we called them *data usage tests*: they verify how the data from an external service is used in the *function under test*).

We are testing both business logic and some data source concerns at once, so it's more of an "end-to-end" test.

```
test("travelGuide should return a search report if it can't find a good-enough guide") {
  // given an external data source with a single attraction,
  // no movies, no artists and no IO failures
  val dataAccess = dataAccessStub(
    IO.pure(List(yellowstone)), IO.pure(List.empty), IO.pure(List.empty)
  )

  // when we want to get a travel guide
  val result: Either[SearchReport, TravelGuide] = travelGuide(dataAccess, "").unsafeRunSync()

  // then we get a search report with bad guides (0 artists, 0 movies means the score is < 55)
  assert(result == Left(
    SearchReport(List(TravelGuide(yellowstone, List.empty)), problems = List.empty)
  ))
}
```

We pass an empty string here because all the data is stubbed to always return the same.

Note that we used two additional helpers: one is dataAccessStub function, which takes three IO values and returns a DataAccess with three functions that return given values, and the second is yellowstone:

Having these helpers makes the test above and the following tests much easier to read.

```
def dataAccessStub(
    attractions: IO[List[Attraction]],
    artists: IO[List[Artist]],
    movies: IO[List[Movie]]
): DataAccess = new DataAccess {
  def findAttractions(name: String, ordering: AttractionOrdering, limit: Int): IO[List[Attraction]] = attractions
  def findArtistsFromLocation(locationId: LocationId, limit: Int): IO[List[Artist]]                  = artists
  def findMoviesAboutLocation(locationId: LocationId, limit: Int): IO[List[Movie]]                   = movies
}

val yellowstone: Attraction = Attraction("Yellowstone National Park", Some("first national park in the world"),
                              Location(LocationId("Q1214"), "Wyoming", 586107))
```

> This helper function creates a DataAccess value, which provides IO programs that always succeed with given values. It's used to focus on different aspects in tests without worrying about side effects. Note that this is still just a function that returns a value we pass to another function!

Red-green-refactor

We have our first test, and it fails because our function returns a SearchReport that doesn't contain any bad guides, even though we know that at least one should be fetched (Yellowstone with no pop culture subjects). We could now implement this functionality in the simplest possible way and then create another test, which should be failing. Then, we would change the implementation in the simplest possible way that satisfies both test cases, refactor the code if we feel there's a better way, and move on to creating the third test case. This iterative process, which is called *red-green-refactor*, continues until we satisfy all the requirements. We could also speed up this process and do it in batches. So let's write two more failing tests before writing our first implementation.

> **THIS IS BIG!**
> Mocking and stubbing are just passing values to functions.

We add a few more helper immutable values that make our tests more understandable.

```
val hatefulEight: Movie = Movie("The Hateful Eight", 155760117)
val heavensGate: Movie  = Movie("Heaven's Gate", 3484331)

test("travelGuide should return a travel guide if two movies are available") {
  // given an external data source with a single attraction,
  // two movies, no artists and no IO failures
  val dataAccess = dataAccessStub(
    IO.pure(List(yellowstone)), IO.pure(List.empty), IO.pure(List(hatefulEight, heavensGate))
  )
```

This is a test that tests the successful path. When there are always some big movies, we can be sure that the travel guide has a high score.

```
  // when we want to get a travel guide
  val result: Either[SearchReport, TravelGuide] = travelGuide(dataAccess, "").unsafeRunSync()

  // then we get a proper travel guide because it has a high score (> 55 points)
  assert(result == Right(TravelGuide(yellowstone, List(hatefulEight, heavensGate))))
}

test("travelGuide should return a search report with problems
      when fetching attractions fails") {
  // given an external data source that fails when trying to fetch attractions
  val dataAccess = dataAccessStub(
    IO.delay(throw new Exception("fetching failed")), IO.pure(List.empty), IO.pure(List.empty)
  )
```
Here, we simulate a failure by stubbing an IO value that describes a failing program.

```
  // when we want to get a travel guide
  val result: Either[SearchReport, TravelGuide] = travelGuide(dataAccess, "").unsafeRunSync()

  // then we get a search report with a list of problems
  assert(result == Left(
    SearchReport(badGuides = List.empty, problems = List("fetching failed"))
  ))
}
```
The list of problems is a list of strings. We decided these strings should be messages extracted from all the exceptions we encounter.

Now we have three failing tests (we are *red*), so let's implement a function that satisfies them all (*green*).

Making tests green

Our new implementation needs to find attractions with a given name (a maximum of three) and then fetch artists and movies for each location. If fetching attractions fails, we need to return a `SearchReport` with the exception message inside. That's what our tests are testing for, and this is what we need to implement. The first step, not shown here, is to create a single `travelGuide` function that satisfies the test without worrying about the design. Then, we refactor it by extracting two functions and naming everything properly. Here's the *green* (and *refactored*) implementation.

Again, we show a version after some refactoring. The first green version was not book material.

```
def travelGuideForAttraction(
  dataAccess: DataAccess, attraction: Attraction
): IO[TravelGuide] = {
  List(
    dataAccess.findArtistsFromLocation(attraction.location.id, 2),
    dataAccess.findMoviesAboutLocation(attraction.location.id, 2)
  ).parSequence.map(_.flatten).map(subjects => TravelGuide(attraction, subjects))
}
```

This function concurrently fetches artists and movies for a location of a given attraction and returns a program that, if successfully executed, returns a `TravelGuide`.

```
def findGoodGuide(guides: List[TravelGuide]): Either[SearchReport, TravelGuide] = {
  guides.sortBy(guideScore).reverse.headOption match {
    case Some(bestGuide) =>
      if (guideScore(bestGuide) > 55) Right(bestGuide)
      else Left(SearchReport(guides, List.empty))
    case None =>
      Left(SearchReport(List.empty, List.empty))
  }
}
```

This function gets a list and returns `Right(TravelGuide)` if there is a guide with a high score or `Left(SearchReport)` otherwise. Note that we can add some additional tests for this function as well!

```
def travelGuide(
  dataAccess: DataAccess, attractionName: String
): IO[Either[SearchReport, TravelGuide]] = {
  dataAccess
    .findAttractions(attractionName, ByLocationPopulation, 3)
    .attempt
    .flatMap(_ match {
      case Left(exception) =>
        IO.pure(Left(SearchReport(List.empty, List(exception.getMessage))))
      case Right(attractions) =>
        attractions
          .map(attraction => travelGuideForAttraction(dataAccess, attraction))
          .parSequence
          .map(findGoodGuide)
    })
}
```

$IO[A]$ Each IO[A] value has the `attempt` function that returns an `Either`.

Look at the new **attempt** function we called on the IO. That's how we can get any exception that would be thrown by the program described in that IO. We use its message in the result.

```
def attempt: IO[Either[Throwable, A]]
```

`attempt` returns the a program that will never fail (i.e.,throw an exception) when executed. Instead, the execution successfully finishes and returns the Throwable wrapped in Left.

`Either[Throwable, A]`

Adding more red tests

As described earlier, after our tests have become green and we have refactored the code so that it looks *good enough*, we face this question: is this enough, or are there any features still missing? If there are missing functionalities, we should add another test that *highlights* one of them by failing (being *red*). In our case, the requirements were that we should not fail if fetching anything fails, but we should gather the exception messages as a list and return them inside a SearchReport value. So far, we have just implemented gathering the exceptions thrown by the findAttractions function (by calling attempt on the IO value it returns), but there are two more data layer functions we still call without protecting against their possible exceptions by calling attempt. Here's the test that shows that.

Remember that when you flatMap ten IO values together to create a sequence, if only one of them describes a program that will fail when executed, the whole IO value describes a program that will fail when executed. A program returned by attempt protects us against that.

```
val yosemite = Attraction("Yosemite National Park",
                    Some("national park in California, United States"),
                    Location(LocationId("Q109661"), "Madera County", 157327))
test("travelGuide should return a search report
        with some guides if it can't fetch artists due to IO failures") {
    // given a data source that fails when trying to fetch artists for "Yosemite"
    val dataAccess = new DataAccess {
        def findAttractions(name: String, ordering: AttractionOrdering, limit: Int) =
            IO.pure(List(yosemite, yellowstone))

        def findArtistsFromLocation(locationId: LocationId, limit: Int) =
            if (locationId == yosemite.location.id)
                IO.delay(throw new Exception("Yosemite artists fetching failed"))
            else IO.pure(List.empty)

        def findMoviesAboutLocation(locationId: LocationId, limit: Int) =
            IO.pure(List.empty)
    }

    // when we want to get a travel guide
    val result: Either[SearchReport, TravelGuide] = travelGuide(dataAccess, "").unsafeRunSync()

    // then we get a search report with one bad guide (< 55) and list of errors
    assert(
        result == Left(
            SearchReport(
                badGuides = List(TravelGuide(yellowstone, List.empty)),
                problems = List("Yosemite artists fetching failed")
            )
        )
    )
}
```

We create yet another immutable value, which holds a small descriptive name and can be used to improve the tests readability.

It's definitely a more complicated test, but it's still a small one! Here our DataAccess stub is defined directly, without any helper, because it does more than just return the same value every time. It returns a failing IO when asked about artists from the location of Yosemite. It doesn't fail when getting artists from the location of Yellowstone. And since there are no artists and movies at all in our stubbed data layer, there is no good guide here to return. That's why we expect a SearchReport back. It needs to contain a guide for Yellowstone and a problem description it encountered when trying to find artists from Yosemite's location. Our current travelGuide function fails when this test runs.

Isn't it a nice API? And remember that it's still just a function returning an immutable value!

The last TDD iteration

To make the test green (without failing any previous tests), we need to change the production code and attempt every IO value in our program, gather all the exceptions, and return them as a part of a SearchReport value.

```
def findGoodGuide(
    errorsOrGuides: List[Either[Throwable, TravelGuide]]
): Either[SearchReport, TravelGuide] = {
  val guides: List[TravelGuide] = errorsOrGuides.collect(_ match {
    case Right(travelGuide) => travelGuide
  })
  val errors: List[String] = errorsOrGuides.collect(_ match {
    case Left(exception) => exception.getMessage
  })
  guides.sortBy(guideScore).reverse.headOption match {
    case Some(bestGuide) =>
      if (guideScore(bestGuide) > 55) Right(bestGuide)
      else Left(SearchReport(guides, errors))
    case None =>
      Left(SearchReport(List.empty, errors))
  }
}
```

> We use collect that takes a function, which uses pattern matching to select which values should be filtered and extracts those values. You can also use a single expression to separate errors from results, using the separate function! Have a look at this chapter's source code to learn more.

```
def travelGuide(
    dataAccess: DataAccess, attractionName: String
): IO[Either[SearchReport, TravelGuide]] = {
  dataAccess
    .findAttractions(attractionName, ByLocationPopulation, 3)
    .attempt
    .flatMap(_ match {
      case Left(exception) =>
        IO.pure(Left(SearchReport(List.empty, List(exception.getMessage))))
      case Right(attractions) =>
        attractions
          .map(attraction => travelGuideForAttraction(dataAccess, attraction))
          .map(_.attempt)
          .parSequence
          .map(findGoodGuide)
    })
}
```

✔ **All tests pass!**

> Note that we attempt on individual IO values, so it needs to be done before parSequence, which now returns an IO of List of Eithers.

As you see, test-driven development can be a good technique to use when dealing with new requirements. We have been able to completely overhaul our previous version and add new, more complicated features step by step while still keeping a somewhat concise implementation. We also have a pretty good test suite that covers the new requirements. We could also use property-based tests for TDD, especially when developing non-IO-based pure functions (like findGoodGuide).

And that's all! As you probably expect, there are a few more cases that we haven't covered here and a few great possible improvements to our pop culture travel guide. We will ask you to implement these things very soon. Make sure you play with the code and try to expand our tests and solutions. The material in chapters 11 and 12 is advanced—grokking it requires practice! Take your time and never stop coding (functionally!)

Note that we have introduced collect and attempt without much explanation in the final pages of the book. This was done on purpose. You now know everything you need to start learning new functions and exploring the world of functional APIs on your own!

Summary

In this chapter we used all the familiar functional programming tools to develop tests that helped us discover some bugs and understand the requirements.

Test pure functions by providing examples

We added some quick and small tests by providing examples of inputs and asserting on expected outputs. We learned that testing in functional programming is mainly about coming up with function input parameters and verifying a function's output value.

Test pure functions by providing properties

We then learned about property-based tests, which helped us find an integer-overflow bug in our chapter 11 guideScore implementation. They are developed by providing specifically generated values and testing whether a function returns output from an expected range. We learned how to provide our own generators (Gen values) and that they also have the flatMap function, which makes them easy to compose. We also learned that coming up with properties is not an easy job, and it's good to base them on requirements.

Test side effects without using any mocking libraries

We then moved over to testing functions that use IO values. There are two approaches to testing such functions: stubbing IO values when a given function just uses the external data or running real servers when its main responsibility is the integration. In our case we used stubbed IO values to test the travelGuide function and a real server to test the DataAccess implementation returned by the getSparqlDataAccess function in the production code. We used a Resource value to make sure our locally run SPARQL server instances are always closed and released properly. We showed that we can use property-based tests in such integration tests as well.

By *stubbing* we mean hardcoding DataAccess functions to always return the same values.

Develop new functionalities in a test-driven way

Finally, we got a new requirement and decided to implement it using the test-driven development approach (TDD). We first created three failing tests (*red*), then we implemented a new version of travelGuide that satisfied those tests (*green*), extracted smaller helper functions from it (*refactor*), and repeated the process to end up with the final version.

We didn't show the version before the refactoring, but you may imagine it wasn't very pretty! Explore the book's code repository for more!

The last dance

Thank you for reading *Grokking Functional Programming*! I am sure that the knowledge and skills you've obtained here will help you grow as a programmer and achieve massive success in your career.

I hope you've had a lot of fun reading all 12 chapters and analyzing their examples. The good news is that all of them can be further expanded to include even more advanced topics. If you strive for more functional programming goodies taught in the spirit of this book, please make sure to visit my web page at https://michalplachta.com.

You can get in touch with me there as well!

And finally, if you've enjoyed all these hard exercises in the book, and you can't get over the fact that it's all over now, I have a surprise for you!

Farewell exercises

1. **API rate limiter**—Wikidata servers have API limits. Our solution from chapters 11 and 12 doesn't keep track of all the requests it makes. Your task is to use your knowledge about functional concurrency to implement a configurable request rate limiter for the whole application (e.g., make no more than five requests a second).

2. **Console user interface**—The application we've implemented in chapters 11 and 12 doesn't have any user interface! Implement a console-based interface that asks for the name of an attraction and returns a travel guide. For example:

   ```
   Enter attraction name:
   > Bridge of Sighs
   Thanks! Preparing your guide...
   Bridge of Sighs is a bridge over a canal in Venice. Before visiting,
   you may want to listen to Talco and watch some movies that
   take place in Venice: "Spider-Man: Far from Home" and "Casino Royale".
   ```

What if one of our users tries to pull a "SPARQL injection" trick on us?

3. **Stream-based asynchronous interface**—Can you expand your implementation of the console-based user interface above and allow the user to search for multiple attractions at once?

   ```
   Enter attraction name:
   > Bridge of Sighs
   Thanks! Preparing your guide...
   Want to search for another one in the meantime?
   > Yosemite
   Thanks! Preparing 2 guides for you...
   ```

4. **Testing**—Did you add proper tests for all the functionalities you've implemented above?

5. **Functional design**—Expand the model we developed for the application in chapter 9 (currency exchange). Can you introduce a better model that doesn't use **BigDecimals** directly?

We use only a basic subset of Scala in the book. Here is the chronological summary of all the Scala features we use in the book. You can look at them in your editor by going to the chA_ScalaCheatSheet.scala file in the book's code repository. Make sure to look at the README.md file, too.

Defining a value

```scala
val x: Int = 2022
val y: String = "YYY"
val z = true
```

You can define the expected type of your value using :, but you don't have to do it, and the compiler will try to infer it for you. Here, the inferred type of z is Boolean.

Defining a function

```scala
def f(a: Int): Int = {
  a + 1
}
```

Semicolons are not required, nor is the return keyword.

```scala
def g(a: Int, b: String): Boolean = {
  a == b.length && z
}
```

Values are compared using ==. Here, the logical && operator is part of the last expression in the function body, which becomes the returned result.

Calling a function

```scala
f(x)
→ 2023
g(x, y)
→ false
```

Creating immutable collections

```scala
val list: List[Int]  = List(1, 2, 3)
val set: Set[String] = Set("Hello", "World")
```

Passing a function by name

```scala
list.map(f)
→ List(2, 3, 4)
```

Passing an anonymous function

```scala
list.filter(i => i > 1)
→ List(2, 3)
```

We define a function using the double-arrow operator.

Passing an anonymous two-parameter function

```scala
list.foldLeft(2020)((sum, i) => sum + i)
→ 2026
```

Defining functions with multiple parameter lists (currying)

```scala
def h(a: Int)(b: List[Int]): Boolean = {
  b.contains(a)
}
```

Applying arguments only for a single parameter list returns another function.

```scala
val foo: List[Int] => Boolean = h(2020)
```

A => B is a type of a function that takes A and returns B.

Math

```scala
Math.max(Int.MinValue, 2022)
→ 2022
```

Math operations are defined in the Math object. Type numerical boundaries can be obtained using the MinValue and MaxValue fields.

Defining a case class (product type) and creating its value

```scala
case class Book(title: String, numberOfChapters: Int)
val grokkingFp = Book("Grokking Functional Programming", 12)
```

The dot syntax for accessing values in a case class

```scala
val books: List[Book] = List(grokkingFp, Book("Ferdydurke", 14))
books.filter(book => book.numberOfChapters > 13)
→ List(Book("Ferdydurke", 14))
```

The underscore syntax for defining anonymous functions

```scala
books.filter(_.numberOfChapters > 13)
→ List(Book("Ferdydurke", 14))
```

This is equivalent to the filter usage in the section above.

Missing implementation: ???

```scala
def isThisBookAnyGood(book: Book) = ???
```

This code compiles, but it will throw an exception if someone calls it (for any book, not just this one!).

String interpolation

```scala
s"Reading ${grokkingFp.title} now!"
→ "Reading Grokking Functional Programming now!"
```

If you want to create a multi-line String value, you can use triple quotes: """text""". String interpolation is possible there, too (add an s before).

Passing a multi-line function

```scala
books.map(book =>
  if (book.numberOfChapters > 12)
    s"${book.title} is a long book"
  else
    s"${book.title} is a short book"
)
→ List("Grokking Functional Programming is a short book",
       "Ferdydurke is a long book")
```

You don't have to use braces if your indentation is correct.

Type inference and empty lists

```scala
val emptyList1             = List.empty[Int]
val emptyList2: List[Int] = List.empty
```

Both definitions of a value holding an empty list of integers are equivalent. You can always help the compiler this way.

Type inference and forcing the type

```
val listOfDoubles1              = List[Double](1, 2, 3)
val listOfDoubles2: List[Double] = List(1, 2, 3)
```

Without setting the type, the compiler would infer a List[Int].

Defining a for comprehension

```
for {
  i    <- List(1, 2)
  book <- books
} yield s"Person #$i read ${book.title}"
→ List("Person #1 read Grokking Functional Programming",
       "Person #1 read Ferdydurke",
       "Person #2 read Grokking Functional Programming",
       "Person #2 read Ferdydurke")
```

Objects as modules and object as "bags" for types and functions

```
object things {
  case class Thing(value: Int, description: String)
  def inflate(thing: Thing): Thing =
    thing.copy(value = thing.value + 2030)
}
```

We can bundle types and functions inside well-named objects.

You can copy a case class value by providing only fields you want to change, using the copy function.

```
things.inflate(things.Thing(3, "Just a thing"))
→ Thing(2033, "Just a thing")
```

They are publicly available using the dot syntax.

Defining an opaque type (newtype)

```
object model {
  opaque type BookRating = Int

  object BookRating {
    def apply(rawRating: Int): BookRating =
      Math.max(0, Math.min(5, rawRating))

    extension (a: BookRating) def value: Int = a
  }
}
```

We can define opaque types that are zero-cost wrappers around primitive types.

In their companion object (object with the same name) we can define the apply function, which is called when creating a new value based on the underlying primitive value.

By default, an opaque type doesn't inherit any functionalities from its underlying type. We can add them by providing extension methods.

Importing everything from an object using underscore

```
import model._
```

Creating and using a value of an opaque type

```
val rating: BookRating = BookRating(5)
rating / 2
→ Error: rating / 2 value / is not a member of model.BookRating
val i = rating.value / 2
→ i: Int = 2
```

Creating a BookRating from an Int value (apply is called)

You need to use an extension method (the value here returns the underlying Int).

You can't use rating as any Int even though it's just an Int underneath.

Defining enums (sum types)

```
enum BookProgress {
  case ToRead
  case Reading(currentChapter: Int)
  case Finished(rating: BookRating)
}
import BookProgress._
```

Each of the three types are subtypes of BookProgress. ToRead is a singleton type, while Reading and Finished are product types with one field. You can create bigger cases.

Pattern matching

```
def bookProgressUpdate(book: Book, bookProgress: BookProgress): String = {
  bookProgress match {
    case ToRead =>
      s"I want to read ${book.title}"
    case Finished(rating) =>
      s"I just finished ${book.title}! It's $rating/5!"
    case Reading(currentChapter) =>
      if (currentChapter <= book.numberOfChapters / 2)
        s"I have started reading ${book.title}"
      else
        s"I am finishing reading ${book.title}"
  }
}
```

We can destructure a value into its internal values.

The compiler checks whether we provided a case for each possible item in the enum. All expressions to the right of the => operator need to have the same type (here, String).

Naming parameters in class constructors and functions

```
val b = Book(title = "Grokking Functional Programming",
          numberOfChapters = 12)
bookProgressUpdate(book = b, bookProgress = Reading(currentChapter = 13))
→ "I am finishing reading Grokking Functional Programming"
```

It's true, you know! And thanks for reading it all!

Using `traits` as bags for function blueprints

```
trait BagOfFunctions {
  def f(x: Int): Boolean
  def g(y: Book): Int
}
```

A value of type BagOfFunctions will provide two functions.

Creating `trait` instances (bags of functions)

```
val bagOfFunctions = new BagOfFunctions {
  def f(x: Int): Boolean = x == 1
  def g(y: Book): Int    = y.numberOfChapters * 2
}
bagOfFunctions.f(2020)
→ false
```

We are creating a value of type BagOfFunctions by using the new keyword and providing implementations for the two required functions.

We can access each of the internal functions using the dot syntax.

Unit **value in Scala**

```
val unit: Unit = ()
```

There is only a single value of type Unit in Scala: (). Nobody can create another value. This type is returned from functions that don't return anything constructive (they usually cause a lot of side effects).

Creating a `Map` immutable type

```scala
val book1 = Book("Grokking Functional Programming", 12)
val book2 = Book("Ferdydurke", 14)
val progressPerBook: Map[Book, BookProgress] = Map(
  book1 -> Reading(currentChapter = 13),
  book2 -> ToRead
)
```

Passing functions that pattern match

You can use the Map.`values` function to return a list of values held in the Map (here, BookStates).

```scala
progressPerBook.values.filter(bookProgress =>
  bookProgress match {
    case ToRead      => false
    case Reading(_)  => false
    case Finished(_) => true
  }
)
→ List.empty
```

We use a subset of Scala syntax in the book because our focus is FP. That's why we usually stick to writing functions using the familiar => operator, even when all they do is pattern matching.

```scala
progressPerBook.values.filter(_ match {
  case ToRead      => false
  case Reading(_)  => false
  case Finished(_) => true
})
→ List.empty
```

Alternatively, you can write exactly the same code using a more concise syntax.

```scala
progressPerBook.values.filter {
  case ToRead      => false
  case Reading(_)  => false
  case Finished(_) => true
}
→ List.empty
```

You can ignore destructured values by not naming them and using the underscore to indicate that.

Not naming values using underscore

```scala
for {
  _    <- List(1, 2, 3)
  book <- List(Book("A", 7), Book("B", 13))
} yield book.numberOfChapters
→ List(7, 13, 7, 13, 7, 13)
```

Durations and big numbers

You can use this concise syntax to create FiniteDuration immutable values, which are used universally in time-based functions and types.

```scala
import scala.concurrent.duration._
val duration: FiniteDuration         = 1.second
val durations: List[FiniteDuration] =
  List(100.millis, 2.seconds, 5.minutes, 500_000.hours)
```

You can use an underscore inside numbers to make them more readable.

Appendix B
Functional gems

We have been highlighting important topics, findings, and conclusions about functional programming using THIS IS BIG! boxes. They are the most important takeaways from this book. We list them all here.

THESE ARE BIG!

Chapter 1: Learning functional programming
- In FP, we tend to focus more on signatures than bodies of functions we use.
- Functions that don't lie are very important features of FP.
- In FP, we focus on *what* needs to happen more often than *how* it should happen.

Chapter 2: Pure functions
- Pure functions are the foundation of functional programming.
- We pass copies of data in FP instead of changing the data in place.
- In FP, we separate concerns into different functions.
- We use three rules to create pure functions, which are less buggy.

Chapter 3: Immutable values
- Avoiding mutability lies at the heart of functional programming.
- We don't use mutable states in FP—we use immutable ones instead.
- In FP, we just pass immutable values around!
- Immutability makes us focus on relations between values.

Chapter 4: Functions as values
- Some mainstream languages expose APIs that embrace immutability (e.g., Java Streams).
- Functions *stored* as values are what FP is really about.
- Functions that take functions as parameters are ubiquitous in FP code.
- Functions that don't lie are crucial for maintainable codebases.
- Functions are treated exactly the same as other values in FP.
- Returning functions is a foundation of designing flexible APIs.

Chapter 5: Sequential programs
- `flatMap` is the most important function in FP.
- You will find a lot of for comprehensions in functional programs.
- FP is programming with expressions, not statements.
- In FP, we build big programs from small functions.
- FP heavily relies on abstracting common features—you learn once and use them everywhere.

Chapter 6: Error handling
- Indicating an error in FP means returning an immutable value that represents an error.
- In FP, you can focus on implementing one small function without worrying about others.
- FP is programming with expressions; functional programmers don't use statements.
- In FP, there usually is a function for every problem in your code.
- Functions and values compose very well together—we use them to build big programs from smaller pieces.
- Handling errors in FP is taking an *error value* and returning a different value.
- In FP, we prefer compilation errors over runtime crashes.

Chapter 7: Requirements as types
- In FP, we model data so that only valid business combinations are possible.
- In FP, each type has many higher-order functions.
- There is a higher-order function available for all the common use cases!
- Sum type + product type combo gives us modeling superpowers.
- In FP, behaviors are separated from the data model.
- In FP, some behaviors can be modeled as data.

Chapter 8: IO as values
- In FP, we push the impurity out of most of our functions.
- In FP, we just pass immutable values around!
- In FP, we treat impure functions as unsafe code.
- When we use a function that returns an IO, we are forced to return an IO as well.
- FP is about transforming immutable values using pure functions, even when handling IO.
- We push the impurity out of the functional core, so it's easier to test and maintain.
- In FP, we strive to put as many essential concerns as possible inside pure functions.
- Functional programmers treat everything as values.
- In FP, we "solve" a signature by providing the function body.

Chapter 9: Streams as values
- In FP, we solve a lot of problems using recursion.
- Lazy evaluation, recursion, and potential infinite executions have a lot in common.
- Types tell a lot about the internals in both IO and streaming programs.
- Streams help to separate concerns in your application.
- Many languages and libraries try to use the power of FP by including stream-like lazy APIs.

Chapter 10: Concurrent programs
- Writing concurrent programs is much easier when we can only deal with immutable values and pure functions.
- In FP, programmers tend to use atomic references a lot when creating concurrent programs.
- We model concurrently accessible shared mutable states as immutable values.
- In FP, a multi-threaded program can be modeled as an immutable list of sequential programs.
- In functional programs we work with fibers instead of OS-level threads.

Chapter 11: Designing functional programs
- Many OO design principles can be used with pure functions and immutable values (FP).
- IO enables you to use well-established imperative client libraries in your functional programs!
- "Outsourcing" a concern by requiring a new parameter is a very common design practice in FP.
- We model releasable resources as values.

Chapter 12: Testing functional programs
- FP tests are just calling functions and asserting on their outputs.
- Property-based tests help us look at our functions more critically.
- In FP, even generating random test values can be described by a single immutable value.
- We use exactly the same techniques in tests as in production code.
- `Resource` and `IO` types help write proper readable and maintainable integration tests.
- Mocking and stubbing are just passing values to functions.

index

T